THE DYNAMICS OF TAXATION

This book brings together a landmark collection of essays on tax law and policy to celebrate the legacy of Professor Judith Freedman. It focuses on the four areas of taxation scholarship to which she made her most notable contributions: taxation of SMEs and individuals, tax avoidance, tax administration, and taxpayers' rights and procedures.

Professor Freedman has been a major driving force behind the development of tax law and policy scholarship, not only in the UK, but worldwide. The strength and diversity of the contributors to this book highlight the breadth of Professor Freedman's impact within tax scholarship. The list encompasses some of the most renowned taxation experts worldwide; they include lawyers, economists, academics and practitioners, from Australia, Britain, Canada, Germany, Ireland, Malta, Portugal, Spain and Ukraine.

The Dynamics of Taxation

Essays in Honour of Judith Freedman

Edited by
Glen Loutzenhiser
and
Rita de la Feria

•HART•
OXFORD • LONDON • NEW YORK • NEW DELHI • SYDNEY

HART PUBLISHING

Bloomsbury Publishing Plc

Kemp House, Chawley Park, Cumnor Hill, Oxford, OX2 9PH, UK

1385 Broadway, New York, NY 10018, USA

HART PUBLISHING, the Hart/Stag logo, BLOOMSBURY and the Diana logo are trademarks of Bloomsbury Publishing Plc

First published in Great Britain 2020

A catalogue record for this book is available from the British Library.

Library of Congress Cataloging-in-Publication data

Names: Freedman, Judith, honouree. | Loutzenhiser, Glen, editor. | La Feria, Rita de, editor.

Title: The dynamics of taxation : essays in honour of Judith Freedman / edited by Glen Loutzenhiser and Rita de la Feria.

Description: Oxford, UK ; New York, NY : Hart Publishing, an imprint of Bloomsbury Publishing, 2020. | Includes bibliographical references and index.

Identifiers: LCCN 2020031746 (print) | LCCN 2020031747 (ebook) | ISBN 9781509929092 (hardback) | ISBN 9781509929108 (ePDF) | ISBN 9781509929115 (Epub)

Subjects: LCSH: Taxation—Law and legislation. | Taxation—Law and legislation—England. | Husband and wife—Taxation—England. | Small business—Taxation—Law and legislation—England. | Tax evasion—Law and legislation—England. | Taxation—Law and legislation—European Union countries. | Freedman, Judith.

Classification: LCC K4460 .D96 2020 (print) | LCC K4460 (ebook) | DDC 343.42—dc23

LC record available at https://lccn.loc.gov/2020031746

LC ebook record available at https://lccn.loc.gov/2020031747

ISBN: HB: 978-1-50992-909-2
ePDF: 978-1-50992-910-8
ePub: 978-1-50992-911-5

Typeset by Compuscript Ltd, Shannon
Printed and bound in Great Britain

To find out more about our authors and books visit www.hartpublishing.co.uk. Here you will find extracts, author information, details of forthcoming events and the option to sign up for our newsletters.

FOREWORD

A *Festschrift* is literally a celebration of writing, and the editors have ensured that this volume more than qualifies for that description. Many distinguished names in the tax world (and I mean the world, not just the UK) have written thought-provoking pieces on Professor Judith Freedman's special interests in tax. These include small businesses (which includes differences in legal forms, and categorisation of employment and self-employment), tax avoidance, taxation of corporations generally, tax administration (including tax authority discretions), taxpayers' rights, taxation of the family (from her early writings in the 1980s), plus some others, like the contribution by Edwin Simpson on the implications of the myth of ownership for tax law and Emma Chamberlain's piece on the future of inheritance tax that are harder to categorise. These are all topics that would benefit from fresh thinking for which academics are well placed to put forward suggestions, particularly when (as with all Judith Freedman's work) realistic policy is as important as theoretical ideals.

On small businesses we have a chapter by David G Duff suitably entitled 'Income Taxation of Small Business: Towards Simplicity, Neutrality and Coherence' (primarily on the lack of them). This topic is well illustrated in another chapter 'Principles and Practice of Taxing Small Business' by Stuart Adam and Helen Miller containing a figure showing the substantial tax differences depending on whether a person is an employee, self-employed, or company owner-manager. Are these differences essential? Adam and Miller consider what might be done to correct them. Does the contribution by Hugh Collins 'Dependent Contractors in Tax and Employment Law' provide a way forward? Addington's original income tax taxed professions and employments in the same way and only slightly differently from trades.

At the other end of the scale of size is John Snape's chapter 'Fiscal Jurisdiction and Multinational Groups. A Perspective from "Political Right"'.

On anti-avoidance, there is Malcolm Gammie's contribution on the use and growth of statutory 'avoidance' language. Rita de la Feria's chapter 'EU General Anti-(Tax) Avoidance Mechanisms' and Wolfgang Schön's chapter 'The Concept of Abuse of Law in European Taxation: A Methodological and Constitutional Perspective' are reminders that one needs to think more widely than domestically, whether or not the EU will continue to restrict us (Anzhela Cédelle's piece on 'The Changing Patterns of EU Direct Tax Integration' reminds us of some of those developments). And if it does not, there is 'The Origins, Development and Future of Zero-Rating in the UK' by Geoffrey Morse.

On the fundamentals of corporation tax is the chapter by Michael P Devereux and John Vella 'Reflections on the Allowance for Corporate Equity After Three Decades.' Was it really that long ago that the IFS Capital Taxes Group started it with a subtitle 'A Corporation Tax for the 1990s'? The relationship between accounting and tax, another of Judith's interests dating from her time at the LSE, is represented by 'True and Fair View and Tax Accounting' contributed by Andrés Báez Moreno.

Family taxation is represented by Glen Loutzenhiser's chapter 'Geoffrey and Elspeth Howe and the Path Towards Independent Taxation of Husbands and Wives: 1968–1980'. Independent taxation surely started off better than the present situation that now attempts, not surprisingly unsuccessfully, to marry pure individual income taxation with pure family social security benefits.

Tax administration is represented by Michael Walpole's chapter 'Trends in Tax Administration' written from an Australian point of view, and Stephen Daly's 'Drawing the Boundaries of HMRC's Discretion'.

I hope that the book will be read and enjoyed, as it deserves to be, by the Treasury, HMRC (and their counterparts outside the UK) and tax practitioners, as well as academics.

I remember first meeting Judith near the start of her academic career when she joined the LSE. She used to take part in a seminar started by Professor Wheatcroft and Professor Prest to try to overcome the gulf in understanding between lawyers and economists who were both writing about tax. I would like to think that her interest in tax policy may date back to that seminar. It is, therefore, a particular pleasure and privilege for me to write this to mark the next milestone in her career. It is obviously premature to join with the authors in wishing Judith Freedman a happy retirement when she still has a Chair (albeit with a different name) in Oxford and has just embarked on a part-time judicial career in the Social Entitlement Chamber. We hope that this volume will encourage her to write more on the topics presented here for which she will now, hopefully, have more time.

John Avery Jones

JUDITH FREEDMAN AS A COLLEAGUE 1982–2020

Heathrow airport, Thursday 7 December 2006. Around 6 pm. I was due to travel to Munich for a conference organised by Professor Wolfgang Schön on 'Tax and Corporate Governance'. I parked my car at the airport, checked in and was walking to the gate to board the flight. Unfortunately, there had been a mini tornado in the London area earlier that day (these things happen occasionally) and it had disrupted the flights. However, my flight appeared to be on time. As I walked to the gate, however, I saw Judith Freedman sitting there looking decidedly unhappy: I'm not certain that the sight of me particularly cheered her up.

Judith had been booked on the earlier flight that day, but it had been cancelled because of the weather conditions. She had been bumped onto the same flight as me and had already been waiting at the airport for several hours when I turned up. I sat down and began chatting to her, probably the first time I'd spoken to her for any substantial length of time outside a tax conference or meeting of tax teachers.

Judith and I had both begun teaching at London University around the same time. She was appointed to the LSE in 1982, and I had begun teaching at the School of Oriental and African Studies from 1979, but my teaching had not shifted into tax law until I had completed my doctorate and began teaching a course in international tax law with Professor David Williams of Queen Mary College in around 1985. At that time, the LLM at London University was taught on an intercollegiate basis with students registering at any one of the five colleges that had law schools and then taking courses offered by any one of the colleges. In the tax field there was a lack of coordination, with four of the colleges, for example, offering competing courses in income taxation, but with no courses in international tax law or VAT.

During the late 1980s and 1990s, Judith and I were both involved in a much-needed project to change this situation, and to introduce collaboration between the various teachers at London University and rationalise the tax courses available. Instead of offering competing courses, we collaborated to teach a new range of courses, each one taught at only one of the law schools. This allowed a far better use of resources, and the introduction of new courses in international tax law, European Community tax law, taxation principles and policy (which Judith led on), VAT and other subjects. This collaboration provided the groundwork on which London was able to develop a powerful offering of tax courses, and to start attracting large numbers of students from overseas who wished to take an LLM focused on taxation.

During this period Judith and I met from time to time at the various coordinating meetings of London tax teachers, usually held at some restaurant in the Covent Garden area chosen by the late (and very sadly missed) Jeff Price. My recollection is that we were both committed to this better use of resources to produce a wider range of options than the colleges could offer acting separately. Though we were collaborating to offer the tax courses, there was a certain element of competition still present in the relationship, however. Each college was still competing for student registrations, and there remained a certain degree of rivalry between colleagues.

So, when I walked towards Judith at Heathrow I wasn't certain that her exasperation was directed only at British Airways. She had moved to Oxford five years previously, but our previous contacts had partly been characterised by the collaboration and rivalry of the LLM. Judith still had strong loyalty to the LSE.

While waiting for the plane, Judith and I began chatting about a whole range of topics: tax, academia, tax in practice, family, publishers etc. We both came from a similar, north London background. Gradually we began to realise that the time had slipped by and our flight had still not been called to board. Several attempts to obtain information from British Airways proved frustrating. The incoming flight had been delayed because of the bad weather; as a result, the crew had exceeded the number of hours that they were permitted to work and a replacement crew was being brought in; the replacement crew was delayed because of the bad weather; there was a concern about whether Munich airport would still be open when the plane arrived; no one was certain if the plane could take off and arrive in time. We continued chatting away.

As the hour approached 10 pm, which would have been around the last time that a plane could have taken off and arrived in Munich before the airport closed, Judith and I had been chatting for four or five hours. She was quite agitated – she was due to present a paper the next day on Financial and Tax Accounting, and she had promised Wolfgang Schön that she would be there to present it.[1] I was simply commenting on another paper, and was rather more relaxed about whether I arrived or not.

Throughout the evening Judith had been in touch with her husband, Lawrence – internationally renowned professor of War Studies at King's College – to see if he had any information on the delay or could find alternative flight tickets. It was quite amusing seeing Judith draft Lawrence in as a travel agent. Eventually, and well after 10 pm, British Airways finally told us that the flight would not be leaving, that we should all collect our luggage and go back to the departure hall to book a flight for the next day. This seemed to have been a cunning plan on the part of British Airways, because by the time we all collected luggage and exited, the counter for booking new flights had just closed for the day. Frankly, at this stage I was prepared to forget about Munich completely and simply go home. Not so Judith: she had promised Wolfgang Schön and she wasn't going to let him down. Lawrence had found us two seats on the first flight out of London City airport for the next morning. I collected my car, and we drove to Judith's house in Wimbledon, arriving in the small hours of the morning. After a few hours' sleep, we went over to London City airport and eventually arrived at the Max Planck Institute in Munich shortly after the conference had begun and in time for Judith's paper and my comments. Judith had honoured her commitment to be there.

[1] See J Freedman, 'Financial and tax accounting: transparency and truth' in W Schön (ed), *Tax and Corporate Governance* (Berlin, Springer Science, 2008).

It is strange how a mini tornado and a delayed flight can turn an acquaintance into a firm friendship.

At the time Judith and I spoke, the intercollegiate nature of the London LLM was beginning to fall apart. Under pressure from individual colleges to offer their own LLMs, gradually the tax teachers had no option but to cease collaboration between the colleges, though none of them was happy with this outcome. I could see that this was going to hit the tax courses very badly as it was exactly this collaboration that had allowed London to offer such a range of courses and compete with established international tax programmes like Leiden and NYU. In an attempt to preserve London's position, I established an MA in Taxation at the Institute for Advanced Legal Studies (IALS) which ran quite successfully for a number of years, despite lacking any administrative support for most of that time. Meanwhile, Judith had moved to Oxford, where she introduced a new tax course on the BCL/MJur programme on business taxation to run alongside the existing, long-standing Personal Tax course. With colleagues she also introduced an undergraduate tax option in Oxford. Successful though these were, however, it was clearly difficult to offer a full range of specialist tax options within the very established BCL/MJur.

I wasn't entirely surprised, therefore, when Judith approached me around 2014 to discuss the establishment of what became the part-time MSc in Taxation at Oxford. Judith knew that the MA was functioning quite efficiently at IALS, but I was frustrated because of the lack of support. On the other hand, securing the long-term future of taxation in Oxford would be greatly assisted by being able to offer a full Master's course in taxation, attracting top quality specialist tax students and helping to cement Oxford's reputation, alongside its existing tax courses and its Centre for Business Taxation, as a centre for excellence in tax teaching and research. The fees from the degree would also assist in funding a further tax teaching post at Oxford. Although Oxford University had a strict limit on student numbers, making creation of a new degree difficult, Judith and her colleagues had discovered the possibility of introducing a part-time degree that was not affected by these rules. I very readily agreed to support her proposal for the new degree.

By this stage, Judith had become expert in the convoluted world of Oxford academic administration. She and her colleagues put their expertise to work, managing the intricate processes of obtaining consent to introduce a new degree course, which involved obtaining approval at college, faculty and university level. I remain lost in admiration at the way in which Judith and her colleagues managed an incredibly complex process in only a year, and managed not only to secure approval for the new degree but also a commitment to ensure there were adequate posts made available to guarantee its future teaching. In this process I was wheeled out from time to time to provide assurances to the faculty that there would be no difficulty in filling the places on the degree with adequately qualified candidates, and obtaining high-quality teaching to match. Judith provided regular updates on the process, displaying her personal frustration with the bureaucracy, but all the time showing how she had mastered it and remained committed to achieving the result she wanted. In truth, despite outward appearances of frustration with the process, I think she rejoiced in the way she had mastered control over it. She was enjoying the challenge presented by the bureaucratic nature of the approval process.

The MSc in Taxation started in 2016, having been oversubscribed by excellent applications. Judith and the Oxford team steered the programme through its very successful first three years, and even in her semi-retirement from Oxford she still participates actively in the degree. There are many legacies that Judith leaves on her semi-retirement from academia, both at the LSE and at Oxford, but I am certain that one of the longest-lasting legacies will be the MSc in Taxation.

Somewhere along this process, and perhaps arising out of our discussions at Heathrow, Judith asked me to join her as deputy editor of the *British Tax Review* (*BTR*). We agreed that I would assume this role on the basis that I had limited time to commit to it but would provide backup to Judith where necessary. It has seldom proved necessary. In practice, I remain astonished at how much time and energy Judith commits to the publication. Frankly, getting every issue out is a labour of love, and it would simply not happen if Judith didn't commit an immense amount of time and personal resources to the process. The publication would have folded several years ago but for Judith's commitment to its continuation. I am not certain that the publishers always recognise exactly how much she contributes to the continued publication of the *BTR*.

Throughout the almost 40 years that I have known her, Judith has been a most excellent colleague to work with. She is utterly reliable in meeting her commitments, but always conscious of the commitments of others. She is very firm in her views, but open to input from others. She has been prepared to stand up to publishers and administrators to secure, for example, the continuation of the *BTR* and the establishment of the new degree at Oxford. At the same time, she is very human and approachable; much of our discussions are about family and friends as about academic topics. It has been a pleasure working with her on a number of projects, and this publication is a mark of the respect and affection held for her by colleagues and friends. I am delighted to have been both.

Philip Baker

CONTENTS

ABOUT THE CONTRIBUTORS

Stuart Adam is a Senior Research Economist at the Institute for Fiscal Studies.

John Avery Jones is a Retired Judge of the Upper Tribunal (Tax and Chancery Chamber) and retired visiting professor, London School of Economics.

Philip Baker OBE QC is a barrister at Field Court Tax Chambers and Visiting Professor of Law at Oxford University.

Anzhela Cédelle is a Counsellor at the OECD's Secretariat of the Global Forum on Transparency and Exchange of Information for Tax Purposes, and teaches on the Oxford MSc in Taxation.

Emma Chamberlain OBE Fellow CTA MA (Oxon) TEP is a barrister at Pump Court Tax Chambers and Visiting Professor of Law at Oxford University.

Hugh Collins is the Cassel Chair of Commercial Law at the London School of Economics and was formerly the Vinerian Professor of English Law at All Souls College, University of Oxford.

Stephen Daly is Lecturer in Corporate Law at the Dickson Poon School of Law, King's College London.

Rita de la Feria is Professor of Tax Law at the University of Leeds, and an International Research Fellow at the Oxford University Centre for Business Taxation.

Michael P Devereux is Director of the Oxford University Centre for Business Taxation, Professor of Business Taxation, Saïd Business School, University of Oxford and Professorial Fellow at Oriel College, Oxford.

David G Duff is Professor of Law and Director of the Tax LLM program at the Peter A. Allard School of Law at the University of British Columbia.

Malcolm Gammie CBE QC is in practice at One Essex Court, and is a deputy Judge of the Upper Tribunal (Tax and Chancery).

Glen Loutzenhiser is Associate Professor of Tax Law, Faculty of Law, University of Oxford and Tutorial Fellow in Law of St Hugh's College, University of Oxford.

Helen Miller is Deputy Director of the Institute for Fiscal Studies and head of their tax sector.

Andrés Báez Moreno is Associate Professor of Tax Law at the Universidad Carlos III de Madrid, and a lawyer at the Madrid Bar.

Geoffrey Morse is the Professor of Corporate and Tax Law at the University of Birmingham, and sometime Professor and Head of the Law School at the University of Nottingham.

Wolfgang Schön is Director at the Max Planck Institute for Tax Law and Public Finance, Honorary Professor at Munich University and an International Research Fellow at the Oxford University Centre for Business Taxation.

Heather Self is a partner in the corporate tax team at Blick Rothenberg.

Edwin Simpson is Barclays Bank Associate Professor of Taxation Law, Faculty of Law, University of Oxford, Official Student in Law of Christ Church, Oxford and a Barrister at New Square Chambers, Lincoln's Inn.

John Snape is Associate Professor of Law at Warwick Law School, the University of Warwick.

John Vella is Associate Professor of Tax Law in the Faculty of Law at the University of Oxford, Assistant Director of the Oxford University Centre for Business Taxation, and a Fellow of Harris Manchester College.

Michael Walpole is Head of School in Tax and Business Law (incorporating Atax) at the University of New South Wales in Sydney.

Introduction: A Tribute to Professor Judith Freedman's Outstanding Career

GLEN LOUTZENHISER AND RITA DE LA FERIA

Planning for this volume of essays in honour of Professor Judith Freedman started nearly four years ago, after Judith informed us of her intention to step down from her position as the statutory Chair of Taxation Law at Oxford University. It is the culmination of years of preparatory work and celebrations, the highlight of which was a conference held on 15–16 May 2019 in Oxford at the Saïd Business School sponsored by the Oxford Law Faculty, Chartered Institute of Taxation and the Oxford University Centre for Business Taxation. It was a tremendous two days, bringing together 60 tax academics and academically minded practitioners from all over the UK, continental Europe, Canada and Australia, to discuss the influence Judith's work has had across a range of topics and to celebrate her remarkable career.

The contributors to this volume presented draft versions of their chapters, and two of Judith's most recent doctoral students – Daigy Ogembo and Diego Quinones – presented on their research. We also benefited from a tremendous group of commentators on each presentation plus some distinguished session chairs, all grateful to lend their efforts to enhancing the works in this volume and to celebrating Judith's career. We wish to extend our sincere thanks to Eduardo Baistrocchi, Michael Blackwell, Steve Bond, Dominic de Cogan, Bill Dodwell, Sandra Eden, Chris Evans, Hans Gribnau, Irem Guceri, Peter Harris, Judith Knott, Geoffrey Loomer, Timothy Lyons, Ray McCann, Lynne Oats, Christiana HJI Panayi, Jonathan Peacock and the other conference participants for their immensely valuable contributions. At the conference dinner held in the spectacular dining hall at Balliol College the conference attendees were joined in the celebrations by other Oxford colleagues of Judith including the current and two former Deans of the Law Faculty, two of Judith's law tutors during her undergraduate studies at Oxford, her long-time colleague on the *British Tax Review*, Jane O'Hare, lawyers from Pinsent Masons LLP,[1] as well as members of Judith's family. It truly was a memorable evening, and a fitting tribute to her.

[1] Pinsent Masons LLP had for many years donated funds to the Oxford Law Faculty in support of tax teaching, first providing funding for the Career Development Fellowship in Tax Law held by Glen Loutzenhiser and later Judith's Chair. Judith's Chair was originally funded by donations from KPMG, so both firms played an important part in supporting the development of tax teaching and research at Oxford. As is usual with chairs funded in this way, the donation was to the University on strict terms ensuring full academic freedom. Judith was appointed to the University in the normal way and was not an employee of either firm.

During the years of preparation leading up to the publication of this volume, what stood out the most for us was the overwhelmingly positive response that we received from everyone we contacted – the warmth and respect that everyone, without exception, expressed towards Judith in their responses. It was with those responses in mind that the word 'dynamic' was chosen for the title of this volume of essays in her honour. It effectively captures those qualities of Judith that those of us who have had the pleasure to work with her know very well – her boundless energy, drive and charisma; her relentless commitment to making a positive impact in taxation research, teaching and policy; her dedication to being a (positive) force for change.

We are grateful to the team at Hart Publishing, now an imprint of Bloomsbury Publishing plc, and in particular Roberta Bassi for commissioning the book, and Linda Staniford for seeing it through to publication. We also want to express our thanks to Daisy Ogembo for her editorial assistance and to Agata Dybisz and Pauline Simpson for their invaluable administrative help in making the Oxford conference such a success.

A General Tribute to Judith's Outstanding Career

After qualifying as a solicitor and working in the corporate tax group at Freshfields in London, Judith found her calling in academia. She joined the University of Surrey as a lecturer in law in 1980 before moving to the LSE where she taught tax and company law, first as a Lecturer in Law and then as Reader. She was also a Senior Research Fellow in Company and Commercial Law at the Institute for Advanced Legal Studies from 1989 to 1992. During her tenure at the LSE she co-founded the undergraduate tax course and the MSc in Law and Accounting. Judith moved to Oxford in 2001 to take up the inaugural Chair in Taxation at the Faculty of Law, University of Oxford and a Fellowship at Worcester College. At Oxford, Judith would go on to play an instrumental role in founding two more successful interdisciplinary masters degrees – the MSc in Law and Finance in 2010 and the part-time MSc in Taxation in 2016. She quickly increased the tax offerings of the Oxford Law Faculty by launching two new courses – a business tax course on the BCL/MJur (to join the long-standing Personal Tax course) and, with the help of other Oxford colleagues, an undergraduate tax law option. She played key roles in the administration of both the Law Faculty and Worcester College as a member of numerous committees, hiring panels and in her time as the Faculty's Associate Dean, Development and Communications.

During her long and distinguished academic career, Judith contributed to the development of the teaching, practice, administration and academic study of tax law in countless ways, in the UK and worldwide. She generated world-leading research primarily but not exclusively in the field of tax law, with an emphasis on corporate and business taxation. Her special interests lay in tax policy and design, small businesses, the interaction between law and accounting, tax avoidance, tax and corporate social responsibility, and the use of discretion in the administration of taxation. These fields of special interest are reflected in the contributions to this volume.

Her impact on the law has been profound. Most notably, Professor Freedman was a member of the 2010 Aaronson study group considering whether the UK should implement a general anti-avoidance rule, which directly led to the introduction of the UK GAAR in the Finance Act 2013. She was a contributor to the 2010 Institute for Fiscal

Studies-led Mirrlees Review and is a long-standing member of the IFS's influential Tax Law Review Committee (and from 2019 is Chair of the Committee). Her work on the Mirrlees Review was cited in the 2017 Taylor Review of Modern Working Practices. In 2020, the Chancellor appointed Judith to the Board of the Office of Tax Simplification. Her regular advisory work to HMRC, HM Treasury, the Office of Tax Simplification and the media has also helped shape the law.

Over her career Judith published widely in numerous tax publications as well as prestigious general law journals such as the *Law Quarterly Review* and *Modern Law Review*. She served on a number of Law Society, DTI and HMRC committees and advisory groups and was a member of the *Company Law Review*'s working party on small companies. She is general editor of and frequent contributor to the leading UK tax journal, the *British Tax Review*, as well as sitting on the editorial boards of the *eJournal of Tax Research*, the *Canadian Tax Journal*, the *Australian Tax Review* and the *Tax Journal*. She has held the Anton Philips Visiting Chair at the University of Tilburg and is an Adjunct Professor in the Australian School of Taxation and Business Law, University of New South Wales.

In 2005, Judith, working with Professor Colin Mayer, then Director of the Oxford Financial Research Centre, bid against other universities for a grant from the 100 Group to set up the Oxford University Centre for Business Taxation, based at the Säid Business School and working in partnership with the Law Faculty tax academics. It was something of a dream of hers to have an interdisciplinary tax research group and now, under the leadership of its first and to-date only director, Professor Michael Devereux, the Tax Centre conducts cutting-edge research in economics and law and is heavily engaged in tax policy debates and tax policy-making across the globe. For many years Judith was the Director of Legal Research at the Tax Centre. She was actively involved in the Centre's research programme, publications, conferences/workshops and grant applications. In 2014 she was involved in founding the Oxford Law Faculty's Oxford Women in Law (OWL) network and then in 2015, she became one of the founding members of the Women in Tax network, which from its initial branch in London has in just four years spread worldwide, with branches from Ireland to Brazil.[2]

Judith was appointed a CBE in the 2013 New Year's Honours List for her services to tax research; as an Honorary Fellow of the Chartered Institute of Taxation in January 2015; and in 2016 she was elected a Fellow of the British Academy. In 2019, after stepping down to a part-time research post at Oxford and taking on the new title of Professor of Tax Law and Policy, Judith became a part-time judge in the Social Security and Child Support Tribunal.

A Personal Tribute to Judith's Mentorship

When discussing Judith Freedman's outstanding career it is easy to lose sight of its human dimension, the impact she has had on the career of so many others, and her role as a mentor of so many young tax academics and professionals. Judith has taught

[2] For more on Judith and the Women in Tax network see the Afterword in this volume by Heather Self.

countless students at the graduate and undergraduate level over her academic career, many of whom have gone on to successful careers in taxation law, including Professor Christiana HJI Panayi (Queen Mary London), Mary Ashley (Old Square), Thomas Chacko (Pump Court), Imran Afzal (Field Court), Michael Jones and Michael Firth (both Gray's Inn), to name just a few. At Oxford, she has also supervised or mentored several research students and junior academics, either through the Law Faculty or through the work of the Centre for Business Taxation, many of whom went on to become successful academics in their own right, in the UK or elsewhere around the world. Those – who we have come to designate during the process of preparing this volume as Judith's academic children – include Dr Anzhela Cédelle (OECD), Dr Stephen Daly (King's College London), Professor Geoffrey Loomer (University of Victoria, Canada), Dr Daisy Ogembo (Oxford University), Dr John Vella (Oxford University) and, of course, the two of us.

Rita: I met Judith Freedman in 2004, as a final year PhD student at Trinity College, Dublin. It was a random encounter: at the EATLP Congress, in Paris, outside a seminar room. I was then a young female wannabe scholar, with no networks in tax law academia, but keen to make a difference. Judith took me under her wing, introduced me to other academics, nurtured – and tested – me, until eventually, three years later, when I was already a lecturer at Queen's University Belfast, she encouraged me to apply for a research fellowship position at the then newly established Oxford University Centre for Business Taxation. At the time, most friends and colleagues advised me against leaving a permanent lectureship to take up a fixed-term post at Oxford, but encouraged by Judith, and keen to learn, I took the risk. It was probably the best decision that I took in my career to date, and one that changed not only that career, but my life, forever. It was also around that time that I started developing what I – privately, until now – call Judith's law: Judith is always right. Even when my instinct is to do something different, I have learnt (from experience) to ignore my instinct and do what Judith says. It is impossible to overstate the impact that Judith has had on my career: I have been lucky enough to have had a few mentors throughout my career, but it is fair to say that, even though I was never technically her student, no one has had a bigger impact on it than Judith Freedman. From advice on what shoes to wear at conferences to job offers, there is rarely a significant decision in my career over the last decade that was not preceded by seeking Judith's advice. Yet, her impact was not restricted to career choices, but also at a personal level: at various key moments in my personal life, Judith was always available to provide not only emotional, but also practical support. That alone is a debt that can never be repaid.

Glen: I also met Judith Freedman in 2004, shortly after finishing the LLM at Cambridge. I was spending my last few weeks post-studies travelling in Europe before returning to practice at my Toronto law firm after a nine-month sabbatical when I heard Oxford was advertising for a Career Development Fellowship in Tax Law. I was delighted to be offered the job a few short weeks later and looked forward to the opportunity to spend some time in academia – blissfully unaware that those three years would stretch into 15 years and counting and also how lucky I was going to be to work closely with Judith Freedman. Judith spent a considerable time in those early days helping me find my feet with my teaching and research. She invited me to lunch and dinner at Worcester College regularly, and even bought me a cake one year when we had to agree BCL exam marks on my birthday. She encouraged me to take up doctoral studies during my Fellowship and was an incredibly knowledgeable and supportive supervisor. She invited me to a party celebrating the fiftieth anniversary of the *British Tax Review* at Middle Temple in 2006 where I happened to meet my now wife Eleanor. Her support and guidance carried on after my appointment as a university lecturer in 2009. Like Rita, I also cannot think of a significant career or life question that I did not seek Judith's advice on. Although I was pleased that Judith wanted to stay on in Oxford in a part-time capacity after stepping down from her Chair, and that I have been able to continue teaching with her on our part-time MSc in Taxation and working with her on the *British Tax Review*, I greatly miss not seeing her and teaching with her as frequently as before. I particularly miss our regular catch-up chats in her amazing office at Worcester College. I simply could not have hoped for a better colleague and mentor.

***

The professional and personal impact that Judith's mentorship has had on our lives is far from unique; Judith has had a similar impact on the life of many of her academic children, most of whom have either written a chapter in this volume or provided invaluable commentary on draft papers at the Oxford Conference in May 2019. There is a reason why so many of us were so keen to honour Judith in this manner. Academic mentor relationships are not always straightforward: they are often emotionally detached, hierarchical and at times even exploitative. Judith's style is none of the above: she is caring, encouraging and selfless with her time.

Today – thanks to a large extent to Judith – we, like many of her academic children, are in a position to help others; we too have become academic gatekeepers. In that role, we actively seek to mimic Judith's style – she is a role model to us in many ways, but not least in how senior academics and academic mentors should behave. So that, beyond the scholarship, teaching, policy impact and all the wonderful things that are part of her outstanding career, this too is part of her legacy: there is now a group of academics, spread around the world, carrying on Judith's mentorship style. Supporting and encouraging young people, aware of unconscious biases, gender and otherwise, and actively working for a tax world that is more diverse, more inclusive and overall a force for good.

That, just in itself, is an extraordinary legacy to leave. We will not let her down.

PART I

Taxing Small Businesses and Individuals

1

Geoffrey and Elspeth Howe and the Path Towards Independent Taxation of Husbands and Wives: 1968–1980

GLEN LOUTZENHISER

I. Introduction

Although Professor Judith Freedman is perhaps best known for her academic writing on tax avoidance, small business and tax administration, at the beginning of her academic career at the London School of Economics and Political Science[1] her writing on taxation initially focused on the family. She has remarked to this writer on more than one occasion over the years that very little attention has been paid to her early work. This chapter is a first step towards filling this lacuna in the literature.

Building upon the work of Freedman and others, and drawing upon recently released archival material, this chapter explores the events leading up to the introduction of independent taxation of married women in the Finance Act 1988 with effect from April 1990. Most importantly, this chapter makes the novel assertion that Baroness Elspeth Howe, former deputy commissioner of the Equal Opportunities Commission (EOC) and also the wife of former Chancellor Geoffrey Howe, played a highly significant and heretofore not fully appreciated role alongside her husband in the move towards independent taxation of married women in the late 1960s and 1970s. In particular, it is argued herein that Elspeth Howe, with Geoffrey Howe's backing, contributed directly and indirectly – especially through her work on the EOC – to the Conservative Party's policy work on independent taxation. The Party's (and the Howes') pursuit of independent taxation was advanced on a number of fronts, including through the work of two internal Conservative Party committees – the 1977 Committee on Women and Tax and

[1] After working as a solicitor at Freshfields in London, Judith Freedman taught tax and company law at LSE, first as a Lecturer in Law and then as Reader. She was also a Senior Research Fellow at the Institute for Advanced Legal Studies. During her tenure at LSE she co-founded the MSc in Law and Accounting. After moving to the University of Oxford Law Faculty in 2001 to take up the Chair in Taxation, she would go on to play an instrumental role in founding two more interdisciplinary masters degrees – the MSc in Law and Finance in 2010 and the part-time MSc in Taxation in 2016.

the 1968 Cripps Committee. These two committees have received scant attention in the prior literature, but this chapter argues that the historical records demonstrate that they were key links in the chain of events leading to independent taxation of married women.

II. Freedman on Tax and the Family

Professor Freedman's early writing on tax and the family included three Finance Act notes related to the tax treatment of married couples for the *British Tax Review* – a journal with which she would later become synonymous as its general editor.[2] Freedman also wrote two articles for the *Journal of Child Law* on childcare costs and the role of the tax system, and examining the merits of child benefit, child tax allowances and other forms of payment to families with children.[3] In these articles Freedman argued, amongst other points, that 'tax relief was not going to meet the problem of lack of resources for childcare' and that the non-deductibility of childcare costs is 'perfectly consistent with the fact that other essential expenditure such as food and travel is also non-deductible'.[4]

Freedman with three co-authors also produced a report in 1988 for the Institute for Fiscal Studies (IFS) entitled *Property and Marriage: An Integrated Report*.[5] This appears to be Freedman's first publication with the IFS, a group with which she would work closely over her career, including as a Research Fellow,[6] a long-standing member and then chair of the IFS's influential Tax Law Review Committee[7] and a contributor to the Mirrlees Review.[8] The report was the end product of a Working Group on Family Property Law established by the IFS in 1985 and comprised of lawyers and economists. It is an impressive, early example of the type of scholarship for which Freedman would become well known.

The report sought to tackle the root causes of a wide range of problems in the operation of aspects of the law concerning property and marriage. The analysis is broad, thoughtful and insightful. As the report title suggests, Freedman et al come at the tax law issues from the perspective that tax law was not 'divorced' from other areas of law

[2] J Freedman, 'Finance Bill Note: Taxation of Husband and Wife' [1985] *BTR* 175; J Freedman, 'Independent Taxation: Lion or Mouse?: Clauses 24, 31–34, 41, 93 and 98 and Schedule 3' [1988] *BTR* 224; J Freedman and R Schuz, 'Settlements – a suitable case for treatment? Clauses 109–110' [1989] *BTR* 204. The first mention of Judith Freedman in the *British Tax Review* is in an editorial note by John Avery Jones at the start of volume 1 of 1984 announcing a new panel of case note writers, which included Freedman. Her first *BTR* publication was a case note on a Schedule E case, *Varnam v Deeble* [1984] STC 336, in volume 5 of that same year: [1984] *BTR* 309.

[3] J Freedman, 'Tax Relief and Childcare Costs – The Re-invention of Child Benefit' (1989) 1 *Journal of Child Law* 74; and J Freedman, 'Paying for Children and the Role of the Tax System: Where to Now' (1992) 4 *Journal of Child Law* 52.

[4] Freedman, 'Paying for Children and the Role of the Tax System' (n 3) 52.

[5] J Freedman, E Hammond, J Masson and N Morris, *Property and Marriage: An Integrated Approach* (London, Institute for Fiscal Studies, 1988).

[6] See, eg, J Freedman, *Employed or Self-employed? Tax Classification of Workers and the Changing Labour Market* (London, The Institute for Fiscal Studies, 2001); and J Freedman and E Chamberlain, 'Horizontal Equity and the Taxation of Employed and Self-Employed Workers' (1997) 18 *Fiscal Studies* 87.

[7] See www.ifs.org.uk/research/TLRC.

[8] C Crawford and J Freedman, 'Small Business Taxation' in S Adam et al (eds), *Dimensions of Tax Design: The Mirrlees Review* (Oxford, Oxford University Press for Institute for Fiscal Studies, 2010).

concerning the family.[9] The Working Group set out to examine the area of family property 'in its widest sense', considering the function and objectives of family law across legal fields generally treated as distinct – property, family, tax, social security and pensions, bankruptcy, succession and intestacy.[10] This view that tax law is not an island became a central theme of Freedman's career, in her writing, teaching and administrative work. The report's main proposal was to call for a new regime of family property for the UK – a so-called 'mixed community of gains' – which took as its starting point equal division of all property acquired during marriage.[11]

III. A Brief Summary of the Movement Towards Independent Taxation

When the IFS Working Group was established in 1985, the UK personal income tax system essentially ignored married women as individuals in their own right.[12] As discussed briefly in this section and in more detail in a doctoral thesis by Brice and a two-part article in the *British Tax Review* by Barr, from the time of the inception of the income tax in 1799, the income of a married woman was almost always simply added to her husband's income and he was taxed on the total.[13] The Income and Corporation Taxes Act 1988, section 279, formerly the Income and Corporation Taxes Act 1970, section 37, provided:

> A woman's income chargeable to income tax shall …, during which she is a married woman living with her husband, be deemed for income tax purposes to be his income and not to be her income.

Some notable procedural changes to the general rule were introduced over time, however, including giving a married woman the right to request to be assessed separately from her husband,[14] and, from 1971, allowing a married woman to be taxed separately on her earned income.[15]

Brice, Barr and Freedman et al also all made the point that by the 1970s treating the income of a wife as that of her husband clearly was deeply offensive to many women – and some men.[16] In so doing they cite the important work by the EOC in this area,

[9] Freedman, Hammond, Masson and Morris (n 5) iii.
[10] ibid 1.
[11] ibid 26–30.
[12] ibid 4.
[13] NA Barr, 'The Taxation of Married Women's Incomes – I' [1980] *BTR* 398 and 'The Taxation of Married Women's Incomes – II' [1980] *BTR* 478; AN Brice, 'The Tax Treatment of the Family Unit' (PhD thesis, University of London, 1982).
[14] ICTA 1988, s 283 formerly ICTA 1970, ss 38–39. For a detailed discussion of the history and operation of separate assessment see Brice (n 13) 112–47.
[15] ICTA 1988, s 287. For a detailed discussion of the option for separate taxation of a wife's earnings see Brice (n 13) 147–66.
[16] In 1982, Brice argued that by 1980 criticism of the aggregation rule had moved from primarily legal reasons (eg, inconsistency with the 1882 changes to the married woman's property regime) to social ones: see Brice (n 13) 404. Brice concludes (at 597) that 'the retention of the aggregation rule cannot be defended and, as it perpetuates an injustice against married persons, should be repealed' and (at 612) 'the repeal of the principle

and especially the 1977 EOC Report *Income Tax and Sex Discrimination*.[17] In fact, Freedman starts her 1988 *BTR* Finance Act note with this opening sentence: 'The Equal Opportunities Commission began pressing the case for reform of taxation of husband and wife in 1977'.[18] This chapter will return to the importance of the EOC's work, and that of its deputy chairman Elspeth Howe, shortly. In 1978 the Meade Committee also recognised that the idea that a woman on marriage becomes dependent on her husband had become less and less relevant with an increasing number of married women working outside the home coupled with changing social attitudes on the relationship between men and women.[19] The Meade Committee devoted a separate chapter in its final report to the subject of 'Tax Unit' and began the chapter by setting out eight conflicting criteria to be considered in choice of individual, spouse of family tax unit.[20]

Two important next steps paved the way for the eventual introduction of independent taxation. The first was Chancellor Geoffrey Howe's 1980 Green Paper *The Taxation of Husband and Wife*,[21] which was inconclusive but stimulated much debate.[22] The second was Chancellor Nigel Lawson's 1986 Green Paper 'Reform of Personal Taxation', which included as its centrepiece detailed proposals on a potential move to independent taxation of married women.[23] Freedman in her 1985 *BTR* Finance Bill asked why Lawson issued another Green Paper on this subject rather than a White Paper to iron out the detailed workings?[24] Nigel Lawson provided an explanation in his 1992 Memoirs:

> When I discussed this with Margaret [Thatcher], however, she made it clear that she did not like the idea at all, and felt that there was nothing really wrong with the status quo. She was emphatic that a White Paper was out of the question.[25]

In his 1988 Budget speech, Chancellor Lawson announced the government would introduce independent taxation of married women with effect from April 1990. Chancellor Lawson described the government's two objectives behind the change: first, it gave married women the same privacy and independence in their tax affairs as everyone else, and second, it brought to an end the way in which the tax system could penalise marriage.[26] The first objective is not one of the eight criteria listed in the Meade Report, but the second objective is reflected in the first criteria that 'the decision to marry or not to marry should not be affected by tax considerations'.[27] As will become

of husband's accountability should also follow, making husbands and wives individually responsible for their own tax affairs'. See also Freedman, Hammond, Masson and Morris (n 5) 114, 119; Barr (n 13) 486–87; and J Tiley, 'Tax, Marriage and the Family' (2006) 65 *CLJ* 289, 291.

[17] Equal Opportunities Commission, *Income Tax & Sex Discrimination* (Manchester, 1977).

[18] Freedman, 'Independent Taxation: Lion or Mouse?' (n 2) 224.

[19] J Meade (ed), *The Structure and Reform of Direct Taxation* (London, George Allen and Unwin, 1978) 377.

[20] ibid 377–78.

[21] HMSO, *Taxation of Husband and Wife* (Cmnd 8093, 1980).

[22] Freedman, Hammond, Masson and Morris (n 5) 119.

[23] HMSO, The Reform of Personal Taxation (Cmnd 9756, 1986).

[24] Freedman, 'Finance Bill Note' (n 2) 175–76. Freedman was also critical of the proposal for transferrable allowances: see Freedman, 'Finance Bill Note' (n 2) 176–80; and Freedman, 'Independent Taxation: Lion or Mouse?' (n 2) 225.

[25] N Lawson, *The View from No 11: Memoirs of a Tory Radical* (London, Corgi Books, 1992) 882.

[26] 15 HC Deb vol 129 col 997 (15 March 1988). See also Lawson (n 25) 881–87.

[27] Meade (n 19) 377, criteria 1.

clear, it is argued in this Chapter that the first objective was the primary driving force behind the change.

Thus, by the time Freedman et al's IFS Working Group Report was published in 1988, a fundamental shift in taxing married women's income was imminent. It will be recalled that the Working Group proposed a new property regime centred on a mixed community of gains. At first glance it might appear that moving away from joint taxation of spouses to independent taxation is incongruous with the Working Group's proposal; however, the authors were clearly aware that change was afoot and argued there was no incongruity. Freedman et al considered how the distinct areas of law could interact with this new property regime in an integrated way,[28] and in the case of tax law this meant aiming for taxation 'on the basis of current property rights of the parties as individuals'.[29] They argued against joint taxation of income based on a questionable assumption that couples share income equally, or taxation of individuals with transferable allowances not tied to actual ownership of property or genuine transfers of income.[30] Freedman repeated this position in her 1988 *BTR* Finance Note, pointing out that it was the underlying law of property not the tax law that was deficient: 'it is difficult to devise and operate a sensible and coherent system of independent taxation when underlying property law does not make clear what are the respective interests of the spouses in any given property'.[31]

The Finance Act 1988, section 32 provided that the Income and Corporation Taxes Act 1988 (ICTA 1988), section 279 (the provision treating the income of a woman living with her husband as his income for income tax purposes) shall not have effect for the year 1990–91 or any subsequent year of assessment. Husbands and wives were also given their own annual allowance for capital gains. Although Lawson's Green Paper proposals had envisioned independent taxation would be accompanied by transferable personal allowances between the spouses[32] – which, as already noted, Freedman criticised for not reflecting actual property rights – the final legislation did not include transferrable allowances. Lawson explains in his memoirs that transferrable allowances were left out of the 1988 reforms because the Inland Revenue said it was too complex to implement them until 1993 at the earliest and Lawson wanted some form of independent taxation up and running during the lifetime of the Parliament that had just begun.[33] Margaret Thatcher in her memoirs stated that she was opposed to fully transferrable allowances because they were too expensive.[34]

The practical 'halfway-house'[35] eventually pursued was independent taxation combined with a Married Couple's Allowance (MCA), which replaced the former

[28] Freedman, Hammond, Masson and Morris (n 5) 106–33.

[29] ibid 2.

[30] ibid 106–09, 128.

[31] Freedman, 'Independent Taxation: Lion or Mouse?' (n 2) 228, and citing the IFS Working Group report for more on this point.

[32] *The Reform of Personal Taxation* (n 23); and see analysis of the Green Paper proposals in Freedman, Hammond, Masson and Morris (n 5) 120–27.

[33] Lawson (n 25) 885. The technical complexity was also highlighted in Freedman, Hammond, Masson and Morris (n 5) 120.

[34] M Thatcher, *The Downing Street Years* (London, Harper Collins Publishers, 1993) 570. The cost was also highlighted as an issue in Freedman, Hammond, Masson and Morris (n 5) 126.

[35] Lawson (n 25) 885.

married man's allowance and was set at an amount equal to the difference between the single allowance and the married man's allowance. The purpose of the MCA apparently was to ensure that no married couple was worse off under the new regime.[36] The MCA was left unindexed and thus eroded in value over time; presently it is available only to those married couples or civil partners living together where at least one of the couple/partners was born before 6 April 1935.[37] In her 1988 *BTR* Finance Note and in her 1992 *Child Law* article, Freedman was highly critical of the MCA and suggested it would be best left to whither on the vine in favour of increasing child benefit 'which was the best method of meeting all the different claims for assistance of those with children, whether based on need or equity'.[38] She had advocated increasing child benefit in her 1989 article[39] and in her 1992 article, Freedman noted 'in fact the position set out [in her 1989 article] was very similar to that later expounded by the Chancellor in his 1991 Budget Statement'.[40] It should be noted that child benefit did increase substantially in the subsequent years, more than doubling from £9.65 for the first child in 1992 to £20.30 in 2010.[41] Since then the rate of increase has been nearly non-existent – the current amount of £21.05 for 2020–21 is just 75 pence higher than in 2010 – and the formerly universal child benefit has been means-tested against income since 2012.[42] Transferable allowances remained a discussion point within the Conservative Party, however, and a partial (10 per cent) transferrable allowance between some married spouses/civil partners eventually was introduced under the Coalition government led by Prime Minister David Cameron.[43]

IV. Elspeth Howe and the Movement Towards Independent Taxation

In this next section I pursue my primary argument – that Baroness Elspeth Howe played a highly significant and heretofore not fully appreciated role alongside her husband Geoffrey Howe in the move towards independent taxation of married women in the late 1960s and 1970s. Her direct and indirect contribution is revealed in the archival records,

[36] B Robinson and G Stark, 'The Tax Treatment of Marriage: What has the Chancellor Really Achieved?' (1988) 9 *Fiscal Studies* 48, 49.

[37] Income Tax Act 2007, ss 45–46.

[38] Freedman, 'Independent Taxation: Lion or Mouse?' (n 2) 225–28; and Freedman, 'Paying for Children and the Role of the Tax System' (n 3) 52.

[39] Freedman, 'Tax Relief and Childcare Costs' (n 3) 78–79.

[40] Freedman, 'Paying for Children and the Role of the Tax System' (n 3) 52.

[41] HM Revenue and Customs, KAI Benefits & Credits, 'Child Benefit Statistics' (28 February 2018), available at: assets.publishing.service.gov.uk/government/uploads/system/uploads/attachment_data/file/684138/Introduction_to_Child_Benefit_Small_Area_Data_2017.pdf.

[42] On means-testing see the high income child benefit charge in Income Tax (Earnings and Pensions) Act 2003, Part 10, Chapter 8, introduced by Finance Act 2012, s 8 and sch 1. See also criticism in G Loutzenhiser, 'Finance Act notes: section 8 and Schedule 1: high income child benefit charge' [2012] *BTR* 370.

[43] Income Tax Act 2007, ss 55A–55E, introduced by Finance Act 2014, section 11. See also criticism of the partially transferrable allowances in G Loutzenhiser, 'Transferable personal allowances: a small step in the wrong direction' [2015] *BTR* 110. For an opposing view see L Beighton and D Draper, 'Transferable personal allowances: a small step in the right direction' [2015] *BTR* 580.

including those related to the work of two significant but previously overlooked internal Conservative Party committees considering this issue – the 1977 Committee on Women and Tax and the 1968 Cripps Committee.

I begin advancing this theory with this remarkable excerpt from Nigel Lawson's 1992 Memoirs in which he suggested that Prime Minister Margaret Thatcher was hostile to Geoffrey Howe's and his proposals for moving to independent taxation of married women, partly (in Lawson's view) because Thatcher believed Elspeth Howe to be the inspiration for them:

> There had already been one Green Paper on the subject of the taxation of husband and wife, produced by Geoffrey in 1980, but the response had been inconclusive. It certainly showed that the status quo had very few friends, but, as so often, there was no agreement whatever over the various options for change that were clearly set out. Despite Geoffrey's strong desire to right this wrong, the unhelpful response to his Green Paper, coupled with Margaret's pronounced hostility to doing anything at all *(partly, I suspect, because she believed it was all inspired by Geoffrey's wife, Elspeth)* ensured that no further action was taken. It therefore fell to me, when I became Chancellor in 1983, to pick up Geoffrey's baton (emphasis added).[44]

This a curious statement – was the move to independent taxation of married women really inspired by Elspeth Howe, as Margaret Thatcher apparently believed? And why would this lead to hostility about the idea on Thatcher's part? On this second point, it does seem that Elspeth Howe and Margaret Thatcher did not have a good personal relationship. In Geoffrey's Howe obituary in *The Guardian* in 2015, Elspeth Howe is described as his 'fiercely strong-minded wife … who notoriously did not get on with Thatcher'.[45] The nature of Margaret Thatcher and Elspeth Howe's relationship is not critical to the central argument advanced in this chapter on Elspeth's role in the move towards independent taxation, however, and is not pursued further here. It is also clear from the archival records that Thatcher was not in favour of the move to independent taxation, as Lawson wrote in his memoirs. For example, in a letter from Lawson to Thatcher dated 26 July 1983 requesting her approval for him to begin working on a new consultative document on independent taxation Thatcher memos 'Yes, but I am very much *against* the proposed changes MT'.[46]

In his 1994 Memoirs, Geoffrey Howe refuted the idea that Elspeth was behind the move to independent taxation, writing that he had been 'personally committed to the idea' for years:

> The wide-ranging reform programme, foreshadowed in our 1987 manifesto, was set in train. I was particularly pleased that Nigel Lawson had at last been able, in his 1988 Budget, to implement the plan on which we had both been working, for the genuinely independent taxation of married women. The previous system had long been resented as unfair. As long ago as 1980 I had published the first Green Paper proposing action to remedy this. Nigel published a second, more fully developed set of proposals in 1986. But Margaret had always been inexplicably hostile to this reform, as to a number of others demanded by her own sex. *Nigel suggests this was because she attributed the whole notion to my 'feminist' spouse, Elspeth* [citing the

[44] Lawson (n 25) 882.

[45] 'Lord Howe of Aberavon obituary' *The Guardian* (10 October 2015).

[46] Letter from N Lawson to M Thatcher dated 26 July 1983, with Thatcher annotations (Records of the Prime Minister's Office: Correspondence and Papers, 1979–1997, National Archives, ref PREM 19/993).

above quote from Lawson's memoirs]. *I had in fact been personally committed to the idea, at least since 1968. For in that year the Cripps Committee, of which I was a member, had recommended just such a change in our report, Fair Share for the Fair Sex.* This is a not untypical example of the pace of the reform process in our country: virtually two decades of sustained effort by people, including Nigel and myself, each with a well-considered personal commitment to the change (emphasis added).[47]

Relying on recently released archive material, the remainder of this chapter proceeds to advance the argument that Elspeth Howe did indeed play a highly significant role in this change, most notably through her work on the EOC but also in supporting the Conservative Party's efforts on this issue in other ways, including the 1968 Cripps Committee that Geoffrey Howe refers to in the above quote from his memoirs. This is not to take away from what is clearly Geoffrey Howe's (and Nigel Lawson's) commitment to this issue; however, it is argued here that the historical records indicate Howe's commitment was more of a team effort with his wife as opposed to the solely personal one he portrays in his memoirs.

Who then is this 'feminist' Elspeth Howe, the alleged inspiration behind the move to independent taxation? Elspeth Rosamund Morton Shand was born 8 February 1932. She married Geoffrey Howe in 1953 and they had three children. Lady Howe served in a number of roles in her career, including on the Broadcasting Standards Commission and as a Justice of the Peace in London from 1964 until 2002. She was appointed a CBE in the 1999 New Year's Honours List and in 2001 she was made a life peer, as Baroness Howe of Idlicote. At the time of writing Baroness Howe continues to serve as a cross-party peer in the House of Lords, with a particular focus on young people and problem gambling.[48] In a newspaper article published at the time of her appointment to the Broadcasting Standards Commission, Baroness Howe was described by family friends as having 'high moral standards and a great sense of right and wrong' and also as 'a feminist – but not a tiresome feminist'.[49] Importantly for present purposes, the writer of that newspaper article goes on to say '[h]er feminism has taken practical form in her membership of bodies such as the Equal Opportunities Commission'.[50]

Elspeth Howe was first deputy chairman of the Equal Opportunities Commission from 1975 to 1979. As noted above, Freedman, Brice and Barr cite the work of the EOC at this time as a highly significant development in the movement towards independent taxation. The EOC had been established in 1975 by the Harold Wilson Labour government, under the chairmanship of Betty Lockwood.[51] In its landmark 1977 publication *Income Tax and Sex Discrimination*, the EOC was highly critical of the tax system and provided many examples of women (and men) unhappy with the tax regime as it applied to married couples. The EOC stated:

[O]ur present income tax system evolved over a period when paid work outside the home was the exception rather than the norm for married women. It also reflects the then pervasive

[47] G Howe, *Conflict of Loyalty* (London, Macmillan, 1994) 566.
[48] See www.parliament.uk/biographies/lords/baroness-howe-of-idlicote/3610.
[49] 'Media: A Tory feminist for TV's watchdog: Michael Leapman profiles Lady Elspeth Howe, the incoming chair of the Broadcasting Standards Council' *The Independent* (9 June 1993).
[50] ibid.
[51] Howe, *Conflict of Loyalty* (n 47) 123.

> social assumption that women, married or single, were essentially dependants, and, if they were not, were likely to become so. This assumption, which is derived from the attitudes dominant for over a century, permeates the entire structure of personal taxation, and is now to be found embodied in s 37 of the Income and Corporation Taxes Act 1970 … It is not surprising that a system based upon this assumption should be regarded as, at best, humiliating, and at worst discriminatory, and occasion mounting criticism and complaint. Indeed, it is fair to say that personal taxation is the one major area of Government policy in which no progress has been registered since the passage of the Sex Discrimination Act two years ago.[52]

The EOC continued:

> Nor, it should be noted, do the complaints come exclusively from women. Naturally, women form the larger group of persons who have written to complain about the humiliation involved in the assumption, at all stages of their dealings with the Inland Revenue, that joint income is the property of the husband, as well as about the anomalies involved (eg, where a working woman whose husband is unemployed is not usually given the reliefs to which she is entitled without considerable correspondence and delay). Men have also written to complain of the burden of having to take responsibility for their wives' financial affairs.[53]

The EOC also cited examples of problems in the Inland Revenue's communications concerning married women's tax affairs:

> Perhaps the most common complaint made by married women about their position concerns the Inland Revenue's practice of conducting correspondence with the husband only:
>
> > I am in receipt of (the Inland Revenue) form relating to my income tax papers and I note the remark 'If you are a married woman living with your husband he should complete the form as if it were addressed to him'. Does the fact that you are 'a married woman living with your husband' pre-suppose that you have relinquished every vestige of intelligence?
>
> …
>
> In the latest print of the form referred to in this case, the Inland Revenue have changed the wording to 'If you are a married woman, living with you husband, will you please ask him to complete this form as if it were addressed to him'. The message is more courteously phrased, but otherwise unchanged.
>
> ….
>
> It may be suggested that such complaints are trivial. But what many married women object to is the assumption that they do not exist as far as the Inland Revenue is concerned.[54]

The EOC outlined a number of possible reforms, most based on separate assessment of married persons but others based on a joint model, and concluded:

> A taxation system for the future, which is based on the proposition that the partners in a marriage are entitled to be treated as individuals in their own right, is not likely therefore to weaken or damage the unity of the family. On the contrary, it will prevent a good deal of the unnecessary humiliation and distress caused by the present arrangements. It is also much more likely to be in tune with emerging social trends.[55]

[52] Equal Opportunities Commission, *Income Tax & Sex Discrimination* (n 17) 4.
[53] ibid 4–5.
[54] ibid 19–20.
[55] ibid 55.

In a follow up document *Responses to EOC Consultative Document Income Tax and Sex Discrimination*,[56] the EOC reported near unanimous support for moving to the individual as basic tax unit:

> The fundamental question posed the Commission's Consultative Document was that of the basic tax unit; should this be the family or the individual. The view that this unit should be the individual was almost unanimous. This is perhaps the only aspect of the response received which shows a consistency throughout almost all the comments made.[57]

The EOC concluded:

> From the response received the Commission is convinced … that there is a marked preference for a revised system which would have the individual as the basic unit. The Commission believes that these opinions can no longer be ignored and hopes that work can commence to speed the prospect of acceptable reform.[58]

In a press release from the EOC in July 1978, Lady Howe was quoted as saying privacy 'was the major remaining problem' and '[t]he only way a woman can have any privacy in her tax affairs, and have access to as much information about her husband's income as he has about hers is through separate assessment'.[59] Lady Howe was further quoted in the press release:

> The Commission still believes that there must be a fundamental reform of the tax system to get rid of the clause stating 'a woman's income chargeable to tax shall be deemed for income tax purposes to be his (her husband's) income, and not her income' (S 37 Tax Act 1970). The Commission's December [1977] booklet 'Sex Discrimination and Income Tax' initiated the public debate and set out three main options for reform, and the task is now for the government to make the basic decision on how to tax married couples. Is the tax unit to be the couple or the individual?[60]

This brings us to Elspeth Howe's contribution to the work of the first internal Conservative Party committee that I argue played an important role in the move to independent taxation but has drawn little attention in the previous literature – the Committee on Women and Tax.

Geoffrey Howe, then Shadow Chancellor, wrote a letter dated 9 September 1977 to Baroness Janet Young at the Conservative and Unionist Central Office asking for Baroness Young's views on establishing a 'semi-detached' study on 'the future balance of the tax system as between the sexes'.[61] Importantly, in this early letter proposing the formation of what would become the Committee on Women and Tax, Geoffrey Howe makes specific reference to the work of Elspeth's Howe's EOC: 'I know that the Equal

[56] Equal Opportunities Commission, *Responses to EOC Consultative Document Income Tax & Sex Discrimination* (Manchester, 1978).

[57] ibid 31.

[58] ibid 37.

[59] Equal Opportunities Commission, Press Release 'EOC response to tax changes for married women' dated 3 July 1978 (Papers of G Howe, Special Collection, Bodleian Library, University of Oxford, Shelfmark MS. Howe dep 154).

[60] ibid.

[61] Letter from G Howe to J Young dated 9 September 1977 (papers of G Howe, Special Collection, Bodleian Library, University of Oxford, Shelfmark MS. Howe dep 154).

Opportunities Commission has produced and is producing some material on this subject and that the [Labour] Government is doing quite a lot of thinking about it'.[62]

In the letter Howe wrote that 'it is a difficult theme slightly outside the main theme of our tax policy work. Yet ideally it should not be ignored by our Party'.[63] He also wrote in the letter 'I am anxious that the field should not be left entirely to feminist organisations on the political left when I know that Conservative women are genuinely concerned about this theme'.[64] Indeed the Conservative Party at this time had a Tax Policy group, which met frequently, but tellingly in the minutes and papers of the period from 1977 to 1979 there is almost no mention of the tax unit generally and no mention at all of a plan to move to independent taxation.[65] Instead, the main focus of the Tax Policy group in this period was on shifting from direct to indirect taxation, corporate tax reform, alleviating capital taxation and reducing tax rates, especially the top rate of income tax.[66] Howe further wrote in his letter of 9 September 1977 that he envisioned the study would produce 'some kind of publishable report which would demonstrate our firm interest without necessarily leading to immediate commitments'.[67]

Howe wrote again to Baroness Young on 17 November 1977 to confirm that Margaret Thatcher, then Party leader and Leader of the Opposition, and Keith Joseph, who had overall responsibility for Conservative Party policy and research, approved the establishment of the Committee on Women and Tax.[68] This letter is also copied to Thatcher. In it, Howe asked Baroness Young to go ahead with inviting the members he mentioned in an earlier letter dated 2 November.[69] Howe's suggestions for members included Shelagh Roberts, who had been a member of the 1968 Cripps Committee – more on that committee later – and she later agreed to become chair of the Committee on Women and Tax.[70] In addition to taking an active role in constituting the committee's membership, Howe was also involved in drafting the committee's terms of reference.[71]

In a letter the following month dated 19 April 1978 to the Right Honourable Lord Thorneycroft at the Conservative and Unionist Central Office, Howe highlighted press campaigns by *Women's Own* magazine and *The Sunday Times* 'which make very clear the

[62] ibid.

[63] ibid.

[64] ibid.

[65] See, eg, letter from G Howe to DG Lindsay dated 17 May 1976 (papers of G Howe, Special Collection, Bodleian Library, University of Oxford, Shelfmark MS. Howe dep 148). On the Tax Policy group and taxation of the family, a brief summary of a 1977 OECD paper on the treatment of the tax unit in OECD member countries was circulated to the group by P Cropper on 2 May 1977 and a short paper by A Sewill on the French quotient system was circulated to the group by P Cropper on 9 June 1977 (papers of G Howe, Special Collection, Bodleian Library, University of Oxford, Shelfmark MS. Howe dep 148, 149).

[66] See, eg, letter from P Hordern MP to P Cropper dated 31 March 1977 with an accompanying outline of policy goals (papers of G Howe, Bodleian Library, University of Oxford, Shelfmark MS. Howe dep 149).

[67] Letter from G Howe to J Young dated 9 September 1977 (n 61).

[68] Letter from G Howe to J Young dated 17 November 1977 with approval confirmed in a letter from K Joseph to G Howe dated 15 November 1977 (papers of G Howe, Special Collection, Bodleian Library, University of Oxford, Shelfmark MS. Howe dep 154).

[69] Letter from G Howe to J Young dated 17 November 1977 (n 68).

[70] ibid.

[71] Letter from J Young to G Howe dated 11 November 1977, in which Baroness Young thanked Howe for sending her the draft terms of reference, and letter from P Cropper to J Young dated 30 November 1977 stating 'Sir Geoffrey Howe has revised the Terms of Reference for the "Taxation of Women" Committee as enclosed' (papers of G Howe, Special Collection, Bodleian Library, University of Oxford, Shelfmark MS. Howe dep 154).

strength of the developing campaign for changes in the tax system which give married women a better deal than at the present'.[72] Howe further noted that the Committee on Women and Tax were studying this issue:

> We shall, of course, be considering their recommendation very carefully and taking advantage of the advice which Arthur Cockfield is also offering on the subject – so that we should be in a position, fairly soon, to bring forward at least some proposals for consideration. There are obviously some landmines in the path about which we shall have to think pretty carefully but it should be possible to find a way through.[73]

Baroness Young and Nigel Lawson MP are also copied into the letter.

Other letters further indicate a close connection between the work of the EOC and the Committee on Women and Tax. Betty Lockwood, then chair of the EOC, wrote to Geoffrey Howe on 13 December 1977, enclosing a copy of their publication *Income Tax and Sex Discrimination* and writing that the EOC 'would be most interested in your own response to the options set out in this document'.[74] Betty Lockwood continued:

> I hope you will agree with us that the case for reform is a substantial one, and I would particularly appreciate your considered opinion on what you think is the most feasible form that a change should take.[75]

Geoffrey Howe replied to Betty Lockwood on 16 December 1977, thanking her for sending him a copy of *Income Tax and Sex Discrimination*.[76] He informed Miss Lockwood that the Conservative Party had set up a Working Party on this general subject, chaired by Shelagh Roberts. Howe also wrote:

> I shall be keeping in close touch with the work of that Group *for whom your document will be essential reading*. In one way or another, we shall be in touch with you along roughly the lines that you suggest in due course (emphasis added).[77]

Howe copied Shelagh Roberts into that letter in order that she may take advantage of Miss Lockwood's offer of extra copies of the EOC publication.[78] Further, on 10 January 1978 the committee member from the Conservative Research Department, Peter Cropper, wrote to his fellow committee member Shelagh Roberts attaching some notes on the EOC booklet *Income Tax and Sex Discrimination*.[79] It is beyond doubt that the committee was well aware of the EOC's work and actively considered it from the earliest stages of the committee's work.

Another fascinating aspect of the contribution of the EOC work to the Conservative Party thinking on this issue is the steps Geoffrey Howe took to ensure the EOC's work

[72] Letter from G Howe to Rt Hon Lord Thorneycroft dated 19 April 1978 (papers of G Howe, Special Collection, Bodleian Library, University of Oxford, Shelfmark MS. Howe dep 154).

[73] ibid.

[74] Letter from B Lockwood to G Howe dated 13 December 1977 (papers of G Howe, Special Collection, Bodleian Library, University of Oxford, Shelfmark MS. Howe dep 154).

[75] ibid.

[76] Letter from G Howe to B Lockwood dated 16 December 1977 (papers of G Howe, Special Collection, Bodleian Library, University of Oxford, Shelfmark MS. Howe dep 154).

[77] ibid.

[78] ibid.

[79] Letter from P Cropper to S Roberts dated 10 January 1978 (papers of G Howe, Special Collection, Bodleian Library, University of Oxford, Shelfmark MS. Howe dep 154).

(ie, Elspeth Howe's work) was properly attributed on the record. This emerges quite clearly in his correspondence with Shelagh Roberts dated 8 August 1978 and 4 January 1979 related to the committee's forthcoming report, wherein Geoffrey Howe specifically requested the committee refer to the EOC's work in its report. On 8 August 1978 he wrote:

> A reference to the EOC discussion document might not come amiss (not because I have any reason to publicise their work but simply to show that your Committee were aware of it).[80]

On 4 January 1979 Geoffrey Howe wrote again to Shelagh Roberts suggesting the committee reference the EOC's work in its final report, which was due to be published imminently, but this time pressing more strongly and, importantly, specifically mentioning Elspeth by name:

> One other thought is prompted in my mind by all the EOC activity on this front. Should not your own report make at least some reference to the EOC consultative document, not least because – I write from memory – pages 4 and 5 of your own Report seem to draw pretty heavily on the text of that document? *I am not, of course, defending Elspeth's copyright, still less her amour propre- but anxious to protect you from possible criticism!* (emphasis added).[81]

Thus, it appears clear from this correspondence that Geoffrey Howe saw the EOC's work as not just his wife's work ('Elsepth's copyright') but her '*amour propre*' – that is to say her sense of pride/self-worth. This is a remarkable and illuminating choice of words. Unsurprisingly, the Committee on Women and Tax's final report published later in January 1979 duly did make reference to the EOC's work: 'The Committee also acknowledge some very helpful information contained in "Income Tax and Sex Discrimination" published by the Equal Opportunities Commission'.[82] The committee's main recommendation was very much in line with Howe's 1980 Green Paper that shortly followed. The committee proposed 'to treat adults as individuals for the purpose of tax on earned income', recommending every adult person have a uniform personal tax allowance, and stating that this proposal 'will remove the major discrimination against women'.[83]

The Conservative Party's 1979 general election manifesto briefing included one reference to the taxation of married women, which specifically referred to the work of the Committee on Women and Tax and promised a consultative Green Paper:

> **Q. What are you going to do about the taxation of women?**
>
> **A.** We recognise the strong feelings aroused by the present tax treatment of married women. However, it will be very difficult to find a system which will please everybody – married women at work, married women at home, single women, widows. We must not rush ahead without very thorough consultation.

[80] Letter from G Howe to S Roberts dated 8 August 1978 (papers of G Howe, Special Collection, Bodleian Library, University of Oxford, Shelfmark MS. Howe dep 154).

[81] Letter from G Howe to S Roberts dated 4 January 1979 (papers of G Howe, Special Collection, Bodleian Library, University of Oxford, Shelfmark MS. Howe dep 154).

[82] *Women and Tax*, Report of the Committee on Women and Tax Established in January 1978 by Baroness Young, Deputy Chairman of the Conservative Party, Under the Ageis of the Women's National Advisory Committee of the Conservative Party and Published by the Committee, 3 (papers of G Howe, Special Collection, Bodleian Library, University of Oxford, Shelfmark MS. Howe dep 154).

[83] Women and Tax (n 82) 8.

> A Party committee under the aegis of the Women's National Advisory Committee, chaired by Miss Shelagh Roberts, GLC, recently (January 1979) produced a discussion paper 'Women and Tax'. This recommended a uniform personal tax allowance for every adult person.
>
> Sir Geoffrey Howe has spoken of the importance of fiscal neutrality between the working wife and the wife who stays at home to look after her family.
>
> **COMMITMENT**
>
> A Conservative government would wish to produce a consultative Green Paper on this subject, as a basis for action.[84]

Howe became Chancellor of the Exchequer on 4 May 1979 in Margaret Thatcher's new Conservative government. A review of the minutes from the Chancellor's regular morning meetings reveals the first mention of the taxation of married women was in the meeting on 18 September 1979: 'It was envisaged that a consultative Green Paper would be issued in mid- or late-1980'.[85] This was followed by a reference to an attached copy of the wording of the 1979 general election manifesto briefing just quoted.

A final and even more remarkable (and more public) example of the Chancellor trumpeting his wife's work on the EOC occurred the following year during his Budget Speech in the House of Commons on 26 March 1980, wherein he announced his plan to issue his Green Paper on the Taxation of Husband and Wife. Howe stated:

> We have also been reviewing the treatment for tax purposes of husband and wife [presumably a reference to the Committee on Tax and Women]. This is a complex and important subject. *I am grateful in particular to the Equal Opportunities Commission for the light which its publications have shed on this aspect of sex discrimination. In view of my relationship with the former deputy chairman of that body I hope that it is not improper for me to mention its work, but, as I have observed, it is easier to define the problems than to find the answers.* Certainly, radical changes should not be made in haste. I propose, therefore, to issue later this year a Green Paper on this subject. I hope that it will stimulate further constructive debate leading us ultimately to acceptable solutions (emphasis added).[86]

Professor John Tiley, writing in the *British Tax Review* in 1998 and without the benefit of access to the archival material just discussed, picked up on Lawson's suggestion that Thatcher thought Elspeth Howe was behind this idea, and made this throw-away comment in a footnote: 'Although Lawson seems to think Thatcher was mistaken as to the provenance of the idea [ie Elspeth Howe] this is perhaps belied by Geoffrey Howe's expression of thanks to the Equal Opportunities Commission in his 1980 Budget speech'![87]

[84] Reproduced in Minutes of Chancellor's Morning Meeting 18 September 1979, prepared by P Cropper (HM Treasury: Private Office of the Chancellor of the Exchequer: Sir Geoffrey Howe's records, Chancellor of the Exchequer's morning meetings 1979, National Archives, ref T 639/3).

[85] Minutes of Chancellor's Morning Meeting 18 September 1979, prepared by P Cropper (HM Treasury: Private Office of the Chancellor of the Exchequer: Sir Geoffrey Howe's records, Chancellor of the Exchequer's morning meetings 1979, National Archives, ref T 639/3).

[86] G Howe, Budget Speech (26 March 1980) Hansard HC [981/1439–91, 1477–78], available at: www.margaretthatcher.org/document/109498.

[87] J Tiley, 'Away from a virtuous tax system?' [1998] *BTR* 317, fn 9.

Lady Howe stepped down from her full-time post as deputy chairman when Geoffrey Howe became Chancellor of the Exchequer in 1979. In his memoirs, Geoffrey Howe described Elspeth's decision to give up her EOC position as a 'disagreeable side-effect' of his becoming Chancellor.[88] Both Howes recognised that the EOC was bound by its nature 'to be controversial from time to time' and 'might have cause to bring enforcement proceedings against government itself'.[89] Thus, 'Elspeth felt obliged, and rightly so, to give up her position as deputy chairman'.[90] Geoffrey Howe recalled that Elspeth 'had much enjoyed the work' and also noted her decision was sharply criticised at the time by 'some "feminist" opinion', who called into question the sincerity of her commitment to the cause of equal opportunities.[91]

In addition to these repeated references to the EOC's work, there are other examples in Geoffrey Howe's personal papers of Elspeth Howe's direct involvement in Conservative Party tax policy discussions. For example, on 21 January 1977, in a letter to Peter Cropper at the Conservative Research Department, Howe wrote that he gave a copy of their paper on married women's tax allowances to Elspeth in order for her to secure comments from others at the EOC on it.[92] Another example is evident from a letter dated 14 March 1978 from Geoffrey Howe to Peter Cropper wherein Howe stated that 'Elspeth has had a quick look at Arthur Cockfield's paper C/Tax 6'.[93] At the time Cockfield is known to be providing advice to the Committee on Women and Tax, as evidenced in Geoffrey Howe's letter dated 19 April 1978 to the Right Honourable Lord Thorneycroft at the Conservative and Unionist Central Office referred to above.[94] Howe set out two questions that Elspeth raised about this document and its impact on families where the mother goes to work and the father stays home to look after the children, and also for single parent families.[95]

Along with these letters, in the archive of Geoffrey Howe's papers from that period is a six-page document entitled 'Sex Discrimination: A Tory attitude for 1978. Some Notes by Elsepth Howe'.[96] In that document reference was made to the Conservative's 'good record not to be cast away', including the 1968 Cripps Committee.[97] The document laid out several reasons for the Conservative Party to pursue women's rights for electoral reasons, and covers a wide range of topics that should be considered, including public appointment of women, employment rights, pensions and taxation.[98] It encouraged

[88] Howe, *Conflict of Loyalty* (n 47) 123.

[89] ibid. Similar reasoning is expressed by G Howe in a 1979 letter to a friend: see letter from G Howe to J Doren dated 3 August 1979 (papers of G Howe, Special Collection, Bodleian Library, University of Oxford, Shelfmark MS. Howe dep 42).

[90] Howe, *Conflict of Loyalty* (n 47) 123.

[91] ibid 123–24.

[92] Letter from G Howe to P Cropper dated 21 January 1977 (papers of G Howe, Special Collection, Bodleian Library, University of Oxford, Shelfmark MS. Howe dep 154).

[93] Letter from G Howe to P Cropper dated 14 March 1978 (papers of G Howe, Special Collection, Bodleian Library, University of Oxford, Shelfmark MS. Howe dep 154).

[94] Text at n 72.

[95] Letter from G Howe to P Cropper dated 14 March 1978 (n 93).

[96] Document entitled 'Sex Discrimination: A Tory attitude for 1978. Some Notes by Elsepth Howe' (papers of G Howe, Special Collection, Bodleian Library, University of Oxford, Shelfmark MS. Howe dep 154).

[97] ibid.

[98] ibid.

the Party to 'take a constructive and generally sympathetic attitude in this field' and 'consider how far society/law should do more for the family'.[99] On taxation, it asked 'is it right for tax returns to be the sole responsibility of the husband or indeed for him to be legally entitled to a wife's tax rebate in certain circumstances?'[100]

What then of Geoffrey Howe's 1994 Memoirs, wherein he downplayed Margaret Thatcher's belief that Elspeth was behind the whole notion by pointing to his personal commitment to this issue dating back to the 1968 Cripps Committee? In his memoirs, Geoffrey Howe discussed the findings of the Cripps Committee:

> The third 'disadvantaged' group which I had the chance to consider was (much too coyly) identified in the title of our report, *Fair Share for the Fair Sex*. This was the product of a committee set up by Ted Heath under the chairmanship of Sir Anthony Cripps QC, to make recommendations to the Conservative Party about legal discriminations against women. Probably our most important recommendations when we reported in 1969 were for the use of the electoral roll (instead of property qualification) as the basis of jury service; and for changes in the discriminatory tax treatment of married women. This last proposal had to wait eleven years before I was able, in my 1980 Budget, to take the first steps towards implementing the change. Eight years later the job was completed by Nigel Lawson.[101]

As Howe described, the Cripps Committee's final report issued in 1969 outlined a number of recommendations aimed at reducing discrimination against women across a wide spectrum of issues.[102] The topics addressed were civic rights and the criminal law, personal rights, family law, property in marriage, and taxation.[103] On taxation, the committee's first recommendation was: 'Married women should be treated for tax purposes as individuals or single persons'.[104] Notably Shelagh Roberts, who would later chair the 1977 Conservative Party on Women and Tax, was also a member of the Cripps Committee.[105] Interestingly, Shelagh Roberts and Elspeth Howe were also both speakers at the 15 June 1966 Conservative Women's Annual Conference.[106]

Although Geoffrey Howe cites his involvement in the 1968 Cripps Committee as evidence of his long-standing 'personal commitment' to addressing the discriminatory tax treatment of married woman in refuting the suggestion that Elspeth Howe was behind the whole idea of the move to independent taxation, Howe's position is undermined by a letter dated 6 May 1969 from the chair of the Cripps Committee, Sir Anthony Cripps, thanking Geoffrey Howe for his work for the committee.[107] At the end of the letter Cripps wrote: 'Please also thank Elspeth from me for much assistance

[99] ibid.
[100] ibid.
[101] Howe, *Conflict of Loyalty* (n 47) 43.
[102] Cripps Committee Report, February 1969 (Conservative Party Archive, Special Collection, Bodleian Library, University of Oxford, Shelfmark CC0 170/9/2/1).
[103] ibid 3.
[104] ibid 46–48, 57. Other recommendations included changes to housekeeper relief, post-war credits, family allowance, maintenance payments, age-related reliefs and child relief: 57–58.
[105] Cripps Committee Report (n 102) 1.
[106] Letter from unnamed writer to E Heath and copied to B Sewill, J Prior and DR Brant dated 8 June 1966 with enclosed conference handbook (Conservative Party Archive, Special Collection, Bodleian Library, University of Oxford, Shelfmark CRD 3/38/2).
[107] Letter from A Cripps to G Howe dated 6 May 1969 (papers of G Howe, Special Collection, Bodleian Library, University of Oxford, Shelfmark MS. Howe dep 37).

in support of you. It really was great fun for us all. And Howe (Geoffrey) and Howe (Elspeth) too, I hope!'[108]

Thus, there is clear evidence that even as early as 1968 the Howes were working together on Conservative Party policies aimed at addressing the discriminatory treatment of women. This included what Howe described in his memoirs as one of the most important recommendations of the Cripps Committee – ending the discriminatory tax treatment of married women.

V. Conclusion

Professor Freedman's early writing on tax and the family may not be as well known as her later writing but exhibited key hallmarks of it. It was often interdisciplinary and focused on solving tax issues by dealing with root problems in the larger legal landscape, such as with property rights in marriage. This chapter used Freedman's work on independent taxation of married women as a springboard to investigate the highly significant and heretofore underappreciated role Baroness Elspeth Howe played in the move to independent taxation during the late 1960s to early 1980s. It is beyond doubt that Geoffrey Howe and Nigel Lawson were the driving forces behind changing the legislation deeming a married woman's income to be her husband's for tax purpose. But despite protestations to the contrary from her husband in his published memoirs, the archival records show that Elsepth Howe's work behind the scenes and with the highly influential Equal Opportunities Commission – work championed by her husband Geoffrey at every opportunity – had a major impact on the Conservative Party's policy work on this topic during this crucial, formative time period.

[108] ibid.

2

Does an Inheritance Tax Have a Future? Practical Options to Consider

EMMA CHAMBERLAIN

I. Background

A. Introduction

The taxation of wealth and transfers of wealth is an issue that excites strong passions. It is sometimes said that inheritance tax (IHT) is 'almost uniquely unpopular'.[1] It has been described as 'Britain's most hated tax'.[2] The first Mirrlees Report on Taxation of Wealth[3] published in 2010 noted the unpopularity of IHT, partly due to the perception that its burden falls disproportionately on the middle classes.

The tax is perhaps most resolutely opposed by those who are least likely to pay it. In a 2015 YouGov poll of UK voters, 59 per cent of respondents felt that IHT was unfair, compared with just 22 per cent who thought it was fair.[4] Academics also seem divided on whether and how to tax wealth.[5]

Despite its unpopularity, IHT raises relatively little revenue. In 1895–96 the £14 million from death duties represented about 35 per cent of Revenue taxes. By 1968,

[1] Office for Tax Simplification, 'Inheritance Tax Review – First Report: Overview of the Tax and Dealing with Administration' (*GOV.UK*, November 2018), available at: assets.publishing.service.gov.uk/government/uploads/system/uploads/attachment_data/file/758368/Final_Inheritance_Tax_report_-_print_copy.pdf. One blog writer commented, 'if you are a well-advised aristocrat with a few 100,000 acres the system is positively generous. If you are a widow in Guildford with only one dormant asset, your home, you will be punished – punished at 40%': John Blundell, 'Inheritance Tax Only Makes the Rich Richer' (Institute of Economic Affairs, 1 May 2005) www.iea.org.uk/in-the-media/media-coverage/inheritance-tax-only-makes-the-rich-richer.

[2] Emma Agyemang, 'Inheritance Tax: What Does the Future Hold?' *Financial Times* (11 July 2019), available at: www.ft.com/content/10370c58-a235-11e9-974c-ad1c6ab5efd1.

[3] R Boadway, E Chamberlain and C Emmerson, 'Taxation of Wealth and Wealth Transfers' in JA Mirrlees et al (eds), *Tax by Design: The Mirrlees Review* (Oxford, Oxford University Press for Institute for Fiscal Studies, 2011).

[4] Stephan Shakespeare, 'Voters in All Parties Think Inheritance Tax Unfair' (*YouGov*, 19 March 2015), available at: yougov.co.uk/topics/politics/articles-reports/2015/03/19/inheritance-tax-most-unfair.

[5] See, eg, N Lee, 'Inheritance Tax – An Equitable Tax No Longer: Time for Abolition?' (2007) 27 *Legal Studies* 678. A pro IHT view is espoused by S White, 'Moral Objections to Inheritance Tax' in M O'Neill and

estate duty produced only about £382 million or about 5.8 per cent of total Revenue receipts. The yield in 2018–19 stands at a record £5.4 billion but now comprises less than 1 per cent of total tax revenues. Fewer than 5 per cent of deaths result in the payment of IHT. There are 588,000 deaths each year, of which 275,500 are required to complete an IHT form; of these only 24,500 result in payment of any tax.[6]

In January 2018 the then Chancellor asked the Office for Tax Simplification (OTS) to review the current arrangements on UK IHT, noting the complexity of the regime. The subsequent consultation garnered more responses than any other OTS review demonstrating the strength of public feeling on this topic.[7] In January 2020 the All Party Parliamentary Group published a report (the APPG Report)[8] on the reform of IHT co-written by the current author discussing some alternatives. One option often discussed is a form of accessions tax (AT). Some of the design issues raised by AT are considered in section II but for reasons of space section III explores two other options – capital gains tax (CGT) and flat rate gift tax.

B. The History of Death Duties in the UK

A brief review of the past may be helpful. From 1694, a succession of different duties arose on death such as probate duty, legacy duty and later succession duty but these did not capture lifetime gifts. In 1894 Harcourt tried to simplify the structure by introducing a new estate duty with rates rising from 1 per cent to 8 per cent (for estates over £1 million), and he abolished all other duties save for legacy and succession duties. Estate duty became chargeable on most property passing on death without regard to the relationship of the beneficiaries to the deceased.[9] By 1949 rates had risen to 80 per cent for estates over £1 million and legacy and succession duty was abolished because, in part, it was perceived to fall disproportionately on the smaller estate. Estate duty peaked in 1969 with the highest marginal rate fixed at 85 per cent for estates in excess of £750,000 provided that total duty did not exceed 80 per cent of the value of the total estate.

CGT was introduced in 1965 and until 1971 was also chargeable on death although it was deductible for estate duty purposes. After 30 March 1971 CGT was no longer charged on death, and a CGT step up was given on death for CGT purposes. By contrast, CGT remains payable on most lifetime gifts (and in general is not deductible against the

S Orr (eds), *Taxation: Philosophical Perspectives* (Oxford, Oxford University Press, 2018). For a US perspective, see DG Duff, 'Alternatives to the Gift and Estate Tax' (2016) 57 *Boston College Law Review* 893. See also, E Chamberlain, 'Capital Taxes – Time for a Fresh Look' [2015] *BTR* 679; and E Chamberlain, 'A Review of Agricultural Property Relief and Business Property Relief' [2016] *BTR* 509.

[6] Office of Tax Simplification, 'Inheritance Tax Review – Second Report: Simplifying the Design of Inheritance Tax' (*GOV.UK*, July 2019), available at: www.assets.publishing.service.gov.uk/government/uploads/system/uploads/attachment_data/file/816521/Final_Inheritance_Tax_2_report_-_print_copy.pdf 4.

[7] ibid.

[8] The All-Party Parliamentary Group, 'Reform of Inheritance Tax' (*STEP*, January 2020), available at: www.step.org/sites/default/files/Policy/Reform%20of%20inheritance%20tax%20report%20Jan%202020%20final%20ALT.pdf.

[9] Real property situated outside the UK was exempt even if owned by a UK domiciliary, and foreign domiciliaries only paid on UK property. From 1910 gifts made within three years of death were caught.

IHT liability that may arise on the donor's death within seven years). Thus, a discrepancy opened up (and remains) between lifetime and death gifts.

In 1972 an important new relief was introduced: property left to a surviving spouse was exempt up to £15,000. Despite the high rates, estate duty raised relatively little revenue: it was not backed up by a general gift tax. Only gifts made in the seven years prior to death were subject to estate duty. To stop people giving their property away and still benefiting from it, anti-avoidance legislation called 'reservation of benefit' rules were introduced giving rise to a string of cases.

The Conservatives toyed with the idea of an accessions tax in 1972,[10] where the donee pays the tax (and the more widely wealth is spread, the less overall tax is paid). In the event, they lost office, and Labour replaced estate duty with capital transfer tax (CTT) in 1975. The comments made then by Denis Healey about estate duty seem remarkably similar to those levied against IHT today:

> Nothing is more offensive to the vast majority of ordinary taxpayers, most of whom are subject to PAYE, than the knowledge that people far better off than themselves are avoiding taxation by exploiting loopholes in the existing law. If the existing estate duty operated effectively, the great concentrations of private wealth would already have been broken up and with them many of the unfair advantages enjoyed by generations of the heirs and relatives of wealthy men.[11]

CTT, therefore, aimed to be 'a comprehensive tax on all transmissions of personal wealth'. Certainly, CTT had a much more coherent structure than estate duty; all gifts of property, whether made during lifetime or on death, were cumulated together and progressive rates of tax applied to the ever-increasing cumulative total of the donor taking into account all lifetime and death transfers. It was described as a 'cradle to the grave' tax. Why, then did it raise less money? Denis Healey noted in his autobiography:

> I replaced the estate duty which had become a laughing stock since no one who could afford an accountant ever paid it, with a capital transfer tax which covered gifts made before death as well. From the start I excluded money inherited by a man's widow from the tax. This piece of natural justice was long overdue … but in the end I had to accept so many other special cases for exclusion that when I left office four years later, the CT was still raising less revenue than the avoidable Estate Duty it replaced.[12]

Perhaps the single most critical reason why CTT raised less money than estate duty was the extension of spouse exemption. Even the limited £15,000 estate duty exemption introduced in 1972 was estimated to cost £60 million. Successive Conservative governments after 1979 steadily eroded many of the basic principles of CTT. Ten-year rather than lifetime cumulation was introduced in 1981 and rates were lowered from 75 per cent to 60 per cent by 1984. In 1986 Nigel Lawson renamed CTT inheritance tax and returned to the estate duty model of tax-free lifetime gifts provided the donor survived seven years. He justified it thus:

> [CTT] has been a thorn in the side of those owning and running family businesses and as such has had a damaging effect on risk taking and enterprise within a particularly

[10] HMSO, *Taxation of Capital on Death: A Possible IHT in Place of Estate Duty* (Cmnd 4930, 1972).
[11] Record of Estate Duty Debate, HC Deb 26 March 1974, vol 871, cols 313–14.
[12] D Healey, *The Time of My Life* (London, Michael Joseph, 1989) 404.

> important sector of the economy … [T]he lifetime gifts tax which the Labour Government introduced … is an unwelcome and unwarranted impost. By deterring lifetime giving it has had the effect of locking in assets, particularly the ownership of family businesses.[13]

In order to stop people giving away assets but still benefiting Lawson was forced to reintroduce the reservation of benefit rules in largely the same form as estate duty. Hence all the old estate duty cases (some of which were Privy Council cases relating to estate duty in Australia!) became relevant again, and a new tax avoidance industry began. Pre-owned assets income tax was introduced in Finance Act 2004 to stop this. More pages of complex anti-avoidance legislation were added. In short UK governments largely gave up trying to tax lifetime transfers of wealth in any meaningful way.

In 1988, IHT was made a two-rate tax: a nil rate band of £110,000 in 1988 and a flat rate of 40 per cent thereafter. In 1992, business property relief (BPR) and agricultural property relief (APR) were increased to 100 per cent. The tax then remained largely unchanged until 2006 when Labour introduced changes to the taxation of trusts and in 2007 introduced the transferable nil rate band – the ability to transfer the nil rate band between spouses and hence use two nil rate bands on the last spouse to die. For the last 11 years since April 2009 that nil rate band has been frozen at £325,000. A new residential nil-rate band was phased in from April 2017. From April 2020 this is £175,000 per individual. The overall effect is that a married couple with an estate of under £2 million leaving their estate to the children will pay no IHT on the first £1 million.

Many Commonwealth countries such as India, New Zealand, Australia and Canada have abandoned estate duty and have no tax on transfers of wealth other than (in some cases) CGT; but IHT has remained in the UK, a curious mix of CTT and estate duty. Cumulation and the allocation of the nil rate band between lifetime gifts and the death estate cause endless confusion as the OTS highlighted in its second report.[14] APR and BPR, the transferable nil rate band, the residential nil rate band, reduced rate charities relief have all further eroded the tax base and created new boundaries for dispute.

The incidence of IHT is currently regressive at higher levels. As the OTS pointed out in its first report, the average rate of tax increases from under 5 per cent for estates with a net value of under £1 million, up to 20 per cent for estates valued at £6–7 million, after which it falls to 10 per cent for estates with a value of £10 million or more. This does not take account of lifetime giving, which probably increases the distortion still further, as people whose main asset is the family home cannot easily give it away during their lifetime.[15]

Should the UK now follow the Commonwealth model and abolish any form of estate duty altogether, perhaps replacing it with CGT on death? The merits of levying CGT instead of IHT on death are discussed in section III. Some common objections to IHT are set out in the APPG Report.[16] Many of these objections relate to the tax *in its current*

[13] N Lawson, Budget Speech (18 March 1986), Hansard HC [94/166–184, 175].

[14] Difficult questions surround liability for failed PETs; liability for tax on the reservation of benefit property; the allocation of the nil rate band to lifetime transfers made within seven years of death to the detriment of the death estate.

[15] See, eg, the recent case of *Shelford (Executors of J Herbert) v HMRC* [2020] UKFTT 53 (TC) where an attempt to do so has failed.

[16] App 1, section 4.

form rather than to the taxation of wealth as such. However, as the APPG Report also discusses, there remain good arguments for taxing wealth if the right method can be found. Sections II and III below explore some options.

II. Design Issues for Wealth Transfer Taxes

Certain key design issues need consideration if a wealth transfer tax (WTT) is to work effectively. However, the correct design is affected by the type of WTT. In this respect, it is helpful to define terms as follows: a system where tax is levied on the donor who makes gifts on lifetime or death is called here 'estate tax'. A system which taxes the donee on gifts and legacies cumulatively over that donee's lifetime is called 'an accessions tax' (AT). The current UK IHT is an estate tax.

A. The Scope of the Charge

Here one has to consider the following factors:

(a) Residence of the donor.
(b) Residence of donee.
(c) Situs of the asset being given.

Currently, the UK offers a rather arbitrary form of relief: foreign domiciled donors who have been here for less than 16 years only pay IHT on UK assets and even after 15 years will not pay IHT on foreign assets settled into a trust before the 16-year deadline. Hence IHT is linked not only to long-term residence but also to the concept of domicile of the donor; the residence or domicile status of the donee is irrelevant, which is logical for an estate tax.

The Canadian model deals with the problem by imposing CGT not IHT on death and rebasing the assets to market value when the donor first arrives in Canada so only post-Canadian residence gains are taxed. An exit charge is then levied if the person becomes non-resident so that gains accruing in the course of Canadian residence are captured. France has a run-off period for new arrivals before full IHT becomes payable on all inheritances.

Question (c) above – situs – is relatively easily solved. Whatever system is adopted, all gifts of UK situated property should potentially be within the scope of estate tax/accessions tax irrespective of the residence or domicile of the donor or donee. That is the current position with a few exceptions.[17] In addition, the current position of taxing UK residential property held in enveloped vehicles should remain.

Questions (a) and (b) are more difficult to answer. It is suggested that domicile is abolished altogether as a relevant concept in taxing transfers of wealth. Liability should depend not on someone's domicile but be linked solely to an objective test of residence.

[17] eg, in relation to government gilts owned by a non-UK resident and authorised unit trusts and OEICs held by foreign doms.

Logically, an estate tax should be charged by reference to the residence status of the donor and AT charged by reference to the status of the donee. However, this could lead to significant avoidance. It is suggested that whatever model is adopted, the tax base should be extended to cover all transfers where *either* the donor or donee is a long-term UK resident (say resident here for more than 10 out of the last 15 tax years).

One problem with this option is that if the donee living here is taxed on gifts received from a foreign resident donor, including a trust, there may well be double taxation as some countries will tax transfers of wealth made *by* persons living in their country. The same could apply in reverse (although less frequently), where the UK-based donor makes gifts to the foreign donee. Double tax relief must be given. However, this would provide a good opportunity to review our 10 existing estate duty/IHT treaties generally. Four of them are pre-CTT, and three treaties still apply to countries that have abolished IHT effectively giving the deceased double non-taxation![18]

Another question is what happens if the long-term resident leaves the UK. It is suggested that the donor/donee should remain within the scope of the tax if UK resident for 10 out of the last 15 tax years to prevent deathbed emigrations. Again the double tax consequences of this would need to be considered carefully as the donor may die subject to death taxes in two countries.

B. Spouses/Cohabitees/Relatives

Most countries provide for some relief, if not outright exemption, on transfers of property between spouses and civil partners, although the UK was almost the last to do so in 1972 under estate duty. In many civil law countries, a lower rate of tax is also levied on transfers to close relatives; the reasoning is that inheritance from a friend rather than a parent should be considered more in the nature of a windfall and therefore taxed more heavily. Ireland's accessions tax levies tax at a lower rate on gifts to children than friends.

Should spouse exemption only apply on death or apply to all lifetime transfers; should the relief be extended to cohabitees? It is suggested that the argument for spouse or civil partner exemption is greater where rates are higher as the hardship suffered on the first death is more. However, the same hardship argument could be raised by cohabitees, although there may be more practical difficulties in monitoring whether someone is a cohabitee as opposed to whether they are married.

A progressive estate tax raises further issues as one estate of £1 million passing on the last spouse to die will end up paying more tax than two estates of £500,000. Hence the deferral of tax on the first death comes at some cost. In the case of AT, there are other complications: if, say, a husband inherits from his wife, and it is spouse exempt, should this inheritance be ignored altogether in calculating the rate of tax on husband's other inheritances? Does it make a difference if the husband inherits from his wife in trust rather than outright?

Another question is whether it is right to tax gifts to distant relatives or friends more heavily than gifts to (say) children. This question is more relevant to a progressive

[18] See Sweden, India and Pakistan. In the latter two cases, a long-term UK resident who is domiciled in one of their countries under their law can escape UK IHT altogether.

AT than a flat rate estate tax. The windfall argument above is not necessarily accurate. A friend or distant relative may well have legitimate expectations if they have been close to the deceased. Moreover, in the case of AT, any differentiation in favour of close family members would arguably increase concentrations of wealth when one of the main objectives of this system is to disburse wealth more widely. The Resolution Foundation and the Institute for Public Policy Research reports both favour AT tax and neither report suggests differential rates.

C. Should Special Reliefs Apply to Different Assets?

Currently, the UK gives very generous tax breaks to trading businesses and agricultural land. Should these continue? Again much depends on the rate of tax. A high rate will generally require greater relief for businesses which will object that, otherwise, family companies will need to be sold to pay tax due on death. Death is not a planned or voluntary event. However, BPR and APR currently do not require the person who inherits on death to retain the asset for any minimum length of time; hence, the business can be sold immediately after death without any CGT or IHT payable at all by the heirs. The rules are different for lifetime gifts increasing distortions in behaviour. However, introducing a minimum period of ownership for the heir who inherits on death is not desirable if it encourages economic inefficiency. In any event, the rule is in practice relatively easily avoided by selling to a buyer who allows the seller to retain preference shares in the business for the required minimum length of time.[19]

D. What Other Exemptions Should Be Given?

Currently, IHT has many other lifetime reliefs: small gifts exemption; gifts in consideration of marriage; annual exemption with carry forward; gifts for family maintenance; normal expenditure out of income exemption; charity exemption; maintenance funds; employee trusts; conditionally exempt transfers for objects or land of pre-eminent or outstanding interest; a nil rate band of £325,000 renewable every seven years. Many of these reliefs date back to estate duty. AT would certainly require their wholescale review as it would be the donee's position that is relevant. There are also reliefs such as residential nil rate band available on death.

Whatever wealth transfer tax system is adopted, it may be sensible to exclude any gift not exceeding £250 in value (reflecting the current small gifts exemption) but also introduce an annual lifetime allowance for the donee (if AT is introduced) or for the donor if estate tax is in point. A level of £20,000 or £30,000 exemption each year with no ability to carry forward that annual exemption could be considered. All other lifetime reliefs other than charity exemption would be abolished (including the nil rate band which causes so many complications and confusion in the current system).

[19] For a fuller discussion of the options on BPR/APR see Chamberlain, 'A Review of Agricultural Property Relief and Business Property Relief' (n 5).

E. Trusts

How do you deal with trusts, foundations, usufructs and other similar structures which do not die and can provide benefits to people without actually transferring wealth to them? In many trusts, income accrues to one group of beneficiaries and capital to another. How should these different interests be taxed? The benefits accruing to beneficiaries are not always capable of being valued as they are contingent or discretionary.

Possible approaches include:

a. Treat the trust as transparent, ie, include the trust fund within the taxable estate of the settlor or the trust's beneficiaries on the basis that HMRC simply 'looks through' the trust. In the US, for example, a grantor trust is a trust whose settlor is treated as the owner of the trust assets for all US tax purposes. As a result, distributions of income or capital to other beneficiaries are treated as gifts from the settlor and not taxable on them.
b. Attribute ownership of capital to income beneficiary. Until 22 March 2006 this was the approach taken by the UK so that the capital interest in a trust fund was attributed to the individual entitled to the income. This approach is now limited to trusts for disabled beneficiaries and certain trusts arising on death.
c. Create a fictional taxpayer. In this case, the trust is taxed as a separate entity and subject to a separate system of rates. This approach is adopted for most UK lifetime trusts for IHT purposes since 2006 with a 6 per cent periodic charge every 10 years and exit charges of lesser amounts plus an entry charge of 20 per cent. A trust set up every seven years broadly has its own nil rate band.

HMRC suggests that taxation should be neutral between outright gifts and gifts in trust so that a donor uses a trust for purely non-fiscal reasons.[20] How to achieve this in the context of wealth transfer taxes and particularly AT is not straightforward. The general effect of trusts is to maintain concentrations of wealth and discourage distributions, which is the opposite of AT's objectives. If you tax a life tenant at the same rate as an outright gift to him, how does this affect that individual's lifetime cumulative accessions total, particularly if he never actually receives any capital but just an income interest? Is it fair to tax the donee at a higher rate on other inheritances simply because he is treated as receiving the underlying capital of the trust fund even if he takes a revocable income interest? If you tax him on the value of his income interest rather than the underlying capital, how is that income interest to be valued given it may be revocable? In commercial terms it would be more or less valueless.

What rate should be imposed on entry into a discretionary trust given it may have no history of inheritances as donee? Even if you cumulate all discretionary trusts set up by the donor, this does not necessarily fulfil the objectives of AT, which is looking at the tax position of the donee.

Trusts are easier to deal with under an estate tax system than under AT. The discretionary trust periodic charge (say every 10 years) can be fixed by reference to the overall

[20] See, eg, HMRC, 'Consultation on the Taxation of Trusts' (*GOV.UK*, 2018), available at: www.gov.uk/government/consultations/the-of-taxation-of-trusts-a-review.

rate levied on the death of a donor. So a 20 per cent death rate might justify something like a 3 per cent 10-year periodic rate. See section III.B below, paragraph 10.

However, in the case of AT, it is less easy to work out a compensating 'neutral' position for trusts. Ireland operates capital acquisitions tax (a form of AT) with no tax on entry into a discretionary trust, capital acquisitions tax on the distribution of capital to a beneficiary and an initial charge of 6 per cent on the later of the death of the settlor or (broadly) the last child of the settlor reaching 21. From then on a 1 per cent annual charge is also imposed while the assets remain in trust. The status of the beneficiary and their history of inheritances is ignored while the property remains in trust. This position is not as such a neutral position.

Another question is, what happens if the trust is non-resident and holds only non-UK property? Should it be subject to tax if none of the beneficiaries has any UK connection? In the case of the estate tax, there is logic in linking the trust's tax status only to that of the settlor. A trust set up by a long-term UK resident settlor would, therefore, be subject to tax at the same rate irrespective of the status of the beneficiaries. But what about AT where the logic is to tax by reference to the status of the beneficiary?

Given that in II.A above it was suggested that tax should be levied in relation to estate tax and AT if either donor or donee were UK resident, one option is to impose WTT on trustees wherever resident if any of the following are satisfied:

(a) The assets of the trust are UK situated.
(b) The settlor is a long term UK resident.
(c) Any beneficiary is a long term UK resident.

Under this route the residence of the trustees (which can easily be manipulated) is irrelevant. However, (c) could raise significant design problems. For example, in the case of a foreign resident settlor who settles foreign assets into a trust, he may be able to avoid the entry or periodic charges for some time by merely ensuring that there are no long term UK resident beneficiaries even if later added. France has adopted this model with limited success. Is it fair that even the presence of one long-term UK resident discretionary beneficiary can subject the whole trust fund to periodic charges?

A better option (at least for estate tax) may be to tax the trust by reference to the status of the settlor. If he is a long-term UK resident, then the trust (whenever established) becomes subject to periodic charges, and the status of the beneficiary is irrelevant unless either (a) a long-term UK resident beneficiary receives a benefit at which point they are taxed or (b) such a beneficiary takes a right to income (in which case the capital could be attributed to them). This system is adopted in section III.B – see paragraph 10.

F. Other Taxes

WTT cannot be treated in isolation. Is there a case for an annual wealth tax in conjunction with a wealth transfer tax? Some of the arguments for and against an annual wealth tax have been considered elsewhere in the APPG Report and the Mirrlees Report on Taxation of Wealth; they are currently the subject of a separate academic study led by Advani, Chamberlain and Summers. See https://ukwealth.tax. For reasons of space, they are not considered further here. The idea was discussed in a Green Paper in 1974 but Healey abandoned it for many of the practical reasons discussed in the APPG Report. It is worth noting that of the 16 OECD countries that operated a wealth tax in 1995, only three still have it on any permanent basis. Sweden and Austria abandoned it; the German federal courts declared it unconstitutional; France has now largely restricted it to real estate.

Even if only an annual tax on high-value property was introduced, significant unfairness could arise if the person who inherited a house free of mortgage pays the same amount as someone who purchased it with a mortgage paid for out of taxed salary. However, levying wealth tax only on the net value of assets may lead to avoidance.

The OECD Report in 2018 concluded that from both an efficiency and equity perspective, there is little need for a net wealth tax in countries with broad-based personal capital income taxes and well-designed inheritance and gift taxes. In short, in their view, a wealth tax is an imperfect substitute for taxes on personal capital income, capital gains or on wealth transfers.

What about CGT? As noted above, when CGT was introduced in 1965, death was also an occasion of charge although deductible against estate duty. The charge was abolished in 1971 and a step-up introduced. The abolition was for the practical reason that (in the government's view) the levy of two taxes on the same event, CGT as well as estate duty, imposed an excessive burden on estates, and particularly family businesses. By contrast, the CGT charge on lifetime gifts remains unless the gifted asset is a qualifying business or is given to a lifetime trust in which case the gain can be held over.[21] In the case of the estate tax, the liability for both CGT and estate tax on gifts will fall on the donor. In the case of AT, the donor bears the CGT, and the donee pays AT. Nevertheless, it is still likely to be perceived as double taxation. Although, in itself, double taxation is not necessarily irrational as the two taxes are doing different things, whether in practice it would be tolerated is doubtful.

A compromise may be to roll over the accrued gain on any gifted asset (whether transferred during lifetime or on death) to the donee. In this way, the gain will be subject to tax in the long run, but the double charge to CGT and WTT on the same occasion is avoided. The pros and cons of CGT are considered further in section III.

G. Rates

Fundamental to tax design is the question of rates. Should tax rates be progressive or flat; at what level should tax start to be levied? If rates are low, this can influence tax design as there is less need for reliefs. However, the type of system also influences rates. The principle of AT, which taxes a donee on all accessions of inheritances, necessarily envisages a progressive system. Some suggest that inheritances should be subject to income tax in the hands of the donee. Others (such as the Resolution Foundation) want a separate rate of up to 30 per cent on inheritances received by the donee with a £125,000 lifetime exemption. This is the model adopted in Ireland.

[21] See Taxation of Chargeable Gains Act 1992, s 260.

III. Two Options for Discussion: CGT or Flat Rate Gift Tax?

A. CGT Not IHT on Death

Currently, there are two major reliefs for CGT (excluding those such as entrepreneurs' relief and rollover relief on businesses which are not discussed here). The first is the principal private residence relief which costs approximately £27.2 billion in lost tax.[22]

The second CGT relief is the effective exemption, and rebasing of all gains on death, sometimes referred to as 'the step-up'. Thus, if someone dies holding an asset pregnant with gain, it is currently rebased to market value on death free of CGT. This opens up a stark contrast between lifetime gifts of assets (where the disposal is treated as taking place at market value, and gains are taxed on the donor)[23] and transfers on death where there is no CGT. Indeed, there can be a double charge, CGT and IHT, on lifetime gifts if the donor dies within seven years and zero CGT and IHT on death if the donor dies holding business property. The cost of the CGT uplift is unknown as HMRC no longer records the figures.[24]

There are two options.

Option 1: No-Gain No-Loss Transfer on Death

This option does not impose CGT on death but simply removes the exemption so that the donee inherits at the donor's base cost. It is an option that has to operate in conjunction with a WTT rather than in isolation and is considered in III.B below.

The OTS recommended in their second report that there should be no CGT uplift on death to the extent that assets were not subject to IHT on death. Instead, the assets would pass on a 'no-gain no-loss' basis. This no-gain no-loss transfer basis would apply in the following situations:

1. Where spouse exemption is given on death. On later sale or disposal by the recipient spouse, CGT would be payable on the original base cost of the deceased.
2. On transfers of assets qualifying for 100 per cent BPR or APR.
3. On the death of a foreign domiciliary where no IHT is paid on the foreign property.

While this option has some significant attractions in terms of eliminating the distortions between lifetime giving and transfers on death, it is not without complications:

1. What if part of a business did not qualify for full BPR relief on death? Would a proportion of the business then get a CGT uplift and how would this be calculated?
2. It means that record keeping is more onerous. Instead of just taking probate value, the person who inherits will need to know the deceased's original base cost. Equally,

[22] Recent papers released from National Archives show Chancellor Lawson and his advisers considering extending CGT to the main residence, possibly combined with abolishing IHT, in the run-up to the 1989 Budget.

[23] Subject to limited reliefs such as hold over relief which applies only if the gift is chargeable to IHT or is a gift of certain business assets.

[24] It was apparently £640 million in 2010/11.

in many, cases HMRC does not currently confirm valuations if the estate is exempt, so probate values are not always certain.

3. What happens where an asset is split between a spouse and a child with some of it chargeable to IHT and some not? Should only the fractional interest received by the exempt beneficiary receive no gain no loss treatment?
4. The position on the main home needs consideration. If it passes on a no-gain no-loss basis, does the donee inherit any of the main residence relief that the deceased might have had? See example 1 in section III.B below.
5. On assets such as farms and businesses that continue for several generations, the CGT bill may become disproportionately large and harder to calculate. Inflationary gains may be taxed.

Of course, it would be possible to roll over accrued gains on all death transfers, not just exempt transfers, and it is an approach recommended in section III.B below, but the same issues arise.

Option 2: Taxing Unrealised Gains on Death and Abolishing IHT

Another option sometimes discussed is to abolish IHT altogether and impose CGT on the death of any UK resident or any individual (wherever resident) who owns UK real estate. This option would follow the Canadian model which abolished gift and estate tax and introduced a tax on capital gains that included a deemed realisation on transfers of property by gift or at death.

The argument in favour of substituting IHT with CGT is that it simplifies the tax system as it means people only have one tax to deal with; it may have more public acceptance in regimes that run this model. CGT taxes gains rather than absolute values, so people do not see it as double taxation. It is not a tax that penalises saving. All the administrative machinery is already in place to collect the tax. The system can relatively easily deal with taxpayers leaving and arriving by rebasing to market value the assets of all persons arriving in the UK and imposing an exit charge on those who leave. Canada broadly adopts this approach.[25]

However, there are practical and theoretical disadvantages in having CGT and not IHT charged on death (as opposed to just rolling over the accrued gain).

Practical Disadvantages of CGT on Death

1. The OTS suggested it would have a substantial Exchequer cost as people's main asset – their home – would effectively not be taxed at all due to main residence relief (PPR). However, the relief does not need to be available on death at all as the deceased no longer needs to be rehoused. Even if PPR was abolished on death, the OTS suggests that replacing IHT with CGT on death would still only raise

[25] An exit charge for the UK would need to take into account the effect of treaties as well as EU law. See, eg, the case of *Trustees of the Panayi A&M Trust v HMRC* [2019] UKFTT 622 in relation to the exit tax imposed on trusts.

£2.8 billion compared with over £5 billion for IHT. Moreover, this would mean those making a lifetime gift of a house would have exemption and those who die owning the house have none. It may, therefore, be necessary to have more fundamental reform of PPR. There are three options:

a. A pure rollover option such that on final lifetime gift or death, roll over is not available. On downsizing, some tax is also paid. Experience of other states such as in the US suggests this can be problematic and complex with extensive record keeping.
b. A fixed lifetime allowance, for example, £500,000 per individual. Thereafter all gains on the main residence are taxed. Again this requires monitoring over a lifetime.
c. A fixed or percentage amount of gain is exempt on each disposal. So if a house was sold for a gain of £500,000 only up to 10 per cent of the gain is exempt. There could be a £50,000 de minimis exemption and a cap of, say, £100,000 per individual disponer. Some form of rebasing would need to be introduced – probably to April 2015 to tie in with the regime for non-residents. This at least avoids recording gains over a lifetime. The charge would apply on lifetime or death transfers in the same way.

2. Imposing CGT on death, particularly in conjunction with restricting PPR, would impact a much larger number of people than IHT currently does as the number of tax-paying estates would rise to 182,000 rather than 28,500, and the number of reported disposals of the house would increase. The threshold to pay CGT is much lower than that of IHT. Presumably, on transfers between spouses on death, there would be no immediate CGT but a deferment so that the assets would pass on a no-gain no-loss basis (as currently occurs on lifetime transfers). However, historical records would still need to be kept. With the introduction of electronic 30-day reporting on disposals of residential property from April 2020 that are not CGT exempt, it may be easier to impose more compliance.
3. For executors making disposals, they would now need to worry about CGT and need two figures: the historic base cost and the value at death. (Rebasing to 2015 would make this easier at least on the main residence.) Even if there was just a deferment of CGT until eventual sale, they would need the historical records. (Having said that the author thinks this objection may be exaggerated given that executors will be saved a vast amount of other trouble such as going through bank statements checking lifetime gifts. In many cases, the acquisition cost will be easily ascertainable.)
4. Unless indexation was reintroduced, it would potentially tax paper gains. (To some extent this is typically dealt with by having a lower rate of CGT, for example, 28 per cent rather than 45 per cent income tax.)
5. There would probably still need to be reliefs for businesses and land which are illiquid and where the historic gains are often significant. The point about taxing a gain realised on death (as opposed to any type of voluntary sale or gift during the taxpayer's lifetime) is that the deemed disposal arises as a result of something over which the taxpayer has no control – his death. It is a dry charge if he cannot sell the asset. Hence businesses will still demand reliefs. In Canada there is a deferral of CGT on death for qualifying businesses although on eventual sale the gain is still taxed.

Theoretical Problems of CGT on Death

1. The position for trusts would need to be considered as trusts do not die. Thus the tax would be avoided on, for example, valuable pictures or houses, simply by retaining these assets in a trust and allowing them to be used by beneficiaries. To stop this sort of tax avoidance, a disposal could be deemed to occur every few years with the trust given a final credit for past tax paid when the asset is sold, but this can become complicated particularly if the asset goes down in value after the deemed disposal.
2. It fails the horizontal and vertical equity tests. First, inherited as opposed to earned income would no longer be taxed at all if received in cash. Second, it is much less redistributive than IHT as it taxes only a fraction of wealth transfers. A person inheriting £1 million cash will pay no CGT on death. The burden is shifted to smaller estates and away from the largest estates, so reducing progressivity.

Many OECD countries, therefore, retain wealth transfer taxes. At least 22 OECD countries have a wealth transfer tax in some form or other today although there are some notable exceptions such as Canada, New Zealand, Austria, Sweden, Australia, India, Pakistan, Hong Kong and most of remaining Asia apart from Japan.

B. Flat Rate Gift Tax

This tax was the APPG's preferred option and is essentially an estate tax levied on the donor although with some modifications to take account of trusts. It is based on the assumption that if rates are low enough and the tax is kept simple, you do not need reliefs; tax avoidance stops. The discussion below incorporates many of the design features discussed in section II.

Key Points

1. All lifetime gifts (other than to spouse or charity) are taxed on the donor when made at 10 per cent, subject to a £30,000 annual allowance.[26] There is a death allowance of something similar to the current nil rate band of £325,000, available only on death to individuals and not to trusts. All the complications of allocating lifetime gifts to the unused nil rate band if the donor dies within seven years disappear, and there is no taper relief as it is irrelevant how long the donor lives. The arbitrary deadline of seven years is abolished. The death allowance can be transferred between spouses.
2. On gifts of cash, 10 per cent is withheld by the donor. On gifts of an illiquid asset, the donor has the option to pay over 10 years in interest-bearing instalments

[26] The level of lifetime allowance is for debate and would need to be indexed.

(although in the case of trading businesses and farms this could be interest-free instalments).[27]

3. The donor has an annual gifts exemption (or annual lifetime allowance) of £30,000. A married couple, therefore, have £60,000 each to give away. All other reliefs such as gifts in consideration of marriage and normal expenditure out of income relief would be abolished although possibly small gifts exemption of £250 could be retained to avoid monitoring very small gifts. Any gifts over £30,000 per annum would be taxed at 10 per cent immediately, and the annual allowance cannot be carried forward. (The annual allowance is set at £30,000 to reduce IHT compliance and record-keeping.) Unlike the current position, lifetime gifts would, therefore, have no effect on the rate of tax payable on death.
4. The reservation of benefit rules and the pre-owned assets (POAT) code are abolished; all lifetime gifts are taxed when made if over the annual lifetime allowance.[28]
5. The loss to estate, cumulation and grossing-up principle are abolished. No nil rate band is given to trusts, so there is no gift of £325,000 tax-free to trusts every seven years. The tax treatment of trusts is discussed further in paragraph 11 below.
6. All pension funds left at death are taxed at the flat rate of 10 per cent (or added to the estate and the excess taxed at 20 per cent to the extent the value of the estate is over £2 million) unless passing to the spouse.
7. Tax is payable on death at 10 per cent on the worldwide estate unless either it is over £2 million (in which case the rate increases to 20 per cent) or exempt due to the spouse/civil partnership and charity exemption. The harsh distinction between no exemption for cohabitees who pay up to 40 per cent IHT tax versus complete exemption for spouses/civil partnership is tempered as rates are lower (see example 2 below).
8. Gifts exemption for charities is retained. A gift to a charity can be seen as, in effect, a voluntary 100 per cent 'tax' on the part of the donor, which ends up in the overall public realm. Many charities rely heavily on legacy-giving and anything which disincentivises charitable legacies is likely to be strongly resisted and counterproductive. The reduced and complex rate of 36 per cent on the remaining chargeable estate where 10 per cent or more of the estate is given to charity is abolished.
9. Foreign domiciliaries. Domicile is abolished as a connecting factor. Donors who have been UK resident for more than 10 out of the last 15 years will pay tax on all subsequent lifetime gifts including gifts into trust and transfers on death on a worldwide basis at 10 per cent/20 per cent. Gifts by donors who are not long-term UK resident are still taxed if the donee is a long-term UK resident, but the donee would then be accountable for the tax. (See section II.A design features).

[27] The disadvantage of offering interest-free instalments to trading businesses is that it sets up an artificial boundary requiring determining of what is a qualifying trading business. It may be better to say that tax on all businesses that is due on death transfers is either interest free or interest bearing without discrimination in favour of trading businesses.

[28] Although there could still be some advantage in making lifetime gifts if it captured the lower 10% for larger estates; this partly depends on the rates set.

10. Trusts. The position operates as follows:
    a. Discretionary trusts set up by a long-stay UK resident settlor are subject to a 10 per cent entry charge if made during his lifetime (in the same way as a gift to an individual) or 20 per cent if made on death from an estate of over £2 million.
    b. Discretionary trusts set up prior to the settlor becoming a long-term UK resident would not be subject to any entry charge.
    c. Discretionary trusts are subject to a periodic tax of 3 per cent every 10 years from the date the settlor first becomes a long-term UK resident (and for as long as the settlor remains a long-term UK resident or if he dies a long-term UK resident). There is no nil rate band, so there would need to be some allowance of, say, £30,000 for each trust so that assets with a value under this would pay no periodic tax. This would take most trusts holding term life policies out of the tax net. The residence status of the beneficiaries is ignored while the assets are held in a discretionary trust.
    d. However, a distribution from any discretionary trust to a long-term UK resident beneficiary would be subject to estate tax at 10 per cent (with a possible credit for the past periodic tax paid) even if the settlor has never had any connection to the UK. The 10 per cent/20 per cent differential between assets passing on death from deceased to an individual versus asset passing via a trust set up in lifetime would need to be carefully calibrated to reduce avoidance.
    e. A life interest trust set up by a long-stay UK resident settlor would be subject to 10 per cent/20 per cent tax on gift into trust irrespective of the status of the life tenant. A trust set up by a settlor with no UK connection would also be subject to 10 per cent on lifetime gift to a life interest trust if the life tenant was a long-term UK resident beneficiary in line with the principle discussed in section II.A that if either donor or donee is a long-term UK resident, tax should be paid. (If the trust set up by a non-resident settlor was initially discretionary and then became interest in possession for a UK resident, the 10 per cent would be charged at that point to reduce avoidance.)
    f. On death or earlier termination of the life interest, 10 per cent tax would be payable if either the life tenant or the settlor was a long-stay UK resident. Hence the current long-term IHT tax-free status of trusts set up by foreign doms for UK resident beneficiaries would be curtailed.
    g. Any discretionary trust of a settlor who dies a long-term UK resident remains within the periodic charge even if set up prior to the settlor taking up long-term UK residence.

11. Finally, the CGT death uplift would be abolished on all assets, and they would pass on a no-gain no-loss basis; gains on all lifetime gifts of assets would also be held over. The playing field between lifetime and death gifts would thus be equalised. The heir would therefore eventually pay CGT on the gain and a small amount of IHT on inheritance. The practical implications of this are set out in example 1.

Comments on the Flat Rate Gift Tax

1. Those who spread lifetime gifts over a number of years at less than £30,000 per annum will be better off under the new regime. Those making larger lifetime gifts would be worse off as they would be paying tax earlier (and more tax than if they made the gift and survived seven years). The OTS considered HMRC research into lifetime giving that suggested that 27 per cent of the population gave £1,000 or more away, with the majority (65 per cent) giving less than £5,000 away. They would be unaffected by the proposed tax on lifetime giving.
2. In 2015/16, 4,860 estates (about 20 per cent of the total number of taxpaying estates) recorded lifetime gifts being made less than seven years before death. HMRC data refers to gifts of £870 million in value being made in the seven years prior to death. There is virtually no meaningful data on gifts made more than seven years before death, and it would not be unreasonable to assume that the majority of larger lifetime gifts are made at a time when the donor *does* survive seven years.
3. As example 3 illustrates below, those with larger estates not held in business property are potentially substantially better off for IHT purposes under the new regime if it is a flat rate of 10 per cent; however, this does not take account of the fact that the CGT uplift on death will no longer be available and that large lifetime gifts are now taxed.
4. As the CGT death uplift would be abolished on all assets, those whose estates show large unrealised gains, but are exempt from IHT on death due to spouse exemption or BPR or APR, will be worse off. See example 4.
5. The married couple with an estate of over £650,000 – £1 million will be slightly worse off under the new regime. See example 1.
6. There is no BPR or APR, on the basis that the 10 per cent (20 per cent for larger estates over £2 million) payable on transfers of family businesses and farms could be funded over 10 years by interest-free instalments. Family businesses and farmers may object to the loss of 100 per cent BPR and APR, but the 1 or 2 per cent charge a year could generally be funded out of net income. This, of course, does mean that the question of what a qualifying business is would still need to be considered.

   As example 4 illustrates, those with farms and businesses are worse off under the new regime, particularly as they will lose the tax-free CGT death uplift, but the overall tax burden is still small. Currently, 16,380 estates are expected to benefit from BPR and APR on death over the next five years at a total cost to the Exchequer of £5.85 billion, but this does not take into account the cost of the reliefs on lifetime transfers. Nor does it measure the cost of the CGT uplift on death (which effectively means a business or farm can be free of both CGT and IHT even if sold shortly after death).
7. The tax treatment of trusts becomes more neutral compared with gifts to individuals. The long-term residence status of either donor/donee or settlor/beneficiary effectively brings the outright or settled gift into tax.
8. Reform PPR? The additional tax on lifetime transfers and the abolition of reliefs may not compensate for the loss of revenue by the reduction in rate from 40 per cent

to 10/20 per cent on death, although, as the level of lifetime giving and the cost of the CGT uplift is unknown, this is speculative.[29] The heirs of those who die with large estates not qualifying for BPR will, on paper at least, be better off. They will only pay 10 per cent/20 per cent rather than 40 per cent over the initial £650,000. See example 3. The *possible* loss of yield is, therefore, a risk. However, as the OTS noted, the average rate actually reduces to less than 20 per cent for larger estates so the risk may be more theoretical than real. One option is to combine the introduction of a flat rate IHT with a reform of CGT main residence relief. See option 2 and the suggestions made there on main residence relief. See also example 1 below.

Practical Examples of the Flat Rate Gift Tax[30]

The impact of any change is best illustrated through the use of examples.

Example 1: The married couple with joint assets of £1 million mainly tied up in the house

Married couple John and Janet die with joint assets of £1 million, of which £650,000 is tied up in their main house. They have each made limited lifetime gifts of £3,000 a year. Janet dies, leaving everything to John. John then dies, leaving everything to their children. No business property or farm is owned. The remaining assets apart from the house comprise shares showing a significant gain on death.

Current position: No tax payable on either death. Janet's estate on her death is covered by spouse exemption; John's estate is covered by two nil rate bands and two residential nil rate bands and all unrealised gains are wiped out on each death. Assets are rebased to market value on each death. Lifetime gifts have no effect on the IHT position as they fall within the annual exemption.

Total tax is nil.

New regime: No tax on first death due to spouse exemption. No CGT uplift so if John sells Janet's shares during his lifetime, he could pay more CGT. On John's death, IHT payable will be £35,000 (being the excess of £350,000 over £650,000 taxable at 10 per cent).

Total tax on death is £35,000. Effective tax rate on death is 3.5 per cent. CGT may be payable not on death but on a later sale of the assets.

CGT position: On John's death, the house would pass at cost to his children, although it is suggested that to align the position with lifetime giving and to reduce compliance

[29] The OTS estimated that abolishing APR and BPR entirely would fund a reduction of the main rate of IHT from 40% to 33.7%, but this assumed that the CGT relief on death remained unchanged and lifetime gifts would remain untaxed. Therefore, the lower rates may not be revenue losing if more people pay.

[30] See also APPG Report, section 1.

costs they can carry forward his main residence relief for the period during which it was John's main residence. For example, if John occupied it throughout his ownership for 10 years as his main residence, and on John's death the children let it and then sold it five years later, then approximately two-thirds of the gain on sale would qualify for main residence relief. If the children sold immediately after he died, there would be no CGT.

The shares would not be rebased to market value on John's death. The children would inherit at the base cost of Janet or John and CGT would be payable on a later sale.

If PPR is reformed in the way suggested at option 2 of CGT, then on sale by the children after John's death only a maximum £100,000 of any gain on the house accruing during its ownership would be exempt. If John sold during his lifetime, the same rule would apply. If Janet and John sold while both were alive, then they each receive up to £100,000 exemption (or 10 per cent of the gain if less).

Example 1A: The married couple with £1 million, but who have made modest annual lifetime gifts

As above, but John had made three lifetime gifts of £30,000 to his children in each of the three years before his death. He dies still holding £1 million.

Current position: No tax payable on any of the lifetime gifts, but (unless normal expenditure out of income could be claimed which is likely to be controversial) there would be more tax payable on John's death as £81,000 was given away in excess of the annual exemption[31] and would, therefore, use up part of his nil rate band. This would mean *£32,400* IHT payable on John's death, assuming his estate is still worth £1 million at death.[32] Note that if the gifts were of assets rather than cash and the assets showed a gain, then John would pay CGT on the gain when making the gift.

Total tax is £32,400.

New regime: No tax payable on any of the lifetime gifts as they do not exceed £30,000 a year. Gains can be held over. On John's death, tax payable will be as in example 1 – £35,000. John's house and other assets would pass at cost to his children and see CGT position above.

Total tax is £35,000.

The above illustrates the relative simplicity of the flat rate option as lifetime gifts have no effect on the tax payable on death but are separately taxed in their own right. More CGT is likely to be payable as the assets are not rebased on each death, and if PPR is curtailed there would be further tax payable on a disposal.

[31] £90,000 less 3 × £3000 = £81,000.

[32] Available NRB is £650k less £81,000 = £569k + RNRB of £350,000, so £919k is not taxed. This leaves £81,000 taxable at 40%.

Example 2: The cohabitees

Peter is single living with his partner George (but not married or in a civil partnership). They each die, leaving everything to each other and then on the last death the joint estate passes to charity. Estate of each is £500,000, mainly held in the jointly owned house and lifetime gifts are £3,000 per annum. George dies first. Total estate is £1 million.

Current regime: No tax on lifetime gifts. £70,000 IHT is payable on George's death (his £500,000 estate gets the benefit of the nil rate band of £325,000 but not of the residential nil rate band as the house does not pass to children. So £175,000 is taxable at 40 per cent). On Peter's death, there is no tax as it passes to charity. NB – it makes no difference if Peter is given a life interest on George's death and then it passes to charity. Charitable exemption is only available on the last death. Base cost uplift in house for CGT purposes on George's death and then Peter's.

Total tax is £70,000 payable only on George's death.

New regime: IHT of £17,500 is payable on George's death (10 per cent of £175,000). No IHT is payable on Peter's death due to charitable exemption.

Total tax is £17,500 payable on George's death.

Note: The above illustrates that under the flat rate regime, there is less distinction between married and unmarried couples. Cohabitees are better off, as the rate of tax is lower than at present and therefore the reliefs available to married couples are worth less. In addition, the burden of tax on the first cohabitee to die, leaving everything to the second is much less, which is important in relation to the family home.

Example 2A: As above, but on Peter's death, everything is left to the relatives of George and Peter

Current regime: £70,000 payable by each of them on each death.[33] CGT uplift.

Total tax is £140,000.

New regime: £17,500 is payable on each death. No CGT uplift.

Total tax is £35,000.

Example 2B: Facts as in example 2A above, but 10 years previously, Peter had given away £300,000 to his relatives

Current regime: No tax on lifetime gifts.

Total tax remains £140,000.

[33] £500,000 – £325,000 NRB = £175,000 chargeable at 40% = £70,000.

New regime: £27,000 payable at date of gift (after deducting annual lifetime allowance of £30,000).

Total tax is £27,000 + £35,000 = £62,000.

Example 2C: Facts as in example 2A above, but Peter gives away £30,000 every year for 10 years prior to his gift = total £300,000 (deduct £3,000 annual exemption each year for the last seven years, leaving a chargeable gift of £189,000)[34]

Current regime: No tax on lifetime gifts as only the last seven gifts are counted, and they fall within the nil rate band (leaving £136,000 nil rate band available on Peter's death). Therefore £364,000[35] is chargeable on Peter's death so tax is £145,600.

Total tax is £215,600.[36]

New regime: No tax on lifetime gifts as they each fall within the lifetime allowance.

Total tax remains £35,000.

Note: The above illustrates the simplicity of the flat rate regime as the death allowance of £650,000 is not deducted against lifetime gifts. These are taxed at 10 per cent if they exceed the £30,000 each year. It also shows the benefits of spreading gifts over a period of time rather than lumping them into one year. In addition, there is no arbitrary cut off point of seven years. The lifetime gifts are all taxable over the annual limit of £30,000, and it does not depend on the gamble of surviving seven years. Taper relief and other complexities become irrelevant.

Example 3: Large estate. Civil partnership and children

Miriam and Jane are in a civil partnership and have a joint estate of £2.5 million. They make no lifetime gifts, and they leave everything to each other and then to their children.

Current regime: Tax of £740,000 payable on last death (deduct two nil rate bands leaving a chargeable estate of £1.85 million taxed at 40 per cent = £740,000). No residential nil rate band is available as their estate is too large.

Total tax is £740,000.

New regime: Tax of £185,000 payable on the last death. Even if tax on values over £2 million was 20 per cent, then tax would remain the same as death allowance reduces estate to £1.85 million.

[34] 7 × £27,000 = £189,000.
[35] £500,000 – £136,000 remaining NRB leaving chargeable estate of £364k.
[36] £70,000 on George's death and £145,600 on Peter's.

Total tax is £185,000.

Note: As in all the examples, it is not clear what the CGT difference would be as the assets would not be rebased on death.

Example 3A: Facts as above except that they each make lifetime gifts of £500,000 in one year to bring their estate under the threshold to qualify for the RNRB. They die within seven years of each other. On last death, the estate is worth £1.5 million

a. Assume they both survive the gift by seven years

Current regime: No tax on lifetime gift. Tax on last death reduced to 40 per cent × £500,000 = *£200,000* as they now qualify for the residential nil rate band, so the first £1 million is not taxed.

Total tax is £200,000.

New regime: Lifetime gift is taxed at 10 per cent = tax of £97,000 (£1m less £30k = £970,000 × 10 per cent). Tax on last death is £85,000.[37]

Total tax is £182,000.

b. Assume they each die within two years of their gifts.

Current regime: Each lifetime gift becomes chargeable as to £175,000. (The first £325,000 of each gift falls within each of their nil rate bands, and the balance is chargeable at 40 per cent.) Tax is £70,000 each. On the last death, there is no available nil rate band. £1,150,000[38] is chargeable at 40 per cent = £460,000 tax.

Total tax is £600,000.

New regime: Position unchanged as lifetime gifts are taxable at 10 per cent and the couple's death allowance is unaffected.

Total tax is £182,000.

Example 4: Very large estate comprising mostly farms and business property

Phil, a widower, dies leaving his son a working farm worth £2 million (currently qualifying for 100 per cent BPR and APR). He leaves his daughter a portfolio of AIM-listed shares worth £3 million owned for two years all qualifying for BPR. The family business worth £1 million is left to both children equally along with some cash and house worth together around £650,000. His deceased wife left everything to him and made no gifts. Total estate is £6.650m.

[37] £1.5 million less £650K = £850,000 × 10%.
[38] £1.5 million less residence nil rate band of £350,000.

Current regime: *No tax on Phil's death.* The chargeable assets of £650,000 (house and cash) fall within the two nil rate bands of him and his widow. The rest of the estate at £6 million qualifies for BPR or APR. Children inherit the assets free of tax and at a rebased CGT value.

New regime: Total estate is £6.650 million. After deducting £650,000 death allowance, 10 per cent is payable on £2 million = £200,000 and the balance of £4 million is taxed at 20 per cent = £800,000 funded over 10 years in interest-free instalments = £100,000 per annum. There is no rebased CGT value so, on a later sale of the business, CGT is payable on the total gain since Phil's acquisition.

Total tax is £1 million payable over ten years compared with nil under IHT regime.

The above illustrates that on a large estate of £6.65 million currently qualifying for reliefs, the tax would be greater, as there are no reliefs and the CGT position would be worse. However, if Phil's wealth was held in an investment portfolio rather than in qualifying assets, the tax on his death currently would be £2.4 million but would be unchanged from the above tax of £1 million under the new regime.

Example 4A: Business property gifted during lifetime.

Estate is £6.650m as above but that Phil makes a lifetime gift of his farm worth £2 million to his son (also a farmer) and survives three years.

Current regime: *No tax on Philip's death.* Although he has died within seven years, full APR is available, provided the son has retained the farm. The gain on lifetime gifts of agricultural assets can be held over. Position on death should be unaffected.

New regime: No CGT on lifetime gift. Gain held over. However, £200,000 tax is payable on the lifetime gift at 10 per cent payable in 10 yearly instalments. After deduction of two nil rate bands, there is £4 million remaining in his death estate that is chargeable to tax: £2 million is charged at 20 per cent, and £2m is taxed at 10 per cent.

Total tax – £800,000.

By handing the business on early, the rate of tax is less than keeping it until death – at 10 per cent rather than 20 per cent. The CGT position is the same on death or lifetime transfers. By contrast, the current tax regime encourages qualifying trading businesses to be retained until death to obtain the CGT death uplift as well as IHT exemption.

Example 5: Taxation of foreign domiciliaries

Foreign-domiciled widower Ajay dies UK resident. He has lived in the UK for 11 years. Therefore he is a long-term UK resident. Ajay dies with a personal estate of £10.650 million, of which only £650,000 is UK situated. He leaves it all to his UK resident domiciled children.

Current regime: *No tax* on his death as foreign assets are excluded from IHT, and £650,000 is covered by his and his late partner's nil rate bands.

New regime: Tax is £200,000 on the first £2m, and £1.6m (being 20 per cent on the remaining 8m chargeable estate) as tax is levied on his worldwide estate of £10m (after deducting the £650,000 death allowance) after ten years of UK residence.

Total tax is £1.8 million.

If Ajay had set up a trust prior to his death then, under the current IHT regime, there would never be a tax on trust assets provided they were non-UK situated. Under the new flat rate regime, Ajay would pay 10 per cent on a gift to trust if the trust was set up after his tenth year of UK residence and the trust pays 3 per cent charges every 10 years. Even if Ajay set up the trust prior to long-term UK residence, on distribution of trust assets to UK resident beneficiaries there would be 10 per cent payable then. If Ajay dies a long-term UK resident the trust will always be subject to periodic charges even if settled prior to UK residence and any distributions even to non-resident beneficiaries would be subject to tax at 10 per cent.

Example 6: Trusts for UK persons

Rakesh is a UK-domiciled widower. He set up a trust 10 years ago for his children during his lifetime from which he can also benefit. He settled £10 million into it during his lifetime, and he dies with £650,000 in his personal free estate. Assume the trust is worth the same amount now.

Current regime: No tax is payable on his free estate due to two nil rate bands. £10 million trust is taxed at 20 per cent on the way in (£2 million) and another 40 per cent on his death under reservation of benefit rules (£4 million). Trust pays 6 per cent on the tenth anniversary = £600,000.

Total tax is £6.6 million.

In practice no well advised widower would ever do the above given the tax bill. The amount of revenue currently collected from the entry charge is miniscule. Under the new regime, as there would be the same tax potentially payable whether on lifetime or death, the entry charge would have some traction.

New regime: No tax payable on his free estate due to death allowance of Rakesh and his widow. One million payable on gift into trust. No tax on his death but trust pays a periodic charge say of 3 per cent and then 10 per cent when capital distributions are made.

Total tax depends on when distributions are made out of trust, but it results in a more neutral tax position under the flat rate tax regime.

Note that if Rakesh was not a long-term UK resident although there would be no tax on his settling assets into trust and no periodic charges, there would be tax on distributions to UK resident beneficiaries or if the trust owned UK assets or if there was a UK resident life tenant (at which point the 10 per cent would be payable).

Note that in moving to a flat rate regime it would be necessary to consider transitional provisions very carefully to forestall avoidance. In addition, it is important to view the flat rate gift tax as a total package combining low rates with few reliefs, removal of options for avoidance and a harsher CGT regime. It will not work if only adopted piecemeal.

3

Should the Suggestion that Ownership is a 'Myth' Have Any Implications for the Structure of Tax Law?

EDWIN SIMPSON

I. Introduction

When I presented an earlier version of this chapter at the conference held for Judith Freedman in Oxford on 15 and 16 May 2019, I began by saying a few words recognising Judith's immense contribution to modern tax scholarship, and delighting in what a pleasure it has been to work and teach with her in the Oxford Faculty of Law for nearly 20 years, since her appointment in 2001. As I said then, and record more permanently now, we used to do a double act in front of our undergraduate and graduate tax students in which Judith would argue powerfully for a UK GAAR,[1] and I would dismiss the idea as unnecessary nonsense that would never happen. We did this repeatedly, and I thought happily enough, for years – until Judith pulled rank and settled the argument once and for all by legislating one![2]

I also paid tribute to the sheer *growth* in tax activity that has occurred in Oxford during Judith's time here. When Judith arrived, the Faculty taught just one tax course (for BCL and MJur students) called 'Personal Taxation', which had been founded in the 1960s by Ash Wheatcroft. The Saïd Business School was just opening; the Oxford University Centre for Business Taxation did not yet exist (it was founded in 2005). As I write now, however, the Faculty offers two BCL and MJur courses: Corporate and Business Taxation and Policy, and the Taxation of Trusts and Global Wealth (the successor to the Personal Taxation course); an undergraduate option in Taxation has been established; and the part-time MSc in Taxation introduced, which draws tax practitioners to Oxford from all over the world. Judith has not of course done all this herself

[1] ie, a legislated, rather than judicially created, general anti-avoidance (or anti-abuse) rule.

[2] The story is of course a little more complicated than that. Judith was one of the seven members of the 'Aaronson Committee' (with Graham Aaronson QC, John Bartlett, Sir Launcelot Henderson, Lord Hoffmann, Howard Nowlan and John Tiley) whose *GAAR Study* of 11 November 2011 led directly to the UK GAAR introduced by Finance Act 2013, pt 5 and sch 43.

(Philip Baker, Emma Chamberlain, Mike Devereux, Glen Loutzenhiser and John Vella deserve honourable mentions), but it would not have happened without her.

I hope that I am right, taking account of Judith's published work, and insights learned from teaching with her, that she would subscribe to two propositions. The first is that tax lawyers must strive to locate their work within that of other disciplines, whether that be the work of economists, accountants, historians, comparative lawyers, or political theorists and philosophers; the second, that they must nevertheless have confidence in the contribution that they can make, as holders of specifically legal expertise. It is in these complementary insights[3] – I will call them Freedman virtues – that the ideas of this chapter originate.[4]

II. The Murphy and Nagel Claim

In their jointly authored book, *The Myth of Ownership*,[5] Liam Murphy and Thomas Nagel claim that 'ownership' may somehow be less than 'real'.[6] This chapter considers whether this claim should be thought to have implications for the way in which *the law* governing taxation and property generally is structured. The conclusion is that it should not do so, because the current legal starting point of some form of 'absolute' property right (the very thing that Murphy and Nagel deny in some sense to be real), subject to democratically mandated taxation by legislation, has proved highly effective in generating, governing and regulating a very sophisticated set of relationships between citizen, property and state (and not only in the context of taxation, but, as we shall see, in wider 'regulatory' contexts and in wider property and public law generally). This has been the case, in particular, because our legal conceptual tools include, alongside the legal notion of 'property', all sorts of other equally fundamental legal concepts, such as 'contract' or 'liability'.[7] In the context of comprehending the legal structures generating,

[3] They have been widely exhibited, eg: J Freedman, 'Five Recommendations for Restoring Trust in HMRC' *Tax Journal* (16 February 2017); J Freedman, 'Tax policy making: beyond simplification' *Tax Journal* (28 May 2015); J Freedman, C Evans and R Krever (eds), *The Delicate Balance: Tax, Discretion and the Rule of Law* (Amsterdam, International Bureau of Fiscal Documentation, 2011); J Freedman, 'Improving (Not Perfecting) Tax Legislation: Rules and Principles Revisited' [2010] *BTR* 717; J Freedman, 'Financial and Tax Accounting: Transparency and "Truth"' in W Schon (ed), *Tax and Corporate Governance* (Berlin, Springer Science, 2008); J Freedman, 'Is Tax Avoidance Fair?' in C Wales (ed), *Fair Tax: Towards a Modern Tax System* (London, The Smith Institute, 2008); J Freedman, 'Interpreting Tax Statutes: Tax Avoidance and the Intention of Parliament' (2007) 123 *LQR* 53; M Lamb, A Lymer, J Freedman and S James (eds), *Taxation: An Interdisciplinary Approach to Research* (Oxford, Oxford University Press, 2004); J Freedman, 'Accounting Standards: A Panacea?' *Tax Journal* (17 October 2004); J Freedman, 'Aligning Taxable Profits and Accounting Profits: Accounting standards, legislators and judges' (2004) 2 *eJournal of Tax Research* 4; and J Freedman, 'Defining Taxpayer Responsibility: In Support of a General Anti-Avoidance Principle' [2004] *BTR* 332.

[4] See too J Waldron, 'Legal and Political Philosophy' in J Coleman and S Shapiro (eds), *The Oxford Handbook of Jurisprudence and Philosophy of Law* (Oxford, Oxford University Press, 2002), urging the importance of such communication.

[5] L Murphy and T Nagel, *The Myth of Ownership: Taxes and Justice* (Oxford, Oxford University Press, 2002).

[6] The precise nature of their claim is considered further in the next section.

[7] This is Peter Benson's trio of fundamental private law concepts see P Benson, 'Philosophy of Property Law' in J Coleman and S Shapiro (eds), *The Oxford Handbook of Jurisprudence and Philosophy of Law* (Oxford, Oxford University Press, 2002) 752 considered further below in section IV.A.

governing and regulating the social practice of taxation, these other private law concepts have equal roles to play, as do statutory liabilities, originating in public law and democratically mandated legislation.[8]

The interplay between such separate basic legal concepts, the one no more fundamental than the other, has enabled the analysis not only of baselines and outcomes, with which the political theorist may be principally concerned when speculating about justice and taxation, but also a sophisticated account of the necessary constitutional structures, checks, balances and so forth, surrounding such outcomes. If the claim argued for by Murphy and Nagel were to be suggested to have implications for the *structure* of tax law, then it would need to be shown how it could meet these challenges at least as well as the law's existing conceptual structure does; and that, this chapter concludes, looks to be quite some task. In essence, the point is that, whilst at a high level of abstraction, the terms 'ownership' and 'property' might be used to refer to what it is that you have left after all other calls on your resources have been settled, the terms are not so used, nor should be so used, in law.

Two other introductory points can be made. The first is that Murphy and Nagel's book has, quite rightly, been deeply influential. In my own teaching of an undergraduate Jurisprudence option (Justice and Taxation) it has equal prominence, within a relatively short course, alongside Rawls, *A Theory of Justice*[9] and Nozick, *Anarchy, State, and Utopia*;[10] and its insights annually challenge, perplex and inform Oxford students. In a recent collection of essays in 2017,[11] its influence on the philosophical foundations of tax law was noted on the first page of Monica Bhandari's introduction to the essays as follow:

> It is this work that starts to bring the strands of the philosophical foundations of tax law together in modern times. The authors consider ideas of justice within the conception of property rights and how taxes fit in with those ideas. It is essential reading … and readers will see many references to the work in this collection, some using it as a springboard for their own ideas.[12]

The second is that this chapter does not seek in any way to undermine, nor to advance, the normative policy positions advocated by Murphy and Nagel. Our existing legal structures are quite capable of accommodating the policy outcomes for which they argue, if they are right to argue for them; but that is a different matter from the subject of this chapter. Its concern is only with any suggestion that our basic legal concepts might be somehow deficient.

[8] This is considered further below in section IV.B in the context of Jeremy Waldron's defence of legislative limits to the measure of property in his 2011 Hamlyn Lectures: *The Rule of Law and the Measure of Property* (Cambridge, Cambridge University Press, 2012).

[9] J Rawls, *A Theory of Justice* (Cambridge, MA, Harvard University Press, 1971).

[10] R Nozick, *Anarchy, State, and Utopia* (New York, Basic Books, 1974).

[11] M Bhandari (ed), *Philosophical Foundations of Tax Law* (Oxford, Oxford University Press, 2017).

[12] ibid 1–2. Within the collection see too J Snape, '"The Sinews of the State": Historical Justifications for Taxes and Tax Law' (ch 1); D de Cogan, 'Michael Oakeshott and the Conservative Disposition in Tax Law' (ch 5); P Emerton and K James, 'The Justice of the Tax Base and the Case for Income Tax' (ch 6); and DG Duff, 'Tax Policy and the Virtuous Sovereign: Dworkinian Equality and Redistributive Taxation' (ch 7).

III. The Nature of the Claim that Ownership is a 'Myth'

The claim that ownership is less than it seems is based on Murphy and Nagel's view that private property rights are *conventional.* The notion of original entitlement to pre-tax wealth, from which the state demands contributions, is (they argue) to misunderstand the reality of the matter, and to be deceived by convention:

> If there is a dominant theme that runs through our discussion, it is this: Private property is a legal convention, defined in part by the tax system; therefore, the tax system cannot be evaluated by looking at its impact on private property, conceived as something that has an independent existence and validity. Taxes must be evaluated as part of the overall structure of property rights that they help to create … It is illegitimate to appeal to a baseline of property rights in, say, 'pre-tax income' for the purpose of evaluating tax policies, when all such figures are the product of a system of which taxes are an inextricable part. One can neither justify nor criticize an economic regime by taking as an independent norm something that is, in fact, one of its consequences … Property rights are not the starting point of this subject but its conclusion.[13]

There is a revealing tension within these remarks. On the one hand, Murphy and Nagel suggest that '[p]rivate property is a legal convention, defined in part by the tax system'; on the other, that it is 'illegitimate to appeal to a baseline of property rights … for the purpose of evaluating tax policies'. The latter claim seems a thoroughly plausible one, but it is not a claim that appears to have implications for the structure of tax (or other) law, nor one which seems to depend upon any 'conventional' nature of legal reasoning. But the former claim can only be regarded as doing both. It may assist to consider in what sense of the 'conventional' the Murphy and Nagel claim may be intended; and, more so still, to consider the level of generality (I will call this the 'register') at which the claim is really intended to operate.

A. The 'Conventional' Aspect of the Claim

Conventionalism is not a straightforward idea. As Nelson Goodman has observed:

> The terms 'convention' and 'conventional' are flagrantly and intricately ambiguous. On the one hand, the conventional is the ordinary, the usual, the traditional, the orthodox as against the novel, the deviant, the unexpected, the heterodox. On the other hand, the conventional is the artificial, the invented, the optional, as against the natural, the fundamental, the mandatory.[14]

To make matters worse, Michael Rescorla notes:

> Adding to the confusion, 'convention' frequently serves as jargon within economics, anthropology, and sociology. Even within philosophy, 'convention' plays so many roles that we must ask whether a uniform notion is at work. Generally speaking, philosophical usage emphasizes

[13] Murphy and Nagel (n 5) 8–10.

[14] N Goodman, 'Just the Facts, Ma'am!' in M Krausz (ed), *Relativism: Interpretation and Confrontation* (Notre Dame, IN, University of Notre Dame Press, 1989).

> the second of Goodman's disambiguations. A common thread linking most treatments is that conventions are 'up to us', undetermined by human nature or by intrinsic features of the non-human world. We *choose* our conventions, either explicitly or implicitly … [A] distinctive thesis shared by most conventionalist theories is that there exist alternative conventions that are in some sense equally good. Our choice of a convention from among alternatives is undetermined by the nature of things, by general rational considerations, or by universal features of human physiology, perception, or cognition.[15]

It may be that basic legal concepts are indeed conventional in some of these senses (for example as being the usual, the orthodox as opposed to the novel, the heterodox; and as having been, in some sense, *chosen*). But it is far less obvious that the legal notion of private property is conventional in the sense that there exist alternative conventions that would be equally as good. To establish that the legal notion of private property is conventional in *that* sense it would be necessary at least to propose an equally promising alternative. Legal theorists tend equally to think that their foundational legal ideas, even if in some sense chosen, have been so chosen for sound supporting reasons.[16] This is so of course at a number of different levels of generality – even within essentially legal discourse. One might be criticising or defending (say) the claimed distinction between private and public law, or between judge-made law and legislation, or between *in rem* rights and *in personam* rights, or between ownership and obligation, or between contract, tort and restitution, and so on. And a similar point can, of course, be made as far as philosophical and political discourse about such questions is concerned. It will be important therefore also to consider the 'register' at which the Murphy and Nagel claim may be intended.

B. The 'Register' of the Claim

Legal and other theorists of course think and write at different levels of generality at different times. One way of thinking about this (although there are certainly others) is, as is so often the case, to draw upon the ideas of John Rawls.[17] As Patrick Emerton and Kathryn James have put it, in the context of their discussion of the tax base:

> [U]nlike Murphy and Nagel, we deploy the Rawlsian idea that the political principles that give effect to ideals of justice are articulated and implemented in *stages*: first, abstract political philosophy, then the formulation of a constitution consistent with the dictates of philosophy, then the enactment of legislation under that constitution etc.[18]

[15] M Rescorla, 'Convention' in EN Zalta (ed), *The Stanford Encyclopedia of Philosophy* (summer 2019 edn), 1.1–1.2, available at: plato.stanford.edu/archives/sum2019/entries/convention/.

[16] Such that the basis (say) of contract in *agreement*, or of tort law and criminal law in *wrongdoing*, or of fiduciary law in *trust and confidence*, or of restitution in *unjust enrichment* within private law is supported by reason, just as much as the more obvious examples from criminal law when (say) the proper extent of defences of provocation or self-defence is being reasoned towards.

[17] Rawls, *A Theory of Justice* (n 9) 195–201.

[18] Emerton and James (n 12) 126. They go on to contend, in the context of discussion of the tax base, that 'principles concerning private law rights that arise at the constitutional stage, and hence that constrain (or ought to constrain) legislative choices, can thereby constrain the choice of the tax base'.

It is not necessary for the argument to be made here to defend the Rawlsian idea of staged implementation. It is enough to make the lesser point that such different levels of theoretical abstraction and technicality, and legal abstraction and technicality, do plainly exist. And one difficulty is to know at which register Murphy and Nagel are making their claim. At times, it seems that they are doing so at quite a high level of abstraction. For example, in their own consideration of the tax base (which Emerton and James question for similar reasons to the concerns of this chapter about the wider Murphy and Nagel claim about tax law generally), Murphy and Nagel write: 'Since justice in taxation is not a matter of a fair distribution of tax burdens measured against a pretax baseline, it cannot be important in itself what pretax characteristics of taxpayers determine tax shares',[19] and, on the following page: 'Once we reject the idea that justice in taxation is a matter of ensuring a fair distribution of tax burdens relative to the pre-tax baseline [then certain things follow]'. At this level of generality, ie, as part of a discussion of 'justice in taxation', apparently broadly conceived, and leaving to one side whether it is right or not, the claim seems a reasonable one to make, just as some versions of the conventionalist claim are plausible.[20] But then there are the passages already set out where they write that '[p]rivate property is a legal convention, defined in part by the tax system'.[21]

This is just plain wrong as a matter of current law. Private property rights *per se* in common law systems are not defined in part or at all by the tax system, although of course they are impinged upon by legislation providing for taxation. But that, unfortunately, is not the end of the matter. For if Murphy and Nagel *were* right about the point at the higher level of abstraction, ie, if questions of 'justice in taxation' *do* need to be approached in the way they suggest (and it has already been conceded that this claim is credible), then legal theorists would have reason at least to think carefully again about whether they have their underlying concepts right. Precisely because these 'choices' of basic concepts are hoped to be underpinned by reason, lawyers would have grounds for concern if they did not in fact reflect the underlying reality they aim to represent. And there can be little doubt that Murphy and Nagel *are* right, in at least some sense, at the level of ultimate entitlement, all things considered. For otherwise the taxation that we have would be illegitimate *in toto* (quite apart from any particular deficiencies or inadequacies its detailed rules might have). The question is whether our legal structures need to change adequately to account for Murphy and Nagel's point, or whether those legal structures, including those that operate beyond the bounds of 'property' as such capture ultimate entitlement perfectly well already.

The argument now proceeds in relatively high register by considering the work of two theorists, chosen, in the first case because of the light thrown on how a legal conception of 'property' operates alongside other equally fundamental private law conceptions; and, in the second, because 'property' also operates alongside, or

[19] Murphy and Nagel (n 5) 98.
[20] See above after n 13.
[21] Murphy and Nagel (n 5): see n 13.

perhaps, better 'subject to' its regulation by public law and statute. It may be helpful first, however, given the breadth and depth of modern theorising about property, and the difficulties of register, to be explicit about some important and vexed questions that this chapter is *not* about.

First, it does not seek to resolve disagreements concerning whether legal property rights are best conceived as being 'rights to things', as 'rights between persons', or as 'rights between persons with regard to things'.[22] This is not to say that such matters are unimportant – very far from it – but they are not in the same part of the register within which Murphy and Nagel's claim needs to be engaged. Nor, and for the same reason, does it seek to resolve whether the 'bundle of rights' view of property remains tenable, or whether it has just about been superseded by views that see the 'right to exclude' as paramount.[23] Nor is it necessary to resolve just how normative the philosophy of law is generally;[24] nor, finally, whether we would do better to jettison concern for private property altogether and replace it with notions (say) of communal or common property. To this extent, although the argument below aims generally to be as neutral as possible about political theory, it does assume the need for a legal concept of private property, *of some sort*, ie, it assumes the existence of something capable of being the subject of the Murphy and Nagel claim. The argument now turns to consider Peter Benson's account of 'property' as part of a wider theory of private law, followed by Jeremy Waldron's defence of the legitimacy of legislation limiting the measure of property.

[22] The literature is vast: see, eg, WN Hohfeld, *Fundamental Legal Conceptions as Applied in Judicial Reasoning* (New Haven, CT, Yale University Press, 1919); AM Honoré, 'Ownership' in G Guest (ed) *Oxford Essays in Jurisprudence* (Oxford, Oxford University Press, 1961); LC Becker, *Property Rights: Philosophical Foundations* (London, Routledge, 1977); LC Becker, 'Too Much Property' (1992) 21 *Philosophy and Public Affairs* 196; SR Munzer, *A Theory of Property* (Cambridge, Cambridge University Press, 1990); SR Munzer, 'A Bundle Theorist Holds On to his Collection of Sticks' (2011) 8 *Econ Journal Watch* 265; SR Munzer, 'Property and Disagreement' in JE Penner and HE Smith (eds), *Philosophical Foundations of Property Law* (Oxford, Oxford University Press, 2013); J Christman, *The Myth of Property: Toward an Egalitarian Theory of Ownership* (New York, Oxford University Press, 1994); JW Harris, *Property and Justice* (Oxford, Oxford University Press, 1996); JE Penner, *The Idea of Property in Law* (Oxford, Clarendon Press, 1997); JE Penner, 'The "Bundle of Rights" Picture of Property' (1996) 43 *UCLA Law Review* 711; E Claeys, 'Property 101: Is Property a Thing or a Bundle?' (2009) 32 *Seattle University Law Review* 617; HE Smith, 'Property as the Law of Things' (2012) 125 *Harvard Law Review* 1691; TW Merrill and HE Smith, *Property: Principles and Policies* (New York, Foundation Press, 2007); B McFarlane and S Douglas, 'Defining Property Rights' in JE Penner and HE Smith (eds), *Philosophical Foundations of Property Law* (Oxford, Oxford University Press, 2013); A Ripstein, 'Possession and Use' in JE Penner and HE Smith (eds), *Philosophical Foundations of Property Law* (Oxford, Oxford University Press, 2013); TP Seto, 'A Forced Labour Theory of Property and Taxation' in M Bhandari (ed), *Philosophical Foundations of Tax Law* (Oxford, Oxford University Press, 2017).

[23] See generally n 22. For example, JE Penner 'Property qua the right of exclusive use stands for the proposition that property is not by its nature some bundled together aggregate or complex of norms, but a single, coherent right' in 'The "Bundle of Rights" Picture of Property' (n 22) 754; SR Munzer 'I maintain that property is a set of relations between the owner and other persons with respect to things, and that a good many normative modalities are involved in property besides the right to exclude' in 'Property and Disagreement' (n 22) 297. See also McFarlane and Douglas, 'Defining Property Rights' (n 22) defending the exclusion view on Hohfeldian grounds, and Smith's 'modular' analysis of property in 'Property as the Law of Things' (n 22).

[24] For a wry note on this, see Waldron's discussion of 'normative positivism', and the apparent contradiction in terms involved: Waldron, 'Legal and Political Philosophy' (n 4) 369–74.

IV. 'Property' within Wider Accounts of Private and Public Law

A. Benson and the Tension between Theories of Property and Private Law

Peter Benson has identified the same tension that exists between the Murphy and Nagel claim and actual tax law in rather broader terms.[25] He notes that the prime concern of recent property theory has been

> the justice of private property as one among several institutions of society that distribute the benefits and burdens which arise through social cooperation.[26] … [Yet] [t]his preoccupation with distribution in holdings contrasts strikingly with the intrinsic orientation of the principles of ownership and acquisition in private law … [where] the question of distribution is not even raised as a relevant consideration.[27]

Benson seeks to resolve this tension through a defence of the orientation of private law, but considered *comprehensively*,[28] so as to include not only a theory of entitlement to 'property', but also theories of 'contract' and of 'liability'. His contention is that property, contract and liability exhaust the 'fundamental categories or elements of private law', taking the latter to embody what he calls 'the juridical conception of rights'.[29] Private law 'can be suitably analysed in its own terms as a distinct ensemble of principles, doctrines and considerations'. It 'has a normative character and integrity of its own'.[30] Benson seeks to make explicit 'a definitive normative conception of private law' and to consider 'what the right of property consists in when it is viewed strictly and solely within the parameters of this conception'.[31]

This points very directly to the *legal* mistake made by Murphy and Nagel. Our legal concept of 'property' need not be expected to do *all* of the work as far as all-things-considered entitlements are concerned. It operates alongside, and with the support of, the other essential elements of private law. Benson defends this trio of 'property', 'contract' and 'liability' by means of a Rawlsian 'public' justification',[32] and argues ultimately that

[25] Benson (n 7).

[26] Citing, in 2002, J Waldron, *The Right to Private Property* (Oxford, Clarendon Press, 1988); Munzer, *A Theory of Property* (n 22) in support and Harris (n 22) and Penner, *The Idea of Property in Law* (n 22), as notable exceptions.

[27] Benson (n 7) 752–53.

[28] It is this comprehensiveness which makes it particularly salient as part of a response to the Murphy and Nagel claim.

[29] Benson (n 7) 777. See also Benson (n 7) 754: '[T]he conception is intended to articulate at a high level of generality pervasive features and requirements that characterise the most basic doctrines of the different parts of private law, as these have been largely settled across most common law jurisdictions'.

[30] Benson (n 7) 753.

[31] ibid fn 1. Benson contrasts his approach with that of Harris (n 22) ch 10: 'the main difference between our respective justifications is that the one I formulate is framed solely in terms that are internal and specific to [a] juridical conception of rights, hence to private law understood as a distinctive normative domain, whereas Harris's is not so limited' (Benson (n 7) fn 3).

[32] '[A] public justification *starts* with principles, doctrines, and values that are pervasive and settled in different parts of the legal and political culture of a given society – for example, in the principles, doctrines,

'it is "reasonableness" that is the animating notion that makes a non-distributive notion of private property in private law capable of operating satisfactorily'. Whether he is right about this does not matter for the point to be drawn from his approach as far as the Murphy and Nagel claim is concerned; but his argument is that within 'the public legal and political culture of a liberal democracy', a normative conception of persons 'as free and equal' will play a pivotal role.[33] And, if people are to be treated equally, then

> how might it be compatible with the freedom and equality of persons that one of them is entitled to exclude others from something – possibly by his or her unilateral action and without their prior assent – when previous to the acquisition, those excluded had equal standing to make the thing their own?[34]

Benson seeks to accomplish this using the well-known departure point of 'first occupancy',[35] aware throughout that there is no need for his account of property to accomplish *everything*:

> [M]any of the topics standardly discussed in property textbooks represent complex, or in James Penner's term, 'hybrid' legal institutions that combine features of more than one elementary kind of legal relation; for example, property and contract. Moreover, the principles … discussed may incorporate considerations that go beyond the juridical conception of rights and that embody social and economic imperatives that can be legitimately pursued only via legislative enactment.[36]

Because able to rely on the separate idea of 'contract' to account particularly for *transfers* of property, Benson is able to focus his juridical concept of property upon only three aspects: first, an exclusive right to possess; next, the exclusive right to use; and, finally, the right to alienate.[37] Again, because he can rely on 'contract' for *transfers*, the right to alienate which forms part of the right of 'property' is strictly limited to abandonment (as opposed to transfer), by which legitimate first occupancy is brought to an end by a resource being again rendered unowned. In this way Benson sees the three core aspects of the juridical conception of property as constituting a form of circle, leading from legitimate first occupancy, through the exclusive right to use, to abandonment and return to non-ownership. These three aspects constitute, so to speak, the 'essence' of the

and historically authoritative writings that make up its private and public law' (Benson (n 7) 757): see J Rawls, *Political Liberalism* (New York, Columbia University Press, 1993); and J Rawls, 'The Idea of Public Reason Revisited' in S Freeman (ed), *Collected Papers: John Rawls* (Cambridge, MA, Harvard University Press, 1999).

[33] Benson (n 7) 757.

[34] ibid 756.

[35] J Locke, *Two Treatises of* Government, book II (New York, Cambridge University Press, 1988); OW Holmes, *The Common Law*, ed M DeWolfe (Boston, MA, Little, Brown, and Company, 1964) Lecture VI; Nozick (n 10); R Epstein, 'Possession as the Root of Title' (1979) 13 *Georgia Law Review* 1221; SR Munzer, 'The Acquisition of Property Rights' (1991) 66 *Notre Dame Law Review* 661.

[36] Benson (n 7) 757. This Dworkin-like turn is considered further below in the discussion of Waldron. Hayek has made a similar point about contract complementing property: 'That other people's property can be serviceable in the achievement of our aims is due mainly to the enforceability of contracts. The whole network of rights created by contracts is as important a part of our own protected sphere, [and] as much the basis of our plans, as any property of our own': F Hayek, *The Constitution of Liberty* (Chicago, IL, University of Chicago Press, 1960) 140.

[37] Based on the three-part Roman Law division between *ius possendi*, *ius utendi* and *ius abutendi*: Benson (n 7) 773.

private law idea of property. Private law's analysis of transfer (as opposed to abandonment) can be left to be the work principally of 'contract', but also, where appropriate, of 'liability' (and of public law).

Returning to Benson's defence of the *reasonableness* of such an account of property, the puzzle is whether property, seen in this way, is 'suited to be part of the legal and political order that honours individuals as free and equal persons'.[38] The question is whether 'the principle is intrinsically reasonable in the sense of articulating norms that are consistent with, and indeed expressive of, this view of individuals'.[39] Again, whether he is right is not the main concern here, but Benson concludes that 'the apparent indifference of the legal conception of property to need is not only consonant with respecting people as free and equal, *but indeed necessary for it*'.[40] 'Ownership represents the exercise of the moral powers that are shared identically by all … indifference towards need is conceptually basic in our understanding of freedom and must be presupposed'.[41] Furthermore, it is an account of freedom of this sort that underlies the legitimacy of private law containing categories of liability between individuals at all:

> In our judgments, both everyday and juridical, we make reference to [this], or at least implicitly suppose [it], when we require that individuals be accountable for their acts … We cannot make sense of our public legal culture unless we view, and are entitled to view, ourselves in this way.[42]

Within this high register there is, of course, disagreement as to how highly to regard freedom in comparison with other values. Legal systems have to provide a forum within which everyday matters can nevertheless be determined whilst such controversies remain unresolved. Democracy, legislative processes and public law are vital complements to the conceptual commitments of private law, and it is to these that the argument now turns.

B. Waldron and the Tension between Theories of Property and Public Law

An account of private law, even one as meticulous and comprehensive as Benson's, is insufficient to provide a conceptual basis for a tax system, which depends equally vitally on an adequate conception of democracy, legislation, and public law. Jeremy Waldron, in his Hamlyn Lectures of 2011, *The Rule of Law and the Measure of Property*,[43] approached such questions through the lens of the Rule of Law[44] and an analysis of the impact of

[38] Benson (n 7) 800.
[39] ibid.
[40] Emphasis added.
[41] Benson (n 7) 814.
[42] ibid 813.
[43] Waldron, *The Rule of Law and the Measure of Property* (n 8).
[44] Capitalised throughout the printed version of the lectures, to distinguish the ideal from the quite separate idea of 'a rule of law': Waldron, *The Rule of Law and the Measure of Property* (n 8) 6.

US environmental regulation on beachfront property rights on a barrier island off the coast of South Carolina. The analysis begins with a discussion of *Lucas v South Carolina Coastal Council*,[45] and Waldron asks 'whether it detracts from the Rule of Law to subject property rights to restriction in the way regulations restricted Mr Lucas'?[46]

The *Lucas* case concerned a property developer who bought expensive beachfront real estate only to see his development intentions thwarted by state environmental regulations whose purpose was to protect the coastline from erosion. Mr Lucas knew at the time of his purchase that there was some such regulation already in place, but it was further legislation following a commission report completed after he had purchased, but before he began construction, that denuded his property of almost all its value. His case, brought against South Carolina under the Fifth and Fourteenth Amendments to the US Constitution, which prohibit the taking of private property for public use without fair compensation, went all the way to the US Supreme Court, which required that he be paid substantial damages. As Waldron notes, there is a huge literature on the 'taking' provisions of the US Constitution, but it was not the focus of his attention.[47] His concern was rather that:

> On the one hand, you have a property right developed presumably in accordance with the Common Law that South Carolina shares with many other jurisdictions – a property right defined by Common Law and circulating according to market principles. On the other hand, you have an environmental determination, made by an administrative body, pursuant to a piece of state legislation: a rule that exists as law because it occurred to some legislators in Columbia, South Carolina, that it might be a good idea to protect the beaches of the barrier islands from erosion. These are two different types of law – Common Law versus statutory regulation – and we may want to ask whether our ideal of the Rule of Law privileges one kind of law rather than the other.[48]

Waldron's argument proceeds by rejecting Locke's 'bottom-up' (to use Epstein's phrase)[49] account of property rights, favouring instead the view that 'modern' property rights are really the result of determinations and allocations made by public law. He uses land allocation in New Zealand as a clear example:

> It was used and cultivated first by a collective group, it's original Maori owners … It was then transferred by the indigenous tribe – whether by respectable or dubious transactions … – to the colonial government as part of that government's right of pre-emption (established under the Treaty of Waitangi). The British government's policy of encouraging white settlement led them to offer the leasehold in this land to enterprising settlers. And their policy of encouraging family farming in New Zealand led them to redistribute some of the leaseholds and then convert leasehold to freehold property … supervised by the state purportedly in the public interest at every stage.[50]

[45] *Lucas v South Carolina Coastal Council* 505 US 1003 (1992).

[46] Waldron, *The Rule of Law and the Measure of Property* (n 8) 3.

[47] He merely observes that 'the *Lucas* decision represented something of a revival of the Supreme Court's willingness to condemn state regulations as takings': Waldron, *The Rule of Law and the Measure of Property* (n 8) 3.

[48] Waldron, *The Rule of Law and the Measure of Property* (n 8) 9–10.

[49] R Epstein, *Design for Liberty: Private Property, Public Administration, and the Rule of Law* (Cambridge, MA, Harvard University Press, 2011) 99.

[50] Waldron, *The Rule of Law and the Measure of Property* (n 8) 29–30.

The New Zealand case may be plainer than some, but Waldron suspects that 'a similar tale can be told in most legal systems, with variations no doubt, but in ways that equally undermine the myth that modern property rights can trace their standing to anything remotely like a Lockean provenance'.[51] Instead, legal property rights are the product of sophisticated, legal process, in much the same way as was the environmental legislation in *Lucas*. There, a federal law, the Coastal Zone Management Act 1972, provided a general framework for the protection of coastlines from erosion, and led the South Carolina legislature in 1977 to enact consequential state law providing for environmental regulation, administrative process, the zoning of some land as requiring particular permission for development and so forth. In turn, in 1988, following a special commission review, further state legislation was enacted which led directly to Mr Lucas's land becoming incapable of development in the way that he had hoped. It appears, as Waldron notes, to have been 'a careful and scrupulous process, both at the various legislative stages and at the administrative stage'.[52]

Such careful and scrupulous due process is hardly new. Returning to the acquisition of private property, the public, legislated nature of the process in South Carolina is in some respects little different from seventeenth- to nineteenth-century inclosure processes in England and Wales. Indeed, the practice of 'general' inclosure consolidation acts from which particular, local inclosure acts could draw their central provisions, mirrors rather closely the interplay between US federal and state legislation. A recent UK Court of Appeal case[53] necessitated consideration of such inclosure processes in some detail. The Parish of Crudwell Inclosure Act 1816 incorporated by reference general provisions from the Inclosure Consolidation Act 1801, supplemented by other provisions required by particular local circumstances. The local Act appointed a Commissioner 'for putting this Act in execution; subject to the Rules, Orders, Directions and Regulations of the [1801 Act] (which shall be applied deemed and taken as part of this Act)'.[54] The preparation of the Inclosure Award appears to have taken 25 years, not being completed until 1841. The scheme of the legislation required the Commissioner to determine the boundary of the lands to be inclosed, which could be subject to appeal to the Quarter Sessions (section 3). The Commissioner was then to survey and value the land, and draw up a plan (section 4). Next, to set our certain roads, ways, ditches, drains etc over the land, before turning to the process of determining specific allotments of land. Once that was completed, the Commissioner was to draw up a formal 'Award in Writing', to be read and executed at a Meeting of the Proprietors, read out in church, and so forth, and ultimately inrolled in one of the Courts at Westminster. This Award, together with its Map, would set out the parcels of land, their size and so forth, as well as the roads, ways, ditches, drains etc to be laid out between the parcels.

Throughout the process, the Commissioner was required to act openly, and many of his determinations could be subjected to legal challenge. For example, the provision for the setting out of major public roads ('the publick Carriage Roads and Highways') over the land concerned (section 8), which was to be done *before* the Commissioner began to

[51] ibid 31.
[52] See the more detailed description in Waldron, *The Rule of Law and the Measure of Property* (n 8) 79.
[53] *R (Andrews) v Secretary of State for Environment Food and Rural Affairs* [2015] EWCA Civ 669.
[54] *Andrews* (n 53) [8].

consider the allotment of parcels, required his initial proposals to be set out on the ground 'by Marks and Bounds', to be shown on a Map which was to be available for inspection by all concerned, for notice to be given of the proposals in the local newspaper, and by affixing the Map to the church door, and required that he hold a Meeting at which the persons concerned could state any objection. Were there to be objections they were to considered by the Commissioner, sitting with any local Justice of the Peace not interested in the land concerned. Provision was made for objection by others to any proposed amendments. Similar, careful procedures were provided at every stage of the process, which, as already indicated, for one reason or another seems to have taken 25 years.

Once completed, the final Award would then 'at all Times be admitted and allowed in all Courts whatever as legal Evidence'; and the

> several Allotments, Partitions, Regulations, Agreements, Exchanges, Orders, Directions, Determinations, and all other Matters and Things therein mentioned and contained, shall … be binding and conclusive … unto and upon the said Proprietors, and all Parties and Persons concerned or interested in the same, or in any of the Lands, Grounds, or Premises aforesaid.

The process was plainly intended to be final, but nevertheless, the Court of Appeal was willing to consider its validity 200 years after the process had begun.

The particular point considered by the Court of Appeal is itself of some relevance to the concern of this chapter in the interplay between private and public entitlement. It concerned whether, following the setting out of 'the Publick Carriage Roads and Highways', the similar procedure for setting out 'private Roads, Bridleways, Footways, Ditches, Drains, etc' permitted the setting out of *public* bridleways and footways, or only *private* ones, ie, easements. There was no other provision in the legislation which justified the Commissioner in doing so, and the provision already referred to providing for the setting out of 'Publick Carriage Roads and Highways' (section 8), required the same to be at least 30 feet wide. And yet the Commissioner concerned, Mr Daniel Trinder, purported to set out a number of such lesser, but public, rights at widths considerably less than 30 feet. There was expert historical evidence before the Court that this was also the practice of a very large number of local commissioners across the country, relying on similar general clauses from the 1801 Act.

The outcome (that, despite not being the natural construction, the adjective 'private' must be taken to apply only to the immediately following word at the start of the list (ie, 'Roads'),[55] such that Mr Trinder *did* have power to set out minor *public* bridleways and footpaths at widths of less than 30 feet) is of less concern than the different 'registers' of allocation evidenced by the inclosure process. These are not well captured by the easy view that such processes *only* concerned suppressing the common interest in favour of creating individual, private landholdings. Of course, such processes did indeed involve doing exactly that, in ways that drastically changed the pattern of land ownership and occupation over the areas of land concerned over a period of more than 300 years;[56] but such processes can also be seen to be characterised by 'careful and scrupulous' due

[55] ie, roads for use by a 'private' class of (say) neighbouring landowners.

[56] Between 1604 and 1914 over 5,200 enclosure Bills were enacted by Parliament, relating to some fifth of the total area of England and Wales, ie, some 6.8 million acres, or 28,000 km2: www.parliament.uk/about/living-heritage/transformingsociety/towncountry/landscape/overview/enclosingland/.

process, and by a concern to provide for the public interest (through the creation of major and minor highways – ie, today, vehicular routes and lesser public rights of way such as footpaths and bridleways – as well as drains and ditches etc) every bit as much as to allocate to individuals the parcels of land bounded and defined by the extent of such public rights.

There may be a risk of becoming distracted by inclosure processes from Waldron's argument about *Lucas*. Waldron's concern was whether it detracts from the Rule of Law to subject property rights to restriction in the way regulations restricted Mr Lucas; and he had taken his argument as far as rejecting, in clear cases such as New Zealand (and we now know from *Andrews* that there may be ground to do so too in land subject to inclosure process) a Lockean 'bottom-up' account[57] of property rights, favouring instead the view that 'modern' property rights are really the result of determinations and allocations made, in many perhaps even all cases, by public law. This move, at first sight, might appear to offer some support for the Murphy and Nagel claim, because such determination and allocation might be made *after* taxation as they suggest they should be (rather as parcels of land in inclosure processes were allocated *after* setting out public rights of way). But Waldron does not offer support for their claim in this way, because his conclusion is that even a 'strong', *substantive* conception[58] of the Rule of Law should not privilege private property in the same way that it might privilege, say, prospectivity, or human rights, or natural justice. Rather, private property's subjection to public law regulation by legislation (just as this regulated its acquisition) is itself *required* by the Rule of Law to further equally important concerns of democracy and freedom. Waldron considers a number of arguments that might be thought to support such a privilege for private property, but (rightly) concludes that none of them does. Such arguments would need to have their origin in some form of concern for legality (to count as Rule-of-Law type arguments at all). Waldron considers in particular two, related candidates, but rejects them both. First, he considers the concern that laws should be reasonably stable. As Raz has observed:

> [P]eople need to know the law not only for short-term decisions … but also for long-term planning. Knowledge of at least the general outlines and sometimes even of details of tax law and company law are often important for business plans which will bear fruit only years later. Stability is essential if people are to be guided by law in their long-term decisions.[59]

The second candidate is again related to stability, but seen through the lens of the 'special considerations about the personal and psychological investment that an individual has in the objects connected to him'.[60] This has led to the view that respect for property

[57] See n 49 above.

[58] ie, one which goes beyond concern (merely) that law should be 'prospective, open and clear' (J Raz, 'The Rule of Law and Its Virtue' in *The Authority of Law: Essays on Law and Morality* (Oxford, Clarendon Press, 1979) 214–15), and comply with requirements of generality, clarity, constancy, publicity, prospectivity and practicability (L Fuller, *The Morality of Law* (New Haven, CT, Yale University Press, 1964); but should require and justify also certain 'substantive' features of legality, such as commitments (say) to protection of human rights, natural justice, human dignity or democracy.

[59] Raz (n 58) 214–15. It is impossible not to think of Judith when reading this passage.

[60] Waldron, *The Rule of Law and the Measure of Property* (n 8) 56.

rights may be bound up with respect for persons.[61] These stability inspired arguments, to allow for planning and for personal attachment, do undoubtedly have a Rule-of-Law flavour about them, but Waldron rejects them as sufficient grounds for insulating, say, Mr Lucas's beachfront property from all legal incursion, and does so without falling into the trap of concluding that all such reasoning need be compressed into our notion of property. Rather:

> Law works holistically. And property rights are not defined in isolation from the rest of the law. What my property rights amount to is partly a matter of how things stand in other areas of law. Robert Nozick once observed that '[m]y property rights in my knife allow me to leave it where I will, but not in your chest'. Property rights live in the shadow of the criminal law. And it will not do to turn the tables and say that property rights constrain the development of the criminal law and place limits on what uses of material goods the legislature may criminalize. (As in: 'I thought this was my gun or my marijuana. Why can't I do with it what I please?')[62]

This is very much the same point against the Murphy and Nagel claim considered above in the context of Benson's theory of private law. 'Property' needs 'contract' to provide for transfer; and property 'lives in the shadow' of taxation, just as much as it does of the criminal law. Intriguingly, in reasoning towards this conclusion, Waldron refers to Murphy and Nagel in a way that might seem to offer some support for their claim, suggesting that perhaps 'we come to identify our personal income in terms of post-deduction payment, net of income tax – this is argued in a book by [Murphy and Nagel]'.[63] But this seems to have their claim the wrong way around: their contention is that the 'conventional' position is the very opposite, but that it should change. More importantly, it cannot fit alongside Waldron's (correct) view that law operates 'holistically'. In the end Waldron concludes that it is just mistaken to seek to privilege concern for property in Rule-of-Law terms:

> Arguing in Rule-of-Law terms for property, markets, and economic freedom is simply too distracting. It bogs us down in debates about substantive conceptions and about the sticks in the bundle that are specially privileged as a matter of legality. And it prevents us saying what we want to say about private property for fear that that will not be something that comes under the auspices of the Rule-of-Law ideal.[64]

Most importantly of all, the Rule of Law provides no sound reason to insulate property from 'legislation'. Indeed, legislation seems particularly clearly to *advance* both procedural and (other) substantive concerns of the Rule of Law. In procedural terms it is 'prospective, open and clear';[65] it seems to comply with Fuller-like requirements of the law's 'internal morality'[66] very much more straightforwardly than do, for example,

[61] See, eg, D Hume, *A Treatise of Human Nature*, eds LA Selby-Bigge and PH Nidditch (Oxford, Clarendon Press, 1978) Book III, Part ii; and M Radin 'Property and Personhood', reprinted in M Radin, *Reinterpreting Property* (Chicago, IL, University of Chicago Press, 1993) 36, both relied on by Waldron, *The Rule of Law and the Measure of Property* (n 8).

[62] Waldron, *The Rule of Law and the Measure of Property* (n 8) 70.

[63] ibid 69.

[64] ibid 75.

[65] Raz (n 58).

[66] Fuller (n 58).

customary or judge-made law. And, in substantive Rule-of-Law terms, it values – indeed gives effect to – democracy.

Waldron suspects that Rule-of-Law type arguments *against* legislation impinging on property might be better grounded in the concern that legislation is willed by the very people that Rule-of-Law concerns are meant to constrain – ie, powerful politicians.[67] More broadly this point concerns the idea that Rule-of-Law concerns are meant to *constrain* the all-powerful state, yet legislation is the very paradigm of the state in action.[68] But these concerns too he (rightly) rejects. We have every bit as much reason to be alarmed, on these sorts of grounds, about judge-made law (where there is the familiar unease about, for example, the modern creation of common law criminal offences).[69] In any event, Waldron is unconvinced that a substantive conception of the Rule of Law should *prioritise* property over democracy.[70] However imperfect legislatures may be, we want them to be well designed and effective to make law, in ways courts simply are not and cannot be expected to be. He concludes:

> In general, legislation has the characteristic that it gives ordinary people a sort of stake in the Rule of Law, by involving them directly or indirectly in its enactment, and by doing so on terms of fair political equality.[71]

This is of course in particular why democratically mandated legislation, as opposed to any other method, is so suited to the imposition of taxation. In tax law, just as in criminal law (although arguably even more strongly), there are strong substantive reasons, and grounding for them in the Bill of Rights 1689, that taxation is *peculiarly* a matter for legislation. Ministers have no authority to impose a tax,[72] and neither do judges.[73]

I want to return to the detail of the taxation constitution in the last section of this chapter, after looking at one final possible analogous incidence of the interplay between the private and public spheres. The UK has no direct equivalent to the taking clauses of the US Constitution.[74] Laying out by inclosure commissioner or more modern statutory process is not, however, the only way that public rights of way over private land can come into being. They can still do so today, and, by analogy with the law of private rights of way (or easements), arise by prescription. Indeed, prescription can provide for

[67] Waldron, *The Rule of Law and the Measure of Property* (n 8) 86. Some of the arguments Judith and I used to stage about the need for a GAAR (see text to n 2 above) were of this type, ie, about whether one could have confidence that Westminster politics would be likely to produce an effective GAAR.

[68] Waldron, *The Rule of Law and the Measure of Property* (n 8) 88.

[69] ibid 91.

[70] ibid 93–95.

[71] ibid 97.

[72] *Attorney-General v Wilts United Dairies Ltd* (1921) 37 TLR 884; not even in war time. This point is considered further below in section VI.

[73] This latter point lies of course at the heart of concern about judge-made anti-avoidance principles, of the type associated with *WT Ramsay Ltd v IRC* [1982] AC 300: see generally E Simpson and B McFarlane, 'Tackling Avoidance' in J Getzler (ed), *Rationalizing Property, Equity and Trusts – Essays in Honour of Edward Burn* (Oxford, Oxford University Press, 2003) considering the matter in the context of both tax and property law. I have argued elsewhere that the judicial role in such contexts is less of a concern than might appear if it can properly be regarded as an application of legislation to facts: E Simpson, 'The Ramsay Principle: A Curious Incident of Judicial Reticence?' [2004] *BTR* 358.

[74] Waldron, *The Rule of Law and the Measure of Property* (n 8) 3.

still more extensive incursion on private ownership than mere rights of way, through the establishment of rights of *recreation* over private property; and legislation in England and Wales has gone further still, by directly creating a right to roam over defined categories of mountain, moor, heath and down land, whatever the landowner's views about it might be.[75]

V. The Prescriptive Acquisition of Public Rights Over Private Land

In the context of prescriptive acquisition of private or public rights over private property, the *Newhaven* case[76] provides an interesting English complement to the *Lucas* case discussed by Waldron. *Newhaven* concerned whether a beach that had formed within the harbour wall of a port on the south coast of England, and had been used for recreation by inhabitants of the town since at least the end of the First World War, could be registered as a 'village green' to protect such user, or whether it could not lawfully be so registered, such that the relevant port authority would be entitled to maintain a fence around it in order to prevent its recreational use from continuing.

The case is reminiscent of *Lucas* (and indeed *Andrews*) in that once again one sees legal process as the context in which the contest between private right and public interest is fought out. The English law of prescription is different from civil law (and indeed from Scottish law), as Lord Hoffmann observed in the *Sunningwell* case:

> Any legal system must have rules of prescription which prevent the disturbance of long-established de facto enjoyment. But the principles upon which they achieve this result may be very different. In systems based on Roman law, prescription is regarded as one of the methods by which ownership can be acquired. The ancient *Twelve Tables* called it usucapio, meaning literally a taking by use … The periods of prescription … were substantially lengthened by Justinian and some of the conditions changed, [but] it remained in principle a method of acquiring ownership. This remains the position in civilian systems today.
>
> English law, on the other hand … did not treat long enjoyment as being a method of acquiring title. Instead, it approached the question from the other end by treating the lapse of time as either barring the remedy of the former owner or giving rise to a presumption that he had done some act which conferred a lawful title upon the person in de facto possession or enjoyment.[77]

We find ourselves in familiar territory. Just as one *could* take account of taxation in defining the extent of property (as Murphy and Nagel claim), or afterwards by legislating to take part of what initially belonged to a private individual away (as common law systems do), equally private or public rights over someone else's land it seems can be analysed as directly impacting upon ownership, or as doing so only indirectly. It is

[75] Countryside and Rights of Way Act 2000. Whereas prescriptive acquisition is concerned with how matters might appear to the landowner: see further below in section V.

[76] *R (Newhaven Port and Properties Limited) v East Sussex County Council* [2015] UKSC 7.

[77] *R v Oxfordshire County Council, ex p Sunningwell Parish Council* [2000] 1 AC 335, 349.

perfectly coherent for a member of the public to have a statutory right to roam (say) over land that remains owned by somebody else, without it being the case that they own anything in consequence of having such a right.

As far as prescriptive acquisition of similar rights over land is concerned, much turns today on the *quality* of the prescriptive use; and it has been clear since *Sunningwell* that the character of use required is the same for the acquisition of a private easement, a public right of way, or recreational use of the sort at issue in *Newhaven*. Lord Hoffmann explains:

> It became established that such user had to be, in the Latin phrase, *nec vi, nec clam, nec precario*: not by force, nor stealth, nor the licence of the owner. The unifying element in these three vitiating circumstances was that each constituted a reason why it would not have been reasonable to expect the owner to resist the exercise of the right – in the first case, because rights should not be acquired by the use of force, in the second, because the owner would not have known of the user and in the third, because he had consented to the user, but for a limited period.[78]

English law has accordingly rooted its approach to prescription in the fact that the use required, for whatever the relevant prescriptive period may be, must be of a kind appropriate to enable the landowner to resist it, such that the landowner might almost be regarded as having impliedly granted the right by failing to take steps to do so. It is accordingly said that such rights 'lie in grant', and this is as true as far as the acquisition of public rights is concerned as it is of the acquisition of private rights:

> Just as the theory was that a lawful origin of private rights of way could be found only in a grant by the freehold owner, so the theory was that a lawful origin of public rights of way could be found only in a dedication to public use.[79]

The key statutory provision as far as the recreational right claimed in *Newhaven* was concerned is now Commons Act 2006, section 15(2) which relevantly provides for land to be registered as a village green where 'a significant number of the inhabitants of any locality, or of any neighbourhood within a locality, have indulged as of right in lawful sports and pastimes on the land for a period of at least 20 years'. 'Land' is defined by section 61(1) to include land covered by water, so it was no barrier to the possible registration of Newhaven beach as a village green that it was entirely covered by the sea twice a day.[80]

All therefore turned in *Newhaven* on whether the use had been without force, stealth or licence (ie, permission), in each case because it would not have been reasonable in such circumstances to have expected the port authority to have taken steps to resist such use. And the port authority was, the Supreme Court held, able to establish that the user had in fact been impliedly permitted, because the port authority had power to make byelaws regulating access to the land, and had done so. In 1931, byelaws had been made regulating access to the harbour for (among other things) fishing, playing sports or games and dog walking. The Supreme Court reasoned that a prohibition can

[78] *Sunningwell* (n 77) 350–51.

[79] ibid 351–52.

[80] It seems to have shared this feature with some at least of Mr Lucas's land (see Waldron, *The Rule of Law and the Measure of Property* (n 8) fn 35, 80). The original framers of the definition of 'land' now contained in the Commons Act 2006 may have had duck ponds in mind, rather than the sea.

be expressed in such a way as to imply a permission. So, for example, a requirement that dogs must be kept on a lead implies a permission to bring dogs into the port.[81] Users reading the byelaws ought accordingly to have known that their access was permitted, because it was regulated. They could bathe or play, but only so long as their activity did not fall foul of the restrictions in the byelaws.[82] And this was held to be so even though users may have been unaware even of the existence of any such byelaws, which it appeared had not been enforced in living memory.

Again, the outcome of the case is not as significant as its form as a contest between public and private interests mediated through underlying notions of private property overlain with statutory concern for legitimate public interest. 'Property' once again does not have to do all of the work, but is supported by statutory concern for public rights within public law, just as it is supported by 'contract' within private law. Such structures certainly mean that all does not need to be achieved 'within' our legal conception of property; and they ensure that equally important weight is given to the moral significance of agreement (in the case of contract) and of democracy (in the case of legislation).

VI. The Constitution of Tax Law

A. The Primacy of Legislation in Taxation (or 'No Taxation without Representation')

Tax lawyers need little reminding that:

> Taxes are creatures of statute and depend for their [legal] validity solely upon the Acts of Parliament creating them; the function of the courts in relation to tax is to interpret those Acts and not to create the law.[83]

The history of this basic constitutional truth is beyond the scope of this chapter,[84] but the doctrine that only Parliament can enact a tax is rooted not only in concern for democracy, but every bit as much in an initial 'absolute' conception of private property complemented by the democratically mandated Parliamentary power to interfere with it. In the particular context of taxation, rather than other legislation, there have developed peculiarly nuanced constitutional rules and conventions, limiting for example the role of the House of Lords in relation to 'money bills'. Parliament Act 1911, section 1(2) defines a Money Bill as:

> (2) [A] Public Bill which in the opinion of the Speaker of the House of Commons contains only provisions dealing with all or any of the following subjects, namely, the imposition, repeal, remission, alteration, or regulation of taxation.

[81] *Newhaven* (n 76) [57]–[58].
[82] ibid [60]–[63].
[83] *Simon's Taxes* (LexisNexis) A1.103. See further nn 72 and 73 above.
[84] See further Bill of Rights 1689, Article 4; and E Simpson, 'Making Sense of the Ramsay Principle: a Novel Role for Public Law?' in J-B Auby and M Freedland (eds), *The Public Law/Private Law Divide: une entente assez cordiale* (Oxford, Hart Publishing, 2006).

Section 1(1) provides that:

> (1) If a Money Bill, having been passed by the House of Commons, and sent up to the House of Lords at least one month before the end of the session, is not passed by the House of Lords without amendment within one month after it is so sent up to that House, the Bill shall, unless the House of Commons direct to the contrary, be presented to His Majesty and become an Act of Parliament on the Royal Assent being signified, notwithstanding that the House of Lords have not consented to the Bill.

The significance of this is clear as respecting the underlying constitutional fundamental[85] that elected members of Parliament (and so not those in the House of Lords) can be said to *consent* on behalf of their constituents to the imposition of taxation every time a Money Bill is enacted. I have argued elsewhere[86] that there is something *somewhat* illusory about this analysis, given the strength of executive control over MPs in such circumstances, but it does run strongly counter to the claim that our legal conception of '[p]rivate property is … defined in part by the tax system', any more than the fact that slavery is unlawful defines in part the law of contract. Our legally recognised concept of ownership is instead subject to the lawful levying of taxation upon it by Act of Parliament in certain defined circumstances.

As Atkin LJ put it in the *Wilts United Dairies* case:[87]

> Though the attention of our ancestors was directed especially to abuses of the prerogative, there can be no doubt that this statute [the Bill of Rights, 1689] declares the law that no money shall be levied for or to the use of the Crown except by grant of Parliament. We know how strictly Parliament has maintained this right – and, in particular, how jealously the House of Commons has asserted its predominance in the power of raising money.[88]

B. Conclusions

This chapter has sought to assess the claim made by Murphy and Nagel that '[p]rivate property is a legal convention, defined in part by the tax system'.[89] The argument has proceeded by doubting that property is conventional in the sense that other notions could be chosen by the law for equally good reason. It also queried the 'register' at which the claim is intended. If it is a claim about our current legal structures, then it is plainly wrong. But even if it is intended at the higher register of the evaluation of tax policy concerns, then it still needs to be met at the legal level, because lawyers have reason to want the design of their everyday conceptual apparatus to reflect underlying realities

[85] The phrase owes its origin to HWR Wade, 'Constitutional Fundamentals' (Cambridge, Hamlyn Lecture Series, 1980).

[86] See nn 73 and 84 above.

[87] *Wilts United Dairies* (n 72) citing *Gosling v Veley* (1850) 12 QB 328 where Wilde CJ said: 'The rule of law that no pecuniary burden can be imposed upon the subjects of this country, by whatever name it may be called, whether tax, due, rate, or toll, except under clear and distinct legal authority, established by those who seek to impose the burden, has been so often the subject of legal decision that it may be deemed a legal axiom, and requires no authority to be cited in support of it.'

[88] The idea that there be no taxation without representation is no less jealously guarded in the United States.

[89] Text to n 13 above.

rather than conceal them. But an analysis of Benson's comprehensive account of private law gives some reason for confidence that 'property', alongside other foundational concepts such as 'contract' can be justified in its currently determinedly absolute from, particularly when it is complemented by Waldron's account of the values of the Rule of Law, and their justification of prospective, open and clear, democratically mandated legislation. These points hold not only against the Murphy and Nagel points, but also against the very different type of claim that taxation is no better than theft. That private rights of property are subject to democratically mandated taxation embodies a sophisticated framework of constitutional analysis that is not lightly to be dismissed. The citizen may be absolutely entitled as a matter of the private law conception of property; but equally[90] (and this word is important) absolutely obliged as a matter of public law to pay over a duly-demanded tax. Taxation sits within the constitution much as environmental regulation does, or the Inclosure Acts do, or the prescriptive acquisition of rights over other people's land does. The richness of the existing complete legal picture gives some cause for hope – although certainly not over-confidence – that tax policy decisions, as they change over time, can be implemented in ways which respect both private law's respect for property, alongside other ideals, and public law's respect for democratically mandated legislation.

[90] In the sense that the obligations of others not to interfere with your property entitlements are no more fundamental than is your statutory obligation to pay tax. Murphy and Nagel are right that you could not, in a modern state, have the former without the latter, but that has no implications for the concept of property within private law, provided that it is complemented by a modern democratic basis for the implementation of taxation through legislation.

4

Income Taxation of Small Business: Towards Simplicity, Neutrality and Coherence

DAVID G DUFF

I. Introduction

Among the many contributions that Judith Freedman has made to tax law and policy in the United Kingdom and around the world, one of the most sustained and significant involves the regulation and taxation of small business. Beginning with her 1994 *Modern Law Review* article on 'Small Businesses and the Corporate Form'[1] and continuing through numerous subsequent publications on the taxation of small business,[2] Professor Freedman has consistently and persuasively argued for simplicity, neutrality and coherence in the design of legal rules for the regulation and taxation of small business.

In her *Modern Law Review* article, Professor Freedman challenged proposals for a separate legal form for small businesses in the United Kingdom,[3] a theme to which she returned in the context of the taxation of small business.[4] In the latter context, she has argued that the taxation of similar economic activities carried on through different legal forms is best addressed not by creating new classifications and complex anti-avoidance provisions to discourage tax-motivated choices among different legal categories, but by structural changes that reduce or eliminate differences between the taxation of similar activities carried on through different legal forms in order to minimise tax-motivated

[1] J Freedman, 'Small Businesses and the Corporate Form: Burden or Privilege?' (1994) 57 *Modern Law Review* 555.

[2] See, eg, J Freedman, 'Why Taxing the Micro-Business is Not Simple – A Cautionary Tale from the "Old" World' (2006) 2 *Journal of the Australasian Tax Teachers Association* 58; C Crawford and J Freedman, 'Small Business Taxation' in S Adam et al, *Dimensions of Tax Design: The Mirrlees Review* (Oxford, Oxford University Press for Institute for Fiscal Studies, 2010); and A Adams, J Freedman and J Prassi, 'Rethinking Legal Taxonomies for the Gig Economy' (2018) 34 *Oxford Review of Economic Policy* 475.

[3] Freedman, 'Small Businesses and the Corporate Form' (n 1).

[4] See, eg, Crawford and Freedman (n 2) 1061–64 (rejecting the creation of new legal categories for the taxation of small business and concluding that 'the best solution will be one that does not rely on defining sub-categories of company or types of shareholder').

incentives to choose among these legal forms.[5] For this and other reasons, Professor Freedman has also questioned the rationale and effectiveness of special tax preferences for small business, particularly if these are delivered in the form of a reduced rate that is available to all small businesses, however defined.[6]

This article reviews Professor Freedman's contributions to tax law and policy regarding small business, and evaluates Canadian experience with the taxation of private companies and their shareholders in light of Professor Freedman's work. Section II summarises Professor Freedman's main conclusions regarding the taxation of small business, addressing both the taxation of similar economic activities conducted through different legal forms and the rationale and effectiveness of special tax preferences for small business. Section III examines Canadian experience with the taxation of private companies and their shareholders, illustrating the ways in which Professor Freedman's concerns about structural tax differentials and tax preferences for small business have played out in the Canadian context. Section IV concludes with a few observations about how best to promote simplicity, neutrality and coherence in the taxation of small business.

II. Judith Freedman on the Taxation of Small Business

Although sometimes viewed as relatively simple and limited in scope, structural issues concerning the taxation of small, owner-managed businesses are, as Professor Freedman's co-authored contribution to the Mirrlees Review emphasises, highly complex and pervasive in the design of the entire tax system.[7]

Because individuals may conduct similar economic activities either as employees or self-employed independent contractors, and small businesses may be carried on in unincorporated form or through a corporate entity, the existence of these different legal categories poses key questions about the rationale (if any) for differences in the tax treatment of income derived through these different legal forms, as well as important issues regarding the effects of any tax differentials on economic behaviour. As a result, while many individuals have no choice other than to provide their services as employees, and incorporation is often commercially necessary for larger businesses wishing to raise external capital, the choice among employment, self-employment and incorporation is, as Professor Freedman observes, uniquely relevant for 'owner-managed businesses at the smallest end of the business sector'.[8]

In addition, deliberate use of the tax system to encourage (or compensate) small business through tax preferences raises further questions about the rationales, if any, for such encouragement (or compensation), the effectiveness of specific tax preferences to address these rationales, and the behavioural impact of these preferences. The following

[5] See, eg, Freedman, 'Taxing the Micro-Business' (n 2); Crawford and Freedman (n 2); and Adams, Freedman and Prassi (n 2).

[6] Freedman, 'Taxing the Micro-Business' (n 2); and Crawford and Freedman (n 2).

[7] Crawford and Freedman (n 2) 1032.

[8] ibid 1029.

sections summarise Professor Freedman's conclusions on each of these issues, beginning with the taxation of similar economic activities conducted through different legal categories before turning to the rationale and effectiveness of special tax preferences for small business.

A. Legal Categories, Tax Differentials and Policy Responses

In the United Kingdom, as in many other countries including Canada, tax rules create key tax differentials between the taxation of employees and self-employed independent contractors on the one hand, and between unincorporated businesses and incorporated businesses on the other.

Employees, for example, are generally highly constrained in their ability to deduct expenses, while deductions for self-employed taxpayers are much more generous.[9] In the United Kingdom, for example, employees must satisfy a strict test of the expense being incurred 'wholly, exclusively and necessarily in the performance of the duties of employment',[10] while self-employed taxpayers may deduct expenses incurred 'wholly, exclusively and necessarily for the purposes of the trade'.[11] In Canada, employees are allowed only those deductions that are expressly allowed under the Income Tax Act,[12] while self-employed taxpayers may deduct 'ordinary and well-accepted' expenses in computing business profits,[13] subject to a specific statutory requirement that the expense is incurred 'for the purpose of gaining or producing income from the business'.[14] In addition to this important tax differential, income paid to employees is typically subject to social insurance contributions and/or payroll taxes, which are generally less substantial or not imposed on income paid to self-employed taxpayers. As well, while income paid to employees is generally subject to withholding at source, this is typically not the case for income paid to self-employed taxpayers.

As a result, as Professor Freedman has explained, tax law offers a number of incentives to treat those who supply services to an engager's business as self-employed taxpayers rather than employees.[15] Since the boundary between these two legal categories depends on detailed assessments of the facts of the particular relationship,[16] it is not surprising that

[9] See, eg, Crawford and Freedman (n 2) 1044–45.

[10] Income Tax (Earnings and Pensions) Act 2005, s 336.

[11] In the UK, see Income Tax (Trading and Other Income) Act 2005, s 34.

[12] Income Tax Act, RSC 1985, c I-1 (as amended), s 8(2) (ITA).

[13] ibid s 9(1) defines a taxpayer's income from a business as the taxpayer's 'profit' from that business. Canadian courts have held that this concept authorises the deduction of business expenses the deduction of which is consistent with 'ordinary principles of commercial trading' and 'well-accepted business practices'. See, eg, *Imperial Oil Limited v Minister of National Revenue* [1947] CTC 353, (1947) 3 DTC 1090 (Ex Ct); and *The Royal Trust Company v Minister of National Revenue* [1957] CTC 32, 57 DTC 1055 (Ex Ct).

[14] ITA, s 18(1)(a).

[15] Freedman, 'Taxing the Micro-Business' (n 2) 480.

[16] Crawford and Freedman (n 2) 1044 (referring to 'characteristics or 'badges' of employment status'). In Canada, see, eg, *Wiebe Door Services Ltd v Minister of National Revenue* [1986] 2 CTC 200, 87 DTC 5025 (FCA), which established a test that looks to 'the total relationship' between the parties, considering traditional factors like control, as well as economic factors such as chance of profit and ownership of tools, and the extent to which the taxpayer is integrated into the engager's business when viewed from the perspective the taxpayer.

this determination is among the most disputed tax issues.[17] It is also not surprising that these tax differentials have contributed to a growing shift toward self-employment over the last two decades, particularly with the rise of the so-called 'gig economy'.[18]

Tax differentials between unincorporated businesses and incorporated businesses are even greater than those between employees and self-employed taxpayers, due to differences in the rates at which income is subject to tax in the hands of individuals and corporations and the ease with which corporate income facilitates the conversion of what would otherwise be higher-taxed labour income into lower-taxed income from capital.

Although corporate income tax rates in many countries were once comparable to the highest marginal rate of income tax for individuals, this is no longer the case as globalisation and capital mobility have placed downward pressure on corporate income tax rates at the same time as growing economic inequalities have created political pressure to increase top marginal rates of personal income tax. In Canada, for example, the average combined federal and provincial tax rate on corporate income that does not qualify for a special 'small business' rate was almost 45 per cent in 2000, which was only slightly less than the average combined federal and provincial top personal income tax rate at the time.[19] Since then, the average combined federal and provincial tax rate on corporate income not eligible for the small business rate has fallen to 26.8 per cent, while the average top marginal federal and provincial income tax rate for individuals has increased to 51.6 per cent.[20] Similarly in the United Kingdom, while the general corporate tax rate fell from 35 per cent in 2000 to 19 per cent in 2017, the top marginal personal tax rate increased from 40 per cent to 45 per cent over this period. Although the ultimate impact of these tax differentials depends on the taxation of corporate distributions and the taxation of gains on the sale or liquidation of corporate shares, dividends or gains may also be subject to tax at reduced rates, and the ability to defer the distribution of corporate income or the sale or liquidation of corporate shares means that lower corporate tax rates can yield both permanent and temporary tax reductions.

In addition to the advantage of a lower income tax rate, incorporation also allows owner-managers to convert what would otherwise be income from labour into income from capital that may be distributed in the form of dividends or realised in the form of gains on the sale or liquidation of corporate shares.[21] Since dividends or capital gains may be subject to tax at lower rates than those applicable to business or employment income,[22] and are generally not subject to social insurance contributions and/or payroll taxes,[23] this ability to convert labour income into capital income creates an additional

[17] See the cases discussed in DG Duff et al, *Canadian Income Tax Law* (Toronto, LexisNexis, 2018) 211–18.

[18] Adams, Freedman and Prassi (n 2).

[19] See, eg, Department of Finance Canada, *Tax Planning Using Private Corporations* (Ottawa, Department of Finance, 2017) 12, chart 5.

[20] ibid.

[21] Crawford and Freedman (n 2) 1049.

[22] This is particularly the case with capital gains, which are subject to entrepreneur's relief in the UK, and also favoured in Canada both by taxing only half the gain and through a 'lifetime capital gains deduction' that currently exempts over $860,000 of gains realised on the disposition of 'qualified small business corporation shares' over the course of a taxpayer's lifetime. See the discussion at text to nn 140–58.

[23] In the UK, on the other hand, recent changes to dividend taxation appear to have been designed to address this differential to some extent. See G Loutzenhiser, 'Where next for small company tax reform in the UK?' [2016] *BTR* 674.

tax advantage for small businesses to incorporate.[24] As well, the conversion of labour income into capital income makes it much easier to split income with non-arm's length persons such as spouses and children who acquire shares in a corporation, creating yet another potential tax benefit to incorporation.[25]

Just as the tax differentials between employees and self-employed taxpayers create incentives for workers to become self-employed, so also do the tax differentials between unincorporated businesses and incorporated businesses create powerful incentives for small owner-managed businesses to incorporate. As a result, it is not surprising that the number of corporations increased dramatically in the United Kingdom after the introduction of a nil rate for small companies in 2000,[26] and that the number of small business corporations in Canada increased by 50 per cent from 2001 to 2014 after the Supreme Court of Canada sanctioned a previously uncertain income-splitting arrangement involving the payment of discretionary dividends by private companies.[27] Nor is it surprising that most of these incorporations have involved owner-managed small businesses with few or no employees,[28] since it is precisely these kinds of businesses that are apt to be most responsive to tax differentials between these different legal categories.

In response to this tax-motivated behaviour, governments often enact complex statutory rules, which as Professor Freedman's co-authored contribution to the Mirrlees Review emphasises, 'attempt, often unsuccessfully, to confine the tax advantages to a subcategory'.[29] Alternatively or additionally, revenue authorities may rely on specific or general anti-avoidance rules to challenge tax-motivated arrangements to obtain tax benefits available through specific legal categories.

In the United Kingdom, for example, the introduction of a nil tax rate on small companies was accompanied by the enactment of personal service company (PSC) rules that are designed to discourage employees from incorporating by subjecting the earnings of these companies to income tax and National Insurance Contributions (NICs) as if the income had been earned directly by the individual performing services.[30] Subsequent rules aimed to deny the benefit of the nil rate to profits that were not reinvested in the business by applying an additional tax on corporate distributions paid out

[24] Crawford and Freedman (n 2) 1049.

[25] ibid.

[26] ibid 1054–56.

[27] Department of Finance Canada, *Tax Planning Using Private Corporations* (n 19) 11, chart 4. The case at issue, and the limited legislative response to the decision are discussed later in this chapter at text accompanying nn 39–42 and 159–67. Although the average combined federal and provincial rate of tax on small business income decreased from 20% to 14.4% during this period, the opportunity to split income was much more significant, particularly when several provincial governments allowed non-medical practitioners to hold shares in professional corporations, thereby effectively offloading part of the cost of negotiating with medical professional on the federal treasury. See also M Wolfson and S Legree, 'Policy Forum: Private Companies, Professionals and Income Splitting – Recent Canadian Experience' (2015) 63 *Canadian Tax Journal* 717.

[28] For evidence from the UK, see Crawford and Freedman (n 2) 1056–58, reporting that the number of companies with no employees increased by approximately 50% from 2000 to 2006, while those with one to nine employees increased by less than 40% and those with 10 or more employees increased by less than 20%. For evidence from Canada, see Department of Finance Canada, *Tax Planning Using Private Corporations* (n 19) 11, reporting that the number of incorporated self-employed individuals doubled between 2000 and 2016 and the number of professional services corporations tripled during this period.

[29] Crawford and Freedman (n 2) 1061.

[30] ibid 1050.

of profits that were taxed at a rate lower than the regular small company rate.[31] Although the latter rules were repealed along with the nil rate in 2006, the PSC rules remain.

Similarly in Canada, where a 'small business deduction' reduces the rate of tax on the 'active business income' of 'Canadian-controlled private corporations',[32] access to this low rate is precluded for personal services businesses (PSBs) in which an 'incorporated employee' performs services on behalf of the corporation.[33] Although the Canadian rules do not look through the corporation to tax this income as if it were earned directly by the individual performing the services, other provisions deny the deduction of most expenses incurred by a PSB other than remuneration and benefits paid to the 'incorporated employee'[34] and subject income that is received by the PSB to a rate of federal income tax equal to the highest federal marginal tax rate imposed on individuals.[35]

In order to challenge income-splitting arrangements involving private corporations, the United Kingdom has generally relied on anti-avoidance rules rather than detailed statutory provisions, invoking the 'settlements provisions' in *Jones v Garnett*.[36] While the taxpayer prevailed at the Court of Appeal and at the House of Lords, the reasons for these judicial decisions differed sharply, leaving some uncertainty as to precisely when these provisions might apply – as borne out at least in one subsequent decision by a Special Commissioner.[37] Although the Labour government of the day introduced draft legislation to address family income-splitting arrangements, implementation of this legislation was postponed and the legislation was eventually withdrawn.[38]

In Canada, on the other hand, where a 1998 decision by the Supreme Court of Canada sanctioned a previously uncertain income-splitting arrangement involving the payment of discretionary dividends by private companies,[39] the government of the day was quick to enact a legislative response in the form of a separate 'tax on split income' (TOSI) which subjected most private company dividends received by individuals under the age of 18 to tax at the top marginal rate of personal income tax.[40] Since this provision applied only to individuals under the age of 18, however, income splitting through private corporations continued to be available for spouses and adult children, contributing to a 50 per cent

[31] Freedman, 'Taxing the Micro-Business' (n 2) 69; and S Ball, 'The Non-Corporate Distribution Rate – Section 28 and Schedule 3' [2004] *BTR* 459.

[32] ITA, s 125. See the discussion at text accompanying n 99–138.

[33] ITA, s 125(7) 'personal services business'.

[34] ITA, s 18(1)(p).

[35] This is accomplished by a number of provisions, beginning with the general corporate rate of 38% in ITA, s 123(1), a 10% deduction for income earned in a province under s 124(1), and an additional tax of 5% under s 123.5. Although provincial corporate and individual rate rates vary, this equivalence generally also applies when provincial income taxes are taken into account.

[36] G Loutzenhiser, 'Tax Avoidance, Private Companies and the Family' (2013) 72 *CLJ* 35–49.

[37] *Buck v Revenue & Customs Commissioners* [2009] STC (SCD) 6, discussed in ibid 43.

[38] Loutzenhiser, 'Tax Avoidance, Private Companies and the Family' (n 36) 42.

[39] *Neuman v The Queen* [1998] 1 SCR 770, [1998] 3 CTC 177, 98 DTC 6297 (SCC), relying on the Supreme Court of Canada's prior decision in *McClurg v The Queen* [1990] 1 SCR, [1991] 1 CTC 169, 91 DTC 5001 (SCC) to conclude that the payment of discretionary dividends on a class of shares held by the taxpayer's spouse was not subject to the attribution rule in ITA, s 56(2). For a critical review of the decision, see DG Duff, '*Neuman* and Beyond: Income Splitting, Tax Avoidance, and Statutory Interpretation in the Supreme Court of Canada' (1999) 32 *Canadian Business Law Journal* 345.

[40] ITA, s 120.4. In order to prevent share sales designed to avoid the provision, it was subsequently extended to capital gains from the sale of private company shares to non-arm's length persons.

rate of growth in the number of Canadian-controlled private corporations (CCPCs) over the following 15 years, with much higher rates of growth for self-employed individuals and professional corporations.[41] The government returned to the issue in 2017, proposing to extend the TOSI rules to adult individuals receiving dividends from and capital gains from the disposition of shares of private companies over which a connected individual exercises significant influence, unless these amounts are reasonable in the circumstances taking into account contributions of labour and capital.[42] After considerable controversy, a substantially revised and considerably more complex version of these rules was enacted effective for the 2018 taxation year.

Reflecting her consistent emphasis on simplicity and neutrality in tax rules, Professor Freedman has been sharply critical of these responses to differences in the tax treatment of similar economic activities carried on through different legal forms. Of the PSC rules, for example, she has written that they are 'complex and uncertain' in their application, relying on the same fact-based tests that are used to distinguish employees from self-employed taxpayers, and that they impose 'a cost and burden on a greater number of business owners than are ultimately subject to the provisions, because many people need to seek advice'.[43] Similar criticisms might be directed at the PSB rules in the Canadian ITA, which also rely on the same fact-based determinations that are used to distinguish employees from self-employed taxpayers.[44]

Professor Freedman has also questioned the use of anti-avoidance provisions to challenge income-splitting arrangements involving private corporations, arguing that this approach 'has created serious uncertainty for many small businesses and a general sense of persecution', and denouncing this response as 'a lazy approach to policy making because the problem is perceived as being too hard to tackle with specific and structural legislation'.[45] At the same time, she also criticised the proposed legislative response to *Jones v Garnett*, maintaining that those provisions were 'complex and fact dependent, leading to justified criticisms that [they] would be heavy in compliance and administrative costs and yet would probably raise little revenue'.[46] Here too, similar criticisms may be directed at Canada's TOSI rules, which are extraordinarily complex and also dependent on fact-based determinations, notwithstanding the existence of specific safe harbours that inevitably add to the complexity.

Rejecting these limited legislative and judicial responses to the existence of tax differentials among similar economic activities carried on through different legal forms, Professor Freedman has instead favoured structural changes that reduce or eliminate

[41] Department of Finance Canada, *Tax Planning Using Private Corporations* (n 19) 11.

[42] ibid 23–28.

[43] Freedman, 'Taxing the Micro-Business' (n 2) 72, adding that: 'This is a source of a great deal of angst for business people, which causes considerable annoyance beyond those in fact subject to the legislation. It also creates a great deal of work for professional advisors, but work which they would perhaps prefer not to have as it is not especially productive or lucrative'. See also Loutzenhiser, 'Tax Avoidance, Private Companies and the Family' (n 36) 43–44.

[44] See the definition of 'personal services business' in ITA, s 125(7), which turns on whether the incorporated employee 'would reasonably be regarded as an officer or employee of the person or partnership to whom or to which the services were provided but for the existence of the corporation'.

[45] Freedman, 'Taxing the Micro-Business' (n 2) 74.

[46] Crawford and Freedman (n 2) 1053.

these tax differentials themselves – arguing that the optimal policy response to tax-motivated responses to these tax differentials is 'to align the tax payable by each group as far as possible, such that the boundaries matter less or, if possible, not at all, for tax purposes'.[47] For this reason, she has argued that 'if it is desired to tax income from incorporated firms as labour income, then it would be preferable to achieve this through structural changes to the tax system' instead of through complicated provisions like the PSC rules that aim to recharacterise corporate income as employment income.[48] For the same reason, she has also argued that responses to the use of private corporations to split income with related individuals should be addressed 'in a holistic way, looking at the rules on family taxation, small business taxation and capital transfers between spouses' as a whole,[49] recognising that the 'fundamental issue' involves the recharacterisation of income from labour as income from capital.[50] In principle, therefore, her preferred approach would be that '[i]ndividuals who are identical in every way except their legal form should not face radically divergent tax incentives'.[51] For this reason, her co-authored contribution to the Mirrlees Review suggests that a possible solution to the existence of tax differentials for small businesses carried on through different legal forms 'might be to treat employees through to companies across the whole small business spectrum in exactly the same way for tax purposes, taxing them on the same receipts at exactly the same rate'.[52]

Notwithstanding this conceptual ideal, however, Professor Freedman has recognised that practical and theoretical considerations may justify some tax differentials for income obtained through different legal forms. Explaining that receipts 'vary in nature' and that 'an employee's wage cannot be equated with the receipts of a business', for example, Professor Freedman's co-authored contribution to the Mirrlees Review suggests that a taxpayer's income from employment must be computed differently from that of a self-employed taxpayer, for whom the computation of business income requires 'the application of rules from which it is possible to derive a profit figure'.[53] As well, observing that globalisation and capital mobility have created downward pressure on corporate income tax rates,[54] Professor Freedman also acknowledges the enduring presence of tax differentials between labour income and capital income, suggesting however that these differentials are best addressed by structural reforms that prevent the conversion of labour income into capital income.[55]

As a result, although Professor Freedman seems to suggest that rules for computing the income of employees and self-employed taxpayers might reasonably differentiate among allowable deductions,[56] she maintains that tax differentials on income derived

[47] Adams, Freedman and Prassi (n 2) 486.
[48] Crawford and Freedman (n 2) 1052.
[49] Freedman, 'Taxing the Micro-Business' (n 2) 74.
[50] Crawford and Freedman (n 2) 1054.
[51] Adams, Freedman and Prassi (n 2) 484.
[52] Crawford and Freedman (n 2) 1032.
[53] ibid.
[54] ibid 1064.
[55] ibid 1033.
[56] Although Professor Freedman is not clear on this point, it appears to be a reasonable inference from the suggestion in her co-authored contribution to the Mirrlees Review that 'an employee's wage cannot be equated with the receipts of a business': Crawford and Freedman (n 2) 1032.

through these different legal forms should be reduced by aligning NICs on income earned by employees and self-employed taxpayers and requiring tax and NIC contributions to be deducted on payments to self-employed taxpayers.[57] Similarly for income derived through incorporated businesses, Professor Freedman has suggested that tax differentials are best addressed by aligning effective tax rates 'after taking into account capital investment'[58] by distinguishing labour income from capital income and subjecting the former to NICs and taxation at the higher rates applicable to individuals. To this end, her co-authored contribution to the Mirrlees Review proposes that the United Kingdom should adopt a dual income tax similar to that in the Nordic countries, including an allowance for corporate equity (ACE) in computing corporate income that would exclude the normal rate of return on corporate assets while taxing other corporate income at higher rates that apply to individuals.[59] Correspondingly, unincorporated businesses would pay the capital income tax rate on an imputed return on business assets, with the remainder taxable at higher rates of tax applicable to labour income.[60] Although this approach would not eliminate the ability of owner-managers to split their income with non-arm's length persons, it would reduce the resulting tax advantages by taxing income other than the normal return to capital at the labour income tax rate.[61] Similar proposals have been made for a dual income tax in Canada,[62] but these recommendations have yet to be adopted in Canada or the United Kingdom.

B. Tax Preferences for Small Business

Consistent with these proposals for structural changes to reduce or eliminate tax differentials for similar economic activities carried on through different legal forms, Professor Freedman has also rejected special tax preferences for small business – particularly if these are delivered in the form of reduced rates such as the short-lived nil rate in the United Kingdom or the small company rate that was eliminated in 2015. Although recognising that market failures may justify tax incentives for certain kinds of behaviour, such as research and development, and that some such incentives might reasonably differentiate between small and medium-sized enterprises (SMEs) and larger corporations,[63] Professor Freedman has challenged each of the three leading arguments in favour of broad-based tax preferences for small businesses: first, that they are necessary to address structural challenges that small enterprises experience obtaining finance; second, that they compensate for structural issues in being small such as the regressive impact of

[57] Adams, Freedman and Prassi (n 2) 493.

[58] Crawford and Freedman (n 2) 1030.

[59] ibid 1067.

[60] ibid 1068.

[61] ibid 1069.

[62] See, eg, K Milligan, *Tax Policy for a New Era: Promoting Economic Growth and Fairness* (Toronto, CD Howe Institute, 2014).

[63] Crawford and Freedman (n 2) 1078–80, noting that smaller enterprises may have fewer opportunities to balance costs against profits from other activities. For this reason, Canadian tax assistance for research and development carried on by private companies is generally provided in the form of refundable tax credits. ITA, ss 127(10) and 127.1(1).

compliance burdens and an inability to set off losses against profits; and more generally that small businesses are important engines of economic growth and job creation, which itself justifies support through the tax system.[64]

Beginning with the last of these arguments, there is little evidence to support the claim that small business is crucial to economic growth or job creation. Although studies suggest that incorporated businesses are more likely to grow than unincorporated businesses,[65] it is unclear whether incorporation is a cause or effect of growth, since businesses that wish to grow are likely to incorporate at some point,[66] while other businesses that do not wish to grow may incorporate primarily for tax reasons.[67] Nor are all small businesses effective vehicles for job creation, since many closely held corporations have no employees and only a minority of small enterprises create jobs.[68] Where small businesses do create jobs, moreover, these jobs may not endure, as studies suggest that only a small percentage of SMEs last for more than 10 years.[69] As a result, Professor Freedman concludes, tax preferences that are conferred on small businesses in order to encourage growth and job creation are apt to be poorly targeted and ineffective, encouraging the tax-motivated incorporation of small businesses more than the economic outcomes that these tax preferences are intended to promote.[70]

Nor is there strong evidence of any pressing market failure in the financing of SMEs. Although it is reasonable to conclude that many new businesses find it more difficult to raise capital than established enterprises,[71] Professor Freedman rightly explains that an effective policy response to this market failure would target newly established businesses, not small businesses as a whole, many of which may not wish to expand and have little or no need for finance.[72] Indeed, by withdrawing tax benefits as new enterprises grow, tax preferences targeted at small businesses may create a barrier to this growth instead of removing one.[73] According to one study, for example, by encouraging economic activity through SMEs rather than larger corporations, Canada's small business deduction may contribute to lower productivity in Canada than in other developed countries.[74] As a result, instead of enhancing economic efficiency by counteracting a market failure, tax preferences for small business may actually impede economic efficiency.[75]

In contrast to a lack of evidence to support arguments that small business is essential to economic growth and job creation and systematically disadvantaged in raising

[64] Crawford and Freedman (n 2) 1074.

[65] See, eg, DJ Story, *Understanding the Small Business Sector* (Abingdon, Routledge, 1994) 140.

[66] Freedman, 'Taxing the Micro-Business' (n 2) 64.

[67] ibid, characterising many of these small businesses as 'life-style businesses' that are carried on for non-tax reasons, but incorporated for tax reasons.

[68] Crawford and Freedman (n 2) 1038, 1075.

[69] K Hendricks, R Amit and D Whistler, 'Business Taxation of Small and Medium-Sized Enterprises in Canada' (October 1997) Working Paper 97–11, Prepared for the Technical Committee on Business Taxation 1, reporting that only 20% of SMEs existed 10 years later.

[70] Freedman, 'Taxing the Micro-Business' (n 2) 64.

[71] ibid.

[72] Crawford and Freedman (n 2) 1078.

[73] ibid 1080.

[74] D Chen and JM Mintz, 'Small Business Taxation: Revamping Incentives to Encourage Growth' (2011) 4:7 School of Public Policy Research Papers 1–29 (University of Calgary School of Public Policy).

[75] Freedman, 'Taxing the Micro-Business' (n 2) 61, concluding that tax preferences for small business 'may distort the market in unintended ways by, for example, resulting in the allocation of resources to small firms in circumstances where larger firms could be used more efficiently'.

finance, there is considerable evidence indicating that small businesses experience a disproportionate burden to comply with tax rules and other regulatory obligations by virtue of their size alone.[76] It is also reasonable to conclude that SMEs may be more constrained than larger enterprises in their ability to set off losses against profits. As Professor Freedman's co-authored contribution to the Mirrlees Review notes, however, this constraint is more likely to apply to new enterprises than more established enterprises, and is probably best addressed by permitting some pass-through treatment for corporate losses, particularly new corporations, than by a broader tax preference for all small businesses in the form of a reduced rate of tax.[77]

Although disproportionate compliance costs may justify some relief provisions, such as reduced reporting requirements or income thresholds for VAT registration,[78] it is also not obvious that this structural disadvantage is best addressed by a reduced rate of income tax for all small businesses. On the contrary, Professor Freedman cautions, since a low corporate tax rate for small business is apt to be accompanied by detailed anti-avoidance rules to prevent abuse, a tax preference along these lines can add to the complexity of the tax system, thereby increasing compliance burdens for enterprises wishing to benefit from the preference.[79] In addition, complexity and compliance costs are often compounded by the fact that these anti-avoidance rules are often revised and extended to address novel forms of abuse.[80]

In the United Kingdom, for example, where a nil rate of tax on the first £10,000 of corporate income was introduced in 2002, complicated anti-avoidance rules were subsequently enacted in order to increase the corporate tax rate on distributions paid out of profits taxed at less than the general corporate tax rates, thereby negating the advantage of the nil rate on these profits.[81] Likewise in Canada, where a small business deduction reduces the rate of corporate tax on the first $500,000 of active business income of a CCPC, numerous and increasingly complicated anti-avoidance rules aim to prevent the multiplication of this deduction through 'associated corporations' and other arrangements.[82] It is ironic, therefore, that those defending the Canadian deduction often point to the costs that businesses bear in order to comply with tax rules as a central rationale for the preservation of a tax preference that greatly contributes to these compliance costs.[83]

[76] See, eg, C Evans, A Hansford, J Hasseldine, P Lignier, S Smulders and F Vaillancourt, 'Small business and tax compliance costs: A cross-country study of managerial benefits and tax concessions' (2014) 12 *eJournal of Tax Research* 453.

[77] Crawford and Freedman (n 2) 1084.

[78] ibid 1081–82.

[79] ibid 1082–83, characterising this outcome as a form of 'complex deregulation'.

[80] Freedman, 'Taxing the Micro-Business' (n 2) 65–67, explaining that compliance and administrative costs are increased not only by the complexity of legal rules, but by frequent changes in legal rules.

[81] ibid 69, citing one commentator who described these anti-avoidance provisions as 'bordering on the surreal'.

[82] See, eg, the associated corporation rules in ITA, s 256, and recently enacted rules denying the small business deduction for income from the provision of services or property to a private corporation where the corporation, one of its shareholders or a person who does not deal at arm's length with the corporation or one of its shareholders holds a direct or indirect interest in the private corporation to which the services or property are provided. ITA, s 125(1)(a) and 125(7) 'specified corporate income' and 'specified partnership income'.

[83] See, eg, T Mallet, 'Policy Forum: Mountains and Molehills – Effects of the Small Business Deduction' (2015) 63 *Canadian Tax Journal* 691.

In addition to the complexity associated with a low corporate tax rate for small business, moreover, experience suggests that this kind of tax preference can be extremely costly in terms of foregone revenues. In the United Kingdom, which offered a reduced corporate tax rate for small companies until 2015, the cost of this tax preference was estimated at £1.585 billion in 2013–14.[84] In Canada, the annual cost of the small business deduction in terms of foregone federal income tax revenue was estimated at $3.75 billion in 2016, an amount that is projected to increase to $5.585 billion in 2019 – making it the second most costly corporate tax expenditure after the partial taxation of capital gains.[85]

Finally, studies indicate that a low corporate tax rate for small business provides the most benefit to high-income shareholders and family members who are able to obtain the greatest advantage from the deferral and income-splitting opportunities that are available when income is derived through private corporations. According to one Canadian study, less than 5 per cent of tax filers in the lower half of the income distribution own CCPC shares versus 65–80 per cent of tax filers in the top 0.1 per cent of the income distribution.[86] Another study documents the extent to which CCPCs have been used for income-splitting purposes, particularly by high-income professionals.[87] For these reasons, it is not surprising that a prominent Canadian economist has reported that 60 per cent of the tax benefit from the small business deduction goes to households with more than $150,000 in income.[88]

Given these criticisms, it is perhaps surprising that several countries, including Canada and the United Kingdom, have provided preferential corporate tax rates for small business, and that these tax preferences have persisted over many years.[89] As Professor Freedman's co-authored contribution to the Mirrlees Review notes, the explanation for this result is largely political, as the small business community is vocal, well-organised and broadly supported by the media and the general public, leading to 'the introduction of reliefs which then become entrenched into the system and are hard to remove even if found unhelpful'.[90] Nonetheless, this study continues, experience with the United Kingdom's nil corporate tax rate in the early 2000s demonstrates that 'business will broadly support simplifying measures where the reliefs have become very complex'.[91] Indeed, it is testament to the influence of the Mirrlees Review's recommendation that the general corporate rate should be aligned with the small business rate,[92] that the United Kingdom eliminated

[84] Her Majesty's Revenue and Customs, 'Estimated costs of principal tax reliefs', available at: www.gov.uk/government/statistics/main-tax-expenditures-and-structural-reliefs.

[85] Canada, Department of Finance, *Report on Federal Tax Expenditures – Concepts, Estimates and Evaluations 2019* (Ottawa, Department of Finance, 2019) 29 (hereafter Canada, *Report on Federal Tax Expenditures*), available at: www.fin.gc.ca/taxexp-depfisc/2019/taxexp-depfisc19-eng.pdf.

[86] M Wolfson, M Veall, N Brooks and B Murphy, 'Piercing the Veil: Private Corporations and the Income of the Affluent' (2016) 64 *Canadian Tax Journal* 1.

[87] See, eg, Wolfson and Legree (n 27).

[88] Jack Mintz, quoted in Bill Curry and Steven Chase, 'Tories to table tax-cut-heavy federal budget plan' *Globe & Mail* (21 April 2015).

[89] For an excellent, though now somewhat dated, survey of small business taxation in Australia, Canada, the United Kingdom and the United States, see N Brooks, 'Taxation of Closely-Held Corporations: The Partnership Option and the Lower Rate of Tax' (1986) 3 *Australian Tax Forum* 381.

[90] Crawford and Freedman (n 2) 1086.

[91] ibid.

[92] ibid 1066, 1071.

the preferential rate for small business in 2015 by reducing the general corporate rate to the lower rate applicable to small business. In Canada, on the other hand, recent efforts to limit the use of private corporations for tax planning produced a political backlash that ultimately led the federal government to actually increase the differential between the general corporate rate and the small business rate.[93]

III. Canadian Experience with the Taxation of Private Companies and their Shareholders

As noted earlier, Canada provides a preferential corporate tax rate for small business, which is delivered in the form of a 'small business deduction' that reduces the federal tax rate on the first $500,000 of active business income earned in a taxation year by a CCPC.[94] It also maintains a preferential regime for capital gains, only half of which are subject to tax,[95] and exempts over $800,000 of capital gains from the disposition of 'qualified small business corporation shares' that are realised by resident individuals over the course of their lifetimes.[96]

Together with other tax benefits resulting from incorporation, such as the ability to convert labour income into capital income and the ability to split income more easily with related persons, these provisions create strong incentives for resident individuals to incorporate otherwise unincorporated enterprises, and for these shareholders to access corporate surpluses in the form of capital gains from the sale or liquidation of shares, rather than the distribution of dividends which are generally taxable at personal tax rates.[97] Instead of pursuing the kinds of structural reforms that Professor Freedman advocates in order to reduce or eliminate these tax differentials, however, Canadian governments have relied on increasingly complicated statutory provisions and anti-avoidance rules in order to limit the scope of these tax preferences. The following sections review Canadian experience with the taxation of private companies and their shareholders, illustrating how Professor Freedman's concerns have played out in the Canadian context.

A. Taxation of Private Companies

The key elements of the small business deduction date from 1972, when the federal government replaced a two-tiered rate structure for all corporate income that had existed since 1949.[98] Although the Canadian Royal Commission on Taxation (Carter Commission) rejected arguments for a preferential small business rate in its

[93] See the discussion at text accompanying nn 134–38.

[94] ITA, s 125.

[95] ITA, s 38, generally limiting the taxable amount of a capital gain and the allowable amount of a capital loss to one-half of the capital gain or loss.

[96] ITA, s 110.6(2.1).

[97] As explained more fully below, n 139 and accompanying text, these dividends are subject to a gross-up and tax credit mechanism designed to integrate corporate and individual income taxes.

[98] See Brooks (n 89) 422–25.

1967 Report,[99] and the federal government's 1969 White Paper recommended that the dual-rate structure should be abolished,[100] political opposition led the government to replace the lower corporate rate with a tax credit that effectively reduces the federal corporate tax rate for qualifying income of eligible corporations.[101] When first introduced in 1972, this credit reduced the corporate tax rate by 25 per cent from a general rate of 50 per cent to a small business rate of 25 per cent.[102] With long-term reductions in the corporate tax rates, however, this rate differential had decreased substantially by 2011, by which time the general federal corporate tax rate was 15 per cent and the federal small business rate was 11 per cent.[103]

In order to target the small business deduction to small businesses, the original provision included three features which remain to this day. First, the credit is available only to private corporations, not public corporations or corporations controlled by one or more public corporations – presumably since private corporations cannot raise capital by issuing shares to the public.[104] Second, the credit is limited to a maximum amount of qualifying income for each taxation year (originally $50,000 but now $500,000), which must be shared among CCPCs that are 'associated' with each other in the year.[105] Finally, the credit applies only to the corporation's income from an 'active business carried on' by it in Canada so as to exclude its use to reduce the rate of tax on income from passive investments held by a private corporation.[106]

In addition to these elements, the original legislation included two other features intended to target the incentive to new small businesses that would use the tax savings to invest in their businesses. First, in order to limit the incentive to new small businesses, the legislation included a 'total business limit' that limited the maximum amount of qualifying income that could benefit from the credit to an aggregate amount.[107] Second, in order to discourage qualifying corporations from using the tax savings to accumulate passive investments, the legislation included a special refundable tax on 'ineligible investments' that effectively eliminated the benefit of the credit when a qualifying corporation made an investment that was not for the purpose of gaining or producing income from the business.[108] Although these features arguably made the

[99] Canada, Royal Commission on Taxation, *Report*, vol 4 (Ottawa, Queen's Printer, 1967) 270–73.

[100] Hon EJ Benson, Minister of Finance, *Proposals for Tax Reform* (Ottawa, Queen's Printer, 1969) 27, paras 4.15–4.18.

[101] See Brooks (n 89) 434–37.

[102] ibid 437.

[103] This rate differential is greatly increased, however, by provincial corporate income taxes, for which general corporate rates current range from 11% to 16% and small business rates range from 2% to 6%. Although all provincial and territorial governments levy their own income taxes, provincial income taxes are generally collected by the federal government under tax collection agreements whereby the provinces agree to adopt the same definition of taxable income as the federal income tax, while maintaining freedom to set their own rates.

[104] The credit is further limited to corporations that are not controlled by one or more non-residents in order to ensure that the benefit flows primarily to residents of Canada. ITA, s 125(7) 'Canadian-controlled private corporation'.

[105] ITA, s 125(2).

[106] ITA, s 125(1)(a).

[107] This aggregate limit was originally set at $400,000, but was increased to $500,000 in 1974, $750,000 in 1976 and $1 million in 1982. Brooks (n 89) 439.

[108] ITA, former Part V.

small business deduction a relatively well-designed tax subsidy,[109] the refundable tax on ineligible investments was retroactively repealed in 1973 before it came into force,[110] and the total business limit was repealed in 1985.[111]

Judicial decisions further undercut the target-effectiveness of the subsidy by interpreting the (originally undefined) concept of an 'active business' expansively to include most activities carried on by a corporation, including investment in income-producing property.[112] Although the federal government responded to these decisions in 1979 by defining the concept of an 'active business' to exclude a 'specified investment business' the 'principal purpose' of which is 'to derive income (including interest, dividends, rents and royalties) from property',[113] this statutory test has been subject to considerable litigation in which courts must engage in a fact-based inquiry to determine whether the taxpayer's core business activity involves the provision of property or the provision of services.[114] This is also the case with an exclusion for a 'personal services business' which turns on whether an incorporated employee 'would reasonably be regarded as an officer or employee of the person or partnership to whom or to which the services were provided but for the existence of the corporation'[115] – thereby relying on the same fact-based determinations that are used to distinguish employees from self-employed taxpayers.[116]

Other elements of the small business deduction have also been subject to frequent litigation and recurring legislative amendments that increase complexity as well as compliance and administrative costs. Although the distinction between a private and a public corporation is easily drawn,[117] the concept of corporate control is less clear and is often disputed.[118] This is particularly the case with concept of de facto control, on which

[109] Brooks (n 89) 441.

[110] SC 1973–74, c 14, s 60(1)(2). According to the Minister of Finance at this time, the refundable tax was not only complex but also unnecessary since 'small corporations … will, in fact, use these tax savings to expand their businesses, to improve their technology and to create more jobs for Canadians'. Canada, House of Commons Debates, 19 February 1973, 1433 (Finance Minister, Hon J Turner).

[111] SC 1984, c 45, s 40.

[112] See, eg, *The Queen v Rockmore Investments Ltd*, 76 DTC 6156 (FCA); *The Queen v MRT Investments Ltd*, 76 DTC 6158 (FCA); and *ESG Holdings Ltd v The Queen*, 76 DTC 6158 (FCA), in which interest income on mortgages held by the taxpayers was characterised as income from an active business; and *The Queen v Cadboro Bay Holdings Ltd*, 77 DTC 5115 (FCTD) at 5123, in which the Court held that any quantum of business activity giving rise to income in a taxation year is sufficient for the income to be characterised as income from an active business.

[113] ITA, s 125(7) 'specified investment business'.

[114] See, eg, *072443 BC Ltd v The Queen* [2015] 1 CTC 2123, 2014 DTC 1208 (TCC), aff'd 2015 DTC 5115 (FCA), in which the Court determined that the principal purpose of a self-storage business was to derive income from the provision of rental space rather than the provisions of services. See also *Rocco Gagliese Productions Inc v Canada* [2018] TCJ No 102, [2019] 3 CTC 2154, 2018 DTC 1099 (TCC), in which the Court held that the taxpayer's principal purpose was to earn income from composing music, notwithstanding that its main source of income was from royalties.

[115] ITA, s 125(7) 'personal services business'. This exclusion was originally introduced in 1979 as one of various 'non-qualifying businesses' (including professional corporations and management service corporations) that were eligible for a reduced credit. The reduced credit for personal services businesses was eliminated in 1981 and the exclusion for other non-qualifying businesses was eliminated in 1985. See Brooks (n 89) 443–49.

[116] See, eg, *Dynamic Industries Ltd v Canada* [2005] 3 CTC 225, 2005 DTC 5293 (FCA).

[117] See the definitions of 'private corporation' and 'public corporation' in ITA, s 89(1).

[118] See, eg, *Duha Printers (Western) Ltd v Canada* [1998] 3 CTC 303, 98 DTC 6334 (SCC); and *Silicon Graphics Ltd v Canada* [2002] 3 CTC 527, 2002 DTC 7112 (FCA).

the statutory definition of a Canadian-controlled private corporation has relied since an amendment to this effect was added to the ITA in 1988.[119] Following contradictory interpretations of this concept,[120] moreover, the ITA was further amended in 2017 to require courts to 'take into consideration all factors that are relevant in the circumstances' in determining de facto control,[121] ensuring that the statutory test depends on a detailed fact-based inquiry.

The concept of corporate control is also relevant to the associated corporation rules, which had accompanied the pre-1972 dual-rate corporate tax and were retained in order to prevent businesses from increasing the amount of income that is eligible for the credit by incorporating multiple entities.[122] Subject to numerous deeming rules[123] and a targeted anti-avoidance rule enacted in 1988 which deems two or more corporations to be associated where 'it may reasonably be considered that one of the main reasons for the separate existence of those corporations in a taxation year is to reduce the amount of taxes that would otherwise be payable',[124] these provisions have been subject to frequent litigation.[125] In order to further prevent multiplication of the small business deduction, moreover, recent amendments have introduced complicated rules that generally deny the small business deduction for income from the provision of services or property to a private corporation where the corporation, one of its shareholders, or a person who does not deal at arm's length with the corporation or one of its shareholders, holds a direct or indirect interest in the private corporation to which the services or property are provided.[126] Yet other amendments have aimed to better target the incentive to small businesses by reducing the amount of income eligible for the deduction to the extent that the equity of the corporation and associated corporations exceeds $10 million,[127] and to discourage the use of tax savings to accumulate passive investments by also reducing the amount of income eligible for the deduction to the extent that investment income of the corporation and associated corporations exceeds $50,000 annually and eliminating the deduction completely if annual income from passive investments reaches $150,000.[128]

[119] ITA, s 256(5.1), stipulating for the purposes of the ITA that a corporation is 'controlled, directly or indirectly in any manner whatever' by a person or group of persons where 'the controller has any direct or indirect influence that, if exercised, would result in control in fact of the corporation'.

[120] See, eg, *Transport ML Couture Inc v Canada* [2003] 3 CTC 2882, 2003 DTC 817 (TCC), aff'd 2004 DTC 6636 (FCA); and *McGillivray Restaurant Ltd v Canada* [2015] 3 CTC 2205, 2015 DTC 1030 (TCC), aff'd [2017] 5 CTC 103, 2016 DTC 5048 (FCA).

[121] ITA, s 256(5.11).

[122] ITA, s 256.

[123] See, eg, the deemed control and share ownership rules in ITA, s 256(1.2)–(1.4) and the deemed association rule for corporations associated with a third corporation in s 256(2).

[124] ITA, s 256(2.1).

[125] See, eg, *Brownco Inc v Canada* [2008] 5 CTC 2123, 2008 DTC 2591 (TCC); *Taber Solids Control (1998) Ltd v Canada* [2010] 1 CTC 2290, 2009 DTC 1343 (TCC); *Maintenance Eurêka Ltée v Canada*, 2011 DTC 1319 (TCC); *Jencal Holdings Ltd v Canada*, 2019 DTC 1019 (TCC); and *Prairielane Holdings Ltd v Canada*, 2019 TCC 157 (TCC).

[126] ITA, s 125(1)(a) and 125(7) 'specified corporate income' and 'specified partnership income'. For a useful explanation of these rules, see K Keung, 'New Small Business Deduction Rules Under Section 125' in *Report of the Proceedings of the Sixty-Eights Tax Conference*, 2016 Conference Report (Toronto, Canadian Tax Foundation, 2017) 27:1–26.

[127] ITA, s 125(5.1)(a) [generally applicable to taxation years after June 1994].

[128] ITA, s 125(5.1)(b) [generally applicable to taxation years after 2018].

As explained earlier, the annual cost of the small business deduction in terms of foregone federal income tax revenue was $3.75 billion in 2016 and is projected to increase to $5.585 billion in 2019 – making it the second most costly tax expenditure after the partial taxation of capital gains.[129] Evidence also suggests that the deduction provides the most benefit to high-income shareholders and family members who are able to obtain the greatest advantage from the deferral and income-splitting opportunities that are available when income is derived through private corporations.[130] Finally, for the reasons that Professor Freedman has identified, a reduced rate for incorporated small businesses is a poorly targeted tax incentive that greatly increases tax complexity for small businesses, as well as compliance and administrative costs.[131]

For these reasons, Canada would be well served to heed the advice of the Mirrlees Review and to follow the example of the United Kingdom by eliminating any differential between the general corporate tax rate and the small business rate. In fact, this possibility seemed tantalisingly close in 2015 when the differential in federal corporate tax rates was only 4 per cent, and a new government was elected on a platform that promised to review all tax expenditures benefiting top income earners[132] and (unlike the other two major political parties) did not promise to reduce the small business rate.[133] Instead of addressing the rate differential directly, however, the government eventually proposed various measures to limit opportunities for tax planning using private corporations, including new provisions to discourage income splitting through private corporations,[134] a specific anti-avoidance rule to prevent the conversion of taxable dividends into tax-preferred capital gains,[135] and other provisions to discourage the use of private corporations to accumulate passive investments.[136] In the face of fierce criticism from professionals and the small business sector, the government ultimately withdrew the specific anti-avoidance rule to prevent the conversion of dividends into capital gains, adopted a much weaker provision to discourage the use of private corporations to accumulate private investments,[137] and lowered the federal small business rate to 9 per cent,[138] thereby increasing the differential between this rate and the general corporate tax rate.

[129] Canada, Report on Federal Tax Expenditures (n 85) 29.

[130] See nn 86–88 and accompanying text.

[131] Text accompanying nn 65–83.

[132] Liberal Party of Canada, 2015 Election Platform, *A New Plan for a Strong Middle Class* (2015) 73, available at: www.liberal.ca/wp-content/uploads/2015/10/New-plan-for-a-strong-middle-class.pdf.

[133] Conservative Party of Canada, 2015 Election Platform, *Protect our Economy* (2015) 19, available at: s3.documentcloud.org/documents/2454398/conservative-platform-2015.pdf; New Democratic Party of Canada, 2015 Election Platform, *Building the country of our dreams* (2015) 15, available at: s3.documentcloud.org/documents/2454378/2015-ndp-platform-en.pdf.

[134] Department of Finance Canada, *Tax Planning Using Private Corporations* (n 19) 18–31.

[135] ibid 55–60.

[136] ibid 32–54.

[137] ITA, s 125(5.1)(b), which reduces the amount of income eligible for the small business deduction to the extent that investment income of the corporation and associated corporations exceeds $50,000 annually, eliminating the deduction completely when investment income is $150,000 per year – thereby allowing passive investments of $1 million with an assumed annual return of 5% without any reduction in the small business deduction and eliminating the small business deduction if passive investments with an assumed annual return of 5% are $3 million.

[138] SC 2018, c 12, s 20(1), amending ITA, s 125(1.1).

B. Taxation of Shareholders

As Professor Freedman rightly notes, the extent to which a tax system encourages individuals to incorporate a small business is influenced not only by reduced rates for corporate income but also by the ability to convert labour income into lower-taxed income from capital and by the ability to split this income with related persons. Although Canada taxes dividends received by individual shareholders at personal tax rates, subject to a gross-up and tax credit regime designed to integrate corporate and individual income taxes,[139] tax preferences for capital gains and the ability to split corporate income more easily than labour income create additional incentives to incorporate otherwise unincorporated businesses and an incentive for individual shareholders to convert otherwise taxable dividends into capital gains from the sale or liquidation of shares. As with the small business deduction, Canadian governments have relied on complex statutory provisions and anti-avoidance rules to limit the extent of these tax benefits, instead of pursuing structural reforms that would reduce or eliminate the tax differentials resulting from different kinds of income.

i. Dividends and Capital Gains

Like the small business deduction, the gross-up and tax credit mechanism for dividends was introduced in 1972, at which time the general corporate tax rate in Canada was 50 per cent, the small business deduction reduced this rate to 25 per cent, and the gross-up and tax credit for individual shareholders offset corporate tax at the small business rate.[140] Under this regime, individual shareholders subject to tax at a marginal rate of 50 per cent paid an effective rate of $33^1/_3$ per cent on the cash amount of the dividends paid out of corporate income.[141] Since one-half of capital gains were taxable at the time, these rules created an incentive to realise corporate surpluses in the form of capital gains, which would be taxable at effective rate of only 25 per cent for individual shareholders subject to tax at a 50 per cent marginal rate.[142]

Because Canada did not tax capital gains before 1972, it had considerable experience with 'surplus stripping' transactions designed to convert otherwise taxable dividends

[139] ITA, ss 82(1) and 121. Until 2005, this gross-up and credit system was designed to integrate corporate and individual income taxes only for corporate income subject to the small business deduction. Since then a separate gross-up and tax credit for 'eligible dividends' integrates corporate and individual income taxes subject to tax at the general corporate rate.

[140] Brooks (n 89) 437.

[141] Assuming $100 of corporate income subject to tax at the 25% small business rate, an individual shareholder taxable at a 50% marginal tax rate who received a dividend of $75 would gross-up the cash amount of the dividend by $25 ($33^1/_3$% of $75), and receive a tax credit of $25 against tax otherwise payable of $50 (50% of $100), resulting in an effective rate of tax on the cash amount of the dividend of $25/$75 = $33^1/_3$%. If the corporate income were subject to the general rate of 50%, the individual receiving a dividend of $50 would gross-up the cash amount of the dividend by $16.67 ($33^1/_3$% of $50), and receive a tax credit of $16.67 against tax otherwise payable of $33.33 (50% of $66.67), resulting in an effective rate of tax on the cash amount of the dividend of $16.67/$50 = $33^1/_3$%.

[142] Assuming that the value of a corporation is increased by the amount of after-tax income retained by the corporation, shareholders of a corporation earning $100 of income subject to tax at the 25% small business rate would realise a gain of $75 on the sale or liquidation of their shares, resulting in a taxable capital gain of $37.50 and tax of $18.75 (25% of the gain) for individuals subject to tax at a 50% marginal rate.

into non-taxable capital gains, and had enacted various rules deeming proceeds from the sale or liquidation of shares to be dividends in specific circumstances.[143] While the taxation of capital gains reduced the incentive to engage in these transactions, the difference in effective tax rates on dividends and capital gains meant that these rules were retained in 1972.[144] Although subsequent amendments in 1990 synchronised the effective rates on capital gains and dividends paid out of corporate income subject to the small business rate by reducing this rate to 20 per cent and increasing the capital gains inclusion rate to three-quarters,[145] this equivalence was not established for corporate income that was subject to the general corporate tax rate, and capital gains became generally more attractive than dividends after 2000 when the capital gains inclusion rate was reduced to one-half.

In 1985, moreover, the federal government increased the incentive for surplus stripping by enacting a lifetime capital gains exemption that exempts a specific amount of capital gains realised by resident individuals over the course of their lifetimes.[146] Although this exemption was capped at $100,000 in 1987 and repealed in 1995, a more generous exemption for capital gains from the disposition of 'qualified small business corporation' shares was introduced in 1988 and remains in place.[147] Originally limited to $500,000, this amount was increased to $750,000 in 2007 and $800,000 in 2014, when this amount was indexed for inflation, as a result of which the value of the exemption had increased to $883,384 by 2020.

Extremely complicated,[148] with multiple limitations,[149] and a targeted anti-avoidance rule that disallows the exemption where among other things 'it can reasonably be

[143] See, eg, Income Tax Act, RSC 1952, c 148, s 81(1), which deemed funds or property distributed or appropriated in any manner whatever to or for the benefit of one or more shareholders on a winding-up, discontinuance or reorganisation of a corporation's business to be a dividend to the extent of the corporation's undistributed income on hand; s 81(2) which deemed a dividend to have been received on the redemption of a share to the extent of the shareholder's undistributed income on hand; and s 138A(1), which deemed amounts received or receivable by a taxpayer as a consequence of a disposition or exchange of property to be a dividend where it could reasonably be considered that 'one of the purposes' of the disposition or exchange was 'to effect a significant reduction of, or disappearance of, assets of a corporation at any time in a manner such that the whole or any part of any tax that might otherwise have been or have become payable … in consequence of any distribution of property of a corporation has been or will be avoided'. For a useful discussion, see HH Stikeman and R Couzin, 'Surplus Stripping' (1995) 43 *Canadian Tax Journal* 1844.

[144] ITA, ss 84(2), 84(3) and former 247(1) (which was repealed in 1988 when Canada's general anti-avoidance rule (GAAR) came into effect).

[145] Assuming $100 of corporate income subject to tax at the 20% small business rate, an individual shareholder taxable at a 50% marginal tax rate who received a dividend of $80 would gross-up the cash amount of the dividend by $25 (25% of $80), and receive a tax credit of $20 against tax otherwise payable of $50 (50% of $100), resulting in an effective rate of tax on the cash amount of the dividend of $30/$80 = 37.5%. Alternatively, if the after-tax income were retained by the corporation, resulting in a gain of $80 on a disposition of the shares, the shareholder would pay tax of $30 (50% of $60, being three-quarters of the gain), also resulting in an effective tax rate of 37.5%.

[146] ITA, s 110.6(3) [repealed in 1995]. As originally enacted, the exemption was to be phased in from $20,000 in 1985 to $50,000 in 1986, $100,000 in 1987, $200,000 in 1988, $300,000 in 1989 and $500,000 in 1990.

[147] ITA, s 110.6(2.1).

[148] See, eg, the definition of 'qualified small business corporation share' in ITA, s 110.6(1), which includes ownership and asset requirements 'at the determination time' and for 24 months preceding this time.

[149] See, eg, the concept of a 'cumulative gains limit' in ITA, s 110.6(1), which reduces the amount that may be deducted under the exemption in a taxation year to the extent of the taxpayer's 'cumulative net investment loss' at the end of the year.

concluded, having regard to all the circumstances, that a significant part of the capital gain is attributable to the fact that dividends were not paid on a share',[150] the lifetime capital gains exemption was also accompanied by specific anti-avoidance rules aimed at surplus stripping through non-arm's length transactions,[151] and through the purchase by a public corporation of shares distributed in the form of a stock dividend.[152] Although the anti-avoidance rule for public corporations has not resulted in any litigation, the anti-avoidance rule for non-arm's length transactions has been subject to considerable litigation, which is not surprising for a provision that depends on the factual determination of a non-arm's length relationship between an individual who sells shares and a corporation that purchases the shares.[153] The lifetime capital gains exemption has also been subject to numerous cases involving the Canadian general anti-avoidance rule, which was also enacted in 1988.[154]

Consistent with Professor Freedman's admonition, therefore, Canadian tax preferences for capital gains have been accompanied by complex statutory provisions that 'attempt, often unsuccessfully, to confine the tax advantages to a subcategory'[155] and by reliance on specific and general anti-avoidance rules to challenge tax-motivated arrangements to obtain tax benefits resulting from specific legal forms. In addition to their complexity, these tax preferences are extremely costly in terms of foregone revenues,[156] uncertain in their economic impact,[157] and disproportionately benefit high-income taxpayers.[158] Here too, therefore, Canada would be well served to heed Professor Freedman's advice to reduce or eliminate the tax differentials resulting from these tax preferences.

ii. Income Splitting

The incentive to incorporate a small business for tax reasons is also driven by opportunities to split income with related persons. Although Canada has a lengthy history with attribution rules that limit opportunities to split income with spouses and related

[150] ITA, s 110.6(8). Potentially quite broad, this provision is limited in scope by an exception for 'prescribed shares'.
[151] ITA, s 84.1.
[152] ITA, Pt II.1.
[153] See, eg, *Brouillette v Canada* [2005] 4 CTC 2013, 2005 DTC 1004 (TCC); *Côte-Létourneau v Canada*, 2007 TCC 91, 2010 DTC 1116 (TCC); and *Poulin v Canada* [2016] 6 CTC 2206, 2016 DTC 1129 (TCC).
[154] See, eg, *McNichol v Canada* [1997] 2 CTC 2088, 97 DTC 111 (TCC); *Geransky v Canada* [2001] 2 CTC 2147, 2001 DTC 243 (TCC); and *McMullen v Canada* [2007] 2 CTC 2463, 2007 DTC 286 (TCC).
[155] Crawford and Freedman (n 2) 1061.
[156] Canada, *Report on Federal Tax Expenditures* (n 85) 30, 34, estimating the annual cost of the lifetime gains exemption in terms of foregone federal income tax revenue as $1.5 billion in 2016, which is projected to increase to $1.81 billion in 2019, and the annual cost of the partial inclusion of capital gains as $12.91 billion in 2016, which is projected to increase to $17.115 billion in 2019.
[157] See, eg, KJ McKenzie and AJ Thompson, 'The Impact of the Capital Gains Exemption on Capital Markets' (1995) 21 *Canadian Public Policy* S100, 2113, concluding that '[i]t is … difficult to draw strong conclusions about the effect of the capital gains exemption on the cost of capital, and, therefore, on investment'.
[158] DG Duff, 'Canada' in M Littlewood and C Elliffe (eds), *Capital Gains Taxation: A Comparative Analysis of Key Issues* (Cheltenham, Edward Elgar Publishing, 2017) 156–57 and 163, reporting that capital gains constitute a much larger share of income reported by high-income taxpayers than middle- and low-income taxpayers and that the tax benefit from the lifetime capital gains exemption is enjoyed overwhelmingly by high-income taxpayers.

minors through transfers of property for consideration less than fair market value,[159] and the revenue authorities have successfully relied on a provision limiting deductions to amounts that are 'reasonable in the circumstances'[160] in order disallow the deduction of excessive salaries paid to related employees,[161] opportunities to split income through private corporations were greatly facilitated by a 1998 Supreme Court of Canada decision allowing the diversion of corporate income to the taxpayer's spouse through a separate class of shares on which dividends could be paid at the discretion of the company's directors.[162]

Although the government of the day responded to this decision with a provision taxing most private company dividends received by individuals under age 18 at the top marginal rate,[163] this TOSI did little to discourage the tax-motivated incorporation of small businesses since it did not apply to spouses or adult children. Indeed, in the 15 years after the TOSI came into effect in 2000, the number of CCPCs increased by 50 per cent, the number of incorporated self-employed individuals doubled, and the number of professional services corporations tripled.[164]

When the government returned to this issue in 2017, it did not – as Professor Freedman would have suggested – address the problem of income splitting 'in a holistic way' considering both the conversion of labour income into capital income and 'the rules on family taxation … and capital transfers between spouses',[165] but instead proposed to extend the TOSI rules to include all resident individuals receiving dividends or capital gains from the disposition of shares of a private corporation over which a 'connected individual' exercises significant influence.[166] After considerable controversy and opposition from professionals and the small business sector, a substantially revised and considerably more complex version of these rules was enacted effective for the 2018 taxation year.[167] Here again, therefore, Canada would have been better served if it had heeded Professor Freedman's advice.

IV. Conclusion

Over the course of a distinguished academic career, Judith Freedman has consistently and persuasively argued that the taxation of similar economic activities carried on through different legal forms is best addressed by reducing or eliminating the tax differentials among these legal forms, instead of through complicated statutory provisions and anti-avoidance rules that attempt to confine the tax advantages associated with particular legal forms to subcategories of these forms. For this and other reasons,

[159] For the current version of these rules, see ITA, ss 74.1–74.5.
[160] ITA, s 67.
[161] See, eg, *Grant Babcock Ltd v Minister of National Revenue* [1985] 2 CTC 2181, 85 DTC 518 (TCC); and *Maduke Foods Ltd v Minister of National Revenue* [1989] 2 CTC 284, 89 DTC 5458 (FCTD).
[162] *Neuman* (n 39).
[163] ITA, s 120.4.
[164] Department of Finance Canada, *Tax Planning Using Private Corporations* (n 19) 11.
[165] Freedman, 'Taxing the Micro-Business' (n 2) 74.
[166] ibid 18–31.
[167] SC 2018, c 12, s 13(5)–(7), amending ITA, s 120.4.

she has also questioned special tax preferences for small business, particularly through a reduced corporate tax rate for small business.

Canadian experience with the taxation of private companies and their shareholders illustrates why Professor Freedman's contributions to tax law and policy regarding small business are so convincing. Instead of minimising tax differentials among different legal forms, Canada provides a preferential tax rate for small business and tax preferences for capital gains, which encourage the tax-motivated incorporation of otherwise unincorporated businesses, the conversion of labour income into capital income and dividend income into capital gains, and income splitting with related persons. In order to limit the scope of these tax preferences, moreover, Canada relies on complicated statutory provisions which are subject to frequent amendment as well as specific and general anti-avoidance rules to challenge perceived abuses. The result is a complex and often uncertain legislative framework the economic merits of which are doubtful, the tax advantages of which are enjoyed disproportionately by high-income taxpayers, and the cost of which in terms of foregone revenues and increased compliance and administrative costs are substantial.

As Professor Freedman notes, the reason why these kinds of tax preferences persist had more to do with politics than policy, since the small business community is vocal, well organised and broadly supported by the media and the general public.[168] At the same time, experience in the United Kingdom suggests that business may support simplifying reforms when tax rules become extremely complex,[169] and that it is possible to align corporate tax rates for small and large businesses – though it is important to note that this result was accomplished by reducing the general corporate rate to the small business rate instead of by increasing the small business rate, which would have been much more challenging politically.

Most importantly, perhaps, experience in the United Kingdom suggests that thoughtful tax policy analysis, particularly when provided through an expert and impartial medium like the Mirrlees Review, can have a positive impact on actual tax policy. Indeed, Professor Freedman's contributions to tax law and policy regarding small business are testament to her conviction that

> in the long run a clear policy based system that can be explained to taxpayers and shown to be equitable and simple to operate may be more successful politically than one which responds to lobbyists and creates complexity, resulting in anti-avoidance provisions and confusion amongst users about the objectives of the system.[170]

[168] Crawford and Freedman (n 2) 1086.
[169] ibid.
[170] ibid.

5

Principles and Practice of Taxing Small Business

STUART ADAM AND HELEN MILLER

I. Introduction

The UK imposes very different tax liabilities on income from work depending on legal form. Primarily as a result of the fact that not all incomes are subject to National Insurance contributions (NICs) and some are subject to preferential rates, employees face a tax penalty relative to those who conduct work through their own business.

The way different incomes are treated for tax purposes is a problem. The system is unfair, complicated and economically inefficient. These problems are not new and not unforeseen. Researchers have been highlighting the problems and predicting that they would grow, including as a result of changing work patterns that blur the lines between employment and self-employment, for more than two decades. As the problems have grown, so too have the costs, including the revenue cost to the government. Official forecasts in 2017 implied that lower tax rates for the self-employed and company owner-managers relative to employees would cost about £15 billion in 2021–22.

This chapter reviews how the UK tax system treats different legal forms, how that has changed in the last two decades, and how the problems have evolved with changing work patterns. We then turn to consider why, given that the problems are known, substantial, long-running and growing, there has been so little progress in fixing them.

We suggest that part of the reason that the current system persists is widespread beliefs that the system is justified – ie, that there are benefits that offset the costs imposed by differentiating tax by legal form. We set out why none of the common arguments holds up. Levying lower taxes on the self-employed cannot be justified by differences in publicly funded benefits (the differences are far smaller than the tax advantages) or by differences in employment rights (which do not act to skew the labour market towards employment). Lower tax rates are also poorly targeted at boosting entrepreneurship.

It has long been recognised that there is a great deal of heterogeneity within the small business population and that not all are 'entrepreneurial'. The latest research using HMRC tax records is allowing the population of the self-employed and company owner-managers to be described in much more detail. The research highlights that most business owners, while conducting perfectly respectable trades, are not employing others, investing or growing – let alone doing anything that produces positive 'spillovers' to wider society and that will, therefore, be underprovided by the market. This serves to demonstrate how poorly targeted the tax breaks are.

Another reason why there has been little progress towards a solution is that the leading solution proposed – which was set out in the IFS-led Mirrlees Review and which required substantial changes to both rates and bases of various taxes – is seen by many as too radical to be workable or even desirable.[1]

This combination of factors – the beliefs that there is a valid reason to apply lower tax rates to business owners or that the solutions are not achievable – has led policymakers to respond to challenges by trying to modify and police the boundaries between legal forms. This approach has been ineffective because it does not tackle the underlying problem: that there are differences in tax rates across groups which cannot be clearly defined because there is no coherent principle underlying the distinction.

We conclude this chapter by discussing how we could approach improving the UK tax system. The first step has to be improving understanding of the system, the problems it creates, and why it does not have advantages that some think it does. To succeed, reform proposals must recognise two factors. First, the problems related to tax and legal form stem from the tax system and will only, therefore, be solved by fixing the tax system. Second, the taxation of employees, the self-employed and company owner-managers sits precisely at the point where many parts of the tax system come together; we must approach the tax system as a system and consider both tax rates and tax bases. This brings challenges, but also benefits. Policymakers around the world have long struggled with a perceived trade-off between, on the one hand, aligning capital income tax rates with labour tax rates to prevent tax avoidance, and on the other hand, applying low tax rates to capital to preserve incentives to save and invest. The trade-off can be escaped by aligning the overall marginal tax rate schedules for capital and labour income while also adjusting the tax *base* to preserve incentives to save and invest.

We propose that progress could be made by studying how manageable steps could be taken towards a solution and how different practical approaches could be taken to achieve economically equivalent outcomes.

II. The UK'S Tax Penalty on Employment

Different sources of income are subject to different taxes and rates of tax, which act to provide preferential rates to the self-employed and those operating through their own companies (see Figure 1). Employees' salaries are subject to income tax and both employee and employer NICs, above certain thresholds.[2] The self-employed also pay income tax and NICs on their earnings, but self-employed NICs are lower than employee NICs and there is no equivalent of employer NICs for the self-employed.

[1] JA Mirrlees et al (eds), *Tax by Design: The Mirrlees Review* (Oxford, Oxford University Press for Institute for Fiscal Studies, 2011).

[2] In discussing employees, we assume they are paid regular wages and not remunerated in other forms, such as stock options or benefits in kind, which are taxed differently.

Company owner-managers face different tax rates depending on how they choose to take their income, which can represent a mix of returns to labour effort and invested capital. Company owner-managers can achieve a lower tax rate than employees or the self-employed by taking income out of their company in the form of dividends or capital gains rather than wages. Specifically, as employees of their business, they can take a salary as an ordinary employee would, thus taking advantage of tax-free allowances in the National Insurance and income tax systems, as well as accruing rights towards the single-tier state pension. They can also pay themselves in dividends, which entails paying corporation tax on business profits (which are net of wages) and then paying income tax (but not NICs) on dividends at the personal level. The combined rates of tax on company profits and dividends are lower than the combined rates of income tax and NICs on salary. A company owner-manager looking to withdraw income from their company in a way that minimises their tax liability should pay themselves the NICs secondary threshold in salary and take any withdrawal above that in the form of dividends.[3] Below we highlight the current scale of tax differences across legal forms and how they have changed over time; Adam, Miller and Pope set this out in more detail.[4]

Figure 1 Tax due on total income generated of £40,000, 2019–20

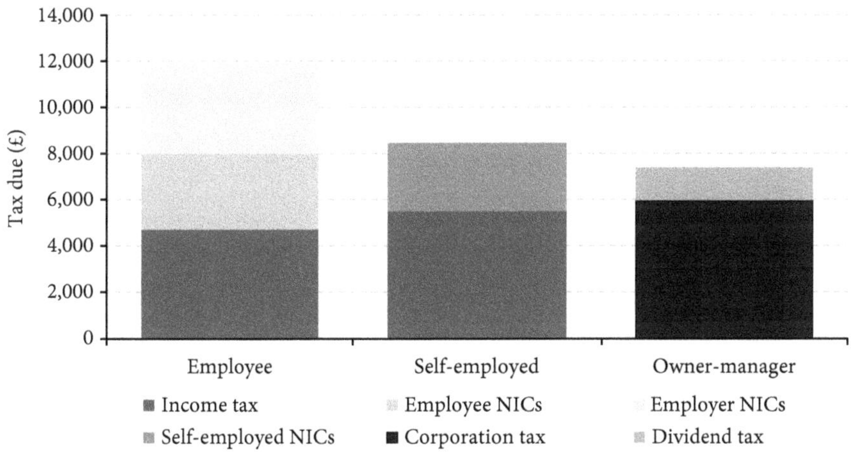

Note: the calculations assume: total income generated and paid out is equal to £40,000 for each legal form; the tax cost for employees includes employer NICs; company owner-managers take a salary equal to the NI secondary threshold and all post-tax profit as dividends. Income tax payments are lower for an employee than for a self-employed person because the employee's taxable earnings are lower as a result of employer NICs.

Figures 1 and 2 illustrate how the tax liability of individuals generating a certain amount of total income (set at £40,000 in Figure 1) varies by legal form; tax liability is highest

[3] For those with stable salaries and no other income, earnings up to the NI secondary threshold are within the personal allowance and therefore not taxed, unless an individual has a high enough income that the personal allowance is withdrawn: the personal allowance is reduced by 50 pence for every pound of income above £100,000, gradually reducing it to zero for those with incomes above £125,000.

[4] S Adam, H Miller and T Pope, 'Tax, Legal Form and the Gig Economy' in C Emmerson, P Johnson and R Joyce (eds), *The IFS Green Budget: February 2017* (London, Institute for Fiscal Studies, 2017), available at: www.ifs.org.uk/publications/8872.

for an employee and lowest for a company owner-manager at all levels of income. NICs treatment explains all of the difference between employees and the self-employed and the majority of the difference between both of these and company owner-managers. When calculating the tax payment for an employee, we include employer NICs, which, much like a wage, is a cost incurred by the employer to employ the individual.

For company owner-managers, we assume that income is taken out of the company in the current year (we return to discuss this below) and in the most tax-efficient way. Miller, Pope and Smith, using HMRC tax records, show that the majority of company owner-managers follow the strategy of paying themselves a small salary and taking any other withdrawals in the form of dividends.[5]

Figure 2 Tax due at different levels of income generated, 2019–20

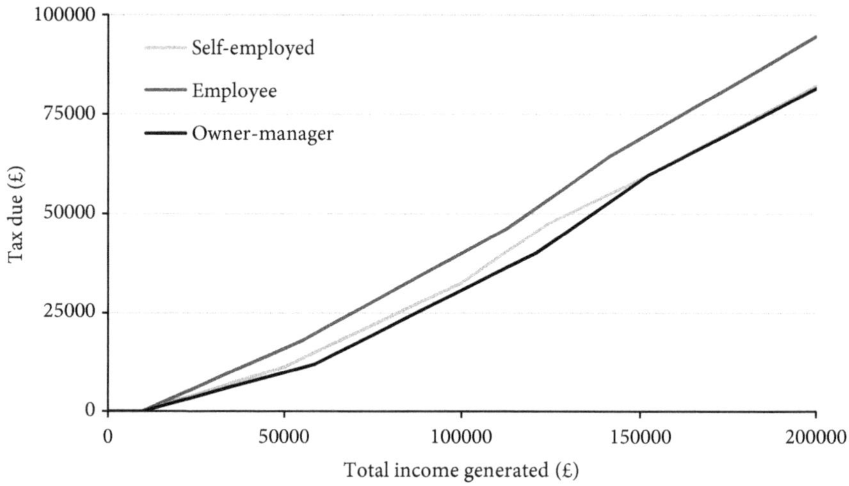

Note: The same assumptions as in Figure 1 hold here at each stated income level.

The preferential treatment of business incomes has long been a part of the UK tax system. Figure 3 shows liabilities since 1999–2000 for the example of a £40,000 income level (expressed in 2019–20 prices and, as in Figures 1 and 2, assuming company owner-managers take out all income in the year it is earned). The relative treatment of different legal forms has varied over time with changes in income tax, NICs, dividend tax and corporation tax regimes. For example, the liability of company owner-managers fell in the early 2000s with the introduction of a 'starting rate' of corporation tax and increased when it was effectively abolished in 2004–05.[6] The tax advantage of incorporation was sharply reduced in 2016–17 as a result of changes in the taxation of dividends.

[5] H Miller, T Pope and K Smith, 'Intertemporal Income Shifting and the Taxation of Owner-managed Businesses' (2019) Institute for Fiscal Studies Working Paper 19/25, available at: www.ifs.org.uk/publications/14475.

[6] A 'starting rate' of corporation tax meant that the first £10,000 of profit was subject to a lower tax rate, set at 10% in 2000–02 and 0% in 2002–06. In 2004–05 and 2005–06, profits distributed to shareholders were subject to a 19% tax rate (equivalent to the small companies' rate), which ended this tax advantage for most owner-managers.

These figures understate the tax advantages associated with self-employment and company owner-management. As well as lower headline tax rates, business owners generally have:

- More scope to deduct work-related expenses from their income than employees do (though there are exceptions to this).[7]
- Opportunities to split business profits among multiple individuals, including by making their spouse a shareholder or partner.[8]
- More scope than employees to (legally) avoid or (illegally) evade taxes.

Figure 3 Tax due on total income generated of £40,000, over time (2019–20 prices)

Note: Converted to 2019–20 terms using the consumer price index (CPI). Takes into account differences in corporation tax, income tax, dividend tax and NICs rates and thresholds. Assumes company owner-manager takes a salary equal to the NICs secondary threshold and all post-tax profit as dividends, except in 2014–15 and 2015–16 (when the employment allowance applied to company owner-managers), in which years we assume the company owner-manager takes a salary equal to the personal allowance and distributes all post-tax profits as dividends. Assumes that the company owner-manager is the only employee of their company and that the employee operates in a sufficiently large company that the employment allowance does not meaningfully affect their employer's NICs liability.

Company owner-managers can reduce their tax liability by adjusting when they take income out of a company because, unlike profits from self-employment, corporate profits are subject to personal income tax only when they are distributed to shareholders.

[7] The core of this difference is that employees' expenses are only deductible if incurred 'wholly, exclusively and necessarily' in the performance of their duties, while self-employment expenses need only be incurred 'wholly and exclusively' for business purposes. But the difference in practical application is bigger than this difference in wording suggests.

[8] J Cribb, H Miller and T Pope, 'Who are Business Owners and what are they Doing?' (2019) *Institute for Fiscal Studies Report*, available at: www.ifs.org.uk/publications/14241. The authors provide indirect evidence that the incentive to split income affects the structure of companies: 75% of two-person partnerships and 70% of two-director companies have one male and one female partner or director respectively (overall, the majority of business owners are male).

Company owner-managers can use the ability to retain income in their companies to defer paying personal tax on it, to shift their taxable income forwards or back in response to policy changes, and to smooth their taxable income (and therefore tax payments) over time. For example, a company owner-manager who usually earns less than the higher-rate income tax threshold but occasionally earns more than that can avoid paying any higher-rate income tax if she retains earnings in the company when she earns more than the threshold and takes them out in a year when she earns less. Miller, Pope and Smith show that a large part of the overall responsiveness of company owner-managers to tax rates can be attributed to this type of income smoothing.[9] That paper also shows that a significant number of company owner-managers retain significant amounts of money within their companies. There is a strong tax incentive to do this because income retained within a company and taken as capital gains when the shares are sold is subject to substantially lower tax liability as a result of entrepreneurs' relief – a preferential 10 per cent rate of capital gains tax (CGT) that most company owner-managers qualify for (for comparison the dividend tax rate for individuals in the higher-rate income tax band is 32.5 per cent).[10] Entrepreneurs' relief was introduced in 2008–09 and exacerbates the difference between the taxation of labour and capital for precisely the group that has the greatest ability to switch their incomes between the labour and capital tax bases.

III. Growing Problems Caused by Differentiating Tax by Legal Form

There are four broad types of problem created by a tax system that differentiates tax treatment according to legal form. They are related to: fairness, economic efficiency, government revenue and administrative costs. None of these is a new problem, and there have been predictions that the problems would grow with changing work patterns.[11] Here we discuss these problems, noting that, arguably, each has grown in recent years as

[9] Miller, Pope and Smith (n 5).

[10] Entrepreneurs' relief was (prior to April 2020) available on the first £10 million of otherwise taxable gains realised over an individual's lifetime. Finance Act 2020, sch 3, reduced the lifetime limit to £1 million on disposals on or after 5 April 2020 and renamed entrepreneurs' relief as 'business asset disposal relief'. The eligible assets are: shares owned by employees or directors with at least 5% of the shares and voting rights; unincorporated businesses; and business assets sold after the closure of a business. Newly issued, unlisted company shares owned for at least three years by external investors now qualify for investors' relief, which is similar in many ways. Entrepreneurs' relief can also be used by the self-employed, although the opportunities here are more limited since it is more difficult for them to defer income for tax purposes. If the self-employed do amass such assets that are later sold, they will only be subject to capital gains tax (without an additional layer of corporation tax) such that the tax treatment is even more generous than for company owner-managers.

[11] Judith Freedman has been at the forefront of this: see, eg, J Freedman and E Chamberlain, 'Horizontal Equity and the Taxation of Employed and Self-Employed Workers' (1997) 18 *Fiscal Studies* 87; J Freedman, *Employed or Self-Employed? Tax Classification of Workers and the Changing Labour Market* (London, Institute for Fiscal Studies, 2001); J Freedman, 'Small Business Taxation: Policy Issues and the UK' in N Warren (ed), *Taxing Small Business: Developing Good Tax Policies* (Australian Tax Research Foundation, 2003); J Freedman, 'Why Taxing the Micro-Business' is Not Simple – A Cautionary Tale from the "Old World"' (2006) 2 *Journal of the Australasian Tax Teachers Association* 58.

a result of (at least one of) three related factors. First, the number of people choosing to work for their own business has been increasing. Business owners (including both the self-employed and those owning closely held companies) have been the fastest growing part of the UK labour force since at least 2000; the number of companies with one or two directors increased by 60 per cent between 2007–08 and 2014–15.[12] Second, there have been changes in the nature of work, including as a result of digital platforms in the 'gig economy' that facilitate the matching of workers to customers.[13] Third, governments have taken additional steps to try to police the boundaries between legal forms (through 'IR35' legislation).

Issues of fairness – specifically, horizontal equity (that is, treating similar people similarly) – arise when two people earning similar incomes are taxed differently. There has always been (and will always be) a grey area between legal forms, such that the work of some employees is not distinctly different from that of some people working for their own business. This grey area has arguably grown as more people have provided their labour services to larger companies or agencies either while being sole traders or operating through 'personal service companies'.

The potential for unfairness is evident when two people earning similar incomes from similar work are taxed differently because they use different legal forms. Yet even when two people earn similar incomes from very *different* activities, it might be considered unfair to tax them differently. The crucial question in applying the principle of horizontal equity is always what dimensions, or criteria, are relevant in assessing whether people are 'similar'. It is doubtful that merely providing different kinds of services obviates the imperative for equal treatment if the services are equally valuable to the people paying for them. Unless there is some other difference between those earning business income and those earning employment income that justifies differential tax treatment – a question we consider in the next section – the current arrangement seems unfair on employees and employers.

Differential tax treatment creates economic inefficiency by distorting a range of individuals' choices. This distortion ultimately reduces society's aggregate output and wellbeing, as where people change behaviour to reduce their tax liabilities, their financial gain in reduced tax payments is mirrored by an equal loss of revenue to the government while there is an additional (financial or non-financial) loss to the individuals from not doing as they would have preferred in the absence of taxation. The tax system favours certain legal forms over others and encourages individuals to behave in certain ways once they have chosen a legal form. There is substantial evidence that these incentives change behaviour.

[12] In 2015–16, 4.9 million people were operating through self-employment, up from 3.9 million in 2000–01. The majority (4.1 million) were sole traders. In 2014–15 there were 1.6 million owner-managers of companies with either one or two directors, up from 0.8 million in 2000–01. Companies with a sole director (most of whom also have only one shareholder) have accounted for all the growth in owner-managed companies since 2006–07 when a legal change made being a one-director company possible. Statistics taken from Cribb, Miller and Pope (n 8), based on HMRC tax records.

[13] The 'gig economy' cannot be directly measured. While there have been many salient examples of 'gig jobs' in recent years, such as Uber, the growth in business ownership is a wider phenomenon (Adam, Miller and Pope (n 4); Cribb, Miller and Pope (n 8); LF Katz and AB Krueger, 'The Rise and Nature of Alternative Work Arrangements in the United States, 1995–2015' (2019) 72 *ILR Review* 382 documents the rise of alternative work arrangements in the US and suggests possible explanations.

The UK provides a clear illustration of how incorporation responds to incentives. Figure 4 shows the number of incorporations over time. Spikes occurred at times when the incentives, or at least the perceived incentives, to incorporate changed.[14] The increase in incorporations in response to the 0 per cent starting rate of corporation tax in the early 2000s was predictable and, indeed, predicted by researchers at the Institute for Fiscal Studies (IFS).[15,16]

Figure 4 Incorporations per week since 1991 (52-week moving average)

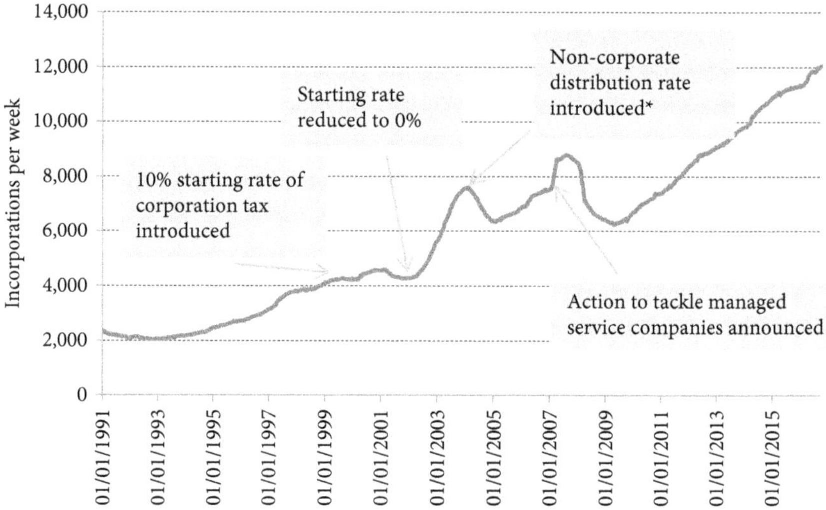

* This effectively marked the end of the tax advantage of the starting rate for most company owner-managers.
Source: Correspondence with Companies House.

Increasing the number of new businesses was an explicit goal of the starting rate of corporation tax.[17] However, having more small companies should not automatically be seen as a positive outcome. This was ultimately recognised by the last Labour government, which unwound the starting rate following concerns that the rapid growth in new companies represented the effects of tax-motivated incorporation. Despite this stark lesson in why it is important not to conflate more incorporations with more entrepreneurship, it continues to be the case that growth in business ownership (including self-employment) is often held up as a success story (for example, in the UK's 2017 Industrial Strategy).[18]

[14] For further discussion, see C Crawford and J Freedman, 'Small Business Taxation' in S Adam et al (eds), *Dimensions of Tax Design: The Mirrlees Review* (Oxford, Oxford University Press for Institute for Fiscal Studies, 2010).

[15] L Blow, M Hawkins, A Klemm, J McCrae and H Simpson, 'Budget 2002: Business Taxation Measures', *IFS Briefing Note 24*, 2002, available at: www.ifs.org.uk/publications/1774.

[16] The structure of companies has changed in response to legal reforms as well as tax incentives. Notably, the Companies Act 2006 removed the requirement for private companies to have a company secretary; since then companies with a sole director (of which there were none before 2006) have accounted for all the growth in owner-managed companies (Cribb, Miller and Pope (n 8)).

[17] See Freedman, 'Taxing the Micro-Business' (n 11).

[18] HM Government, *Industrial Strategy: Building A Britain Fit for The Future* (White Paper, 2017), available at: assets.publishing.service.gov.uk/government/uploads/system/uploads/attachment_data/file/664563/industrial-strategy-white-paper-web-ready-version.pdf.

As well as distorting choices over whether to adopt a particular legal form, the UK tax system distorts the behaviour of those in a given legal form, including over how much to invest and how to withdraw income from a company. As highlighted above, recent research uses HMRC tax records to show that company owner-managers readily switch between capital and labour tax bases.[19] Income is almost always taken out of a company in the way that minimises tax payments – usually in the form of dividends, if the income is being taken annually, or capital gains if the income is taken when a company is closed or sold. Despite the significant amount of money that is retained within companies – on average a sole director generating £150,000 each year retains £50,000 in the company – there is no evidence that tax-motivated retention leads to higher investment in assets for use in the business; instead the earnings are held in cash or equivalent assets.

These effects on behaviour matter. They mean that people are not doing what they would ideally like to, and resources are not being put to their most productive use. And to the extent that they reduce people's tax payments, they mean that tax rates elsewhere must be higher – increasing the cost to other taxpayers – to provide the revenue that the government needs.

Government revenues are reduced substantially as a result of providing reduced tax rates for business owners, relative to the tax that would be levied if they were employees. Based on official statistics, it is possible to say the following:[20]

- The cost of reduced rates of NICs for the self-employed (relative to employees) was expected to be £5.6 billion in 2019–20.[21] This amount equates to around £1,100 per self-employed person. Revenue raised from self-employed NICs in the same year is estimated at £3.4 billion,[22] ie, less than 40 per cent of what would be due if the self-employed and employed were treated comparably.
- The Exchequer cost of applying lower tax rates to the population of closely held company owner-managers was forecast in 2017 to rise to over £9.5 billion by 2021–22.[23]

[19] Miller, Pope and Smith (n 5).

[20] These numbers are based on data from before the COVID-19 crisis. The crisis will have changed the magnitude of these costs as a result, for example, of changes in employment and income levels. At the time of writing it is not clear how the economy will recover and therefore how the revenue costs of various tax breaks will be impacted.

[21] See HMRC, 'Estimated cost of Structural Tax Reliefs', October 2019, available at: gov.uk/government/statistics/minor-tax-expenditures-and-structural-reliefs.

[22] Appendix D of Government Actuary's Department, 'Report by the Government Actuary on the draft Social Security Benefits Up-rating Order 2019 and the draft Social Security (Contributions) (Rates, Limits and Thresholds Amendments and National Insurance Funds Payments) Regulations 2019, available at: gov.uk/government/publications/report-to-parliament-on-the-2019-re-rating-and-up-rating-orders.

[23] This forecast comprises two parts. In 2017 HMRC estimated that the cost, in 2021–22, of providing lower taxes to the existing population of closely held companies (relative to taxing them as employees) would be more than £6 billion (HM Treasury, Spring Budget 2017, fn 3, available at: assets.publishing.service.gov.uk/government/uploads/system/uploads/attachment_data/file/597467/spring_budget_2017_web.pdf). The Office for Budget Responsibility forecast that this annual cost would rise by an additional £3.5 billion by 2021–22 as a result of a rise in owner-managed companies' share of the total workforce (OBR, November 2016, Box 4.1, available at: obr.uk/box/the-effect-of-incorporations-on-tax-receipts/). These are the most recent published forecasts; changes since then (such as the reduction in the dividend allowance from £5,000 to £2,000, the reduction in the lifetime limit in entrepreneurs' relief from £10 million to £1 million and the shift in

- In 2017–18 (the last year for which we have data on the number of claimants), the estimated cost of entrepreneurs' relief was £2.3 billion, or £53,500 per claimant – though this will fall markedly as a result of the reduction in the lifetime limit from £10 million to £1 million, not to mention the fall in asset prices caused by the COVID-19 crisis.[24] Note that this tax advantage will typically relate to capital gains built up over many years (it is not the tax saving made each year by a claimant) and is the cost relative to the case in which these capital gains are taxed under the main capital gains tax regime (not relative to a world in which they are taxed as salary or dividend income).

Revenues will additionally be affected because evasion and avoidance are higher among business owners than employees (which also further exacerbate the problems of unfairness, inefficiency and diverted resources). HMRC estimates that the 'tax gap' for income tax, NICs and CGT in 2017–18 – the gap between the tax that 'ought' to have been paid (as HMRC defines that) and the tax actually paid – was 1 per cent or £2.9 billion for PAYE (which covers the vast majority of employees) but 15 per cent or £7.4 billion for self-assessment taxpayers (including business owners). In 2015–16, 28 per cent of sole traders and small partnerships under-declared tax, the majority by more than £1,000.[25]

The presence of boundaries in the tax system creates the need to devise, administer, comply with and police rules to distinguish the different legal forms. These, in turn, impose costs by diverting officials, taxpayers, accountants and occasionally the courts from more productive activities – all to a greater extent, the bigger the tax differential on either side of the boundary. The UK government's main tool for trying to prevent tax-motivated changes in legal form has been the 'IR35' rules, initially introduced in 2000, which essentially set out when corporate income should be treated as employment income for tax purposes.[26] These rules created additional administration and compliance costs yet were largely seen as ineffective and have repeatedly been reformed. In 2017, responsibility for enforcing the rules switched from the individuals operating companies to their engagers, if the latter were in the public sector. In 2020 this was due to be extended to large and medium-sized engagers in the private sector, though with the onset of the COVID-19 crisis this was delayed until 2021. Wherever the boundaries dictated by IR35 and similar rules are placed, and however they are enforced, they face the fundamental underlying problem that there are grey areas that mean that different types of people cannot be placed neatly into categories. Moreover, it is not even clear which types of people/businesses the government thinks should or should not have access to preferential (ie, business) tax rates.

responsibility for complying with IR35 from the worker to the engager and the wider economic effects of the COVID-19 crisis) might be expected to reduce these numbers somewhat. The OBR's most recent Fiscal Risks Report concluded that the fiscal risk involved 'has not changed materially', available at: OBR, Fiscal Risks Report 2019, paragraph 4.24 (obr.uk/frr/fiscal-risks-report-july-2019/), but this assessment pre-dated the 2020 Budget reforms and the COVID-19 crisis.

[24] See HMRC, 'Estimated costs of non-structural tax reliefs', October 2019, available at: www.gov.uk/government/statistics/main-tax-expenditures-and-structural-reliefs.

[25] See HMRC, 'Measuring tax gaps', August 2019, available at: www.gov.uk/government/collections/measuring-tax-gaps.

[26] Freedman, 'Taxing the Micro-Business' (n 11).

IV. Three Arguments that do not Support Tax Differences

The discussion above highlights that problems around fairness, economic efficiency, revenue loss and administrative costs arise because people are taxed very differently according to whether they are an employee, self-employed or working through their own company. However, we accept many tax differentials across the system because there are benefits which outweigh the costs. Concerning legal form, those defending differential tax rates broadly tend to agree that genuinely similar work should be taxed in the same way regardless of legal form but argue that there are important differences between people in different legal forms that justify different tax treatment. There are three common arguments put forward in support of tax differences (ie, in support of the idea that the benefits outweigh the costs): that lower tax rates reflect lower state benefit entitlements, lower employment rights, or the value of promoting entrepreneurship. Here we lay out why none of these arguments stands up to scrutiny. Even if there were no grey areas between legal forms, and employees, the self-employed and company owner-managers were very different, we maintain that the current tax differentials across different legal forms would be unjustified.

First, the argument for lower taxes on the self-employed to reflect their reduced benefit entitlements has merit in principle, but in practice, **the difference in entitlements is far too small to justify their current tax advantages**.

If the benefits system creates a bias in favour of employment over self-employment, there is a case for an offsetting tax rate differential to level the playing field. National Insurance is presented as a contributory system, with contributions paid in return for entitlements. In principle, lower NIC rates on the income of the self-employed can, therefore, be seen as a quid pro quo for lower entitlements.[27] However, today there are just two publicly funded 'contributory' benefits that employees can access but the self-employed cannot: contribution-based jobseeker's allowance and statutory maternity/paternity/adoption/shared parental pay. The value of these reduced entitlements is small: we estimate that they would only justify setting the self-employed NIC rate less than one percentage point lower than the combined employer and employee rates.

The difference in access to contributory benefits was more significant in the past (although still smaller than the tax differences) but has substantially shrunk as benefits have been extended to the self-employed (and more broadly the contributory nature of NICs eroded). What was until recently the biggest difference in entitlements – the fact that the self-employed accrued rights to the basic state pension, but not to the earnings-related top-up (state second pension) – was removed in April 2016; now both the self-employed and employees accrue rights to a single-tier pension. Formerly 'contracted-out' (of the state second pension) employees must now pay the full rate of

[27] In so far as other tax and benefit policies also have the net effect of favouring one legal form over another, there is a similar case for offsetting it through differential tax rates to level the playing field. This applies, for example, to the rules that allow more generous deductibility of work-related expenses for the self-employed than for employees, and to tax-advantaged forms of remuneration, such as redundancy pay, that are only available to employees. Of course, the prior question is whether some legal forms should be favoured in the first place. As far as possible, it would be better to apply the same benefit entitlement rules, expense deductibility rules, etc across different legal forms than to offset such differences with differential tax rates.

NICs in return for this entitlement, while the self-employed have seen an increase in entitlement with no such increase in their NIC rate. HMRC estimates that this reform increased the aggregate tax advantage of self-employment relative to employment by about £2 billion.[28]

The most significant disadvantage now faced by the self-employed in the benefits system comes from universal credit, a new benefit currently being rolled out (amid much delay) as a replacement for six major existing means-tested benefits and tax credits. Unlike its predecessors, universal credit treats the self-employed as earning at least a certain amount (after a year's grace period) even if they report earning less than that and gives them correspondingly less support. This reduction in entitlements was forecast to save the Exchequer £1 billion a year by 2023–24:[29] a substantial amount, but still nowhere near big enough to justify the £5.6 billion NICs advantage of self-employment. The combined main rates of employer and employee NICs is 22.7 per cent.[30] At most, the lower universal credit entitlement might justify a self-employed NICs rate about three percentage points below this – still more than double the current 9 per cent rate. Yet in any case the argument is (so far, at least) not made as often in respect of universal credit, perhaps because, rightly or wrongly, universal credit is not seen as part of a 'contributory' system in the same way as some other benefits.

Even this difference in universal credit entitlements has been put into question by the COVID-19 crisis. The spring 2020 Budget announced that the practice of assuming a minimum income for the self-employed would be suspended for the duration of the outbreak, so at the time of writing the self-employed are treated in the same way as other universal credit claimants. The policy was controversial even before the crisis, so there must be at least a chance that it will not be reinstated in quite the same form after the crisis.

The response to COVID-19 also demonstrated that the government provides comparable income protection for employees and the self-employed in hitherto unseen ways. The Self-Employed Income Support Scheme (SEISS), which provided grants to the self-employed whose profits were reduced by the COVID-19 crisis, was designed to provide government support that was comparable to that provided to employees through the Coronavirus Job Retention Scheme (CJRS).[31] The crisis showed that, not only are standard state benefits almost as generous to the self-employed as to employees, but the unspoken promise of emergency support the government provides to the self-employed is comparable to that for employees. When announcing the SEISS, Chancellor Sunak said that

> in devising this scheme – in response to many calls for support – it is now much harder to justify the inconsistent contributions between people of different employment statuses. If we all want to benefit equally from state support, we must all pay in equally in future.[32]

[28] See HMRC, 'Estimated cost of structural tax reliefs' (n 21).

[29] Source: Table 4.28 of Office for Budget Responsibility (2018), *Economic and Fiscal Outlook October 2018*, available at: obr.uk/efo/economic-fiscal-outlook-october-2018/.

[30] This is appropriately measured as the total marginal tax rate on an additional pound paid out by the employer, not on an additional pound of nominal salary: that is (0.12 + 0.138) ÷ 1.138.

[31] See S Adam, H Miller and T Waters, 'Income Protection for the self-employed and employees during the coronavirus crisis', *IFS Briefing Note BN277*, 2020, available at: www.ifs.org.uk/publications/14786.

[32] See S Adam and H Miller, 'Covid-19: will tax reform be the silver lining or the missed opportunity?' *Tax Journal* (7 May 2020), available at: www.taxjournal.com/articles/covid-19-will-tax-reform-be-the-silver-lining-or-the-missed-opportunity-.

Second, **lower tax rates for the self-employed cannot be used to offset differences in employment rights** between different legal forms.

A common – and understandable – misconception is that the self-employed should get lower taxes because they do not get employment rights (and conversely those who do get employment rights should be taxed at higher rates).[33] This logic behind this line of argument is incorrect and has always been incorrect.

The first thing to note is that employment rights are not a benefit given by the government to employees (ie, are not like state benefit entitlements), but a benefit that the government requires employers to give to their employees. The second thing to note – and the reason, in a nutshell, why the logic fails – is that employment rights affect both sides of the labour market: employees and employers. Employment rights make employment more attractive (relative to self-employment) to the worker, but they simultaneously make it less attractive for employers to choose employees over the self-employed.[34] Employment rights are not favouring employment over self-employment overall in a way that might justify an offsetting tax differential; they merely redistribute between the two parties within an employment relationship. Because of this, employment rights do not (and cannot) act to skew the labour market in favour of employment relative to self-employment. In contrast, our tax system does skew the market in favour of getting work done through self-employment. Add these two effects together, and you have a situation that skews the market in favour of self-employment, not a market with a level playing field. Miller sets out this argument in detail, including showing that it does not depend on any specific assumption about how labour markets operate or how wages adjust.[35]

Third, **lower tax rates for business owners cannot be justified as a way to incentivise entrepreneurship**.

People running their own businesses may be doing something fundamentally different from employees, including investing, employing others, innovating, taking risks and other such 'entrepreneurial' activities. In principle, one can make an argument in favour of using tax policy to address the market failures that can arise in relation to entrepreneurship. But blanket reductions in tax rates for all the self-employed and company owner-managers are poorly targeted at that objective.

The business owner-manager population encompasses a large variety of business models: people using a business legal form include everyone from taxi drivers, plumbers

[33] Employees are entitled to certain legal rights (sometimes only after a minimum employment period), including the relevant minimum wage, statutory minimum holiday, sick and redundancy pay, protection against unlawful discrimination and unfair dismissal, and statutory maternity/paternity/adoption/shared parental leave and pay. 'Workers' who are not employees have fewer rights. The self-employed are not covered by employment law. See Adam, Miller and Pope (n 4) for a summary. See also H Miller, 'Lack of employment rights doesn't justify lower taxes for the self-employed' (London, Institute for Fiscal Studies, 2019), available at: www.ifs.org.uk/publications/13079.

[34] Some rights or benefits can be provided in a way that is mutually beneficial for both employer and employee (because they are valued by employees and relatively cheap for employers to provide). For example, many employers provide healthcare, which they may be able to access at preferential rates relative to individual employees. However, we would expect employers to provide these types of benefits regardless of whether they are mandated in employment law; employment laws do not instigate mutually beneficial trades.

[35] H Miller, 'Lack of Employment Rights doesn't Justify Lower Taxes for the Self-employed', *IFS Observation*, 19 June 2018, available at: ifs.org.uk/publications/13079.

and local shop owners, to IT consultants, doctors and lawyers, to those running genuinely innovative businesses that will go on to grow and employ others. A recent analysis of HMRC tax records shows that, to the extent that it is possible to describe the stereotypical closely held business, it is not one that makes substantial investments or goes on to grow.[36] Key findings include:

- Sole traders (the large majority of business owners) generated an average of £12,100 from their business in 2015–16, substantially below employees' average earnings (£30,100). Partners and company owner-managers have significantly higher average incomes than employees.
- Most sole traders do not employ anyone; around 70 per cent have total business costs (including wages and capital investment) below £10,000. Median costs for owner-managed companies are £24,000, although with significant variation across different types of business. The share of both sole traders and owner-managed companies using any capital allowances has fallen substantially in the past decade.
- Most sole traders exit quickly: 60 per cent have ceased trading within five years of setting up. The overall annual growth in self-employment is the net result of high rates of entry and exit. For example, between 2014–15 and 2015–16 the sole trader population grew by almost 70,000, but this was a net effect of 650,000 sole traders starting up and 580,000 exiting.
- Remarkably, while the number of sole traders grew by 800,000 between 2007–08 and 2015–16, their *aggregate* profit fell over the same period. This was driven by large falls in profits of those sole traders who remained in business (ie, it was not the result of low income among new businesses). The proportion of sole traders with profits above £40,000 halved between 2007–08 and 2015–16.

In any case, the mere fact of investing, taking risks or employing people does not justify preferential tax rates on the entrepreneur's income.

It is true that those running businesses sometimes employ people, and that we would like to reduce the extent to which taxation discourages employment. But if that is the aim, it would surely be better pursued by making it cheaper to hire people. It is a bizarre twist of logic to argue that the best way to promote employment is to impose higher tax rates on employment than on profits.

More seriously, it is important to note that (contrary to widespread belief) there should be no presumption for the government to promote investment or risk-taking per se: if the market does not provide sufficiently high rewards for such activities, they should not be undertaken. But nor should the government aim to discourage these activities, and at present the UK tax system does discourage risk-taking and some forms of investment:

- The effect of the tax system on incentives to invest depends on how the investment is financed and the type of asset invested in. Broadly, there is neutral treatment of equity-financed investment covered by the Annual Investment Allowance (AIA); a disincentive for equity-financed investment not covered by the AIA; and a subsidy to debt-financed investment covered by the AIA.[37]

[36] Cribb, Miller and Pope (n 8).
[37] Mirrlees et al (n 1).

- The tax system discourages risk-taking because profits and losses are treated asymmetrically: the government penalises successful projects (by taxing the profits) more than it cushions unsuccessful ones (through loss offsets, which are incomplete, especially for new businesses that fail).[38]

Lower rates of tax on income do lessen these problems – the lower the tax rate, the less the peculiarities of the tax base matter for firms' tax liabilities – but they are an expensive and poorly targeted approach. Lower tax rates cannot eliminate the distortions completely unless the tax rate falls to zero, and the giveaway from reduced tax rates tends to be concentrated on the most profitable investments, where additional incentives are least needed.

A better approach would be to address the underlying source of the problem directly. Fully symmetrical treatment of profits and losses is not practical but reforming the current rules on loss offsets would be a sensible focus of policy reform. Likewise, removing the distortions to investment decisions requires adjusting the tax base – capital allowances and the treatment of debt and equity finance – not tax rates. Indeed, even if there were a policy goal to incentivise investment (ie, to provide subsidies), this would be better achieved through the tax base than by giving lower tax rates.

Entrepreneurs' relief – a reduced (10 per cent) rate of capital gains tax on owner-managed businesses – is particularly poorly targeted if the goal is to encourage entrepreneurs to make risky investments in their own business, for two main reasons. First, any incentive effects are only present for those who make a profit and can afford to retain profits in their business – and are larger for more profitable investments, targeting the money on those investments that would be worthwhile even in the absence of tax breaks rather than on the borderline-worthwhile investments where incentives really matter. Second, while the relief does increase the incentive to hold capital in the business, it does not increase the incentive to invest those retained earnings within the business. This is because it does not affect the relative incentives to invest in fixed assets *versus* holding the retained profits in cash. If, in the absence of a tax incentive to retain earnings, a business is undertaking the optimal amount of investment, there is no reason additional retained earnings would lead them to invest more: if additional investments are not profitable then they will prefer to keep the retained earnings in cash (or equivalent assets). Miller, Pope and Smith set this out in more detail and show empirically that there is no evidence that UK company owner-managers who retain more earnings as a result of tax incentives make more use of capital allowances.[39]

The case for government intervention is strongest where markets fail to provide the appropriate incentives. For example, there may be too few new ideas tried out because innovators do not reap all the rewards (some 'spill over' to other businesses that can learn from the experiences of the innovator). Alternatively, some small or new firms may find it prohibitively expensive to raise external finance because potential lenders have less information than would-be borrowers about the firm's prospects. However,

[38] Losses can only be set against other income, with significant restrictions (which differ between companies and the self-employed) on what income they can be used to offset. Losses carried forward get no compensation for the delay, and there is a risk that the losses can never be used.

[39] Miller, Pope and Smith (n 5).

neither of these examples provides a compelling case for lower tax rates on business income.

Lower tax rates once a project is successful do little to help new firms to raise finance, or to address the immediate cash-flow concerns that are central to so many new businesses. Other approaches, such as enhanced investment allowances or loan guarantees, may be more effective.

And where there are spillovers, it is better, if possible, to target the specific activities that generate them, as the R&D tax credit, for example, attempts to do. This is not always possible: not all the innovative activities that bring wider social benefits can be pinpointed and subsidised in that way. Yet most small businesses do not generate significant spillover benefits to wider society. From newsagents to IT contractors, they consist of people quietly going about the (perfectly honourable) business of making a living by providing valuable goods and services to others – much as most ordinary employees do. There is little evidence that the gains from using across-the-board lower rates to promote those socially beneficial activities that cannot be targeted more directly are big enough to justify scattering tax benefits so widely and creating the problems of boundaries in the tax system highlighted above.

Finally, we note that **one pragmatic argument for taxing the self-employed and company owner-managers at lower rates than employees is that the former two groups are more responsive to tax** (as shown by, for example, Adam et al).[40] The more a tax reduces taxable income, the lower the revenue yield from the tax, and the greater the loss of taxpayer welfare per pound of revenue raised. So it can be efficient to set lower tax rates for more responsive groups. The self-employed and company owner-managers are more responsive to tax in part because they have more ways to manipulate their incomes for tax purposes, rather than simply because of 'real' economic responses such as the amount of effort they put in.[41] The first way to deal with this, therefore, is to reduce the options that the self-employed and company owner-managers have to avoid (or evade) taxes – for example, by taxing capital gains at the same rates as ordinary income. Sensible policy changes would reduce the extent to which the self-employed and company owner-managers can escape tax more easily than employees, though not entirely eliminate the difference in responsiveness. But any potential efficiency gains that remained would have to be weighed against the costs of differentiation. And there are clearly equity concerns over a policy of providing lower tax rates to one group because they can more easily avoid or evade tax.

V. An Old Solution: Fix the Tax System

The problems highlighted above stem from the differential rates of tax placed on different legal forms. It is only by evening out relative tax rates that we can hope to solve those problems. This is not a new insight: Crawford and Freedman, for example, concluded

[40] S Adam, J Browne, D Phillips and B Roantree, 'Frictions and Taxpayer Responses: Evidence from Bunching at Personal Tax Thresholds' (2019) IFS Working Paper W17/14, available at: ifs.org.uk/publications/9679.
[41] Miller, Pope and Smith (n 5).

that 'alignment or equalization of tax rates across legal forms is necessary to achieve a sensible system for taxing small owner-managed businesses'.[42]

Instead, there have been attempts to address these problems by writing and policing rules that determine what should fall on each side of a legal boundary. These approaches have been largely ineffective, in part because there are not neat definitions of which types of people/business should get preferential tax treatment, either conceptually or in practice. If definitions around the boundaries are adjusted, the new definitions will quickly come under pressure.

More importantly, and as we have argued, the current tax system would not be justified even if there were clear distinctions between legal forms. Even if all arguments about horizontal equity were put to one side (because we were happy to give some groups lower tax rates than others) and even if there were no tax-motivated changes in legal form, there would still be other distortions to behaviour (including to how company owner-managers arranged their activities and to investment incentives), there would still be additional administration costs, and there would still be a revenue cost. It is hard to justify accepting any of these costs given that there is little justification for favouring one legal form over another in the first place. We have managed to create a system that is costly (in various dimensions) but that still disincentivises (some forms of) investment and provides very little support to some genuine entrepreneurship. That is, the costs can't even be argued to be the unfortunate side-effect of a system that is successfully targeting a worthwhile objective.

The solution to the problems laid out above is known. Building on the work of many others, this was brought together and laid out by Crawford and Freedman and more broadly by the Mirrlees Review of the UK tax system undertaken for the IFS.[43] One key message from that work is that any reforms in this area must be mindful that the taxation of employees, the self-employed and company owner-managers sits precisely at the point where many parts of the tax system come together. Incentives to switch between legal forms depend on the bases and rates of income tax (including the treatment of dividends), NICs, corporation tax and CGT. Changing any one of these has far-reaching effects: tax rates on earnings affect all employees, not just those who might otherwise set up a business; corporation tax affects all companies, from one-man bands to multinationals; taxation of dividends and capital gains affects portfolio shareholders and buy-to-let landlords as well as business owner-managers. Addressing this by introducing a special regime for 'small businesses' (however defined) would add another boundary to the tax system that would create problems of its own and not reflect any underlying principle. It might replace one big tax differential with two smaller ones, but the underlying problem would still be there. Such policies are sometimes better than nothing. But they are at best a sticking plaster rather than a solution to the underlying tensions in the tax system, and at worst can create more problems than they solve. The tax treatment of different legal forms should always be seen in the context of the whole tax system. Attempting to solve one narrow problem in isolation – such as by adjusting

[42] Crawford and Freedman (n 14).
[43] ibid; Mirrlees et al (n 1).

only the treatment of one legal form or of introducing different tax regimes for a subset of small businesses – is the policy equivalents of 'whack-a-mole': the particular problem may be fixed but at the expense of another one popping up elsewhere in the system.

The Mirrlees Review proposes a design for the whole tax system which aligns the taxation of different legal forms as just one part of a broader plan. Essentially, it argues that the same overall tax rate schedule should apply to income from all sources, but with full allowances given (at both the personal and corporate tax levels) for amounts saved and invested to avoid discouraging those activities.

Aligning the treatment of different legal forms requires applying the same overall tax rate schedule to income derived from employment, self-employment and companies – bearing in mind that this overall rate schedule currently involves varying combinations of income tax, NICs, CGT and corporation tax, depending on the income source. Broadly, this could be achieved by (i) aligning the NICs paid by self-employed individuals with those paid by employers and employees combined (preferably in the course of integrating NICs with personal income tax) and (ii) taxing dividend income and capital gains at the same rate schedule as earned income (including employee and employer NICs), with reduced tax rates for dividends and capital gains on shares to reflect corporation tax already paid. This process would include removing entrepreneurs' relief, though in many cases the reduced capital gains tax rates for shares would limit the increase in the tax rate that this entails. Note that alignment does not necessarily require an increase in the corporation tax rate, which would raise valid concerns around making the UK less competitive. Instead, overall rate alignment could be achieved at the personal level by adjusting dividend and capital gains tax rates while keeping a relatively low corporation tax rate (which could be set with reference to multinationals). Aligning the treatment of these income sources would also mean reversing the recent trend towards having a large separate allowance in each tax, a feature that favours incorporation since a company owner-manager, unlike an ordinary employee, can benefit from additional tax-free allowances for dividends and capital gains as well as from the main income tax personal allowance.

One valid concern with aligning rates on total income is that, in isolation, higher tax rates on income from self-employment and companies (which reflect a mix of rewards for labour and capital) produce disincentives to save and invest. This, in turn, creates an apparent trade-off that policymakers around the world have struggled with for decades: on the one hand, they want to align capital tax rates with labour tax rates to prevent tax avoidance that arises because labour income can be converted into capital income, but on the other hand, they want low capital tax rates to preserve incentives to save and invest. The result has usually been an awkward compromise, with regular changes in tax rates (such as the roller coaster of UK CGT rates – see Adam et al (2017)) as policymakers give different weight to those competing concerns. In most countries, capital income tends to be taxed at reduced rates relative to labour income (often with different forms of capital income taxed at different rates), leaving some disincentive effects and some scope for avoidance. However, the trade-off can be escaped by **aligning the overall tax rates for capital and labour income *while giving a full deduction for capital costs*.** Adjusting the tax base allows the incentives to save and invest to be preserved while also removing incentives to switch across tax bases.

In a nutshell, designing the tax base to avoid disincentives to save and invest is achieved by giving full allowances (at both personal and corporate tax levels) for amounts saved and invested. There are two ways to go about doing this:[44]

- Cash saved or invested can simply be deducted from taxable income/profits at the point it is saved/invested. This approach is currently applied to pension contributions by the income tax system, and to business investment where 100 per cent first-year allowances are available (as in the case of the AIA).
- A deduction could be given each year for an imputed risk-free rate of return to capital previously saved/invested. This is the rate-of-return allowance (RRA) treatment of saving and the allowance for corporate equity (ACE) treatment of business investment, neither of which has ever been used in the UK although both are now used in other countries.

Timing aside, these two treatments are equivalent. With stable tax rates, the stream of allowances given each year under the second approach is worth the same as the upfront deduction given under the first approach. Both avoid discouraging saving and investment, since an asset that (in the absence of taxation) yields just enough of a return to be worth the upfront cost will see the tax on income generated exactly offset (in present value terms) by the tax deduction for the investment cost. Only returns in excess of that level will yield a net tax liability, and since only a fraction of the excess will be taxed away, assets that yield such high returns will still be worthwhile investments. And in both cases the deduction depends only on the amount saved/invested, irrespective of the actual return it generates; each extra pound of income is taxed in full regardless of the form in which it is taken, so there is no tax incentive to choose one legal form over another or to dress up one form of income as another.

This solution does not solve all problems. It does not, for example, remove the ability or incentive for business owners to split income with family members. But it also solves many more problems than are highlighted in this chapter, including the bias towards debt financing, the sensitivity of savings incentives to inflation and the lock-in effect currently present in CGT.

VI. How to Make an Old Solution Work

Given that the problems with taxing legal forms in very different ways are large, long-running, well known and growing and that no one seems happy with the current system, it is perhaps surprising that so little progress has been made in fixing the system. There would seem to be at least two broad reasons for this.

The first is misunderstanding. It is still a commonly held belief that lower rates of tax for business owners are justified by some combination of lower rates of benefit entitlement, a lack of employment rights or the desirability of promoting entrepreneurship.

[44] These approaches and their properties – including other advantages not discussed here – are explained in Mirrlees et al (n 1). For brevity, we do not discuss here how debt and equity finance should be treated – another thorny area that could be largely resolved as part of a reform like this.

There is also misunderstanding about who business owners are. Broadly, debates tend to focus either on entrepreneurs or the low-income self-employed. This makes increasing tax rates on business income difficult because there is widespread support for lower taxes on entrepreneurs and because tax rises on the self-employed can be portrayed as penalising those on low incomes (as was the case in 2017 when the Chancellor Philip Hammond 'U-turned' on his proposal to increase NICs on the self-employed as a result of political pressure).[45] It is only by better understanding the heterogeneous nature of the business population that one can better appreciate how poorly targeted tax breaks are. Better empirical evidence – notably from HMRC tax records, which allow us to say much more about the business owner population than has been possible from surveys – and greater appreciation of the problems that can be caused by tax-motivated changes in legal form (for example, when employers reshape the jobs they offer to the detriment of workers) may be steps towards raising awareness.

The second reason is that the comprehensive solution proposed is seen as too radical (either to be worth it or to be feasible) and too theory driven. Freedman notes that, in response to a suggestion that it would be worthwhile to examine approaches to small business that are quite different from the current system, Accountingweb commented that '*it seems dangerous to allow academics to decide tax policy as they lack hands on experience*'.[46] The Mirrlees Review has been described as 'academic'; it was not intended as a compliment. However, the approaches to date – essentially tinkering with tax boundaries to try to prevent some forms of avoidance – have failed and will continue to fail because they do not address the underlying problem. The question, then, is how we can realistically transition to a more fundamental solution.

Current work at the IFS focuses on breaking the Mirrlees Review's radical reform proposals into smaller, more manageable steps. Even small steps can be hard politically, as evidenced by the 2017 U-turn on a minor change to NICs for the self-employed. Designing a pathway towards the end solution is also tricky because implementing only part of a full solution risks exacerbating some problems even while alleviating others. However, packages of reforms can be designed for which the benefits outweigh the costs even if the ultimate intended destination is never reached. If the logic of the approach is agreed, there is ample scope for academics and practitioners to work together to find practical ways to improve the tax system.

[45] H Miller, 'Tax in a Changing World of Work' (20 April 2017) *Tax Journal*, available at: taxjournal.com/articles/tax-changing-world-work-20042017.

[46] J Freedman, 'Small Business Tax: Where do we go from here?' (June 2008) *Tax Adviser* www.ifs.org.uk/mirrleesreview/press_docs/taxadviserfinal.pdf.

6

Dependent Contractors in Tax and Employment Law

HUGH COLLINS

I. The Binary Divide

When Judith Freedman and I were colleagues at LSE in the 1990s, we realised that we were working on a similar or at least an overlapping problem.[1] Both tax law and employment law rely for various purposes on a binary division between contracts of employment and independent contractors, or, in other words, between the employed and the self-employed. This method of applying a legal distinction between contracts of service and contracts for services is a creation of the common law that was developed by judges over several centuries. The distinction has applications in many branches of the law and has also been used to interpret regulations and statutes such as the Master and Servant Acts.[2]

In tax law, the classification of the contract affects the amount of the employee's income tax and an employer's obligation to collect it through the PAYE system. It also has a significant effect on liability for national insurance for both employer and employee, and on possible liability to pay VAT for the self-employed. In employment or labour law, many key protective rights in the Employment Rights Act 1996 (ERA 1996), such as the right to protection against unfair dismissal, are only accorded to persons working under a contract of employment. Therefore, tax liabilities and employment protection rights can depend crucially on the issue of employment status that is determined by the legal classification of this binary division of contracts for the personal provision of services. In both tax law and employment law, the binary divide represents a cliff edge: tax liabilities for the performance of work and the application of employment law turn on this common law distinction.

[1] J Freedman and E Chamberlain, 'Horizontal Equity and the Taxation of Employed and Self-Employed Workers' (1997) 18 *Fiscal Studies* 87; J Freedman, *Employed or Self-Employed? Tax Classification of Workers and the Changing Labour Market* (London, Institute for Fiscal Studies, 2001); H Collins, 'Independent Contractors and the Challenge of Vertical Disintegration to Employment Protection Laws' (1990) 10 *Oxford Journal of Legal Studies* 353.

[2] H Collins, KD Ewing and A McColgan, *Labour Law* (Cambridge, Cambridge University Press, 2012) 189.

Although this legal classification is a shared concern for tax and employment lawyers, the policy issues surrounding its application differ somewhat. The binary divide raises various tax policy considerations; however, perhaps the main issue is whether the differences in tax treatment that arise from the legal classification facilitate a fair distribution of the burden of taxation and avoid distortions created by manipulations of legal forms.[3] Turning employees into independent contractors by changing the terms of their contracts could produce significant savings in liability for taxation and national insurance contributions for both the employer and the employee, without either party incurring significant detriments such as loss of entitlements for workers to social security benefits. Similarly, turning employees into employees of personal service companies or other kinds of legal intermediaries could transform income into capital gains and dividends, with potential savings in the burden of taxation. Whilst there may be some good reasons to give tax breaks to small businesses and start-ups, in the 1990s there was clearly a trend for the parties to consider a change in the legal form of the work relationship purely to avoid taxation. Switches from the status of employment to an independent contractor without any change in the real substance of the obligations to perform work personally in exchange for wages frequently appeared to be a tax avoidance strategy. This reduction of taxation could be achieved by adjustments to the terms of the contract for work with a view to producing a conclusion under the common law's binary divide that the worker was an independent contractor. Such adjustments were initially made by the crude device of an express declaration in the contract that the worker was an independent contractor. Since such statements were often unconvincing in the context of the contract as a whole, the courts decided that such statements could not be determinative; for classification, the courts would have to look at the substance of the contract as a whole.[4] More elaborate modifications to contracts were therefore required to reduce liability for taxation and national insurance contributions.

This growing incidence of the replacement of integrated businesses with outsourcing arrangements provided by independent contractors also raised key policy concerns in employment law. Although Parliament had decided that employees require legislative protection on a growing number of issues such as dismissal and redundancy, by turning these employees into self-employed contractors, most of the statutory obligations of employers under employment rights law could be eliminated at a stroke of the pen. While the avoidance of employment law may not always have been the main purpose of employers' decisions to turn employees into freelancers, consultants, casual workers and other kinds of independent contractors, it was clearly not an unwelcome side-effect for employers. When combined with the possible savings in taxation and administration, the strategy of turning employees into dependent contractors sometimes became almost irresistible. Indeed, given the possible incentives from the differences in taxation, it became reasonable to ask why there were any employees at all.[5] The concern of employment lawyers was not only that perhaps the bulk of the nation's workforce would be excluded from most

[3] C Crawford and J Freedman, 'Small Business Taxation' in S Adam et al (eds), *Dimensions of Tax Design: The Mirrlees Review* (Oxford, Oxford University Press for Institute for Fiscal Studies, 2010).

[4] See, eg, *McMeechan v Secretary of State for Employment* [1997] ICR 549 (CA).

[5] H Collins, 'Why Are There Contracts of Employment?' (1993) 149 *Journal of Institutional and Theoretical Economics* 762.

employment protection rights, but also that, to achieve the objective of having employees reclassified as dependent contractors, the terms of the contracts would have to be altered to transfer major risks onto the shoulders of the workers. For instance, if employees were turned into casual workers, as required, and only paid when and if they performed work, this precarious form of work would not only significantly reduce job and income security for the worker, but also greatly increase the chance of exclusion from employment protection rights. This exclusion might happen either because the contract might be classified as a contract for services, or because the worker would lack sufficient continuity of employment to qualify for the main employment protection rights.[6]

What tax and employment law have in common, therefore, is a concern that by manipulation of legal forms through alterations in the terms of contracts for the personal performance of work, the parties will unfairly reduce their tax liability and thwart the policy of Parliament to accord workers certain mandatory statutory rights. The question then arises whether the common law's binary division is fit for the purpose of drawing the boundary in the right place from the perspective of public policy without being vulnerable to strategies of avoidance of tax and employment law responsibilities. If it is not fit for this purpose, the question becomes: what are the alternatives?

An anti-avoidance strategy in this context can take three forms. The first form adjusts the existing legal test of the common law for the binary division in order to make it less prone to manipulation through the terms of contracts for the performance of work. Minor adjustments can almost certainly be achieved by the judges through a reinterpretation of the precedents in the common law and policy sensitive determinations in particular cases on a close study of the facts. We have noted already, for instance, that the judges decided not to take express statements of employment status in the contract for work as determinative of the issue. A second anti-avoidance strategy is to invent a new supplementary legislative category for the classification of contracts. This category would identify particular types of workers who are classified as independent contractors under the binary division of the common law, but who would be treated the same as employees at least for specific purposes under tax law or employment law. This group are often called 'dependent contractors' because though they may appear to be self-employed as a result of their contractual arrangements, in practice, like employees, they are significantly dependent on one employer for work and remuneration. As we shall see below, this strategy has been adopted in employment law (but not tax law) by the invention of the statutory category of 'worker'. The third strategy is to attempt to replace the common law with a new statutory framework that would provide new statutory tests for the classification of workers into categories for the purposes of tax law and employment law. Under this third strategy, the statutory classifications could differ for tax law and employment law in accordance with policy considerations that might, for instance, want tax law to minimise those who would be excluded from the regular PAYE system, but prefer certain employment law rights to be confined to a narrow category of workers who are fully integrated into a business organisation. The Taylor Report *Good Work* made proposals for a statutory intervention along those lines.[7]

[6] *O'Kelly v Trusthouse Forte* [1984] QB 90 (CA); *Carmichael v National Power* [1999] ICR 1226 (HL).
[7] M Taylor et al, *Good Work: The Taylor Review of Modern Working Practices* (UK, Gov.UK, 2017).

The choice between these three anti-avoidance strategies is a vast topic because any particular approach is likely to have many ramifications. As regulators know from experience, blocking one anti-avoidance strategy may merely serve to encourage the development of other strategies that from a policy point of view may turn out to be even worse than the original problem that was addressed. In this chapter, what will be attempted is the more modest task of reflecting on the question of the legal form of the legal regulation that attempts to classify contracts for the performance of work for the application of both tax law and employment law. This issue is, therefore, about the design of the form of the regulation rather than its precise substance. We will therefore not conclude that one of the three anti-avoidance strategies is the best one to choose.

Nevertheless, the argument will tend to endorse the approach of the common law judges under the first anti-avoidance strategy. Although that endorsement does not rule out any kind of statutory intervention, it does indicate the pitfalls of departing from the common law's approach that has evolved over several centuries. To demonstrate some of those pitfalls, we will examine how the use of the statutory concept of 'worker' in employment law has fared. This example of the second anti-avoidance strategy can teach us some salutary lessons that apply both to employment law and tax law.

The first part of the argument distinguishes two forms that the law governing the process of classification might adopt. These are called binary and multivariate analysis.[8] Having described those two forms in the abstract, we shall observe how they work in the context of drawing the binary divide between employees and independent contractors. Both approaches have strengths and weaknesses. Binary analysis seems likely to be more predictable in its outcomes, whereas multivariate analysis seems more likely to succeed as an anti-avoidance strategy. This prediction can be tested, to some extent, by an examination of the interpretation of the statutory concept of 'worker', introduced into employment law. My argument will be that although in form the statutory concept of worker adopts a binary analysis, the courts have in practice had to interpret the statute to introduce a multivariate analysis in order to prevent the statutory reform from being thwarted by avoidance strategies. This example points to the superiority of multivariate analysis for the purpose of determining the application of the binary divide (or a similar classification scheme under a new statute) in a way that obstructs the manipulation of legal forms for the avoidance of tax liabilities and employment protection rights.

II. Binary and Multivariate Analysis

In order to explain the distinction between binary and multivariate analysis that I have in mind, let me offer a couple of examples before offering a functional definition.

Consider the characteristics of an elephant. Let us say that there are five distinguishing characteristics – a trunk, big ears, tusks, leathery skin and four legs. Now imagine

[8] 'Multivariate' is a term drawn from statistics involving a calculation using several distinct, though not usually independent, random variables. Lawyers often use the phrase 'multifactor analysis' in the same sense, but it is less precise and, as will be seen below, it does not distinguish clearly this approach from binary analysis.

a case of a person accused of killing an elephant. The accused person points out that this dead creature does not have tusks (probably because someone has cut them off); although the accused has killed an animal, the accused claims that it is not an elephant because it lacks tusks. If we approach the question whether the person can be accused of killing an elephant in a binary way of thinking, we would say that the five characteristics are all necessary features of being a thing that we call an elephant. In the absence of one of those items such as tusks, therefore, there is no dead elephant, but some other kind of dead animal. On a multivariate analysis, in contrast, the reasoning might say that each of the five characteristics should be considered and it should be carefully assessed whether and to what extent the thing has those characteristics. On this approach, the dead animal scores highly on four of the variables – trunk, ears, skin and legs – so there is at least an 80 per cent chance that it is an elephant. That degree of probability should be good enough to call the creature an elephant for the purposes of determining whether the accused has killed an elephant or a different kind of animal.

This contrast between a binary analysis and a multivariate analysis is typical in medical diagnosis. For lots of medical conditions, a doctor will examine the patient to discover whether or not the standard list of symptoms (or risk factors) is present or not. For the common cold, the doctor might examine whether there is a high temperature, and look for a runny nose, a cough, bleary eyes, and ask the patient whether he is suffering. The absence of one of these features, such as high temperature, will not in itself prevent a doctor from reaching a diagnosis of a common cold. The doctor is carrying out a multivariate analysis, so no symptom is a necessary or sufficient condition. If none of the symptoms, except claims by the patient of suffering greatly, are present, the doctor is unlikely to diagnose anything except malingering, not because other symptoms are necessary, but rather, given the paucity of symptoms, on balance, the correct diagnosis is likely to be (based on statistical probability) something other than a common cold – perhaps a hangover. In the middle, where the patient has some but not all the normal symptoms of a cold, a doctor has to make a judgement based on knowledge and experience whether there are sufficient indications of a common cold to justify the diagnosis, recognising at the same time that there is a margin of error and that a positive diagnosis may turn out to be wrong. The doctor might also include an assessment of whether the patient is attempting to avoid some unpleasant duty, such as an obligation to go to work. At the other extreme, when there are very severe cases of all the symptoms, the doctor is likely to conclude that the patient has indeed at least got a cold, but may be suffering from something worse such as pneumonia. This example illustrates the typical case of multivariate medical diagnosis. For some illnesses, however, there will be some kind of biological marker. In other words, a procedure like a blood test or a urine test will immediately confirm or disprove a diagnosis. In such a case, binary reasoning holds sway: subject to errors in performing the test, the diagnosis is concluded by satisfying this necessary and sufficient condition.

What are the key differences between binary and multivariate reasoning? Binary reasoning is always looking for something that is a necessary feature so that its absence rules out a possibility. In relatively simple questions, the factor may be one that is a sufficient condition, so that its presence will determine the outcome. Binary analysis may also include an item that, if found to be present, will rule out the possible classification. If the animal has wings, for instance, from a binary point of view, it is not an elephant.

Multivariate reasoning examines a number of characteristics, assesses the degree to which they are present, and draws a conclusion about the most probable classification. It does not function with necessary or sufficient conditions. Like a computer programme, binary classification uses rules with yes or no outcomes. Multivariate analysis looks for statistical probabilities: an animal with wings is extremely unlikely to be an elephant, but a statistical improbability does not necessarily completely rule out the possibility. It is possible to combine these kinds of analysis in the sense that there might be one necessary condition, but it is not a sufficient condition, so a multivariate analysis will determine whether additional factors justify a particular classification.

III. Classification of Contracts for the Performance of Work

The law could approach the task of determining whether a contract for the personal performance of work is a contract of employment or a contract for services by using either a binary method or a multi-factor perspective. The common law has experimented with both. Many tests using binary reasoning have been proposed and applied by the courts in the past. The most commonly used of those tests have been the 'control test' and the 'business in his own account test'. The 'control test' asks:

> [W]ho lays down what is to be done, the way in which it is to be done, the means by which it is to be done, and the time when it is done? Who provides (ie hires and fires) the team by which it is done, and who provides the material, plant and machinery and tools used?[9]

On a binary approach, if the employer decides these matters, or at least has the right to decide them, it is a contract of employment; and vice versa. The 'business risk' or 'economic reality'[10] test asks:

> [I]s the person who has engaged himself to perform these services performing them as a person in business on his own account? … [F]actors, which may be of importance, are such matters as whether the man performing the services provides his own equipment, whether he hires his own helpers, what degree of financial risk he takes, what degree of responsibility for investment and management he has, and whether and how far he has an opportunity for profiting from sound management in the performance of his task.[11]

If the worker assumes these risks, it is likely to be a contract for services; and vice versa. Lawyers often tried to turn these tests into the conditions of binary reasoning. In other words, it was said that if there is no control, there can be no contract of employment. Similarly, it could be said that if the worker took no business risks, the worker had to be an employee; in contrast, if the worker took a risk in remuneration or the availability of work, the worker would be classified as an independent contractor.

The multivariate approach to classification insists instead that there are a number of criteria or factors that need to be taken into account, without any one of them being

[9] *Lane v Shire Roofing Company (Oxford) Ltd* [1995] IRLR 493 (CA) 16 (Henry LJ).
[10] *United States v Silk*, 331 US 704 (1946) (US Supreme Court).
[11] *Market Investigations v Minister of Social Security* [1969] 2 QB 173 (HC) 185 (Cooke J).

determinative on its own. Indicative factors favouring the finding of a contract of employment under a multivariate or multi-factor approach might be:

- The employer exercises control over the content and manner of the work done.
- The employer agrees to pay wages and accepts the business risk of profit and loss.
- The worker is integrated into the organisation.
- The employer supplies capital, raw materials, tools and equipment.
- The worker is required usually to perform work personally, rather than use substitutes.
- The business accepts the allocation of other risks such as sickness and health and safety responsibility.

Using a multivariate approach, a court would examine all of these features of the work arrangement and conclude that there is a contract of employment if a majority of the factors are present or substantially present, even though perhaps one factor is absent altogether and others less clearly present. For instance, it would be possible to reach the conclusion that there is a contract of employment even though the worker brings her own tools and exercises control over how work is done provided that the employer exercises general control over the tasks to be performed and takes virtually all the risk of profit and loss.

What approach have the common law courts used in order to operate the binary divide between employees and independent contractors? Many judges have been tempted towards a binary analysis because of its simplicity and predictability. At first, the control test was regarded as determinative, probably because in tort law it had seemed to be especially pertinent to the issue of whether the employer should be vicariously liable for the negligence of a worker. Later, originating in cases connected to taxation and social security, the business risk or economic reality test was treated as determinative, though many factors had to be considered when assessing the allocation of risk between the parties.[12]

In recent times, a much-cited approach is that presented by MacKenna J in *Ready Mixed Concrete (South East) Ltd v Minister of Pensions and National Insurance* in which he identified three conditions for a finding of a contract of service:

(1) the worker agrees to provide his or her own work and skill in exchange for remuneration;
(2) the worker agrees to be subject to the employer's control; and
(3) 'other provisions of the contact are consistent with it being a contract of service'.[13]

Whilst it is clear that the first and second conditions are regarded as a binary analysis that must be satisfied for a finding of a contract of employment, the third condition is ambiguous between a binary and a multivariate analysis. It can be interpreted to mean either that a single term that is inconsistent with a finding of a contract of employment

[12] *Market Investigations v Minister of Social Security* (n 6); *O'Kelly v Trusthouse Forte* (n 6).
[13] *Ready Mixed Concrete (South East) Ltd v Minister of Pensions and National Insurance* [1968] 2 QB 497 (HC).

should exclude that relationship from the classification of a contract of employment, or it may merely mean that a court should consider all the terms of the contract to assess whether on balance they support the finding of a contract of employment. This test has supported the argument that the presence of a term that permits a worker to provide a substitute is inconsistent with the finding of a contract of employment because it appears to contradict the first condition that the worker must promise to perform the work personally.

Despite the tendency of this test presented as three necessary conditions to tempt courts towards a binary analysis with respect to each condition, courts usually stress today that no single factor should be determinative and that a court should examine all aspects of the relationship and the terms of the contract before classifying the contract.[14] In other words, the modern tendency, though far from uniform, is to approach the question of classification by using a multivariate methodology.

IV. Avoidance by Drafting

Whichever approach is used, either binary or multivariate, lawyers can draft the terms of contracts to avoid the conclusion that workers should be classified as employees. They can include terms that expressly deny or undermine any conclusion that the first and second conditions in *Ready Mixed Concrete* have been met. The first condition can be avoided by insisting either that there is no obligation on either side to offer work or take it, or that the employee can substitute another worker and is therefore not obliged to perform the work personally. Similarly, the second condition can be made less probable by again insisting that the worker is a casual, who can take work offered as he or she pleases, or by insisting that the worker should take all the risks of not achieving a particular task. Some contracts read as if a lawyer has sat down to place a bunch of terms in a contract that are designed to produce the conclusion that there is no contract of employment. As Elias J once observed, we should not forget the risk that 'Armies of lawyers will simply place substitution clauses, or clauses denying any obligation to accept or provide work in employment contracts as a matter of form, even where such terms do not begin to reflect the real relationship.[15] Some of these elaborate contracts have been so obviously mere avoidance devices that the courts have treated the terms as shams. In such cases, written terms in the small print of standard form contracts have been regarded as fictions that do not correspond to the intentions of the parties or their real agreement. Following *Autoclenz Ltd v Belcher*,[16] such false terms can be ignored for the purpose of employment status classification. For instance, the contract in the *Autoclenz* case had been carefully amended, in order to state expressly that the valeters in the hand car wash were responsible for their taxes, that the work was casual, as required, that suitably

[14] See, eg, J Riley, 'The Definition of the Contract of Employment and its Differentiation from Other Contracts and Other Work Relations' in M Freedland (Gen ed), *The Contract of Employment* (Oxford, Oxford University Press, 2016) 330.

[15] *Consistent Group v Kalwak* [2007] IRLR 560 (EAT) [57].

[16] *Autoclenz Ltd v Belcher* [2011] UKSC 41; [2011] ICR 1157 (SC).

qualified substitutes were permitted, and that the valeters would supply their cleaning equipment. In practice, however, there was no expectation that the valeters would not usually work full-time, there was no realistic prospect that they could use a substitute, and they would certainly not use their own equipment. Taking into account the point that the contract had been drafted by the employer's lawyers in a one-sided way, the Supreme Court was able to conclude that the written terms were a fiction and did not correspond to the actual agreement that was intended and carried out in practice.

Although the courts have combated some of the more obvious instances of avoidance of employment rights by recognising that some of these terms in contracts are shams, it remains possible and entirely lawful for lawyers to continue to try to present terms for jobs that tend to negative a finding of a contract of service. But such a task appears to be considerably harder if the courts adopt a multivariate approach towards the classification of employment status. On a multivariate approach, the fact that the contract includes terms that point in a direction away from a contract of employment is not determinative. The balance of indications from the terms of the contract may weigh in favour of a finding of a contract of employment. For instance, suppose the contract includes a term that permits the worker to find a suitable substitute in the event that the worker is sick, such a term does point towards the status of independent contractor because the worker is not always required to perform the work personally, but it would be outweighed if the other factors predominantly favoured the status of employee.

In contrast, if this list were used within a binary approach, it might well elevate the presence of one factor to exclude a finding of a contract of employment. If the contract permits, for example, the worker to find a substitute when the worker is sick or the delivery bicycle has a puncture, binary reasoning leads inexorably to a finding that the worker is an independent contractor owing to the ability to provide a substitute, even though all the other indications are that the worker is correctly classified as an employee. Under the multivariate approach, however, one factor or term in a contract cannot be determinative.

If it is true that the multivariate approach to classification makes it harder to use complex drafts of contracts to avoid employment rights, that conclusion suggests that binary reasoning should be avoided if the dominant policy concern is to have an effective anti-avoidance regulatory strategy. The binary analysis presents a much more tempting invitation to employers to attempt to contract out of their obligations under employment law. Although binary analysis appears to lead to the conclusion possibly suggested in the third condition of *Ready Mixed Concrete* that a single term that negatives a finding of employment will be effective to avoid employment law rights, multivariate analysis looks at all the terms to consider, on a balance of probabilities, what employment status was created by the contract. As in the earlier example of the elephant, binary analysis produces false classifications because it can too easily be manipulated.

It must be conceded, however, that binary analysis cannot be avoided altogether during this process of the classification of employment status. Before the question of the proper classification of the contract arises, there is a prior issue of whether indeed there is a contract between the parties at all. Concerning that preliminary issue, the general law of contract of the common law provides a binary answer: there is no contract unless there is an agreement supported by consideration. At common law, the existence of contracts is not regarded as a matter of degree or probability. There is either a contract between the parties or not. The first condition stated in *Ready Mixed Concrete* that 'the worker agreed to provide his or her own work and skill in exchange for remuneration' represents the common law's requirements of agreement and consideration. The requirement of consideration is sometimes described as 'mutuality' in the context of contracts of employment. Mutuality is, therefore, a necessary condition for a contract and, therefore, binary reasoning is appropriate. But the concept of mutuality (at least in this sense) throws no light whatsoever on the question of classification, because there must be mutuality or consideration for both contracts of employment and contracts for services.

V. The Statutory Concept of Worker

To try to prevent workers from falling outside statutory protections for employees, in some recent legislation, Parliament extended the statutory employment protections to some independent contractors.[17] This definition of the statutory concept, which was called, perhaps confusingly 'workers', includes employees, but extends to some who would be classified as independent contractors, provided that in some sense they are economically dependent or integrated into another business. The statutory definition is set out in the Employment Rights Act 1996, section 230(3):

> (3) In this Act 'worker' means an individual who has entered into or works under (or, where the employment has ceased, worked under) –
>
> (a) a contract of employment; or
>
> (b) any other contract, whether express or implied and (if it is express) whether oral or in writing, whereby the individual undertakes to do or perform personally any work or services for another party to the contract whose status is not by virtue of the contract that of a client or customer of any profession or business undertaking carried on by the individual.

The most important of the employment rights that are extended to 'workers' include the National Minimum Wage Act 1998,[18] the Working Time Regulations 1998,[19] unauthorised deductions from wages,[20] protections for whistle-blowers,[21] and rights in connection with trade unions, collective bargaining, and industrial action.[22] The extension of protection to the statutory concept of 'worker' does not apply to other important employment rights such as unfair dismissal and redundancy payments. Discrimination law has its own rules derived from EU law, which according to Lady Hale, though

[17] In fact, this practice started in the Employers and Workmen Act 1875.
[18] National Minimum Wage Act 1998, s 54.
[19] Working Time Regulations 1998, reg 2.
[20] ERA 1996, s 13.
[21] ERA 1996 s 47(B)(1).
[22] Trade Union and Labour Relations (Consolidation) Act 1992, s 296(1).

expressed differently, extend to the same or a very similar class of employees and independent contractors as described by the statutory concept of 'worker'.[23]

The question to be considered here is whether this third statutory category of 'worker' helps to solve problems arising from employers' attempts to avoid the application of employment law rights by manipulating the terms of contracts for the personal performance of work. The main purpose of extending some rights to the statutory concept of 'worker' or dependent contractors was to fulfil the general purpose of the protective law. For instance, if a minimum wage law aims to place a floor on wage levels below which no one should fall, an extension to independent contractors who in practice obtain all their work and remuneration from one employer is a necessary step to satisfy the aim of the legislation. But it was also hoped that the introduction of this middle category might defeat or discourage some of the more obvious strategies of avoidance that mostly consisted of tweaking a few terms of the contract and telling the workers that they were self-employed. Did the statutory concept of worker help to defeat employers' avoidance measures?

At present, it must be admitted that this question cannot be answered with confidence. One of the most high-profile litigated topics in employment law in recent years has been the interpretation of the concept of 'worker' in the Employment Rights Act 1996. The Supreme Court has been called upon to interpret the concept of a 'worker' in *Bates van Winkelhof v Clyde & Co LLP*,[24] (a case that decided that partners in an LLP could be workers), *Pimlico Plumbers Ltd v Smith*,[25] and in *Uber BV v Aslam*.[26] The meaning of the statutory concept of 'worker' was also the key issue in the decision of the Central Arbitration Committee (CAC) concerning the Deliveroo riders' attempt to obtain recognition for a trade union.[27] All this litigation is not necessarily a sign that the legislation is not working properly and that it is not preventing attempts to avoid employment law rights. On the contrary, the fact that employers such as Pimlico Plumbers were prepared to fight their case that their plumbers were not 'workers' within the statutory definition all the way to the Supreme Court, losing in every tribunal and court along the way, perhaps demonstrates that the legislation is fulfilling its purpose. Yet this litigation does demonstrate that preventing anti-avoidance measures by the technique of a supplementary statutory category is far from being a straightforward fix.

Why does the statutory concept of worker not solve the problem of avoidance? My argument is that this statutory reform and indeed, any statutory reform, runs the risk of falling into the trap of mandating binary reasoning about the binary divide. In my view, the reason why the litigation is complex and unpredictable in its outcomes is that the courts are having to reinsert a multivariate analysis into what on its face is a statutory requirement for a binary analysis in order to achieve the purpose of the statutory employment rights.

[23] *Bates van Winkelhof v Clyde & Co LLP* [2014] UKSC 32, [2014] ICR 730, [31]–[32].
[24] *Bates van Winkelhof v Clyde & Co LLP* [2014] UKSC 32, [2014] ICR 730.
[25] *Pimlico Plumbers Ltd v Smith* [2018] UKSC 29, [2018] ICR 1511.
[26] *Uber BV v Aslam* UKSC 2019/0029 (hearing 29 July 2020) on appeal from [2018] EWCA Civ 2048.
[27] *Independent Workers' Union of Great Britain (IWGB) v RooFoods Limited T/A Deliveroo* TUR1/985(2016) 14 November 2017.

VI. Multivariate Reasoning in the Statutory Concept of Worker

This development of a return to binary reasoning may have been almost inevitable. In order to extend the statutory protection beyond employees, Parliament had to state which group of independent contractors would be included in the concept of worker. Therefore, a definition was needed. The use of the concept of employee in statutes did not require a definition because there was significant case law which, as it had evolved over more than a century, on the whole, pointed to the use of a multivariate analysis as the preferred method of classification. Now, however, when a court is invited to decide whether an independent contractor is a worker within the statutory definition, the judgment has to go through the elements of the new statutory definition by applying the words of the text. By providing a definition, albeit a loose one, the text creates the conditions for a binary analysis, because each element of the definition has to be satisfied in order to bring the case within the concept of 'worker'.

First, the statutory concept of worker requires the 'personal performance of work'. It appears to follow that as soon as a person manages and pays others to perform the work rather than performing it personally, this managerial role is likely to take the person outside the statutory concept of a worker. Equally, an unfettered contractual right to use substitutes instead of performing the work personally appears to exclude a person from the statutory category of worker. In the Deliveroo riders' application for trade union recognition, for instance, they were excluded from the category of workers because they had an unrestricted right to use substitutes, which meant that they did not have to perform work personally.[28] Because the work does not require special skills except the ability to ride a bike or a motor scooter, Deliveroo permitted riders, if they wanted, to take a break and get a friend to do the delivery instead. According to the CAC, the consequence of this flexibility in the contract was to exclude these low-paid workers from invoking the statutory procedure to obtain recognition for a trade union on the ground that they could not be workers because under the contract they did not have to perform the work in person. If this judgment is correct, the consequence is that the Deliveroo riders are also excluded probably from the national minimum wage, other statutory rights, and almost certainly discrimination law as well.

In order to limit the damage of this kind of binary reasoning that says 'if there is a substitution clause, this cannot be a worker', in *Pimlico Plumbers Ltd v Smith*,[29] the Supreme Court smuggled back into the definition of the concept of worker some of the old multivariate analysis that had been used in the common law with respect to employees.[30] The Court held that where the 'dominant feature' of the contract is personal performance, even though substitutions are permitted, the test for the statutory concept of worker would be satisfied. In that case, because the right to substitute other workers

[28] ibid.

[29] *Pimlico Plumbers Ltd v Smith* (n 25). M Ford, 'Pimlico Plumbers: Cutting the Gordian Knot of Substitution Clauses?' (*UK Labour Law Blog*, 19 July 2018), available at: wordpress.com/view/uklabourlawblog.com.

[30] *Byrne Bros (Formwork) Ltd v Baird* [2002] ICR 667 (EAT).

was limited to other approved Pimlico Plumbers, the Court concluded the dominant feature of the contract was personal performance so that the plumber could be classified as a worker. Similarly, in *James* v *Redcats (Brands) Ltd*,[31] the contract provided that a courier had the right to find an alternative courier if she was 'unable to work'. Elias J held that, since the right to provide a substitute only arose when she was unable to work, perhaps through sickness, rather than leaving the matter to her discretion according to whether or not she wished to do the job personally, this arrangement meant that the claimant was obliged to do the work personally. The 'dominant feature' test tries to remove the sting from the binary structure of reasoning set up by the statute by permitting it to be satisfied by a contract that does not, strictly speaking, demand personal performance. The dominant purpose test permits other terms of the contract that indicate that the work will be done in person, such as requirements of obedience, reporting and disclosure, to raise the probability that it is a contract to perform work personally.

The second part of the statutory definition of worker that invites binary reasoning is the exclusion of contracts where the putative employer is merely a client or customer of the person performing the service. If the person performing work has a variety of clients and customers, or who at least has a realistic option of working for other clients and markets the business in that way, the contract is likely to be characterised as one of independent contracting rather than one that satisfies the statutory definition of a worker. In contrast, if the person has been recruited by the core business to work for it as an integral part of its operations, they are likely to be classified as a 'worker'.[32] Several terms of the contract are likely to be important in identifying cases where the independent contractor is performing the work for the other business. For instance, if the contract prohibits working for other clients, or requires full-time work, or requires the contractor to comply with a wide range of organisational rules and accounting practices, it is likely that the contractor will be classified as a worker.

Again, in my view, tendencies towards binary reasoning in the application of the words of the statute have been thwarted to some extent by importing reasoning from the common law for the classification of employees and independent contractors. Even though it is not mentioned in the statutory definition, the idea of control or subordination is used to avoid the description of the employer as a mere client or customer. In *Pimlico Plumbers*, for instance, the plumber had to wear the company's uniform, hire a van with logos from the business, work for about 40 hours each week, and comply with a restrictive covenant preventing work as a plumber in London on termination of the contract. These contractual requirements that were evidence of the sort of control that is typically found in contracts of employment were sufficient to indicate that the core business was not a customer or client of the plumber, but rather his employer. This device of retrieving the common law factor of control or subordination risks confusion, because the statutory concept of worker is supposed to include independent contractors who are not usually supposed to satisfy the common law test of control. The risk can be avoided by recognising that the court is not re-invoking a binary test of employment status based

[31] *James v Redcats (Brands) Ltd* [2007] ICR 1006 (EAT).
[32] *Cotswold Developments Construction Ltd v Williams* [2006] IRLR 181 (EAT); *Hospital Medical Group Ltd v Westwood* [2012] EWCA Civ 1005, [2013] ICR 415.

on the concept of control, but is rather trying to transform the statutory test for a worker into a multivariate analysis. The court draws on factors that indicate dependence and subordination to establish, on the balance of probabilities, that the provider of work is closer to being an employer than a client or customer.

These interpretations of the statutory concept of 'worker' have the merit that they make it harder to avoid statutory employment rights by inserting terms in the contract that negative the two main conditions of the statutory definition of a worker. The technique being used is one that draws on the common law's multivariate analysis of the binary divide for the new purpose of forging an interpretation of the statutory concept of worker that is resistant to avoidance. Many years ago, Mr Recorder Underhill QC (as he then was) was criticised for suggesting that the statutory concept of a worker was only a modified version of the multivariate analysis of the binary divide that was commonly used by courts. Regarding the distinction between workers and genuine independent contractors, he said:

> Drawing that distinction in any particular case will involve all or most of the same considerations as arise in drawing the distinction between a contract of service and a contracts for services – but with the boundary pushed further in the putative worker's favour … The basic effect of limb (b) is, so to speak, to lower the passmark, so that cases which failed to reach the mark necessary to qualify for protection as employees might nevertheless do so as workers.[33]

As an interpretation of the words of the statutory definition of 'worker', this statement seemed inventive and perhaps incorrect at the time. Yet in the light of subsequent decisions in the Supreme Court, it describes what has become the correct approach.

VII. Conclusion

The common law has always approached the task of classifying contracts with one hand tied behind its back. By granting almost complete freedom of contract, it enables the parties to choose terms that neatly avoid unwelcome regulation, be it tax liabilities, environmental responsibilities, or employment rights. The task for reform of the way the common law draws the divide between employees and the self-employed must confront two issues. The first is that the place where the common law places the binary divide does not appear to fit very well with contemporary contractual arrangements for the personal performance of work that have evolved in the modern division of labour, especially those in the 'gig economy'. Although many people work under contracts that appear to make them self-employed, their degree of dependence and subordination is sufficiently similar to the position of employees to justify a similar treatment in tax and employment law. The second task for reform is to discover the best form for regulation to take that will best obstruct attempts by employers (and sometimes employees as well) to avoid tax liabilities and employment rights.

My main point has been that the method of providing a statutory extension, as has been attempted in the statutory concept of 'worker', runs the inevitable risk that it

[33] *Byrne Bros (Formwork) Ltd v Baird* (n 30) [17].

will reintroduce the binary reasoning that once distorted the common law's drawing of the binary divide. If a statutory extension is to be developed, it has to be drafted in the form of multivariate analysis, so that it lists the factors that should be taken into account when making the classification, whilst making sure that none can be treated as determinative of the issue. That point was supported by the observation that to prevent avoidance and manipulation, the courts have inserted a multivariate analysis into the statutory concept of a 'worker' even though the statute appears to set up a binary analysis. A further implication of my main point is that it is not possible to reduce the task of classification of contracts to the form of some kind of simplified computerised questionnaire, as in CEST,[34] because the classification process should be conducted not through binary analysis but multivariate analysis.

[34] HMRC's Check Employment Status for Tax (CEST) (April 2017).

PART II

Tax Avoidance

7

Tackling Tax Avoidance: The Use and Growth of Statutory 'Avoidance' Language

MALCOLM GAMMIE

I. Introduction: What is Avoidance?

Across the world, there can surely be few topics that have attracted such an extensive tax academic literature as that of avoidance. In recent times, curbing tax avoidance has been proclaimed by every UK political party as the source of untold amounts of additional revenue, sufficient to fill the funding gap in their promises of additional spending on public services, benefits and infrastructure. No current Budget or subsequent Finance Bill would be complete without a raft of new measures designed to counter, curtail and penalise tax avoidance. 'Twas ever thus?

To answer that question, a chapter on tax avoidance should perhaps start with some description of the subject matter: 'What is tax avoidance?' The search for a definition may make sense within the context of a particular study of the subject matter: the asserted definition of tax avoidance framing the research and the scope of the writing. An answer to the question, however, might simply be, 'You know it when you see it'. Such an answer could be said to acknowledge that definitions of avoidance may tend to reflect its author's preconceptions or prejudices about the subject matter. On the other hand, setting such issues aside, such an answer might be regarded as acknowledging that avoidance can only be identified through its statutory context. One has to know precisely what it is that a person is said to be avoiding and why they are doing so.

Judicial consideration of this question casts little light on the issue. Lord Clyde famously said that:

> No man in this country is under the smallest obligation, moral or other, so to arrange his legal relations to his business or to his property as to enable the Inland Revenue to put the largest possible shovel into his stores.[1]

The quotation is perhaps better known than the subject matter of the case in the course of which Lord Clyde made his observation. The case does not appear to have concerned anything that might ordinarily be thought of as tax avoidance. It involved the

[1] *Ayrshire Pullman Motor Services and DM Ritchie v IRC* (1929) 14 TC 754, 763–64.

straightforward question whether or not a motorbus business operated by a father and his children was being carried on by them in partnership.

In what is perhaps among the best-known tax avoidance cases, Lord Tomlin remarked that:

> Every man is entitled if he can to order his affairs so that the tax attaching under the appropriate Acts is less than it otherwise would be. If he succeeds in ordering them so as to secure this result, then, however unappreciative the Commissioners of Inland Revenue or his fellow taxpayers may be of his ingenuity, he cannot be compelled to pay an increased tax.[2]

Even when establishing the *Ramsay* principle, Lord Wilberforce reaffirmed the principle that:

> A subject is entitled to arrange his affairs so as to reduce his liability to tax. The fact that the motive for a transaction may be to avoid tax does not invalidate it unless a particular enactment so provides. It must be considered according to its legal effect.[3]

As Lord Wilberforce went on to note, however, the legal nature of an arrangement for tax purposes may emerge, 'from a series or combination of transactions intended to operate as such'.[4] As to the legal effect of the transactions involved in the *Duke of Westminster's* case, Lord Templeman would subsequently put it more robustly, and briefly, on the basis that, 'gardeners do not work for Dukes on half-wages'.[5]

While suggesting the limits of action that may be effective to avoid tax, none of the above statements assist in answering the question of what avoidance is. Furthermore, the truth of any of those statements critically depends upon there being no specific anti-avoidance language involved; 'unless a particular enactment so provides', as Lord Wilberforce noted. That is the focus of this chapter: when and in what way has Parliament so provided by referring explicitly to the concept of 'avoidance'?

On that basis, no answer is required or attempted to the question, 'What is tax avoidance?' The only question is when, since income tax was reintroduced by Peel in 1842, has Parliament resorted to using the words 'avoid' or 'avoidance' in the annual Finance Act?[6]

II. The Characteristics of Avoidance

Nevertheless, where Parliament chooses to use such language, some conception of what amounts to 'avoidance' may be useful in reaching a conclusion on the

[2] *IRC v Duke of Westminster* [1936] AC 1, 19–20.
[3] *WT Ramsay Ltd v IRC* [1982] AC 300, 323.
[4] ibid 324.
[5] *Ensign Tankers (Leasing) Ltd v Stokes* [1992] 1 AC 655, 669.
[6] In fact, it was not until the early twentieth century that the use of an annual Finance Act (FA) became firmly established, see JHN Pearce, 'The Rise of the Finance Act: 1853–1922' in P Harris and D de Cogan (eds), *Studies in the History of Tax Law*, Vol 7 (Oxford, Hart Publishing, 2015).

arrangements under review. Lord Nolan sought to provide a basic definition of tax avoidance in *IRC v Willoughby* when he said:

> Tax avoidance within the meaning of s741 is a course of action designed to conflict with or defeat the evident intention of Parliament.[7]

In reaching his conclusion, Lord Nolan was adopting Revenue Counsel's submission that:

> The hallmark of tax avoidance is that the taxpayer reduces his liability to tax without incurring the economic consequences that Parliament intended to be suffered by any taxpayer qualifying for such reduction in his tax liability. The hallmark of tax mitigation, on the other hand, is that the taxpayer takes advantage of a fiscally attractive option afforded to him by the tax legislation, and genuinely suffers the economic consequences that parliament intended to be suffered by those taking advantage of the option.

Focusing on the intention of Parliament might not be thought especially groundbreaking. Indeed, one of the earliest explicit references to tax avoidance in the official Reports of Tax Cases reflects that need. In *Seaman v Lee*, Grantham J noted in relation to the exemption of houses for artizans' dwellings under section 26(2) of the Customs and Inland Revenue Act 1890 that:

> if we look at the language which the legislature has adopted, it seems to me that there can be no doubt as to what their intention was. There are four things which they provide for here to insure there being no trick, if I may use the term, upon the Legislature, because it is very possible that builders might for the purpose of avoiding the inhabited house duty so treat dwellings that in one sense they were separate and in another not. Therefore, the Legislature has four provisions here to take care that the Revenue is not defrauded, and that any alteration is not made for the purpose of defrauding the Revenue.[8]

Lord Templeman, for his part, suggested that a tax avoidance scheme could be recognised by 'the apparently magical result' that it purported to achieve, whereas:

> [t]here is nothing magical about tax mitigation whereby a taxpayer suffers a loss or incurs expenditure in fact as well as in appearance.[9]

The problem with that characterisation is that not every member of the judiciary is a Hogwarts alumnus, trained to recognise and counter Lord Voldemort's sinister schemes or to answer easily the riddles that Parliament may formulate in response. While 'magic' may be an appropriate epithet to describe the results claimed in some cases, many other tax avoidance arrangements are more prosaic.

If there is one certainty about the subject matter of avoidance, it is that, as night follows day, wherever there is tax, there will be tax avoidance or, perhaps more accurately, the accusation of tax avoidance, depending upon the accuser's particular perspective of what amounts to tax avoidance. When examined, 'avoidance' in much literature – especially in journalistic and political writing – may mean no more than

[7] *IRC v Willoughby* [1997] STC 995, 1004c.
[8] *Seaman v Lee* (1899) 4 TC 67, 75.
[9] *Ensign Tankers (Leasing) Ltd v Stokes* (n 5) 676. Lord Templeman was adopting the description used by Lord Fraser in *Ramsay* [1982] AC 300, 337 and in *IRC v Burmah Oil Co Ltd* (1981) 54 TC 200, 221.

that someone else is not (or is thought not to be) paying as much tax as their 'accuser' thinks they ought to be paying. In other words, that some transaction, arrangement or course of action should carry with it a greater liability to pay tax than has actually been suffered by one or more of the actors involved in that process.

This is not necessarily a modern trend. In *Singer v Williams*, Viscount Cave observed that:

> It appears to have been found by experience that the limitation of the tax on foreign income to income received in the United Kingdom led to transactions by which the liability to tax was avoided; for it was within the power of a person resident in the United Kingdom to cause his foreign income or some part of it to be paid to his account abroad and invested or expended there, so that the liability to Income Tax should not attach to it. It was no doubt for this reason that the Legislature enacted Section 5 of the Finance Act 1914.[10]

In the years leading up to 1914, commentators with a particular view of such matters may well have regarded as tax avoidance the retention of income offshore by those UK resident individuals who were in a position to do so, just as many today continue to regard the use of the remittance basis as avoidance by the far more limited category of individuals for whom that basis remains available. On the other hand, if the legislature chooses to allow individuals to place their income outside the scope of current taxation, what is it that characterises their action as tax avoidance?[11]

As Lord Hanworth MR noted in *Dewar v IRC:*

> Now I want to make two observations in reference to Income Tax and Sur-tax generally. As has often been pointed out, if the subject is within a charging section, he must pay; if he is not within the charging section he has not got to pay. No doubt there can be cases in which some specious documents have been executed for the purpose of appearing to have effected a disposal of money or property so as to, what is called, evade a tax which ought to be paid. But where there is no such device resorted to, it is not true to say that a man who does not pay is evading the tax. You have got to show that the tax is exigible in the facts of the case, and if it is not exigible it is not a case of evasion at all … 'evasion' is not an accurate word to use with regard to cases where the facts do not bring the charge down upon the subject.[12]

Those who are entitled and able to take advantage of the opportunity that Parliament makes available to organise their affairs to reduce the Exchequer's demands on their resources may (depending upon your point of view) be thought foolish not to do so or, by not doing so, as unnecessarily generous to the public purse.

[10] *Singer v Williams* [1921] 1 AC 41, 47–48.

[11] In contrast, perhaps, to the adoption of particular steps that are designed to remit foreign income or gains to the UK but without that triggering any charge to tax, see, eg, *Hall v Marians* (1935) 19 TC 582; *Timbrell v Lord Aldenham and Others* (1947) 28 TC 293.

[12] *Dewar v IRC* [1935] 2 KB 351, 19 TC 561. This was said by reference to *Bullivant v The Attorney General for Victoria* [1901] AC 196 which noted that 'evasion' is not limited to dishonest or fraudulent evasion (see further below). *Dewar* concerned whether unpaid interest should be included in total income and could be assessed to surtax. Perhaps Lord Hanworth was responding to the Inland Revenue's suggestion that the omission of the interest from the taxpayer's return bordered on evasion, but the Court concluded that the interest had first to be received and not just accrue. Lord Hanworth need not have had a sham transaction in mind in referring to the execution of 'specious documents', but merely a transaction entered into with the intention of avoiding tax, see further below.

III. Evasion or Avoidance: What is the Difference?

In the mid-1950s, Professor Wheatcroft suggested that the shortest definition of tax avoidance that he knew was: 'The art of dodging tax without actually breaking the law', and commented that, 'A more precise definition is not easy to frame'.[13] Nevertheless, Professor Wheatcroft went on to suggest that 'a tax avoidance transaction is one which would not be adopted if the tax-saving element had not been present'; he concluded that tax avoidance should be defined as a transaction that (a) avoids tax, (b) is entered into for the purpose of avoiding tax or adopts some artificial or unusual form for the same purpose, (c) is carried out lawfully, and (d) is not a transaction which the legislature has intended to encourage.[14]

Although open to criticism,[15] at the time that he was writing, there was some substance to Professor Wheatcroft's mid-1950s formulation of tax avoidance, and in two particular respects, it can be thought of as having been adopted by those responsible for formulating the UK's tax laws. First, nowadays, in 2020, a tax avoidance purpose will often be fatal to the tax avoidance design of the whole arrangement – no new legislative measure is adopted without there being attached to it some such limitation or something similar. Second, the existence of an artificial or unusual form of transaction in order to avoid tax – even if otherwise successful in doing so – may well attract the application of the general anti-abuse rule of the Finance Act 2013. In neither case is the transaction likely to be successful in avoiding tax nor, it might be suggested, can it, therefore, be carried out lawfully.

The concept of 'lawfulness' that Professor Wheatcroft had in mind was undoubtedly the distinction that for many years and certainly by the 1950s has been drawn between avoidance and evasion: as he put it, 'Avoidance is legal: evasion illegal'.[16] In 2020, the distinction generally continues to hold good in Professor Wheatcroft's terms: he illustrated evasion as involving an element of fraud or concealment. Failure to declare income or deliberately understating income remain particular categories of 'evasion' that are still ordinarily distinguished from 'avoidance'.

Lord Justice Robert Walker referred to this distinction in giving judgment on the original challenge to the IR35 legislation in *R v IRC ex parte Professional Contractors Group Ltd and Others* when he noted that, 'The Judge saw the objectives of IR35 as preventing not only tax evasion but also (and more importantly) widespread tax

[13] GSA Wheatcroft, 'The Attitude of the Legislature and the Courts to Tax Avoidance' (1955) 18 *Modern Law Review* 209. This was the text of a University of London Special Lecture in Laws delivered at the London School of Economics and Political Science on 21 February 1955. It has been referred to in a number of contexts, notably in J Avery Jones, 'Nothing Either Good or Bad, But Thinking It Makes It So – The Mental Element in Anti-Avoidance Legislation-I' [1983] *BTR* 9, and see also n 15 below.

[14] Wheatcroft (n 13) 209.

[15] See P Harris, 'The Profits Tax GAAR: An Aid in the "Hopeless" Defence Against the Dark Arts' in P Harris and D de Cogan (eds), *Studies in the History of Tax Law*, Vol 8 (Oxford, Hart Publishing, 2017).

[16] Wheatcroft (n 13) 209. As Lord Templeman put it in *IRC v Challenge Corporation Ltd* [1987] 2 WLR 24: 'Evasion occurs when the Commissioners is not informed of all the facts relevant to an assessment of tax. Innocent evasion may lead to a re-assessment. Fraudulent evasion may lead to a criminal prosecution as well as a re-assessment. In the present case the taxpayer fulfilled its duty to inform the Commissioner of all the relevant facts … the material distinction in the present case is between tax mitigation and tax avoidance'.

avoidance by persons who saw themselves as legitimately exploiting a gap in the law'.[17] In the many IR35 cases that have followed, it has not normally been true that individuals who have been found to fall foul of such legislation, having failed in their attempt to escape its ambit, are characterised as 'tax evaders'.[18]

The reverse, however, is not always true. 'Evade' and 'evasion' are not limited to dishonest, fraudulent or illegal conduct. In *Bullivant v The Attorney General for Victoria*,[19] the House of Lords had to consider the issue of legal professional privilege in the context of an order to produce a deceased person's instructions to his solicitor to prepare a conveyance where section 115 of the Administration and Probate Act of Victoria 1890 applied to conveyances etc, 'with intent to evade the payment of duty'. As Lord Lindley noted:

> [T]here are two ways of construing the word 'evade': one is, that a person may go to a solicitor and ask him how to keep out of an Act of Parliament – how to do something which does not bring him within the scope of it. That is evading in one sense, but there is nothing illegal in it. The other is, when he goes to his solicitor and says, 'Tell me how to escape from the consequences of the Act of Parliament, although I am brought within it.' That is an act of quite a different character.[20]

Lord Lindley's explanation of the two potential meanings of 'evade' offers an interesting perspective on a variety of tax avoidance arrangements. An individual who is entitled to and takes advantage of the remittance basis to ensure that their foreign income and gains remain outside the scope of UK taxation clearly falls within the first category: the income or gains never come within the scope of the Act unless and until remitted. In many cases, however, the advice that taxpayers seek is how to escape the consequences of the Act, in the sense that they already have taxable income or gains and what they are seeking is some way to avoid having to pay the tax that they would otherwise have to pay if they did nothing. They may have no intention of dishonestly concealing their income or gains, but the arrangements that are then devised and that they enter into might well be thought to amount to 'an act of quite a different character'.

Given the ambivalent nature of the word, it is unsurprising that reference to 'evasion' might easily be referring to 'avoidance', without any suggestion of illegality. It was only over time that the distinction between 'legal avoidance' and 'illegal evasion' became more firmly established.[21] Nevertheless, there are many examples of 'evade' and 'evasion' continuing to be used judicially to describe legal avoidance and, in particular, to describe the type of arrangements or transactions that Parliament had chosen to identify in legislation as specifically targeted against tax avoidance.

[17] *R v IRC ex parte Professional Contractors Group Ltd and Others* [2001] EWCA Civ 1945, [2002] STC 165, [84].

[18] Although HMRC may still argue for penalties on the grounds that there has been a loss of tax due to the taxpayer's carelessness, see, eg, *RALC Consulting Ltd v HMRC* [2019] UKFTT 702 (TC).

[19] [1901] AC 196.

[20] ibid 207. The House accordingly upheld the deceased's privilege on the basis that, without expressing any view on the meaning of s 115, no fraud had been alleged or proved and accordingly there were no grounds for holding that privilege had been lost.

[21] See J Frecknell-Hughes, 'Historical and Case Law Perspective on Tax Avoidance' in N Hashimzade and Y Epifantseva (eds) *The Routledge Companion to Tax Avoidance Research* (London, Routledge, 2017).

Lord Russell in *FPH Finance Trust Ltd (in liquidation) v IRC (No 1)*[22] observed that, 'the devices resorted to by people who wished to evade liability for Sur-tax were many and ingenious' and noted that section 21 of the Finance Act 1922 had sought to defeat one of those devices by apportioning a close company's retained profits to its participators.[23] Similarly, Atkinson J in *Lattilla v IRC (No 2)*[24] talks about 'defeating the evasion of payment of Super-tax' in the context of section 21. That section had been enacted explicitly, 'with a view to the avoidance of the payment of super-tax through the withholding from distribution of income of a company which would otherwise be distributed'.

Lord Reid, in particular, was prone to use 'evade' and 'evasion' to describe arrangements that did not involve any element of fraud, dishonesty or concealment but which had been targeted by specific anti-avoidance provisions. In *IRC v Bates*, in an early illustration of more recent avoidance involving loans that might never be repaid,[25] he described the particular avoidance arrangements against which the legislation was targeted, as follows:

> These provisions were first enacted in 1938. The mischief against which they were directed appears to have been that some taxpayers, intending to avoid paying surtax, transferred to trustees of settlements shares in companies controlled by them: then they borrowed money from the trustees, who used the dividends on these shares to make the loans. In that way the settlors got possession of the income from the shares which they had settled in the form of capital payments which did not attract surtax. And if the trustees were complacent the settlors might never repay these 'loans'. The reason why some companies were brought in appears to have been that some settlors had devised rather more elaborate schemes. A settlor might form a company, controlled by him, to which he transferred assets yielding income. He would then put the whole, or the greater part, of the shares of that company in the settlement, and then he would cause that company to lend to him the whole or a part of its income, thereby diminishing the dividends which would otherwise have gone to the settlement trustees. He would not repay these loans during his lifetime, and in that way he would receive and enjoy the income of the assets which he had transferred to the company without being liable to pay surtax in respect of it. Of course it was necessary to stop that kind of tax evasion, and of course it was necessary to try to anticipate and forestall more complicated variations of this plan.[26]

In the later case of *Greenberg v IRC*, also dealing with legislation targeted specifically against tax avoidance, Lord Reid observed that:

> We seem to have travelled a long way from the general and salutary rule that a subject is not to be taxed except by plain words. But I must recognise that plain words are seldom adequate to anticipate and forestall the multiplicity of ingenious schemes which are constantly being devised to evade taxation. Parliament is very properly determined to prevent this kind of tax

[22] *FPH Finance Trust Ltd (in liquidation) v IRC (No 1)* [1944] AC 285. See *also FPH Finance Trust Ltd (in liquidation) v IRC (No 2)* [1946] AC 38.

[23] As he went on to note s 21 itself had proved capable of 'evasion' by the expedient of putting the company into liquidation and this had to be addressed by s 14(3) FA 1937.

[24] *Lattilla v IRC (No 2)* (1949) 32 TC 159.

[25] See *RFC 2012 plc (in liquidation) (formerly The Rangers Football Club plc) v Advocate General for Scotland* [2017] UKSC 45, [2017] 1 WLR 2767.

[26] *IRC v Bates* [1968] AC 483, 503D–504D. See also Lord Reid in *IRC v De Vigier* [1964] 1 WLR 1073; *Jamieson v IRC* [1963] 3 WLR 156 and *IRC v Countess of Kenmare* [1957] 3 WLR 461.

> evasion and, if the courts find it impossible to give very wide meanings to general phrases, the only alternative may be for Parliament to do as some other countries have done, and introduce legislation of a more sweeping character which will put the ordinary well-intentioned person at much greater risk than is created by a wide interpretation of such provisions as those which we are now considering.[27]

More succinctly, he noted in *Saunders v IRC* that:

> If the words of a Statute are reasonably capable of two interpretations it is right to adopt that which will prevent evasion provided that this course does not lead to some other difficulty or injustice.[28]

More recently in the early development of the *Ramsay* case law, Lord Scarman in *Furniss v Dawson* said this:

> Speeches in your Lordships' House and judgments in the appellate courts of the United Kingdom are concerned more to chart a way forward between principles accepted and not to be rejected than to attempt anything so ambitious as to determine finally the limit beyond which the safe channel of acceptable tax avoidance shelves into the dangerous shallows of unacceptable tax evasion … What has been established with certainty by the House in *Ramsay's* case is that the determination of what does, and what does not, constitute unacceptable tax evasion is a subject suited to development by judicial process.[29]

IV. Early Legislative Use of Evasion and Avoidance Language: 1842–1921

But what of Parliament's use of explicit avoidance language? The term 'evasion' is found in the Income Tax Acts back to 1842. Section 55 of the Income Tax Act 1842 provided that any person who had refused or neglected to deliver any list, declaration or statement as required, or who had wilfully delayed doing so, might be subject to a penalty. Section 129 of the Act permitted a person who had delivered an incorrect statement to avoid a penalty by delivering an additional statement or schedule rectifying an omission or error before any penalty was charged. Furthermore, if proceedings had been commenced to recover a penalty, such proceedings could be stayed, 'on due proof that no fraud or evasion whatever was intended'.[30]

This reference in the 1842 Act to 'evasion' might well have been regarded as including 'avoidance' but can be contrasted with the absence of the word 'avoid' or 'avoidance'

[27] *Greenberg v IRC* [1972] AC 109, 137D–F.

[28] *Saunders v IRC* [1958] AC 285 297. Nevertheless, he went on to reject the idea that a 'strained' construction should be put on the legislative words or that they should be construed according to the spirit of the law to bring the case within the mischief at which the law was aimed.

[29] *Furniss v Dawson* [1984] AC 474, 513F–H. At first glance, Lord Scarman may be thought to be distinguishing lawful avoidance and unlawful evasion. The reference to what is 'acceptable' and what is 'unacceptable', however, indicates that the distinction he is really drawing is between avoidance that 'works' and avoidance that the *Ramsay* principle defeats. He went on to suggest that Lord Diplock's formulation of the *Ramsay* principle in *Burmah*, above n 9, provided the best way forward.

[30] See *Attorney-General v Till* [1910] AC 50 and in relation to the same provision in s 25(3) of the Income Tax Act 1952, see *IRC v Hinchy* [1960] AC 748.

in the tax avoidance sense. Indeed, the Income Tax Act 1918, being the first income tax consolidation, contains no use of the word 'avoid' or 'avoidance' in that sense. Similarly, although there are over 100 uses of the word 'purpose' in the 1918 Act, none of them is directed to the issue of the taxpayer's purpose in the way now associated with a 'tax avoidance purpose'.

It is not that income tax avoidance was an unrecognised phenomenon at the time. Indeed, the absence of any explicit reference to avoidance in the 1918 Act can be contrasted with the provisions of section 44(3) of the Finance (No 2) Act 1915, which provided as follows:

> A person shall not, for the purpose of avoiding payment of excess profits duty, enter into any fictitious or artificial transaction or carry out any fictitious or artificial operation, and, if he has entered into any such transaction or carried out any such operation before the commencement of this Act, shall inform the Commissioners of Inland Revenue of the nature of the transaction or operation. If any person acts in contravention of, or fails to comply with, this provision, he shall be liable on summary conviction to a fine not exceeding one hundred pounds.[31]

This language was adopted by section 55(4) of the Finance Act 1920, which similarly provided that:

> A person shall not, for the purpose of avoiding payment of corporation profits tax, enter into any fictitious or artificial transaction. If any company acts in contravention of this provision, the company, and in the case of a foreign company the agent, manager, factor, or other representative of the company, shall be liable on summary conviction to a fine not exceeding five hundred pounds.

For its part, the 1920 Royal Commission on the Income Tax was of the view that:

> it would strengthen the position of the authorities in their dealings with the taxpayer who seeks to avoid the tax by so arranging his business that the intention of the law is defeated, if power were given similar to that now existing under the provisions of the Excess Profits Duty Act, that is to say, the power of ignoring, for the purposes of assessment, any fictitious or artificial transaction entered into for the purpose of evading or avoiding Income Tax.[32]

V. Legislative Use of Avoidance Language: 1922–51

Parliament afforded no such power to the Inland Revenue for income tax purposes but section 21 of the Finance Act 1922 did explicitly acknowledge the avoidance of super-tax in these terms:

> With a view to preventing the avoidance of the payment of super-tax through the withholding from distribution of income of a company which would otherwise be distributed, it is hereby enacted as follows: …

[31] See P Ridd, 'Excess Profits Duty' in J Tiley (ed), *Studies in the History of Tax Law*, Vol 1 (Oxford, Hart Publishing, 2004).

[32] Royal Commission on the Income Tax, *Report of the Royal Commission on the Income Tax* (Cmd 615, 1920) para 635.

This initial statutory reference to avoidance was descriptive only of Parliament's purpose in legislating and was unrelated to whatever purpose the company or its participators had in withholding the company's income from distribution. As Lord Sands noted in *David Carlaw & Sons Ltd v IRC*:

> The object of Section 21 of the Finance Act of 1922 is to prevent the avoidance of payment of Super-tax … In the case of certain companies provision is made that if a reasonable proportion of the profits of the year is not distributed in dividends, then it is within the power of the Commissioners to direct that the whole income of the company shall be treated as income of the members for the purposes of Super-tax. Now, as it appears to me, the direction is plain and is not subject to the qualification that the Commissioners must be satisfied that the motive was the avoidance of Super-tax. I can quite understand the reason for the motive being so treated. Human motives are obscure, difficult of ascertainment, sometimes conjectural, and their ascertainment cannot appropriately be allowed to enter into the matter of the collection of the public revenue … It would be quite a reasonable provision that, where Commissioners are satisfied that a certain retention would have been justifiable and reasonable but that the sum retained is excessive, only the excess amount retained should be treated as if it had been distributed as profits to the shareholders. But it is not so provided. On the contrary, where there is an excess, then the whole income, even including that part which might reasonably have been retained, is treated as if it had been distributed. I think, however, there is probably an intelligible reason for the matter being so treated. As I indicated, the object is to prevent the avoidance of Super-tax, and I can quite conceive that the Legislature may have deemed that those who were disposed to devise means for the avoidance of this tax would think it worthwhile to try it, at all events if they were to suffer nothing more than that the margin was to be rendered subject to the tax, if they were found to have acted unreasonably as regards that margin. It may be that there will be cases where prudent and careful shareholders with an eye to the future of their business, such as Mr Robertson I have no doubt justly represents his clients to be, will suffer what no doubt will be hardship under this general rule. But I think that the policy of the Legislature was to allow no holes in the net, because if any holes were left there was no guarantee but that some of the fish that were really wanted would pass through these holes.[33]

By contrast, section 20 of 1922 Act introduced provisions that would eventually develop into part of the anti-avoidance code dealing with settlements, but without Parliament feeling the need to describe the purpose of that section as designed to prevent the avoidance of income or super-tax.

Five years later, section 33 of the Finance Act 1927 was enacted as, 'Provisions for preventing avoidance of super-tax by sales cum dividend etc'. Subsection (3) provided as follows:

> If it appears to the Special Commissioners by reference to all the circumstances in relation to the assets of any such individual … that the individual has thereby avoided or would avoid more than ten per cent of the amount of the super-tax for any year which would have been payable in his case if the income from those assets had been deemed to accrue from day to day and had been apportioned accordingly and the income so deemed to have been apportioned to him had been treated as part of his total income from all sources for the purposes of super-tax, then those assets shall be deemed to be asset to which subsection (4) of this section applies.

[33] *David Carlaw & Sons Ltd v IRC* [1926] SC 870, 880–81.

Subsection (4) provided that income from any assets to which the subsection applied should be treated as accruing day to day and to be received as it accrued. However, the proviso to subsection (4) incorporated this qualification:

> Provided that an individual shall not be liable to be assessed to super-tax under this section in respect of any such income if he proves to the satisfaction of the Special Commissioners that the avoidance of super-tax was exceptional and not systematic, and that there was not in his case in any of the three next preceding years any such avoidance of super-tax as is described in the provisions of the last preceding subsection.

Then, in the Finance Act 1936, section 18 provided as follows:

> For the purposes of preventing the avoiding by individuals ordinarily resident in the United Kingdom of liability to income tax by means of transfers of assets by virtue or in consequence whereof, either alone or in conjunction with associated operations, income becomes payable to persons resident or domiciled out of the United Kingdom, it is hereby enacted as follows: …

Again, 'avoidance' was used to describe the purpose of the legislation, but there was a proviso to the effect that:

> this subsection shall not apply if the individual shows in writing or otherwise to the satisfaction of the Special Commissioners that the transfer and any associated operations were effected mainly for some purpose other than the purpose of avoiding liability to taxation.

Two years later, section 28 of the Finance Act 1938 amended section 18 to introduce specific provisions dealing with the receipt of capital sums and substituting the following provision for the proviso to section 18(1):

> (1B) The last two foregoing subsections shall not apply if the individual shows in writing or otherwise to the satisfaction of the Special Commissioners either:
>
> (a) That the purpose of avoiding liability to taxation was not the purpose or one of the purposes for which the transfer or associated operations or any of them were effected; or
>
> (b) That the transfer and any associated operations were bona fide commercial transactions and were not designed for the purpose of avoiding liability to taxation.

In the intervening year, section 12 of the Finance Act 1937 had been headed as dealing with the 'prevention of avoidance of tax by certain transactions in securities' but without the need to resort to specific avoidance language to identify the type of transactions in question.[34]

Come the Second World War and the reintroduction of an excess profits tax, section 35 of the Finance Act 1941 provided that:

> Where the Commissioners are of the opinion that the main purpose for which any transaction or transactions was or were effected (whether before or after the passing of this Act) was the avoidance or reduction of liability to excess profits tax, they may, if they think fit, direct that such adjustments shall be made as respects liability to excess profits tax as they consider

[34] Essentially repo transactions.

> appropriate so as to counteract the avoidance or reduction of liability to excess profits tax which would otherwise be effected by the transaction or transactions.[35]

Section 35 was subsequently amended retrospectively by section 33 of the Finance Act 1944 so that it had effect, and was deemed always to have had effect, as if it referred to 'the main purpose or one of the main purposes' being the avoidance or reduction of liability to excess profits tax. Furthermore, section 33(3) provided as follows:

> If it appears in the case of any transaction or transactions, being a transaction which involves, or transactions one or more of which involve:
>
> (a) the transfer or acquisition of shares in a company; or
>
> (b) a change or changes in the person or persons carrying on a trade or business or part of a trade or business,
>
> that, having regard to the provisions of the law relating to excess profits tax, other than the said section thirty-five and this section, which were in force at the time when the transaction or transactions was or were effected, the main benefit which might have been expected to accrue from the transaction or transactions during the currency of excess profits tax was the avoidance or reduction of liability to the tax, the avoidance or reduction of liability to excess profits tax shall be deemed for the purposes of the said section thirty-five to have been the main purpose or one of the main purposes of the transaction or transactions.

Section 32 of the Finance Act 1951 replicated section 35 (as amended) for the purposes of profits tax. Section 32(3) contained a similar deeming provision to that of section 33(3) of the 1944 Act. Section 69 of the Finance Act 1952 extended section 32 to excess profits levy.

Finally, in this period of development, section 36 of the Finance Act 1951 was headed, 'Restriction of certain transactions leading to the avoidance of income tax or profits tax', and provided that:

> all transactions of the following classes (being classes of transaction which result or may result, directly or indirectly, in the avoidance of liability to income tax or the profits tax) shall be unlawful unless carried out with the consent of the Treasury.

There was no requirement, however, that the classes of transaction in question should, in fact, have been designed with avoidance of income or profits tax in mind.

VI. Legislative Use of Avoidance Language: 1952–70

By the time of the next consolidation in 1952, there were no more than half a dozen or so occurrences of the words 'avoid' and 'avoidance' in the Income Tax Act 1952. None of the Finance Acts in the following years to the time of Professor Wheatcroft's lecture in 1955 contained any provisions explicitly referring to avoidance. Indeed, the Finance Acts for the rest of the decade are devoid of any such provisions.

[35] See P Ridd, 'Excess Profits Tax Litigation' in J Tiley (ed) *Studies in the History of Tax Law*, Vol 2 (Oxford, Hart Publishing, 2007).

The 1960s, however, started in different vein with section 28 of the Finance Act 1960 tackling avoidance through certain transactions in securities and introducing the new concepts of 'tax advantages' and 'bona fide commercial reasons'.[36] Thus, section 28(1) provided:

> Where –
>
> (a) in any such circumstances as are mentioned in the next following subsection, and
> (b) in consequence of a transaction in securities or of the combined effect of two or more such transactions,
>
> a person is in a position to obtain, or has obtained, a tax advantage, then unless he shows that the transaction or transactions were carried out either for bona fide commercial reasons or in the ordinary course of making or managing investments, and that none of them had as their main object, or one of their main objects, to enable tax advantages to be obtained, this section shall apply to him in respect of that transaction or those transactions.

Notwithstanding that start to the decade, 1960s Finance Acts illustrate little further use of explicit avoidance language. Section 83(11) of the Finance Act 1965 dealt with the transition from income and profits tax to corporation tax and dividends paid in the year 1965–66. Dividends greater than the standard amount could be exempted under section 83 provided the company could show that 'it was not the company's main purpose or one of its main purposes' in paying the excess to avoid or reduce a liability under section 47(3) of the Act in respect of dividends paid in later years.

The Finance Act 1968 introduced a 'special charge' and section 50(1) provided:

> Where, as a result of any action or decision taken by any person on or after 19th Match 1968, an individual's aggregate investment income is, apart from this section, less by any amount than it would have been but for that action or decision, his aggregate investment income shall for the purposes of this Part of this Act be increased by that amount unless it is shown to the satisfaction of the Board that avoidance of, or reduction of liability to, the special charge was not the main object or one of the main objects of the action or decision.

Subsection (2) described a number of actions or decisions as a result of which an individual's investment income might be less and subsection (3) then provided that:

> If it appears that the main benefit which might have been expected to accrue from the action or decision was the avoidance or reduction of liability to the special charge, or to the special charge and surtax together, the avoidance or reduction of liability to special charge shall be deemed for the purposes of this section to have been the main object, or one of the main objects, of the action or decision.

The Finance Act 1969 contained two particular anti-avoidance provisions: the first in section 31 dealing with the sale by an individual of income derived from his personal activities. Section 31(1)(c) required that the main object or one of the main objects, of the transactions or arrangements must be the avoidance or reduction of liability to income tax. The second in section 32 dealt with artificial transactions in land and subsection (1) provided that 'This section is enacted to prevent the avoidance of tax

[36] The expression 'bone fide commercial transaction' had been used in s 18 FA 1936 by s 28(2) FA 1938.

by persons concerned with land or the development of land'. Again, however, this was merely descriptive of the purpose of the legislation and was not effective to limit its application to transactions designed with that purpose in mind.[37]

Thus, by the time of the next consolidation in 1970, matters had developed legislatively to the point where the Income and Corporation Taxes Act 1970 could include Part XVII entitled 'Tax Avoidance'. This incorporated the Finance Act 1960 provisions (as amended) dealing with transactions in securities, the repo provisions that had originated in the Finance Act 1937, the 1936 provisions dealing with transfers of assets abroad and a number of miscellaneous provisions, including those derived from the 1951 Finance Act and sections 31 and 32 of the Finance Act 1969. As Part XVII illustrates, however, it was not a prerequisite for legislation to be included in that Part that the provision should contain an explicit reference to avoidance. Furthermore, the 1927 provisions for sales cum dividend were located in section 30 of the Act and the successor to the apportionment provisions of section 21 of the Finance Act 1922 could be found in a separate part of the Act dealing with close companies.[38] Come the 1988 consolidation. Part XVII of the 1970 Act became Part XVII of the 1988 Act.

VII. Legislative Use of Avoidance Language in 2020

It may have taken more than 100 years to lay the foundations for legislative avoidance language, but construction on those foundations has continued at breakneck pace come the twenty-first century. Tax avoidance language has become commonplace in legislative terms. It is not the purpose of this chapter to provide a comprehensive guide to the variety of legislative formulations that can currently be found in the main Acts. Some examples will serve to demonstrate the main building blocks.[39]

Section 3A of the Taxation of Chargeable Gains Act 1992 defines 'connected to avoidance' as the disposal, acquisition or holding of an asset which forms part of 'a scheme or arrangements of which the main purpose, or one of the main purposes, was avoidance of liability to capital gains tax or corporation tax'.[40] On a few occasions,

[37] See *Yuill v Wilson* [1980] STC 460; *Chilcott v IRC* [1982] STC 1; *Page v Lowther* [1983] STC 61.

[38] As also the settlements code.

[39] The illustrations do not include statutory references to tax avoidance or tax advantage that appear in administrative provisions such as penalty provisions, disclosure of tax avoidance schemes, advance payment notices, follower notices, the promoters or enablers of tax avoidance provisions, etc. The following abbreviations are used in referring to the various Acts: Finance Act [year] (FA [year]); Income and Corporation Taxes Act 1988 (ICTA); Taxation of Chargeable Gains Act 1992 (TCGA); Capital Allowances Act 2001 (CAA); Income Tax (Earnings and Pensions) Act 2003 (ITEPA); Income Tax (Trading and Other Income) Act 2005 (ITTOIA); Income Tax Act 2007 (ITA); Corporation Tax Act 2009 (CTA 2009); Corporation Tax Act 2010 (CTA 2010); Taxation (International and Other Provisions) Act 2010 (TIOPA).

[40] For the same or similar formulations, see s 3G(5)(cb) TCGA; s 14H(1)(b) TCGA; s 30(4) TCGA; s 103KG(10), (13) TCGA; s 105K(1) TCGA; s 137(1) TCGA; s 139(5) TCGA; s 140B(1) TCGA; s 140E(8) TCGA; s 151A(2)(c) TCGA; s 169LA(7) TCGA; s 169S(3B) TCGA; s 169VV(3) TCGA; s 179(2AB) TCGA; para 1(2)(d) Sch 5B TCGA; s 38(5) FA 1999; paras 14, 21(4), (5), 23A(3)(b), 24(2), (4), 38, 40(5), (6), 71(1) and 83(3) Sch 15 FA 2000; s 165D(5) CAA; s 165E(3) CAA; s 215(3) CAA; s 236(4A)(d), (5A)(d) FA 2004; s 236A(3) FA 2004; para 2A(4) Sch 28 FA 2004; para 22(7A)(b), (7B(b) Sch 36 FA 2004; para 14 Sch 35 FA 2009; para 22(1)(b) Sch 61 FA 2009; para 14(1)(b) Sch 1 FA 2010; para 15L(5) Sch 19 FA 2011; para 47(1)(b)

reference is made to the 'object' rather than to the 'purpose' of the arrangements.[41] The 'tax' that may not be avoided will usually be specified in the relevant provision[42] and will vary according to the provision in question: it may be specific to the provision[43] or cast the net far wider. Where the provision just refers to 'tax' the context may have to provide an answer.[44]

A slightly different formulation is to refer to arrangements 'the main purpose, or one of the main purposes, of which is to obtain a tax advantage'.[45] Such provisions may not be expressed in terms of 'purpose' but may instead require that the tax advantage

Sch 19 FA 2011; s 86(3) FA 2015; s 40(5) FA 2016; para 3(7) Sch 12 F(no2)A 2017; para 15E(6) Sch 25 ICTA; s 100B(4) ITEPA; s 289E(4) ITEPA; s 346(2A) ITEPA; s 402D(11) ITEPA; s 420(8) ITEPA; s 424(2) ITEPA; s 428(10) ITEPA; s 429(1A) ITEPA; s 430A(1)(d) ITEPA; s 431B(a) ITEPA; s 437(2) ITEPA; s 443(1A) ITEPA; s 446A(2)a) ITEPA; s 446K(2)(a) ITEPA; s 446R(1A) ITEPA; s 446U(1)(c) ITEPA; s 446UA(1) ITEPA; s 447(4) ITEPA; s 449(1A) ITEPA; s 451(2) ITEPA; s 453(2) ITEPA; s 479(8)(a) ITEPA; s 489(4) ITEPA; s 519(1)(c), (3A)(g) ITEPA; s 524(1)(g) ITEPA; s 524(2E)(g) ITEPA; s 554AC(2) ITEPA; s 554Z(15) ITEPA; s 556A ITEPA; s 701(2)(c)(iii) ITEPA; para 4 Sch 5 ITEPA; para 11(5)(b), (7), (9) Sch 5 ITEPA; s 369B(5) ITTOIA; s 404A(5) ITTOIA; s 577A(4) ITTOIA; s 709(6) ITTOIA; s 770(4) ITTOIA; s 128(5A) ITA 2007; s 138(2), (4) ITA; s 165 ITA; s 176 (4)(b)(ii), (5)(b) ITA; s 178 ITA; s 182(2), (4) ITA; s 183(6) ITA; s 191(3), (4), (5) ITA; s 257BE ITA; s 257CE ITA; s 257DB(2), (4) ITA; s 257DC(6) ITA; s 257LE ITA; s 257MK(2), (4) ITA; s 257MM(5)(b)(ii), (6)(b) ITA; s 257MN(5) ITA; s 257MU(2)(b), (3), (4)(b) ITA: s 257MV(5)(b), (6), (7)(b) ITA; s 257QE(5)(b) ITA; s 261(3)(a)(ii) ITA; s 292(2) ITA; s 294(5) ITA; s 302(3)(b), (4), (5)(b) ITA; s 312(b) ITA; s 320(1)(c) ITA; s 321(1)(b) ITA; s 330(1)(b), (1A)(b) ITA; s 353 ITA; s 809EZDB(8)(b) ITA; s 809VA(7) ITA; s 809YA(11) ITA; s 18D(3) CTA 2009; s 426(1)(b) CTA 2009; s 437(1)(b) CTA 2009; s 677(1)(b) CTA 2009; s 686(1)(b) CTA 2009; s 789(1)(c) CTA 2009; s 831(1)(b) CTA 2009; s 1016(1A)(e) CTA 2009; para 4(2)(c), (3)(c) Sch 35 FA 2009; para 6(1) Sch 35 FA 2009; s 80(2), (4)(a) CTA 2010; s 235 CTA 2010; s 269BDN(1)(b) CTA 2010; s 357KEA(4) CTA 2010; s 357WBC(4) CTA 2010; s 1013(2) CTA 2010; s 1088(6) CTA 2010; s 1092(2)(b) CTA 2010; s 1096(3)(a) CTA 2010; s 117(3)(b) TIOPA; s 119(3)(b) TIOPA; s 371BI(3)(b), (6)(c) TIOPA; Reg 8A(3)(d), (4)(d) Individual Savings Account Regs 1998; Reg 12(a) Venture Capital Trust (Exchange of Shares & Securities) Regs 2002; Reg 4(2) Income Tax (PAYE) Regs 2003; Reg 9(3)(a) Venture Capital Trust (Winding up and Mergers) (Tax) Regs 2004; Reg 5(3) Pension Schemes (Reduction in Pension Rates) Regs 2006.

[41] See, eg, s 864(2) CTA 2009; s 773(2)(b) ITA; s 734(3) CTA 2010.

[42] For a provision that just refers to 'tax', see s 789(1)(c) CTA 2009; s 1016(1A)(e) CTA 2009.

[43] Examples include para 2A(4) Sch 28 FA 2004; s 18D(3) CTA 2009; s 864(2) CTA 2009; s 556A ITEPA; s 709(6) ITTOIA; s 165 ITA 2007; s 257BE ITA 2007; s 235 CTA 2010; in certain provisions, the tax is or may be a foreign tax, see s 357BP(8)(b) CTA 2010.

[44] Thus, s 1119 CTA 2010 defines 'tax', where neither income tax nor corporation tax is specified, means either of those taxes.

[45] See, eg, s 270IB (4) CAA. For the same or similar formulations, see s 16A(1)(b) TCGA; s 31(1)(b), (6)(b) TCGA; s 144ZD(7) TCGA; s 151C(3) TCGA; s 151D(3) TCGA; s 169SC TCGA; s 169VU TCGA; s 184A(1)(c) TCGA; s 184B(1)(c) TCGA; s 184G(5) TCGA; s 184H(4) TCGA; para 11(1) Sched 1A TCGA; para 2(7) Sched 4AA TCGA; para 14(1) Sch 232 FA 1995; para 15(b) Sch 22 FA 1995; s 70V(2) CAA; s 104(1)(d) CAA; s 104E(1)(d) CAA; s 165D CAA; s 165E(3) CAA; s 197(1)(d) CAA; s 212M(1) CAA; s 215(3); s 270IB(4) CAA; s 313A(1)(d) CAA; s 416ZE(5) CAA; s 488(5) CAA; s 567(4) CAA; s 570A(3) CAA; s 196F((1)(e) FA 2004; s 70(9)(ca) FA 2006; s 5A(1) CTA 2009; s 51(4) CTA 2009; s 214(3A) CTA 2009; s 311(7) CTA 2009; s 347(3) CTA 2009; s 442(5) CTA 2009; s 455A(5) CTA 2009; s 455C(3) CTA 2009; s 465(4) CTA 2009; s 475C(9) CTA 2009; s 486D(1) CTA 2009; s 492(1)(c) CTA 2009; s 521E(1) CTA 2009; s 550(2)(b) CTA 2009; s 599A(7) CTA 2009; s 629(3) CTA 2009; s 650(9) CTA 2009; s 691(5) CTA 2009; s 695A(4) CTA 2009; s 698A(5) CTA 2009; s 698C(3) CTA 2009; s 849B(9) CTA 2009; s 864(2) CTA 2009; s 879L(4)(a) CTA 2009; s 931V CTA 2009; s 1217LA(2) CTA 2009; s 1217RL(2) CTA 2009; s 1218ZCM(2) CTA 2009; s 1220(3) CTA 2009; s 1248(2) CTA 2009; s 1305A(1)(d) CTA 2009; s 124(3)(d) FA 2009; s 207(1) FA 2013; s 63(1) Revenue Scotland and Tax Powers Act 2014; s 81B(1) Tax Collection and Management (Wales) Act 2016; para 9(1)(d) Sch 2 FA 2015; s 103(1) FA 2016; s 19(4) F(no2)A 2017; s 291B(1) FA 2018; s 482(5), (6) ITTOIA; s 74B(3) ITA 2007; s 98A(2) ITA 2007; s 357YI(3) CTA 2010; s 464A(6) CTA 2010; s 937C(2) CTA 2010; s 130A(7) TIOPA; s 259M(5) TIOPA; s 461(4) TIOPA; para 2(2)(b) Sch 4 FA 2019; para 49(1) Sch 5 FA 2019; Reg 12(2) Taxation of Securitisation Companies Regs 2006; Reg 5(4), (6) Taxation of Insurance Securitisation Companies Regs 2007.

be the main benefit that could reasonably be expected to arise from the transaction.[46] The concept 'tax advantage' is also used in connection with a series of anti-avoidance provisions that are expressed in terms of an 'unallowable purpose'.[47]

The 'tax advantage' may be specific to the provision[48] or cast in more general terms. Section 1139 of the Corporation Tax Act 2010 defines 'tax advantage' as a relief or increased relief from tax, a repayment or increased repayment of tax, the avoidance or reduction of a charge to tax or an assessment to tax or the avoidance of a possible assessment to tax.[49] Similar definitions can be found elsewhere.[50] The advantage may accrue to a specified person or any party to the arrangement or any other person.[51]

'Arrangements' are commonly defined as including 'any agreement, understanding, scheme, transaction or series of transactions (whether or not legally enforceable)'.[52] The Revenue Scotland and Tax Powers Act 2014 has a more elaborate definition, as 'any transaction, scheme, action, operation, agreement, grant, understanding, promise, undertaking or event (whether legally enforceable or not)' and an arrangement 'may comprise one or more stages or parts'.[53] The Tax Collection and Management (Wales) Act 2016 is slightly different still. An 'arrangement' includes 'any transaction, scheme, action, operation, agreement, grant, understanding, promise, undertaking, event or series of any of those things (whether legally enforceable or not)'. In addition, references to an 'arrangement' are to be read as including a series of arrangements and any part or stage of an arrangement comprised of more than one part or stage.[54]

Finally, a variety of provisions couple the requirement that there be no tax avoidance purpose or tax advantage with the requirement that the arrangement or transactions in question should have a 'bona fide commercial purpose' or 'genuine commercial reasons'.[55]

[46] See, eg, s 151C(3) TCGA; s 151D(3) TCGA; para 14(1)(b), 15(b) Sch 22 FA 1995; s 567(4) CAA; s 431(2)(c) ITTOIA; s 449(1)(b) ITTOIA; s 452G(1)(b) ITTOIA.

[47] See s 151C(3) TCGA; s 151D(3) TCGA; s 212M(1) CAA; s 442 CTA 2009; s 521E(1) CTA 2009; s 691 CTA 2009; s 1220 CTA 2009; s 132(3) FA 2012; para 17(2) Sch 17 FA 2012; s 398E(3) CTA 2010; Reg 8(6) CT (Treatment of Unrelieved Surplus ACT) Regs 1999; Reg 52E(6) Authorised Investment Funds (Tax) Regs 2006; Reg 12(2) Taxation of Securitisation Companies Regs 2006; Reg 5(3) Taxation of Insurance Securitisation Companies Regs 2007; Reg 35(3) Mutual Societies (Transfer of Business) (Tax) Regs 2009; Reg 105(6) Offshore Funds (Tax) Regs 2009.

[48] See, eg, s 196F(1)(e) FA 2004.

[49] This includes a charge under the controlled foreign company provisions, the bank levy and the diverted profits tax.

[50] eg, s 608W(5) ITTOIA which provides that a 'tax advantage' includes relief or increased relief from tax, repayment or increased repayment of tax, avoidance or reduction of a charge to tax or an assessment to tax, avoidance of a possible assessment to tax, deferral of a payment of tax or advancement of a repayment of tax and avoidance of an obligation to deduct or account for tax. This definition is adopted in para 11(6) Sch 1A TCGA but a narrower definition may apply elsewhere in the TCGA. Thus, s 16(2) TCGA defines the 'tax advantage' as relief or increased relief from tax, repayment or increased repayment of tax, avoidance or reduction of a charge to tax or an assessment to tax, avoidance of a possible assessment to tax. s 577(4) CAA defines a tax advantage for the purposes of the CAA as obtaining an allowance or greater allowance or avoiding a charge or securing the reduction of a charge.

[51] See, eg, s 16A(3)(b) TCGA.

[52] See, eg, s 14H(3) TCGA.

[53] s 63(2) Revenue Scotland and Tax Powers Act 2014.

[54] s 81B(3)(a), (b) Tax Collection and Management (Wales) Act 2016.

[55] See, eg, s 103K(1) TCGA; s 103KG(13) TCGA; s 137(1) TCGA; s 139(5) TCGA; s 140B(1) TCGA; s 140D(1) TCGA; s 140E(8) TCGA; s 151A(2)(c) TCGA; s 169SC(5)(b) TCGA; s 169VU(1)(d) TCGA; s 169W(3) TCGA; s 181(1)(c) TCGA; para 1(2)(c) Sch 5B TCGA; para 14(1)(a), 15(a) Sch 22 FA 1995; s 426(1)(a)

VIII. Some Reflections on Avoidance Legislation in 2020

Faced with the blizzard of avoidance legislation, it becomes increasingly difficult to characterise as 'lawful avoidance' transactions which are knowingly entered into with the aim of avoiding tax in a legislative world in which an avoidance purpose may be fatal to the objective of avoiding tax. Thus, disclosing the entirety of an arrangement but misstating its purpose or overstating its commercial or non-tax purposes or benefits may be thought to be tantamount to concealing its true nature and therefore little different from concealing elements of the arrangement itself. The same may be true of artificial or unusual transactions, the nature of which characterises them as open to countermeasures; and especially in either case when coupled with the imposition of penalties for an inaccurate return.

In a world in which 'purpose' or 'main purpose' has been adopted as a principal indicium of avoidance, and where an arrangement is viewed with suspicion when it incorporates artificial or unusual steps that are difficult to explain apart from the tax results they are claimed to produce, it is unsurprising that measures aimed at curbing 'avoidance' and 'evasion' are now spoken about in the same breath.

'Avoidance' may certainly be associated with artifice, which may involve an element of deception; deception in the sense of something that does not immediately reveal its true self. In this sense, avoidance may involve a form of 'concealment' that can verge on illegal evasion. Being 'less than open' might be an appropriate description for such avoidance but, in general, it is still the case that 'avoidance' is not normally associated with anything that can be regarded as dishonest conduct. 'Evasion' is usually the more appropriate moniker for anything that can be so regarded. Nevertheless, the current tendency to elide 'avoidance' with 'evasion' takes one back to a time when the distinction between 'legal avoidance' and 'illegal evasion' was not firmly established.

Accordingly, in terms of Professor Wheatcroft's definition of tax avoidance, all that remains is the question whether the transaction is one that the legislature wishes to encourage. The difficulty here is that of discerning the legislature's purpose. On occasion, the legislative purpose can seem clear enough. If you cross the river Thames using the Dartford Crossing you pay a toll. If you choose the Blackwall Tunnel, you do not. A person who picks a route that uses the Blackwall Tunnel necessarily avoids the toll, and they may choose to do so even though the Dartford Crossing would be equally

CTA 2009; s 437(1)(a) CTA 2009; s 677(1)(a) CTA 2009; s 686(1)(a) CTA 2009; s 789(1)(b) CTA 2009; s 831 CTA 2009; s 1217LB CTA 2009; s 1217RM(1) CTA 2009; s 1218ZCN(1) CTA 2009; para 22 Sch 61 FA 2009; s 357UE Corporation Tax (Northern Ireland) Act 2015; s 19(6) F(No2)A 2017; s 709(6) ITTOIA; s 138(2), (4) ITA; s 165 ITA; s 176(4)(b)(i), (5)(b)(i) ITA; s 178 ITA; s 182(2), (4) ITA; s 183(6) ITA; s 191(3)(a), (4), (5)(a) ITA; s 247(1)(f)(i) ITA; s 257BE ITA; s 257CE ITA; s 257DB(2), (4) ITA; s 257DC(6) ITA; s 257HB(1)(f)(i) ITA; s 257MK(2), (4) ITA; s 257MM(5)(b)(i), (6)(b)(i) ITA; s 257MN(5) ITA; s 257MU(2)(a), (3), (4)(a) ITA; s 257MV(5)(a), (6), (7)(a) ITA; s 257QE(5)(b) ITA; s 261(3)(a)(i) ITA; s 292(2) ITA; s 294(5) ITA; s 302(3)(a), (4), (5)(a) ITA; s 312(b) ITA; s 320(1)(c) ITA; s 321(1)(b) ITA; s 326(3)(a) ITA; s 330(1)(b), (1A)(b) ITA; s 412I(2)(a) ITA; s 737(4)(a) ITA; s 739(4)(a) ITA; s 80(2), (4)(a) CTA 2010; s 357UE CTA 2010; s 734(2)(a) CTA 2010; s 1088(4)(a) CTA 2010; s 1089(4)(a) CTA 2010; s 117(3)(a) TIOPA; s 119(3)(a) TIOPA; Reg 8A(3)(c) Individual Savings Accounts Regs 1998; Reg 12(a) Venture Capital Trusts (Exchange of Shares and Securities) Regs 2002; Reg 9(3)(a) Venture Capital Trusts (Winding up and Mergers) (Tax) Regs 2004; Regs 3(1)(c), 5(3) Qualifying Private Placement Regs 2015.

convenient (but less cost effective solely as a result of the toll). Indeed, their choice of route may be one that is arrived at with that very aim in mind, and without regard to the possible traffic conditions involved.

In that respect, Professor Wheatcroft's suggestion that 'a tax avoidance transaction is one which would not be adopted if the tax-saving element had not been present'[56] must surely be understood by reference to his definition of 'tax avoidance'. The Blackwall Tunnel route is one that would not – or, at least, may not – have been chosen (having regard, for example to traffic conditions) but for the toll. But the origins and aim of the Dartford Crossing toll may be assumed to have been to defray the cost of construction.[57] Motorists pay for their use of the facility of the Dartford Crossing rather than a levy on their action of crossing the river Thames. You do not have to pay the toll – and are therefore not avoiding the toll in the relevant sense – if you are not using the facility.[58]

The legislature, however, rarely acts with a single purpose in mind. It may choose to levy a tax on cigarettes at a particularly high rate because it believes that smoking is a risk to health and an anti-social activity. At the same time, however, it aims to raise a certain amount of tax from those prepared to accept the risk and indulge in the activity. It might ban smoking altogether – as it does with Class A drugs – but instead, it taxes the activity. A person may avoid paying the duty by choosing not to smoke, but that may have nothing to do with either the social policy or tax avoidance. The social policy may achieve its purpose in the case of a smoker who smokes less or gives up smoking because of the cost involved and consequently avoids paying as much duty. The Border Force's activities in enforcing the law, however, are not just a matter of delivering a particular social policy but are principally aimed at collecting tax from those who engage in the activity (or supply those who do) but would otherwise seek to avoid or evade payment.

Tobacco and similar duties in their social function are designed to disincentivise particular behaviour. To the extent that they succeed in that objective, they are not especially problematic: no duty will be levied or paid. The problematic aspects derive from those who are not disincentivised and who persist in the socially discouraged activity but seek to avoid or evade payment of the resulting duty.

What is particularly problematic, however, in terms of ascertaining the legislature's purpose are measures that are designed to encourage or incentivise positive behaviour; not to desist or refrain from particular action but rather to indulge in certain action. Here, the legislature's purpose may be particularly opaque: legislatively, it offers on various conditions to reduce the tax that a person would otherwise have to pay, but not if the person concerned enters into the arrangement or transacts solely or mainly for the purpose of reducing the tax they would otherwise have to pay.

The contradiction is readily apparent: in essence, the legislature says, 'if you do this, we will reduce your tax bill; but if you are doing this to reduce your tax bill, you will

[56] Wheatcroft (n 13) 209.

[57] A toll has been charged for the Dartford Crossing since the first tunnel opened on 18 November 1963 and was not introduced just to defray the cost of constructing the Queen Elizabeth bridge.

[58] This reasoning begs the question whether the choice of an alternative route to avoid the toll becomes tax avoidance once the toll has become a general revenue-raising measure rather than one aimed at defraying the costs of construction, operation or maintenance of the Dartford Crossing. Or are the 'toll profits' that accrue to the Exchequer just a reflection of the facility's value to its users?

not qualify for any reduction'. But if taxpayers would choose to do something anyway for reasons apart from the tax incentive, why offer them a tax incentive to do it? And if they would only do it because they are offered a tax incentive to do it, and therefore are doing it to get the tax reduction, in what way is their purpose, or one of their purposes, not a tax purpose?[59]

A similar contradiction may arise in the case of artificial or unusual transactions. At one level, any transaction that taxpayers would not otherwise enter into except to achieve a particular tax result might be said to be artificial or unusual in the circumstances. On another level, such a transaction may be the necessary gateway to the tax advantage that the legislature has crafted.

Writing on avoidance in 1979, Professor John Kay noted that the legislative response to the particular avoidance arising from the distinction between income and capital had not been to get to the heart of the problem but to attack the mechanisms of particular avoidance schemes.[60] As he noted:

> The final exasperated outcome is the buttress of a rather vague and general provision which leaves doubt in the mind of honest and dishonest taxpayer alike; and which may well create difficulties for those who have no thought of tax avoidance.

As he also observed that

> legislators unable to deal with avoidance in more appropriate ways, seek to inhibit it by passing laws which require taxpayers to observe the spirit as well as the letter of the code by means of very general anti-avoidance provisions. This means attempting to distinguish tax avoidance mechanisms from similar or identical actions which are bona fide transactions. This second type of provision is more common abroad than in the United Kingdom.

No more, it seems.

[59] And the task of discerning the legislative purpose is not assisted when the Revenue is prepared to deny the taxpayer's entitlement to rely on the consultative material that preceded the introduction of the incentive in question, as they did in *London Luton Hotel BPRA Property Fund LLP v HMRC* [2019] UKFTT 212 (TC).

[60] J Kay, 'The Economics of Tax Avoidance' [1979] *BTR* 354.

8

EU General Anti-(Tax) Avoidance Mechanisms

RITA DE LA FERIA*

I. Introduction

The EU principle of prohibition of abuse of law has been developing within the jurisprudence of the Court of Justice of the European Union (CJEU), through a process of reverberation, since the mid-1970s, and should now be recognised as a principle of EU law. Whilst the intensity of application of the EU principle of prohibition of abuse of law may vary depending upon the area of law at stake, its general applicability has been well defined since the CJEU decision in *Halifax*, namely: it applies to all areas of law, and to all types of legal instruments, whatever the legal source, and even in the absence of national legislation; and its scope is defined through the fulfilment of two cumulative conditions, namely purpose and artificiality. It is argued therefore that, as it stands, this principle cannot be regarded as a mere interpretative principle, but rather displays all the key characteristics of a general principle of EU law.[1]

This chapter explores the consequences of such a characterisation insofar as taxation is concerned. First, it is argued that the recent decision in *Cussens and Others*,[2] where the principle was held to apply in a purely domestic situation, and in the absence of domestic provisions, confirms that, within taxation, the principle is now operating as a general anti-avoidance principle (GAAP); second, it is contested that this is not a merely interpretative GAAP, but rather a general principle one; third, it is asserted that the recent approval of an EU general anti-abuse rule (GAAR) should be seen as a codification of the principle,[3] and that this raises the question of whether the coexistence

* I am grateful for the many comments received at the conference, and particularly those of the discussant, Eduardo Baistrocchi. This chapter was finalised during a research visit to McGill University, Faculty of Law; I would like to thank the Faculty for hosting me, and particularly Allison Christians for the many discussions held during my visit. Any remaining errors are my own.

[1] As first proposed in R de la Feria, 'Prohibition of Abuse of (Community) Law – The Creation of a New General Principle of EC Law Through Tax' (2008) 45 *Common Market Law Review* 395.

[2] Case C-251/16, *Cussens and Others*, ECLI:EU:C:2017:881.

[3] Council Directive (EU) 2016/1164 of 12 July 2016 laying down rules against tax avoidance practices that directly affect the functioning of the internal market [2016] OJ L193/1, 1–14.

of the two – GAAP and GAAR – is problematic or redundant; fourth, it is argued that this is a natural development, which can be seen in various other jurisdictions where the approval of a GAAR followed from the existence of a GAAP, either with the nature of an interpretative principle such as in the UK,[4] or of a general principle, such as substance over form;[5] finally, it is claimed that there are no obvious obstacles to their coexistence, if a hierarchy of norms is followed, whereby the level of generality increases with each step. Following this approach an interpretative GAAP would be applied in the first instance, with a GAAR acting as a residual provision; or the GAAR would apply in the first instance, as a manifestation of a wider general GAAP, which will then act as the default anti-avoidance mechanism. Indeed, conceptually, there should be no obvious impediment to the coexistence of these three levels of general anti-avoidance mechanisms: an interpretative GAAP, a GAAR and a general GAAP, applied in that order, as visually represented in Figure 1 (below). On the contrary, such a structure can present significant advantages in terms of anti-avoidance protection and, as opposed to what may be the intuition, legal certainty.

This chapter is structured as follows. In section II the process of co-constitutive reverberation that characterises the jurisprudential development of the EU principle of prohibition of abuse of law is analysed; section III provides an in-depth examination of the nature and scope of that principle, and presents the arguments as to why it

Figure 1 EU General Anti-(Tax) Avoidance Mechanisms by Level of Generality

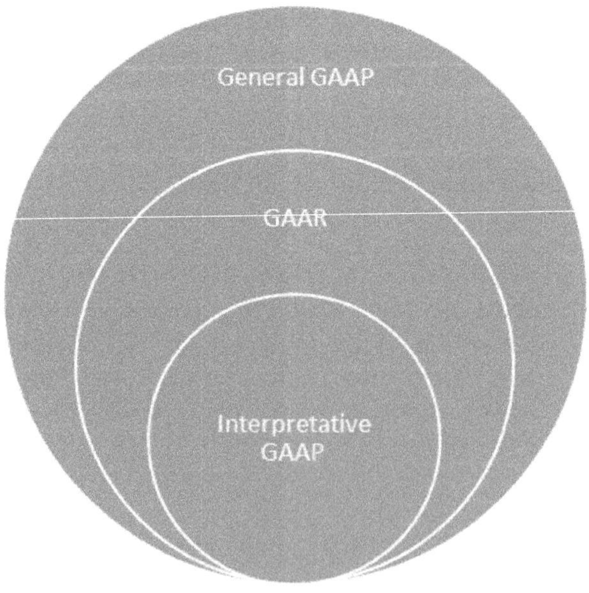

[4] The so-called *Ramsay* principle, as discussed in section IV below.

[5] F Zimmer, 'Form and Substance in Tax Law – General Report' (2012) *IFA Cahiers de Droit Fiscal International* 87A.

should now be regarded as a GAAP, which exhibits the characteristics of a general legal principle; in section IV attention turns to the rationale for the approval of the new EU GAAR, and its key characteristics, arguing in favour of its characterisation as a natural process of codification, and presenting the parallels between that process, and the one that has been witnessed in other jurisdictions, such as the UK. Section IV concludes with considerations over the advantages of the coexistence of these different general anti-avoidance mechanisms, and their hierarchical application.

II. Developing the EU GAAP

The CJEU had been alluding to abuse and abusive practices in its rulings for more than 40 years.[6] For a long time, however, the significance of these references was unclear. Several factors might have contributed to this lack of clarity, including the Court's failure to adopt a coherent terminology – using words such as 'avoidance',[7] 'evasion',[8] 'circumvention',[9] 'fraud'[10] and 'abuse',[11] in an apparently interchangeable fashion – as well as the absence of clear guidelines as to the scope, and the applicability, of the concept.[12] This state of affairs changed radically, however, in the early 2000s with two developments: first, the introduction by the Court of an abuse test in *Emsland-Stärke* in 2000;[13] and second, the subsequent emergence of an intense debate as to whether the Court would apply this new test to the field of taxation,[14] followed by the landmark decision in *Halifax*.[15] Together these two cases confirmed not only the criteria for determining the existence of abuse, but, more importantly, confirmed prohibition of abuse of law as an emerging general principle of EU law.

General principles of EU law do not appear in fully-fledged form. They are unwritten principles, detected and recognised by the CJEU and extrapolated through a creative exercise, which often involves a deductive approach whereby the principle is derived from the objectives of the law and its underlying values.[16] As such, creation and

[6] Case 33/74, *Van Binsbergen*, ECLI:EU:C:1974:131.
[7] Case C-23/93, *TV10*, ECLI:EU:C:1994:362, para 21.
[8] Case 115/78, *Knoors*, ECLI:EU:C:1979:31, para 50.
[9] Case 229/83, *Leclerc*, ECLI:EU:C:1985:1, para 27.
[10] Case C-367/96, *Kefalas and Others*, ECLI:EU:C:1998:222, para 20.
[11] Case C-441/93, *Pafitis and others*, ECLI:EU:C:1996:92, para 68.
[12] de la Feria, 'Prohibition of Abuse of (Community) Law' (n 1) 395–98.
[13] Case C-110/99, *Emsland-Stärke*, ECLI:EU:C:2000:695.
[14] P Harris, '*Abus de droit* in the field of Value Added Taxation' [2003] *BTR* 131; and P Farmer, 'VAT Planning: Assessing the "Abuse of Rights" Risk' *Tax Journal* (27 May 2002) 15.
[15] Case C-255/02, *Halifax*, ECLI:EU:C:2006:121.
[16] See T Tridimas, *The General Principles of EU Law* 2nd edn (Oxford, Oxford University Press, 2006) 4–6; B de Witte, 'Institutional Principles: A Special Category of General Principles of EC Law' in U Bernitz and J Nergelius (eds), *General Principles of European Community Law* (The Hague, Kluwer Law International, 2000); M Herdegen, 'General Principles of EU Law – the Methodological Challenge' in U Bernitz, J Nergelius and C Cardner (eds), *General Principles of EC Law in a Process of Development* (Alphen aan den Rijn, Kluwer Law International, 2008); and X Groussot and HH Lidgard, 'Are There General Principles of Community Law Affecting Private Law?' in U Bernitz, J Nergelius and C Cardner (eds), *General Principles of EC Law in a Process of Development* (Alphen aan den Rijn, Kluwer Law International, 2008).

development of these principles is better characterised as a co-constitutive process,[17] the result of a dialectical interaction between national laws and EU law, were both the outcome and the source of a long process of cross-fertilisation, back and forth, between the national legal orders and the EU legal order.[18] The origins of this process, which can be witnessed in the development of all general principles, can be traced back to the early days of the Court in cases decided under the Coal and Steel Community. Both the general principle of proportionality and general principle of equal treatment were first mentioned in the case law of the 1950s,[19] and the general principle of the right to defence is found in staff cases dating back to the early 1960s.[20] As the European integration process evolved, the application of general principles expanded with a proliferation of cases in the 1970s, where the basic features of principles such as proportionality and equal treatment were laid down.[21] Today these general principles are amongst the most prominent general principles of EU law, regularly applied by the CJEU in its case law across all areas of EU law.

This judicial evolution can be better understood in the context of a theoretical framework, which distils the various elements of the co-creation and the co-development of general principles of EU law. Words usually applied in the context of the extensive literature on diffusion of law, such as 're-transplantation' and 'reception', have been employed in association with the whole or part of this dynamic process.[22] Nevertheless, it is argued that a better designation would be of a co-constitutive process of reverberation,[23] which can be distilled into three stages.

The process starts at the pre-cognisance level with similar principles or legal concepts applied within different Member States' jurisdictions – not necessarily all – being cast into the centre of questions referred to the CJEU. Often these principles or concepts are similar only to the extent that at their core they express an identical legal essence, even though its particular characteristics, such as scope and criteria for application and name or designation, differ from Member State to Member State. This vagueness that results from the discrepancies between Member States also gives the Court a higher level of flexibility to use the concept in whatever context it feels more appropriate, providing it with a specific scope and criteria for application, definition, etc. The concept or principle

[17] On co-constitutive theory generally, see J Nice, 'The Emerging Third Strand in Equal Protection Jurisprudence: Recognizing the Co-Constitutive Nature of Rights and Classes' (1999) 4 *University of Illinois Law Review* 1209.

[18] W van Gerven, 'Two Twin-Principles of EU Law: Democracy and Accountability, Consistency and Convergence' in U Bernitz, J Nergelius and C Cardner (eds), *General Principles of EC Law in a Process of Development* (Alphen aan den Rijn, Kluwer Law International, 2008) 28–29.

[19] On proportionality see Case 8/55, *Fédération Charbonnière de Belgique*, ECLI:EU:C:1956:7; on equal treatment, see Case 14/59, *Société des fonderies de Pont-à-Mousson v High Authority of the European Coal and Steel Community*, ECLI:EU:C:1959:31.

[20] See Case 32/62, *Maurice Alvis v Council of the European Economic Community*, ECLI:EU:C:1963:15.

[21] Tridimas, *The General Principles of EU Law* (n 16) 7–8.

[22] See respectively G de Búrca, 'Proportionality and Subsidiarity as General Principles of Law' in U Bernitz and J Nergelius (eds), *General Principles of European Community Law* (The Hague, Kluwer Law International, 2000); and J Usher, 'The Reception of General Principles of Community Law in the United Kingdom' (2005) 16 *European Business Law Review* 489.

[23] On the concept of reverberation, see R de la Feria, 'Introducing the Principle of Prohibition of Abuse of Law' in R de la Feria and S Vogenauer (eds), *Prohibition of Abuse of Law: A New General Principle of EU Law?* (Oxford, Hart Publishing, 2011).

is then used in different judgments, reiterated and added to, without full awareness of its significance, scope or meaning. Realisation of the process of creation of a new principle of EU law is at that point unavoidable, with cognisance being not necessarily triggered internally within the CJEU itself, but often externally, either by national courts or legal commentators – or both. Once made aware of the process, the Court has to decide on whether to proceed or not – thus, whilst the process involves various agents, the Court is in essence the sole cognisance-agent.

As the stage of post-cognisance, the intensity of the dialectic debate increases significantly, with the interaction also becoming more focused: the CJEU tends to frame its decisions differently, imposing a new structure in light of the new legal principle; whilst national courts' requests for preliminary rulings also become more specific and targeted around the principle.[24] As the new principle develops, legal commentators focus their attention more closely on the topic and national legislatures may also react by imposing new rules which better reflect – or respect – the new principle of EU law. At this stage the dialectic process is no longer solely vertical, but also horizontal, with national courts and even legislatures responding both to doctrinal and jurisprudential developments in other Member States.[25] Figure 2 below provides an illustration of the co-constitutive reverberation process through its different stages.

This co-constitutive process of reverberation in its different stages can be observed as regards the co-creation and co-production of various principles relevant to tax law, including most recently, the principle of third-party liability for fraud.[26] As discussed below, it can also be clearly observed as regards the principle of prohibition of abuse of law.

A. Pre-Cognisance Period: From *Van Binsbergen* to *Halifax*

The pre-cognisance stage can be said to extend from the first references by the CJEU to abuse and abusive practices in *Van Binsbergen* in the 1970s, to the ruling in *Halifax* in 2006. During this period, the Court made consistent reference to prohibition of abuse and abusive practices in response to questions referred to it by national courts. Similar to other principles and legal concepts, the concept of abuse was present within the legal systems of many – it has been argued that in all – Member States,[27] but its particular characteristics, such as the scope and criteria for application and designation,

[24] On this collaboration and mutual deference between the CJEU and national courts, see CF Sabel and O Gerstenberg, 'Constitutionalising an Overlapping Consensus: The ECJ and the Emergence of a Coordinate Constitutional Order' (2010) 16 *European Law Journal* 511.

[25] J Usher, 'General Principles and National Law – A Continuing Two-Way Process' in U Bernitz, J Nergelius and C Cardner (eds), *General Principles of EC Law in a Process of Development* (Alphen aan den Rijn, Wolters Kluwer, 2008) 393, 415.

[26] R de la Feria and R Foy, '*Italmoda*: the birth of the principle of third-party liability for VAT fraud' [2016] *BTR* 270.

[27] A Sayde, *Abuse of EU Law and Regulation of the Internal Market* (Oxford, Hart Publishing, 2014) 32 et seq; see also A Lenaerts, 'The General Principle of the Prohibition of Abuse of Rights: A Critical Position on Its Role in a Codified European Contract Law' (2010) 18 *European Review of Private Law* 1121, 1125.

Figure 2 Co-Constitutive Process of Reverberation

Phase I: Pre-Cognisance

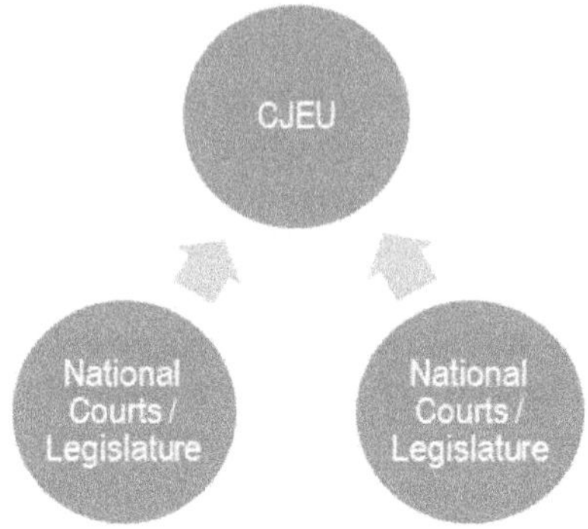

Phase II: From Pre-Cognisance to Cognisance

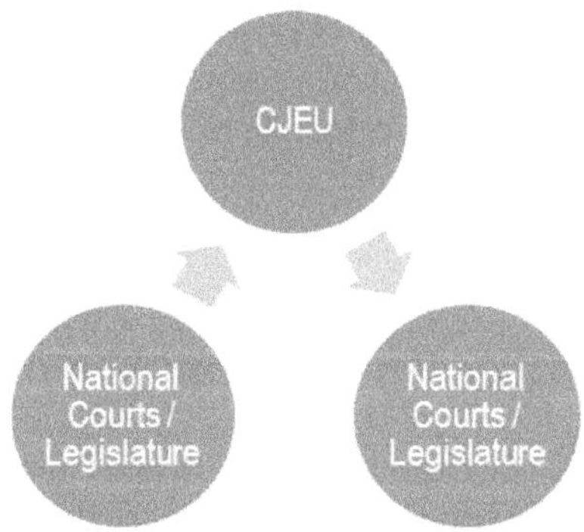

Phase III: From Cognisance to Post-Cognisance

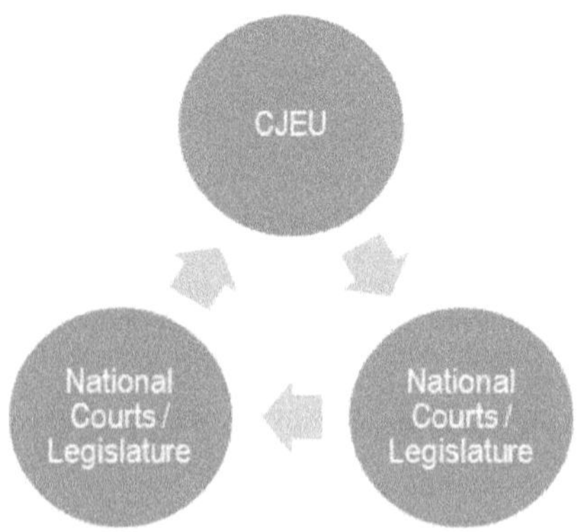

differed from Member State to Member State.[28] The vagueness resulting from these discrepancies gave the Court the freedom to slowly and progressively develop – via the dialectic process between the CJEU and the national courts – a new EU concept of abuse, with a specific meaning, scope and criteria for application.

Van Binsbergen concerned free movement of services,[29] and whether rules preventing a Dutch lawyer, who had moved to Belgium, from appearing before the Dutch courts, were justified to prevent the circumvention of Dutch professional rules. The Court, in a landmark statement, which has been consistently cited in later rulings, concluded:

> Likewise, a Member State cannot be denied the right to take measures to prevent the exercise by a person providing services whose activity is entirely or principally directed towards its territory of the freedom guaranteed by article [49] for the purpose of avoiding the professional rules of conduct which would be applicable to him if he were established within that state; such a situation may be subject to judicial control under the provisions of the chapter relating to the right of establishment and not of that on the provision of services.[30]

In the early 1990s a number of cases were referred to the CJEU concerning circumvention transactions within the field of broadcasting.[31] The cases, which became known as the broadcasting cases, focused on the interpretation not only of the treaty provisions on free movement of services, as well as the provisions of the Television Without Frontiers Directive.[32] In all cases, the Court was essentially asked whether restrictions imposed by Member States on free movement of broadcasting services could be justified in light of the Court's approach to abuse and abusive practices, as set out in *Van Binsbergen*; and in all cases the Court considered that it did indeed apply. Apart from reiterating the decision in that case, the cases were particularly significant as regards the development of the principle of prohibition of abuse of law as a result of the opinion of Advocate General Lenz in one of them, *TV10*.[33] Indeed two aspects of this opinion can potentially be regarded as constituting a precursor of, or a basis for, the development by the CJEU of the abuse doctrine in later rulings, as follows:

a. The view expressed in the opinion that an activity, even if abusive, should be regarded as falling within the scope of the free movement provisions, with the abuse principle seen as 'an exception' to those provisions, could arguably be regarded as the theoretical framework behind the *Centros* line of case law.
b. The reference in the opinion to the need for the establishment of criteria for the determination of the existence of abuse, and in particular to the possible use of objective and/or subjective criteria, could arguably be regarded as the origin of the abuse test, set out by the some years later in *Emsland-Stärke*.

[28] J Freedman, 'The Anatomy of Tax Avoidance Counteraction: Abuse of Law in a Tax Context at Member State and European Union Level' in R de la Feria and S Vogenauer (eds), *Prohibition of Abuse of Law: A New General Principle of EU Law?* (Oxford, Hart Publishing, 2011), ch 25.

[29] Case 33/74, ECLI:EU:C:1974:131.

[30] ibid para 13.

[31] Cases C-211/91, *Commission v Belgium*, ECLI:EU:C:1992:526; C-148/91; *Veronica*, ECLI:EU:C:1993:45; C-23/93, *TV10*, ECLI:EU:C:1994:362.

[32] Council Directive 89/552/EEC of 3 October 1989 on the coordination of certain provisions laid down by Law, Regulation or Administrative Action in Member States concerning the pursuit of television broadcasting activities [1989] OJ L298/23.

[33] Case C-23/93, *TV10*, ECLI:EU:C:1994:251.

The CJEU decision in *Centros*,[34] although not completely surprising from an abuse of law perspective,[35] gave rise to immense controversy in the context of company law.[36] Like prior cases, *Centros* was a circumvention case, it concerned a company, owned by Danish citizens, but incorporated in the UK, allegedly with the sole aim of avoiding the application of Danish rules on minimum capital. The Court started by reinstating that Member States were entitled to introduce national measures to prevent abuse, but then went on to introduce the concept of legitimate circumvention by affirming that a move to another Member State is not in itself abusive. Under this new approach, the previous broad – and perhaps simplistic – conceptualisation of abuse, under which all circumvention situations were regarded as abusive, was therefore substituted for a narrower – and perhaps more sophisticated – conception of it, under which not all circumvention situations would be tantamount to an abuse of EU law.

Emsland-Stärke concerned the interpretation of Regulation 2730/79 on export refunds on agricultural products.[37] The factual circumstances of the case were relatively straightforward: Emsland-Stärke, a German company, exported a potato-based product to Switzerland, for which it received export refund; however, immediately after their release for use in Switzerland, the products were transported back to Germany unaltered, by the same means of transport, and released for use therein.[38] The question for the CJEU was essentially whether in these circumstances the emerging principle of abuse could preclude Emsland-Stärke's right to export refund. At the hearing, the European Commission argued that, although the Court had not expressly recognised it as a general principle of EU law, a general legal principle of abuse of rights existed in almost all the Member States and had, in practice, already been applied in the case law of the CJEU. Without charactering its previous jurisprudence as a 'general principle' (yet), the Court agreed. It then went on to set out the abuse of law test, as follows:

> A finding of an abuse requires, first, a combination of objective circumstances in which, despite formal observance of the conditions laid down by the Community rules, the purpose of those rules has not been achieved. It requires, second, a subjective element consisting in the intention to obtain an advantage from the Community rules by creating artificially the conditions laid down for obtaining it. The existence of that subjective element can be established, inter alia, by evidence of collusion between the Community exporter receiving the refunds and the importer of the goods in the non-member country.[39]

The debate over the implications of the new abuse test for other areas of EU law was directly associated with the Court's rationale in *Emsland-Stärke*. Although the ruling provides no express statement in this regard, it was assumed by many immediately after the judgment that the fact that agricultural levies constituted a Community's

[34] Case C-212/97, *Centros*, ECLI:EU:C:1999:126.

[35] The case emerged in the context of the so-called Greek Challenge Cases on company law rules, see Cases C-367/96, *Kefalas and Others*, ECLI:EU:C:1998:222; C-441/93, *Pafitis and others*, ECLI:EU:C:1996:92; C-373/97, *Diamantis*, ECLI:EU:C:2000:150.

[36] Reflected in the fact that the decision is one of the most commented upon in the history of the CJEU.

[37] Commission Regulation (EEC) No 2730/79 of 29 November 1979 on the application of the system of export refunds on agricultural products [1979] OJ L317/1.

[38] Case C-110/99, ECLI:EU:C:2000:695.

[39] ibid paras 52–54.

own resource had played a major role.[40] Indeed, a few years before, the European Commission had put forward a proposal on the protection of the Community's own resources, which included a definition of 'abuse of Community law',[41] and whilst following negotiations soften the language used and limited the scope of the clause,[42] the final version did include a general anti-abuse provision.[43] On this basis it was argued by some Member States' tax authorities that, as VAT was also part of the Union's own resources,[44] the abuse test should apply within the field of that tax.[45] Thus, it was in this manner that the then emerging general principle of prohibition of abuse of law, firmly arrived to taxation.

B. From Pre-Cognisance to Cognisance: *Halifax*

Almost 30 years later, the passage from dormant status to full consciousness, from pre-cognisance to cognisance, finally came with *Halifax*. Engulfed in an intense stream of legal commentary, the reference by the London VAT and Duties Tribunal arrived at the CJEU in 2002; it was the first of several referrals which arrived at the Court between 2002 and 2004,[46] on the application of what was designated then by the national referring courts as the doctrine or principle of abuse of rights to VAT cases.[47] Yet, the case was not decided until 2006, and in the intervening period, the Court decided on some of the other references.

The first of these judgments delivered by the CJEU was *RAL*, a case concerning the determination of the place of supply of services, where the supplier, the RAL Group, had – through a restructuring scheme – located its place of business outside EU territory for VAT purposes, with the sole aim of avoiding output VAT. Although the potential application of the principle of abuse of law had been specifically raised by HMRC and covered by the referring court in its question, the Court refused to answer, adopting instead what was regarded at the time as a novel interpretation of the VAT Directive's rules on place of supply of services.[48] Soon after, the Court decided in *Centralan*, which concerned transactions entered into by the University of Central Lancashire allegedly with the exclusive aim of maximising the recovery of input VAT incurred on the

[40] See Harris (n 14).

[41] European Commission, 'Proposal for a Council Regulation (EC, Euratom) on protection of the Community's financial interests' COM(94) 214 final, 7 July 1994.

[42] Sayde (n 27) 44 et seq.

[43] Council Regulation (EC, Euratom) No 2988/95 of 18 December 1995 on the protection of the European Communities financial services [1995] OJ L312/1.

[44] There is a substantial amount of legislation in this area, see R de la Feria, *A Handbook of EU VAT Legislation*, Vol III (The Hague, Kluwer Law International, 2004–) table V.A.1.

[45] Harris (n 14); D Ladds and M Chowdry, 'Debenhams Retail Plc v Commissioners of Customs and Excise' [2004] *BTR* 26, 32.

[46] On the proceedings in the UK courts that preceded the preliminary references, see P Pincher, 'What is avoidance?' [2002] *BTR* 9.

[47] Cases C-419/02, *BUPA*, ECLI:EU:C:2006:122; C-223/03, *University of Huddersfield*, ECLI:EU:C:2006:124; C-452/03, *RAL (Channel Islands)*, ECLI:EU:C:2005:289; and C-63/04, *Centralan Property*, ECLI:EU:C:2005:773.

[48] For an analysis of this decision and its implications, see R de la Feria, '"Game Over" for aggressive VAT planning?: *RAL v Commissioners of Customs & Excise*' [2005] *BTR* 394.

construction costs of one of its buildings.[49] Whilst the questions referred by the national court concerned solely the interpretation of the VAT Directive's provisions, in its written observations, the European Commission raised the issue of the potential application of the principle of abuse of rights to the case. Once again, however, as it had done in *RAL*, the Court avoided answering on this point, preferring instead to adopt a teleological interpretation of the provisions in the Directive.

The delay in issuing its judgment in *Halifax*, as well as in providing a definite answer in any of the above cases is indicative of the Court's transition to a cognisance stage in the process of creating a new legal principle. Finally, in 2006, following the comprehensive opinion of Advocate General Maduro, the Court finally delivered its decision in *Halifax*. The factual circumstances, by now well known, can be summarised as follows: Halifax, a financial institution with a limited right to deduct input VAT, engaged in a series of transactions with the main aim of being allowed to deduct the totality of the VAT incurred in the construction of its new call centres.[50] In the judgment, the CJEU confirmed that the principle of prohibiting of abuse also applied to the sphere of VAT, and therefore the VAT Directive should be interpreted as precluding any right of a taxable person to deduct input VAT where the transactions from which that right derived constituted an abusive practice. In order to determine whether an abusive practice has taken place, the Court then set out a two-part test, an abusive practice will be found to exist where:

1. The transactions concerned, notwithstanding formal application of the conditions laid down by the relevant provisions of the [VAT Directive] and the national legislation transposing it, resulted in the accrual of a tax advantage, the grant of which would be contrary to the purpose of those provisions.
2. It is apparent from a number of objective factors, such as the purely artificial nature of the transactions and the links between operators involved in the scheme, that the essential aim of those transactions concerned was to obtain a tax advantage.[51]

According to the CJEU, it is for the national courts to verify in each specific case, and in light of the evidence presented, whether these conditions are fulfilled and consequently, whether an abusive practice has taken place. Once such practice has been established, the transactions involved 'must be redefined so as to re-establish the situation that would have prevailed in the absence of the transactions constituting that abusive practice'.[52] Whilst no one doubted the landmark status of the *Halifax* decision,[53] it was also clear from the outset that further guidance would be required on the application of the abuse principle to VAT, and thus, that new cases were likely to arise in this area.[54]

[49] Case C-63/04, *Centralan*, ECLI:EU:C:2005:773.

[50] For a detailed analysis of the facts in the case, see R de la Feria, 'Giving themselves extra (VAT)? The ECJ ruling in *Halifax*' [2006] *BTR* 119.

[51] C-255/02, ECLI:EU:C:2006:121, paras 74, 75 and 81.

[52] ibid para 94.

[53] It has even been argued that 21 February 2006, nicknamed 'Halifax Day', marked the beginning of a new stage of evolution for the EU VAT system, see J Swinkels, 'Halifax Day: Abuse of Law in European VAT' (2006) 19 *International VAT Monitor* 173.

[54] As the Court itself acknowledged in *Halifax*, para 77. See also comments in R de la Feria, 'The European Court of Justice's solution to aggressive VAT planning – further towards legal uncertainty?' (2006) 15 *EC Tax Review* 27.

C. Post-Cognisance: From *Halifax* to *Cussens and Others*

Since the decision in *Halifax* we have entered the post-cognisance period, with the intensification of vertical interaction between the EU judicial arm and the courts and legislatures of the Member States, and horizontal interaction between courts and legislatures of different Member States amongst themselves.[55] National legislation of various Member States was altered as a result of the Court's rulings, and national courts reportedly started to apply the EU principle of abuse of law to purely internal situations, including in France,[56] Italy,[57] the Netherlands[58] and the UK.[59] At EU level the number of cases referred to the CJEU on the new EU principle of prohibition of abuse of law increased significantly.

In direct taxation the significance of *Cadbury Schweppes*, which concerned the compatibility of controlled foreign companies (CFC) rules, can hardly be overstated. This significance did not rest in the statement by the CJEU that establishing subsidiaries in another Member State, for the purpose of benefiting from the favourable tax regime which that establishment enjoys, did not in itself constitute abuse; the legitimacy of so-called 'tax location shopping' could have already been inferred from the *Centros*' line of case law.[60] Nor in the Court's reference in the judgment to 'wholly artificial arrangements'; in *ICI* the Court had already held that national legislation, which restricts the exercise of the freedom of establishment, could only be justified where it had 'the specific purpose of preventing wholly artificial arrangements'.[61] Rather, the novelty of *Cadbury Schweppes* rested in the definition of 'wholly artificial arrangement' given by the Court, namely its alignment with the principle prohibition of abuse of law, as set out in *Halifax*. Significant as well, was the decision in *Kofoed*,[62] which concerned the interpretation of an anti-abuse clause set out in the Merger Directive.[63] In its judgment the Court refers

[55] As Freedman, 'The Anatomy of Tax Avoidance Counteraction' (n 28) commented, 'the traffic is not one-way but multi-directional'.

[56] L Leclercq, 'Interacting Principles: The French Abuse of Law Concept and the EU Notion of Abusive Practices' (2007) 61 *Bulletin for International Taxation* 235; S de Monès et al, 'Abuse of Tax Law Across Europe (Part One)' (2010) 2 *EC Tax Review* 85.

[57] Italy is said to be a paradigmatic example of the reverberation process, see D Carolis, 'The Reverberation Effect on the EU Notion of Abuse of Law on the Italian Tax Legal System: Towards and Enhanced Horizontal Interaction Among National General Anti-Abuse Rules?' (2017) 45 *Intertax* 169. See also C Garbarino, 'The Development of a Judicial Anti-Abuse Principle in Italy' [2009] *BTR* 186; and S de Monès et al, 'Abuse of Tax Law Across Europe (Part Two)' (2010) 3 *EC Tax Review* 123.

[58] Case C-352/08, *Modehuis A Zwijnenburg*, ECLI:EU:C:2010:282.

[59] R de la Feria, '*HMRC v Weald Leasing Ltd.* Not Only Artificial: The Abuse of Law Test in VAT' [2008] *BTR* 556.

[60] C Panayi, *Double Taxation, Tax Treaties, Treaty Shopping and the European Community* (Eucotax Series, Kluwer Law International, 2007) 179–93; see also T O'Shea, 'The UK's CFC rules and the freedom of establishment: Cadbury Schweppes plc and its IFSC subsidiaries – tax avoidance or tax mitigation?' (2007) 16 *EC Tax Review* 13.

[61] Case C-264/96, *ICI*, ECLI:EU:C:1998:370, para 26. This approach was confirmed in later cases, see Cases C-324/00, *Lankhorst-Hohorst*, ECLI:EU:C:2002:749, para 37; C-9/02, *de Lasteyrie*, ECLI:EU:C:2004:138, para 50; and C-446/03, *Marks & Spencer*, ECLI:EU:C:2005:763, para 57.

[62] Case C-321/05, *Kofoed*, ECLI:EU:C:2007:408.

[63] Council Directive 90/434/EEC of 23 July 1990 on the common system of taxation applicable to mergers, divisions, transfers of assets and exchanges of shares concerning companies of different Member States [1990] OJ L225/1.

for the first time to the principle of prohibition of abuse of law as a 'general Community law principle'.

Since those first decisions in direct taxation in the post-cognisance area, more cases continued to be decided by the CJEU on the basis of the EU principle of prohibition of abuse of law. Developments to the application of the principle to VAT cases were also fast coming. Soon after *Halifax*, the Italian courts forwarded *Part Service*, in which the Court was essentially asked whether

> there can be a finding of an abusive practice when the accrual of a tax advantage is the principal aim of the transaction or the transactions in question, or if such a finding can only be made if the accrual of that tax advantage constitutes the sole aim pursued, to the exclusion of other economic objectives.[64]

The Court seemed to confirm its – English version – decision in *Halifax*, stating that obtaining a tax advantage need not be the sole aim of the transaction, but merely the principal aim, thus significantly broadening the scope of the abuse of law principle. In 2008 the UK courts, perhaps unsurprisingly given the level of litigation at national level which followed *Halifax*,[65] referred two more cases to the CJEU. *Weald Leasing* and *RBS Holdings* concerned arrangements entered into by financial institutions with the sole aim of obtaining a tax advantage.[66] In *Weald Leasing*, the most significant of the two decisions, the focus was upon three aspects of the principle of prohibition of abuse of law, as applied to VAT, as follows: the interpretation of the first element of the abuse of law test; the meaning and significance of the expression 'normal commercial operations' in the context of the test; and the redefinition of abusive transactions. In an unequivocal judgment the Court reinstated the need for the fulfilment of the first element of the test in order to establish the existence of abuse, denied significance to the expression 'normal commercial operations' for the purposes of that test, and reiterated previous statements as regards the redefinition of abusive transactions.

The decision in *Weald Leasing* seemed to have sufficiently clarified the scope of the principle of prohibition of abuse of law for VAT purposes. A few years later, however, the CJEU was asked to decide in *Newey* (*Ocean Finance*),[67] which concerned a loan broker setting up a structure that involved a company in Jersey, with the aim of avoiding paying input VAT on advertising services. The arrangements had been challenged by HMRC on the basis – amongst other aspects – that they were contrary to the principle of prohibition of abuse of law; indeed, on the facts, case appeared to fulfil both elements of abuse of law test, as set out in *Halifax*, and reinstated in *Weald Leasing*. In a rather surprising decision, however, the Court stated that

> the contractual terms, even though they constitute a factor to be taken into account are not decisive … They may in particular be disregarded if it becomes apparent that they do not reflect economic and commercial reality, but constitute a wholly artificial arrangement

[64] Case C-425/06, *Part Service*, ECLI:EU:C:2008:108, para 40.

[65] For an analysis of the UK cases decided in the interim period see de la Feria, 'Prohibition of Abuse of (Community) Law' (n 1) and R de la Feria, '*Weald Leasing*. Application of the abuse of law test in the VAT sphere. Court of Justice' [2011] *Highlights & Insights on European Taxation* 3.

[66] Case C-103/09, *Weald Leasing*, ECLI:EU:C:2010:804; and Case C-277/09, *RBS Holdings*, ECLI:EU:C:2010:810.

[67] Case C-653/11, *Newey* (*Ocean Finance*), ECLI:EU:C:2013:409.

> which does not reflect economic reality and was set-up with the sole aim of obtaining a tax advantage, which it is for the national court to determine.[68]

The decision raises various questions, in particular over the scope of the principle insofar as VAT is concerned: does the scope of the principle encompass only transactions which fulfil the two elements of the test, namely purpose and artificiality, or is only artificiality enough? Is it necessary for abuse to be found that the transactions are wholly artificial, or only that the principal aim is to obtain a tax advantage? Does the expression 'normal commercial operations' have a role in defining the scope of the abuse of law principle? Overall, either purposely or unwillingly, there was an apparent departure from previous case law, the ratio of which was unclear, although the language used was reminiscent of previous judgments on the application of the principle of prohibition of abuse of law to direct taxation cases.[69] The decision in *WebMindLicences* confirmed, however, that the apparent language departure in *Newey (Ocean Finance)* did not in fact reflect a real departure in case law.[70] Reiterating its previous decisions, in particular those in *Halifax* and *Weald Leasing*, and clearly inspired by *Centros* and *Cadbury Schweppes*, the Court went back to applying the two-part test for determining the existence of abuse of law to the circumstances of the case, namely: whether a transaction, such as that in the main proceedings, results in the accrual of a tax advantage contrary to the objectives of the VAT Directive;[71] and, whether the essential aim of a transaction is solely to obtain that tax advantage.[72]

As this discussion was unfolding within VAT, interesting developments were also happening within direct taxation cases concerning the interpretation of the principle of prohibition of abuse of law. One of the most significant decisions, which has since framed much of the debate, was that in *3M Italia*.[73] In this case, concerning the taxation of dividends, asked about the applicability of the principle, in light of *Halifax* and *Cadbury Schweppes*, the Court stated that 'no general principle exists in European Union law which might entail an obligation of the Member States to combat abusive practices in the field of direct taxation'.[74] The statement was interpreted as indicating a limited scope of application of the principle within the field of non-harmonised direct taxation,[75] and even confirming the non-existence of an EU GAAP insofar as non-harmonised taxes were concerned.[76] Whether the Court would have decided the same way today is difficult to say. It is worth noting that in one of its most recent decisions on the principle, *Cussens and Others*, the Court confirmed that the principle 'displays

[68] ibid para 52.

[69] For an analysis see R de la Feria and M Silva Costa, 'O Impacto de *Ocean Finance* no Conceito de Abuso de Direito Para Efeitos de IVA' (2013) 6 *Revista de Finanças Públicas e Direito Fiscal* 321.

[70] Case C-419/14, *WebMindLicences*, ECLI:EU:C:2015:832.

[71] ibid paras 37, 40 and 41.

[72] ibid paras 42–44.

[73] Case C-417/10, *3M Italia*, ECLI:EU:C:2012:184.

[74] ibid para 32.

[75] L de Broe and D Beckers, 'The General Anti-Abuse Rule of the Anti-Tax Avoidance Directive: An Analysis Against the Wider Perspective of the European Court of Justice's Case Law on Abuse of Law' (2017) 26 *EC Tax Review* 133, 138. See also R Szudoczky, '*3M Italia*: Tax Amnesty Aimed at Concluding Tax Litigation Prolonged for an Unreasonable Time Does Not Constitute State Aid' (2013) 12 *European State Aid Law* 162.

[76] C Panayi, *European Union Corporate Tax Law* (Cambridge, Cambridge University Press, 2013) 337 et seq.

the general, comprehensive character which is naturally inherent in general principles of EU law',[77] and in *Argenta Spaarbank*, it stated that the special anti-avoidance rule (SAAR) in the Parent–Subsidiary Directive (PSD) 'reflects the general EU law principle that abuse of rights is prohibited'.[78] Regardless of whether this is the case, however, the decision in *3M Italia* does not deny the existence of the principle, but merely indicates a possible sliding scale of judicial review, which is also evident in others areas of EU law, particularly as regards free movement of persons and citizenship.

As the development of the EU principle of prohibition of abuse of law continued within tax, arguably only one area remained relatively unaffected by the principle, namely that of free movement of persons and citizenship. Whilst the principle had often been invoked in the context of cases in these areas of EU law,[79] and the Court had never expressly rejected the application of the principle per se, it had indeed failed to find abuse of law in any of these cases,[80] leading many commentators to reject the relevance of the principle to free movement of persons and citizenship rights.[81] However, whether there should be full convergence between free movement of persons and the other freedoms,[82] was not fundamental for the debate: indeed, one could easily envisage a situation where the Court – perhaps justifiably – did not apply the principle for the purposes of judicial review uniformly across all areas of EU law, and the intensity of judicial review exercised varied depending on the subject matter.[83]

In that context, it is also interesting to note the range of European law areas in which the EU principle of prohibition of abuse of law has been invoked, which include, inter alia: contractual liability;[84] free movement of workers and recognition

[77] Case C-251/16, ECLI:EU:C:2017:881, para 31.

[78] Case C-39/16, *Argenta Spaarbank*, EU:C:2017:813, para 60. On the relevance of the principle in direct taxation directives, see A Cordewener, 'Anti-Abuse Measures in the Area of Direct Taxation: Towards Converging Standards Under Treaty Freedoms and EU Directives' (2017) 26 *EC Tax Review* 60.

[79] It has even been used by the UK to justify the deportation of EU citizens, see *Gunars Gureckis v Secretary of State for the Home Department* [2017] EWHC 3298.

[80] See in particular Cases C-413/01, *Ninni-Orasche*, ECLI:EU:C:2003:600; C-109/01, *Akrich*, ECLI:EU:C:2003:491; C-200/02, *Chen*, ECLI:EU:C:2004:639; C-138/02, *Collins*, ECLI:EU:C:2004:172; C-147/03, *Commission v Austria*, ECLI:EU:C:2005:427.

[81] See KS Ziegler, '"Abuse of Law" in the Context of the Free Movement of Workers' in R de la Feria and S Vogenauer (eds), *Prohibition of Abuse of Law: A New General Principle of EU Law?* (Oxford, Hart Publishing, 2011); E Spaventa, 'Comments on Abuse of Law and the Free Movement of Workers' in R de la Feria and S Vogenauer (eds), *Prohibition of Abuse of Law: A New General Principle of EU Law?* (Oxford, Hart Publishing, 2011); C Costello 'Citizenship of the Union: Above Abuse?' in R de la Feria and S Vogenauer (eds), *Prohibition of Abuse of Law: A New General Principle of EU Law?* (Oxford, Hart Publishing, 2011); and M Dougan, 'Some Comments on the Idea of a General Principle of Union Law Prohibiting Abuses of Law in the Field of Free Movement for Union Citizens' in R de la Feria and S Vogenauer (eds), *Prohibition of Abuse of Law: A New General Principle of EU Law?* (Oxford, Hart Publishing, 2011).

[82] See P Oliver and WH Roth, 'The Internal Market and the Four Freedoms' (2004) 41 *Common Market Law Review* 407; and C Barnard, 'Fitting the Remaining Pieces into the Goods and Persons Jigsaw?' (2001) 26 *European Law Review* 35.

[83] The 'sliding scale of judicial review' is a well-known phenomenon within constitutional law literature. See D Doukas, *Werbefreiheit und Werbebeschränkungen: Eine europa- und grundrechtliche Untersuchung der Kontrollmaßstäbe für Beschränkungen der kommerziellen Kommunikation, dargestellt am EG-Recht, an der EMRK, am deutschen Grundgesetz und an der griechischen Verfassung* (Baden-Baden, Nomos, 2005).

[84] Case T-271/04, *Citymo*, ECLI:EU:T:2007:128.

of professional qualifications;[85] freedom of establishment and company law;[86] social policy;[87] competition;[88] common customs tariff;[89] agricultural policy;[90] and EU citizenship.[91] Even more interestingly perhaps, the principle has also been invoked within the area of freedom, security and justice,[92] and in a case concerning external relations where its applicability was implicitly accepted by the Court, even though the claim of abuse of law was rejected in the case.[93] More cases are pending at the CJEU where the principle has been invoked, expanding it to new areas, such as criminal procedure,[94] and employment law.[95] Equally noteworthy is the fact that, from the 1990s onwards, the EU legislator started enacting legislative provisions codifying the principle in various areas of EU law,[96] including: EU citizenship;[97] use of EU budget resources;[98] cross-border transmission of broadcasting services;[99] international civil procedure;[100] and enforcement of intellectual property rights.[101] To these sporadic references in secondary legislation, perceived by the Court itself as 'codifications' or 'reflections' of its case law[102] – a trend common to other general principles of EU law[103] – the EU legislator added, in 2000, a broader provision, Article 54 of the Charter of Fundamental Rights of the European Union, under the heading 'Prohibition of abuse of rights'.

As the EU principle of prohibition of abuse of law is increasingly densified, as well as invoked across a greater diversity of contexts, the co-constitutive process of reverberation, in its post-cognisance stage, continues, and its status as a general principle of EU law solidifies.

[85] Case C-311/06, *Consiglio Nazionale degli Ingegneri (CNDI)*, ECLI:EU:C:2009:37; and Joined Cases C-58/13 and 59/13, *Torresi*, ECLI:EU:C:2014:265.

[86] Case C-210/06, *Cartesio*, ECLI:EU:C:2008:723.

[87] Cases C-396/07, *Mirja Juuri*, ECLI:EU:C:2008:656; and C-222/14, *Dikaiosynis*, ECLI:EU:C:2015:473.

[88] Case C-260/07, *Total España*, ECLI:EU:C:2009:215.

[89] Cases C-7/08, *Har Vaessen Douane Service*, ECLI:EU:C:2009:417; C-607/13, *Cimmino and Others*, ECLI:EU:C:2015:448; and C-131/14, *Cervati*, ECLI:EU:C:2016:255.

[90] Case C-434/08, *Harms*, ECLI:EU:C:2010:285.

[91] Case C-202/13, *McCarthy and Others*, ECLI:EU:C:2014:2450.

[92] Cases C-168/08, *Hadady*, ECLI:EU:C:2009:474; C-C-254/11, *Shomodi*, ECLI:EU:C:2013:182; and C-352/13, *CDC Hydrogen Peroxide*, ECLI:EU:C:2015:335.

[93] Case C-16/05, *R*, ECLI:EU:C:2007:530.

[94] Case C-612/15, *Kolev and Others*, ECLI:EU:C:2018:392.

[95] Case C-423/15, *Kratzer*, ECLI:EU:C:2016:604.

[96] As noted by S Vogenauer, 'The Prohibition of Abuse of Law: An Emerging General Principle of EU Law' in R de la Feria and S Vogenauer (eds), *Prohibition of Abuse of Law: A New General Principle of EU Law?* (Oxford, Hart Publishing, 2011).

[97] Article 35 of Directive 2004/38/EC on the right of citizens of the Union and their family members to move and reside freely within the territory of the Member States.

[98] Article 4(3) of Regulation 2988/95 on the protection of the European Communities financial interests [1995] OJ L312/1.

[99] Article 3 of Council Directive 89/552/EEC of 3 October 1989 on the coordination of certain provisions laid down by Law, Regulation or Administrative Action in Member States concerning the pursuit of television broadcasting activities [1989] OJ L298/23, as amended by Directive 2007/65/EC of the European Parliament and of the Council of 11 December 2007 [2007] OJ L332/27.

[100] Article 6(2) of Council Regulation (EC) No 44/2001 of 22 December 2000 on jurisdiction and the recognition and enforcement of judgments in civil and commercial matters [2001] OJ L12/1.

[101] Article 3(2) of Directive 2004/48/EC of the European Parliament and of the Council of 29 April 2004 on the enforcement of intellectual property rights [2004] OJ L195/16.

[102] Vogenauer (n 96).

[103] As explained by Tridimas, *The General Principles of EU Law* (n 16) 11 et seq.

III. EU Principle of Prohibition of Abuse of Law as an EU General GAAP

Within taxation, despite the ongoing densification of the principle of prohibition of abuse of law, it is argued that its status as a de facto GAAP can hardly be contested. The question that arises then is as regards the nature of that GAAP, namely as an interpretative principle or as a general principle; the answer is in turn dependent on the characterisation of the principle of prohibition of abuse of law as a general principle, or as an interpretative principle. It is true that in many cases the exact nature of the principle will be, from a practical perspective, irrelevant,[104] as two of the main functions of general principles is to operate as interpretative aids, and gap fillers.[105] There are, however, many situations where the distinction is legally, and practically, relevant: beyond their role as interpretative aids, general principles can also act as overriding rules of law,[106] and can therefore trigger *contra legem* interpretation, acting as instruments of judicial review, and apply directly at national level, in the absence of domestic legislation to the effect. General principles have, therefore, all the legal functions of interpretative principles, as well as others.

It is the presence of those other legal functions which makes the characterisation of principle of prohibition of abuse of law as a general principle, or as an interpretative principle, crucial for taxation. An interpretative GAAP is only applicable in the presence of EU legislation, and it is limited by its wording; whilst, a general GAAP can be applied in the absence of EU legislation, and act as an instrument of judicial review. It is argued that it should now be regarded as settled case law that the principle, as developed by the Court, displays the key characteristics of a general principle of EU law, and consequently, within taxation, it should be regarded as a general GAAP. Table 1 provides an overview of the principle as it stands, with reference to key CJEU case law in taxation.

Of course, it could have been argued that the Court itself settled the matter by characterising the principle as a general principle of EU law in *Kofoed*.[107] This, however, would have amounted to a strictly formalist approach of one single case, which is difficult to justify, particularly in the context of previous terminological confusions in this area. Whilst relevant, therefore, the wording used by the Court cannot be the sole determining factor in the characterisation of this principle as a general one,[108] and indeed

[104] Farmer (n 14) 15–17.

[105] X Groussot, 'The General Principles of Community Law in the creation and development of due process principles in competition law proceedings: From Trans ocean Marine Paint (1974) to Montecatini (1999)' in U Bernitz and J Nergelius (eds), *General Principles of European Community Law* (The Hague, Kluwer Law International, 2000).

[106] J Nergelius, 'General Principles of Community Law in the Future: Some Remarks on their Scope, Applicability and Legitimacy' in U Bernitz and J Nergelius (eds), *General Principles of European Community Law* (The Hague, Kluwer Law International, 2000).

[107] Case C-321/05, ECLI:EU:C:2007:408, para 38.

[108] Arguing event against its necessity, see S Prechal and M de Leeuw, 'Transparency: A General Principle of EU Law?' in U Bernitz and J Nergelius (eds), *General Principles of European Community Law* (The Hague, Kluwer Law International, 2000).

Table 1 EU Principle of Prohibition of Abuse of Law as General GAAP

Applicability	Scope	Consequences
Applies to all types of legal instruments, including to primary EU legislation (*Cadbury Schweppes*), and to secondary EU legislation (*Halifax*) Applies to purely domestic situations, and in the absence of national legislation (*Cussens and Others*)	Applies where two cumulative conditions are fulfilled: (1) despite formal observance of the law, tax advantage obtained is against its purpose; and (2) principal aim of transactions, as established by objective factors, is to obtain tax advantage (*Halifax, Part Service, Weald Leasing, WebMindLicences*)	Right conferred by the legal provision is removed, and any advantage obtained must be object of restitution (*Halifax*) Transactions to be redefined so as to re-establish the situation in the absence of the abusive transactions (*Halifax*), even where redefinition results in a less favourable tax treatment (*WebMindLicences*), applied with retroactive effect (*Halifax*)

such designations of the CJEU have in the past been questioned.[109] The core issue therefore is whether or not the principle displays the key characteristics of a general principle of EU law. It is argued not only that it does, but that this is now settled case law.

Although there is no full doctrinal agreement on what constitutes a general principle of EU law,[110] the main characteristics usually attributed to them, namely generality, weight and non-conclusiveness, are all present in the jurisprudence of the CJEU regarding the principle of prohibition of abuse of law.[111] Beyond these key characteristics, however, there are several other factors that confirm the principle – and by consequence the GAAP – as it stands today, as general, rather than merely interpretative.

First, as it has rightly been argued,[112] the conceptualisation of the principle of prohibition of abuse of law as interpretative ignores the second element of the abuse of law test – which many have sought to argue, in cases such as *Weald Leasing*, as its main element – namely artificiality, that the principal aim of the transaction is to obtain an advantage. A finding that the application of the rule in question is contrary to its purpose is not regarded as sufficient; the reliance of those invoking the rule must be abusive – this is more than reading down the relevant rule through interpretation. This reality was acknowledged by Advocate General Mazak in *RBS Holdings*,

[109] J Raitio, 'The Principle of Legal Certainty as a General Principle of EU Law' in U Bernitz and J Nergelius (eds), *General Principles of European Community Law* (The Hague, Kluwer Law International, 2000).
[110] As reported by X Groussot, *General Principles of Community Law* (Groningen, Europa Law Publishing, 2006) 129–30.
[111] For a detailed analysis see de la Feria, 'Prohibition of Abuse of (Community) Law' (n 1).
[112] ibid.

who stated that interpreting a provision of EU law and establishing an abusive practice were 'conceptually distinct and should accordingly be dealt with one after the other'.[113]

Second, the principle has been used by the CJEU on various occasions as an instrument of judicial review of national legal provisions. It was arguably in that capacity that the principle was applied in *Cadbury Schweppes* and other direct taxation cases regarding non-harmonised areas: in these cases the principle of prohibition of abuse of law does not influence the interpretation of the scope of the freedom of establishment, which is deemed to apply, but on the contrary, it is used as a stand-alone exception to the applicable free movement right; this then resulted in the disapplication of the national provisions, as per the principle of supremacy of EU law, *not* in an interpretation of the national provision in conformity with EU, as per the principle of indirect effect.

Third, it is clear from the CJEU jurisprudence that the principle applies in the absence of national legislation to the same effect. Arguably, it was this characteristic that sparked the various preliminary references to the Court coming from the UK courts, following the decision in *Emsland-Stärke*: it is hardly coincidental that these cases emerged from the UK, which lacked at that time a general anti-avoidance, or anti-abuse provision; it rather reflects the willingness of HMRC to invoke what was then known as the abuse of rights doctrine against VAT avoidance schemes, in the absence of national legislation to that effect. It does not result necessarily from either the statement in *Kofoed* – according to which, in the absence of the transposition of a specific anti-avoidance provision in the Merger Directive, the principle should not substitute it – or that in *3M Italia* – according to which there is no obligation upon the Member States to combat abusive practices in the field of direct taxation – that the principle does not apply in the absence of national legislation. Yet, to the extent that it could have been interpreted in that manner, the decision has been arguably reversed in *Italmoda*, *Cussens and Others*, *N Luxembourg 1*, *and T Danmark*.[114] In *Italmoda* the Court asserted that 'express authorisation cannot be required in order for the national authorities and courts to be able to refuse a benefit under the common system of VAT',[115] and relying on that statement, the Court finally settled the matter in *Cussens and Others* expressly stating that 'the principle that abusive practices are prohibited may be relied on … even in the absence of provisions of national law'.[116] As the Court indicated in that judgment, this characteristic of the principle entails more than interpretation; it implies direct applicability, which is a feature of general, rather than interpretative, principles. This judgment has now been confirmed in *N Luxembourg 1*, where the Court stated that 'even if it were to transpire, in the main proceedings, that national law does not contain rules … Member States must, therefore, refuse to grant the advantage resulting from [Mergers Directive], in accordance with the general principle that abusive practices are prohibited'.[117]

[113] Case C-277/09, *RBS Holdings*, ECLI:EU:C:2010:566, para 29.

[114] On the constitutional significance of *Cussens and Others* see D Leczykiewicz, 'Prohibition of abusive practices as a "general principle" of EU law' (2019) 56 *Common Market Law Review* 703.

[115] Case C-131/13, *Italmoda*, ECLI:EU:C:2014:2455, para 59. For an analysis of the case, see de la Feria and Foy (n 26).

[116] Case C-251/16, ECLI:EU:C:2017:881, paras 33–34.

[117] Case C-115/16, *N Luxembourg 1*, ECLI:EU:C:2019:134, paras 117–21.

Finally, whilst the terminology used within CJEU is still not uniform, it is noteworthy that there are now several – and growing – numbers of statements confirming the nature of the principle of prohibition of abuse of law as a general principle of EU law, not only made by several Advocates General, but also by the Court itself, the most recent of which in *Cussens and Others*, *Argenta Spaarbank*,[118] *N Luxembourg 1*,[119] and *T Danmark*.[120] Indeed a brief analysis of the various statements on the general versus interpretative nature of the principle of prohibition of abuse of law, as summarised in Table 2 below, highlights the fact that not since 1998 has an Advocate General expressly supported the characterisation of the principle as interpretative – although in 2004 the Advocate General in *Chen* did express some reservations as to its characterisation as general;[121] on the contrary, not only have there been multiple references to the principle as a general principle of EU law, but these have grown in intensity during the post-cognisance period starting in *Halifax*. In this regard, it is also significant to note that, as it is acknowledged within the EU constitutional law doctrine, one of the most significant roles of Advocates General has been their contribution to the development of general principles of EU law.[122]

Over the last decade various arguments have been presented against the characterisation of the principle of prohibition of abuse of law as a general principle of EU law. Most of these have now been expressly addressed by the jurisprudence of the CJEU,[123]

Table 2 CJEU References to Nature of EU Principle of Prohibition of Abuse of Law

General Principle	**Interpretative Principle**
Centros (Advocate General La Pergola), 1999	*Kefalas* (Advocate General Tesauro), 1998
Diamantis (Advocate General Saggio), 2000	*Chen* (Advocate General Tizzano), 2004?
Halifax (Advocate General Maduro), 2006	
Kofoed, 2007	
Bozkurt (Advocate General Sharpston), 2010	
Oberto and O'Leary (Advocate-General Mengozzi), 2014	
***CASTA and Others*, 2016**	
***Cussens and Others*, 2017**	
***Argenta Spaarbank*, 2017**	
***N Luxembourg 1*, 2018**	

[118] Case C-39/16, EU:C:2017:813, para 60.

[119] Case C-115/16, ECLI:EU:C:2019:134, paras 96–97. See also, in the area of free movement of workers, Case C-359/16, *Ömer Altun*, ECLI:EU:C:2018:63, para 49.

[120] Case C-116/16, *T Danmark*, EU:C:2019:135, paras 70–71.

[121] Case C-200/02, *Chen*, ECLI:EU:C:2004:307, para 111.

[122] N Burrows and R Greaves, *The Advocate General and EC Law* (Oxford, Oxford University Press, 2007) 7; and T Tridimas, 'The role of the Advocate General in the development of Community Law: Some reflections' (1997) 34 *Common Market Law Review* 1349, 1386.

[123] de la Feria, 'Prohibition of Abuse of (Community) Law' (n 1) 436–37.

but two arguments are arguably still relevant, and thus merit closer scrutiny. The first is that the principle is inconsistently applied by the Court, and that this lack of uniform application somehow prevents its characterisation as a general principle of EU law.[124] The answer to this argument, however, is that uniformity of application is not a fundamental characteristic of general principles, due to their inherent structural generality and scope-related generality.[125] It is not surprising therefore that, as mentioned above, the intensity and the scope of application of a general principle may vary depending on the subject matter,[126] and that this is a phenomenon present as regards other (uncontested) general principles of EU law, such as the principle of proportionality.[127]

The second argument is that characterising the prohibition of abuse of law as a general principle carries significant risks of undermining the general principle of legal certainty.[128] The characterisation as a general principle does indeed carry risks to legal certainty, as expressly acknowledged by Advocate General Maduro in *Halifax*,[129] which should not be underestimated. The principle of legal certainty is inherent to any legal system and in essence requires that the application of the law to a specific situation must be predictable.[130] Within the EU context, the principle was first invoked by the CJEU in 1961,[131] has long been recognised as general principle of EU law,[132] and often features in the case law of the CJEU, with reportedly over 2,500 decisions of the Court making express reference to it.[133] Despite its notorious ambiguity and vagueness,[134] it is said to encompass several other principles, and in particular the principle of legitimate expectations, which requires that those who act reasonably and in good faith on the basis of the law should not see those expectations defrauded.[135]

The contra-argument to the contention that the principle of prohibition of abuse of law should not be characterised as a general principle of EU law because it undermines legal certainty is twofold. First, acknowledging the risks which characterising the principle of prohibition of abuse of law as a general principle of EU law, does not – indeed cannot – equate to denying its existence; disagreeing with a specific legal development, cannot mean denying that the development ever took place. Second, the principle of prohibition of abuse of law must be balanced against other principles, and

[124] N Brown, 'Is there a general principle of abuse of rights in European Community Law?' in T Heukel and D Curtin (eds), *Institutional Dynamics of European Integration*, Vol II (Dordrecht, Martinus Nijhoff Publishers, 1994) 511.

[125] C Semmelmann, 'General Principles in EU Law between a Compensatory Role and an Intrinsic Value' (2013) 19 *European Law Journal* 457, 461.

[126] See section II above on the sliding scale of judicial review.

[127] TI Harbo, 'The Function of the Proportionality Principle in EU Law' (2010) 16 *European Law Journal* 158.

[128] A Arnull, 'What is a General Principle of EU Law?' in R de la Feria and S Vogenauer (eds), *Prohibition of Abuse of Law: A New General Principle of EU Law?* (Oxford, Hart Publishing, 2011) 22–23.

[129] Case C-255/02, *Halifax*, ECLI:EU:C:2005:200, para 77.

[130] Raitio (n 109) 52.

[131] Case 42/59, *SNUPAT*, ECLI:EU:C:1961:5.

[132] See amongst many others, Cases 52/69, *Geigy*, ECLI:EU:C:1972:73; C-323/88, *Sermes*, ECLI:EU:C:1990:299; C-154/05, *Kersbergen-Lap*, ECLI:EU:C:2006:449; C-345/06, *Heinrich*, ECLI:EU:C:2009:140; C-337/07, *Altun*, ECLI:EU:C:2008:744; C-201/08, *Plantanol*, ECLI:EU:C:2009:539; C-72/10, *Costa*, EU:C:2012:80.

[133] J Van Meerbeeck, 'The principle of legal certainty in the case-law of the European Court of Justice: from certainty to trust' (2016) 41 *European Law Review* 275.

[134] ibid.

[135] Raitio (n 109) 54.

vice versa, other principles must be balanced against the principle of prohibition of abuse of law; indeed conflicts between two or more general principles is not uncommon, and a balance must always be achieved between different principles that 'form part of the Community legal system'.[136] Despite its status as a general principle of EU law, the principle of legal certainty is not absolute and should not be safeguarded at all costs, but rather outweighed by other legal principles.[137] As demonstrated by the CJEU case law, often resource to other general principles will undermine legal certainty:[138] paradigmatic examples of this phenomenon would be cases involving the general EU principle of proportionality,[139] or the general EU principle of equal treatment.[140]

It is therefore in this context that the discussion as regards the risks to legal certainty presented by the EU principle of prohibition of abuse of law should be held. Those risks are often raised in the context of general anti-avoidance mechanisms;[141] however, as it has been argued, these principles 'cut(s) across an immemorial debate between two legitimate objectives of any legal order: legal certainty (the tendency to yield predictable legal outcomes) and legal congruence (the tendency to yield equitable legal outcomes)';[142] or put a different way, the principle of prohibition of abuse of law should be set in the context of the wider debate over security versus justice. Blind respect for legal certainty and the rigid respect of the letter of the law will lead to inequity, and jeopardise what has been designated as 'legal congruence'.[143] This is particularly true in the context of EU law, not least since hard law is often difficult to approve, so that reliance on judicial discretion in its application is particular necessary in the context of changing realities.[144]

All the above leads to the inescapable conclusion that the principle of prohibition of abuse of law is now a general principle of EU law, and as such a general GAAP, rather than an interpretative one, with all the legal consequences which being characterised as such entails. In particular, general principles are regarded as primary EU law, and described by the CJEU as having constitutional status.[145] They therefore carry significant legal force, and their significance within the development of the EU legal system

[136] Case C-255/02, ECLI:EU:C:2005:200, para 84.

[137] Raitio (n 109) 58.

[138] On the balancing of the principle of legal certainty with that of legality, see, eg, X Groussot and T Minssen, '*Res judicata* in the Court of Justice case-law: balancing legal certainty with legality?' (2007) 3 *European Constitutional Law Review* 385.

[139] T Lyons, 'State Aid, Taxation and Abuse of Law' in R de la Feria and S Vogenauer (eds), *Prohibition of Abuse of Law: A New General Principle of EU Law?* (Oxford, Hart Publishing, 2011).

[140] Joined Cases C-402/07 and C-432/07, *Air France*, ECLI:EU:C:2009:716; and C-581/10 and C-629/10, *Deutsche Lufthansa and Others*, ECLI:EU:C:2012:657.

[141] J Freedman, 'The UK GAAR' in M Lang et al (eds), *General Anti-Avoidance Rules (GAARs) – A Key Element of Tax Systems in the Post-BEPS World* (Amsterdam, IBFD, 2016). See also M Gammie, 'Moral Taxation, Immoral Avoidance – What Role for the Law?' [2013] *BTR* 577.

[142] Sayde (n 27) 167.

[143] ibid 168 et seq.

[144] As discussed in R de la Feria, 'EU VAT Principles as Interpretative Aids to EU VAT Rules: The Inherent Paradox' in M Lang et al (eds), *Recent VAT Case Law of the CJEU* (Vienna, Linde, 2016).

[145] Cases C-101/08, *Audiolux and Others*, ECLI:EU:C:2009:626, para 63; C-174/08, *NCC Construction Denmark*, ECLI:EU:C:2009:669, para 42.

has been profound.[146] Given their constitutional status they obviously take precedence over EU secondary legislation, by virtue of the hierarchy of EU norms, and over national legislation, by virtue of the principle of supremacy of EU law;[147] they are directly applicable, and they are regularly applied by the CJEU, in the absence of national or EU law to that effect, often producing a decisive effect on the outcome of a case, by helping to define the scope of rights granted by legislation. It is against this background that the approval of the EU GAAR should be read.

IV. From EU GAAP to EU GAAR

Whilst relatively new within the EU legal system, GAAPs and GAARs have played a central role within tax systems worldwide for over a century.[148] It is, however, undeniable that over the last two decades general anti-tax avoidance mechanisms have become increasingly popular around the globe,[149] and that this trend intensified in the wake of the financial crisis in 2008–09, as the public's reaction to tax avoidance at a time of austerity created a political momentum which favoured the approval of new (general) anti-avoidance mechanisms.[150] Within the EU, by 2002, only a few EU Member States had neither a GAAP, nor a GAAR, in their legal systems,[151] and those that did not have approved one since, either independently,[152] or as result of EU jurisprudential,[153] and legislative developments.[154] This trend is also evident internationally, and the multiplication of anti-avoidance mechanisms witnessed in the last decade has now culminated with the introduction of a GAAR at treaty level: the Principal Purpose Test.[155] It is against this background that the approval of an EU GAAR should be considered.

[146] As pointed out by Arnull (n 128) 18.

[147] Case C-2/08, *Olimpiclub*, ECLI:EU:C:2009:506.

[148] The first GAAR is thought to be the New Zealander, which dates back more than 130 years, see C Ellife, 'New Zealand's General Anti-Avoidance Rule – A Triumph of Flexibility Over Certainty' (2014) 62 *Canadian Tax Journal* 147. In Europe, the German GAAR is also over 100 years old now, see G Staringer, 'GAAR-dians of the Tax Galaxy. A 100-year GAAR Journey from Germany to Austria and Back to the EU' (2019) 47 *Intertax* 986.

[149] C Waerzeggers and C Hillier, 'Introducing a General Anti-Avoidance Rule (GAAR)' (2016) *IMF Technical Note – Tax Law* 1; and I Mosquerra et al, 'Tools Used by Countries to Counteract Aggressive Tax Planning in Light of Transparency' (2018) 46 *Intertax* 140.

[150] J Freedman, 'GAAR as a process and the process of discussing a GAAR' [2012] *BTR* 1, 22–27. See also see generally RC Christensen and M Hearson, 'The new politics of global tax governance: taking stock a decade after the financial crisis' (2019) 26 *Review of International Political Economy* 1068.

[151] Zimmer (n 5) 37–38.

[152] Such as the UK, see Freedman, 'GAAR as a process' (n 150).

[153] This was the case in Italy, see Carolis (n 57).

[154] As was the case in Greece, see V Athanasaki, 'A Critical Approach to GAARs in the Greek and the EU Tax Law' (2019) 4 *EC Tax Review* 183.

[155] For an analysis of this new GAAR, which is outside the scope of this chapter, see C Palao Toboada, 'OECD Base Erosion and Profit Shifting Action 6: The General Anti-Abuse Rule' (2015) 69 *Bulletin of International Taxation* 602; A Baez Moreno, 'GAARs and Treaties: From the Guiding Principle to the Principal Purpose Test. What Have We Gained from BEPS Action 6?' (2017) 45 *Intertax* 432; and D Duff, 'Tax Treaty Abuse and the Principal Purpose Test: Part II' (2018) 66 *Canadian Tax Journal* 619.

A. Developing the EU GAAR

The process of partial codification of the principle of prohibition of abuse of law took place in stages, even if arguably rather quickly. The first step came in 2012, with the release of the European Commission's recommendation on aggressive tax planning, which advised Member States to adopt general anti-avoidance rules to counteract avoidance that falls outside the scope of SAARs, 'adapted to domestic and cross-border situations'.[156] Three key elements stand out as regards this recommendation.

First, the recommendation constitutes an implicit acknowledgement of the contested nature of the principle of prohibition of abuse of law, as recently as 2012. Whilst it could be – and was – argued that by then the principle already exhibited the key characteristics of a general principle of EU law,[157] and thus applied to domestic situations, in the absence of national legislation, the decision in *3M Italia* that same year had cast doubts over the applicability of the EU GAAP to non-harmonised areas. Second, the recommendation is also indicative of the Commission's emerging concerns over creating a level playing field on anti-avoidance rules, which was arguably the key motivator for the ATAD proposal a few years later. Finally, although it has been contested that the recommendation clearly attempts to conform, and partially codify, with the CJEU case law on the principle of prohibition of abuse of law,[158] the proposed GAAR was arguably less clear than the case law. Whilst ostensibly soft law, the recommendation had an immediate and concrete effect, triggering legislative changes in various Member States.[159]

The next significant development came soon after the 2012 recommendation, with the appearance of EU SAARs: rules that similar to GAARs are designed to combat avoidance schemes, regardless of their specific characteristics or methods, but in the context of a specific area of taxation.[160] Both the proposal for a Financial Transactions Tax (FTT),[161] and the proposal amending the PSD, included SAARs, and in both cases the rationale presented by the Commission was to ensure a level playing field. Although the FTT proposal was never approved, the SAAR in the PSD has been in force since 2015,[162]

[156] Commission Recommendation 2012/772/EU of 6 December 2012 on aggressive tax planning [2012] OJ L338, 41–43.

[157] See de la Feria, 'Prohibition of Abuse of (Community) Law' (n 1).

[158] AP Dourado, 'Aggressive Tax Planning in the EU Law and in the Light of BEPS: the EC Recommendation on Aggressive Tax Planning and BEPS Action 6' (2015) 42 *Intertax* 43.

[159] Carolis (n 57); and Athanasaki (n 154).

[160] Distinct from TAARs, anti-avoidance rules that targeted specific types of avoidance, such as thin-capitalisation or transfer pricing rules. The terminology is not always consistent however, and at times authors refer to TAARs, as SAARs and vice versa, or as 'proper' and 'improper' SAARs, see J Zarnoza and A Baez, 'Spanish Report' in M Lang et al (eds), *General Anti-Avoidance Rules (GAARs) – A Key Element of Tax Systems in the Post-BEPS World* (Amsterdam, IBFD, 2016).

[161] European Commission, 'Proposal for a Council Directive Implementing Enhanced Cooperation in the Area of Financial Transaction Tax' COM(2013) 71 final. See J Englisch et al, 'The financial transaction tax proposal under the enhanced cooperation procedure: legal and practical considerations' [2013] *BTR* 223; and G Maffini and J Vella, 'Evidence-Based Policy Making? The Commission's Proposal for an FTT' (2015) Oxford University Centre for Business Taxation Working Paper WP15/15.

[162] Council Directive (EU) 2015/121 of 27 January 2015 amending Directive 2011/96/EU on the common system of taxation applicable in the case of parent companies and subsidiaries of different Member States [2015] OJ L21, 1–3.

and it is broadly regarded as the inspiration for the EU GAAR in the ATAD.[163] There are two key elements to that SAAR: the definition of what constitutes abuse, with reference to artificiality, and purpose of the law; and stipulation of the basic consequences of finding that abuse, namely the removal of the benefits granted by the Directive. Whilst it could reasonably be argued that that definition of what constitutes abuse closely follows the CJEU case law on the principle of prohibition of abuse of law, and as such should be regarded as a codification – albeit partial, insofar as it only applies to one area of taxation – of the EU GAAP, the criteria set out therein for determining artificiality is problematic. In the first instance the provision defines artificiality by reference to 'an arrangement or a series of arrangements … put in place for the main purpose or one of the main purposes of obtaining a tax advantage', but it then goes on to state that those arrangements 'shall be regarded as not genuine to the extent that they are not put into place for valid commercial reasons which reflect economic reality'. Although the references to economic reality and commercial reasons, or normal commercial operations, do appear frequently within the case law of the Court, it is difficult to know what is meant by them,[164] and on at least one occasion the Court went so far as to expressly reject the significance of one of those expressions as a criterion for determining abuse.[165] It would have been preferable, therefore, if the Directive defined artificiality solely with reference to 'the main purpose or one of the main purposes'. Nevertheless, one year later, a similar approach was adopted by the ATAD.

In early 2016, the European Commission presented its legislative proposal for a new ATAD,[166] reportedly as a vehicle to implement the Base Erosion and Profit Shifting (BEPS) project: the new directive would impose legally binding obligations upon Member States to incorporate the conclusions of Action 2 on hybrid mismatches, Action 3 on CFC rules, and Action 4 on interest deductibility.[167] Yet, even if the proposed directive was reportedly aimed at cross-border practices, in the framework of BEPs, some of the proposed rules had a broader focus, including the proposed EU GAAR, which would apply both to domestic and cross-border situations. According to the Commission, the key aim was to limit tax competition and ensure a level playing field: national GAARs might make certain Member States less attractive than those without a GAAR, or with a less strict GAAR,[168] an issue often designated as the early adopters problem;[169]

[163] F Debelva and J Luts, 'The General Anti-Abuse Rule of the Parent–Subsidiary Directive' (2015) 55 *European Taxation* 223; and D Weber, 'The New Common Minimum Anti-Abuse Rule in the EU Parent–Subsidiary Directive: Background, Impact, Applicability, Purpose and Effect' (2016) 44 *Intertax* 98.

[164] Freedman, 'The UK GAAR' (n 141). Similarly, M de Wilde, 'The ATAD's GAAR: A Pandora's Box?' in P Pistone and D Weber (eds), *The Implementation of Anti-BEPS Rules in the EU: A Comprehensive Study* (Amsterdam, IBFD, 2018).

[165] Case C-103/09, *Weald Leasing*, ECLI:EU:C:2010:804. See also de la Feria and Silva Costa (n 69).

[166] European Commission, 'Proposal for a Council Directive laying down rules against tax avoidance practices that directly affect the functioning of the internal market' COM(2016) 26 final.

[167] A Cédelle, 'The EU Anti-Avoidance Directive: a UK Perspective' [2016] *BTR* 490. See also R de la Feria, 'Harmonising Anti-Tax Avoidance Rules' (2017) 3 *EC Tax Review* 140.

[168] G Sinfield, 'The *Halifax* principle as a universal GAAR for tax in the EU' [2011] *BTR* 235; T Lyons, 'The financial crisis, tax avoidance and an EU GAAR' [2013] *BTR* 111; and T Franz, 'The General Anti-Abuse Rule Proposed by the European Commission' (2015) 43 *Intertax* 660.

[169] Cédelle (n 167).

an EU GAAR would therefore ensure that national GAARs applied uniformly within the Union and vis-à-vis third countries.

Although EU harmonisation within direct taxation has traditionally been slow, with proposals lingering for years on the EU policy agenda, the ATAD was adopted merely six months after it was proposed. The speed at which the proposal was approved is undoubtedly symptomatic of the trend towards, and political momentum behind, the introduction of new general anti-tax avoidance mechanisms,[170] but it is also indicative of how little scrutiny its provisions were subject to. From a technical perspective, although, the ATAD was not automatically accepted, and the final text does reflect some political compromise, the EU GAAR, as set out in Article 6 of the ATAD, is said to have been mostly settled as from the start of the negotiations,[171] and it reads, as follows:

1. For the purposes of calculating the corporate tax liability, a Member State shall ignore an arrangement or a series of arrangements which, having been put into place for the main purpose or one of the main purposes of obtaining a tax advantage that defeats the object or purpose of the applicable tax law, are not genuine having regard to all relevant facts and circumstances. An arrangement may comprise more than one step or part.
2. For the purposes of paragraph 1, an arrangement or a series thereof shall be regarded as non-genuine to the extent that they are not put into place for valid commercial reasons which reflect economic reality.
3. Where arrangements or a series thereof are ignored in accordance with paragraph 1, the tax liability shall be calculated in accordance with national law.

The speed of approval has also resulted in concerns being raised over the lack of scrutiny, namely comprehensive technical discussions, and an impact assessment, to which the new EU GAAR was subject.[172] From a constitutional perspective, questions have also been raised over its compatibility with the EU principles of conferral of powers, subsidiarity and proportionality, on the basis that the Directive was not necessary in order to ensure the effective functioning of the internal market.[173] Whilst the argument is not necessarily convincing, as the concept of the internal market, as devolved by the CJEU since *Titanium Dioxide*,[174] includes elimination of distortions to competition, which lack of harmonisation of anti-avoidance rules does arguably cause, the matter merited, nevertheless, higher scrutiny.

B. EU GAAP Versus EU GAAR

The introduction of the GAAR in the EU legal system raises various questions over its interaction with the principle of prohibition of abuse of EU law, in its role as EU

[170] ibid.

[171] A Rigaut, 'Anti-Avoidance Directive (2016/1164): New EU Policy Horizons' (2016) 56 *European Taxation* 502.

[172] de Broe and Beckers (n 75); and Cédelle (n 167).

[173] I Lazarov and S Govind, 'Carpet-Bombing Tax Avoidance in Europe: Examining the Validity of the ATAD Under EU Law' (2019) 47 *Intertax* 852.

[174] For a detailed analysis of the Court's case law on the concept of internal market, see R de la Feria, 'VAT and the EU Internal Market: The Paradoxes of Harmonisation' in D Weber (ed), *Traditional and Alternative Routes to European Tax Integration* (Amsterdam, IBFD, 2010).

GAAP. According to the explanatory memorandum to the ATAD, the new EU GAAR is 'designed to reflect the artificiality tests of the CJEU', and thus the stated objective is clearly one of (partial) codification: the EU general principle of prohibition of abuse of law, the EU GAAP, is codified for direct taxation purposes. The first question which arises, therefore, is whether, as implied by the Commission, this is truly a codification act. For those that argued that the principle of prohibition of abuse of law did not constitute a general principle of EU law, but merely an interpretative principle, which did not apply in the absence of national provisions, and did not constitute therefore an EU GAAP, the new EU GAAR goes beyond codification, significantly enlarging the scope of application of the principle to (now) apply to domestic situations.[175] Significantly, this seems also to be the opinion of Advocate General Kokott, as expressed in *N Luxembourg 1*.[176] Yet, for those who argued that the principle of prohibition of abuse of law already displayed the characteristics of a general principle of EU law, and thus applicable to domestic situations, and in the absence of national provisions, the new EU GAAR constitutes indeed a partial codification of the principle for the purposes of direct taxation.

The question is then, what does codification add, and how should the interaction between the EU GAAP and the EU GAAR be conceptualised? The main advantage of codification is legal certainty: whilst before there was a debate on whether the EU principle of prohibition of abuse of law should apply characterised as an EU GAAP, applied to non-harmonised areas of direct taxation, in the absence of domestic provisions, now this debate has been settled by statute; equally, where there was debate about the main elements of the EU GAAP, now those elements (test, consequences) are set in hard law. It is also noteworthy that this evolution from GAAP to GAAR is not unique to the EU, and there are significant parallels between the EU process and that in the UK – or in the US.[177] At the time of the decision in *Halifax*, it was often stated that the judgment was to the EU legal system, what *Ramsay* had been for the UK one,[178] and whilst there are significant differences, not least the fact that, as opposed to the principle of prohibition of abuse of law, the so-called *Ramsay* principle has been confirmed by the courts as merely an interpretative principle, or a principle of statutory construction,[179]

[175] de Broe and Beckers (n 75); Franz (n 168); C Brokelind, 'Legal Issues in Respect of the Changes to the Parent–Subsidiary Directive as Follow-Up to the BEPS Project' (2015) 43 *Intertax* 816; and G Bizioli, 'Taxing EU Fundamental Freedoms Seriously: Does the Anti-Tax Avoidance Directive Take Precedent Over the Single Market?' (2017) 26 *EC Tax Review* 167.

[176] I Lazarov, '(Un)Tangling Tax Avoidance Under the Interest and Royalties Directive: The Opinion of AG Kokott in *N Luxembourg 1*' (2018) 46 *Intertax* 873.

[177] For a detailed analysis of the process in the UK, see Freedman, 'GAAR as a process' (n 150); for an overview of the US process see R Prebble and J Prebble, 'General Anti-Avoidance Rules and the Rule of Law' in N Hashimzade and Y Epifantseva (eds), *The Routledge Companion to Tax Avoidance Research* (London, Routledge, 2017), citing also C Pietruszkiewicz, 'Economic Substance and the Standard of Review' (2009) 60 *Alaska Law Review* 339, and A Likhovski, 'The Duke and the Lady: Helvering v Gregory and the History of Tax Avoidance Adjudication' (2004) 25 *Cardozo Law Review* 953.

[178] *WT Ramsay Ltd v IRC* [1982] AC 300. See R Lyal, '*Cadbury Schweppes* and Abuse: Comments' in R de la Feria and S Vogenauer (eds), *Prohibition of Abuse of Law: A New General Principle of EU Law?* (Oxford, Hart Publishing, 2011).

[179] J Freedman, 'Interpreting Tax Statutes: Tax Avoidance and the Intention of Parliament' (2007) 123 *LQR* 53; and M Gammie, 'The Judicial Approach to Avoidance: Some Reflections on *BMBF* and *SPI*' in J Avery

there is some truth to this statement. Both the *Ramsay* principle and the EU principle of prohibition of abuse of law are jurisprudentially constructed GAAPs, broadly developed to address similar concerns, and applying a similarly criteria / test. Despite the different internal market dynamics, namely the need to ensure a level playing field, the approval of the UK GAAR speaks to a large extent to the same concerns as the approval of the EU GAAR: with *Ramsay* confirmed as an interpretative principle, its effectiveness was, by nature, limited by the wording and context of any given provision; and whilst a case could, and was, made since *Halifax* that the EU principle of prohibition of abuse of law did not display the characteristics of a mere interpretative principle, doubts remained in some quarters, which the Commission was clearly keen to remove.

The partial codification in the form of the EU GAAR does not, however, alter the nature of the EU principle of prohibition of abuse of law as a general principle of EU law, with all constitutional consequences which that characterisation entails. In particular, the EU GAAP will continue to hold the two key functions of any general principle of EU law, namely as a default provision, and as an instrument of judicial review. As a gap filler, the principle will continue to hold its relevance despite the new EU GAAR, acting as a default mechanism, applicable not only to areas outside taxation, but in any taxation matter that may possibly fall outside the scope of the EU GAAR, under the standard *lex specialis derogat legi generali* rule.[180] As an instrument of judicial review, the principle will – in theory – be the standard against which secondary legislation, either domestic or EU, can be assessed. This function is particularly important in the context of the new EU GAAR: the principle of prohibition of abuse of law, as a general principle of EU law, constitutes primary legislation, and thus, under the EU hierarchy of norms, the GAAR must comply with it.[181] Yet, despite the express references to the CJEU case law in the ATAD proposal, there are not insignificant differences between that case law and the new EU GAAR.

The first key difference between the principle of prohibition of abuse of law as a GAAP, and the new GAAR, is the relevance afforded to 'economic reality', which from passing references, seemingly *obiter dictum*, in the case law,[182] is now elevated into one of the key criteria for assessing artificiality, without any guidance as to its meaning. The second, probably more significant, difference is the use of 'main purpose or one of the main purposes' as another key criterion for assessing artificiality. This is a very different artificiality threshold from that used by the Court in direct taxation cases, where the criterion under the principle of prohibition of abuse of law has tended to be 'wholly artificial transactions', a much higher artificiality threshold. Why the preference for a lower threshold in the new GAAR one can only speculate: a lower threshold is used in VAT, where the standard artificiality test has been, since *Part Service*, the 'principle aim', and the new SAARs in the PSD and the Merger Directive also include a lower threshold, so it is possible that some contamination across tax areas was at play. In any event, such

Jones, P Harris and D Oliver (eds), *Comparative Perspectives on Revenue Law: Essays in Honour of John Tiley* (Cambridge, Cambridge University Press, 2008) 25.

[180] On the application of this rule in the context of anti-avoidance mechanisms, see also Zarnoza and Baez (n 160).

[181] As currently pointed out by Lazarov and Govind (n 173).

[182] See discussion above on the Court's references to economic reality and normal commercial operations.

differences raise the question as to whether the GAAR could be tested against – and ultimately be regarded as incompatible with – the GAAP.

This risks of judicial review of the GAAR appears to have been one of the reasons behind Advocate General Kokott's opinion in *N Luxembourg 1*, denying the principle of prohibition of abuse of law the status of general principle of EU law, directly applicable in the absence of relevant domestic rules.[183] Others have highlighted the possibility of such a review under the EU hierarchy of norms, welcoming the potential scrutiny.[184] It is indeed true that, under the EU hierarchy of norms, the new GAAR can indeed be subject to review against general principles of EU law, including the principle of prohibition of abuse of law. This constitutional truth, however, ignores the practical reality that, within taxation, the Court has been extremely reluctant to review secondary EU legislation in light of EU primary legislation, be it treaty provisions or general principles of EU law.[185] Whether the Court will depart from this so-called tax exceptionalism, and assess the compatibility of the GAAR with the GAAP, only time will tell – but on the basis of its previous case law, the opposite seems rather more likely, namely that the GAAP will evolve in line with the GAAR.

V. Conclusion

In the last two decades, general anti-avoidance mechanisms have become increasingly popular around the globe. Yet this global trend hides significant variation: anti-avoidance mechanisms are not uniform, but rather differ significantly in design, function, scope and choice of legal instrument. Whilst there is now significant literature on the design of specific general anti-avoidance mechanisms, such as GAARs, limited attention has been paid to how these mechanisms actually develop over time, and to how they interact with each other. The aim of this chapter is to start filling this gap, by considering the process of co-constitutive development of general anti-tax avoidance mechanisms within the EU: identifying the various stages of legal principle formation, and its manifestation within taxation as a jurisprudential GAAP; tracing the natural process that led to the eventual approval of the GAAR; and finally considering the interaction between these different types of general anti-avoidance mechanisms.

The EU principle of prohibition of abuse of law has been developing within the jurisprudence of the CJEU, through a co-constitutive process of reverberation, since the mid-1970s. Despite its wider scope of application, it is argued that within taxation the principle has assumed the role for the last 15 years as a de facto GAAP, with the characteristics of a general legal principle, rather than merely an interpretative one. It is further asserted that the approval of an EU GAAR constitutes a natural progression in the development of general anti-tax avoidance mechanisms within the EU, which is

[183] Case C-115/16, *N Luxembourg 1*, ECLI:EU:C:2018:143.

[184] Lazarov and Govind (n 173); and Lazarov (n 176).

[185] de la Feria, 'VAT and the EU Internal Market' (n 174); and R de la Feria and D Doukas, 'The Constitutional Role of the CJEU in Taxation Post-Harmonisation' (Workshop on Fiscal Federalism in the EU, Cambridge University, July 2017).

identical to that witnessed in other jurisdictions around the globe: from the jurisprudential creation of the EU GAAP, to the eventual approval of the EU GAAR. It is argued moreover that this progression is not only natural, but also a positive one, so long as the EU GAAR is conceptualised as a partial codification of the EU GAAP, and that its application follows the standard hierarchy of legal norms rules. If so, the importance of the EU general principle of prohibition of abuse of law does not decrease, either generally – as its scope of application continues to expand to new areas of law – or in its role as GAAP, as it will continue to fulfil its role as gap filler, and as a (potential) instrument of judicial review. The coexistence of an EU GAAR and a general principle GAAP thus present significant advantages, increasing legal certainty, whilst maintaining the flexibility that naturally results from jurisprudential constructs.

This chapter seeks to make a catalysing contribution to the development of a general theory of anti-avoidance mechanisms. Its ambition has been to stimulate much needed tracing of the global development and spread of anti-avoidance rules; identification of types, common patterns, and trends in their origin, design, function and scope; establishment of principles for their interplay, both within and between jurisdictions; and examination of legitimacy concerns. Only through such research will this global trend be properly understood, in its full legal complexity.

9

The Concept of Abuse of Law in European Taxation: A Methodological and Constitutional Perspective

WOLFGANG SCHÖN

I. Introduction: The Danish Directive Shopping Cases

'Abuse of law'[1] is a concept omnipresent both in the area of taxation and in the area of European law. It comes as no surprise that the jurisprudence of the European Court of Justice (the Court) and the accompanying literature are full of cases where tax authorities have rejected a taxpayer's position as 'abusive'.[2] This is mirrored by a wealth of judgments and rulings delivered by domestic courts, tribunals and fiscal authorities, which deal with the concept of 'abuse of law' under the national fiscal legislation[3] of all Member States of the European Union[4] and under international

[1] The varying terminology has been laid out by Advocate General Bobek in Case C-251/16, *Cussens*, ECLI:EU:C:2017:648, opinion of 7 September 2017, paras 23–31. For a critical assessment of the myriad of concepts being consistently conflated in this context see C Öner, 'Is Tax Avoidance the Theory of Everything in Tax Law? A Terminological Analysis of EU Legislation and Case Law' (2019) 27 *EC Tax Review* 96.

[2] A Saydé, *Abuse of Law and Regulation of the Internal Market* (Oxford, Hart Publishing, 2014); D Weber, *Tax Avoidance and the EC Treaty Freedoms: A Study of the Limitations under European Law to the Prevention of Tax Avoidance* (The Hague, Kluwer Law International, 2005); R Guski, 'The re-entry paradox: Abuse of EU law' (2018) 24 *European Law Journal* 422; S Kamanabrou, 'Abuse of law in the context of EU law' (2018) 43 *European Law Review* 534; A Lenaerts, 'The Role of the Principle Fraus Omnia Corrumpit in the European Union: A Possible Evolution Towards a General Principle of Law?' (2013) 32 *Yearbook of European Law* 460, 485 et seq; K Lenaerts, 'Le juge d l'Union, promoteur de la lute contre l'abus de droit en matière fiscale' (2019) 6 *Revue Générale du Contentieux Fiscal* 433; S Vogenauer, 'The Prohibition of Abuse of Law: An Emerging General Principle of EU Law' in R De la Feria and S Vogenauer (eds), *Prohibition of Abuse of Law: A New General Principle of EU Law?* (Oxford, Hart Publishing, 2011).

[3] For a recent analysis of the UK GAAR in the international context see J Freedman, 'The UK General Anti-Avoidance Rule: Transplants and Lessons' (2019) 73 *Bulletin for International Taxation* 332.

[4] A comparative view in the area of taxation is presented by J Freedman (ed), *Beyond Boundaries: Developing Approaches to Tax Avoidance and Tax Risk Management* (Oxford, Oxford University Centre for Business Taxation, 2008); M Lang et al (eds), *General Anti-Avoidance Rules (GAARs) – A Key Element of Tax Systems in the Post-BEPS World* (Amsterdam, IBFD, 2016); C Osterloh-Konrad, *Steuerumgehung – eine rechtsvergleichende und rechtstheoretische Analyse* (Berlin, Mohr Siebeck, 2020); P Rosenblatt and ME Tron, 'Anti-avoidance measures of general nature and scope – GAAR and other Rules, General Report' in (2018) 13a *Cahiers de droit fiscal international* 11; B Arnold, 'A comparison of statutory anti-avoidance rules and judicial

tax treaties.[5] In recent years, this ongoing stream of judicial output has been complemented by efforts at the level of OECD and the European institutions to require states to fight abusive structures under a common heading. Today, Action 6 of the (Base Erosion and Profit Shifting) BEPS Action Plan[6] and Article 6 of the Anti-Tax Avoidance Directive[7] mandate tax legislators to introduce provisions to establish a common concept of tax avoidance fighting a large number of cross-border structures established by multinational enterprises.[8] Back in 2008, in the *Festschrift* for Professor John Tiley, this author had the pleasure to present a first take on 'Abuse of Rights and European tax law'.[9] He is delighted to have the opportunity to follow up on that earlier work in this *Festschrift* celebrating the retirement of Professor Judith Freedman who next to John Tiley represents the best tradition of taxation law in the United Kingdom.

When it comes to the definition and application of the concept of 'abuse of law' in situations covered by EU (tax) law, two major issues stand out. The first issue is of a methodological and constitutional nature. It refers to the legal basis for this concept under European law, the methodological prerequisites for its application, its rank within the hierarchy of European law (primary versus secondary law) and its direct or indirect effect on domestic law (in particular domestic law implementing European law). The second issue refers to the substantive scope and content of the concept, the objective and subjective elements of its meaning, in particular whether it should be understood in a narrow fashion (confined to artificial arrangements solely established with a view to avoid taxes) or in a broader fashion (including real arrangements which might (also) fulfil a commercial purpose).

This chapter is devoted to the first issue: the role and rank of the concept of 'abuse of law' within the institutional framework of European taxation. This is a burning issue, given the fact that the Court has substantially expanded the impact of this concept in recent years. The Court's recurring statement that 'European law cannot be relied upon for abusive or fraudulent ends'[10] has by now been recognised as a

general anti-avoidance doctrines as a means of controlling tax avoidance: Which is better? (What would John Tiley think?)' in J Avery Jones, P Harris and D Oliver (eds), *Comparative Perspectives on Revenue Law: Essays in Honour of John Tiley* (Cambridge, Cambridge University Press, 2008).

[5] D Duff, 'Tax Treaty Abuse and the Principal Purpose Test: Parts 1 and 2' (2018) 66 *Canadian Tax Journal* 619, 947; see most recently *Conseil d'État, Re Verdannet* (no 396954), Judgment of 25 October 2017, (2019) 20 *International Tax Law Reports* 832; M Sadowsky, 'France: Tax Treaty Abuse as *Fraus Legis*' in E Kemmeren et al (eds), *Tax Treaty Case Law around the Globe 2018* (Amsterdam, IBFD, 2019).

[6] Duff (n 5) 948–1006; A Martin Jimenez, 'Tax Avoidance and Aggressive Tax Planning as an International Standard – BEPS and the "New" Standards of (Legal and Illegal) Tax Avoidance' in AP Dourado (ed), *Tax Avoidance Revisited in the EU BEPS Context* (Amsterdam, IBFD, 2017) 25, 48–59.

[7] Council Directive (EU) 2016/1164 of 12 July 2016 laying down rules against tax avoidance practices that directly affect the functioning of the internal market [2016] OJ L193/1; for an overview see A Cédelle, 'The EU Anti-Tax Avoidance Directive: A UK Perspective' [2016] *BTR* 490.

[8] The notion of 'tax avoidance' in the BEPS context is laid out in AP Dourado (ed), *Tax Avoidance Revisited in the EU BEPS Context* (Amsterdam, IBFD, 2017).

[9] W Schön, 'Abuse of Rights and European tax law' in J Avery Jones, P Harris and D Oliver (eds), *Comparative Perspectives on Revenue Law: Essays in Honour of John Tiley* (Cambridge, Cambridge University Press, 2008).

[10] Case C-255/02, *Halifax*, ECLI:EU:C:2006:121, judgment of 21 February 2006, para 68; Case C-196/04, *Cadbury Schweppes*, ECLI:EU:C:2006:544, judgment of 12 September 2006, para 35; Case C-321/05, *Kofoed*, ECLI:EU:C:2007:408, judgment of 5 July 2007, para 38; Joined Cases C-131/13, C-163/13, C-164/13, *Italmoda*, ECLI:EU:C:2014:2455, judgment of 18 December 2014, paras 43, 46, 56; Case C-356/15, *Commission v Belgium*,

'general principle of European law' with sweeping consequences for the practice of European taxation. According to the Court, Member States are no longer just allowed to fight abusive behaviour – they are obliged to do so. As regards substance, a narrow reading of the concept as advocated in earlier judgments has over time given way to a broad-brush 'general' understanding, permeating both the application of the fundamental freedoms and the directives in the area of taxation. Last but not least, the existence or non-existence of specific anti-abuse legislation under European law or domestic law hardly seems to play a role any more: neither does the lack of such provisions prevent the courts and the tax authorities from rejecting the taxpayer's claims nor does the existence of such explicit provisions pre-empt the concurring or even overriding application of the emerging general principle.

This has become visible most clearly in the widely anticipated Danish directive shopping cases decided in early 2019:[11]

> The claimants are Danish companies owned by Luxemburg parent companies whose shareholders are resident outside the European Union. The Luxemburg companies fulfill the conditions for a withholding tax exemption on outbound dividends and interest payments required under the relevant provisions of Danish law. These national provisions implement the withholding tax exemptions granted for intra-European cross-border participations under the Parent–Subsidiary Directive[12] and the Interest Royalty Directive.[13]
>
> Nevertheless, the Danish tax authorities reject the parent companies' claims for withholding tax relief on cross-border dividends. They contend that the Luxemburg companies have been established to circumvent the material requirements of these directives. The taxpayers argue that this is not a valid ground for rejecting the claims as the Danish legislator has not made use of the authorizations laid down in Art 1 par 2 (now Art 1 par 4) of the Parent–Subsidiary Directive and Art 5 of the Interest Royalty Directive, which allow Member

ECLI:EU:C:2018:555, judgment of 11 July 2018, para 99; Case C-251/16, *Cussens*, ECLI:EU:C:2017:881, judgment of 22 November 2017, para 27; Joined Cases C-116/16 and C-117/16, *T Danmark*, ECLI:EU:C:2019:135, judgment of 26 February 2019, paras 70, 90; Joined Cases C-115/16, C-118/16, C-119/16, C-299/16, *N Luxembourg 1*, ECLI:EU:C:2019:134, judgment of 26 February 2019, para 96.

[11] *T Danmark*, judgment (n 10); *N Luxembourg 1*, judgment (n 10); see PA Hernández González-Barreda, 'Holding Companies and Leveraged Buy-Outs in the European Union Following BEPS: Beneficial Ownership, Abuse of Law and the Single Taxation Principle' (2019) 59 *European Taxation* 409; CFE ECJ Task Force, 'Opinion Statement ECJ–TF 2/2019 on the ECJ Decisions of 26 February in *N Luxembourg I et al* (Joined Cases C-115/16, C-116/16, C-119/16 and C-299/16) and *T Danmark et al* (Joined Cases C-116/16 and C-117/17), Concerning the "Beneficial Ownership" Requirement and the Anti-Abuse Principle in the Company Tax Directives' (2019) 59 *European Taxation* 487; A Linn and B Pignot, *Unionsrechtliche Bedeutung des Nutzungsberechtigten, Internationale Wirtschaftsbriefe* (2019) 386–92; T O'Shea, '*N Luxembourg 1*: CJEU Finds Directive Benefits Can Be Denied in Abusive Situations' (22 April 2019) *Tax Notes International* 335; LC van Hulten and JJAM Korving, 'Svig og Misbrug: The Danish Anti-Abuse Cases' (2019) 47 *Intertax* 793; J McLoughlin, 'EU Law Sufficient to Deny Tax Breaks in Cases of Abuse, CJEU Says' (4 March 2019) *Tax Notes International* 978; D Ury, 'La definition de l'abus de droit "non-authentique" par la CJUE' (2019) 6 *Bulletin Francis Lefebvre* 341; N de Boynes, 'La CJUE donne son éclairage sur la notion d'abus de droit' (2019) 21 *Revue de droit fiscal* 44.

[12] Council Directive 2011/96/EU of 30 November 2011 on the common system of taxation applicable in the case of parent companies and subsidiaries of different Member States [2011] OJ L345/08 as amended by Council Directive (EU) 2015/121 of 27 January 2015 amending Directive 2011/96/EU on the common system of taxation applicable in the case of parent companies and subsidiaries of different Member States [2015] OJ L21/1.

[13] Council Directive 2003/49/EC of 3 June 2003 on a common system of taxation applicable to interest and royalty payments made between associated companies of different Member States [2003] OJ L157/49.

States to introduce fiscal provisions against abusive transactions. The Court nevertheless holds that the Danish authorities are not only entitled, but obliged to reject the taxpayers' claims in order to give the general anti-abuse principle under EU law full effect, thus letting the fabric of both the directive and domestic law completely out of the picture.

These judgments are built on a series of earlier decisions in the context of VAT starting in 2006 with the celebrated *Halifax* judgment.[14] In this case, the Court emphasised the substantive impact of the general notion of 'abuse of law' in the area of VAT notwithstanding a lack of an explicit legal basis both under the Directive and the relevant domestic legislation. In a series of later judgments, in particular in *Italmoda*[15] and *Cussens*,[16] the Court established step by step the sweeping role and impact of a general principle that no one can rely on EU law for fraudulent or abusive purposes in the area covered by the VAT directives.

When it comes to secondary EU legislation on direct taxation, on the other hand, the Court had so far limited the impact of the concept of abuse of law to cases covered by specific provisions under the relevant directives – Article 1(2) now Article 1(4) of the Parent–Subsidiary Directive and Article 11(1) now Article 15(1) of the Merger Directive – as these provisions require specific and voluntary implementation by national legislators and judges.[17] Against this background, in 2007, the Court questioned in *Kofoed* the Danish tax authorities' request to apply Article 11(1) of the Merger Directive to a potentially abusive arrangement given the alleged lack of anti-abuse legislation under Danish tax law.[18]

In her two opinions delivered in the above-mentioned recent Danish cases, Advocate General Kokott referred to this strand of jurisprudence when she defended the view that the anti-abuse provisions under Article 1(2) of the Parent–Subsidiary Directive and Article 5 of the Interest Royalty Directive require explicit or implicit implementation under Danish law.[19] But in their judgments the European judges decided that neither the elective character of the anti-abuse provisions under the Directive nor the evident lack of specific or general anti-abuse clauses under Danish law mattered at all. In the Court's view, the paramount nature of the general anti-abuse principle under European law overrides both the limitations of the

[14] *Halifax*, judgment (n 10) paras 67–74; on the 'road to *Halifax*' see R de la Feria, 'Prohibition of Abuse of (Community) Law – The Creation of a New General Principle of EC Law Through Tax' (2008) 45 *Common Market Law Review* (2008) 395, 419.

[15] *Italmoda*, judgment (n 10) paras 54–59.

[16] *Cussens*, judgment (n 10) paras 25–44.

[17] Case C-6/16, *Eqiom*, ECLI:EU:C:2017:641, judgment of 7 September 2017, paras 24–30; Joined Cases C-504/16 and C-613/16, *Deister Holding*, ECLI:EU:C:2017:1009, judgment of 20 December 2017, paras 51–61; in 2015, the Parent–Subsidiary Directive was amended in order to introduce an obligation for the Member States to combat abusive arrangements (Council Directive (EU) 2015/121 of 27 January 2015 amending Directive 2011/96/EU on the common system of taxation applicable in the case of parent companies and subsidiaries of different Member States [2015] OJ L 21/1); F Debelva and J Luts, 'The General Anti-Abuse Rule of the Parent–Subsidiary Directive' (2015) 55 *European Taxation* 223.

[18] *Kofoed*, judgment (n 10) paras 40–46.

[19] Advocate General Kokott in Case C-116/16, *T Danmark*, ECLI:EU:C:2018:144, opinion of 1 March 2018, paras 94–100; AG Kokott in Case C-115/16, *N Luxembourg, 1* ECLI:EU:C:2018:143, opinion of 1 March 2018, paras 98–104; I Lazarov, '(Un)Tangling Tax Avoidance Under the Interest and Royalties Directive: The Opinion of AG Kokott in *N Luxembourg 1*' (2018) 46 *Intertax* 873; van Hulten and Korving (n 11) 797.

Directive itself and of national legislation.[20] This striking statement should give rise to an analysis of the rank and role of the general anti-abuse principle both from a methodological and from a constitutional perspective.

II. The Legal Basis of General Principles

The notion of general principles is well entrenched in European Law.[21] Starting in the early 1970s, the Court has continuously identified a fair number of general principles which are derived both from the common constitutional traditions of the Member States and from the overall set-up of primary and secondary EU law.[22] To start with, all Member States have recognised general principles of law being a natural part of their own legal orders. Their creation is part of the powers of the judiciary, which derives those general principles from the overall panorama of national legislation and jurisprudence. In the European treaties, Article 340(2) of the Treaty on the Functioning of the European Union (TFEU) explicitly refers to these national traditions when it states:

> In the case of non-contractual liability, the Union shall, in accordance with the *general principles common to the laws of the Member States*, make good any damage caused by its institutions or by its servants in the performance of their duties (emphasis added).

The most prominent examples for general principles 'discovered' by the Court are the fundamental rights awarded to all European citizens, protecting them against undue interference by the European institutions.[23] These fundamental rights have been developed by the Court over a number of decades in a broad line of jurisprudence building both on the common constitutional traditions of the Member States, international treaties and European law itself. Finally, they made their way into the Treaty on the European Union (TEU). Today, Article 6(3) TEU reads:

> Fundamental rights, as guaranteed by the European Convention for the Protection of Human Rights and Fundamental Freedoms and as they result from the constitutional traditions common to the Member States, shall constitute *general principles of the Union's law* (emphasis added).

While Article 6(3) TEU presents a clear example for a major set of general principles of EU law, it is by no means exclusive in nature. In recent years, the Court has boldly moved into ever more areas where general principles seem to exist. These principles can be of a substantive or procedural character. To give two examples: in the widely discussed *Mangold* line of judgments, the Court established the material principle,

[20] *T Danmark*, judgment (n 10) paras 77, 83, 89; *N Luxembourg 1*, judgment (n 10) paras 98, 104, 111; concurring K Lenaerts (n 2) 446–48.

[21] T Tridimas, *The General Principles of EU Law*, 2nd edn (Oxford, Oxford University Press, 2006); K Lenaerts and JA Gutiérrez-Fons, 'The Constitutional Allocation of Powers and General Principles of EU Law' (2010) 47 *Common Market Law Review* 1629.

[22] Tridimas, *The General Principles of EU Law* (n 21) 7 et seq.

[23] Case 11/70, *Internationale Handelsgesellschaft*, ECLI:EU:C:1970:114, judgment of 17 December 1970, paras 3–4; Case 4/73, *Nold*, ECLI:EU:C:1974:51, judgment of 14 May 1974, paras 12–15.

that age discrimination is per se prohibited under European law, and enforced this principle vis-a-vis national legislation which explicitly allowed employers to distinguish between junior and senior employees.[24] This line of judgments shows some resemblance to the current jurisprudence on abuse of law in direct and indirect tax matters as the Court not only declared this general principle of non-discrimination to supersede both the limitations of secondary EU law and conflicting domestic legislation. The Court also held in *Mangold* that this principle per se constrains the exercise of rights by private actors.[25] Another strand of judgments, which has recently been extended to the fiscal area, concerns the various 'rights of defence' as regards administrative procedures initiated by the European institutions and procedures under national law in harmonised fields.[26]

Taken as a whole, the creation of general principles of European law has not been viewed as ultra vires as such. It is true that according to the principle of 'conferral' laid down in Articles 4(1), 5(1)–(2), and 13(2) TEU neither the European Union at large nor the European institutions in particular may assume competences not conferred upon them under the European treaties. But as long as the Court's jurisprudence stays within the legal areas covered by the European treaties and as long as the Court cautiously seeks to employ a traditional methodological toolbox when creating general principles, even critical observers like the German Constitutional Court do not see a reason to fundamentally reject the creation and enforcement of general principles by the European Court of Justice.[27]

III. The Rank of General Principles in the European Constitutional Order

What is the impact of a general principle of European law? In *Kücükdeveci*, Advocate General Bot summarised its effect in a case concerning the prohibition on age discrimination:

> As a general principle of Community law, that principle performs several functions. It permits the Community judicature to fill gaps, which might appear in secondary legislation.

[24] Case C-144/04, *Mangold*, ECLI:EU:C:2005:709, judgment of 22 November 2005, paras 74–78; Case C-555/07, *Kücükdeveci*, ECLI:EU:C:2010:21, judgment of 19 January 2010, paras 19–27; for a critical view see T Tridimas, 'Horizontal Effects of General Principles: Bold Rulings and Fine Distinctions' in U Bernitz, X Groussot and F Schulyok (eds), *General Principles of EU Law and European Private Law* (The Hague, Kluwer Law International, 2013); M Herdegen, 'General Principles of EU Law – the Methodological Challenge' in U Bernitz, J Nergelius and C Cardner (eds), *General Principles of EC Law in a Process of Development* (Alphen aan den Rijn, Kluwer Law International, 2008).

[25] The impact of 'general principles of law' on the legal relations between private citizens has been extensively reviewed by Advocate General Cruz Villalon in his opinion of 18 July 2013, Case C-176/12, *Association de médiation sociale*, ECLI:EU:C:2013:491, paras 28–42; see also Lenaerts and Gutiérrez-Fons (n 21) 1641.

[26] Case C-298/16, *Ispas*, ECLI:EU:C:2017:843, judgment of 9 November 2017, paras 25–39; see also Case C-617/10, *Akerberg Fransson*, ECLI:EU:C:2013:105, judgment of 26 February 2013, paras 17–23; Tridimas, *The General Principles of EU Law* (n 21) 370.

[27] Case 2 BvR 2661/06, *Honeywell*, German Constitutional Court, judgment of 6 July 2010, paras 58–66.

> It is also an instrument of interpretation clarifying the meaning and scope of provisions of Community law, and a means of reviewing the validity of Community acts.[28]

The last mentioned function – 'reviewing the validity of Community acts' – points to a dimension, which is not self-evident when we address the concept of general principles under European law. The Court is consistently of the opinion that general principles of European law automatically share the primary rank of the European treaties.[29] Thus, they can be relied upon to call into question the compatibility of lower-ranking legislative and administrative acts, which have been issued by the European institutions.[30]

This analysis holds certainly true where the Court derives these general principles from the overall framework of the treaties themselves, namely the TEU and the TFEU. It is also sensible to award the rank of primary EU law to those principles which can be traced back to the constitutional traditions of the Member States and which are meant to protect European citizens and businesses against overly intrusive legislative and administrative acts issued by the European institutions. Both sources point to a constitutional character of these general principles, which should be able to override lower-ranking acts of law. In this vein, the fundamental rights as established by the Court and today recognised under Article 6(3) TEU clearly deserve to rank above secondary European law like directives or regulations. The political background for this line of jurisprudence taken by the Court is quite evident: the Court wants to ensure that secondary European law can be reviewed in the context of primary European law on the basis of overarching principles in order to avoid interference by constitutional courts established by the Member States.[31]

Contrary to current Court practice, these findings do not necessarily imply that all general principles of European law automatically enjoy the full force of primary law.[32] Rather, the opposite is true. As a starting point we have to recognise that all general principles are derived from a given specific context of legislation and jurisprudence. Consequently, the rank of the principles emerging from this individual context should reflect the respective level of legislation. Thus, it is sensible to assume that there are general principles under primary EU law, which have emerged from the European treaties and the constitutional traditions of the Member States. But this

[28] AG Bot in Case C-555/07, *Kücükdeveci*, ECLI:EU:C:2009:429, opinion of 7 July 2009, para 80; A Lenaerts (n 2) 463; Tridimas, *The General Principles of EU Law* (n 21) 29–35.

[29] *Kücükdeveci*, judgment (n 24) paras 19–27; Case C-101/08, *Audiolux and Others*, ECLI:EU:C:2009:626, judgment of 15 October 2009, para 63; Lenaerts and Gutiérrez-Fons (n 21) 1669; A Lenaerts (n 2) 463; J Temple Lang, 'Emerging European General Principles in Private Law' in U Bernitz, X Groussot and F Schulyok (eds), *General Principles of EU Law and European Private Law* (The Hague, Kluwer Law International, 2013) 65–68; A Arnull, 'What is a General Principle of EU Law?' in R de la Feria and S Vogenauer (eds), *Prohibition of Abuse of Law: A New General Principle of EU Law* (Oxford, Hart Publishing, 2011) 12; Lenaerts and Gutiérrez-Fons (n 21) 1647.

[30] Tridimas, *The General Principles of EU Law* (n 21) 50.

[31] *Internationale Handelsgesellschaft* (n 23) paras 3–4; S Douglas-Scott, 'The European Union and Fundamental Rights' in R Schütze and T Tridimas (eds), *Oxford Principles of European Union Law, Vol 1: The European Union Legal Order* (Oxford, Oxford University Press, 2018).

[32] For a cautious view on this matter see S Besson, 'General Principles and Customary Law in the EU Legal Order' in S Vogenauer and S Weatherill (eds), *General Principles of Law: European and Comparative Perspectives* (Oxford, Hart Publishing, 2017) 113.

does not exclude the existence of general principles under secondary EU law, which have their background in the context of directives and regulations.

The fallacy underlying the theory that general principles of EU law always share the rank of the European treaties became evident in the Court's judgment in *Audiolux*, a company law case.[33] In the underlying proceedings before a Luxemburg court, a shareholder in a public company tried to rely on a general principle of equality of shareholders against an action taken by a dominant shareholder. Both Advocate General Trstenjak[34] and the Court[35] approached this case under the assumption that a general principle recognised under EU law must be awarded the constitutional rank of primary EU law. From this starting point they concluded that the threshold for the establishment of such a general principle has to be very high.[36] Accordingly, neither Advocate General Trstenjak nor the Court recognised a general principle of equal treatment of shareholders – notwithstanding the fact that a fair number of directives in the field of company law and capital markets law refer to such a principle. While everybody will accept this specific outcome (namely that there is no 'primary' European principle of equal treatment of shareholders which would even override and invalidate conflicting European legislation), it would have been clearly possible to recognise such a principle at the level of secondary legislation. Such a 'second-tier' general principle would not have the power to invalidate conflicting European legislation but it would have been able to assist the Court and the national judges with the interpretation of existing directives and to fill gaps in the field of company law and capital markets law.[37]

In a similar vein, general principles in other areas of European private law do not necessarily have to be promoted to the rank of the European treaties. In a later case, Advocate General Trstenjak discussed (and dismissed) at length the notion of a general principle concerning employees' rights to unpaid leave[38] – again this should never be a matter of 'constitutional' principles. Rather, these second-tier principles should be regarded as part and parcel of the overall fabric of European private law, which is to a large extent not built on the treaties themselves or the constitutional traditions derived from all Member States but rather emanating from European directives and regulations or from the common core of sub-constitutional statutory law and case law of the Member States.

[33] *Audiolux* (n 29).

[34] AG Trstenjak in Case C-101/08, *Audiolux*, ECLI:EU:C:2009:410, opinion of 30 June 2009, para 81 et seq.

[35] *Audiolux* (n 29) para 63.

[36] Concurring S Weatherill, 'From Myth to Reality: The EU's "New Legal Order" and the Place of General Principles Within It' in S Vogenauer and S Weatherill (eds), *General Principles of Law: European and Comparative Perspectives* (Oxford, Hart Publishing, 2017) 35; *Arnull* (n 29) 18.

[37] J Basedow, '*Mangold, Audiolux* und die allgemeinen Grundsätze des europäischen Privatrecht' in S Grundmann et al (eds), *Festschrift für Klaus Hopt zum 70. Geburtstag*, Vol 1 (Berlin, Walter de Gruyter, 2010) 41; W Schön, 'Allgemeine Rechtsgrundsätze im Europäischen Gesellschaftsrecht' in S Grundmann et al (eds), *Festschrift für Klaus Hopt zum 70. Geburtstag, Vol 1* (Berlin, Walter de Gruyter, 2010) 1349–54; Vogenauer (n 2) 567.

[38] Case C-282/10, *Dominguez*, ECLI:EU:C:2011:559, opinion of 8 June 2011, paras 110–43; see also Case C-176/12, *Association de mediation sociale*, ECLI:EU:C:2014:2, judgment of 15 January 2014, paras 41–48.

We shall see that this analytical shortcut committed by the Court – confusing the general nature of these principles with its constitutional rank in the hierarchy of European norms – also has a destructive impact on the finely tuned balance of European tax law as regards the fight against abusive arrangements.

IV. Principle of Interpretation or Principle of Substantive Law?

When we examine the general principle that rights conferred under European law must not be employed for abusive or fraudulent ends, another major distinction comes to the fore:[39] is this a methodological principle to be applied by courts and authorities when they interpret existing European law? Or is this a self-standing principle of substantive law, which materially restricts the exercise of rights? This dichotomy is not confined to the area of European law. The notion that the prohibition of abusive behaviour is nothing other than an emanation of the method of 'purposive' or 'teleological' interpretation of written law has been put forward in many jurisdictions, going far beyond cases of abusive transactions by taxpayers. On the other hand, in many legal orders we find either self-standing anti-abuse principles and doctrines (ranging from *fraus legis* to *substance over form*) or written anti-abuse provisions (ranging from the 100-year-old German provision on abuse in tax law to the recently enacted General Anti-Avoidance Rule (GAAR) for the United Kingdom). The same can be shown in matters of European taxation – both at the level of primary law and of secondary law.

A. Abuse and Fundamental Freedoms

When it comes to the controlling role of the fundamental freedoms with regard to national tax legislation, Member States habitually defend discriminatory or restrictive provisions by the necessity to fight cross-border 'abuse' or 'avoidance' committed by taxpayers. In its jurisprudence, the Court has consistently recognised the public interest of Member States to fight tax-driven 'artificial arrangements' which are devoid of economic substance or a commercial purpose. Yet it remains unclear to this day whether this is in the first place a matter of interpretation concerning the scope and content of the fundamental freedoms as such or whether this is a self-standing principle providing a 'ground of justification' for coercive measures taken by national governments.[40]

This ambiguity became evident in *Cadbury Schweppes* where the Court by and large accepted the validity of the UK's controlled foreign companies (CFC)

[39] Kamanabrou (n 2) 542 et seq.
[40] Vogenauer (n 2) 552–54.

legislation on foreign subsidiaries established in low-tax jurisdictions.[41] On the one hand, the Court held in this case and in later judgments that the foreign subsidiary has to meet a certain threshold of economic activity to qualify as a genuine 'establishment' protected under Article 49 TFEU.[42] Following this approach, the lack of economic substance is relevant when interpreting the scope of the fundamental freedom as such. On the other hand, the Court in *Cadbury Schweppes* and in later judgments recognised the right of the Member States to fight tax avoidance in order to 'justify' its restrictive measures.[43] Thus, the judgment leaves open the issue of whether the prohibition on abusive behaviour is an inherent limitation to the scope of the fundamental freedom or a specific and substantive justification.

A similar argument was put forward in *Thin Cap* and *Société de Gestion Industrielle* where the Court accepted the right of tax authorities to adjust cross-border intra-group transactions not compliant with the arm's length standard.[44] On the face of it, the Court discussed this as a matter of justification.[45] But on substance, the Court made clear that non-arm's length transactions are not protected against fiscal measures by Member States, as these transactions are not in line with the general economic assumptions of the internal market about cross-border business, ie, the efficiency-enhancing effects of free competition.[46] On the other hand, if it can be shown that a transaction was not executed at arm's length for good commercial reasons, it cannot be disregarded as abusive.[47] This makes clear that the Court interprets the notion of 'abuse' in the light of the general purpose of the fundamental freedoms in the wider context of the internal market.

[41] *Cadbury Schweppes* (n 10); on the impact of the separation of legal entities inside corporate groups on tax avoidance see J Dine and M Koutsias, 'The Three Shades of Tax Avoidance of Corporate Groups: Company Law, Ethics and the Multiplicity of Jurisdictions Involved' (2019) 30 *European Business Law Review* 149.

[42] *Cadbury Schweppes* (n 10) para 54 ('actual pursuit of an economic activity through a fixed establishment'), para 68 ('ficititious establishment not carrying out any genuine economic activity'); see also Case C-201/05, *Test Claimants in the CFC and Dividend Group Litigation*, ECLI:EU:C:2008:239, judgment of 23 April 2008, para 78 ('the objective pursued by freedom of establishment has not been achieved') and para 81 ('actually established in the host state and carries on genuine economic activities there'); for the most recent statement in this direction see Case C-135/17, *X GmbH*, ECLI:EU:C:2019:136, judgment of 26 February 2019, paras 82–84; this analysis applies in 'U Turn' cases where a number of economic transactions cancel each other out: see Guski (n 2) 427 et seq.

[43] *Cadbury Schweppes* (n 10) para 51; *X GmbH* (n 42) para 73; J Kokott, *Das Steuerrecht der Europäischen Union* (2018) § 2 para 76; de la Feria (n 14) 438 reads *Cadbury Schweppes* as confirming the constitutional nature of the anti-abuse principle as it 'was used to strike down a domestic legal provision on the basis that it did not comply with the Community abuse of law concept'. This is only half right. The domestic CFC legislation examined by the Court was declared invalid as it did not comply with the freedom of establishment under (now) Article 49 TFEU. The freedom of establishment is enshrined in the Treaty as such and thus part of primary law. The concept of abuse of law had only been introduced to possibly justify the Member States' legislation in question.

[44] Case C-524/04, *Test Claimants in the Thin Cap Group Litigation*, ECLI:EU:C:2007:161, judgment of 13 March 2007; Case C-311/08, *Société de Gestion Industrielle*, ECLI:EU:C:2010:26, judgment of 21 January 2010; see also Case C-282/12, *Itelcar*, ECLI:EU:C:2013:629, judgment of 3 October 2013.

[45] *Test Claimants in the Thin Cap Group Litigation* (n 44) para 72; *Société de Gestion Industrielle* (n 44) para 65.

[46] *Test Claimants in the Thin Cap Group Litigation* (n 44) para 87; *Société de Gestion Industrielle* (n 44) para 71–72; *Itelcar* (n 44) para 42.

[47] *Itelcar* (n 44) para 37; Case C-382/16, *Hornbach Baumarkt*, ECLI:EU:C:2018:366, judgment of 31 May 2018, para 49.

Does it make a difference whether we regard the principle that 'European law cannot be relied upon for fraudulent of abusive ends' as a matter of interpretation of the scope of the respective fundamental freedom or as a matter of a self-standing ground of justification? Yes and no! If we discuss the abusive nature of a transaction solely as a matter of interpreting the scope and content of the fundamental freedoms, we are bound to look to the objective features of the economic activity in place and whether it falls under some – more or less restrictive – definition of 'establishment' under Article 49 TFEU or the material scope of another freedom under the treaties. If we discuss the abusive nature of a transaction as a matter of justification we do not only have to clarify to what extent this requires the taxpayer's intention to minimise the tax burden, we also have to examine whether the measures taken by the national legislator are appropriate, necessary and proportionate as the interest of the taxpayers to exercise their freedoms and the interests of the state to fight abusive arrangements have to be balanced.[48]

But this does not mean that this dichotomy is relevant when it comes to the rank of the anti-abuse principle from a constitutional point of view: the fundamental freedoms are part of primary EU law and enjoy direct effect. The notion that the fundamental freedoms cannot be relied upon for fraudulent or abusive ends clearly shares the rank of the fundamental freedoms – irrespective of whether the prohibition on abusive behaviour is construed as a pre-emptive limitation of the scope and content of the fundamental freedoms or as a ground of justification acting as a counterbalance in the interests of the Member States. Against this background, the Court was able to leave open to this day the true nature of the principle that fundamental freedoms cannot be exploited in an abusive fashion.

B. Abuse and Directives

The situation is different when we examine the role of the general anti-abuse principle with respect to secondary EU law, in particular directives in the field of taxation. Again, the Court reiterates the statement that rights granted to taxpayers under directives cannot be relied upon for fraudulent or abusive ends. And again, the issue has to be addressed whether this is just a matter of interpretation or whether we are dealing with a self-standing anti-abuse principle, which constrains the rights of taxpayers under the directive.[49] Moreover, we have to take into account that some directives contain anti-abuse clauses (employing non-uniform language), which allow or require Member States to introduce anti-abuse legislation at the domestic level in order to counter abusive arrangements by taxpayers. Therefore, one has to discuss the interaction between the general anti-abuse principle and these specific provisions.

[48] *Cadbury Schweppes* (n 10) para 47; *Test Claimants in the Thin Cap Litigation* (n 44) para 78; *Société de Gestion Industrielle* (n 44) paras 70–75; *Itelcar* (n 44) paras 35–38; *X GmbH* (n 42) paras 78–88.

[49] Vogenauer (n 2) 558–60; van Hulten and Korving (n 11) 795 discuss this as a matter of 'access' versus 'justification' also in the context of directives. This seems to disregard the fact that the notion of justification plays a very specific role in the context of infringements on the fundamental freedoms but does not show up when it comes to the implementation and application of directives.

i. Anti-Abuse Principle and the Interpretation of Directives

As regards the first point, the theoretical foundation has been laid by Advocate General Maduro in *Halifax*, where he clearly stated, that the general anti-abuse principle as applied in the VAT area is a principle of *interpretation*.[50] For him, the purpose of VAT legislation at the European level requires a limitation of its effects to genuine economic transactions which excludes those arrangements which aim at enjoying unwarranted benefits (like tax credits) not covered by the teleology of the VAT system. Starting from this premise, Advocate General Maduro was not confronted with the issue of the specific rank of this general principle at the level of primary or secondary EU law. If this principle just serves as a methodological tool to interpret a given set of tax provisions in a purposive manner, it is clear that the outcome of this interpretation can only share the rank of the legal instruments subject to this kind of interpretation. This view seems to have been shared by the Court in a number of judgments in the area of VAT legislation.[51]

As regards the second point, the relationship between a general anti-abuse principle (framed as a principle of interpretation) and specific anti-abuse provisions in the relevant directives has to be explored on a case-by-case basis. In the area of VAT, Advocate General Maduro had to deal with the fact that the Sixth VAT Directive contained a specific provision under which the Member States were required to apply for clearance from the European Commission and the Council with respect to unilateral anti-abuse measures introduced under domestic law.[52] He (and the Court) held that this provision did not pre-empt the application of a general anti-abuse principle. While the clearance procedure applied under the Directive aims at preventing inconsistencies between Member States as regards the application and enforcement of VAT provisions, its existence cannot hinder an EU-wide ban on abusive constructions on the basis of a general principle homogeneously applied throughout the European Union. This is convincing, as the levying of VAT is not only mandatory for Member States under the Directive to create a level playing field on the territory of the European Union governed by the principle of neutrality but also important for the financing of the European Union and its institutions.[53] Against this background it makes sense that in the VAT area the full enforcement of VAT debt and the fight against abusive structures should not be dependent on the individual willingness of

[50] AG Maduro in Case C-255/02, *Halifax*, ECLI:EU:C:2005:200, opinion of 7 May 2005, paras 69, 71, 74; see also AG Szpunar in Joined Cases C-131/13, C-163/13, C-164/13, *Italmoda*, ECLI:EU:C:2014:2217, opinion of 11 September 2014, para 63; AG Bobek in *Cussens* (n 1) paras 25, 46, 48, 56; J Englisch in H Schaumburg and J Englisch (eds), *Europäisches Steuerrecht* (2015) 562–63; Kokott (n 43) § 2 para 74; J Freedman, 'The Anatomy of Tax Avoidance Counteraction: Abuse of Law in a Tax Context at Member State and European Union Level' in S Vogenauer and R de la Feria (eds), *Prohibition of Abuse of Law: A New General Principle of EU Law?* (Oxford, Hart Publishing, 2011) 367–70.

[51] *Halifax*, judgment (n 10) paras 71, 85; Case C-425/06, *Part Service*, ECLI:EU:C:2008:108, judgment of 21 February 2008, paras 40–45; Case C-132/06, *Commission v Italy*, ECLI:EU:C:2008:412, judgment of 17 July 2008, para 46; *Italmoda*, judgment (n 10) para 42.

[52] Art 27 of the Sixth VAT Directive; this provision has been replaced by the (largely identical) Art 395 of the VAT System Directive.

[53] *Commission v Italy* (n 51) paras 37–38; Case C-500/10, *Belvedere Costruzioni*, ECLI:EU:C:2012:186, judgment of 29 March 2012, paras 20–22.

Member States to introduce anti-abuse measures by themselves and to seek clearance in that regard under Article 27 of the Sixth VAT Directive / Article 395 of the VAT System Directive.[54]

The situation is different in the field of direct taxation. Here, most existing directives contain specific provisions empowering the Member States to deviate from the provisions of the directive in order to reject abusive claims by taxpayers – be it claims for withholding tax exemptions under the Parent–Subsidiary Directive and the Interest Royalty Directive or claims for tax-free reorganisations under the Merger Directive. Given these specific provisions, there is no need and – in my view – no room for the application of a general principle.[55] Moreover, the Merger Directive and the Interest Royalty Directive deliberately do not require Member States to introduce anti-abuse legislation under their national laws.[56] Moreover, these directives do not establish – unlike the VAT directives – a full and mandatory tax system in its own right.

The difference vis-à-vis the VAT case law becomes evident when we look at withholding tax exemptions under the Parent–Subsidiary Directive[57] and the Interest Royalty Directive. These waivers refer to withholding taxes levied on dividends, interest and royalties paid to foreign affiliated companies under domestic law. Therefore, these withholding tax waivers under European law only apply if domestic legislation in a Member State provides for withholding taxation of outflowing payments in the first place. But this is not always the case. Some countries (like Germany) long ago unilaterally decided not to levy any withholding taxes on outflowing interest payments. Moreover, many countries have successively agreed under a multitude of double tax conventions not to levy withholding taxes on outflowing interest and royalty payments in a generalised fashion (see Articles 11 and 12 of the OECD Model Tax Convention) and sometimes even on cross-border dividends paid to shareholders exceeding a certain minimum participation.[58]

Against this background the draftsmen of these directives had no reason to pressure the Member States into mandatory anti-abuse legislation. Rather, they wanted to suppress the Member States' inclination to defend their revenue interests by introducing over-extensive anti-abuse measures. Until quite recently, the jurisprudence of the Court therefore aimed at constraining far-reaching fiscal measures going beyond truly abusive arrangements.[59] This specific purpose of anti-abuse clauses in the directives should not be overridden by a general principle of law. When it comes

[54] AG Maduro in *Halifax* (n 50) paras 76–80.

[55] Vogenauer (n 2) 551.

[56] *Eqiom* (n 17) paras 17–18; *Deister Holding* (n 17) paras 45, 53; Case C-14/16, *Euro Park Service*, ECLI:EU:C:2017:177, judgment of 8 March 2017, paras 21–24.

[57] In 2015, the Parent–Subsidiary Directive was amended in order to oblige Member States to introduce anti-abuse instruments under their domestic law; existing jurisprudence of the Court refers to the earlier non-mandatory version.

[58] See Art 10(3) Double Tax Conventions Germany/Sweden and Germany/Switzerland.

[59] Case C-352/08, *Modehuis A Zwijnenburg*, ECLI:EU:C:2010:282, judgment of 20 May 2010, para 46–47; *Eqiom* (n 17) paras 24–27; *Deister Holding* (n 17) paras 52, 59; *Euro Park Service* (n 56) paras 48–49; A Cordewener, 'Anti Abuse Measures in the Area of Direct Taxation: Towards Converging Standards Under Treaty Freedoms and EU Directives?' (2017) 26 *EC Tax Review* 60, 63–65; J Bundgaard et al, 'When are Domestic Anti-Avoidance Rules in Breach of Primary and Secondary EU Law? Comments Based on Recent ECJ Decisions' (2018) 58 *European Taxation* 130.

to the impact of a general anti-abuse principle as a tool for interpreting the relevant directives, precedence should be given to the existing specific anti-abuse provisions being part of secondary legislation and a narrow reading should be applied. In this context one should even doubt the recurring statement[60] that general notions of abuse or 'substance over form' under national law can serve as a substitute for explicit anti-abuse legislation implementing the anti-abuse clauses of the directives at the national level. If the wording of the European directives states that national legislators are free to decide whether or not to introduce anti-avoidance provisions countering the abuse of directive benefits, it depends on the will of the Member State's legislature whether the general statutory or judicial anti-abuse tools provided by domestic law can be employed. The national legislator should clarify in the implementation process that it regards these general notions or rules to implement the option granted under the directive in the context of national tax law.

ii. Anti-Abuse Principle as a Self-Standing Concept

The Court, in its recent judgments, takes a different view.[61] From the perspective of the European judges, the general anti-abuse principle is not only a self-standing concept, which cannot be reduced to an interpretative tool. Moreover, it has been promoted by the Court to the rank of primary EU law, which stands above secondary EU law – in particular above directives. As such, its scope and impact is held not to depend on the specific content of secondary legislation, in particular the existence and/or design of anti-avoidance provisions as laid down in the directives.

In this vein, the Court not only pressed for full application of the general anti-abuse principle in the field of fully harmonised VAT.[62] In the recent Danish directive shopping cases, the Court also declared the limitations of the specific anti-avoidance provisions enshrined in the Parent–Subsidiary Directive and the Interest Royalty Directive to be irrelevant when it comes to the effectuation of the general anti-abuse principle.[63] The fact that these provisions leave it to the Member States whether or not to introduce anti-abuse legislation was brushed away by the Court with sweeping statements. The overall tendency of these directives, namely to abolish double taxation of cross-border income in order to help create large European enterprises, is turned on its head. The reader gets the impression that the Court deliberately rides on the current global wave of anti-tax avoidance policies,[64] leaving behind the fine-grained structure of European legislation as well as the underlying theory of free establishment in the internal market.

[60] *Deister Holding* (n 17) para 55; AG Kokott in Case C-321/05, *Kofoed*, ECLI:EU:C:2007:86, opinion of 8 February 2007, para 62; AG Kokott in *T Danmark* (n 19) para 104; AG Kokott in *N Luxembourg 1* (n 19) para 108.

[61] *Cussens*, judgment (n 10) paras 27–28; *T Danmark*, judgment (10) para 75; *N Luxembourg 1*, judgment (n 10) para 101; see also K Engsing Sorensen, 'What is a General Principle of EU Law? A Response' in S Vogenauer and R de la Feria (eds), *Prohibition of Abuse of Law: A New General Principle of EU Law?* (Oxford, Hart Publishing, 2011).

[62] *Cussens*, judgment (n 10) paras 27–28.

[63] *T Danmark*, judgment (n 10) paras 77, 83; *N Luxembourg 1*, judgment (n 10) paras 104–05.

[64] Hérnandez González-Barreda (n 11) 416.

Taking a closer look, this is not only a major policy shift in the jurisprudence of the Court. It is also a categorical error. Even if we accepted that the principle that 'nobody can rely on European law for fraudulent or abusive ends' ranks at the level of primary EU law, this would not entail that the specific emanations of this principle share the same rank.

To give an example of how to avoid this mix of categories: it is widely recognised that the principle *pacta sunt servanda* is a fundamental principle of customary international law.[65] But it is also widely accepted that the application of this general principle does not promote specific international treaties to the same rank.[66] Rather, the general notion *pacta sunt servanda* serves as a basis for the interpretation and enforcement of these treaties; it is a background concept, which provides a foundation for conventions and agreements to be concluded between states. Yet the nature and standing of the conventions and agreements is not elevated as such to the rank of international customary law.

In a similar vein, the application of the general anti-abuse principle in the area of European law does not transform the rights and obligations in question to the rank of primary EU law. The requirement, that rights conferred by a directive in the fiscal area must not be relied upon for fraudulent or abusive ends, works as a constraint on these rights and obligations – but insofar as it shares the constitutional rank of these rights and obligations.[67] Thus, the application of the anti-abuse principle in the area of the fundamental freedoms takes place at the level of primary EU law. Conversely, the application of the anti-abuse principle with regard to regulations or directives takes place at the level of secondary EU law. Therefore, even if one assumes that the general anti-abuse principle under EU law cannot be reduced to a mere interpretative tool, it should be clear that the relationship between the general anti-abuse principle and written secondary EU law cannot be construed as a conflict between higher-ranking and lower-ranking EU law (secondary EU law conferring rights on taxpayers and primary EU law constraining its exercise). Rather, one should ensure that the application of the general anti-abuse principle is performed at the exact same level where the specific entitlements which are held to be abused are enshrined.

Taking a step back, it seems evident that in the Danish directive shopping cases the Court over-extended its own jurisprudence on the role and rank of general principles as part of the European legal order. In this respect one has to take into account the different roles played by different general principles in the context of European law. In its jurisprudence on fundamental rights the Court rightly held that these fundamental rights can be invoked against measures issued by the European institutions and that the Court has the power to invalidate conflicting legislation.[68] These fundamental rights constitute important material principles, which given their foundational character have to be recognised at the level of primary law. Things are more uneasy with respect to the Court's highly criticised line of judgments on age

[65] A Aust, *Pacta sunt Servanda, Max Planck Encyclopedia of International Law* (2007), available at: opil.ouplaw.com.

[66] German Constitutional Court, judgment of 15 December 2015 1 BvL 1/12, paras 42, 47.

[67] The opposing view is explicitly taken by the Court in *Cussens*, judgment (n 10) para 30.

[68] See text at n 23.

discrimination where the judges went so far to enforce a general principle against private actors even before the implementation period for the Member States under the relevant directive had expired.[69] Yet in these cases one would still have to admit that the anti-discrimination principle established by the Court carries a self-standing value judgement, which is amenable to being enforced against contradicting lower-ranked provisions. The anti-abuse principle – on the other hand – is of an abstract nature. It has no substantive meaning if not applied to a specific set of rules.[70] One might even call this principle to be 'accessory' in character as it serves as a means to counteract a 'use' made by agents in respect of a given and specific legal instrument. As Advocate General Bobek put it nicely in his opinion in *Cussens*:

> (29) I consider that it is fair to acknowledge the existence of (that) diversity and not to claim that there is a monolithic EU principle of prohibition of abuse of law. Does that then mean that there still is one single principle of prohibition of abuse of law that is applied differently in different areas? Or does it rather mean that there are multiple area-specific principles?
>
> (30) Intriguing as that question is, I do not consider it necessary to address it in detail here. In practical terms, answering it is essentially a question of definition and the correlating level of abstraction to be chosen for that purpose. At a high level of abstraction, there might indeed be one unifying proto-idea of the principle of abuse, its blurry shadows flickering somewhere on the wall of Plato's allegorical cave. However, once one seeks to gain a sharper picture, and looks in particular into the individual conditions of abuse in the specific areas of law, then considerable diversity becomes apparent.[71]

If we apply this way of thinking to the cases decided by the Court it is easy to concur with the Court in the *Halifax* line of judgments on abusive behaviour under VAT law. As the European legislator intended to establish a full and irredundant set of rules to govern VAT legislation at full scale, securing revenue for the Member States and the European Union as well as ensuring fiscal neutrality between competitors, an unwritten limitation of benefits with regard to abusive behaviour seems to be legitimate.

But if we apply this approach to the Danish directive shopping cases, the Court's findings lack persuasive power. Rather, the Court should have accepted that (1) the Parent–Subsidiary Directive and the Interest Royalty Directive do not establish a full and binding framework for withholding taxation throughout the European Union, and (2) that the European institutions themselves did not see a reason to force Member States to legislate against abusive behaviour. The outcome of the Danish directive shopping cases, namely to partially invalidate the clear wording and intention of the directives' specific anti-abuse provisions and to transform the options awarded to the Member States to fight abusive behaviour into mandates to do so, cannot be accepted. It is telling that the Court in these two judgments explicitly rejects the freedom of the Member States to frame their domestic tax system as they consider best in order to benefit from tax competition as well as the freedom of taxpayers to benefit from

[69] Text at n 24.

[70] Vogenauer (n 2) 567–68.

[71] AG Bobek in *Cussens* (n 1) paras 29–30.

this competition between Member States.[72] This statement goes to the heart of fiscal sovereignty in the overall framework of the European Union.

V. The General Anti-Abuse Principle and National Tax Law

What is the impact of a general anti-abuse principle established at the level of EU law on national tax legislation and court practice? This question deserves a differentiated answer.

A. National Legislation in Conflict with the Fundamental Freedoms

With regard to the fundamental freedoms, it is clear that the anti-abuse principle shares not only the rank but also the direct effect awarded to the freedoms. This follows from the way the freedoms work: according to long-standing jurisprudence of the Court, the four fundamental freedoms constituting the internal market carry direct effect, ie, conflicting national laws must not be applied by domestic authorities and courts. If the Member States in question can show that discriminatory or restrictive national tax provisions are necessary to counteract taxpayers' abuse of the fundamental freedoms, this will (depending on the 'theory' applied to abuse of law) either materially reduce the scope of protection available under the treaty freedom or provide the Member State with a 'ground of justification' validating restrictive domestic legislation. Either way, the anti-abuse principle works as a restriction on the impact of the direct effect awarded to the fundamental freedoms in the first place.

B. National Legislation Implementing Directives

i. Implementation and Interpretation

When it comes to directives, the central issue concerns the question whether the material impact of a general anti-abuse principle under EU law at the national level depends on its implementation by national courts and tax authorities. Again, this is dependent on the theory underlying the role and rank of this general principle.

If we start from the assumption that the anti-abuse principle is in fact a principle of interpretation, then we have to check whether (a) the directive in question can be construed in such a way as to incorporate this principle and (b) whether national legislation can be understood in the same manner. This requires a closer look both

[72] *T Danmark*, judgment (n 10) para 80; *N Luxembourg 1*, judgment (n 10) para 108.

at explicit anti-abuse clauses under national laws and general principles or modes of interpretation amenable to an implementation of the European principles. In the *Halifax* line of judgments, the Court found that both the VAT directives and national VAT legislation can be construed in order to give full effect to the general European anti-abuse principle. This jurisprudence seems to call for purposive interpretation of both secondary EU law and national law, insofar as this is possible under the canons of interpretation awarded by the domestic methodological toolbox and the constitutional limits of the powers of the judiciary.[73] In the Danish directive shopping cases, on the other hand, the lack of national legislation and the dearth of general principles to be invoked under Danish law renders the application of the general anti-abuse principle under EU law futile: if Danish law cannot be construed in such a way as to implement anti-abuse provisions or principles under EU law, taxpayers are free to rely on the domestic tax provisions for abusive ends.

If we start from the assumption that the anti-abuse principle is a self-standing material principle, we first have to agree on the rank of the principle in the hierarchy of European law. If – as this chapter posits – the anti-abuse principle shares the rank of the legislation to be protected against abuse, then the fight against abusive arrangements under the directive requires implementation of the general principle by the Member States as well.[74] For the *Halifax* line of judgments, one might again plead for a purposive interpretation of domestic VAT legislation in order to give full effect to the underlying VAT directives. For the Danish directive shopping cases, on the other hand, the situation under domestic Danish law does not support the recognition of anti-abuse instruments at the national level.[75]

This is where the Court comes in with full force. Starting from the assumption that the general anti-abuse principle ranks at the level of primary law, the Court concludes that it can be employed to reject taxpayers' illegitimate claims irrespective of whether the national legislator explicitly introduced anti-abuse provisions and whether national judges are in the position to construe the law accordingly. Following the Court's perspective on the matter, the impact of the general anti-abuse principle resembles the impact of the fundamental rights: conflicting national law is simply disregarded in order to ensure the full effect of the overarching principle under European law.[76]

This is where the 'categorical error' committed by the Court with respect to the rank of the general anti-abuse principle renders its least desirable consequences: It infringes on the principle of 'legal certainty' which enjoys full protection under

[73] *Italmoda*, judgment (n 10) paras 52–53; AG Szpunar in *Italmoda* (n 50) para 57.

[74] This point was made succinctly by Freedman, 'The Anatomy of Tax Avoidance Counteraction' (n 50) 377: 'There are limits on the extent to which EU law can be applied to modify the domestic law of Member States, however, and it would seem that a general principle of EU law, like a rule imposed by a directive, is subject to those limitations.'

[75] This distinction between the VAT cases and the cases in the area of direct taxation is highlighted by AG Kokott in *T Danmark* (n 19) paras 101–03, 105–07; concurring Lazarov (n 19) 883; dissenting P Pistone, 'Abuse of Law in the Context of Indirect Taxation: From (Before) *Emsland-Stärke 1* to *Halifax* (and Beyond)' in S Vogenauer and R de la Feria (eds), *Prohibition of Abuse of Law: A New General Principle of EU Law?* (Oxford, Hart Publishing, 2011) 389–91.

[76] *Mangold* (n 24) paras 74–78; *Kücükdeveci*, judgment (n 24) paras 44–56.

both EU law and national law. In the Danish cases, national tax legislation did not contain any provision implementing Article 1(2) of the Parent–Subsidiary Directive or Article 5 of the Interest Royalty Directive. Given the fact that the relevant directives emphasise the elective character of the aforementioned anti-avoidance clauses, and given the fact that the Danish legislator deliberately did not apply this election, it seems strange to rewrite the clear situation under domestic law by recurring to a general anti-abuse principle which has been falsely promoted to the rank of the fundamental rights and the fundamental freedoms.

ii. The Concept of Agency[77] *and its Limitations*

Taking a closer look, there seems to be a further institutional argument for the Court's statement that the general anti-abuse principle under EU tax law can be employed directly in domestic courts like in the Danish directive shopping cases. The Court emphasises that not only European law as such but also legislative measures taken by the Member States in order to implement European law are covered by the prohibition against awarding benefits to abusive arrangements. The principle that 'European law cannot be relied upon for fraudulent or abusive ends' has to be applied – according to the Court – also to national measures as the underlying tax benefit ultimately derives from European law. It does not apply where the national legislator acts outside an area covered by European law.[78] This may lead to the theory that the national legislators and courts merely act as 'agents' of the European Union, thus tearing down the institutional divide between the Union and its Members.

This notion of agency has been explicitly enshrined in Article 51(1), section 1 of the European Charter on Human Rights where it is stated that 'The provisions of this Charter are addressed to the institutions and bodies of the Union with due regard for the principle of subsidiarity and to the Member States only when they are implementing Union law'. If – as the Court has confirmed several times by now – European citizens can rely on the fundamental rights (representing general principles of European law) with respect to measures taken by the domestic legislators and courts when they implement European law,[79] it seems viable to assume that the Member States themselves can rely on countervailing general principles as regards the fulfilment of their European mandate. In this respect one might regard it to be overly formalistic to make the protection of the European citizen dependent on whether European law is self-executing (like a regulation) and is administered by an EU institution (like EU competition law) or whether European law requires

[77] JHH Weiler, *The Constitution of Europe* (Cambridge, Cambridge University Press, 1999) 120; U Haltern, *Europarecht*, 3rd edn, Vol II (Tübingen, Mohr Siebeck, 2017) paras 1565–69; Lenaerts and Gutiérrez-Fons (n 21) 1657.

[78] Case C-529/10, *Safilo*, ECLI:EU:C:2012:188, judgment of 29 March 2012, paras 21–24; Case C-417/10, *3M Italia*, ECLI:EU:C:2012:184, judgment of 29 March 2012, paras 30–32; Case C-417/10, *Bartsch*, C-427/06 ECLI:EU:C:2008:517, judgment of 23 September 2008, paras 14–18; see also AG Bobek in Case C-298/16, *Ispas*, ECLI:EU:C:2017:650, opinion of 7 September 2017, paras 29–65; L de Broe and D Beckers, 'The General Anti-Abuse Rule of the Anti-Tax Avoidance Directive: An Analysis Against the Wider Perspective of the European Court of Justice's Case Law on Abuse of Law' (2017) 26 *EC Tax Review* 133, 136–39.

[79] *Akerberg Fransson* (n 26) paras 16–23; *Ispas* (n 26) para 27.

implementation (like a directive) and is administered by the Member States and their executive bodies. Is it really necessary to require Member States to 'transform' the general anti-abuse principle into domestic law in order to reject abusive claims raised by taxpayers in areas covered by the European directives?

From this point of view, one must take a closer look at the issue of whether and when domestic law implements European law. There seems to be a substantial divide between cases under VAT law and cases under the Parent–Subsidiary Directive, the Interest Royalty Directive or the Merger Directive.

The VAT directives establish a full and comprehensive framework for value-added taxation. Member States are required to introduce VAT and to apply a minimum tax rate; exemptions and credits can only be awarded to taxpayers if the VAT directives say so. Against this background, the notion that specific tax benefits in the VAT area are granted under European law, makes sense: the Member States are not in the position to decide whether to have a VAT or not, how to define the tax base and how to design the credit and exemption systems. The *Halifax* line of jurisprudence, in particular its later judgments in *Italmoda* and *Cussens* can be defended in part by this argument.[80]

The situation is completely different when it comes to the withholding tax exemptions under the Parent–Subsidiary Directive and the Interest Royalty Directive.[81] First, the Member States are not required to levy a withholding tax on outflowing payments under their domestic tax legislation at all. Second, the Member States have to a large extent over time decided to reduce or abolish withholding taxation on cross-border payments of dividends, interest and royalties unilaterally or under a multitude of tax treaties – irrespective of their obligations under the directives. From this legal background one can conclude that the withholding exemptions granted under Danish law in the Danish directive shopping cases do not simply represent a mandatory 'agency' on behalf of the European institutions.[82] It may well be that the national legislators would have (or even had) abolished withholding taxes in these cases irrespective of the influence of the European legislator.

This analysis is confirmed by the fact that the majority of these directives authorise the Member States to introduce anti-abuse legislation but explicitly do not require them to act accordingly.[83] Thus, it cannot be said that the European anti-abuse principle must prevail over the taxpayers' claims at all costs. But even if – as under the 2015 version of the Parent–Subsidiary Directive – there is an obligation for Member States to introduce anti-avoidance instruments, this would not as such render this provision of the Parent–Subsidiary Directive directly applicable.[84] Rather, one should accept that if the national legislator is (under secondary European law) free to decide whether to levy a withholding tax at all, European law cannot set aside this

[80] AG Maduro in *Halifax*, judgment (n 10) para 81.

[81] For the opposing view see *T Danmark*, judgment (n 10) paras 71–72; *N Luxembourg 1*, judgment (n 10) para 117.

[82] CFE ECJ Task Force (n 11) 496–97.

[83] M Lang, '*Cadbury Schweppes* line of Case Law from the Member States' Perspective' in S Vogenauer and R de la Feria (eds), *Prohibition of Abuse of Law: A New General Principle of EU Law?* (Oxford, Hart Publishing, 2011) 455–57.

[84] Debelva and Luts (n 17) 230.

discretionary power under the heading of the general anti-abuse principle. Again, the remark made by the Court in the Danish directive shopping cases, that there is no space left for tax competition in this area,[85] misses the point: the Court applies the general anti-abuse principle in order to force Member States to levy a tax which they are free to introduce given the current division of competences between the European institutions and the national legislators. This is simply one step too far.

iii. Ensuring Legal Certainty for European Taxpayers

Moreover, the delineation between European law and implementation measures under the Member States' domestic law is of high importance when it comes to the general principle that legal certainty has to be ensured. In this respect, the position awarded to taxpayers differs from the position awarded to the Member States. This becomes evident when a directive has not been implemented correctly (or not at all) by a Member State. While taxpayers can rely on the benefits granted under the underlying directives if the relevant provisions are clear, unequivocal and specific, the Member States are never entitled to rely on the directives' provisions directly against the taxpayer as it is up to the Member States to transform this legislation into national law.[86] There is no symmetry between the position of a Member State that is in charge of implementation and the citizen who has to rely on the validity of the legal framework provided under national law.

The Court tries to brush these objections away by stating that the anti-abuse principle 'has to be complied with by individuals'[87] and that it does not confer an additional 'obligation'[88] on taxpayers but rather defines the circumstances for exercising rights. This is misleading insofar as being subject to a withholding tax on outflowing dividends clearly works to the detriment of the taxpayer and goes beyond a waiver of benefits. It does not matter whether this financial disadvantage is technically framed as an extension of a fiscal 'obligation' or a constraint on a 'right' under national tax law. Moreover, it is oversimplifying to reject the taxpayers' claims for legal certainty by pointing to the alleged abusive nature of their claim.[89] It is one of the enduring features of 'abuse' in the area of taxation that the borderline between legitimate and illegitimate behaviour by the taxpayer is extremely hard to draw.[90] Taxpayers deserve legal certainty particularly as they cannot foresee how the judges will apply vague and nebulous concepts like 'abuse' or 'avoidance'.[91] Many countries – like the United Kingdom – have for many decades shied away

[85] Text at n 72.

[86] AG Kokott in *Kofoed* (n 60) para 66.

[87] *Cussens*, judgment (n 10) para 38; *T Danmark*, judgment (n 10) para 71; *N Luxembourg 1*, judgment (n 10) para 97; see also Case C-359/16, *Ömer Altun*, ECLI:EU:C:2018:63, judgment of 6 February 2018, paras 48–49; concurring K Lenaerts (n 2) 446–48.

[88] *Italmoda*, judgment (n 10) para 57; *Cussens*, judgment (n 10) para 32; *T Danmark*, judgment (n 10) para 91; *N Luxembourg 1*, judgment (n 10) para 119.

[89] *Italmoda*, judgment (n 10) para 60; *Cussens*, judgment (n 10) para 43; *T Danmark*, judgment (n 10) paras 86–89; *N Luxembourg 1*, judgment (n 10) paras 114–17.

[90] Lord Reed, 'Anti-Avoidance Principles Under Domestic and EU Law' [2016] *BTR* 288; Saydé (n 2) 192–210.

[91] Vogenauer (n 2) 545–46.

from introducing a general anti-avoidance principle (GAAP) or a GAAR given the lack of certainty and the multiple ramifications for legitimate tax planning and homogeneous application of the tax code.[92] At the European level, it cannot be said that the jurisprudence of the Court has so far delivered a reliable framework for the application of the anti-abuse principle.[93]

If a Member State decided to honour the value of legal certainty and not to employ specific or general anti-abuse instruments under its national tax law (including both statutory law and judge-made law), this decision by the national lawmakers should not give way to sweeping statements by the Court about dismantling the legitimate expectations of taxpayers just because – from a very abstract perspective – there might be an element of more or less aggressive tax planning visible in their arrangements.

Last but not least, the legitimate expectation of the taxpayer that he or she is only subject to taxation laws formally enacted by the Member States in question should not be overridden by the claim that the general anti-abuse principle under European law enjoys the constitutional status of primary law.[94] The notion of direct effect awarded to general principles of European law has been developed in order to strengthen the rights of citizens (in particular the fundamental rights but also procedural rights like the rights of defence). It has not been established in order to allow Member States to reject claims by taxpayers, which are well founded under domestic law. If there is no explicit anti-abuse provision in place under domestic law and if no general principle or other interpretative tool can be applied at the level of domestic law against abusive arrangements, the tax authorities of the Member State in question should not be in the position to invoke the European anti-abuse principle vis-à-vis the taxpayer. If the directive as such requires implementation, the same should be said about the anti-abuse principle constraining its effects.

iv. The General Anti-Abuse Principle and Article 6 of the Anti-Tax Avoidance Directive

This leads us to the final issue, the coexistence of the general anti-abuse principle under European law and Article 6 of the Anti-Tax Avoidance Directive (ATAD) enacted in 2016. The first paragraph of this Article reads as follows:

> For the purposes of calculating the corporate tax liability, a Member State shall ignore an arrangement or a series of arrangements which, having been put into place for the main purpose or one of the main purposes of obtaining a tax advantage that defeats the object or purpose of the applicable tax law, are not genuine having regard to all relevant facts and circumstances. An arrangement may comprise more than one step or part.

[92] J Freedman, 'Designing a General Anti-Abuse Rule: Striking a Balance' (2014) 20 *Asia-Pacific Tax Bulletin* 167.

[93] P Pistone, 'The Meaning of Tax Avoidance and Aggressive Tax Planning in European Union Tax Law: Some Thoughts in Connection with the Reaction to Such Practices by the European Union' in AP Dourado (ed), *Tax Avoidance Revisited in the EU BEPS Context* (Amsterdam, IBFD, 2017) 78–83.

[94] Kamanabrou (n 2) 545–46; Ury (n 11) 344.

This newly introduced general anti-abuse provision has been discussed at large by a multitude of writers[95] – in particular with regard to its content and its relationship with the jurisprudence of the Court in the area of taxation. In this chapter, the question, whether the general anti-abuse principle as developed by the Court and Article 6 of the ATAD concur in scope and meaning, is left out of the picture.

Rather, in our context it seems pertinent whether and to what effect Article 6 of the ATAD requires implementation. Starting with the judgments of the Court in the Danish directive shopping cases, one might come to the conclusion that measures of implementation are largely unnecessary.[96] If – as the Court stated in these decisions – the general principle requires full effect even if the relevant directives leave it to the Member States whether to introduce anti-abuse legislation at all, this will be all the more true if – as under the ATAD – Member States are required to introduce such a general provision in their domestic laws.

It is true that under the ATAD, it is mandatory to introduce instruments against abusive transactions by taxpayers. But does this mean that no implementation is necessary at all? In this context it still makes sense to distinguish between European legislation in the VAT area and European legislation in the area of corporation tax. As has been said above, Member States are obliged to introduce a VAT in line with the detailed outline of the tax base laid down in the VAT System Directive. Moreover, there exists a minimum tax rate applicable throughout Europe. Last but not least, part of the revenue has to be forwarded to the European Union as part of its 'own resources'. In the area of corporation tax, none of these features applies. There is (still) no general mandate to levy a corporation tax, there is (still) no minimum corporate tax rate, and there is clearly not yet a common definition of the corporate tax base. Against this background, the prohibition on abusive arrangements under Article 6 of the ATAD refers in general terms to benefits available under the 'applicable tax law' which is the corporate tax law of the Member State in question. The respective tax advantages are therefore no benefits granted under European law as in the *Halifax* line of jurisprudence.[97] The general anti-abuse principle developed by the Court with respect to the abusive pursuit of benefits grounded in European legislation does not apply. This means that transformation of Article 6 of the ATAD into domestic law is required and cannot be substituted by the direct recourse to a general anti-abuse principle under EU law.

VI. Conclusion

Fighting tax avoidance has become one of the mainstays of international tax policy. Yet the overwhelming political trend against any form of tax planning should not

[95] A Garcia Prats et al, 'EU Report in Anti-avoidance measures of general nature and scope – GAAR and other Rules in (2018) 103a IFA *Cahiers de Droit Fiscal International* 55, 65–72; A Báez Moreno and J Zornoza Pérez, 'The General Anti-Abuse Rule of the Anti-Tax Avoidance Directive' in JM Almudí Cid, JA Ferreras Gutiérrez and PA Hernandez González-Barreda (eds), *Combating Tax Avoidance in the EU: Harmonization and Cooperation in Direct Taxation* (The Hague, Kluwer Law International, 2019).

[96] Hernández González-Barreda (n 11) 419.

[97] van Hulten and Korving (n 11) 798–99.

divert our view from the substantial drawbacks of the sweeping statements and vague notions employed in this area. As Judith Freedman has taught us many times, there is hardly a concept in the law which requires more caution and diligence than the notion of abuse. Legislators and judges should hesitate to interfere with the finely woven fabric of a legal system governed by personal freedoms and the rule of law. In its recent judgments in the Danish directive shopping cases, the Court clearly overstepped its mandate, brushing aside both the limitations of secondary EU law and national legislation. The categorical position taken by the Court – elevating the general anti-abuse principle under European law to the rank of primary law – should give way to a more sophisticated analysis of the role and rank of this principle in the context of fundamental freedoms and directives.

PART III

Corporate Tax Reform

10

Fiscal Jurisdiction and Multinational Groups. A Perspective from 'Political Right'

JOHN SNAPE

> Was du bist,
> bist du nur durch Verträge;
> bedungen ist, wohl bedacht deine Macht.[1]

This chapter argues for fiscal jurisdiction – who gets to tax what – to be analysed in terms of the Enlightenment concept of 'political right'. It does so to support, and indeed to underline, some salient conclusions of Judith Freedman's scholarship on Brexit and corporate and commercial tax reform. As will be demonstrated, political right can provide a powerful analysis of tax law and policy. It focuses attention on the political rationale for the kind of law that shapes and sustains the state, in this case, for tax law. A collateral purpose of the chapter is to explore how, in the prism of political right, the strategic tensions between governments and multinational groups might be better understood. The intention is to illuminate the scope for political and diplomatic initiatives on the taxation of economic activities that have some highly mobile and/or cross-border element. The chapter develops, without repetition, themes in the writer's previous work. The discussion is prompted by the pronouncedly prudential strand in Judith Freedman's scholarship.

Furthering these objectives, the chapter argues for a reassessment of the relationship between tax law as public law and the public international law of taxation.[2]

[1] 'Only treaties make you what you are; your power is carefully constrained and calculated', as freely translated (otherwise, see, eg, R Sabor (ed and trans), *Richard Wagner:* Das Rheingold (London, Phaidon, 1997) 67–69. I have benefited from conversations with Dominic de Cogan, Michael Sutton and Andrew Summers. Detailed comments were made by Dominic, by Hans Gribnau and by Marc Stauch. I am responsible for any remaining infelicities, errors or omissions.

[2] A Qureshi, *The Public International Law of Taxation: Text, Cases and Materials* (London, Graham and Trotman, 1994) 1–8.

'The fisc', that artfully-Latinised term originally denoting the principal imperial treasury,[3] is, as Freedman emphasises, a *national* repository.[4] Jurisdiction, the right to prescribe, adjudicate on and enforce a state's laws,[5] is part of what it means to be sovereign. Each of these terms is instinctive to modern lawyers. Not so political right. By political right, the chapter means public law, but understood in the way excavated, elaborated and advocated by Martin Loughlin: the substantive law ('canons and maxims') as well as the procedural law ('customs, usages and manners') that shape 'the activity of governing the state'.[6] National tax laws, whether in the liabilities, reliefs and exemptions that they create, or in their procedures of legislation, adjudication and enforcement, provide major instances – perhaps the *prime* instance – of political right. Fiscal jurisdiction, it is here argued, describes political right's sphere of operation in the tax context. By public international law, the chapter refers to a treaty system constituting, not merely a web of contracts, but a (now threatened) international legal order.[7] This order, in the tax context, is primarily embodied in double taxation conventions (DTCs). The reach of the international legal order, for tax, stops where the state's reach – the ever-shifting fiscal jurisdiction of the state – begins. To pick up the strands in Freedman's work, and also for brevity, the focus of this chapter will be the UK. The arguments made are generally applicable, however. The aim is to examine familiar ideas through new lenses and, as stated, to highlight the political prudence in Freedman's work.

Opinions differ on whether, at a high level of abstraction, a state is restricted in exercising its fiscal jurisdiction. The prism of political right, as will be explained, reveals an underlying paradox: that, if there are any such restrictions, they could well facilitate political action and that high-level abstractions are fatally incomplete. In practice, on fiscal judgement, arguments must be tested in the context of the order constituted by the UK's devolution settlement, by its 130+ DTCs, by the European treaties, by GATT1994/WTO, and by the OECD's Multilateral Convention to Implement Tax Treaty Related Measures to Prevent Base Erosion and Profit Shifting (the MLI), pursuant to BEPS Action 15. It is within this order that groups' strategies, especially capital-allocation decisions and tax planning, are devised. In order to explain the government–group relationship, the chapter clarifies why even trade treaties and DTCs involve politics. The chapter, therefore, asserts the limitations of 'jurisdiction' as the term has traditionally been used. 'Power', as a synonym for jurisdiction, will hardly do. The focus should instead be on effectiveness. One of the keys

[3] C Webber and A Wildavsky, *A History of Taxation and Expenditure in the Western World* (New York, Simon and Schuster, 1986) 124.

[4] J Freedman, 'Defining Taxpayer Responsibility: In Support of a General Anti-Avoidance Principle' [2004] *BTR* 332, 334.

[5] C Ryngaert, *Jurisdiction in International Law* (Oxford, Oxford University Press, 2008) 9.

[6] M Loughlin, *Foundations of Public Law* (Oxford, Oxford University Press, 2010) 10; J Snape, *The Political Economy of Corporation Tax: Theory, Values and Law Reform* (Oxford, Hart Publishing, 2011) esp 10–11, 33, 38–39, 45–46. Loughlin usefully summarises his arguments for understanding public law generally in terms of political right in M Loughlin, 'Political Jurisprudence' (2016) 16 *Jus Politicum: Revue de Droit Politique* 15, available at: juspoliticum.com/article/Political-Jurisprudence-1105.html.

[7] A Bianchi, *International Law Theories: An Inquiry into Different Ways of Thinking* (Oxford, Oxford University Press, 2016) 44–45; J Bew, 'Revenge of the Nation State' *New Statesman* (9–15 November 2018) 24.

to effectiveness, in a rule-of-law state, is legality. Reconsidering the idea of jurisdiction, and thereby illuminating group strategies and governmental responses, we must recognise the politics *within* and *informing* the law and, in talking of fiscal jurisdiction, think of it rather as fiscal sovereignty. Such a reconsideration offers a realistic approach, both to prospective national policymaking and to the (re)negotiation of treaties. Such an approach requires a disposition to political prudence. That, in turn, necessitates both moral sense and realistic understanding and from each can come an awareness of the analytical potential of political right. The chapter, to reiterate, looks at familiar things through new lenses.

The argument unfolds in four main stages. Next, the chapter *justifies* the analysis of fiscal jurisdiction in terms of political right. Then the chapter shows how, whether groups articulate it or not, this is how they interpret their relationships with national governments. The consequence is, as is then argued, that fiscal sovereignty rather than fiscal jurisdiction, is the appropriate lens. On those terms, it is possible to assess the relative roles of principle and pragmatism in exercising fiscal jurisdiction, whether against the assets of groups or in their favour.

I. Fiscal Jurisdiction, Prudence and Problems

Regarding fiscal jurisdiction as being about political right focuses attention on what is *prudent* when governments decide whether and what to tax and, indeed, at what rate(s). Obviously *imprudent* would be HM Government levying corporation tax on, say, the Chinese income of a China-resident corporation.[8] Such fanciful abstractions rightly attract lawyerly disparagement. A considered realism, though, means understanding *why* such an exercise of fiscal jurisdiction would lack political prudence.

A. Problems with Fiscal Jurisdiction

Canonical secondary literature on fiscal jurisdiction is frustratingly abstract. Only broad outlines and highly selective references are possible here. Arnold Knechtle, eliding the niceties raised by the Chinese example, concludes that 'in principle there are no externally imposed legal limits on the fiscal jurisdiction of States'.[9] Michael Akehurst, by contrast, writes that a state might 'levy taxes only if there is a genuine connection between the State and the taxpayer (nationality, domicile, long residence, etc), or between the State and the transaction or property in respect of which the tax is levied'.[10] Ignoring

[8] A Fairpo and D Salter (eds), *Revenue Law: Principles and Practice*, 36th edn (London, Bloomsbury, 2018) 595, adapted (echoing an illustration of parliamentary sovereignty: 'if … [Parliament] enacts that smoking in the streets of Paris is an offence, then it is an offence' (I Jennings, *The Law and the Constitution*, 5th edn (London, University of London Press, 1959) 170–71).

[9] A Knechtle, *Basic Problems in International Fiscal Law* (WE Weisflog tr, Deventer, Kluwer, 1979) 37, 41.

[10] M Akehurst, 'Jurisdiction in International Law' (1972–73) *British Yearbook of International Law* 179, 179–80. The role of domicile in UK tax law is nowadays diminished, though it is not dead. The alleged 'genuine connection' is sometimes formalised as a 'doctrine' or 'concept' of 'economic allegiance' (see P Harris, *International Commercial Tax*, 2nd edn (Cambridge, Cambridge University Press, 2020) 61–62).

the *kind* of law by which fiscal jurisdiction is asserted implicitly excludes politics from the analysis. Politics is excluded even though Akehurst acknowledges some role for customary international law or even, perhaps, for natural law. Moreover, whilst these and other commentaries discuss *what* and *who* may lawfully be taxed, nothing is said about *how* rates are applied. This failure to discuss tax rates is odd, both because hazily held popular notions of *failures* to exercise fiscal jurisdiction focus on tax rates rather than the tax base, and also because – as Freedman points out – rates-reduction demands tend to head-up sovereignty arguments.[11] Clearly, then, a consideration of fiscal jurisdiction must embrace politics. In addition, since the nineteenth century,[12] and especially since the 1920s,[13] DTCs have remodelled whatever abstract limits on jurisdiction there may, or may not, be. In the process, Asif Qureshi writes, DTCs have actually *manifested* 'the basic freedom of a State to legislate in fiscal matters'.[14] That is why the reference above is to 'ever-shifting fiscal jurisdiction'. Qureshi also says that, in his view, fiscal jurisdiction is not about international law, which 'tends not [to] deliberate on … [fiscal jurisdiction] as it does not impinge on another State's sovereignty'.[15] Qureshi's view, that fiscal jurisdiction is more about the public law of individual states, and less about public international law, feels correct. Jurisdictional boundaries form, as it were, the defences beyond which the ocean breaks. William W Bishop Jr, however, says jurisdiction is, 'that part of international law which distinguishes the situations in which a state may lawfully take action with respect to things, persons, and events, from those situations in which it may not legally take action'.[16] On this understanding, jurisdictional boundaries form, so to speak, the sea beyond which is the defence. This latter view is problematic because it suggests the defence is shaped by the sea, rather than the other way round. Regarding, instead, legal rules on fiscal jurisdiction as being sustained by what is both lawful and politically prudent locates fiscal jurisdiction in the state itself. Political right can thus explain both adherence to constitutional and treaty norms and both action and inaction in tax policy. The key is in the concept itself: 'political' because it relates to the state; 'right' because it embodies prudent judgement. Tax law is neither the legal texts without context, nor is it mere social regulation.[17] Freedman never loses sight of this reality. After Brexit, she writes, 'great care will need to be taken' if the UK wants to create an ultra-competitive taxation regime, since 'such a move could become counter-productive in terms of reaching agreement on wider issues and relationships'.[18]

[11] J Freedman, 'Tax and Brexit' (2017) S1:33 *Oxford Review of Economic Policy* S79–S90.

[12] J Hattingh, 'On the Origins of Model Tax Conventions: Nineteenth-Century German Tax Treaties and Laws Concerned with the Avoidance of Double Tax' in J Tiley (ed), *Studies in the History of Tax Law*, Vol 6 (Oxford, Hart Publishing, 2013).

[13] S Picciotto, *International Business Taxation: A Study in the Internationalization of Business Regulation* (London, Weidenfeld and Nicolson, 1992) 18–27.

[14] AH Qureshi, 'The Freedom of a State to Legislate in Fiscal Matters under General International Law' (1987) *Bulletin for International Fiscal Documentation* 16, 19.

[15] ibid 16.

[16] WW Bishop, Jr, *International Law: Cases and Materials*, 3rd edn (Boston and Toronto, Little, Brown, 1971) 531, quoted by RSJ Martha, *The Jurisdiction to Tax in International Law: Theory and Practice of Legislative Fiscal Jurisdiction* (Deventer, Kluwer, 1989) 60n.

[17] M Loughlin, 'Excavating *Foundations*' in MA Wilkinson and MW Dowdle (eds), *Questioning the Foundations of Public Law* (Oxford, Hart Publishing, 2018) 270.

[18] Freedman, 'Tax and Brexit' (n 11) S80.

B. Realism, Not Bealism

The need for more than a devoutly lawyerly approach is suggested by Freedman's warning just quoted. Such an approach without context is a kind of 'Bealism', where law is, inter alia, 'pure', an abstract analytical system entire of itself.[19] In characterising jurisdiction as 'the power of a state to create rights such as will be recognized by other states as valid', and describing jurisdiction as 'a common conception of all nations', Joseph Beale typifies this lawyerly but narrow view.[20] 'Within its jurisdiction a state may levy such taxes as it chooses', he says, 'while outside its jurisdiction it may levy no tax whatever'.[21] Thus do lawyers think. Unreflectively, the practitioner checking the tax section of a Eurobond offering circular will, as the hours creep towards midnight, no doubt accept a definition of 'tax jurisdiction' that encompasses 'the United Kingdom or any political subdivision or any authority thereof or therein having power to tax'.[22] The wording works well enough for the practitioner, but it should not satisfy the jurisconsult or the academic.[23] Freedman has never been content with such abstractions, as witnessed for instance, in her sensitivity to the 'tax avoidance culture' and the impact of this on 'taxpayer thinking'.[24]

Following Freedman's lead, deeper thought is needed. In the direct taxation of corporate income, customary international law has, so Reuven Avi-Yonah argues,[25] created a residence and a source jurisdiction and, crucially, a worldwide sweep for the former.[26] The cosmopolitan, terse and realist wisdom of the Chancery-tax specialist, Lord Wrenbury, explains this:

> [t]he [UK resident] is taxed because (whether he be a British subject or not) he enjoys the benefit of our laws for the protection of his person and property. The [non-UK resident] is taxed because in respect of his property in the United Kingdom he enjoys the benefit of our laws for the protection of that property.[27]

Both residence and source assume one existential precondition of the state: absolute control of a precisely designated territory. The concept of 'territoriality', indeed, implies as much. Groups' legal structures and economic activities both acknowledge

[19] N Duxbury, *Patterns of American Jurisprudence* (Oxford, Clarendon, 1995) 22–24; A Mumford *Taxing Culture: Towards a Theory of Tax Collection Law* (Aldershot, Ashgate, 2002) 14–17.

[20] JH Beale, *A Treatise on the Conflict of Laws*, vol 1 (New York, Baker Voorhis, 1935) 274; Martha (n 16) 59–60. Drawing out the contrast with Beale was suggested by a conversation with my student Jordan Sangha.

[21] Beale (n 20) 518.

[22] Offering Circular, easyJet plc … unconditionally and irrevocably guaranteed by easyJet Airline Company Limited … £3,000,000,000 Euro Medium Term Note Programme, available at: www.londonstockexchange.com/exchange/news/market-news/market-news-detail/EZJ/12650726.html.

[23] '[O]n n'y trouve point assez le jurisconsulte nourri des principes du droit public', as the Marquis de Monclar, a provençal judge, wrote of Montesquieu (see R Shackleton, *Montesquieu: A Critical Biography* (Oxford, Oxford University Press, 1961) 253, quoted).

[24] J Freedman, 'The Tax Avoidance Culture: Who is Responsible? Governmental Influences and Corporate Social Responsibility' in J Holder and Colm O'Cinneide (eds) (2006) 59 *Current Legal Problems* (Oxford, Oxford University Press) 387.

[25] RS Avi-Yonah, *International Tax as International Law: An Analysis of the International Tax Regime* (Cambridge, Cambridge University Press, 2007) esp 28.

[26] Harris (n 10) ch 2.

[27] *Whitney v CIR* (1926) 10 TC 88 (HL) 112, quoted in Fairpo and Salter (n 8) 595.

and deny states' control of their territories. Incorporating subsidiaries in low-tax jurisdictions[28] and (especially easy for the 'tech giants') avoiding creating permanent establishments,[29] have been favoured techniques. In the indirect taxation of goods, such customary law has accumulated the residue of destination and origin principles, plus customer-residence- and place-of-performance-rules in the indirect taxation of services.[30] There is a close association between the direct and indirect tax rules, residence corresponding to origin and destination to source and place of performance. Source, residence, destination and origin, together constitute the most fundamental building blocks of a state's tax base. 'Coordinating' legal authority to tax has long been a principal aim of DTCs.[31] Any theory of fiscal jurisdiction must, therefore, take account both of them and more recent multilateral initiatives (via the EU's and the OECD's (anti-) Base Erosion and Profit Shifting (BEPS) projects).

II. Groups, Governments and Treaties

So, the realistic concept of political right, it is maintained, can explain fiscal jurisdiction more fully than a narrowly focused 'Bealist' approach to jurisdiction. Moreover, groups' decisions to allocate capital to one state or another demonstrate a particular understanding of constitutional and treaty orderings. This understanding can only be mapped by unpacking the political aspects of commercial treaties and DTCs. In the UK, this seems obvious, post-Brexit, but its elements need unpacking.

A. Group Strategies and Political Right

Whether or not lawyers accept a political-right analysis, groups assume it, though they do not refer to it as such: capital-allocating and tax-planning decisions must take account of investors, customers and employees, *as well as* governments and their laws. It is not just a matter of one government, either. 'Given that shareholders will be international', writes Freedman, 'and that duties to pay tax will be owed by the group to a multiplicity of revenue authorities, the picture is very much more complex'[32] than a simple government–group dichotomy might suggest. Investors are primarily concerned about their equity returns.[33] Hence the appeal of the UK's 'planned [but unlikely to be

[28] R Barrera and J Bustamante, 'The Rotten Apple: Tax Avoidance in Ireland' (2018) 32 *International Trade Journal* 150.

[29] Public Accounts Committee, *19th Report: HM Revenue & Customs: Annual Report and Accounts 2011–12* (HC 2012–13, 716); Public Accounts Committee, *9th Report: Tax Avoidance–Google* (HC 2013–14, 112).

[30] L Oats and E Mulligan, *Principles of International Taxation*, 7th edn (Haywards Heath, Bloomsbury, 2019) ch 20.

[31] Qureshi, 'The Freedom of a State to Legislate in Fiscal Matters' (n 14) 16.

[32] Freedman, 'The Tax Avoidance Culture' (n 24) 383.

[33] S Picciotto, *Regulating Global Corporate Capitalism* (Cambridge, Cambridge University Press, 2011) 233–37.

achieved] reduction of the corporation tax rate to 17 per cent by 2020'.[34] Customers value high-speed delivery of sophisticated products, although they claim to be concerned about the impact on high streets.[35] Employees value work, though increasingly with unease about working conditions and job insecurity.[36] Hans Gribnau argues that groups may themselves be moral agents and, reconciling these claims, embrace corporate social responsibility (CSR) for tax.[37] The assertion in this chapter is something much harder-edged than CSR, yet possibly more acceptable to all because of its recognition of uncomfortable realities. Managing a group can be more complicated than governing a state. 'Jurisdictions', Freedman writes, 'may have competing calls on profits' and issues may arise around profit-allocation between those jurisdictions.[38] The very idea of 'management', unlike government, conveys '[t]he sense of less than total control … [implying] coping, dealing with a state of affairs that … [can] never fully be controlled'.[39] Much, if not the whole, of management theory is ultimately about this. Additionally, as Christiana Panayi remarks, 'technically', a UK-resident parent cannot control the business of its subsidiary 'unless' the former's 'articles so provide'.[40] Reconciling these interests is too complex to allow for anything but the thinnest morality. 'CSR in relation to international tax [is] a very difficult argument', Freedman writes, 'because more than one government may be involved and taxpayers may be caught in between two or more governments who have failed to reach sensible agreements between themselves or who are arguing over profit allocation under transfer pricing rules'.[41] Thin it may be, but profit-earning through lawful investment is nonetheless a morality. Groups' central constituent must be their shareholders, cost reductions their chief concern. 'In this context', Freedman concludes, 'the most that can be expected is transparency in reporting'.[42] The writer shares Freedman's CSR misgivings. Compliance with the law is a minimum: the impulse-for-change must come from elsewhere.

B. The Politics of Trade/Commercial Treaties and DTCs

Jurisdiction arguments cross over political and legal ideas. Crucially, the political question is whether and, if so, how, the various factors just mentioned relate to a state's power to act. To choose among tax policy options, and to act on those choices, is to practise

[34] Freedman, 'Tax and Brexit' (n 11) S80. At the date of the final draft of the chapter, HM Treasury has confirmed that 'the headline corporation tax rate will remain at 19% in 2020, the lowest in the G20': see HM Treasury, *Budget 2020: Delivering on our Promises to the British People* (HC 2019–2020, 121) para 1.211.

[35] World Economic Forum, *Shaping the Future of Retail for Consumer Industries* (Insight Report, 2017), available at: www3.weforum.org/docs/IP/2016/; Anna Gross and Alice Hancock, 'Chain Store Closures To Top 1,000 Over Two Years As High Street Crisis Mounts' *Financial Times* (22 April 2019) 1. CO/WEF_AM17_FutureofRetailInsightReport.pdf.

[36] Sarah O'Connor, 'Amazon Unpacked' *FT Weekend Magazine* (London, 9/10 February 2013) 14–19.

[37] H Gribnau, 'The Integrity of the Tax System after BEPS: A Shared Responsibility' (2017) 10 *Erasmus Law Review* 12.

[38] Freedman, 'The Tax Avoidance Culture' (n 24) 383.

[39] L Freedman, *Strategy: A History* (Oxford, Oxford University Press, 2013) 461.

[40] CHJI Panayi, 'Cadbury Schweppes and Cadbury Schweppes Overseas (2006): CFC Rules Under EU Tax Law' in J Snape and D de Cogan (eds), *Landmark Cases in Revenue Law* (Oxford, Hart Publishing, 2019) 425n.

[41] Freedman, 'The Tax Avoidance Culture' (n 24) 383.

[42] ibid.

politics or – as the case may be – diplomacy. Diplomacy, as Edmund Burke implied, is to practise politics – to choose – in the context of international negotiations.[43] In choosing, it is a mistake to isolate national tax issues from international ones, to make a distinction between 'interior' and 'exterior' dimensions to a tax system.[44] Freedman emphasises the impossibility of such a distinction in relation to tax avoidance.[45] It is '[u]pon foreign affairs', says Benjamin Disraeli, that issues so 'diverse as the levels of taxation and the health of industry … [depend]'.[46] A similar observation is Tsilly Dagan's starting point in her recent study:[47] '[t]ax policy goals are no longer tailored to a set group of constituents, but rather, the group of taxpayers and the tax regime to which they are subject are shaped simultaneously'. As Simon Schama has recently reminded us, in relation to the 1860 Cobden–Chevalier Treaty,[48] decisions taken in trade-treaty negotiation can impact significantly at home.[49] A deepening understanding of this point has become a feature of UK politics. The 1860 treaty is the progenitor of such bilateral trade treaties into which the UK might now seek to enter.[50] The issue is whether, in so acting, a government is legally free so to do. This is to act within the rule of law. So to act is required both by the constitutional law and by the treaty law. How that freedom should be exercised is a matter of political assessment. Ceding, by treaty, legal authority to act was long abhorred[51] but it was pioneered, significantly, in relation to indirect taxes, by the 1860 treaty.[52] *Each of* the Emperor of the French and 'England' 'reduced French duties on coal and most English manufactured goods to rates not exceeding 30 per cent.: Great Britain lowered the duties upon French wines and brandy'.[53] The General Agreement on Tariffs and Trade 1947 did similarly, albeit multilaterally, in extending a 'most-favoured nation' status.[54] By contrast, earlier moves on duties, such as the 1846 repeal of the Corn Laws,[55] tended to be unilateral.[56] Bilateral moves were made in the

[43] Noted by D Armitage, *Foundations of Modern International Thought* (Cambridge, Cambridge University Press, 2013) 41, where it is stated that it was Burke who introduced this sense of 'the terms "diplomatic" and "diplomacy" into the English language' in 1797, 'in his *Letters on a Regicide Peace*'.

[44] RBJ Walker, *Inside/Outside: International Relations as Political Theory* (Cambridge, Cambridge University Press, 1993) 176.

[45] Freedman, 'The Tax Avoidance Culture' (n 24) 383.

[46] Quoted in J Charmley, *Splendid Isolation? Britain, the Balance of Power and the Origins of the First World War* (London, Hodder and Stoughton, 1999) 16.

[47] T Dagan, *International Tax Policy: Between Competition and Cooperation* (Cambridge, Cambridge University Press, 2018).

[48] S Schama, 'When Britain Chose Europe' *Financial Times Life and Arts* (London, 2–3 March 2019) 1. Treaty text (Bases d'un Traité de Commerce entre la France et l'Angeterre en 5 Parties' (Archives Nationales is reproduced in AL Dunham, *The Anglo-French Treaty of Commerce of 1860 and the Progress of the Industrial Revolution in France* (Ann Arbor, MI, University of Michigan Press, 1930) 369–72.

[49] See, eg, W Hinde, *Richard Cobden: A Victorian Outsider* (New Haven, CT, Yale University Press, 1987) 293.

[50] Freedman, 'Tax and Brexit' (n 11) S80.

[51] Hinde (n 49) 285.

[52] AA Iliasu, 'The Cobden–Chevalier Commercial Treaty of 1860' (1971) 1 *Historical Journal* 67, 68.

[53] Dunham (n 48) 369–370; L Woodward, *The Age of Reform 1815–1870*, 2nd edn (Oxford, Clarendon, 1962) 179n.

[54] JH Jackson, *The World Trading System: Law and Policy of International Economic Relations*, 2nd edn (Cambridge, MA, MIT Press, 1997) 142, 157.

[55] Woodward (n 53) 124; and, see, on the supposed joys of unilateralism, David Davis, 'If May's Deal Fails, We Must Embrace No Deal' *Sunday Telegraph* (24 March 2019) 19.

[56] Dunham (n 48) ch 1; B Hilton, A *Mad, Bad, and Dangerous People? England 1783–1846* (Oxford, Clarendon Press, 2006) 555.

decades after the Second World War, in relation to direct taxes, through the negotiation of DTCs. These 'allocated rights to tax specific income flows': source states got to tax subsidiary's and branch profits, while those of residence got 'to tax … worldwide income from all sources, subject at least to a credit for valid source taxes'.[57] It is not therefore surprising that, in the context of Brexit, a correspondent with the *Financial Times*, exhorted – ironically – hard Brexiters not to overlook the threat of DTCs and a range of other treaties to sovereignty.[58] In short, '[a] strong element of practical reality inevitably permeates this area'.[59] 'Little revenue would be raised', as has been said, 'by laying a tax on a Chinese-resident's Chinese income.[60]

III. Banishing Power: Rethinking Jurisdiction as Sovereignty

To breathe new life into the concept of fiscal jurisdiction, by thinking of it in terms of political right, involves banishing any idea of jurisdiction as 'power' and thinking instead in terms of 'capacity', of 'competences'/'authorities'[61] and – in combination – of 'sovereignty'. 'Power', though convenient, is no more than an image, ultimately unintelligible.[62] Capacity, however – historically called 'constituent power' – enables greater linguistic precision, focusing attention on effectiveness and enabling the relationship between governments and groups to be mapped symbiotically. Competences delineate spheres of lawful legislative activity. The distinction might well equate to that between 'can' (denoting capacity) and 'may' (denoting competence) in everyday speech. Jurisdiction as political right sees the capacity under the competence and illuminates jurisdiction as sovereignty.

A. Not 'Power' But 'Sovereignty'

The expression political right unites law and politics, not to corrupt law, but to indicate, with telescopic precision, that a particular type of law – political right – stabilises and regulates the practices of tax politics.[63] The boundaries of what is politically possible, in terms of taxing group economic activity, is usefully rendered as *capacity*. The limits of what is lawful, in terms of observing constitutional and treaty norms, are appropriately characterised as *competences*. Politically effective legislation and federation, within constitutional and treaty competences, is no more and no less than *sovereignty*, a term describing an effective *relationship* between government and governed. Jurisdiction, by contrast, denotes only one of these, that is to say, competences.

[57] Picciotto, *International Business Taxation* (n 13) 3.
[58] Richard K Gordon, 'Brexit is only the glorious new beginning' (letter) *Financial Times* (18 March 2019) 22.
[59] Fairpo and Salter (n 8).
[60] ibid.
[61] Martha (n 16) 59.
[62] MA Wenman, 'Power' in I MacKenzie (ed), *Political Concepts: A Reader and Guide* (Edinburgh, Edinburgh University Press, 2005) 371–72.
[63] Snape, *The Political Economy of Corporation Tax* (n 6).

B. Not Private But Public

Equating jurisdiction with power, as Beale does, may work for the private lawyer but, frankly, it makes no sense to public lawyers. Private lawyers can speak intelligibly of powers within – say – a pension fund trust deed, because their exercise is subject to judicial oversight.[64] Though the same may be true for public lawyers in judicial review cases, seeing public law as political right requires a vision of capacity animating legal texts. 'Power', writes Hannah Arendt, 'is always … a power potential and not an unchangeable, measurable, and reliable entity like force or strength'.[65] Instead, effectiveness is the central legitimating value. Even in a Bealist mode of speech, 'power' can hardly be imagined unless it is capable in fact of being exercised. Effectiveness requires even the international aspects of tax law to be considered in terms of sovereignty, notably with regard to political possibilities. Such a view, embodying the political in the legal, is appropriate because, whether envisaged from the defence or from the ocean, fiscal jurisdiction is an example of political right. Political right is what forms the state. One of Burke's intellectual mentors, the *Président* Montesquieu, emphasises the unique function of political right and the radical difference between it and private law. Tellingly, Montesquieu writes that,

> [i]t is ridiculous to pretend to decide the rights of kingdoms, of nations, and of the whole globe by the same maxims on which (to make use of an expression of Cicero)[66] we should determine a drainage right between individuals.[67]

Political right intelligibly explains what is, unreflectively, described merely as power.

C. Capacity and Trust: Forwards, Not Backwards

Capacity – this ability to act – generates trust, manifests political skill, gives expression to democracy, and implies an ultimate threat of force. Capacity is 'the generative principle of public law',[68] in the sense that it transmutes social energies (associated with economic activity) 'into institutional forms through will, consent, and allegiance'.[69] Unless groups and their investors, customers and employees support it, the tax system will not work. Capacity's hallmark is the ability of a tax system 'to generate trust between governors and governed'[70] and thereby to raise revenue.[71] Dominic de Cogan

[64] See, eg, *Mettoy Pension Trustees Ltd v Evans and Others* [1990] 1 *WLR* 1587 (Warner J).

[65] H Arendt, *The Human Condition*, 2nd edn (Chicago, IL, Chicago University Press, 1998) 200.

[66] See MT Cicero, 'On the Laws' in *The Republic* and *The Laws* (N Rudd and JGF Powell eds, c 43BC, Oxford, Oxford University Press, 2016) 102 (Book I).

[67] Baron de Montesquieu, *The Spirit of Laws* (T Nugent tr, first published 1748, New York, Hafner, 1949) II, 75 (Book XXVI, ch 16), adapted: 'Il est ridicule de prétendre décider des droits des royaumes, des nations et de l'univers, par les mêmes maximes sur lesquelles on décide, entre particuliers, d'un droit pour une gouttière, pour me servir de l'expression de Cicéron' (quoted in Loughlin, *Foundations of Public Law* (n 6) 383n).

[68] M Loughlin, *The Idea of Public Law* (Oxford, Oxford University Press, 2003) 113.

[69] ibid 113.

[70] ibid 104.

[71] M Stewart, 'Global Trajectories of Tax Reform: The Discourse of Tax Reform in Developing and Transition Countries' (2003) 44 *Harvard International Law Journal* 139; D Bräutigam, 'Building Leviathan: Revenue, State Capacity and Governance' (2002) 33 *IDS Bulletin* 10.

and May Hen rightly say 'that trust [in tax systems] is not easily measured, verified or even defined'[72] and that two elements are always required: transparency and effectiveness. A tax system's effectiveness relies on the implementation of 'the will of the majority'.[73] Most of the time, this can barely even be guessed at, though, in a representative system, the majority consent of elected representatives is enough. However the system must be effective.[74] In capitalist economies, the social order transmuted into institutional form is created by property relations.[75] Capacity is political, not in a corrupt or partisan sense, but as 'the source of modern political authority'.[76] Capacity is constitutive in the sense that it 'is the juristic expression of the democratic impetus'.[77] It is, so to speak, the wind in the sails of the ship of state.[78] Capacity is 'material', in the sense that it involves coercion, though it cannot be coercive only, since (unlike the force of a mob), it 'must take some representational form'.[79] Capacity is about governing a particular state, but it has regard to other states. If Dagan's thesis, 'that tax competition seriously impacts classic tax-policy goals', is sustainable,[80] this is where it comes into play. Such competition being imperfect, redistributive tax policies will be sacrificed in international struggles to 'recruit' inward investment and desirable citizens. In recruiting inward investment, a low rate of corporation tax, in particular, has long been seen as crucial.[81] Such recruitment has ever been the central nostrum of economic globalisation. So, too, has been fidelity to 'OECD norms', which, after all, as Freedman attests, the UK 'has helped to build'.[82] The Cobden–Chevalier Treaty made this explicit by containing a specific provision 'de rendre la réforme' effected by the treaty 'populaire'.[83] Reflectively, the tax challenge presented by the tech giants is, in some sense, like the threat that the Roman Catholic Church was perceived to present, first to England, then to Great Britain, then to the UK, from 1534 to 1850. The Church's capacity to draw revenues from Crown subjects, its congeries of congregations and corporations, and its ability to transcend territory, suggest material similarities. Attitudes to the EU have some of the same characteristics: those committed to the EU have recently been compared to Jacobites,[84] British subjects who remained faithful to the Stuart cause after the Hanoverian succession. The electronic, networked, challenge to capacity heralded by Michael Hardt and Antonio Negri at the Millennium[85] and manifested in 2011–12 by the Occupy movement,[86] as well as

[72] D de Cogan and M Hen [2018] *CLJ* 656, 656 (review of B Peeters, H Gribnau and J Badisco (eds), *Building Trust in Taxation* (Oxford, Intersentia, 2017)).
[73] Loughlin, *The Idea of Public Law* (n 68) 104.
[74] See the story of the faithful but stupid dog, 'Greyfriars Bobby' (my colleague, Gary Watt, uses this story to illustrate fiduciary duties in equity).
[75] Loughlin, *The Idea of Public Law* (n 68) 106–07.
[76] ibid 99.
[77] ibid 100.
[78] ibid 109.
[79] ibid 113.
[80] Dagan (n 47) 14.
[81] Freedman, 'Tax and Brexit' (n 11) S80.
[82] ibid.
[83] Dunham (n 48) 371.
[84] Robert Tombs, 'I Can't Think of Any Time Britain's Been so Ridiculed' *Mail on Sunday* (7 April 2019) 21.
[85] M Hardt and A Negri, *Empire* (Cambridge, MA, Harvard University Press, 2000).
[86] N Chomsky, *Occupy* (London, Penguin, 2012).

by Extinction Rebellion,[87] are, in a way, similar again. '[T]here is a clear continuity of thought between us and Occupy Wall Street', wrote Occupy London, 'as there is with Spanish *indignados* and the other grassroots movements that spread throughout 2011'.[88] Tax law as political right must embody an interlocking capacity (what *can* be achieved, what is politically possible) and legality (what may be achieved, what is legally permissible).

D. Competences and Legal Authority: Backwards, Not Forwards

The divisions of legal authority, or the right to act, are referred to as 'competences', and they provide a map of lawful interactions between governments, multinational groups and their assets, their investors, their employees and their customers. When designing a new tax, any rule-of-law government must work within its spheres of competence: under constitutional provisions; under the terms of all applicable DTCs; under the European treaties;[89] under GATT1994/WTO; and under the MLI. It is the last of these, together with 'the UK's commitment to BEPS' more generally, Freedman writes, that means 'that the impact of Brexit will be limited'.[90] Group directors know all this, and it reassures them. Competences observed, UK tax legislation may be crazy, but it will not be *so* crazy. Instead of relying on allegiance, consent and will, competences distribute *existing* legal authority between states and political institutions. A government knows *who* is authorised to do *what*. Groups know where to express dissatisfaction. Instead of being political, competences are *legal*, in the sense that they take legal form in legislation and treaties. 'Although addressing the concerns of the present', writes Loughlin, 'law is orientated to the past. Law seeks the closure of that which democracies try to keep open'.[91] Law's strength, for groups, is the fact of at least a temporary closure of the tax treatment. Valhalla has been built – but on compromised terms. Law's weakness is apprehension about what has yet been left open. Beale's definition of jurisdiction – in reality, a description of competences – occludes this ongoing anxiety. Instead of being constitutive, competences are *already* constituted, though capacity means they are constantly under siege. Instead of being material, competences are *formal*. Competences distribute legal authority within states as they distribute it *between* states.[92] On the latter, whilst governments cannot be seen to act vainly, neither can they overstep the bounds of lawful action.[93] Examples successfully combine capacity

[87] Camilla Cavendish, 'Climate Protesters Are Telling Us the Deadly Truth' *Financial Times* (20–21 April 2019) 10.

[88] Occupy London, 'How Hayek Helped Us to Find Capitalism's Flaws' *Financial Times* (26 January 2012) 15.

[89] HM Government, *Review of the Balance of Competences Between the United Kingdom and the European Union: Taxation* (2013).

[90] Freedman, 'Tax and Brexit' (n 11) S81.

[91] Loughlin, *The Idea of Public Law* (n 68) 100.

[92] These contrasting points, as between capacity and competence, appear in Loughlin, *The Idea of Public Law* (n 68) 99–100.

[93] See the Salic Law: 'King thou wilt be if thou followest the law. If thou dost not follow the law, thou wilt not be king' (quoted in HJ Morgenthau, *Scientific Man vs Power Politics* (London, Latimer House, 1947) 152, adapted).

and competence, the point being that capacity is greater when clearly demarcated by competences than it would be otherwise. One set is provided by the jurisdiction exercised in relation to the – mostly indirect – environmental levies introduced in the UK and other EU Member States, mainly during the early 2000s, at both national and regional levels. Justified on welfare-economics grounds, by reference to the need to internalise negative externalities, and mostly reliant on proxies for those externalities,[94] they were in tune with the technocratic mood of the time, such that they tended to consolidate, rather than undermine, trust in the tax system. Also, except for the much-litigated aggregates levy,[95] they adhered closely to complex patterns of competences conferred, not only by the EU treaties and (occasionally) GATT1994/WTO law but also by EU environmental and energy measures.[96] A second set is provided by the bank balance-sheet levy introduced in 2011.[97] Trust in the tax system required some such levy, both because of the systemic threat posed by banks and as retribution for the banks' role in the financial and fiscal crisis, the latter meaning that banks were escaping corporation tax because they were carrying heavy trading losses.[98] It was thus that the bank levy was introduced in the UK with none-too-nice a regard to its conformity with the competences conferred by EU law.[99] Corporation tax anti-avoidance measures provides a third set. Of these, the UK's remodelled Controlled Foreign Companies (CFC) code[100] of 2012 was untypical since rather than drawing what capacity it had from popular outrage, it was designed to address groups' concerns about the lawfulness of the old regime after the *Cadbury Schweppes* case.[101] A distinct tax, designed to restore some trust, and arguably actually having this effect, was the 2015 diverted profits tax (DPT),[102] with early concerns about its lawfulness under EU law, as Freedman has written, now seeming overstated 'for post-Brexit periods at least'.[103] The unilateral digital services tax (DST) contained in Finance Bill 2019–21 provides a fourth – and highly topical – example. A well-designed DST might help to restore some measure of trust in the system and adherence to competences would contribute to its effectiveness. So, for groups, competence provides assurances, but capacity creates tensions. A successful exercise of fiscal jurisdiction means prudently reconciling these.

[94] J Snape and J de Souza, *Environmental Taxation Law: Policy, Contexts and Practice* (Aldershot, Ashgate, 2006) 115–20.

[95] See HM Treasury, Review of the Aggregates Levy: Discussion Paper (13 March 2019), available at: www.gov.uk/government/publications/review-of-the-aggregates-levy/review-of-the-aggregates-levy-discussion-paper.

[96] Snape and de Souza (n 94) chs 8, 12.

[97] Finance Act 2011, s 73, sch 19.

[98] J Snape, 'Tax and the City: The UK's Proposals for a Bank Levy' in JR LaBrosse, R Olivares-Caminal and D Singh (eds), *Managing Risk in the Financial System* (Cheltenham, Edward Elgar Publishing, 2011).

[99] F Amtenbrink and H Raulus, 'Contribution to: Fiscal Policy in the European Union Context – The Semi-detached Sovereignty of Member States in the European Union' in SJJM Jansen (ed), *Fiscal Sovereignty of the Member States in an Internal Market* (Alphen aan den Rijn, Wolters Kluwer, 2011) esp 13–20.

[100] Taxation (International and Other Provisions) Act 2010, Part 9A, as inserted by Finance Act 2012, s 180, sch 20, para 1.

[101] Case C-196/04, *Cadbury Schweppes plc and Another v CIR* [2006] STC 1908; Panayi (n 40).

[102] Finance Act 2015, ss 77–116.

[103] Freedman, 'Tax and Brexit' (n 11) S85.

E. Fiscal Sovereignty: Backwards *and* Forwards

Conceived as political right and embodying both capacity and competence, jurisdiction is thus exactly synonymous with sovereignty. Jean Bodin says that competence to tax is one of sovereignty's main attributes.[104] Montesquieu emphasises that 'political liberty does not consist in an unlimited freedom … [but rather] a right of doing whatever the laws permit'.[105] For, as he explains, 'if a citizen could do what they forbid he would be no longer possessed of liberty, because all his fellow-citizens would have the same power'.[106] Sovereignty as political right, expressed through the division of competences, suggests that Akehurst's 'genuine connection' theory discussed earlier might just be plausible. This is not, as such, because of a principle of natural law, or by virtue of the 'law of nations', or of customary international law. Instead, it is about the accumulated prudence of national governments in designing their tax laws and political (tax) institutions.[107] Qureshi expresses this well when he writes that '[t]he situation is not one of total chaos or the complete anti-thesis of reason, but rather a competitive environment where State astuteness [that is, political prudence] is the order'.[108] The idea that there is a logic to the relations between states, or a related, insight, is what Dagan develops. States compete, she argues, in a global market of commoditised tax regimes, regimes that well-advised multinational groups can pick and choose from, not only as regards jurisdictions, but also as regards components of their corporate tax codes.[109] Freedman fears that Brexit will lead to imprudence. 'The danger', she writes, 'is that Brexit will offer temptations to politicians to react quickly to new-found freedoms in the tax area and to respond to pressure for special treatment without sufficient thought about the consequences'.[110] The division of competences is invariably figured as the denial of sovereignty. However, the idea that sovereignty is diminished by agreed, or self-imposed, restrictions on competences, as Freedman implies, is back-to-front. Sovereignty is enhanced, not denied, by constraints (which is why, in line with the writer's approval of Freedman's prudence, this chapter concurs in her argument that the European treaties and the decisions of the Court of Justice of the European Union impose 'constraints'[111] on UK tax policy). Recall that Homer explains how the goddess Circe, having urged Odysseus to 'avoid/the voices of the otherworldly Sirens', advised him to urge his crew to bind him to the ship's mast, with instructions to 'chain … [him]

[104] J Bodin, *On Sovereignty: Four chapters from* The Six Books of the Commonwealth (JH Franklin tr, first published 1576, Cambridge, Cambridge University Press, 1992) (i.10), referenced in Loughlin, *The Idea of Public Law* (n 68) 80.

[105] Montesquieu (n 67) I, 150 (Book XI, ch 3): 'la liberté politique ne consiste point à faire ce que l'on veut … [but rather] le droit de faire tout ce que les lois permettent' (quoted in Loughlin, *The Idea of Public Law* (n 68) 383n).

[106] Montesquieu (n 67) I, 150 (Book XI, ch 3): 'si un citoyen pouvait faire ce qu'elles défendent, il n'aurait plus de liberté, parce que les autres auraient tout de même ce pouvoir'.

[107] J Freedman, 'Creating New UK Institutions for Tax Governance and Policy Making: Progress or Confusion?' [2013] *BTR* 373, 381.

[108] Qureshi, 'The Freedom of a State to Legislate in Fiscal Matters' (n 14) 18.

[109] Dagan (n 47) 13–14, 23 and 31.

[110] Freedman, 'Tax and Brexit' (n 11) S89.

[111] ibid S80, S85.

even tighter' every time he commanded them to free him.[112] Lashed to the ship's mast, Odysseus cannot be drawn by the song of the sirens, so his and his sailors' ship is not destroyed. Sovereignty, as Loughlin holds, means the sovereignty of public law, of political right, because it is through public law that the general will is exercised. Loughlin quotes Georg Jellinek's idea that sovereignty *both* imposes legal restraints on itself *and* defines itself, to the exclusion of all else.[113] This repays careful thought. Tax law is part of a much larger relationship. As political right, it is not confined to positive law – though it includes that – it relates, too, to institutions and processes, anything, in short, that structures the practice of politics, namely, governing.[114] 'Fiscal jurisdiction' is serviceable, as an expression, but it is not an 'attribute of sovereignty'[115] (as Lord Macmillan, reading Beale, once asserted) – rather, it is *drowned* in sovereignty, altogether merged in it. The constant pull of attractive but unwise tax policy ideas and their tempering by political judgement and legal restraint provides one explanation of why tax law is so edgy, even in rule-of-law states. Nor, with jurisdiction as political right, is any distinction needed between legislative, judicial and enforcement jurisdictions. Due process should mean that all of these are embodied in its exercise.[116]

IV. Political Pragmatism and Moral Principles

Rethinking the approach to fiscal jurisdiction involves weighing up both the appropriate intellectual disposition of those involved in promoting national measures (a DST, the DPT and the (re)negotiation (of DTCs)) against states of affairs as they seem to be and governmental responses as they should be. Some disposition to political prudence is needed, regarding, not only the interaction of the UK's tax system with DTCs and other treaties but with populist movements and groups' tax strategies. Invoking a moral sense is one aspect of that frame of mind, while an understanding of realistic outcomes is another. The key point is the potential of political right: the exercise of fiscal jurisdiction cannot, even for a lawyer, be collapsed into an account of competences alone.

A. A Prudential Disposition

All of the foregoing examples of actual, or proposed, tax measures (whether environmental levies, the bank levy, corporation tax anti-avoidance measures or a DST) express responses to specific contingencies. Fiscal jurisdiction is, loosely, an adverbial phrase. It describes the exercise of political right in the context of tax. It, therefore, focuses

[112] Homer, *The Odyssey* (E Wilson tr, c600–c500BC, New York, WW Norton, 2018) 306 [Book xii]. I claim no originality for referring to the sirens in this context (Snape, *The Political Economy of Corporation Tax* (n 6) 221).

[113] Quoted in Loughlin, *The Idea of Public Law* (n 68) 88.

[114] MA Wilkinson and MW Dowdle (eds), *Questioning the Foundations of Public Law* (Oxford, Hart Publishing, 2018).

[115] *Vascongado v Steamship Cristina and Others* [1938] AC 485, 496 (HL).

[116] Snape, *The Political Economy of Corporation Tax* (n 6) 173–74.

attention on intellectual dispositions. It is about prudence. It makes us ask why, for instance, a rather inept political calculation has, in a series of moves, made corporation tax more territorial and weakened the UK's CFC regime. In all cases, the issue is whether any of these were wise moves, not merely whether they were successful, but rather whether they might be justified with some hindsight as coherent, non-self-contradictory and internally consistent, bearing in mind the circumstances prevailing when each judgement was made. As Cedric Sandford writes: '[w]e have to accept that in the last resort pragmatism is likely to prevail over economic principle, perceived political rationality over economic rationality'.[117] Alternatively, as Nicholas Kaldor put it: '[Tax reform] does not depend merely … on the correct intellectual appreciation of the technical problems involved. It is predominantly a matter of political power'.[118] This reality, going forward, will, among other things, shape the effectiveness or otherwise of the MLI.

B. Moral Sense and Realistic Assessments

For an appreciation of realistic outcomes, it is possible to turn to what has become known as 'political risk', in a strand that draws on Hans Morgenthau. Morgenthau was one of a group, not now so fashionable in an era dominated by Behaviouralism, who had something to say about political risk. His understanding of the lack of interior/exterior dimensions to foreign policy and the centrality of states in the global order, made it possible, perhaps, for him to talk about 'politics among nations'. '[W]hat is at stake … is not who is right and who is wrong but what ought to be done to reconcile the particular interests of individual nations with the general interest in peace and order'.[119] 'The question to be answered', Morgenthau wrote, in a once-famous passage

> is not what the law is but what it ought to be, and this question cannot be answered by the lawyer but only by the statesman. The choice is not between legality and illegality but between political wisdom and political stupidity.[120]

This idea, that a particular political or diplomatic choice might myopically be made with full attention to its legality but neglecting its imprudence, has an obvious application to corporate tax measures. Morgenthau, an American exile from Nazi Germany,

> opposed … not any appeal to international law per se so much as the idea (previously dominant through the teachings of the Austrian giant of the discipline (Hans Kelsen) that law could and should be detached from the realm of politics.[121]

[117] C Sandford, *Why Tax Systems Differ: A Comparative Study of the Political Economy of Taxation* (Bath, Fiscal Publications, 2000) 195.

[118] N Kaldor, 'Will Underdeveloped Countries Learn to Tax?' (1963) 41 *Foreign Affairs* 410, 418, quoted in M Stewart, 'Tax Policy Transfer to Developing Countries: Politics, Institutions and Experts' in H Nehring and F Schui (eds), *Global Debates about Taxation* (Basingstoke, Palgrave Macmillan, 2007) 182.

[119] HJ Morgenthau, 'Diplomacy' (1946) 55 *Yale Law Journal* 1067, 1079.

[120] ibid 1079.

[121] M Mazower, *Governing the World: The History of an Idea* (London, Allen Lane, 2012) 238–239 (quoting Morgenthau (n 119)); Bianchi (n 7) 44, 110–13.

Central to Morgenthau's thought, as taken up by John Hulsman,[122] though not necessarily labelled as such, is prudence. The combination of moral sensibility and realistic assessments steers a middle channel between Machiavelli and Jürgen Habermas.[123] A key historical figure in this mindset, and foregrounded by Hulsman, is Lord Salisbury.[124] He 'saw the world', Hulsman writes, 'in starkly realist terms. His job was to secure Britain's place in the world, no more and no less'.[125] '"[T]he only bond of union that endures" among nations [he believed] is "the absence of all clashing interests"'.[126] He might have added the furtherance of the national interest. In his role as a diplomat, Salisbury's 'hero' was Lord Castlereagh. Of Castlereagh, Salisbury wrote the following salutary words:

> [H]e [Castlereagh] cared for nationality not at all; for the theoretic perfection of political institutions, very little; for the realities of freedom, a great deal; and for the peace, and social order and freedom from the manifold curses of disturbance, which can alone give to the humbler masses of mankind any chance of tasting their scanty share of human joys – for the sake of this, he was quite ready to forego all the rest.[127]

Good tax laws, good treaties, embody and express such an awareness of political risk. Serious commentators still indeed worry about the UK's 'international standing'.[128] More specifically, Dagan seeks to shift the focus away from ideas such as 'inter-nation' equity and what, instead, is necessary to protect a state's tax base.

Understated in political risk analysis, but an essential feature of Morgenthau's work is a certain idea of natural law and natural right in arriving at principle. Examples are environmental protection (internalising externalities, repairing market failures), bank taxes, tax avoidance, which all rely on natural law – that is, economic – incentives. The idea of free trade between nations itself rests on natural law foundations. Natural law does not explicitly form part, for example, of Gribnau's theory asserting the moral responsibility of 'multinationals'. Nor is natural law to be found in Habermas, though it does, in a more ancient guise, form part of the broadly Aristotelian and Kantian tradition to which Habermas belongs. Habermas, who would probably be bewildered to find himself being discussed by a tax specialist, is significant in this context because his work has been invoked by Peter Essers, though, surprisingly, not Habermas' theory of international law.[129] There is a new role for Enlightenment natural law as providing coherent ex-post economic explanation resilient to ideological pulls and, for this, we need Hugo Grotius, perhaps as filtrated via Hersch Lauterpacht.[130] The forms and constraints

[122] JC Hulsman, *To Dare More Boldly: The Audacious Story of Political Risk* (Princeton, NJ, Princeton University Press, 2018) 28–31.

[123] P Essers, 'International Tax Justice Between Machiavelli and Habermas' in B Peeters, H Gribnau and J Badisco (eds), *Building Trust in Taxation* (Oxford, Intersentia, 2017).

[124] See, eg, Hulsman (n 122) ch 8.

[125] ibid 192.

[126] Salisbury, quoted in HJ Morgenthau, *Politics Among Nations: The Struggle for Power and Peace*, brief edn (New York, McGraw-Hill, 1993) 10.

[127] R Gascoyne-Cecil, 'Lord Castlereagh' (1862) 111 *Quarterly Review* 201, quoted in Charmley (n 46) 64.

[128] Bronwen Maddox, 'The Brexit Challenge to Britain's Standing in the World' *Financial Times* (4 April 2019) 11.

[129] See, eg, Bianchi (n 7) 45–46.

[130] J Snape, 'Tulips and Jute: Grotius, Smith and an Enlightenment Ethos in International Taxation Law' (2009–10) 4–5 *Irish Yearbook of International Law* 29.

of this approach, its political expedients – somewhat in the manner of Odysseus being tied to the mast – highlights, rather than diminishes, the role of law in this most arcane area of international politics. For David Hume, though he was a different kind of thinker from Hobbes, treaties were advantageous to princes.[131] The choice in making the tax policy choices available to the UK after Brexit is not between Machiavelli and Habermas. There is a *via media*, as Freedman implies. Clear-sighted policymaking will be needed when the temptation for the UK to renounce its international tax commitments presents itself. Moreover, even if the temptation is resisted, the MLI still leaves room for negotiation, its mechanism for the automatic updating of DTCs far from comprehensive. As Lynne Oats and Emer Mulligan demonstrate, even allowing for the fact that the UK and EU 27 are signatories to the MLI,[132] 'treaty negotiators will still have a significant job of work'.[133] Whilst the MLI largely bypasses 'the time-consuming and costly negotiation stage of updating' DTCs, '[t]here are still administrative and legal formalities to be completed'.[134] In addition, changes negotiated in 2017 to DTC provisions introduced in 2008, for example, will need to be renegotiated where DTCs have not been updated for several decades. Not only that but, as they explain, states in these circumstances may 'refuse to update' DTCs even having signed the MLI.[135] What is valid for the UK is true too for other states, especially – perhaps – for those nurturing developing economies. For them, it might be a matter of knowing when to begin with the UN model DTC or possibly even to follow Dagan's argument to its conclusion and to shun or repudiate DTCs altogether.[136]

C. The Potential of Political Right

The combination of these two (disposition and principle) tells us why some measures in this field have stalled – or are doomed – as proposals and others, having become a reality, have failed. This type of enquiry has always been central to Freedman's work. The UK never ceded to the EU institutions the extravagant competence that would be needed to create an EU-wide Common Consolidated Corporate Tax Base, nor did it do so in relation to DSTs. However, as Freedman points out, were it to proceed by way of enhanced cooperation', the UK would be no worse off after Brexit than before. Competence had already been ceded by treaty in the situations to which enhanced cooperation applies. The same would hold for any conceivable radical reform of corporate income tax with the UK outside the EU. One example of a case in which the UK ceded too great a competence was in relation to the US Foreign Account Tax Compliance

[131] D Hume, 'Of the Laws of Nations' in LA Selby-Bigge and PH Nidditch (eds), *A Treatise of Human Nature*, 2nd edn (1739–1740, Oxford, Clarendon, 1978) 567.

[132] See Deloitte, *OECD Multilateral Instrument Status Tracker* (place of publication not given, Deloitte Touche Tohmatsu Ltd, 2019) 3 (1 June 2019).

[133] Oats and Mulligan (n 30) 120. A similar observation might be made about the distinct, though related, issue of whether and how to contribute to the OECD's agenda on digital taxation, especially as regards the first of its 'pillars' designed to build an international 'consensus' on the issues (ibid 48).

[134] ibid 120.

[135] ibid.

[136] Dagan (n 47) 78–79, ch 4.

Act 2014. This did nothing to enhance the UK's capacity in countering international tax evasion. Whether it enhances American capacity in this respect remains to be seen. The difference between the UK General Anti-Abuse Rule in its original form and as enacted, provide a further example. CFC in the UK was a triumph of competence over capacity. As Freedman says, the experience of UK corporate tax reform suggests that Brexit may yet prove to be the exact opposite: capacity may be exercised in such a way, unrestrained by limited competences, as to contain the seeds of its failure:

> Generally, the increased discretion available to the government over tax matters could result in gimmicks and unwarranted changes unless great care is taken. Temptation needs to be resisted. As with all tax policy-making, post-Brexit changes should follow a holistic road map, consult widely about changes, which can have unintended consequences, and not make changes too rapidly.[137]

Freedman makes similar points in relation to a post-Brexit escape from the strictures of the EU ban on state aid relative to taxation. There will still be GATT1994/WTO 'constraints',[138] though they are 'not so expansively or effectively applied', and the self-discipline just cited will continue to be needed. In reaching this conclusion, though she does not say so, Freedman's approach is framed squarely in terms of political right.[139] Sandford ended his comparative study thus:

> Perhaps the art of statesmanship in tax policy-making is to convince the population, or at least a majority, of the rightness of the tax reform proposals so that good economics does become good politics ... This is no easy task. It may well require ... some 'sheer dumb luck'.[140]

For Freedman, this is never enough. A prudential disposition requires more. To say that the exercise of fiscal jurisdiction is an exercise of fiscal sovereignty, in terms of political right, provides ample, internally coherent, justification.

V. Conclusions

If the considerations argued for here are sustainable, then four forward-looking conclusions follow. The first is that tax law with some cross-border implication is not a category separate from 'politics among nations' but, rather, a practice of international politics. Law, indeed, expresses the ad hoc outcomes of that practice. In the Dickens novel, the lady at the races waves aside the fortune-teller, saying her fortune is 'told already'.[141] The writer asks Professor Freedman not to wave him away but, instead, to reflect on the analytical potential of this proposal. It provides a strong unifying, justification for the approaches that she has taken in her work on corporate and commercial tax reform and on Brexit. It provides a way of looking at familiar things through new lenses.

[137] Freedman, 'Tax and Brexit' (n 11) S82.
[138] ie, under the WTO Agreement on Subsidies and Countervailing Measures 1994.
[139] Freedman, 'Tax and Brexit' (n 11) S88.
[140] Sandford (n 117) 196.
[141] See Angus Wilson on 'Little Nell at the racecourse in *The Old Curiosity Shop*', illustrated by a detail from William Frith's *Derby Day* (1858) (see A Wilson, *The World of Charles Dickens* (Harmondsworth, Penguin, 1972) 140).

The second conclusion is that political right provides a way of understanding the interactions of groups with the exercise of fiscal jurisdiction and the relationship between law and politics in relation to jurisdiction. These considerations seem to shape Freedman's speculations on Brexit. The third conclusion is that with fiscal jurisdiction recharacterised as fiscal sovereignty and regarded as political right, it becomes possible to understand the ever-shifting qualities of this law, expressing, as it does, both the limits on action presented by practical politics and the limits on the reach of individual states created by the division of competences within treaties. Constituent and constituted, these are never settled, always becoming. Whether Verträge, in Fasolt's admonition quoted in the epigraph, stands for 'treaties', or for 'deals', its significance is clear. Such transactions modify what would otherwise be the natural law governing the relationships between states. The contractors have built an imperfect Valhalla, and they like it so much that they have decided to stay.[142] There is always something to be done.

The fourth conclusion, the most important of all, is that the characterisation of fiscal jurisdiction as political right does not denigrate or deny the role of law and lawyers. Rather, it gives a specific role to law, and the rule of law, as stabilising political expedients. Tax legislation and DTCs, their study and their interpretation, become 'political jurisprudence', actual and imperfect manifestations of political right, more or less plausibly understood. Treaties and laws themselves are doubtful politics, of doubtful morality. Yet they might be the best we can do. To revert to the themes suggested by the epigraph, when Wotan begins to alter by 'treaties' the natural law relationships between people(s), he is drawn into treachery, injustice and harm, despite his good intentions.[143] This illustrates as clearly as may be that, if many people had forgotten about political right, by the late nineteenth century, as Loughlin maintains,[144] others (Richard Wagner, Lord Salisbury and Hans Morgenthau among them) had not. Neither, it seems, in an understated yet forceful way has Judith Freedman, in our time. Politicians must act lawfully, for sure, but the exercise of fiscal jurisdiction must also be *prudent*, in order for it to amount to an exercise of fiscal sovereignty.

[142] Though, as the writer's friend Dr George Harrison points out, in Wagner's opera, the builders cannot live with each other, such that one (Fasolt) is slain by the other (Fafner).

[143] 'Unwissend trugvoll,/Untreue übt ich,/band durch Verträge,/was Unheil barg:' (see R Sabor (ed and trans), *Richard Wagner*: Die Walküre (London, Phaidon, 1997) [Act II, Sc 2] 88: 'Unknowingly treacherous/ I acted unfairly,/ and bound by treaties/ what made for harm' (this not Sabor's translation but Magee's, the latter using it to make precisely this point (see B Magee, *Wagner and Philosophy* (London, Penguin, 2000) 115).

[144] Loughlin, 'Political Jurisprudence' (n 6).

11

Reflections on the Allowance for Corporate Equity After Three Decades

MICHAEL P DEVEREUX AND JOHN VELLA [1]

I. Introduction

The debate on reforming fundamental features of the corporation tax has been a constant in Judith Freedman's career. The same questions are asked time and again. How should profit be defined for corporate tax purposes? Should the tax treatment of equity and debt be equalised and, if so, how? Should the corporate tax system follow accounting rules? Should corporate profit be taxed at the corporate and the investor level? How should small businesses be taxed? Should a group of companies be considered as one entity or as separate entities? How should the profit of multinational companies be allocated among countries? But the context in which these questions have been addressed has changed as a result of globalisation, technological advancement, shifting political and public expectations and other factors. Furthermore, practical experimentation and academic work have refined and nuanced some possible answers to these questions. Judith has made important contributions to these fundamental questions over the course of her career, and we are honoured to contribute to this *Festschrift*.

The Allowance for Corporate Equity (ACE) is a response to the first two fundamental questions posed above: how should profit be defined for corporate tax purposes? And should the tax treatment of equity and debt be equalised and, if so, how? In answer to the first question, the ACE narrows the definition of taxable profit to economic rent. By doing so it removes the traditional corporate tax system's distortionary impact on decisions on whether and how much to invest. In answer to the second question, the ACE equalises the treatment of debt and equity at the corporate level by providing a notional deduction for the opportunity cost of equity which matches the deductibility of interest payments.

[1] The authors would like to thank Peter Harris and participants at 'The Dynamics of Taxation' conference for their comments.

The ACE was first proposed by the Institute for Fiscal Studies (IFS) Capital Taxes Group in 1991[2] and has been a staple in discussions on corporate tax reform ever since. It has been considered in reports on corporate tax reform by the OECD[3] and the IMF,[4] and in individual countries' tax policy reviews, including the UK (Mirrlees Review)[5] and Australia (Henry Review).[6] Unlike a number of corporate tax reform proposals – including competing proposals such as the Comprehensive Business Income Tax (CBIT)[7] – the ACE, or variations of the ACE, have also been translated into practice. In fact, it has been adopted – and in some cases also repealed – in at least 11 countries.

The IFS Capital Taxes Group proposed the ACE as a way of addressing two of the main economic distortions created by a traditional corporate tax system: the distortion to investment decisions (whether to invest and how much to invest); and to financing decisions (whether to finance corporate activity with debt or with equity). Addressing these distortions may appear uncontroversial at first glance from a policy perspective, but it raises questions on closer examination, which we address in section III. The ACE addresses distortions to investment decisions by excluding the 'normal' return from the corporate tax base. Can this be justified in broader tax policy terms, particularly at a time of increasing inequality? The ACE addresses distortions to investment decisions by neutralising the tax treatment of debt and equity at the corporate level. Does this not ignore the investor level? Can the tax bias for debt at the corporate level be offset at the investor level?

Different countries' experiences with the ACE over the past 30 years have provided the setting and data to undertake empirical research into its economic impact along different margins. They have also brought to the fore some administrative and possible tax planning problems, especially of forms of the ACE that have been introduced in practice. Furthermore, while the ACE was proposed in the context of a source-based corporation tax, thought has been given to the ACE in the context of other international tax arrangements. For example, academic work has explored the introduction of an ACE on a destination basis and the EU Commission has proposed an ACE in the context of a formulary apportionment system. Section IV of this chapter reviews developments related to the ACE over the past 30 years. Section V of this chapter concludes.

Before addressing these questions, though, we first set out the mechanics of the ACE.

II. Mechanics of the ACE

The ACE provides a notional deduction at the corporate level for the opportunity cost of a company's equity finance. To understand the operation of an ACE, and why it

[2] Institute for Fiscal Studies, *Equity for Companies: A Corporation Tax for the 1990s* (London, Institute for Fiscal Studies, 1991).

[3] OECD, *Fundamental Reform of Corporation Income Tax* (Paris, OECD Publishing, 2007).

[4] R de Mooij, 'Tax Biases to Debt Finance: Assessing the Problem, Finding Solutions' (2012) 33 *Fiscal Studies* 489.

[5] JA Mirrlees et al (eds), *Tax by Design: The Mirrlees Review* (Oxford, Oxford University Press for Institute for Fiscal Studies, 2011).

[6] K Henry et al (eds), *Australia's future tax system: report to the Treasurer* (Canberra, Commonwealth of Australia, 2009).

[7] United States Department of the Treasury, *Integration of the Individual and Corporate Tax Systems: Taxing Business Income Once* (Washington DC, Bureau of National Affairs, 1992).

results in a tax base that is limited to economic rent, it is useful to start by describing the mechanics of a different tax that produces the same result: an R-base cash flow tax (CFT) as proposed by the Meade Committee in 1978. The tax base for an R-base CFT for a given tax period consists in all real inflows less all real outflows in that period.[8] The main difference from a traditional corporation tax is that under an R-base CFT all business expenses are deducted in full as they are incurred (this treatment is often called 'expensing'). Therefore, even capital expenditure that would be deductible over time following a depreciation schedule under a traditional corporate tax is deducted in full as it is incurred under a CFT.

Consider a simple example where an equity-financed company invests 100 in an asset in period 1 (T1) and generates revenues of 112 in period 2 (T2).[9] Assuming that the asset has a value of 0 at the end of T2, the company makes a profit of 12 before tax in T2 – this represents a 12 per cent return on its investment. In deciding whether to undertake the investment the company's management would consider whether the investment is expected to meet its minimum required rate of return. Assuming that the minimum required rate of return given the risk of the investment is 10 per cent, then, in the absence of tax, the return on the investment exceeds the company's minimum required rate of return and the company should undertake the investment. The economic rent of the investment is the excess of the return generated (12) over the minimum required return (10) – that is, 2.

Under an R-base CFT, the company has a negative tax base of 100 in T1 (inflows of 0 less outflows of 100). Assuming that the tax rate is 50 per cent, under a pure CFT the company would receive a refund of 50 in T1. Assuming that the investor can earn the normal rate of return of 10 per cent, the refund of 50 in T1 will have a value of 55 in T2. In T2 the company has a positive tax base of 112 (inflows of 112 less outflows of 0) and a tax liability of 56. Once the refund is taken into account, therefore, that leaves the company with an after-tax profit of 1. In effect, economic rent of 2 is taxed at 50 per cent.

An R-base CFT results in a tax base equivalent to economic rent by allowing all business expenses to be deducted in full as they are incurred. The ACE achieves the same result while keeping existing depreciation rules (or using any other depreciation schedule), meaning that the costs of certain assets are deductible over time according to specific depreciation schedules. The notional allowance for the cost of equity financing compensates for this difference.[10] The base for the allowance in any period is the base at the beginning of the previous period, plus new equity issued in the previous period, less any equity (re)purchased in the previous period, plus retained profits as computed for tax purposes in the previous period.

Assume, for example, that the corporation tax regime allows a deprecation allowance of 20 per cent starting from the first year of purchase. Note that we assume that the asset in fact loses all its value by the end of T2. In T1 the company has a depreciation

[8] Meade Committee, *The Structure and Reform of Direct Taxation, report of a committee chaired by Professor JE Meade* (London, George Allen & Unwin, 1978). See also Department of Treasury, *Blueprints for Basic Tax Reform* (Washington DC, US Government Printing Office, 1977).

[9] If the investment is debt financed and the depreciation schedule reflects true economic depreciation of an asset, the tax base would be narrowed to economic rent.

[10] The equivalence of expensing and a rate of return allowance was first shown in R Boadway and N Bruce, 'A general proposition on the design of a neutral business tax' (1984) 24 *Journal of Public Economics* 231.

allowance of 20 giving it a negative tax base of 20 and a negative tax charge of 10. Following the same approach as above, this is worth 11 in T2. The base for the ACE allowance is 0 in T1 (this is because in our example there is no activity before T1, and the base for the ACE allowance for any period is set at the end of the previous period) and 80 in T2. Assuming that the rate of allowance for the ACE in T2 is also 10 per cent then the value of the allowance is 10 per cent of 80. In T2 the company therefore has a corporate tax base of 24 [equal to 112 (revenues) less 20 (depreciation allowance) less 60 (write off of asset) less 8 (ACE allowance at a rate of 10 per cent)]. The company thus has a tax liability of 12 (50 per cent of 24) in T2. That, combined with the value of the rebate of 10 in T1 leaves the company with after-tax profit of 1 in T2. This is equivalent to the result under an R-base CFT – economic rent of 2 taxed at 50 per cent.

Note that this result would have been achieved whatever the depreciation schedule for the asset. Assume, for example, that a depreciation allowance of 50 per cent is allowed in T1 rather than 20 per cent. This would give the company a higher negative tax in T1 but it would be compensated by a lower ACE allowance in T2. The tax base in T2 now would be 57 [112 (revenues) less 50 (depreciation allowance) less 5 (ACE allowance)] implying a tax charge of 28.5. The negative tax of 25 in T1 has a value of 27.5 in T2, again leaving the company with after-tax profit of 1, measured in T2 values. As the IFS Capital Taxes Group showed, therefore, it is possible for a tax to fall on economic rent with any schedule of depreciation allowances, as long as the measure of retained profits used in calculating the base for the ACE allowance is that computed for tax purposes.

In our example we used the normal rate of return of 10 per cent as the ACE rate. Bond and Devereux[11] show that using the nominal risk-free interest rate would neutralise the treatment of debt and equity and narrow the base to economic rent if the authorities guaranteed the allowance in all states of the world so that receiving the ACE allowance would indeed be risk-free. This would imply providing the company with a refund in the event that the company goes into insolvent liquidation. In practice such a generous treatment is unlikely, and, therefore, a risk premium should be given to account for this specific risk.

The risk premium should not reflect the underlying risk of the company, or the specific investment project, however. Rather it should reflect only the possibility that the company finds itself in a situation in which it does not receive the ACE allowance. This is most likely the case when the company is liquidated, though that would depend on the precise details of the particular scheme introduced. In general, the risk of liquidation would imply a lower rate of return than the normal return required on the company or investment as a whole.

Note, too, that the required rate of relief under the ACE may not be the same as the interest rate that the company pays on its debt. The rate of interest should reflect the underlying risk of the lenders to the company. The fact that the rate of relief for the ACE is not equal to the interest rate does not in any way imply that the tax system is not neutral with respect to the choice of finance; as long as the different rates properly reflect the underlying risk of each.

[11] SR Bond and MP Devereux, 'Generalised R-based and S-based taxes under uncertainty' (2003) 87 *Journal of Public Economics* 1291; and SR Bond and MP Devereux, 'On the design of a neutral business tax under uncertainty' (1995) 58 *Journal of Public Economics* 57.

III. Revisiting Policy Goals and Basic Mechanics

The ACE seeks to achieve neutrality along two dimensions: corporate investment (whether and how much to invest); and corporate finance (whether to use equity or debt finance).

A. Investment Neutrality

Broadly, the traditional corporate tax base is reached by deducting interest and costs (depreciation costs for certain assets) from revenues. The base is thus equivalent to the profit available for distribution to shareholders,[12] which is why the corporate tax is at times described as a tax on the return to equity. In economic terms, this base comprises both the 'normal' return as well as 'economic rent' or 'supernormal' or 'inframarginal' returns. The normal rate of return is the rate of return that the investor could earn on the next best investment option, after adjusting for risk.[13] The normal rate of return therefore includes any premium required by the investor to compensate for the risk of the project. The normal rate of return can also be thought of as the minimum 'required' rate of return on an investment project. If the investor does not expect to earn at least this rate of return, then the investment should not go ahead. Economic rent is any return that an investor receives in excess of this normal rate of return. In this chapter we refer to a corporate tax base that includes both the normal return and rent as a 'traditional' or 'ordinary profit' corporate tax base.

A tax on ordinary profit distorts a company's decisions whether and how much to invest. To see this, return to the example set out above, in which a company invests 100 in T1 and has revenues of 112 in T2 assuming a depreciation allowance of 50 per cent per annum. Tax in T1 is then −25 (50 per cent of 50) and tax in T2 is then 31 (50 per cent of 112–50). In this case, the investment costs 75 after tax in T1, and yields a return of 81 after tax in T2. That represents an after-tax rate of return of 8 per cent, less than the required rate of return of 10 per cent. In this case, the company would not go ahead with the investment. By depressing investment, a tax on ordinary profit imposes a cost on society. There is a vast economic literature estimating the impact of taxes on investment decisions.[14]

This distortion to investment can be avoided if the normal return is excluded from the corporate tax base, thus narrowing the tax base to economic rent. Returning to our example above, the company's return of 12 can be split into two parts: a normal return of 10 (equivalent to the amount the company would have earned by investing in the next best alternative) and economic rent of 2 (the amount above the normal return).

[12] This phrase is not used in the technical sense given under the company law maintenance of capital regime.

[13] Note that in the literature some distinguish between risk-free 'normal' returns, returns to risk and economic rent. In this chapter we use the term 'normal return' to include an adjustment for risk.

[14] Recent papers include E Zwick and J Mahon, 'Tax Policy and Heterogeneous Investment Behavior' (2017) 107 *American Economic Review* 217; E Ohrn, 'The Effect of Corporate Taxation on Investment and Financial Policy: Evidence from the DPAD' (2018) 10 *American Economic Journal: Economic Policy* 272; and MP Devereux, G Maffini and Jing Xing, 'Corporate tax incentives and capital structure: new evidence from UK tax returns' (2019) 11 *American Economic Journal: Economic Policy* 361.

The company should invest if its investment is expected to earn a return that is equal to or more than the normal rate of return. A tax on economic rent does not affect the normal return and, therefore, it should not affect the investment decision. In the presence of a tax on economic rent, the only consideration will be whether the investment is expected to make the minimum required rate of return or not. If an investment is worth undertaking in the absence of tax, it will still be worth undertaking in the presence of a tax on economic rent. A tax of 50 per cent on the economic rent of 2 would not distort the decision to invest in our example. The investment should still take place because the return on the investment exceeds the minimum required rate of return.

While taxes on economic rent would not distort decisions as to whether and how much to invest, if levied on an origin basis they could still distort decisions on *where* to invest. Suppose a company were choosing whether to locate its investment in State A or State B, and that the pre-tax economic rent it would earn is the same in each state. Suppose also that State A and State B both levy origin-based taxes on economic rent, but the rate in A is lower than that in B. In this case, the company would have a tax incentive to invest in A rather than B. Although both states would tax economic rent, the company's after-tax income would be higher in A.[15] This is one of the reasons that in recent years led to the development of taxes on economic rent levied on a destination basis, as discussed in section IV below.

i. Can the Exclusion of Normal Returns be Justified?

An ACE excludes the normal return from the corporate tax base. This removes the distortion to corporate investment present under traditional corporation taxes but may raise questions on broader tax policy grounds. In particular, it may appear to provide individuals with a straightforward shelter for the normal return to capital, which may be seen as particularly troubling in a period of growing inequality. Can the exclusion, on efficiency grounds, of the normal return under an ACE be justified in the face of these concerns?

This issue takes us back to first principles.[16] One of the standard rationales given for a tax on corporate profit is that it provides a backstop for personal income tax. This rationale is based on two propositions that we discuss in more detail below. They are that the normal return to saving *should be* taxed, and that the return on all other forms of saving *is* indeed taxed. It is far from clear that these two propositions actually hold. But let us suppose for now that they do. In that case, in the absence of a corporation tax, or if the corporate tax rate is lower than the personal income tax rate, a corporation may be used to shelter both labour and capital income, and it can be extremely hard to distinguish – both conceptually and practically – between the two. Sheltering labour income is a particular concern for smaller businesses, a topic on which Judith Freedman has made seminal contributions.[17] But our focus here is on capital income.

[15] See MP Devereux and R Griffith, 'Taxes and the location of production: evidence from a panel of US multinationals' (1998) 68 *Journal of Public Economics* 335.

[16] The analysis presented here is set out at greater length in MP Devereux et al, *Taxing Profit in a Global Economy* (Oxford, Oxford University Press, forthcoming) ch 2.

[17] See, eg, C Crawford and J Freedman, 'Small Business Taxation' in S Adam et al (eds), *Dimensions of Tax Design: The Mirrlees Review* (Oxford, Oxford University Press for Institute for Fiscal Studies, 2010).

This sheltering also applies if the corporate tax base is smaller than the full personal income tax base. An ACE would result in the normal return to capital being untaxed at the corporate level; and so, given the second condition above, individuals would benefit by earning such returns in the corporate form. Consider a simple example where individual A invests £1,000 for 10 years earning a pre-tax return of 10 per cent per annum (which is here the normal rate of return). Assume both a personal income tax (at 20 per cent) and a corporation tax with an ACE allowance. If A invested through a company, there would be no corporation tax to be paid because the investment yields only a normal return. A's investment would be worth £1,594 after 10 years. If it is distributed after 10 years and taxed at 20 per cent he would incur a personal tax charge of £319, leaving him with an after-tax income of £1,275. On the other hand, if A invested directly, he would have been taxed every year at 20 per cent, leaving him, after 10 years, with an after-tax income of £1,159.

The introduction of an ACE allowance would thus offer individuals the opportunity to earn a normal return to capital without paying tax as that return accrues. But whether this is a concern depends crucially on whether these returns *should* be taxed as a matter of policy and whether they *are* taxed in practice. Let us now consider each of these in turn.

Whether the normal return to capital[18] (often – and somewhat confusingly – referred to in the literature as simply 'capital income') should be taxed is a hotly debated question among academic economists and lawyers alike. Classic optimal tax theory papers suggested that capital income should not be taxed, on efficiency grounds.[19] But economic theory moved on. The theoretical literature has investigated many cases where the assumptions underlying the classical results do not hold.[20] The Mirrlees Review (2011) identified several situations where the optimal capital income tax rate might be positive. They include cases where there is a positive correlation between earnings capacity and willingness to save to consume at a later date, and cases where there is underinvestment in human capital due to borrowing constraints. These theoretical arguments do not give a clear prescription for the rate at which capital income should be taxed – or even in some cases whether it should be positive or negative. It is certainly not the case that this literature necessarily supports the view that capital income should be taxed at the same rate as labour income.

[18] Investment in capital should here be interpreted broadly, and thus to include investment in businesses, government or corporate bonds, pension funds, housing, art, wine and so on.

[19] AB Atkinson and JE Stiglitz, 'The structure of indirect taxation and economic efficiency' (1972) 1 *Journal of Public Economics* 97; C Chamley, 'Optimal Taxation of Capital Income in General Equilibrium with Infinite Lives' (1986) 54 *Econometrica* 607; KL Judd, 'Redistributive taxation in a simple perfect foresight model' (1985) 28 *Journal of Public Economics* 59. The basic idea is that a tax on capital income creates a wedge between the pre-tax and post-tax rate of return to saving, and hence a disincentive to save and consume in the next period instead of this period. Over time, due to compounding of the rate of return, this wedge grows at a constant rate. In order to avoid tax compounding that grows without limit as the horizon extends, the optimal rate must go to zero, strictly asymptotically: see Chamley (1986) and Judd (1985). In a two-period model, Atkinson and Stiglitz (1976) show that, given various assumptions about preferences, a tax on capital income is redundant in designing an optimal tax structure: see AB Atkinson and JE Stiglitz, 'The Design of Tax Structure: Direct versus Indirect Taxation' (1976) 6 *Journal of Public Economics* 55.

[20] See J Banks and P Diamond, 'The Base for Direct Taxation' in S Adam et al (eds), *Dimensions of Tax Design: The Mirrlees Review* (Oxford, Oxford University Press for Institute for Fiscal Studies, 2010) for an excellent review of this literature. For a recent example see L Straub and I Werning, 'Positive Long Run Capital Taxation: Chamley–Judd Revisited' (2020) 110(1) *American Economic Review* 86.

The case for taxing capital income on the grounds of fairness grounds is not straightforward either. The normal return can be seen as compensation for deferred consumption. Individuals earning income in period 1 can either consume or invest (save) that income. If they choose to invest the income, they will earn a (normal) return in period 2 which they can then consume together with the income from period 1. Taxing the normal return would thus lead to a higher overall burden on the same quantum of income for individuals who choose to consume in period 2 relative to those who choose to consumer in period 1. On the other hand, as the rich save a higher proportion of their income, taxing capital income should have a redistributive effect.

The debate on both grounds is extensive and complex. We do not attempt to summarise its main findings here; we simply report that there does not appear to be a straightforward answer whether to tax capital income from either an economic efficiency or fairness perspective.

But even if we were to conclude that it *should* be taxed, we then have to ask if it *is* actually taxed in the hands of individuals in practice. If it is not actually taxed in the hands of individuals, that would undermine the case for taxing it at the corporate level. Now we need to be a little more precise as to what taxing capital income actually means. We take it to mean that the return to saving is taxed, as it accrues.

There are three potential points at which personal taxation can affect the post-tax return to saving and investment, which makes this a little more complicated. First, when the income that is to be saved, or invested, is earned. Second, when the investment earns a return. Third, when the gains from the investment are realised and the funds spent. We take 'taxing capital income' to mean that the initial saving from income has already been taxed, and that the return is also taxed as it accrues.

However, this form of taxation is not common in practice. It is used for basic bank accounts. For example, a simple means of saving is to put some taxed labour income into a bank account. Depending on the tax regime, any interest on that saving would also be taxed. This is sometimes thought of as double taxation, although that term is not usually very helpful. There is generally no taxation when the accumulated (taxed) savings are withdrawn.

Many forms of capital income are not taxed in this way. Compare, for example, two common forms of investment – a pension fund and owner-occupied housing. Income invested in a pension fund is often exempt from tax, so that pre-tax income can be invested in a pension fund. Further, income accruing in the fund is typically not taxed either, but the pension is taxed when withdrawn. This is rather similar to the treatment under a CFT, described above, though applied at the individual level. Purchases of owner-occupied housing, by contrast, are typically made out of taxed income. But the return to owning the property (the imputed rent) is generally not taxed as it accrues, nor is any gain made on a sale of the property. Not surprisingly, the most popular forms of saving tend to be those that have these tax benefits. The fact that capital income is often not taxed – and is certainly not taxed consistently – in the hands of individuals significantly weakens the case for taxing it at the corporate level on the grounds that this is necessary as a backstop to personal income tax.

But – to give the argument that the normal return earned inside a company *should* be taxed its best shot – let us set these considerations to one side, and assume that we *should*, and in fact *do*, tax capital income in the hands of individuals. In that case, should we then tax the normal return at a corporate level as a backstop to personal income tax? In other words, would such a setting militate against the adoption of an ACE?

To answer these questions, we need to make distinctions along two dimensions. First, we need to distinguish between closed and open economy settings (international trade and investment being present in the latter but not the former). Second, we need to distinguish between the location of personal taxes: specifically, we distinguish where states levy income tax on the worldwide income of residents and where states levy income tax on the domestic source income of non-residents.

Given the assumptions just set out, a case can be made for taxing the normal returns at the corporate level in a closed economy setting. In the absence of such a tax, individuals could indeed shelter their capital income in the corporate form. State A should tax Company A (resident in A) on its normal return because if not individual A (resident in A) could defer tax on her income by leaving it in corporate form. The case of small, closely held companies might be addressed (with challenges) through pass-through treatment, where profit is allocated directly to the owners of the business. But such treatment would be impractical for large companies. There is thus a reasonable case for taxing the normal returns at the corporate level in a closed economy setting, at least for larger companies; but few economies in the world today are closed economies.

The case for taxing the normal return at the corporate level is much weaker in an open economy setting. Recall that the contention here is that such a tax is necessary as a backstop for personal income tax. In an open economy setting, individual A invests in Company A which in turn can invest in State A or State B. To act as a backstop to individual A's tax in State A, State A would have to tax the normal return earned by Company A whether it arises in State A or State B. Individual A can also invest directly in Company B, resident in State B. Again, to act as a backstop to individual A's tax in State A, State A would not only have to tax the normal return earned by Company A but also that earned by Company B. The difficulty here arises from issues of implementation rather than normative consideration. As a small and decreasing number of countries tax the worldwide income of resident companies, and they do not – as a general rule – tax the normal returns of non-resident companies owned by resident individuals, existing corporation taxes provide very incomplete backstop for residence-based income taxation. As a result, the case against the ACE on the grounds that a tax on the normal return at the corporate level is necessary as a backstop for income taxation is weak, even under the two conditions set out above.

In an open economy, Company A can also be owned by individual A or individual B, resident in State B. The inconclusive discussion on taxing capital income above concerned taxation of resident individuals. The grounds for taxing capital income of non-residents are unclear. The ability to pay and benefit principles do not provide strong justifications for taxing the normal return or even the rent earned by non-residents. Despite this, if a state were to tax the normal return of non-residents, then there is a reasonable case for also taxing the normal return at the corporate level as a backstop.

B. Debt Bias

Debt financing enjoys a favourable treatment over equity financing for corporate tax purposes in most jurisdictions. Interest tends to be deductible at the corporate level, but there is generally no equivalent relief for the opportunity cost of equity finance. The extent of this benefit has been decreasing over time as many countries have imposed restrictions on the amount of interest that can be deducted at the corporate level and because of the widespread decline in corporate tax rates, due in part to competitive pressures. The tax advantage of debt relative to equity falls with the corporate tax rate. At a corporate tax rate of 35 per cent an interest payment of £100 results in a deduction of £35 from the corporate tax base, at 21 per cent it results in a deduction of £21.

While the extent of the advantage of debt over equity for corporate tax purposes differs among jurisdictions and has declined over time, it does generally hold true and causes significant problems. We focus on two problems here.

Before doing so, it should be noted what – broadly – equivalent treatment would imply. It is sometimes taken that relief for dividend payments would be equivalent to relief for interest payments. This is not the case. The return to equity finance can be kept in the company as retained earnings or distributed to shareholders as dividends. This is a choice of the company. The total return may include a normal return and an economic rent. Dividends do not measure the normal return to equity finance – they could be above or below the normal return.

There are two important distinctions here with debt finance. First, the entire return to lenders to the company is usually paid out in the form of interest – so there is no equivalent to retained earnings for debtholders. Second, in a competitive market for debt finance, the interest rate should reflect the normal rate of return required by lenders, commensurate with the risk of lending to that particular company. Together, these mean that the deductibility of interest payments is equivalent to relief for the normal return on borrowing.

Equivalent treatment for equity finance would imply relief on the normal return to equity finance, commensurate with the risk of purchasing shares in the company (and noting that the risk premium on equity finance is unlikely to be the same as the risk premium on debt finance). But deductibility of dividends would not make the tax treatment of debt and equity equivalent. Unlike for debt, there is no cash flow that equates to the normal return to equity. Any relief for the normal return to equity finance must instead be calculated by applying an estimate of the normal return to the amount of equity that has been invested. This is essentially the approach used by the ACE.

The asymmetric treatment of debt and equity results in higher corporate leverage. This is supported by extensive empirical evidence. One consensus estimate, based on a meta-analysis, suggests that a 10 per cent point lower corporate tax rate reduces the debt asset ratio by 1.7–2.8 per cent.[21] Increased leverage implies an increased default probability. This has a negative social impact because of the resources wasted through bankruptcy costs and the possible exacerbation of business cycle fluctuations. Empirical evidence shows that the corporate tax debt bias also results in over-leverage by financial firms and therefore increases the probability of default.[22] The social costs caused by the failure of financial firms are significantly higher than those caused by the failure of non-financial firms. The failure of financial firms can produce massive negative

[21] de Mooij (n 4).

[22] M Keen and R de Mooij, 'Debt, taxes and banks' (2016) 48 *Journal of Money, Credit and Banking* 5.

externalities to the economy as a whole, for example, through the contraction in credit and the disruption of payment systems.[23]

The asymmetric treatment of debt and equity also creates significant tax planning opportunities. This causes revenue loss, but it also gives rise to social costs. Revenue authorities expend time and resources trying to shut down these opportunities, and the legislation introduced in response increases the complexity of and uncertainty around corporate tax legislation.

To take one example, the preferential tax treatment of debt provides companies with an incentive to create securities that are classified as debt for tax purposes but exhibit characteristics commonly associated with equity.[24] The UK legislator's response to this problem is to provide detailed legislation targeting specific instances of perceived abuse.[25] Returns typically associated with equity rather than debt are thus recharacterised as 'distributions' for tax purposes, with the consequence that they are not deductible by the borrowing company. This approach is not entirely satisfactory. Seeking to manage the boundary between debt and equity by means of detailed legislation recharacterising instruments that are deemed to fall on the wrong side of the boundary tends to create a fresh set of problems. The detailed legislation can lag behind developments in finance meaning that it can lead to the recharacterisation of unobjectionable transactions merely because they were not known at the time the relevant legislation was promulgated. Further legislation is thus required to exempt them. Developments in finance and practitioner ingenuity also usually mean that the detailed legislation is circumvented by new products, thus again requiring further legislation. To compound matters, the legislation designed to exempt unobjectionable instruments or to catch new products can itself create fresh planning opportunities which would again need to be closed by further legislation. A seemingly interminable and socially wasteful cat and mouse game thus ensues.

i. Is the Debt Bias at the Corporate Level Addressed at the Personal Level?

Having two potential layers of taxation for profit earned in a company complicates the analysis of the extent to which debt finance has a tax preference. When both layers are considered, the tax preference for debt is most pronounced in a classical system of taxation where profits are taxed at two levels – at the corporate level when earned and again at the investor level when paid up as dividends. In contrast, interest is generally only taxed once at the investor level. It is deducted from the corporate tax base and may be taxed in the hands of investors (creditors). Many countries have moved away from

[23] See, eg, M Brunnermeier et al, *The Fundamental Principles of Financial Regulation* (Geneva Reports on the World Economy, 2009); W Wagner, 'In the Quest of Systemic Externalities: A Review of the Literature' (2010) 56 *CESifo Economic Studies* 96; Independent Commission on Banking, *Final Report* (London, 2011).

[24] See, eg, J Vella, 'The asymmetrical treatment of debt and equity finance under UK tax law' in A Reisberg and D Prentice (eds), *Corporate Finance Law: UK and EU Perspectives* (Oxford, Oxford University Press, 2011).

[25] Corporation Tax Act 2010, s 1000 et seq. See G Loutzenhiser, *Tiley's Revenue Law*, 9th edn (Oxford, Hart Publishing, 2019) ch 61.

the classical system by giving relief for double taxation through a variety of methods.[26] For example, dividend income may be taxed at a lower rate or shareholders can receive a credit reflecting the tax paid at the corporate level. These methods appear to offset at the investor level – at least to some extent – the tax preference for debt at the corporate level. But if so, is there really a need to address the tax bias at the corporate level through an ACE?

To answer this question, we need to distinguish, once again, between a closed and an open economy setting. In a closed economy setting the tax treatment of debt and equity could in principle be equalised in different ways. First, they could both be taxed fully at the corporate level, and not at the personal level. This approach has the advantage that a single tax rate – the corporation tax rate – applies to both forms of return. It also offers the possibility of not taxing the normal return earned by the company – by offering relief for the normal return to both debt and equity finance.

Second, the return to debt could be relieved at the corporate level, but an equivalent tax levied at the personal level on the receipt of the interest. Note here though that it is possible to design financial instruments that have some characteristics of debt finance (for example, that that pay a fixed rate of return), but which do not necessarily make regular payments to lenders. More accurately, then, as noted above, this second option could apply to any return which could be taxed in the hands of the provider of finance; and in principle this could be an interest payment or a dividend payment. However, if the dividend represented a payment based on the prior year's profits which had already been taxed at the level of the company, then an adjustment for the prior year's tax would need to be made. It should perhaps also be noted that lenders may or may not be taxed in practice on their receipt of interest. Banks are likely to be taxed; pension funds are generally not taxed; and individuals may or may not be taxed, depending on whether their lending is in a tax preferred account of some form. On the basis of actual practice, we cannot rely on interest paid by companies being subject to tax in the hands of the recipient.

This analysis changes in the setting of a small open economy, in which the investor must pay an investor-level tax on the receipt of income from investing in any assets worldwide.[27] Since the investor is small relative to the world market, any change in her investment would not affect the rates of return earned by companies (or other assets) in which she invests. If some asset expected to pay a higher return, she may invest more in that asset. As she does so, her portfolio would become less diversified, and hence more risky. In principle, she should allocate her portfolio such that the post-tax, risk-adjusted, rate of return is the same for all her investments. If she indeed faces the same tax rate on the returns to all investments, then that is equivalent to receiving the same pre-personal-tax, risk-adjusted, rates of return across all assets. A higher personal tax rate would reduce this post-tax rate of return, but – by the assumption of a small open economy – would not affect the pre-tax rate of return. The incidence of this tax on worldwide income is therefore on the investor.[28]

[26] See, eg, the discussion in P Harris, *Corporate Tax Law: Structure, Policy and Practice* (Cambridge, Cambridge University Press, 2013) 229–311.

[27] This analysis is set out at greater length in MP Devereux et al, *Taxing Profit in a Global Economy* (Oxford, Oxford University Press, forthcoming) ch 2.

[28] For a thorough theoretical treatment of this point, see SR Bond, MP Devereux and A Klemm, 'The Effects of Dividend Taxes on Equity Prices: A Re-examination of the 1997 UK Tax Reform' (2007) Oxford University Centre for Business Taxation Working Papers.

The other side of this analysis is that the rate of return that companies in small open economies must pay to their investors is also fixed on world markets. If companies offered a lower rate of return than investors could earn elsewhere then those investors would indeed invest in other companies in the global market. In this context, a tax on corporate profit on an origin basis (very broadly, where the company has its activities) cannot lower the rate of return offered to investors. Instead, the origin-based tax must result in the company having to earn a higher pre-tax rate of return in order to pay the tax and also pay the same post-tax rate of return to investors. They may do so by becoming more productive, or by forcing up the prices they charge to their customers, or by reducing the prices they pay to suppliers, or by reducing the wages that they pay. The basic point is that taxes levied on corporate profit on an origin basis in a small open economy cannot (in principle, at least) be passed onto shareholders. In this setting, origin-based corporate taxes are likely to fall on individuals other than shareholders, including employees or consumers.[29]

This analysis suggests that the incidence of investor-level and corporate-level taxes on the return to corporate profit are likely to be very different in open economies. If that is true, then it cannot be true that equivalent treatment of debt and equity could be achieved by taxing the return to debt at the investor level and taxing the return to equity at the corporate level. These taxes at different levels would have very different effects.[30]

In turn, this suggests that the two levels of tax cannot simply be aggregated in comparing the effects of the treatment of debt and equity finance. Levying an individual tax on the receipt of interest would not affect the company at all but would reduce the post-tax rate of return earned by the lender. Levying a tax on the normal return to equity finance at the level of the company would not affect the post-tax rate of return earned by the shareholder but would push up the pre-tax rate of return required of the company.

In this context, an ACE would mean that the company level tax fell only on economic rent. Since the tax would not fall on the normal return earned by the company, this would leave the required (normal) rate of return unaffected. Combined with relief for interest payments, this would treat debt and equity equally at the corporate level.

By contrast, in this setting, there is no easy way to equate the treatment of debt and equity and the individual level. Dividends and interest can be taxed at the same rate, but capital gains arising from earnings being retained in the company cannot easily be taxed at the investor level. Some proposals for taxing capital gains on an accruals basis have been made, but these are likely to be difficult to implement for all capital gains made by resident individuals.[31]

[29] RH Gordon, 'Taxation of Investment and Savings in a World Economy' (1986) 76 *American Economic Review* 1086.

[30] This analysis is not limited to large corporations that have international and widely dispersed share ownership. In an open economy, investors in small businesses, be it banks or entrepreneurs, are also plugged into the world market which determines the worldwide rate of return and hence their return.

[31] See, eg, H Grubert and R Altshuler, 'Shifting the burden of taxation from the corporate to the personal level and getting the corporate tax rate down to 15 percent' (2016) 69 *National Tax Journal* 643; and E Toder and AD Viard, *Major Surgery Needed: A Call for Structural Reform of the US Corporate Income Tax* (New York, Peter G Peterson Foundation, 2014).

IV. The Past Thirty Years

A. ACE Adoption

Variants of the ACE – at times called a notional interest deduction – have been adopted in at least 11 countries: Austria, Belgium, Brazil, Croatia, Cyprus, Italy (twice), Latvia, Liechtenstein, Malta, Portugal and Turkey.[32]

A few broad points can be made about the practical experiences with the ACE.

(i) The base for the allowance adopted in most countries departs from that of a textbook ACE in a number of ways. For example, most countries failed to include retained profits – as computed for tax purposes – in their ACE base. Such a departure hinders the ACE's ability to achieve its dual policy goals. Also, all 11 countries listed above included incremental equity rather than the full stock of equity (Belgium switched to incremental equity in 2018). This reduces the revenue cost of introducing the ACE (which is estimated to be approximately 15 per cent of corporate income tax (CIT) revenues or .5 per cent of GDP).[33] It also prevents a windfall being received by existing equity holders, without producing any economic benefit. However, this opens the door to tax planning, as discussed below.

(ii) The rate of the ACE allowance has varied but not to a great extent – the top end being around 7 per cent. As explained, in principle, to achieve the dual goals of an ACE the rate need only be set at the risk-free nominal interest rate if the allowance is guaranteed in all states of the world. As this is unlikely to be offered in practice, the rate should be increased to reflect the risk of the allowance not being utilised due to insolvency. But this rate is not easily observed, and is not the same as the rate required on the business' investment (and would generally be lower).

(iii) At a given tax rate, an ACE can improve a country's competitive position for attracting inward investment, as it effectively narrows the corporate tax base and hence reduces the effective average tax rate. Although concerns have been raised that this could constitute a harmful tax practice,[34] the EU's Code of Conduct Group has found that a number of regimes are not harmful. When asked for the reasons behind the introduction of these regimes, these countries could point to the policy goal of equalising the treatment of debt and equity. In its formal response to the Code of Conduct Group on its newly adopted notional interest deduction regime, Malta, for example, submitted that it introduced the regime in response to the European Council's recommendation to address the debt/equity distortion found

[32] For a summary of the regimes see S Hebous and A Klemm, 'A Destination-Based Allowance for Corporate Equity' IMF Working Paper WP/18/239.

[33] R de Mooij, 'Tax Biases to Debt Finance: Assessing the Problem, Finding Solutions, International Monetary Fund Staff Discussion Note' (3 May 2011) SDN/11/11.

[34] See, eg, the opening statement by Oxfam at a session on Harmful Tax Practices. J Langerock, 'Opening Statement for the TAX3 committee public hearing on the fight against harmful tax practices within the European Union and abroad', available at: www.europarl.europa.eu/cmsdata/147402/5%20-%2005%20Opening%20Statement%20Johan%20Langerock_TAX3%20hearing%2015th%20of%20May.pdf.

under its then existing corporate tax regime. It helpfully cited a report by the European Council which had found that:

> Tax incentives for companies to take on debt are still very high. In 2012, Malta stood out as the country with the second highest gap between the tax treatment of debt and equity financing of new investment. This debt bias may lead to excessively high corporate leverage and inefficient allocation of capital. Malta is among the few Member States without any provisions to counter the debt bias.[35]

Despite countries having this justifiable policy cover, the Code of Conduct Group has issued guidance on notional interest deduction regimes which 'presents a non-exhaustive list of elements and characteristics which indicate that a Notional Interest Deduction Regime may be harmful when assessed against the criteria of the Code of Conduct'.[36] As a general matter, we question the distinction between 'harmful' and 'non-harmful' tax practices and competition. Clearly, however, a country could seek to gain a competitive advantage by broadening the base and increasing the rate beyond what is necessary to achieve the ACE's dual goals.

(iv) A number of planning opportunities have come to light in practice.[37] Some planning opportunities exist under traditional CIT systems but can be more attractive under an ACE. Other planning opportunities are particular to the ACE. Some of these opportunities arise only if an ACE does not follow a textbook design. The Guidance on notional interest deduction regimes produced by the EU Code of Conduct Group, emphasises the need to include anti-avoidance measures in regimes to tackle tax planning opportunities.[38]

We describe four strategies here by way of illustration of what might be thought of as planning.

(a) **Incremental equity**. As noted above, one way of reducing the revenue cost arising from the introduction of an ACE is to apply the ACE to incremental – rather than the full stock of – equity. Companies would then have an incentive to convert old equity into new equity, for example, by transferring the assets of a company to a new company and then winding up the old one. This planning could entail significant transaction costs, as well as capital gains tax charges, but Italy introduced specific anti-avoidance rules to combat it[39] and the guidance by the EU Code of Conduct Group identifies this as a planning structure

[35] Code of Conduct Group (Business Taxation), *Malta's notional interest deduction regime (MT014)*, Brussels, 20 November 2018.

[36] General Secretariat of the Council, *Report to the Council on the Code of Conduct Group* (Business Taxation), Brussels, 25 November 2019.

[37] See S Hebous and M Ruf, 'Evaluating the Effects of ACE Systems on Multinational Debt Financing and Investment' (2017) 156 *Journal of Public Economics* 131; E Zangari, 'Addressing the debt bias: a comparison between the Belgian and Italian ACE systems' (2014) EU Commission Taxation Working Papers; and IMF, *Tax Policy, Leverage and Macroeconomic Stability*, October 2016.

[38] General Secretariat of the Council, *Report to the Council on the Code of Conduct Group (Business Taxation)* (n 36).

[39] E Zangari, 'Addressing the debt bias: a comparison between the Belgian and Italian ACE systems' (2014) EU Commission Taxation Working Papers.

that may be addressed through special anti-abuse rules.[40] Note though, that such measures are not required as a matter of principle; implementing the ACE only for incremental equity reduces the revenue cost, but invites planning around what is 'incremental'.

(b) **Double counting**. As the IFS Capital Taxes Group noted in its 1991 Report, to avoid double counting the base for the ACE allowance should exclude equity purchased in other companies.[41] If this is not done, then multiple ACE allowances could be created through a single injection of equity at the parent level. If P raises 100 in equity finance, but then invests it in S1 which in turn invests it in S2, the investment in S1 and S2 should be deducted from the ACE base in P and S1 respectively. This would leave P and S1 with an ACE base of 0, and S2 with an ACE base of 100. Only if this principle is not followed would there be a clear planning opportunity.

(c) **Planning as result of ACE caps.**[42] Some countries – such as Belgium, Italy and Liechtenstein – cap their ACE base at zero and thus do not allow negative ACE bases. This is done for fear that a negative ACE base and hence an ACE *positive charge* would make the regime unattractive, especially for holding companies. But this does create a planning opportunity.

Suppose that P raises 100 of equity and 200 of debt, all of which it invests in S. In principle, P should have a negative ACE base of 200 (injection of equity of 100 less an outflow of equity of 300), which would balance the ACE base of 300 in S. The negative tax base in P would thus ensure that the cumulative ACE base for the group is equal to the outside equity injected into the group. However, if the ACE base is capped at zero, with negative ACE bases not possible, then the group as a whole would have an inflated ACE base of 300. Alternative measures are then necessary to address this planning opportunity. For example, Belgium caps the total allowance if the arrangement is deemed to be artificial and driven by a tax motive. Alternatively, interest deductions may be denied if, for example, the debt–equity ratio exceeds a certain ratio.

(d) **International tax planning**. Planning opportunities can arise if an ACE is introduced in some countries but not others. Consider the following example. P in Country A raises 200 of equity finance. It uses this to fund subsidiary S1, with 100 of equity and 100 of debt. S1 in turn provides 200 of equity finance to a production subsidiary, S2. Assume also that the interest rate and ACE allowances are both 10 per cent.

If all the three parts of the multinational group were in countries with an ACE allowance, and there were no restrictions on the ACE base being less than zero, then there should be no problem:

- S2 pays tax on profit after an ACE allowance of 20 and distributes the net profit to S1.

[40] General Secretariat of the Council, *Report to the Council on the Code of Conduct Group (Business Taxation)* (n 36) section 4.4.

[41] Institute for Fiscal Studies, *Equity for Companies* (n 2) 74.

[42] Examples (c) and (d) are taken from an IMF report. International Monetary Fund, *Tax Policy, Leverage and Macroeconomic Stability*, Staff Report, October 2016, 61–65.

- S1 has a negative ACE allowance of -10 which exactly matches its deduction for the interest payment of +10.
- P has an ACE allowance of 10 (based on equity issued of 200, less equity purchased of 100), which exactly matches its interest received of 10.

However, suppose that S1 is resident in a country which does not have an ACE. Then the situation in S1 is similar to the case in which there is a cap on the ACE allowance being negative. In this case, S1 would receive a deduction for its interest, but there would be no offsetting effect for the negative ACE allowance.

As the IMF notes, it is the country that does not adopt the ACE that is worse off as a result of this planning.[43] Taking a step back, it is clear that this strategy bears considerable resemblance to traditional debt shifting. The introduction of an ACE in some countries thus gives rise to debt-shifting opportunities out of countries with traditional corporate tax systems. Interest limitation rules will thus be of even greater importance for non-adopting countries.

(v) A number of countries have repealed their ACE schemes, including Austria, Croatia and Italy (twice).[44] The repeal of the Croatian tax appears to have been part of a broader reform aimed at reducing CIT rates, rather than technical or administrative difficulties.[45] Broader tax reforms in 2003 also appear to have led to the repeal of the first ACE introduced in Italy.[46] Italy reintroduced an ACE in 2012, but it was repealed in 2019. The repeal was widely criticised by academics and business associations, but, once again, it was undertaken (together with the repeal of other parts of the CIT regime) in the context of a broader tax reform which included a tax rate cut for specific items of profit.[47]

B. Economic Impact

Empirical economic work on the economic impact of ACE has taken different forms. De Mooij and Devereux use an applied general equilibrium model for Europe to assess quantitatively the effects of ACE, CBIT and combined reforms in EU countries.[48] They find that – if the introduction of the ACE is accompanied by higher taxes on labour or consumption or by lower transfers to households[49] – the ACE improves efficiency by removing the distortion between debt and equity finance and by reducing the cost of capital, thereby improving welfare. However, if the ACE is accompanied by higher

[43] ibid 65.

[44] See A Klemm, 'Allowances for Corporate Equity in Practice' (2007) 53 *CESifo Economic Studies* 229 for more on the first three.

[45] M Keen and J King, 'The Croatian Profit Tax: An ACE in Practice' (2002) 23 *Fiscal Studies* 401.

[46] F Massimi and Carlo Petroni, 'Real-World ACE Reforms and the Italian Experience. Towards a General Trend?' (2012) 40 *Intertax* 11.

[47] Paolo Panteghini and Francesca Pighetti, 'Italy Proposes Major Business Tax Reforms for 2019' (*Tax Analysts*, 14 December 2018).

[48] R de Mooij and MP Devereux, 'An applied analysis of ACE and CBIT reforms in the EU' (2011) 18 *International Tax and Public Finance* 93.

[49] This is done to achieve a revenue neutral proposal.

corporate tax rates,[50] the corporate tax base erodes due to profit shifting and adverse effects on discrete location of profitable investment. Under strong responses to higher statutory tax rates, De Mooij and Devereux find that ACE reforms combined with a higher statutory rate would be welfare reducing for most Western European countries. Most Eastern European countries would still benefit from an ACE due to a small multinational sector.

The introduction of the ACE in various jurisdictions has provided an opportunity to investigate empirically whether the ACE achieved its dual policy goals. There is a growing number of studies that examine the impact of an ACE on firm leverage, most finding that the ACE does indeed reduce leverage.[51] Princen[52] and Panier et al[53] find that the Belgian ACE had an effect of 10 and 7–8 percentage points on financial leverage respectively. Hebous and Ruf find an effect of 11 percentage points for the Belgian affiliates of German multinationals,[54] although this decreased once Belgium reduced the ACE base to incremental equity. Petutschnig and Rünger found that the Austrian ACE could have increased corporate equity ratios by 5.5 percentage points.[55] And finally, Branzoli and Caiumi find that the Italian ACE introduced in 2012 reduced leverage ratios by 9 percentage points on average.[56]

C. The ACE in an International Context

The ACE was proposed and has been implemented in the context of an origin-based corporation tax. In recent years, however, there has been some experimentation and thought given to the ACE in the context of other international tax arrangements. For example, elements of the ACE have been introduced in residence-based tax systems – most notably the United States' new GILTI provision. The ACE has also been considered in the context of more fundamental reform.

Academic work has considered the application of an ACE on a destination basis. As noted earlier, an ACE is equivalent to an R-base CFT, and extensive academic work has been undertaken on the adoption of a CFT on a destination basis (destination-based cash flow tax – DBCFT).[57] In principle, this proposal would have significant advantages

[50] As above, this is done to achieve a revenue neutral proposal.

[51] For an overview of this literature see Hebous and Klemm (n 32).

[52] S Princen, 'Taxes Do Affect Corporate Financing Decisions: The Case of Belgian ACE' (2012) CESifo Working Paper.

[53] F Panier, F Pérez-González and P Villanueva, 'Capital structure and taxes: What happens when you (also) subsidize equity?' (unpublished manuscript, 2015).

[54] Hebous and Ruf (n 37).

[55] M Petutschnig and S Rünger, 'The effects of a tax allowance for growth and investment: Empirical evidence from a firm-level analysis' (2017) WU International Tax Research Paper.

[56] N Branzoli and A Caiumi, 'How effective is an incremental ACE in addressing the debt bias? Evidence from corporate tax returns' (2 January 2018), available at: SSRN: ssrn.com/abstract=3048367.

[57] SR Bond and MP Devereux, 'Cash flow taxes in an open economy' (2002) Centre for Economic Policy Research Discussion Paper Series; AJ Auerbach and MP Devereux, 'Cash-Flow Taxes in an International Setting' (2018) 10 *American Economic Journal: Economic Policy* 69; AJ Auerbach, MP Devereux, M Keen and J Vella, 'Destination-Based Cash-Flow Taxation' (2017) Oxford University Centre for Business Taxation Working Paper.

over the existing system for taxing corporate profit in an international setting. In particular, if adopted globally, it would be more efficient (removing distortions to scale of investment, financing and location decisions), more robust to tax planning,[58] and it would bring tax competition among countries to a halt. Interest in this proposal has spread to policy circles too, with a version of the DBCFT being proposed in the House Republican Senate Plan of June 2016.[59]

In the light of these developments, but also the broader debates about moving – even if only partially – to a destination basis of taxation,[60] Hebous and Klemm explore the adoption of an ACE on a destination basis (DBACE).[61] They find that implementing a DBACE does not appear to cause major technical difficulties beyond those related to an origin-based ACE and a DBCFT. In fact, the DBACE may offer some administrative advantage over a DBCFT in that the number of transitory arrangements could be smaller given that it is closer to the existing system than a DBCFT. On the other hand, while it is more robust to tax planning than an origin-based ACE, a DBACE is not as robust as a DBCFT. Similarly, tax competition would be reduced under a DBACE, but is eliminated under a DBCFT. Overall, therefore, they conclude that given the major political cost of switching from an origin to a destination basis of taxation, the advantages of a DBCFT (in terms of robustness to profit shifting and eliminating tax competition) outweigh the transitional advantages of a DBACE.

Another possible option for radically reforming the international tax system is moving to a system of unitary taxation and formulary apportionment. This option has been studied extensively in academic circles[62] and has been proposed twice by the European Commission – in 2011 and again in 2016.[63] The 2016 proposal includes an Allowance for Growth and Investment (AGI) which features many characteristics of an ACE but falls short of a pure ACE on a number of grounds.[64] Significantly, in June 2018 France and Germany expressed their opposition to the inclusion of the AGI in the common consolidated corporate tax base (CCCTB).[65]

[58] AJ Auerbach, MP Devereux, M Keen and J Vella, 'International Tax Planning under the Destination-Based Cash Flow Tax' (2017) 70 *National Tax Journal* 783; and MP Devereux and J Vella, 'Gaming destination-based cash flow taxes' (2018) 71 *Tax Law Review* 477.

[59] Ways and Means Committee of the House of Representatives, *A Better Way Forward: Our Vision for a Confident America* (2016).

[60] See, eg, OECD, *Addressing the Tax Challenges of the Digitalisation of the Economy* (2019).

[61] Hebous and Klemm (n 32).

[62] See, eg, W Hellerstein, 'The Case for Formulary Apportionment' (2005) 12 *International Transfer Pricing Journal* 108; R Avi-Yonah and I Benshalom, 'Formulary Apportionment: Myths and Prospects – Promoting Better International Policy and Utilizing the Misunderstood and Under-Theorized Formulary Alternative' (2011) 3 *World Tax Journal* 371; M Kobetsky, 'The case for unitary taxation of international enterprises' (2008) *Bulletin for International Fiscal Documentation* 62; R Krever and F Vaillancourt (eds), *The Allocation of Multinational Business Income: Reassessing the Formulary Apportionment Option* (Alphen aan den Rijn, Wolters Kluwer, 2020).

[63] European Commission, 'Proposal for a Council Directive on a Common Corporate Tax Base' COM(2016) 685 final; European Commission, 'Proposal for a Council Directive on a Common Consolidated Corporate Tax Base' COM(2016) 683 final.

[64] C Spengel et al, 'Addressing the Debt-Equity Bias within a Common Consolidated Corporate Tax Base (CCCTB) – Possibilities, Impact on Effective Tax Rates and Revenue Neutrality' (2018) 10 *World Tax Journal* 165.

[65] German–French Position Paper on the CCTB (19 June 2018).

V. Conclusion

Thirty years have passed since the ACE was first proposed. This chapter revisited the justifications for the ACE. It argued that the economic efficiency case for the ACE is not undermined by concerns relating to growing inequality. The ACE narrows the corporate tax base to economic rent and thus excludes the normal return from taxation at the corporate level. Even if one were to assume that the normal return should be, and is, taxed (and both assumptions are questionable) then a tax on the normal return at the corporate level still cannot easily be justified as a backstop to the tax on the normal return of individuals. The chapter also argued that the case for an ACE to neutralise the tax treatment of debt and equity is still compelling. In particular, it argued that the asymmetrical treatment of debt and equity at the corporate level cannot be easily addressed at the investor level because of a difference in incidence. In a small open economy, a tax on the return to investors is likely to be borne by investors, while an origin-based tax on companies is likely to be borne by individuals other than shareholders. The chapter also briefly reviews the international experience with the ACE, which overall appears to have been positive.

12

The Changing Patterns of EU Direct Tax Integration

ANZHELA CÉDELLE*

Few questions have generated as much disagreement as the one concerning the extent of direct tax integration that is necessary for the establishment and smooth functioning of the internal market. Over the decades, the policy vision and regulatory approaches have been changing. This process has not been linear. In other words, EU direct tax integration has not progressed smoothly from one phase to the next in a gradually evolving and logical way. Instead, this process is characterised by sometimes sudden changes, triggered by a variety of political and economic factors. The first Programme for the Harmonization of Direct Taxes, published by the European Commission (the Commission) in 1967,[1] was more ambitious than most modern-day policies. Yet, the current direct tax policy agenda is wider than what was under consideration just a decade ago. Without understanding these flunctuations, the interpretation of the past and present of EU direct tax law and policies can be challenging.

This chapter aims at aiding the navigation through the changing patterns of EU direct tax integration. It draws a macro-picture of the integration process, covering both the evolving policy vision and regulatory approaches, and makes an attempt to rationalise its changing patterns. The analysis builds upon the key programme documents of the Commission on the internal market and tax policy. It shows that throughout history, the successes and failures of tax policies have corresponded with the evolution or crisis of the European integration project more generally. At times, however, this field appears to take its distinct path. The current phase in the EU direct tax integration stands out as one such distinct period, influenced by wider developments in international tax cooperation.

* This chapter is built upon the author's doctoral thesis 'Direct Taxation and the Internal Market: Assessing Possibilities for a More Balanced Integration' (University of Oxford, 2013), co-supervised by Professor Judith Freedman. The opinions expressed and arguments employed are those of the author and do not represent the official views of the OECD or of its member countries.

[1] Commission Memorandum to the Council of 8 February 1967 on Tax Harmonization Programme [1967] Supplement to the Bulletin of the EEC 8/3; Commission Memorandum to the Council of 26 June 1967 on Programme for the Harmonization of Direct Taxes [1967] Supplement to the Bulletin of the EEC 8/5, 3 (Commission, 'Programme for the Harmonisation of Direct Taxes').

I. The First Phase (The 1960s to the Mid-1980s): From Full Harmonisation to 'Absolutely Indispensable' Legislative Measures

In 1951, Belgium, Germany, France, Italy, Luxembourg and the Netherlands signed the Treaty establishing the European Coal and Steel Community. This cooperation was furthered by the treaties establishing the European Economic Community (EEC Treaty, 1957) and the European Atomic Energy Community (EURATOM Treaty, 1957), where Member States committed to the idea of the Common Market and the progressive approximation of economic policies.[2] Chapter 2 of the EEC Treaty was fully dedicated to fiscal matters, but its scope was limited to the harmonisation of indirect taxes. There was no treaty reference to direct taxation.

Whilst the Commission did not have explicit competence in this field, it was able to intervene through its associated functions, such as its responsibility for the abolition of obstacles to the free cross-border movement of persons, services and capital (Article 3(c) of the EEC Treaty); the establishment of a system ensuring that the competition between Member States is not distorted (Article 3(f) of the EEC Treaty); and the approximation of national laws to the extent necessary for the functioning of the Common Market (Article 3(h) of the EEC Treaty). The legislative basis for harmonisation measures was to be found in Article 100 of the EEC Treaty: a general clause provided for the approximation of laws with 'a direct incidence on the establishment or functioning of the Common Market', which was subject to a unanimous vote. Article 93 of the EEC Treaty contained a prohibition of state aid able to obscure trade between Member States.

Despite this limited treaty coverage, the initial vision of direct tax harmonisation was ambitious. The Report on EEC Tax Harmonization (the Neumark Report), prepared by the committee chaired by Fritz Neumark in 1962, contained a number of far-reaching proposals for the coordination of Member States' tax regimes.[3] The Neumark Report called for: (i) partial harmonisation through a split-rate corporate tax system; (ii) harmonisation of withholding tax provisions for dividends and interest payments, as well as a uniform taxation of capital gains; (iii) the revision of double taxation treaties between Member States, and the conclusion of a multilateral convention to eliminate double taxation; and (iv) the establishment of common information services to ensure efficient tax administration.[4] These measures were envisaged for adoption in several stages, reflecting the gradual development of fiscal cooperation. Although the harmonisation goals were set quite high, the absolute unification of tax systems was not considered to be a feasible objective, 'since experience proves that on many grounds *moderate* differences *limited to* the nature (structure) and to the rate of taxes

[2] 'It shall be the aim of the Community, by establishing a Common Market and progressively approximating the economic policies of Member States, to promote throughout the Community a harmonious development of economic activities, a continuous and balanced expansion, an increased stability, an accelerated raising of the standard of living and closer relations between its Member States' (Article 2 of the EEC Treaty).

[3] H Thurston (tr), *The EEC Reports on Tax Harmonization: The Report of the Fiscal and Financial Committee and the Reports of the Subgroups A, B, and C* (IBFD 1963) (Neumark Report).

[4] ibid 154–56.

do not hinder the free play of competition'.[5] The next study, the Segré Report (1966), developed recommendations for the better integration of capital markets, including some measures related to the elimination of fiscal obstacles that may distort investment decisions.[6] Among other proposals, the Segré Report supported the adoption of a multilateral convention between Member States, changes in withholding taxes on interest payments and tax credits provided to domestic shareholders to remove the discrimination of cross-border operations.

The first tax harmonisation programme, which was published by the Commission in 1967, largely reflected the conclusions drawn in these studies.[7] In the long term, it aimed 'to arrive at an approximation of the structures, at a certain approximation of the rates and at the total elimination of double taxation'.[8] In the short term, the programme focused on the approximation of tax liabilities of parent companies and their foreign subsidiaries, cross-border company mergers and acquisitions, and the harmonisation of withholding taxes on dividends and interests. Should these measures leave any room for double taxation, the adoption of a multilateral convention was proposed to address the problem.[9] The Commission also acknowledged the need for establishing administrative cooperation between tax authorities.

These far-reaching harmonisation objectives should be seen as part of the general evolution of the process of European integration. The Common Market was expected to be established within 20 years, by 1 January 1970.[10] The 1960s are often described as the golden era, which saw significant progress in removing the obstacles to cross-border trade, for instance, by setting a common VAT system.[11] The tax harmonisation programme was presented as a tool to ensure fair competition between Member States: the costs of production and capital income should not be determined by differences in taxation that were 'too wide'; investment decisions should not be solely defined by fiscal considerations; and the structural changes in enterprises that adjust their activities to the Common Market should be facilitated rather than hampered by tax provisions.[12]

Pursuing this agenda, the Commission proposed the Merger Directive and the Parent–Subsidiary Directive (1969) for adoption.[13] These two proposals were considered to be components of the wider harmonisation of corporate tax systems.

[5] ibid 102 (emphases added).

[6] Commission, *The Development of a European Capital Market: Report of a Group of Experts Appointed by the EEC Commission* (November 1966) (Segré Report).

[7] Commission, 'Programme for the Harmonisation of Direct Taxes' (1967).

[8] ibid 7.

[9] ibid 9.

[10] Article 8 of the EEC Treaty, see also Case 2/74 *Reyners* [1974] ECR 631.

[11] A common VAT system was established in 1967 (Council Directive 67/227/EEC of 11 April 1967 on the harmonisation of legislation of Member States concerning turnover taxes [1967] OJ 71/1301 (First VAT Directive). For a comprehensive historical overview see R de la Feria, *The EU VAT System and the Internal Market* (Amsterdam, IBFD 2009) 45–88. For a description of other important developments initiated at this stage refer to, eg, LW Gormley, 'The Internal Market: History and Evolution' in N Nic Shuibhne (ed), *Regulating the Internal Market* (Cheltenham, Edward Elgar Publishing, 2006).

[12] Commission, 'Programme for the Harmonisation of Direct Taxes' (1967) 7.

[13] Commission, 'Proposal for a Directive on Cross-Border Company Mergers' COM(69) 5 final [1969] OJ 39/1; Commission, 'Proposal for a Directive on the Tax Treatment of Parent Companies and Subsidiaries from Different Member States' COM(69) 6 final [1969] OJ 39/7. In 1968, the Commission also prepared a preliminary draft of the multilateral treaty, but due to political disagreement further work was not undertaken.

Since disagreement with the proposal made by the Neumark Report was evident, the Commission invited Professor AJ van den Tempel to investigate other potentially acceptable models. The Tempel Report (1970) considered three options: the classic system; the system of a double rate; and the system of credit; it recommended the classic approach as the most appropriate choice.[14] None of these proposals, however, found political support at this early stage of integration.

In 1975 the Commission published a new action programme for taxation, expressing its frustration with the lack of cooperation in fiscal matters.[15] Seeking a solution, the Commission changed its strategy to concentrate on measures that were 'absolutely indispensable'.[16] The long-term projects, such as the harmonisation of corporate tax bases, were suspended. The priority measures concerned: (i) the tax treatment of mergers, divisions and contributions of assets between companies located in different Member States; (ii) the tax liabilities of parent companies and their foreign subsidiaries; (iii) the withholding of taxes on dividend and interest payments; and (iv) the exchange of information between tax authorities. Pursuing these priorities, the Commission proposed several new legislative initiatives.[17] However, all but one directive failed to reach the unanimity threshold. The successful directive provided grounds for the cross-border exchange of information between tax authorities, but it can hardly be considered as groundbreaking.[18] Member States continued to rely upon double tax treaties.[19]

This lack of progress can be explained by the legal and economic context. The EU decision-making process was fully controlled by national governments: any harmonisation measures were subject to a cost benefit analysis. The abolition of tariffs and quantitative restrictions was prioritised and pursued more actively than the elimination

[14] AJ van den Tempel, *Corporation Tax and Individual Income Tax in the European Communities* (Commission of the European Communities 1970) 41 (Tempel Report).

[15] Commission, 'Action Programme for Taxation' (Communication) COM(75) 391 final.

[16] ibid para 4.

[17] The following four initiatives were under consideration: (i) company taxation and withholding taxes on dividends: Commission, 'Proposal for a Council Directive concerning the Harmonization of Systems of Company Taxation and of Withholding Tax on Dividends' COM(75) 392 final [1975] OJ C253/2. This proposal was withdrawn in 1990; (ii) arbitration procedure: Commission, 'Proposal for a Council Directive on the Elimination of Double Taxation in connection with the Adjustment of Transfers of Profits between Associated Enterprises (Arbitration Procedure)' COM(76) 611 final [1976] OJ C301/4. It was substituted by the Arbitration Convention, which was adopted in 1990; (iii) collective investment: Commission, 'Proposal for a Council Directive on the Application to Collective Investment Institutions of the Council Directive concerning the Harmonization of Systems of Company Taxation and of Withholding Taxes on Dividends' COM(78) 340 final [1978] OJ C184/8, withdrawn in 1993; and (iv) income tax: Commission, 'Proposal for a Council Directive concerning the Harmonization of Income Taxation Provisions with respect to Freedom of Movement for Workers within the Community' COM(79) 737 final [1980] OJ C21/6. It was withdrawn in 1992.

[18] Acting upon the proposal from the Commission, the Council adopted a resolution of 10 February 1975 on the measures to be taken by the Community in order to combat international tax evasion and avoidance [1975] OJ C35/1 and subsequently voted for Council Directive 77/799/EEC of 19 December 1977 concerning mutual assistance of tax authorities in the field of direct taxation and taxation of insurance premiums [1977] OJ L336/15 (repealed by Council Directive 2011/16/EU of 15 February 2011 on administrative cooperation in the field of taxation [2011] OJ L64/1).

[19] CM Harris, 'The European Community's Parent–Subsidiary Directive' (1994) 9 *Florida Journal of International Law* 111, 124.

of non-tariff barriers to trade.[20] The Court of Justice of the European Union (the Court) was demonstrating a proactive approach towards market integration by establishing the key principles of interaction between EU law and national legal systems, such as direct effect and supremacy.[21] Governments were slow in digesting these fast-moving and complex transformations of legal systems, which made legislative developments in directions that were not considered essential for the operation of the Common Market much harder. The position of the Commission – the only participant in the legislative process that could potentially see the advantages for the Common Market as a whole behind the curtain of national fiscal interest – was too weak to change this perception. Besides, soon after the Commission published its tax harmonisation programme, Europe faced the difficulties of enlargement and was hit by the economic recession of the 1970s.

To summarise, the first two decades of European direct tax integration can be described as a period of ambitious plans for far-reaching legislative harmonisation with very limited success. This stage demonstrated a mismatch between what was desirable and what was achievable through the legislative route in the given legal, political and economic conditions. It was obvious that either the scope of the harmonisation measures or the regulatory instruments needed to be adjusted. Since then, progress has been made in both directions.

II. The Second Phase (The Mid-1980s to 1992): Reinforcing the Internal Market – A Breakthrough in Positive and Negative Harmonisation

The Report on the Scope for Convergence of Tax Systems (1980) reflected the failure of fiscal integration at the initial stage. The Commission acknowledged: 'a further lesson that experience has taught is that the Community interest is generally disregarded when national tax policies are being framed'.[22] This pessimistic conclusion reflected the general state of affairs with the European project: the progress towards the Community objectives was hampered by differences in the state of national economies and policy objectives. As Craig describes,

> [i]t was … this very sense that the Community was falling behind its agenda which generated a feeling of pessimism in the Community in the late 1970s and early 1980s. There seems to be no ready way in which the Community would ever attain its goals, and the reality of single-market integration appeared to be as far away as ever.[23]

[20] See, eg, M Egan, 'Single Market' in E Jones et al (eds), *The Oxford Handbook of the European Union* (Oxford, Oxford University Press, 2012) 408–09.

[21] See, eg, JHH Weiler, 'Transformation of Europe' (1991) 100 *Yale Law Journal* 2403; A Easson, 'Legal Approaches to European Integration: The Role of Court and Legislator in the Completion of the European Common Market' (1989) 12 *Journal of European Integration* 101.

[22] Commission, 'Report from the Commission to the Council on the Scope for Convergence of Tax Systems in the Community' (Communication) COM(80) 139 final [1980] 1/80 Supplement to the Bulletin of the European Communities, para 109.

[23] P Craig, 'The Evolution of the Single Market' in C Barnard and J Scott (eds), *The Law of the Single European Market: Unpacking the Premises* (Oxford, Hart Publishing, 2002) 11.

The Commission made an attempt to strengthen its internal market strategy, rethinking the steps that were required to create one global market with its participating countries, providing impetus for its growth and stimulating competition.[24] The action plan, prepared by the Commission in 1985 (White Paper on the Internal Market), contained approximately 280 items of legislation that would be required to establish the internal market.[25] The Single European Act (1986) set some institutional changes that were vital for this development.[26] In particular, Article 100a of the EEC Treaty Commission introduced a qualified majority voting system for measures that have as their objective the establishment and functioning of the internal market, and Article 7a of the EEC Treaty stated that this ambitious project should be completed by the end of 1992. Subsequently, all items included in the White Paper on the Internal Market were adopted.[27]

The harmonisation of national direct tax systems, however, found very limited attention in the programme of legislative actions required for completing the integration project. The removal of barriers for cross-border trade was at the centre of attention. The White Paper on the Internal Market distinguished three types of barrier: physical (part I), technical (part II) and fiscal (part III); yet, the fiscal section dealt solely with indirect taxation. The latter was viewed as an essential component that *directly affected the trade* between Member States and thus also the internal market.[28] The discussion on direct taxes was limited to two paragraphs in the context of facilitating cooperation between businesses, where the Commission called for the adoption of the Merger and Parent–Subsidiary directives that had been under consideration since the late 1960s.[29] The qualified majority voting set by Article 100a of the EEC Treaty was not applicable to fiscal matters. The Article contained the explicit restriction that it could not be used in relation to fiscal provisions, provisions relating to the free movement of persons and those relating to the rights and interests of employed persons. This provision was introduced because some Member States preferred to retain ultimate control over sensitive policy areas: the special status of fiscal matters became even more apparent with this amendment.

Christiane Scrivener, the European Commissioner at that time, stated that the European tax strategy needed to be 'ambitious', but kept 'realistic'.[30] The Guidelines for Company Taxation (1990) (the Guidelines) demonstrated a clear departure from the uniform approach and vision of a tax neutral internal market, which had been strongly

[24] Commission, 'White Paper on Completing the Internal Market' (Communication) COM(85) 310 final, para 8.

[25] Commission, 'White Paper on Completing the Internal Market' (Communication) COM(85) 310 final.

[26] See, inter alia, R Dehousse and G Majone, 'The Institutional Dynamics of European Integration: From the Single Act to the Maastricht Treaty' in S Martin (ed), *The Construction of Europe – Essays in Honour of Emile Noël* (Dordrecht, Kluwer Academic Publishers 1994); S Weatherill, 'Supply of and Demand for Internal Market Regulation: Strategies, Preferences and Integration' in N Nic Shuibhne (ed), *Regulating the Internal Market* (Cheltenham, Edward Elgar Publishing, 2006).

[27] Commission, XXVIth General Report on the Activities of the European Communities 1993 (Office for Official Publications of the European Communities, 1994) 35; Commission, XXVIIth General Report on the Activities of the European Communities 1993 (Office for Official Publications of the European Communities, 1994) 36.

[28] Commission, 'White Paper on Completing the Internal Market' (Communication) COM(85) 310 final, para 17.

[29] ibid paras 142–43.

[30] C Scrivener, 'Corporate Taxation in Europe and the Single Market' (1990) 18 *Intertax* 207, 207.

present in its first harmonisation programme.[31] The Commission admitted that 'any form of company taxation is liable to bring about economic distortions (lack of neutrality) because it may give rise to decisions on the location, nature and financing of investment'.[32] The investor's choice may depend on a Member State's tax base, rate and other characteristics of the tax system and this could explain the need for the harmonisation of Member States' tax systems to safeguard 'complete tax neutrality'.[33] Discussing it further, however, the Commission concluded that the principle of subsidiarity holds back such comprehensive measures: 'Member States should remain free to determine their tax arrangements, *except* where these would lead to *major distortions*'.[34] Admitting the importance of tax neutrality, the Commission did not see the possibility of considering it to be an ultimate goal and decided to focus on the gradual elimination of key fiscal obstacles. This balancing exercise, which was described by Graetz and Warren as 'somewhat schizophrenic',[35] was inescapable. Yet, the new tax strategy acknowledged in the Guidelines fitted well into wider European debates on the division of competences between the EU and its Member States – as a result of which the principle of subsidiarity was formalised in the Treaty of Maastricht (1992).[36] Considering the lack of consensus between the Member States, the high appraisal of subsidiarity concerns was also a matter of practical necessity.

Declaring that the coordination and approximation of policies should prevail over the 'systematic use of harmonization', the Guidelines largely repeated the priorities articulated previously by the White Paper on the Internal Market, namely: (i) the proposal for a directive on a common system of taxation applicable to mergers, divisions and contributions of assets involving companies from different Member States; (ii) the proposal for a directive on a common system of taxation applicable to parent companies and subsidiaries from different Member States; and (iii) the proposal for a directive introducing an arbitration procedure for eliminating double taxation in the event of the adjustment of profits between associated enterprises.[37] Drafted by the Commission at the first stage of the integration process, all three proposals were revised to have a more modest scope, and they were subsequently adopted.[38]

The new version of the Merger Directive provided the possibility of deferring capital gains taxes paid upon some cross-border transactions associated with the restructuring of companies, but it excluded the possibility of the relief (or deferral) of

[31] Commission, 'Programme for the Harmonisation of Direct Taxes' (1967).

[32] Commission, 'Guidelines on Company Taxation' (Communication) SEC(90) 601 final, para 3 (Commission, SEC(90) 601).

[33] ibid para 4.

[34] ibid para 5 (emphasis added).

[35] MJ Graetz and AC Warren, 'Income Tax Discrimination and the Political and Economic Integration of Europe' (2006) 115 *Yale Law Journal* 1186, 1228.

[36] For some reflections on the Treaty of Maastricht, which explain the historical context and changes, see a special issue of the *Journal of European Integration*, 'The Maastricht Treaty: Second Thoughts after 20 Years', in particular on the legitimacy problems discussed by JHH Weiler, 'In the Face of Crisis: Input Legitimacy, Output Legitimacy and the Political Messianism of European Integration' (2012) 34 *Journal of European Integration* 825.

[37] Commission, SEC(90) 601 final, paras 17–22.

[38] Refer to a brief overview in BJM Terra and PJ Wattel, *European Tax Law*, 5th edn (Alphen aan den Rijn, Wolters Kluwer Law & Business, 2008) 475–77; (Parent–Subsidiary Directive) 517–18; (Merger Directive) 563–67 (EU Arbitration Convention).

taxes in the circumstances which generated disagreements between Member States.[39] The Parent–Subsidiary Directive dealt with the double taxation of cross-border dividend payments between parent companies and subsidiaries that meet certain substantive requirements (for example, ownership criteria).[40] The new version of the Directive did not require a Member State to introduce an exemption method, but provided a choice between two internationally accepted practices: exemption or credit. Another important exclusion concerned the tax treatment of losses: the old version allowed optional fiscal consolidation for foreign subsidiaries by a domestic parent company, making the status of a subsidiary comparable to that of a branch. The 1976 proposal for a directive on the elimination of double taxation in the case of transfers of profits between associated enterprises in different Member States was replaced by the intergovernmental convention.[41]

The Guidelines also acknowledged two forthcoming proposals, on the carry-over of losses and the withholding of taxes on interest and royalty payments between parent companies and subsidiaries.[42] These draft directives were less successful: published in 1990, they were subsequently withdrawn.[43] The Commission's initiative for the harmonisation of corporate tax bases (1988) was never tabled due to the lack of political support.

At the same time, the Commission began to explore non-binding instruments for the purpose of stimulating cooperation on fiscal matters. Three communications were adopted: addressing the problems of international tax evasion and avoidance (1984);[44] encouraging cooperation between undertakings of different Member States through fiscal measures (1985);[45] and liberalising tax arrangements for capital movements (1989).[46]

[39] Council Directive 90/434/EEC of 23 July 1990 on the common system of taxation applicable to mergers, divisions, transfers of assets and exchanges of shares concerning companies of different Member States [1990] OJ L225/1 (Merger Directive).

[40] Council Directive 90/435/EEC of 23 July 1990 on the common system of taxation applicable in the case of parent companies and subsidiaries of different Member States [1990] OJ L225/6 (Parent–Subsidiary Directive).

[41] Commission, 'Proposal for a Council Directive on the Elimination of Double Taxation in connection with the Adjustment of Transfers of Profits between Associated Enterprises (Arbitration Procedure)' COM(76) 611 final [1976] OJ C301/4; Convention 90/436/EEC of 23 July 1990 on the elimination of double taxation in connection with the adjustment of profits of associated enterprises [1990] OJ L225/10.

[42] Commission, SEC(90) 601 final, paras 23–26.

[43] In fact, a draft directive on losses was initially proposed in 1984 (Commission, 'Proposal for a Council Directive on the Harmonization of the Laws of the Member States relating to Tax Arrangements for the Carry-over of Losses of Undertakings' COM(84) 404 final [1984] OJ C253/5), as amended by Commission, 'Amendments to the Proposal for a Council Directive on the Harmonization of the Laws of the Member States relating to Tax Arrangements for the Carry-over of Losses of Undertakings' COM(85) 319 final [1985] OJ C170/3 and subsequently withdrawn. The new directive had a wider coverage. See Commission, 'Proposal for a Council Directive concerning Arrangements for the Taking into Account by Enterprises of the Losses of their Permanent Establishments and Subsidiaries Situated in other Member States' COM(90) 595 final [1991] OJ C53/30, withdrawn in 2001. For the proposal on withholding taxes on interest and royalty payments see Commission, 'Proposal for a Council Directive on a Common System of Taxation Applicable to Interest and Royalty Payments Made between Parent Companies and Subsidiaries in Different Member States' COM(90) 571 final [1991] OJ C53/26, withdrawn in 1994.

[44] Commission, 'Community Action to Combat International Tax Evasion and Avoidance' (Communication) COM(84) 603 final.

[45] Commission, 'Fiscal Measures Aimed at Encouraging Cooperation between Undertakings of Different Member States' (Communication) COM(85) 360 final.

[46] Commission, 'Tax Measures to be Adopted by the Community in Connection with the Liberalization of Capital Movements' (Communication) COM(89) 60 final.

Acting upon the proposal from the Commission, the Council adopted an action plan for small to medium-sized enterprises (SMEs) in 1986.[47]

Another important development that took place at this stage was the first direct tax judgment delivered by the Court. The gateway for negative harmonisation was opened by the Commission. In 1984 France failed to amend its legislation in response to a reasoned opinion sent by the Commission in the framework of the infringement procedure, which resulted in the case (Case 270/83 *Avoir Fiscal*)[48] being referred to the Court in Luxembourg.[49] This first example did not result in a rapidly growing number of referrals by the Commission.[50] Enforcement actions in this field remained exceptionally rare: all but the single infringement case mentioned in the first Commission's report on the application of Community law concerned indirect taxes.[51] The reports published in the 1980s even used the heading 'Customs Union and Indirect Taxation' rather than a more general 'Taxation'.[52] Member States' courts also maintained a passive position: in the 1980s only one judgment was delivered in response to the request for a preliminary ruling (Case 81/87 *Daily Mail*).[53]

This stage can thus be regarded as transitional: the Commission achieved a certain degree of progress towards positive harmonisation as part of its strategy to reinforce the internal market. It also made the first steps in involving non-binding instruments and infringement proceedings as a means of addressing fiscal obstacles. Although none of these tools became a prevailing and well-established practice at this stage, they laid the groundwork for future developments.

III. The Third Phase (The 1990s): The Increasing Role of Article 267 TFEU in the Field of Direct Taxation

When the priority measures were adopted in 1990, the Commission asked the Ruding Committee to explore the possibilities for further tax integration. This committee of

[47] Council Resolution of 3 November 1986 concerning the action programme for small and medium-sized enterprises (SMEs) [1986] OJ C287/1.

[48] Case C-270/83 *Commission v France* ECLI:EU:C:1986:37 (*Avoir Fiscal*).

[49] Commission, '1st Annual Report on Commission Monitoring of the Application of Community Law (1983)' (Report) COM(84) 181 final, para 60.

[50] *cf* Gormley (n 11) 17.

[51] The first direct tax infringement case was reported under the category 'Bank, Insurance, etc' rather than 'Taxation', which was used for indirect tax cases. In paras 73–74, the report stated that 'on taxation generally, the Commission decided to transmit reasoned opinions in 17 cases in which Member States have failed to meet their obligations. Of these cases, ten relate to the incorrect application of the sixth VAT Directive and seven to infringements of Article 95 of the EEC Treaty'.

[52] See Commission, '2nd Annual Report on Commission Monitoring of the Application of Community Law (1984)' (Report) COM(85) 149 final; Commission, '3rd Annual Report on Commission Monitoring of the Application of Community Law (1985)' (Report) COM(86) 204 final; Commission, '4th Annual Report on Commission Monitoring of the Application of Community Law (1986)' (Report) COM(87) 250 final; Commission, '5th Annual Report on Commission Monitoring of the Application of Community Law (1987)' (Report) COM(88) 425 final; Commission, '6th Annual Report on Commission Monitoring of the Application of Community Law (1988)' (Report) COM(89) 411 final; Commission, '7th Annual Report on Commission Monitoring of the Application of Community Law (1989)' (Report) COM(90) 288 final.

[53] Case 81/87 *Daily Mail* ECLI:EU:C:1988:456.

experts was asked to examine if the existing differences in corporate income taxation, particularly in relation to corporation tax rates, cause distortions of competition and investment decisions, and whether any special measures are required at the EU level to eliminate these distortions.[54] If a need for action were found, the experts were to suggest measures that should be taken (for example, addressing the differences in tax bases or rates) and to specify how far these measures should go (for example, harmonisation, approximation or the establishment of a uniform framework).[55]

The Ruding Report (1992) was drafted in line with the shift towards minimum harmonisation that could be observed in the EU.[56] It concluded that tax measures should be limited to those addressing the major market distortions, allowing Member States to maintain flexibility in exercising their taxing competences. The Ruding Committee recommended focusing on three objectives: (i) removing discriminatory practices that hamper cross-border investment and shareholding; (ii) introducing measures promoting the transparency of tax incentives; and (iii) adopting the minimum level of corporate tax rates and harmonise the income tax bases in order to eliminate harmful tax competition.[57] The Commission accepted only some of these recommendations, refusing the proposals that had no realistic prospects of gaining political support, such as the harmonisation (even to a minimum extent) of corporate tax rates.[58] The Council's response to the Ruding Report emphasised the importance of observing the principle of subsidiarity and the fiscal sovereignty of Member States,[59] and the European Parliament (the Parliament) further echoed these concerns.

In 1996 the Commission prepared a review of the remaining fiscal obstacles for the Informal Meeting of the Council of Ministers for Economics and Finance (ECOFIN), where it acknowledged that the single market required some additional steps to be taken.[60] The review emphasised the shortcomings of cross-border economic liberalisation and national autonomy over fiscal matters. One of the key objectives of the White Paper on the Internal Market was the stimulation of competition: 'ensuring that the market is flexible so that resources, both of people and materials, and of capital and

[54] Commission, *Conclusions and Recommendations of the Committee of Independent Experts on Company Taxation* (Office for Official Publications of the European Communities 1992) (Ruding Report).

[55] ibid.

[56] For more about this tendency see, eg, Craig (n 23) 25; M Dougan, 'Minimum Harmonization and the Internal Market' (2000) 37 *Common Market Law Review* 853 (and other sources cited); S Weatherill, 'Maximum versus Minimum Harmonisation: Choosing between Unity and Diversity in the Search for the Soul of the Internal Market' in N Nic Shuibhne and LW Gormley (eds), *From Single Market to Economic Union* (Oxford, Oxford University Press, 2012). In the tax context see, eg, CE McLure, 'Coordinating Business Taxation in the Single European Market: The Ruding Committee Report' (1992) 1 *EC Tax Review* 13.

[57] The Ruding Report, part III.

[58] Commission, 'Subsequent to the Conclusions of the Ruding Committee Indicating Guidelines on Company Taxation Linked to the further Development of the Internal Market' (Communication) SEC(92) 1118 final. See also Commission, 'Proposal for a Council Directive amending Directive 90/434/EEC of 23 July 1990 on the Common System of Taxation Applicable to Mergers, Divisions, Transfers of Assets and Exchanges of Shares concerning Companies of Different Member States' [1993] OJ C225/3; Commission, 'Proposal for a Council Directive amending Directive 90/435/EEC of 23 July 1990 on the Common System of Taxation Applicable in the Case of Parent Companies and Subsidiaries of Different Member States' [1993] OJ C225/5.

[59] ECOFIN, Council Meeting Conclusions of 23 November 1992 (1621st Council Meeting).

[60] Commission, 'Taxation in the European Union' (Discussion Paper for the Informal Meeting of ECOFIN Ministers) SEC(96) 487 final.

investment, flow into the areas of greatest economic advantage'.[61] In 1996, however, the Commission warned that tax competition between Member States had intensified as a result of the liberalisation of capital movements and the lack of accompanying tax measures.[62]

To find an acceptable solution to this problem, the Council created a high-level tax group under the coordination of Mario Monti.[63] The group was advised not to 'seek harmonisation of taxation systems for harmonisation's sake' and to take due account of the principles of subsidiarity and proportionality.[64] In response, the Monti Report (1996) proposed 'a new European fiscal strategy', which was based upon the combination of binding and non-binding measures. The Monti Package consisted of legislative proposals on the tax treatment of interest, royalties and savings in cross-border situations, as well as a non-binding instrument, the Code of Conduct for Business Taxation, which addressed the problem of harmful tax competition.[65] This regulatory approach should not be considered in isolation from developments in other policy areas: the evolution of the single market was developing towards an effective combination of binding and non-binding measures contributing to the same policy goal.[66] In 1996 the Commission published a general report on the impact and effectiveness of the single market, which was followed by an inventory of steps required by 1 January 1999.[67] The Commission's action plan (1997) mentioned the Monti Package among the priority measures.[68] The debate during the Internal Market Councils (March and May 1997) demonstrated that the tax package was considered to be 'too ambitious' and, as Mortelmans noted: '[i]t could already be inferred from the cautious reaction of the Internal Market Council to the Commission's proposals on taxation that the European Council would not show much initiative on this point'.[69] Indeed, although the Amsterdam European Council supported the action plan,[70] the direct tax initiatives, with the exception of the Code of Conduct for Business Taxation that was adopted by ECOFIN in 1997, were delayed.[71]

[61] Commission, 'White Paper on Completing the Internal Market' (Communication) COM(85) 310 final, para 8.

[62] Confirmation can be found in a number of economic studies such as M Devereux et al, 'Do Countries Compete over Corporate Tax Rates?' (2008) 92 *Journal of Public Economics* 1210. On the positive aspects of regulatory competition see J-M Sun and J Pelkmans, 'Regulatory Competition in the Single Market' (1995) 33 *Journal of Common Market Studies* 67, 82–83.

[63] ECOFIN, Council Meeting Conclusions of 13 April 1996 (informal meeting).

[64] Commission, 'Taxation in the European Union: Report on the Development of Tax Systems' (Report) COM(96) 546 final, para 6.2.

[65] Commission, 'Towards Tax Co-ordination in the European Union – A Package to Tackle Harmful Tax Competition' (Communication) COM(97) 495 final.

[66] See, eg, Craig (n 23) 31.

[67] Commission, 'Impact and Effectiveness of the Single Market' (Communication) COM(96) 520 final; Commission, 'The 1996 Single Market Review' (Staff Working Paper) SEC(96) 2378.

[68] Commission, 'Action Plan for the Single Market (1997–1999)' (Communication) CSE(97)1 final.

[69] Mortelmans then concluded that the progress in relation to the four priority targets set by the Action Plan was different: some proposals were adopted without delay, ie, mainly target 1 (effective rules) and 3 (sectoral distortions to market integration), while others were much less successful, ie, target 2 (tax barriers and anti-competitive behaviour harmonisation) and target 4 (liberalisation of service markets). See K Mortelmans, 'The Common Market, the Internal Market and the Single Market, What's in a Market?' (1998) 35 *Common Market Law Review* 101, 114 and 135.

[70] European Council Conclusions of 16–17 June 1997, point 8.

[71] ECOFIN, Council Meeting Conclusions of 1 December 1997 concerning taxation policy (Annex 1: Resolution of the Council and the Representatives of the Governments of the Member States, meeting within the Council of 1 December 1997 on a code of conduct for business taxation) [1998] OJ C2/1. The Interest and Royalty Payments Directive and the Savings Taxation Directive were only adopted in 2003.

With very limited success in positive harmonisation, the third period was characterised by the increasing role of the Court.[72] The vast majority of cases were referred to Luxembourg by national courts, making Article 267 TFEU a dominant tool of tax integration. The Commission was inert in using its enforcement powers: by 2001 only three judgments were delivered under the infringement procedure framework.[73] The number of investigated cases was low: in 1999, for instance, the Commission issued only two reasoned opinions on direct taxation.[74]

This stage demonstrated that the effectiveness of regulation in the EU was no longer associated with the uniformity of legislative harmonisation, but was considered to require a more complex combination of binding and non-binding instruments. Considering the limited success beyond the non-binding domain, the Commission passed the leading role in this field to the Court.

IV. The Fourth Phase (The Early 2000s): Strengthening the Alternative Regulatory Tools – A More Proactive Enforcement Strategy and Non-Binding Coordination

The regulatory aspect became one of the central issues discussed in the Communication 'Tax Policy in the European Union – Priorities for the Years Ahead' (2001).[75] The Commission stated that the ambitious Lisbon Agenda required tax policy to be considered with 'a new perspective', which would entail more effective tools for policy delivery.[76] Rejecting the need for broad tax harmonisation measures, the Commission concluded that the mobility of tax bases needed 'a certain degree of co-ordination' to eliminate the remaining obstacles to the internal market, particularly double taxation and unintentional non-taxation.[77] Four potential tools were discussed: legislative acts, enforcement actions, 'soft legislation' and enhanced cooperation.[78] In relation to the legislative process, the Commission expressed the view that a qualified majority voting system should be introduced for certain tax matters, in particular those creating severe distortions to the freedom of movement. But since the prospect of this procedural change was questionable, the Communication focused on strengthening the Commission's role as guardian of the Treaties, broadening the range of policy instruments and making the

[72] Notably, MP Maduro, *We the Court: The European Court of Justice and the European Economic Constitution: A Critical Reading of Article 30 of the EC Treaty* (Oxford, Hart Publishing, 1998).

[73] Based on DG TAXUD, 'CJEU Cases in the Area of, or Particular Interest for, Direct Taxation' (updated to 19 December 2019), available at: ec.europa.eu/taxation_customs/sites/taxation/files/20191212_court_cases_direct_taxation_en.pdf.

[74] Commission, '17th Annual Report on Monitoring the Application of Community Law (1999)' [2001] OJ C30/1, 24–25.

[75] Commission, COM(2001) 260 final.

[76] ibid section 2.1. The substantive policy priorities included tackling tax obstacles for cross-border economic activities, combating harmful tax competition and promoting closer cooperation between tax administrations.

[77] EU Member States 'are free to choose the tax systems that they consider most appropriate and according to their preferences' (ibid section 2.4).

[78] ibid section 4.

use of variable geometry under Article 20 TEU.[79] The main emphasis was put on better compliance and coordination.[80]

The enhanced role of infringement proceedings was associated with making the Commission's actions more targeted, in particular through the proactive initiation of its own cases, which were exceptionally rare compared with the infringement files opened in response to complaints from citizens and businesses. The need for a more rigorous approach was explained as follows. First, the Commission noted that the increased number of requests for preliminary rulings indicated that the level of non-compliance was high. The market-led integration, where the development of case law was left to taxpayers in the expectation that the matter of EU law would be raised by litigants, was criticised as a wrong way to ensure stable progress towards the agreed Community objectives. Second, the Commission was facing an 'asymmetrical' effect of the Court's case law.[81] Due to the differences in national tax systems, the application of judgments was often uncertain and many Member States were adjusting their laws to ensure better compliance with EU requirements 'in vastly differing ways'.[82] As guardian of the Treaties, the Commission was foremost concerned with the proper implementation of case law, particularly in relation to rulings with wide horizontal importance.

The non-legislative approach (so-called 'soft legislation' or 'soft law') was considered as another route for taking cooperation in the field of direct taxation to a new level. As discussed earlier, these instruments had been in limited use for the purpose of direct tax policies before 2001. The Commission stated that non-binding instruments (for example, communications, recommendations, guidelines and interpretative notices) could explain the application of EU law in a specific context, contributing to better compliance. As a follow-up to the Court rulings, these instruments could offer new policy solutions if the existing tax provisions were found to infringe EU law, and could thus contribute to more coordinated responses from Member States. Soft law could also fulfil a preventive function by communicating potential legal conflicts between national tax provisions and EU law, and identifying ways of resolving them without costly litigation. This approach, however, was not considered to have universal application. The Commission mentioned that non-binding instruments could be appropriate in cases with firm legal foundations, such as treaty provisions and the Court's jurisprudence. In other cases, soft law could consume substantial resources without making an evident difference due to the lack of direct enforceability.

The regulatory agenda with regard to tax matters corresponded with the messages contained in the programme documents defining the strategy of the single market. As the process of integration advanced, the Commission's attention shifted from the elimination of barriers to making the single market operate more efficiently and enhancing the competitiveness of the European economy.[83] All three generations of the single market's programme documents, which covered the period from 1999 to 2009, devoted

[79] ibid.

[80] For an analysis see, eg, A Fortuin, 'The Influence of European Law on Direct Taxation – Recent and Future Developments' (2007) 47 *European Taxation* 144.

[81] Communication, COM(2001) 260 final, section 4.2.

[82] ibid.

[83] Commission, 'The Strategy for Europe's Internal Market' (Communication) COM(1999) 624 final.

substantial attention to effective policy delivery.[84] The new strategy continued the move from systematic legislative harmonisation to a fuller integration of non-binding instruments.[85] According to the Commission, this approach reflected 'the characteristics of a more mature Internal Market'.[86]

The White Paper on European Governance (2001), which set the direction for changes in EU policymaking, also reflected this regulatory tendency.[87] Its key targets included: (i) a wider and more coherent use of different policy tools, particularly non-legislative instruments, either to complement a legislative approach or to encourage cooperation and progress towards common targets in those policy areas 'where there is little scope for legislative solutions'; (ii) more effective enforcement strategies based on clear selection criteria, allowing a focus on priority cases; and (iii) a higher quality of drafting ensured by minimum consultation standards and the impact assessment of legislative and policy proposals.[88]

In 2006 the Communication 'A Citizens' Agenda – Delivering Results for Europe' called for 'a fundamental review' of the single market.[89] The key 'modernisation' message for 2006–09 concerned the choice of regulatory instruments: the Commission's 'toolbox' should be more strategic (to engage the most suitable tool) and flexible (to accommodate differences between Member States and changes over time).[90] The Staff Working Document 'Instruments for a Modernised Single Market Policy', which accompanied the Communication 'A Single Market for 21st Century Europe' (2007), defined specific recommendations for the better use of non-binding tools and enforcement powers.[91] In 2009 the Commission published a set of measures that could further improve the functioning of the single market.[92] It emphasised the importance of strengthening enforcement policies and alternative problem-solving tools (for example, SOLVIT and EU Pilot), as well as communication policies, particularly through interpretative communications. This brief overview illustrates the post-1999 shift from 'what' (recognising the direction for substantive changes) to 'how' (putting in place measures to ensure that existing laws are correctly transposed, applied, enforced and monitored).

In the view of these priorities, it does not come as a surprise that the scope of legislative changes in the field of direct taxation was modest. The Strategy for Europe's Internal Market for 1999–2003 stressed the importance of the legislative component

[84] Communication, 'The Strategy for Europe's Internal Market' (Communication) COM(1999) 624 final; Commission, 'Internal Market Strategy – Priorities 2003–2006' (Communication) COM(2003) 238 final; Commission, 'A Single Market for 21st Century Europe' (Communication) COM(2007) 724 final.

[85] For more see N Bernard, 'Flexibility in the European Single Market' in C Barnard and J Scott (eds), *The Law of the Single Market: Unpacking the Premises* (Oxford, Hart Publishing 2002); Craig (n 23).

[86] Commission, 'The Strategy for Europe's Internal Market' (Communication) COM(1999) 624 final.

[87] Commission, 'White Paper on European Governance' (Communication) COM(2001) 428 final.

[88] ibid section 3.2.

[89] Commission, 'A Citizens' Agenda – Delivering Results for Europe' (Communication) COM(2006) 211 final.

[90] Commission, 'A Single Market for 21st Century Europe' (Communication) COM(2007) 724 final, section 1.

[91] Commission, 'Instruments for a Modernised Single Market Policy' (Communication) SEC(2007) 1518 final accompanying ibid.

[92] Commission Recommendation of 29 June 2009 on measures to improve the functioning of the single market [2009] OJ L176/17.

of the Monti Package.[93] The annual reviews published in 2000–02 confirmed that the 'tax package' was vital, but the deadline was postponed.[94] Both directives were adopted only in 2003.[95] The Internal Market Strategy for 2003–06 included two sets of priority tax measures.[96] The short-term goals included the revision of the Parent–Subsidiary and Merger directives, which were agreed in 2003 and 2005 respectively. As a long-term strategy, the Commission focused on the Common (Consolidated) Corporate Tax Base (CCCTB) for providing companies with the consolidated tax base for their EU-wide activities and the 'Home State Taxation' pilot scheme for SMEs.[97] The Single Market Strategy for 2006–09 retained these long-term objectives: the Commission confirmed its intention to tackle the fragmentation of the single market through the CCCTB proposal and to further examine how the cross-border operation of SMEs is affected by tax policies.[98]

Thus, during this phase, to respond to the increasing number of requests for preliminary rulings from domestic courts to the Court, the Commission declared that it should intervene more effectively in the field of direct taxation. In practice, this led to the increasing flow of infringement cases pursued by the Commission and several attempts of using non-binding instruments for coordination purposes.[99] The choice of a proactive enforcement strategy and non-binding coordination reflected the general regulatory tendencies in the Single Market Strategy of that period.

V. The Fifth Phase (Beyond 2009): A Perfect Storm to Revamp the EU's Direct Tax Policy Agenda?

The next phase was triggered by the financial crisis which brought austerity measures and budget deficits. A string of tax scandals generated widespread public and political

[93] Commission, 'The Strategy for Europe's Internal Market' (Communication) COM(1999) 624 final; see also Commission, 'Company Taxation in the Internal Market' (Staff Working Paper) SEC(2001) 1681 final.

[94] Commission, '2000 Review of the Internal Market Strategy' (Communication) COM(2000) 257 final; Commission, '2001 Review of the Internal Market Strategy – Working Together to Maintain Momentum' (Communication) COM(2001) 198 final; Commission, '2002 Review of the Internal Market Strategy – Delivering the Promise' (Communication) COM(2002) 171 final.

[95] Council Directive 2003/48/EC of 3 June 2003 on taxation of savings income in the form of interest payments [2003] OJ L157/38 (Saving Directive); Council Directive 2003/49/EC of 3 June 2003 on a common system of taxation applicable to interest and royalty payments made between associated companies of different Member States [2003] OJ L157/49 (Interest and Royalty Directive).

[96] Commission, 'Internal Market Strategy – Priorities 2003–2006' (Communication) COM(2003) 238 final, followed by two subsequent implementation reports: Commission, 'Report on the Implementation of the Internal Market Strategy (2003–2006)' (Communication) COM(2004) 22 final; and 'Second Implementation Report of the Internal Market Strategy 2003–2006' (Communication) COM(2005) 11 final.

[97] Commission, 'Towards an Internal Market without Tax Obstacles – A Strategy for Providing Companies with a Consolidated Corporate Tax Base for their EU-wide Activities' (Communication) COM(2001) 582 final.

[98] Commission, 'The Single Market: Review of Achievements' (Staff Working Document) SEC(2007) 1521 final accompanying 'A Single Market for 21st Century Europe' (Communication) COM(2007) 724 final.

[99] See, in particular, Commission, 'Co-ordinating Member States' Direct Tax Systems in the Internal Market' (Communication) COM(2006) 823; Commission, 'Tax Treatment of Losses in Cross-Border Situations' (Communication) COM(2006) 824; Commission, 'Exit Taxation and the Need for Co-ordination of Member States' Tax Policies' (Communication) COM(2006) 825 final.

attention to the problem of tax avoidance and evasion. Much of the discussions on how to address the loopholes in the existing international tax system were taking place at the level of the Organisation for Economic Co-operation and Development (OECD) and G20, transforming into an unprecedented coordination of action at the global level in the field of tax transparency and anti-base erosion and profit shifting (BEPS) measures. This drive for coordinated actions found its reflection at the EU level, yet again changing the pattern of the integration process in direct taxation.

Initially, the post-2009 period had continued to develop in the direction set in the previous years. In 2009 the new Barosso Commission relaunched the single market as a strategic objective that had to be pursued 'with renewed political determination'.[100] Mario Monti was asked to prepare a report that would answer 'whether, and how, the single market may be turned from a perception of being "yesterday's business" into a key political priority, to meet the growing challenges of European integration'.[101] The Monti Report (2010) did not propose any revolutionary changes in relation to tax policies. It argued for stricter enforcement of the single market requirements and further progress with tax coordination measures to stimulate market integration. Tax coordination was praised as being able to 'safeguard national tax sovereignty as market integration proceeds'.[102] The idea of tax harmonisation was rejected again.[103]

Following the Monti Report, the Commission published the Single Market Act (2011) to relaunch the single market by its twentieth anniversary and to contribute to the objectives of the Europe 2020 Strategy.[104] The Commission's focus shifted back from the instruments delivering effective policies to the substantive policy targets. The Single Market Act defined 12 priority projects for the coming 18 months. In the field of direct taxation, it highlighted the legislative proposal for a CCCTB and non-legislative measures addressing cross-border taxation problems for citizens.[105] The Single Market Act II, presented in October 2012, did not include any new substantive items on direct taxation.[106] The most notable outcome of this period was the adoption of the Administrative Cooperation Directive, which repealed the previous act from 1977.[107]

The Commission's proposal for the CCCTB Directive was published in March 2011. However, its adoption under Article 115 TFEU, which requires unanimity voting in the Council, remained doubtful. In April 2012 the CCCTB proposal was approved with some amendments by the Parliament following the consultation procedure. The Parliament explicitly stated that once it was confirmed by the Council that the legislative proposal lacks the political support of all governments, an alternative procedural arrangement with the participation of a smaller group of Member States should be

[100] JM Barosso, 'Political Guidelines for the Next Commission' (3 September 2009).

[101] M Monti, *A New Strategy for the Single* Market (9 May 2010), section 1.1 (Monti Report).

[102] ibid; see 'Executive Summary'.

[103] ibid.

[104] Commission, 'Europe 2020: A Strategy for Smart, Sustainable and Inclusive Growth' (Communication) COM(2010) 2020 final.

[105] Commission, 'Single Market Act: Twelve Levers to Boost Growth and Strengthen Confidence "Working together to Create New Growth"' (Communication) COM(2011) 206 final, section 2.9.

[106] Commission, 'Single Market Act II: Together for New Growth' (Communication) COM(2012) 573 final.

[107] Council Directive 2011/16/EU of 15 February 2011 on administrative cooperation in the field of taxation, which repealed the previous act from 1977 (Administrative Cooperation Directive).

initiated 'without delay'.[108] The first application of the enhanced cooperation procedure was already on its way in relation to another tax initiative proposed under Article 113 TFEU. In 2012, when 10 Member States had officially expressed their willingness to establish closer cooperation, the Council gave the green light to Article 20 TEU as 'a last resort' option for introducing a financial transactions tax.[109] At that time, Article 20 TEU had been relied upon only twice (ie, in relation to bi-national divorce and EU patents), which turned the tax field into one of the potential frontrunners in the application of this procedure. The proposed use of the enhanced cooperation appeared at the time as a bold policy move, necessitated by strong political backing for this step in some Member States and equally strong opposition in other countries. The financial crisis therefore created the context which pushed the differentiated integration out of the toolbox of possible regulatory tools into the world of real politics. These attempts, however, have not been successful. Whilst subsequently amended and relaunched, both proposals remain pending on the EU tax policy agenda.

Alongside, in the non-binding tax coordination domain, the eurozone crisis triggered another development: Member States agreed upon closer coordination of their budgetary and economic policies through a new model of governance, 'the European Semester' (2010).[110] Assessing the first annual cycle, the European Council concluded that it should integrate a 'pragmatic coordination of tax policies', particularly 'to ensure the exchange of best practices, avoidance of harmful practices, and proposals to fight fraud and tax evasion'.[111] In 2011 the Commission published the Annual Growth Survey, which included the Annex on Growth-Friendly Tax Policies in Member States and Better Tax Coordination in the EU.[112] This step established certain coordination of tax policies by setting guidance for Member States' tax reforms.[113] In parallel, several communications have been issued to address the cross-border taxation problems for citizens.[114]

In 2012 it appeared that the EU direct tax policy would continue developing in the same direction, being dominated by non-binding coordination and possibly an attempt at enhanced cooperation. However, this prediction failed to deliver. Triggered by a growing political drive for changes aiming at enhancing tax transparency and tackling BEPS, the subsequent years have become the most dynamic and productive period to the date.

[108] European Parliament Legislative Resolution 2011/0058(CNS) of 19 April 2012 on the proposal for a Council Directive on a Common Consolidated Corporate Tax Base (CCCTB Directive).

[109] See Commission, IP/12/1138; confirmed in Council Decision 2013/52/EU of 22 January 2013 authorising enhanced cooperation in the area of financial transaction tax [2013] OJ L22/11.

[110] Commission, 'Enhancing Economic Policy Coordination for Stability, Growth and Jobs – Tools for Stronger EU Economic Governance' (Communication) COM(2010) 367/2.

[111] European Council Conclusions of 23–24 June 2011, point 6.

[112] Commission, 'Growth Friendly Tax Policies in Member States and Better Tax Coordination' (Annex IV to the Annual Growth Survey 2012) COM(2011) 815 final.

[113] Communication, 'Annual Growth Survey 2013' (Communication) COM(2012) 750 final, section 1. For an outline of key tax-related issues also refer to Commission, MEMO/12/915.

[114] Commission, 'Removing Cross-Border Tax Obstacles for EU Citizens' (Communication) COM(2010) 769 final; Commission, 'Double Taxation in the Single Market' (Communication) COM(2011) 712 final; Commission, 'Tackling Cross-Border Inheritance Tax Obstacles within the EU' (Communication) COM(2011) 864 final; Commission Recommendation 2011/856/EU of 15 December 2011 regarding relief for double taxation of inheritances [2011] OJ L336/81; Commission, 'Non-Discriminatory Inheritance Tax Systems: Principles Drawn from EU Case-Law' (Staff Working Paper) SEC(2011) 1488 final.

Whilst the leading role in defining the direction of travel was left to the international arena, the EU has become a pioneer in adopting many measures, often taking them forward faster and further than other jurisdictions across the world. Consequently, a number of legislative measures have been adopted at the EU level:

- The Administrative Cooperation Directive has been amended several times between 2014 and 2018 to enable automatic exchange of financial account information, cross-border rulings and country-by-country reports.[115] It also opened the access by tax authorities to the beneficial ownership information collected under anti-money laundering rules and set mandatory disclosure rules on tax planning cross-border arrangements, including automatic exchange of this information.[116]
- The Anti-Tax Avoidance Directive was adopted in 2016 at an unprecedented speed. It sought to ensure a coordinated implementation of the conclusions reached as part of the G20/OECD BEPS project on interest limitation, hybrid mismatches and controlled foreign companies, in addition to two distinct measures driven by the EU's own tax policy agenda, ie, exit taxation and a general anti-abuse rule.[117] The amendments of the Parent–Subsidiary Directive also aimed at enhancing its anti-BEPS features.[118]
- To facilitate the effective resolution of disputes, the EU also adopted Council Directive (EU) 2017/1852 of 10 October 2017 on tax dispute resolution mechanisms in the EU.[119]

In parallel to this dynamic legislative process, other regulatory measures have also gained in speed and reach. Since 2013, the Commission has been investigating individual tax rulings or rulings granted under tax schemes of Member States under EU state aid rules, which resulted in a number of high-value and high-profile cases landing at the Court. Furthermore, in 2016, the Commission published its Communication on an External Strategy for Effective Taxation which laid down a common EU approach to listing third countries that refuse to respect the so-called 'tax good governance standards'.[120] This process led to a large number of political commitments made by jurisdictions around the world to adhere to the set principles. Both processes have generated significant international attention and impact, providing further reasons for recognising the current phase in the EU direct tax integration as the most eventful to the date. Unlike the previous phases, which largely reflected a wider context of the market integration beyond tax, the rapid progress of the past few years is better explained by the influence

[115] Administrative Cooperation Directive, as amended Council Directive 2014/107/EU of 9 December 2014 [2014] OJ L359/1, Council Directive 2015/2376 of 8 December 2015 [2015] OJ L332/1, Council Directive 2016/881 of 25 May 2016 [2016] OJ L146/8, Council Directive 2016/2258 of 6 December 2016 [2016] OJ L342/1, Council Directive 2018/822/EU of 25 May 2018 [2018] OJ L139/1.

[116] ibid.

[117] Council Directive (EU) 2016/1164 of 12 July 2016 laying down rules against tax avoidance practices that directly affect the functioning of the internal market [2016] OJ L193/1, amended by Council Directive (EU) 2017/952 of 29 May 2017 [2017] OJ L144/1 (Anti-Tax Avoidance Directive).

[118] ibid.

[119] Council Directive (EU) 2017/1852 of 10 October 2017 on tax dispute resolution mechanisms in the European Union [2017] OJ L265/1.

[120] Commission, 'An External Strategy for Effective Taxation' (Communication) COM(2016) 24 final.

of external factors. It has built upon the policy dialogue taking place at other intergovernmental arenas and successfully leveraged the political momentum created by the financial crisis, tax scandals and public demand for change.

VI. Concluding Remarks

This retrospective overview has presented the evolution of EU direct tax integration as a process that is composed of five phases. The first phase (from the 1960s to the mid-1980s) was characterised by the move from the initial vision of a full harmonisation model to a more limited focus on several priority measures. During the second stage (from the mid-1980s to 1992), the EU took certain steps seen as essential for the reinforcement of the internal market more generally, which facilitated a breakthrough in legislative harmonisation in the domain of direct taxation. The third stage (the 1990s) brought significant development in the role played by the Court, and the first direct tax rulings were delivered by the Court. Towards the end of the decade, Article 267 TFEU became a dominant route for removing barriers to the freedom of movement in the field of direct taxation. During the fourth stage (the early 2000s), the Commission actively sought alternative tools to stimulate European tax integration, choosing to rely on infringement proceedings to enforce compliance with EU law and non-binding coordination. Finally and most recently (post-2009), the global financial crisis and a series of tax scandals have help to foster closer legislative cooperation between Member States in tackling tax avoidance and evasion. The Commission has also started using its enforcement powers, in particular in the domain of fiscal state aid, and coordination measures more forcefully.

Seventy years of European integration have been a fascinating journey, which could only be sketched out in this brief overview. The EU's direct tax laws and policies have been evolving through the variety of regulatory tools and the search for the measures which could be pursued jointly by EU Member States, as well as the optimal model of direct tax integration for the internal market, continues. Whilst this analysis represents just an attempt at rationalising the history of EU direct tax integration, it offers a convenient framework which may aid the interpretation of its past and present.

13

The Origins, Development and Future of Zero-Rating in the UK

GEOFFREY MORSE

I. Introduction

One of the compelling arguments used by the vote leave campaign in the run-up to the 2016 Brexit referendum was that, as a result of Brexit, the UK would be free to set its rates of VAT.[1] In particular, it was suggested that certain additional items could then be made 'VAT-free'. These items are what might be perceived as necessities, for example, fuel bills.[2] This suggestion plugged into the UK's long-held practice that any form of indirect taxation on goods and services should not as a matter of policy include necessities (whatever they might be). This practice was applied initially to goods excluded from purchase tax, and some services treated favourably by Selective Employment Tax (SET), and was continued, somewhat downsized, into the UK's version of VAT in 1973 through zero-rating such supplies. This policy has over the years become in effect a de facto UK taxpayers' right.[3] As recently as April 2019 it was argued that house plants should be made tax free as being a necessity rather than a luxury.[4]

The effect of making such supplies free of tax for purchase tax simply meant that no tax was payable by anyone in the supply chain, thus reducing the retail price.

[1] Or, it was suggested, even abolish VAT altogether.

[2] In a speech by Michael Gove on 31 May 2016: see 'EU Referendum: Vote Leave wants power to axe fuel VAT' *BBC News* (31 May 2016), available at: www.bbc.co.uk/news/uk-politics-eu-referendum-36414761.

[3] 'The choice of supplies that are zero-rated is obviously dictated by policy considerations. For example, food is a necessity and its cost can be said to fall disproportionately on the poor by comparison with the rich because it absorbs a greater part of their resources. Books promote learning and literacy; newspapers promote knowledge of current affairs. The cost of transport and children's clothing can be said, as with food, to represent a necessity which falls disproportionately on the poor. Residential property is another necessity … Care homes are accorded the same treatment as residential property because they amount in practice to the provision of residential accommodation for those who through age or disability are unable to care for themselves' (Lord Drummond Young in *Balhousie Holdings Ltd v HMRC* [2019] CSIH 7 [26]).

[4] 'Are Plants a Necessity or a Luxury?' *BBC News* (20 April 2019), available at: www.bbc.co.uk/news/av/health-47970728/are-plants-a-necessity-or-a-luxury. This idea was also suggested but rejected by the government in the whole House committee debate on the introduction of VAT in the Finance Bill 1972 – HC Deb 16 May 1972, vol 37, cols 246–471.

For VAT, of course, it also means not only that the ultimate consumer pays no VAT but also that the suppliers to such consumers can recover the VAT they paid on such supplies to them. Because they are making taxable supplies, albeit for 0 per cent tax, they are taxable persons entitled to register as such[5] and so can set off their input tax against a zero-output tax. Recovery of such input tax means that they become what are known as 'repayment traders', receiving significant rebates from HMRC.[6] Such supplies are thus not only tax-free but also subsidised supplies, which increases their importance.

The requirement for tax-free (ie, zero-rated) supplies in the national conscience has had profound political and practical consequences, albeit to the tax purist they are anomalous. This chapter, therefore, examines where the categories of such supplies originated and how they were translated into VAT, principally, initially, as domestic, not Community law. Then it considers why those categories have produced endless interpretative litigation, how this 'domestic' law has slotted into EU law relating to the European framework for the tax as a whole, and finally, briefly, how the categories might be interpreted, at least in the short term,[7] following the still (in January 2020) largely unchartered waters of Brexit.

II. The Origins of Zero-Rated Categories: Purchase Tax

When VAT was introduced into the UK with effect from April 1973, two existing taxes were repealed, purchase tax and SET. In his Budget Speech in 1971, the Chancellor, Anthony Barber, described SET as 'a thoroughly bad tax' and one which 'is almost universally disliked'.[8] SET had been introduced in 1966,[9] as a means of restraining consumer demand, broadening the tax base and manipulating the distribution of labour. In essence, all employers were required to pay an additional amount for each employee at a flat rate, using the national insurance system,[10] but some categories of employer subsequently received that amount back whilst others actually received a premium on top as well.[11] The intention, roughly, was to target the service rather than the manufacturing industries.[12] But even those employers receiving repayments had in effect to make an interest-free loan to the government in between payment and repayment. It was, said Barber in 1971, perceived as unfair and arbitrary and its distinctions he regarded as indefensible.[13] It was also rather cumbersome.[14] So it had to go.

[5] Under s 3 of the VAT Act 1994.

[6] One of the many anomalies of VAT is that zero-rating is preferable to making exempt supplies where any input tax relief is very restricted and so it becomes a cost-component of the further supply. See, eg, *Royal Bank of Scotland Group plc v CEC* [2002] STC 575 CS (IH); [2002] SLT 664.

[7] The lack of a crystal ball still prevents any detailed further evaluation.

[8] HC Deb 30 March 1971, vol 814, col 1393.

[9] By the Finance Act 1966, s 44 and sch 11, and the Selective Employment Payments Act 1966.

[10] The rate for female employees and those under 18 was half that for male employees.

[11] At 130% of the original charge.

[12] See generally 1967 *NILQ* vol 18 365; [1966] *BTR* 171 and 243. For the economic consequences of the tax see WB Reddaway, *Effects of Selective Employment Tax: Final Report* (Cambridge, Cambridge University Press, 1973).

[13] HC Deb 30 March 1971, vol 814, col 1393.

[14] By 1971, some £2,000 million was collected, but nearly £1,500 million was given back: HC Deb 30 March 1971, vol 814, col 1393.

Purchase tax, by way of contrast, said the Chancellor, bore too heavily on a limited number of goods and not at all on services.[15] Accordingly, VAT was to be introduced as a replacement for both taxes as from 1973.[16] Broadening the tax base was the intention at that time, but exceptions for perceived necessities such as food were promised even then, as was 'special treatment in other cases'.[17] The categorising of goods, the lack of uniformity in the proposed rates of VAT and the inevitable consequential problems of interpretation were, in fact, present in purchase tax, so it is to that tax that we must look for the origins and some of the complications of zero-rating.

Purchase tax was introduced as a wartime emergency measure[18] by Part V of the Finance (No 2) Act 1940 as from 21 October 1940, originally as a way of curbing demand for goods although also as a revenue-raising tax.[19] It was a charge 'on the wholesale value of all chargeable goods bought under chargeable purchases'.[20] From the point of view of future zero-rating, the critical point, therefore, is that only some goods were so chargeable – it was never a uniform tax.[21] Those that were chargeable were taxed at the wholesale stage and levied on the wholesale seller[22] on the wholesale value of the goods at an *ad valorem* rate.[23] No distinction was made between domestic or imported goods. There were many differential rates between categories of chargeable goods which could all be changed by statutory instrument.[24] Purchase tax was, therefore, part of the overhead costs of the retailer who could suffer if a rate reduction occurred after the wholesale transaction but before the retail sale.[25] It never applied to services, which were, instead, targeted by SET.

The different classes of chargeable goods and the rates applied to them varied considerably during the lifetime of the tax, the lowest being 5 per cent and the highest 125 per cent.[26] Originally there were only two rates, but thereafter the different rates generally varied in number between three and four, although between 1955 and 1958 there were six or seven.[27] Towards the end of the tax, by then restated in the Purchase Tax Act 1963, there were three general rates, 10 per cent, 15 per cent and 25 per cent[28] applied to 35 groups, many of those applying differential rates within the group. But by 1971 the rates had altered again to four: 13.75 per cent, 22 per cent, 36.67 per cent and

[15] HC Deb 30 March 1971, vol 814, col 1393.

[16] At that stage, the UK was not a member of the EEC, although of course by 1973 it was, and the introduction of VAT was by then a condition of membership.

[17] HC Deb 30 March 1971, vol 814, col 1394.

[18] Which, true to form, lasted for 33 years.

[19] See '*The Reform of Purchase Tax*', Conservative Political Centre, 1959; CW McMahon, *The British Purchase Tax* (London, Fabian Publications, 1952) 11; A Grieve, *Purchase Tax* (London, Sweet & Maxwell, 1958) 1.

[20] Finance (No2) Act 1940, s 18(1).

[21] See AR Prest, *The Future of Purchase Tax* (London, Institute of Economic Affairs, 1961) 7.

[22] Who, as taxable persons, were required to register and were liable to pay the tax if they were required by law to do so: Finance (No 2) Act 1940, s 18(2). Originally the qualification threshold was £2,000 pa, but that was reduced to £500 a year later.

[23] ibid s 21. See Prest (n 21) 8.

[24] Even changing goods from one class to another.

[25] See McMahon (n 19) 9. There were also problems with sale or return transactions, second-hand goods. Like VAT the tax was invoice based, with inspections.

[26] For gas water heaters for part of one tax year in 1947/48 in response to the fuel crisis.

[27] See Prest (n 21) app II.

[28] Cars were always treated separately (30%) and when VAT was introduced an additional car tax was imposed in addition to VAT which lasted until 1992.

55 per cent. Prior to this partial rationalisation, the complexity gave rise to inexplicable distinctions much exploited by opponents during the 1955 to 1958 period of multi-rates. In 1958, the MP, Gerald Nabarro, asked: 'Why are eyelash curlers subject to purchase tax at 90%, whereas eyebrow combs are chargeable only at 30%, and artificial eyelashes are free from tax?'[29] These 'caprices' of purchase tax were, of course, the consequence of the differential rates and classes. As commerce evolved, the classes being out of date was also a problem, although far less of a problem than in the years since 1973. Changes were made by means of a Treasury Order. To take just a few of the later changes, the Purchase Tax (No 1) Order 1971[30] dealt with ceramic tiles and the Purchase Tax (No 6) Order 1971[31] with disposable tables etc. The use of such orders did allow for a quick response,[32] so that the list of drugs and medicines exempt from purchase tax set out in the 1971 Purchase Tax (No 5) Order[33] was updated the next year in the Purchase Tax (No 1) Order 1972.[34]

There are two aspects of purchase tax which are particularly germane to the study of zero-rating and which resonate in VAT today. The first aspect concerns the items which were exempted from purchase tax and therefore tax-free before 1973.[35] The second is the problem of the application of the various classes to the myriad of goods sold, which involved the courts in litigation. One significant difference between the scope of purchase tax and that of VAT is that only the goods specified in the chargeable groups were subject to purchase tax, everything else was excluded. Thus, no tax was the default position. For VAT all goods and services are included, but some are singled out for zero-rating[36] and, of course, some, currently set out in the Principal VAT Directive,[37] are either exempt or eligible for a reduced rate. Otherwise, standard rated is the default position. As a result, several of the current zero-rated supplies, such as books, were simply never subject to purchase tax at all. But we can find correlation in other areas such as transport[38] and children's' clothes.[39] One feature which was not carried forward

[29] Prest (n 21) 7.

[30] SI 1972/155.

[31] SI 1972/1781.

[32] Another pro-leave argument?

[33] SI 1971/3428.

[34] SI 1972/1745.

[35] In the debates on zero-rating during the passage of the Finance Act 1972 which introduced zero-rating, MPs frequently raised the point in argument that the particular item under discussion had been excluded from purchase tax but was now to be taxed.

[36] VAT Act 1994, sch 8.

[37] Council Directive 2006/112/EC of 28 November 2006 on the common system of value added tax [2006] OJ L347/1, Arts 131–66.

[38] Group 27 of the schedule to the Purchase Tax Act 1963 which taxes road vehicles, excludes from the charge, inter alia, vehicles constructed to carry not less than 12 passengers, a current requirement for zero-rating: see, eg, *Cirdan Sailing Trust v CEC* [2005] EWHC 2999; [2006] STC 185. That group also excludes caravans from the charge to purchase tax. Caravans also now benefit from zero-rating – a peculiarly British obsession.

[39] Group 1 of the schedule to the Purchase Tax Act 1963 which taxed 'Garments, headgear, footwear and gloves' had many exclusions including 'garments and footwear of a kind suitable for young children's wear' but not if they were more than 20% made of fur.

into VAT was the exclusion from purchase tax of those goods such as alcohol and tobacco, which are subject to excise duty.

Food, in general, was never subject to purchase tax and it is similarly generally zero-rated for VAT purposes. The current list of which foodstuffs are and are not zero-rated in Group 1 of Schedule 8 to the VAT Act 1994 is both complex, and at times controversial[40] and in consequence, much litigated. Its origins can, however, be found in purchase tax. For purchase tax it was simply a question of which 'luxury' foods should be included as there was no general group relating to food; food thus being generally excluded. Three food items were, however, included. Under group 28 of the Schedule to the Purchase Tax Act 1963, there was a 15 per cent charge on: 'Ice-cream, ice lollies, water ices and similar frozen products, and prepared mixes and powders for making such products'.[41] These words are still found today. Similarly, group 34 imposed a 15 per cent charge on 'Chocolates, sweets and similar confectionery'. This charge also applied to chocolate biscuits but not cakes coated in chocolate. That puzzling distinction between chocolate-covered biscuits and chocolate-covered cakes is preserved in the current zero-rating rules.[42] The distinction is currently explained, somewhat unconvincingly, as the difference between a snack and food, but since, unlike VAT, other 'snacks' were not subject to purchase tax, that was not the reason in 1963.

Beverages were also subject to purchase tax by virtue of group 35 in the Schedule to the 1963 Act. This charged 'manufactured beverages, including fruit juices and bottled waters, and syrups, concentrates, essences, powders, crystals or other products for the preparation of beverages'. But 'tea, mate, herbal teas, cocoa, coffee, and preparations of meat, yeast, egg or milk' were among those items excluded from the charge. That charge and its exemptions are now mirrored in VAT under the VAT Act 1994 Schedule 8 Group 1's Pinteresque structure by 'Excepted Item No 4' and in 'Items overriding the exceptions', numbers 4–7.[43]

The other feature of the purchase tax groups which has followed through into zero-rating in VAT is that they were complex, often providing within a single group for four possibilities. These were: generic items within the group, specific items chargeable at a different rate, exemptions, and goods not comprised within one of the specific sub-groups.[44] Such detailed provisions inevitably spawned litigation as to the ambit of each delineator. Similar to VAT the most productive area of litigation related to those items of food which were subject to purchase tax.[45] One area of dispute was what amounted to 'similar confectionary' to chocolates and sweets chargeable under group 34. In *Candy Maid Confections Ltd v CEC*,[46] the dispute related to toffee apples.

[40] The attempt to introduce the so-called 'pasty tax' on certain takeaway foods in 2012 caused a public outcry. See n 97 below.

[41] That is repeated in Excepted Item 1 in Group 1 of sch 8 to the VAT Act 1994.

[42] See Excepted Item 2 in Group 1 of sch 8 to the VAT Act 1994.

[43] Items 2 and 3 overriding the exceptions are also excluded from the purchase tax charge in Group 34.

[44] Which may then be chargeable under another group.

[45] Litigation was then by way of seeking a declaration from the court as to whether an item was included in a chargeable group or not.

[46] *Candy Maid Confections Ltd v CEC* [1968] 1 Ch 611.

The judge described these as fresh dessert apples dipped into a mixture of sugar, glucose and water, the mixture forming between 17 and 30 per cent of the total weight. Cross J held that the Commissioners had not discharged the onus of showing that they came within the group. The ordinary man would not regard them as confectionary similar to sweets as the apple was not altered in any way; the apples being perishable could not be bought in confectioners' shops, and they had not been included specifically in the group as had crystallised fruits.[47]

But in *CEC v Clark's Cereal Products*,[48] a year later, Sales J granted a declaration that sweetened popcorn,[49] was similar confectionary to sweets and so chargeable. He followed an earlier, as then unreported, case, *CEC v Popcorn House Ltd*.[50] There Lawton J had analysed the manufacturing process as putting dried maize grains into a machine containing heated edible oil to which sugar was added.[51] The maize grains were then heated and 'popped' to about 30 times their original size. Lawton J ventured a definition of the word 'confectionary' as meaning 'any form of food normally eaten with the fingers and made by a cooking process other than baking which contains a substantial amount of sweetening matter'. Those were the characteristics of both sweets and chocolate. As such sweetened popcorn was caught. Such a precise definition could not include toffee apples as they were not cooked. That definition, however, was later expressly rejected as not applicable to VAT law, where any process applied to a sweet product was held to be sufficient. The sweetness could be inherent rather than added.[52] The purchase tax definition was distinguished as applying to a different statutory context.

Accordingly, purchase tax set the scene for the introduction of zero-rating into the UK's version of VAT in 1973. This was evidenced when, in 2018, the Upper Tribunal in *Nestle UK Ltd v HMRC*[53] referred expressly to purchase tax when holding that two flavours of Nesquik products were powders for the preparation of beverages and so excluded from the zero-rating of food.[54] The fact that they were applied to milk did not avail them.[55] The Tribunal analysed the position under purchase tax as being that there was no indication in that tax that all things which might be associated with or added to milk should be excluded. The Tribunal regarded the purchase tax regime as having formed the basis for the UK's VAT concept of zero-rating in that case and one which in that case should be followed.

It is important to remember, of course, in all these incredibly mundane and, on the face of it mildly, humorous micro decisions, just how much money is at stake, especially now given the subsidising effect of zero-rating.

[47] Reminiscent of the then pre-*Ramsay* approach to tax legislation in *Russell v Scott* [1948] AC 422.
[48] *CEC v Clark's Cereal Products* [1969] 1 QB 755.
[49] Sold under the trade name 'Butterkist'.
[50] Decided in 1965 and reported as a Note in *CEC v Popcorn House Ltd* [1969] 1 QB 760.
[51] Salt was the alternative to make salted rather than sweetened popcorn.
[52] *HMRC v Premier Foods (Holdings) Ltd* [2007] EWHC 3134 (Ch); [2008] STC 176.
[53] *Nestle UK Ltd v HMRC* [2018] UKUT 29 (TCC); [2018] STC 575.
[54] As Excepted Item 4 in Group 1 of sch 8 to the VAT Act 1994.
[55] Milk itself is zero-rated as an overriding item to the excepted items.

III. Introduction of VAT and Zero-Rating

The Customs and Excise Department began contingency planning for the introduction of VAT in 1970.[56] A Green Paper was published in that year,[57] and, as promised by the government in 1971, VAT was introduced into the UK in 1973, originally by Part 1 of the Finance Act 1972.[58] 'Tax-free', ie, zero-rated supplies, were there from the start, originally consisting of 14 groups set out in Schedule 4 to that Act.[59] In the Budget debate of 1972, Mr Barber promised, somewhat optimistically that VAT would 'end the ridiculous anomalies' of purchase tax'.[60] Schedule 4 was the subject of three days of debate by the whole House in committee during the passage of the Finance Act 1972 as MPs sought, usually in vain, to extend the categories in the Schedule.[61] Although children's footwear ultimately succeeded, professional sporting events,[62] musical instruments, learning resources, microfilm, 'essential' household appliances, theatrical and concert performances and hearing aids[63] were among those which failed to make the grade. The change from purchase tax to VAT, ie, from a tax on only selected goods to one on the majority of goods and services emphasised the importance of those escaping the tax by means of zero-rating. In the third reading of the Finance Bill in 1972, the Shadow Chancellor, Denis Healey, highlighted the fact that in 1970 the two higher rates of purchase tax, on luxuries such as furs and perfumes, raised £587 million more than the same volume of those same goods would raise under VAT. That money would have to come from tax on less luxurious items.[64]

At present, there are 16 extant groups of zero-rated supplies now contained in Schedule 8 to the VAT Act 1994.[65] This is not the place to itemise all the changes over the years, although it is worth pointing out that fuel and power were originally zero-rated in 1973,[66] whereas children's clothing and footwear was not. Zero-rating has therefore existed in the UK for 46 years within the European framework of the tax, surviving the

[56] For an authoritative account of the introduction of the UK's VAT see Dorothy Johnstone, *A Tax Shall be Charged* (Civil Service Studies, HMSO, 1974). Unfortunately for this paper, she was part of the team charged with designing the machinery of VAT and not its scope (a second team had that brief). Accordingly, it throws little light on the consideration of zero-rating at that time.

[57] *Value Added Tax* (Cmnd 4621, 1970).

[58] Following a White Paper on the new tax in March 1972: *Value Added Tax* (Cmnd 4929, 1972). Provision was made for the transition from purchase tax to VAT to avoid double taxation. It is salutary to note that the original registration threshold was £5,000.

[59] These were: food; water; books; talking books for the blind; newspaper advertisements; news services; fuel and power; construction of buildings; services to overseas traders for overseas purposes; transport; caravans; gold; banknotes; and drugs etc.

[60] In the HC debates on the Finance Bill, many such anomalies were highlighted. See, eg, HC Deb 19 July 1972, vol 841, col 639.

[61] May 11, 12 and 16 1972. See HC Deb 11 May 1972 vol 836, cols 1580–1692; HC Deb 15 May 1972, vol 837, cols 105–80 and 246–471

[62] Which required consideration as to whether professional wrestling was a sport

[63] It was pointed out that only privately acquired aids would be subject to the tax.

[64] See HC Deb 19 July 1972, vol 841, col 638.

[65] There are 19 groups set out in numerical order, but two no longer exist. One group, 19, relating to women's sanitary products, is not yet in force. See below.

[66] It became subject to VAT in 1994 at a reduced rate, although the original intention was to charge the standard rate. That was stopped by a Commons revolt.

successive harmonising VAT directives and the development of the concept of direct effect.[67] The question is how this phenomenon was managed at the outset and how it has largely remained unscathed ever since.

IV. Zero-Rating as Hybrid Domestic/Community Law: Legality and Limitations

At the outset, zero-rating was considered mainly in the context of UK domestic law, if the issue was ever really considered at all. The various EC/EU treaties have each required the harmonisation of turnover taxes in the EU,[68] which in the case of VAT has been activated by a series of directives, addressed to the Member States. But in 1973 there was no comprehensive directive on VAT harmonisation; that would have to wait until 1977, so that little attention appears to have been paid to Community rules at that time.

Further, the concept of direct effect as applied to directives had not been formulated by the Court of Justice of the European Union (CJEU) by that stage, although it was under discussion.[69] European law was simply not seen as an issue in relation to zero-rating; linking it to purchase tax was. The sea-change came in 1977 when the Sixth EC VAT Directive[70] provided common criteria for the VAT base.[71] That Directive concentrated minds on the need to comply with European law, which was particularly true of the list of exempt supplies which were set out in Article 13 of the Sixth Directive. That list is mandatory and cannot be altered by UK law; the UK was obliged to amend its list of exempt supplies to comply with Article 13 after the Commission brought infraction proceedings against the UK.[72]

There is no such list of zero-rated supplies in the Sixth Directive. But that Directive was nevertheless of significance in relation to zero-rating since, in Article 28(2), it provided for its existence 'until a date which shall be fixed by the Council acting unanimously'. That Article allowed a Member State to maintain what the Directive called 'exemptions with refund of tax paid at the preceding stage' provided they complied with the last indent of Article 17 of the Second VAT Directive of 1967.[73] That indent only allowed such exemptions 'for clearly defined social reasons and for the benefit of the final consumer'.[74] Article 28(2) also restricted such exemptions to those in force originally

[67] See, eg, *Finanzampt Munchen III v Mosche* [1997] ECR 1-2615; [1997] STC195 ECJ.

[68] Currently Art 113 of the 2009 Treaty.

[69] The concept of direct effect as applied to the Treaty had been applied in *Van Gend en Loos v Administrie der Berlastingen* [1963] ECR 1; [1963] 2 CMLR 128. It does of course now apply to the VAT directives.

[70] Sixth Council Directive 77/388/EEC of 17 May 1977 on the harmonization of the laws of the Member States relating to turnover taxes – Common system of value added tax: uniform basis of assessment [1977] OJ L145/1.

[71] Although not the rates actually charged.

[72] Case 353/85, *Commission of the European Communities v The United Kingdom* [1980] ECR 817; [1981] STC 251.

[73] Second Council Directive 67/228/EEC of 11 April 1967 on the harmonisation of legislation of Member States concerning turnover taxes – Structure and procedures for application of the common system of value added tax [1967] OJ 71/1303.

[74] The 1967 requirement that the total incidence of such measures must not exceed that of the reliefs under the present system was not carried into the Sixth Directive.

on 31 December 1975. From that Article, as originally drafted, we can, therefore, take four of the five characteristics of zero-rating from the perspective of Community law: (i) the UK was allowed to continue to have zero-rated supplies; (ii) this was, however, a temporary derogation; (iii) the categories could only be justified for clearly defined social reasons and for the benefit of the final consumer; and (iv) they could not be expanded beyond the wording of such supplies at a given date (they were in effect frozen). A fifth, significant, requirement that they must be 'in accordance with Community law' was added by an amendment to Article 28(2) in 1992.[75] Zero-rating was therefore permitted, but it was subject to clear boundaries under Community law.[76]

Those characteristics continued to operate in the pre-Brexit world.[77] The current manifestation is in Article 110 of the 2006 Principal VAT Directive.[78] Zero-rating is still in theory only permitted, although the temporary nature of that permission has in effect de facto become permanent.[79] The requirements for social reasons and the benefit of the final consumer were, however, tested by infraction proceedings brought by the Commission against the UK for failure to fulfil its treaty obligations in respect of certain zero-rated categories. The case was heard by the CJEU under the name *Commission of the European Communities v United Kingdom*.[80] The Commission considered that certain of the zero-rated categories did not comply with the social reasons/final consumer requirements of the Sixth Directive. The Court first rejected an argument that the Commission's case was political and an attempt to bypass the legislative procedure for any such amendments. As the Court had previously decided, the question of compliance with treaty obligations was purely an objective one; it was not concerned with any other objectives of the Commission.[81]

The Commission did not, however, challenge zero-rating as such. They had after all already provided for it in Article 28(2) of the Sixth Directive and considered zero-rating to be essentially equivalent to an 'exemption with refund of tax paid at the preceding stage'.[82] The Court instead first considered the question of 'clearly defined social reasons'. It was accepted by both the UK and the Commission that a category could be challenged only if the reasons for it were not clearly defined or they could not justify the measure, or if the measure lacked proportionality. The Court agreed;[83] identification of social reasons was a matter of political choice, which could only be subject

[75] Council Directive 92/77/EEC of 19 October 1992 supplementing the common system of value added tax and amending Directive 77/388/EEC (approximation of VAT rates) [1992] OJ L316/1. That Directive also changed the cut-off date to 31 January 1991.

[76] Eventually, this has since had consequences which have taken the courts deciding zero-rating issues to apply a European as well as a purely domestic law approach. See the next section below.

[77] But a sea change may be coming from a European initiative. See the final part of this chapter.

[78] Council Directive 2006/112/EC of 28 November 2006 on the common system of value added tax [2006] OJ L347/1.

[79] Despite regular reviews and reports nothing definitive has emerged from the Commission on this point. See, eg, 'VAT Harmonisation' Research Paper 97/31, HC Library.

[80] Case 416/85, *Commission of the European Communities v United Kingdom* [1988] ECR 3127; [1990] 2 QB 130.

[81] See Case 203/87, *Commission of the European Communities v Italy* [1989] ECR 371 (unauthorised use of zero-rating).

[82] Given that understanding, there is little to be gained from an analysis of whether that is strictly true as a matter of semantics.

[83] [1988] ECR 3127, para 14.

to supervision at the Community level if the concept was distorted.[84] None of the categories of zero-rating were in fact challenged on that ground.

The real challenges came on the basis that certain identified supplies were not for the benefit of final consumers. This challenge was not, therefore, a challenge to the general categories but as to elements within them. The Court's decisions on the specified items was based on the decision that: 'the final consumer is the person who acquires goods or services for final use, as opposed to an economic activity, and thus bears the tax'.[85] Use for an economic activity would not, therefore, be use by the final consumer. On that basis, a number of the existing sub-categories of zero-rated supplies were held to be outside the final consumer requirement.[86] The Court added a further refinement, however, which would allow the provision of goods or services at a stage higher in the production or distribution chain which 'is nevertheless sufficiently close to the consumer to be of advantage to him'.[87] This refinement saw off challenges to the zero-rating of seeds etc for the propagation of zero-rated foodstuffs and live animals of a kind generally used as, or yielding or producing food for human consumption. Supplies of news services to undertakings which were providing exempt supplies (such as banks) as opposed to those providing zero-rated supplies (newspapers) were, however, struck down. There was no such criterion as 'incidental benefit' in the scope of zero-rating.

The final aspect of the permissive criteria under Article 28(2) of the Directive was the fixing of a 'cut-off' date beyond which no new categories (or sub-categories) would be allowed. In the Sixth Directive, this was the 31 December 1975, but that was updated in 1992 to 1 January 1991,[88] which date is currently found in Article 110 of the Principal 2006 VAT Directive. The effect of this temporal requirement means that although the UK can reduce the list of zero-rated supplies, it cannot increase them. The UK has itself excluded some items of zero-rated supplies over the years,[89] and reduced the scope of others.[90] It has also removed whole groups such as supplies of power and fuel. None of those exclusions has, however, involved any input from European law. The inability to increase the categories, on the other hand, has proved more of a problem as public opinion moves on. The most obvious example of the former concerns eBooks and e-newspapers, which could not be added to the existing group 3 on physical books and newspapers.[91] The most public example of changes in public opinion concerns women's sanitary products. Originally given a reduced rate status, the government bowed to public pressure (the necessities imperative again) by moving them into zero-rating as Group 19 of Schedule 8 in 2016.[92] However, that provision is not yet in force, awaiting either movement on the issue by the Commission[93] or Brexit.[94]

[84] By leading to measures which, because of their effects and their real objectives, lie outside its scope.

[85] [1988] ECR 3127, para 17.

[86] These included: the supply of water etc, fuel and power to industry; construction of industrial buildings, etc; and supplies of protective boots and helmets to employees.

[87] [1988] ECR 3127, para 17.

[88] By Directive 92/77/EEC amending the Sixth Directive accordingly.

[89] Such as sports drinks in 2012.

[90] Such as the clarification of 'for consumption on the premises' in 2012 by the addition of Note 3A to Group 1 of sch 8 to the VAT Act 1994, following decisions such as *Compass Contract Services UK Ltd v HMRC* [2006] EWCA Civ 867; [2006] STC 1991.

[91] *News Corp UK and Ireland v HMRC* [2018] UKFTT 129 (TC).

[92] By s 126(4) Finance Act 2016.

[93] Which is on the horizon. See the final part of this chapter.

[94] This issue was used specifically by leave supporters.

On the other hand, the Upper Tribunal, in a classic example of the hybrid EU/UK status of zero-rating, has recently held that e-newspapers could be zero-rated although they did not of course exist in 1991.[95] The point was that newspapers were included in Group 3 (having satisfied the EU criteria) and e-newspapers were in fact just newspapers in a different format. The Tribunal applied the doctrine of 'always speaking' statutory construction.[96] The Tribunal summed up their decision as follows:

> The question … is whether as a matter of UK principles of statutory interpretation (which include the 'always speaking' doctrine) the term 'newspapers' is to be construed as including the digital versions that have come into existence since 1991. It will be so construed … if it is found to be within the same genus of facts as those which the expressed policy of the relevant legislation has been formulated. Accordingly while it might be correct to observe that a decision that the digital versions of the newspapers are zero-rated under UK domestic law would result in an item being zero-rated that was not zero-rated in 1991, this is solely because (1) that item did not exist in 1991 and (2) the item is properly to be characterized (according to principles of UK law) as within the genus of things that the pre-1991 legislation did exempt. In such circumstances, we do not think that this would constitute an extension of the category of zero-rated items so as to offend article 110.[97]

The Tribunal were careful to point out that other digital products such as rolling news services would not be newspapers as they were significantly different. It is interesting to note the Tribunal's constant reference to UK law as applicable to the wording of zero-rated categories.[98]

V. Applying Zero-Rating as Hybrid Domestic/Community Law

The categories of zero-rated supplies pre-Brexit are therefore a matter for the UK subject to the parameters laid down in Article 110 of the 2006 Principal VAT Directive. But as a descendant of purchase tax, in doing so, VAT inherited the problem of interpreting and applying complex group structures to establish precisely what each category does and does not include.[99] Unlike purchase tax, there are also additional issues concerning how zero-rating relates to the general mechanism of VAT operations, including the question of multiple supplies. Unlike purchase tax, therefore, zero-rating disputes are sometimes not resolved simply by applying domestic law;[100] there are European considerations as well.

[95] *News Corp UK and Ireland v HMRC* [2019] UKUT 0404.

[96] See *R (Quintavelle) v Secretary of State for Health* [2003] UKHL 13, [2003] 2 All ER 113; *and Royal College of Nursing of the UK v Department of Health and Social Security* [1981] AC 800 (Lord Wilberforce).

[97] *News Corp UK and Ireland v HMRC* [2019] UKUT 0404, [50]–[51]. HMRC has indicated that it will appeal this decision.

[98] Contrasting with the application of EU canons of construction in the Sub One litigation. See below n 121. It is an interesting point, not argued in *News Corp*, as to whether applying a UK canon of construction is in accordance with Community law as required by Art 110.

[99] The law reports are full of such disputes. Given the subsidising effect of zero-rating, the incentives for litigation are strong.

[100] Similar problems arise in connection with both exempt and reduced-rate supplies, but they are subject entirely to European law as they are listed in the directives. Zero-rating is simply allowed.

The complexity and propensity for litigation in the groups is nowhere more prevalent than in Group 1 of Schedule 8, which relates to food. The group is structured to start with one of four general zero-rated categories (for example, food suitable for general consumption) which are then subject to a number of excepted items which are thus standard rated but then there are items overriding those exceptions, which thereby switch back to zero-rated status.[101] The clear intention is to exclude necessities from the tax but not indulgences such as ice cream and crisps.[102] In addition, there is a general exclusion from zero-rating for supplies 'in the course of catering' so that food supplied in restaurants or hot takeaway food is standard rated.[103] Applying that test involves considering such matters as what amounts to 'hot food' and whether it is 'for consumption on the premises'. The proposed amendments to the former in 2012 which would have applied standard rating to any hot take-out food[104] at the time it was provided to the customer, produced a public outcry against what became labelled as 'the pasty tax'. Instead, a more elaborate definition was inserted, which excluded food left to cool naturally.[105] Taking their cue from purchase tax, there is an almost inexhaustive list of disputes about the minutiae of Group 1, but, as with purchase tax, it is important to remember the amount of money involved in each of them.

A. Issues of Construction

Many of disputes as to whether a particular supply falls within zero-rating have involved relatively straightforward issues of construction[106] or of fact, which are settled by a domestic law approach.[107] But gradually the courts have had to involve European elements in such disputes, even as to the meaning of specific words, given that although the categories of zero-rating[108] are contained exclusively only in a domestic statute, their existence derives from the directives on a permissive and restricted basis. This mirrors the development of Community law since 1973, in particular the decision of the CJEU in *Marks & Spencer plc v HMRC*,[109] that although there was no directly enforceable

[101] For the approach as to how to apply this sequence, see *Nestle v HMRC* [2018] UKUT 29 (TCC); [2018] STC 575.

[102] The purchase tax distinction between chocolate biscuits and chocolate cake was continued, which led to the famous Jaffa Cake litigation. The prohibition of any increase in the scope of zero-rating has caused problems with regard to new products. See, eg, the problem of classifying Pringles as similar to crisps: *Proctor & Gamble UK v HMRC* [2009] EWCA Civ 407; [2009] STC 1990.

[103] 'The policy seems clear … human beings have to eat, but they don't have to eat in restaurants or have their food cooked by others', McCombe LJ in *Sub One Ltd v HMRC* [2014] EWCA Civ 773 [3]; [2014] STC 2508.

[104] As being above the ambient air temperature.

[105] See Note 3B to Group 1 of sch 8. There was also substantial public opposition to a proposal to tax static holiday caravans at the standard rate and so exclude them from zero-rating. The compromise was to tax them at the reduced rate.

[106] My favourite example being *CEC v Blackpool Pleasure Beach* [1974] STC 138 where the roller-coaster was held not be transport as it ended where it had started from.

[107] See the guidance from the CA in *Proctor & Gamble UK v HMRC* (n 102) where the 'mind-numbing legal analysis' of the judge below was rejected in favour of a short practical answer as to whether 'Pringles' were made from potato and similar to crisps so as to be standard and not zero-rated.

[108] Unlike those of exempt and reduced-rate supplies

[109] Case 309/06, *Marks & Spencer plc v HMRC* [2008] ECR 1-02283; [2009] STC 452.

community right to have supplies taxed at a zero-rate, general principles of Community law would apply to the operation of such supplies within the harmonised VAT system.[110]

Helpful guidance on the issue of EU construction was, however, given by the Court of Appeal in *Sub One Ltd v HMRC*.[111] This dispute arose from the then wording as to what amounted to hot take-out food and so constituted a supply in the course of catering undeserving of zero-rating.[112] The relevant requirement was that the food 'has been heated *for the purposes of* enabling it to be consumed at a temperature above the ambient air temperature'.[113] In 1988 the Court of Appeal in *John Pimblett and Sons Ltd v CEC*,[114] had established that the test for determining 'the purposes' was a subjective one. As a result, there was a plethora of tribunal cases, often arising from similar situations, which all depended upon an investigation as to the motives of each supplier. In the case of the *Subway* franchisees, such as the appellant, alone there were some 1,200 cases pending, mainly involving the supply of take-out toasted sandwiches. The appellant now claimed that this subjective approach was contrary to European law as applied to zero-rating and that it had suffered damage as a result of the UK's failure to apply European law principles. The Court of Appeal,[115] agreeing with the Upper Tribunal,[116] decided that there was no valid claim in the circumstances, but they did accept that such principles could apply to zero-rating cases. Thus, although the Court would otherwise have been bound by the 1988 subjective test decision, the impact of 'developed' European law required a reconsideration.[117]

The Court of Appeal considered that it was clear that the *Marleasing* principle was universal and could be used to import an objective test.[118] The requirement in Article 110 that the 'exemptions' must be 'in accordance with community law' having been expressly added in 1977.[119] In addition, however, the principle of fiscal neutrality was also applied to the construction of Schedule 8, albeit it in a slightly modified way.[120] The position was set out in the following passage from that judgment of Arnold J in the Upper Tribunal,[121] which was adopted by the Court of Appeal:[122]

> I accept counsel for HMRC's submission to the extent that the starting point is that it is for the UK to determine the boundary between zero-rated supplies and standard-rated supplies. I also accept that the CJEU's judgments in *Rank*[123] and *Isle of Wight*[124] demonstrate that the principle of fiscal neutrality cannot be relied upon as depriving the UK [of] its discretion in

[110] ibid [28] and [33]. See also Case 251/06, *Talacre Beach Caravan Sales Ltd v HMRC*, [2006] ECR 1-6269; [2006] STC 1671 CJEU, [25]. Both those cases are considered in more detail below.

[111] *Sub One Ltd v HMRC* [2014] EWCA Civ 773; [2013] STC 2508, affirming [2012] UKUT (TCC) 34; [2013] STC 318.

[112] The wording was changed in 2012. See n 95 et seq, above.

[113] Note 3A to Group 1 of sch 8 as it was at the time. Italics added.

[114] *John Pimblett and Sons Ltd v CEC* [1988] STC 358.

[115] In the judgment of McCombe LJ with whom the other members of the Court agreed.

[116] Arnold J.

[117] *Sub One Ltd v HMRC* [2014] EWCA Civ 773, para 41.

[118] ibid para 49.

[119] By Directive 92/77/EEC.

[120] Arnold J had also considered that the subjective test was contrary to the principle of objective assessment following the decision of the CJEU in *BLP Group plc v CEC* [1995] ECR 1-1001; [2012] UKUT 34, [105].

[121] [2012] UKUT 34 (TCC), para 80.

[122] [2014] EWCA Civ, para 60.

[123] *Rank Group plc v HMRC* [2011] ECR 1-10947, [53]–[54].

[124] *HMRC v Isle of Wight Council* [2008] ECR 1-7203, [44].

> this respect. It does not follow that the UK can draw the line in such a way as to discriminate between objectively similar supplies. On the contrary Article 110 is explicit that exemptions must be in accordance with Community law.

Thus, supplies which are identical from the point of view of the consumer cannot be distinguished by the UK by the wording of a zero-rated supply. It is clear that the principle of legal certainty would also apply within the same parameters.

It is interesting to reflect that the use of the UK 'always speaking' doctrine to include e-newspapers in zero-rating[125] does not necessarily fit easily with the *Sub One* approach. Fiscal neutrality might have produced a similar result – are newspapers and e-newspapers objectively similar supplies? On the other hand, does the 'always speaking' doctrine fulfil the requirement of being in accordance with Community law if it has no counterpart in that law?

In any event, In *Balhousie Holdings Ltd v HMRC*,[126] the Inner House of the Court of Session regarded the general principles of construction applicable to VAT as applying to the question as to whether a sale and leaseback of a care home should be regarded as a single or as two separate transactions. The latter would retrospectively lose the company's zero-rating status on its initial acquisition of the property.[127] The Court made no distinction between the zero-rated supply and an exempt supply. It regarded an objective approach to the analysis of the transactions used by the taxpayer (sic) as being settled by case law.

B. Other Community Law Aspects

Zero-rating does not, therefore operate in a Community law-free zone. This point was brought sharply into focus in *Marks & Spencer plc v HMRC*.[128] That case was the latest in a long-running saga resulting from the fact that chocolate-covered teacakes sold by the company had initially been subject to standard-rated VAT whereas they should have been zero-rated.[129] The company now sought repayment of some £3.5 million which they had paid in error. HMRC refused most of that amount on the basis that most of it had been passed on to its customers by the company and so repayment to the company would amount to unjust enrichment.[130] They also applied the then rule that all such claims were limited to three years. That time limit was then held to be contrary to Community law,[131] but the unjust enrichment restriction was maintained by HMRC. It was that issue which now came before the CJEU.

The Court held that the company had an enforceable Community right to recover sums mistakenly charged in respect of a zero-rated supply by applying the principle of fiscal neutrality. Rights conferred directly on individuals by Community law were

[125] See *News Corp UK and Ireland v HMRC* [2019] UKUT 0404, n 95 above.
[126] *Balhousie Holdings Ltd v HMRC* [2019] CSIH 7.
[127] See Group 5, Item 1 in sch 8 to the VAT Act and pt 2 of sch 10 to that Act.
[128] Case 309/06, *Marks & Spencer plc* (n 109).
[129] Being cakes and so, for historical reasons, tax-free.
[130] Under s 80(3) of the VAT Act.
[131] *Marks & Spencer plc v HMRC* [2002] ECR 1-6325. No issue specific to zero-rating was involved in that case.

available to charges levied in breach of national legislation allowed by the Directive. They could, therefore, be relied on against a national provision which failed to have regard to those principles.[132] Thus, zero-rating was equated with all other supplies in relation to those principles. But in fact, zero-rating also had an effect on the question as to whether the defence of unjust enrichment applied to the company's claim. One of the consequences of zero-rating is that some traders become what are called 'repayment traders'. Unlike exempt supplies, those making zero-rated supplies are making taxable supplies and are therefore like all taxable persons entitled to set-off their input tax. Since they have little or no output tax, they receive a repayment of the input tax instead of having only to set it off against their output tax as 'payment traders'. In effect, they are creditors and not debtors vis-à-vis the Treasury.

As a result, the CJEU held that although the principles of equal treatment and fiscal neutrality were not infringed by a refusal based on unjust enrichment, the fact that it operated differently between 'payment traders' and 'repayment traders' did involve those two principles:

> [T]he principle of fiscal neutrality precludes the prohibition of unjust enrichment from being applied only to taxable persons such as 'payment traders' and not to taxable persons such as 'repayment traders', in so far as those taxable persons have marketed similar goods … Furthermore the general principle of equal treatment, the infringement of which may be established, in matters relating to tax, by discrimination affecting traders who are not necessarily in competition with each other but are nevertheless in a similar situation in other respects, precludes discrimination between 'payment traders' and 'repayment traders', which is not objectively justified.[133]

So, zero-rating not only carries with it general Community law principles as to its operation, but it can also, by virtue of its unique nature, influence their application.

C. Multiple Supplies

Zero-rating, in common with exempt and reduced-rate supplies, sometimes raises the question of composite or multiple supplies. In essence, this is where a supply consists of more than one element, which if treated separately, would be taxed at different rates or be exempt. The case law of the CJEU has established that whilst each supply is ordinarily to be treated as distinct and separate, a single supply from an economic point of view should not be artificially split so as to distort the functioning of the VAT system and the rate applicable to the principle element should be applied.[134] In *EC Commission v France*,[135] however, the CJEU upheld the specific application by France of a reduced rate to one element of a composite supply.[136] The particular reduced rate fell within the

[132] ibid [33]–[34].

[133] ibid [54].

[134] Principally Case 349/96, *Card Protection Plan Ltd v CEC* [1999] ECR 1-073; [1999] 2 AC 601; and Case 41/04, *Levob Verzekeringen BV v Staattssecretaris van Financien* [2005] ECR 1-9433; [2006] STC 766. There are many other examples in both domestic and Community case law.

[135] *EC Commission v France* [2003] ECR 1-4395.

[136] One aspect of the charge for electric and gas supplies.

terms of the Directive. Then in a further *EC Commission v France*,[137] the CJEU upheld the application of a discretionary reduced rate to one 'concrete and specific' aspect of a specific composite supply.

But the Court of Appeal in *Colaingrove Ltd v HMRC*,[138] held that does not apply where there is no such specific exclusion. If two supplies, A+B would be a composite supply under EU principles then the fact that B on its own would be a reduced rate supply does not affect the composite standard-rated supply – in that case, the reduced rate is subsumed into the composite supply both on the wording of the Act and 'on EU general principles'.[139] There is no doubt that the fact that one element of a composite supply (A+B) is zero-rated rather than at a reduced rate does not affect the application of that principle so that it can be subsumed into a single exempt, reduced or standard-rated supply. That restricts rather than extends zero-rating.[140] The point was specifically argued in *HMRC v The Ice Rink Co Ltd*,[141] but the Upper Tribunal applied the reasoning in *Colaingrove* on reduced-rate supplies where in a composite supply of A+B, supply B on its own was instead a zero-rated supply.

But it also seems that other forms of supply can be subsumed into a zero-rated composite supply and that it does not seem to have been argued that that would extend the categories of zero-rating beyond those allowed.[142] Thus, a fancy tin of biscuits was held by the Court of Session to be subsumed into a single zero-rated supply of biscuits,[143] airline meals on domestic air flights were held by the Court of Appeal to be integrated into a single zero-rated supply of transport,[144] and more recently, the Upper Tribunal regarded the prostheses fitted by the company to be subsumed into a zero-rated supply of medical services.[145]

But the issue which did arise in relation to zero-rating concerned a different situation. Could the doctrine override a specific exclusion from zero-rating? Group 9 of Schedule 8 to the VAT Act provides for zero-rating for mobile caravans but specifically excludes their removable contents. In *Talacre Beach Caravans Ltd v HMRC*,[146] the company argued that the caravan and its contents constituted a single zero-rated supply. Thus, it was an attempt to negate rather than apply a specific exclusion. The CJEU[147] refused the application. To extend zero-rating to the contents of the caravan would be to extend a category of zero-rated items beyond those in force in January 1991 as required, at that time, by Article 28 of the Sixth Directive. As such, it would be contrary

[137] Case 94/09, *EC Commission v France*, [2010] ECR 1-4261; [2012] STC 573 CJEU.

[138] *Colaingrove Ltd v HMRC* [2017] EWCA Civ 731; [2017] STC 1287.

[139] s 29A of the VAT Act 1994 only applies to supplies 'of a description' ie, B taken on its own. A+B is not such a supply.

[140] See, eg *Dr Beynon v HMRC* [2004] UKHL 53 [2005] STC 55; *Purple Parking Ltd v HMRC* Case 117/11, [2012] STC 1680 CJEU; *HMRC v The Honourable Society of Middle Temple* [2013] UKUT 0250 (TCC); [2016] STC 2520.

[141] *HMRC v The Ice Rink Co Ltd* [2019] UKUT 108 (TCC).

[142] The Upper Tribunal did not address a possible argument to that effect in in *HMRC v The Ice Rink Co Ltd* [2019] UKUT 108 (TCC), [45].

[143] *CEC v United Biscuits plc* [1991] STC 325 CS(IH).

[144] *CEC v British Airways plc* [1990] STC 643 CA.

[145] *General Healthcare Group Ltd v HMRC* [2016] UKUT 315 (TCC); [2016] STC 2520.

[146] *Talacre Beach Caravans Ltd v HMRC* Case 251/06, [2006] ECR 1-629; [2006] STC 1671 CJEU.

[147] And the Advocate General, J Kokott. There was no such exclusion in the *News Corp* case, see n 91 above.

to the objectives of that Article.[148] The CJEU also relied on the fact, that as a derogation, zero-rating must be restrictively construed, although that does not seem to have added much to the decision.

VI. The Brexit Effect

The effect of leaving the European Union on the categories and operation of zero-rated supplies is clearly part of the wider impact on UK VAT itself.[149] Leaving the EU VAT area, if we do on 31 December 2020, will clearly have the most significant impact on cross-border transactions[150] but in relation to domestic supplies, the initial intention of the government is to continue as before until changes are made. Thus, in general, all direct EU legislation[151] in force immediately before withdrawal implementation day is to form part of domestic law.[152] That will not, under current proposals, however, include direct EU legislation relating to VAT.[153] But EU rights, powers, liabilities, obligations, restrictions, remedies and procedures applicable before exit day will continue to apply,[154] subject to a power of exclusion or modification by regulations in the case of VAT.[155] In relation to the wording of Schedule 8 to the VAT Act 1994, therefore, it seems that it will become wholly domestic law. In terms of the freedom of Parliament to alter, restrict or expand the categories of zero-rated supplies, the restrictions of Article 110 of the Principal VAT Directive will be removed. It is not 'retained EU law' under the European Union (Withdrawal) Act 2018, as amended.[156] New categories could, for example, be zero-rated,[157] 'Pringles' be made taxable, etc. The Treasury will no longer be able to hide behind Article 110 to preserve its tax base. Similarly, it will be able to expand that base on its own volition.[158]

Ironically, this freedom of defining the different categories of supply comes at the time when the EU is itself proposing to loosen the shackles on the permissible rates

[148] [2006] STC 1671 CJEU, [22].

[149] See J Cape and M Schofield, 'VAT and Brexit: The Past, Present and Future' (2018) 27 *EC Tax Review* 290.

[150] VAT will in such cases be replaced by export and import duty under the Taxation (Cross-border Trade) Act 2018, if and when that Act is brought into force. All references to that Act should be read subject to that caveat.

[151] This does not include directives.

[152] European Union (Withdrawal) Act 2018 s 4, as amended by the 2020 Bill (EUWA).

[153] Taxation (Cross-border Trade) Act 2018 s 42(1) (TCBTA). See also the Value Added Tax (Miscellaneous Amendments and Revocations) (EU Exit) Regs SI 2018/59.

[154] EUWA, s 4.

[155] TCBTA, s 42(2). Any such regulations must be made before 1 April 2023.

[156] But it, and its implementing regulation 282/2011, will still have a function in litigation if it is 'relevant' for interpretation purposes: see below. That would not include legislative changes.

[157] The European Council has in fact already agreed to a proposal to that effect, on 2 October 2018. The difference in tax rates between physical and e publications was upheld by the CJEU in the Case C-174/11, *Zimmerman*, but see M Lamensch, 'Different Rates for Digital and Paperback Publications in the EU, A Breach of Fiscal Neutrality? A Tentative Answer and Broader Reflection on the Coherence of the EU Rules Prohibiting Indirect Tax Discrimination' (2015) 4 *World Journal of VAT/GST Law* 1.

[158] That will probably apply more to the application of exempt and reduced-rate supplies which are specifically prescribed by the Directive.

of VAT. Following its 2016 VAT Action Plan,[159] in January 2018 the Commission put forward a proposal for an amending directive to the Principal Directive as regards the rates of VAT. This amendment would allow Member States more flexibility in setting VAT rates whilst maintaining all existing reduced and zero rates.[160] Under the proposed new Article 98 of the Principal Directive, Member States will be able to have up to two reduced rates with a minimum of 5 per cent, a further reduced rate with no minimum of 5 per cent and a zero-rate. The only restriction is that the overall weighted average rate must be no lower than 12 per cent.[161] Zero-rating would, therefore, be preserved although, strangely, Article 110 of the Principal Directive does not appear to have been repealed by the proposal. It appears therefore that the categories of zero-rating would continue to be limited to the January 1991 wording, but presumably, a new category of supplies with a reduced rate of 0 per cent could be used?[162]

The other Brexit issue affecting zero-rating is how the courts will interpret Schedule 8 immediately after exit day. Section 5(2) of the EUWA preserves the supremacy of pre-exit EU law and principles over pre-exit domestic legislation so that if there is a conflict, the Directive prevails.[163] In terms of VAT, this applies particularly to questions of interpretation. That will be of particular importance in relation to exempt and reduced-rate supplies where the Directive has definitive provisions.[164] But in terms of zero-rating, the major issue is whether the domestic courts will continue to apply the general principles of EU law such as proportionality, legal certainty and, above all, in the VAT context, fiscal neutrality.[165] Section 6 of the EUWA relates to the interpretation of retained EU and domestic case law and principles[166] generally, and section 6(3) requires any question to be decided in accordance with such retained principles and pre-exit EU decisions[167] where relevant. Under the TCBTA, section 6 is expressly referred to in section 42(3) and the EU principle of abuse of rights, used to counter VAT fraud,[168] is expressly continued post exit day as 'one of the consequences' of section 6.[169] Further, s 42(5) of the TCBTA

[159] Communication from the Commission to the European Parliament, the Council and the European Economic and Social Committee on an action plan on VAT. Towards a single EU VAT area – Time to decide COM(2016) 148 final.

[160] Proposal for a Council Directive amending Directive 2006/112/EC as regards rates of value added tax COM(2018) 20 final. This followed from the proposal to change the system of fixing the appropriate rate from the state of origin to the state of destination within the VAT area, which requires less harmonisation.

[161] Proposed new Art 99a of the Principal VAT Directive.

[162] Although the categories of reduced rate would still be set out in the Principal VAT Directive, the UK has a right under Art 113 to transfer any category of zero-rated supplies to the reduced rate list, which could presumably then have a 0% rate.

[163] This includes any amendments to pre-exit legislation where that accords with the intention of the modifications.

[164] Pre-exit decisions of the CJEU will remain binding until 31 December 2020. After that, the situation will be complex: see EUWA, ss 5 and 6, as amended.

[165] As used, eg, in Case 309/06, *Marks & Spencer plc v HMRC* (n 109); and *Sub One Ltd v HMRC* [2014] EWCA Civ 773 affirming [2012] UKUT 34, discussed above.

[166] As defined in s 6(7) of the Act.

[167] There is a complex procedure in the 2020 amending withdrawal bill as to which and when UK courts may depart from previous CJEU decisions. That will be for future articles to dissect.

[168] See Case 255/02, *Halifax plc v HMRC* [2006] ECR 1-2006, [2006] Ch 387; *Kittel v Belgium*, Case 439/04, [2006] ECR 1-6161, [2008] STC 1537.

[169] TCBTA 42(4).

provides for the situation where 'the principal VAT directive remains relevant for determining the meaning and effect of the law relating to value added tax'.

It seems therefore in the aftermath of a hard, medium or soft Brexit on or before 31 December 2020, the application, as distinct from the wording, of Schedule 8 will continue much as before, subject to any regulations. As history shows, the concept and difficulties of tax-free supplies under the 'necessity imperative' will continue into the sunset; it will simply have been repatriated, although it was never really offshore.

PART IV

Tax Administration

14

Drawing the Boundaries of HMRC's Discretion

STEPHEN DALY*

I. Introduction

A core function of HMRC and every other tax authority is to collect taxes prescribed as due.[1] To perform the task, HMRC is vested with a managerial discretion, which allows HMRC to take decisions which are conducive to the collection and management of taxes and credits,[2] such as engaging in cooperative compliance,[3] settling disputes[4] and producing guidance for taxpayers.[5] Judith Freedman, in her writings with John Vella, repeatedly pointed out that the boundaries of this discretion are unclear.[6] At what point can it be said that HMRC has used it unlawfully? The courts have given only fleeting advice. In the case of *R (Davies) v HMRC; R (Gaines-Cooper) v HMRC* (*Gaines-Cooper*),[7] Lord Wilson noted that HMRC is entitled 'to apply a cost–benefit analysis' in the context of exercising its managerial discretion.[8] However, would it follow then, Freedman and Vella asked, that if Parliament were to introduce a tax which raised a low amount of revenue but was expensive to collect, 'HMRC would be justified in overlooking its collection in order to concentrate efforts on other taxes if the overall result would be

* Immense thanks to César Palacios-González, Chris Evans and Iain Campbell for help on the chapter. An earlier version of this chapter also received incredibly helpful comments from attendees at a presentation in the Max Planck Institute for Tax Law and Public Finance in Munich, during a funded visit to the Institute.

[1] Commissioners for Revenue and Customs Act 2005 (CRCA 2005), s 5.

[2] See below in text at n 16.

[3] See J Freedman, G Loomer and J Vella, 'Analysing the Enhanced Relationship between Corporate Taxpayers and Revenue Authorities: A UK Case Study' in L Oats (ed), *Taxation. A Fieldwork Research Handbook* (Abingdon, Routledge, 2012).

[4] See J Freedman and J Vella, 'HMRC's Relationship with Business' (2014) Oxford University Centre for Business Taxation Working Paper.

[5] See J Freedman and J Vella, 'Revenue Guidance: The Limits of Discretion and Legitimate Expectations' (2012) 128 *LQR* 192.

[6] ibid 197; J Freedman and J Vella, 'HMRC's Management of the UK Tax System: The Boundaries of Legitimate Discretion' in C Evans, J Freedman and R Krever (eds), *The Delicate Balance – Tax, Discretion and the Rule of Law* (Amsterdam, IBFD, 2011).

[7] *R (Davies) v HMRC; R (Gaines-Cooper) v HMRC* [2011] UKSC 47, [2012] 1 All ER 1048 (*Gaines-Cooper*).

[8] ibid [26].

higher overall revenue'?[9] Whilst it is beyond dispute that HMRC cannot purposefully ignore the collection of such a tax, HMRC is not obliged to allocate a distinct level of resources to its collection. Freedman and Vella's query accordingly raises issues about what HMRC *may* do with the discretion – a legal question; what HMRC *ought* to do – a normative question; and what HMRC *can* do – a practical question.

The purpose of this chapter consequently is to consider the exercise of this discretion first legally, then normatively and finally practically. The underlying thesis advanced is that the resulting boundaries of discretion are neither distinct, nor identical, but rather are interwoven. Each section, however, seeks to make a discrete contribution. The legal boundaries of discretion are elucidated in order to make clear the scope of the legal choices that may be made. The normative boundaries highlight that different ethical choices are available and that each will have its limitations. Maximising revenues due, for instance, is just one of these choices, whereas other ethical theories lead us elsewhere. Finally, practical limits are placed on HMRC by virtue of its relationship with HM Treasury (the Treasury), thereby rendering misleading the oft-cited assertion that HMRC has a 'wide managerial discretion'.

This chapter concerns itself specifically with the exercise of managerial discretion by HMRC in carrying out the function of collecting taxes due, rather than its other functions such as administering the system for tax credits[10] or specific obligations such as the duty to provide notice to a taxpayer of any assessment to tax.[11]

II. How HMRC May Act

When we speak of legal discretion, what we are referring to is the ability to choose between a range of options, though that choice is not unlimited. Legal discretion duly operates as a function of the relationship between autonomy and its boundaries,[12] and requires that it is the entity vested with the discretion that determines which choice should be made. In this way, legal discretion should be distinguished from instances where some entity undoubtedly has power or influence, but the ultimate decision is vested in a different actor. For instance, the power to definitively interpret statutes ordinarily[13] resides with the tribunals and courts though the public authorities that operate the statutes will be required to operate on the basis of working interpretations[14] and such working interpretations can influence judicial interpretation.[15]

[9] Freedman and Vella, 'Revenue Guidance' (n 5) 195.

[10] CRCA 2005, s 5(1)(c).

[11] See for instance Taxes Management Act 1970, s 29(5).

[12] For this reason, Dworkin once likened discretion to a 'hole in a doughnut'. See R Dworkin, *Taking Rights Seriously* (Cambridge, MA, Harvard University Press, 1978) 31.

[13] There are some instances where interpretation can involve an element of judgement for public authorities, as in the case of *Moyna v Secretary of State for Work and Pensions* [2003] UKHL 44, [2003] 1 WLR 1929.

[14] Sometimes extra-statutory concessions are regarded as discretionary exercises of power when in reality some may arise from purposive interpretation. See S Daly, 'The Life and Times of ESCs: A Defence?' in P Harris and D de Cogan (eds), *Studies in the History of Tax Law*, Vol 8 (Oxford, Hart Publishing, 2017) 177–78.

[15] See G Weeks, *Soft Law and Public Authorities: Remedies and Reform* (Oxford, Hart Publishing, 2016) 1–2; Freedman and Vella, 'HMRC's Management of the UK Tax System' (n 6) 112–15.

Any legal discretion which HMRC holds should be understood in terms of these basic building blocks. Whilst HMRC is vested with some specific discretions by statute, as in the case of HMRC's discretion to mitigate penalties,[16] the concern of this chapter is with the overarching 'managerial discretion' which HMRC exercises. This pervasive discretion allows HMRC to determine how to go about the task of tax collection. It is derived from section 5 of the Commissioners for Revenue and Customs Act 2005 (CRCA 2005), which provides that HMRC has responsibility for the collection and management of taxes, duties, national insurance contributions and credits. Section 5 CRCA is supplemented by section 9 of the Act which provides that HMRC may do anything which it considers (a) necessary or expedient in connection with the exercise of their functions, or (b) incidental or conducive to the exercise of their functions. However, section 5 does not specify how HMRC should go about performing this task and correspondingly it provides legal discretion as to how the task is to be performed.[17] The fact that a legal discretion arises means that the courts will respect decisions taken by HMRC pursuant to the discretion provided that the limits or boundaries of the discretion are not breached.

In order to fully appreciate the boundaries of legal discretion in the UK, it is necessary to start as Freedman and Vella do[18] by considering the fundamental constitutional principle of parliamentary sovereignty, which at its least controversial means that Parliament has legislative supremacy and may *legally* enact or remove any piece of legislation. At its extreme, this means that Parliament can pass legislation which has no enforceable content, such as a law banning smoking on the streets of Paris.[19] The principle provides both the source of any power that HMRC may have, given that it is a body created by statute, and a source of limits. The provision granting the discretion itself places limitations on HMRC's managerial discretion, as do other provisions in CRCA 2005 along with other Acts of Parliament.[20] The courts impose other restrictions though they might be less evident from the reading of statutes.[21] Provided that HMRC does not cross these statutory and judicially developed boundaries, then it shall have open to it a range of choices any one of which will be considered lawful if chosen.

A. Legal Boundaries

The provision granting the discretion imposes a *duty* on HMRC to collect taxes due, which at a minimum requires that HMRC not act in a way directly contrary to that provision, for instance by agreeing not to investigate or challenge a taxpayer's future

[16] See for instance Taxes Management Act 1970, s 102; Value Added Tax Act 1994, s 70.

[17] This provision is to be contrasted with statutes which do express how the discretion is to be exercised. See, for instance, ss 6 and 6A of the Taxes Administration Act 1994 (New Zealand).

[18] Freedman and Vella, 'HMRC's Management of the UK Tax System' (n 6) 87.

[19] I Jennings, *The Law and the Constitution*, 5th edn (London, University of London Press, 1959) 170–71.

[20] This section is heavily influenced by the discussion of the limits in Freedman and Vella, 'HMRC's Management of the UK Tax System' (n 6) 83–108.

[21] Indeed, there is a debate about whether judicial review is grounded in common law or parliamentary sovereignty. See C Forsyth (ed), *Judicial Review & the Constitution* (Oxford, Hart Publishing, 2000).

affairs in return for a fixed sum of money.[22] As notoriously put by Walton J, 'one should be taxed by law, and not untaxed by [administrative] concession'.[23] At the same time, should Parliament seek to raise a tax which is not practically collectable – for instance such as a levy for smoking in Parisian streets, or as in *Vestey v IRC* where the legislation was drafted so broadly that Parliament's attempt 'to impose a tax … ha[d] failed'[24] – there is no duty on HMRC to collect the tax, as the purported duty in such an instance is without substance. Though the precise requirements of the duty to collect are not certain, practicality dictates that the duty should not be interpreted overly expansively. The duty would be unrealisable if it required every penny of tax due to be collected. It would mean that the duty is flouted every time a penny of tax is not paid[25] – regardless of the fact that the failure to pay may lie with the taxpayer or that mistakes in a large organisation are inevitable. Others view this restriction on the duty to collect tax as not being dictated by practicality, by rather by the countervailing duty to *manage*.[26] The result under either interpretation is that the duty to collect is restricted.

In sum, short of instances where the content of the legislation is not enforceable, HMRC has a duty not to ignore taxes prescribed as due, though this duty to collect does not extend to ensuring that every penny of any such tax is collected. HMRC's Litigation and Settlement Strategy exemplifies this distinction.[27] HMRC holds a discretion as to whether to engage in a tax dispute.[28] But, once it does, HMRC must consider each dispute on its merits, rather than as part of a package if there are a number of disputes between a taxpayer, and cannot split the difference between its view and the taxpayer's view of the law.[29]

Other provisions of CRCA 2005 restrict how HMRC may act when seeking to exercise its managerial discretion, such as the prohibition on disclosing confidential taxpayer information.[30] Hence, HMRC cannot disclose taxpayer information even if it considers that it would be conducive to the process of tax collection. Instead, it would seem that the disclosure of taxpayer information could only be justified by reference to the duty to collect tax if the non-disclosure would prevent or undermine the collection of tax, as where the media would sabotage a dawn raid if not told confidential information.[31] Notably, section 11 of CRCA 2005 provides that HMRC shall comply with any directions of a general nature given to them by the Treasury. The discretion thus must be exercised in a manner compatible with directions of the Treasury for instance in respect of HMRC strategies (though it does not extend to allowing the Treasury to

[22] For instance, *Al-Fayed v IRC* [2004] STC 1703 (IH).

[23] *Vestey v IRC* [1979] Ch 198 (Ch), 197.

[24] *Vestey v IRC* [1980] AC 1148 (HL), 1173 (Lord Wilberforce).

[25] See the point conceded by the taxpayer in *IRC v National Federation of Self-Employed and Small Businesses Ltd* [1982] AC 617 (HL) 660 (*Fleet Street Casuals*).

[26] See, for instance, *Gaines-Cooper* (n 7) [26] (Lord Wilson).

[27] See HMRC, *Resolving Tax Disputes: Commentary on the Litigation and Settlement Strategy* (30 October 2017), available at: www.gov.uk/government/publications/litigation-and-settlement-strategy-lss.

[28] ibid para 8.

[29] ibid paras 16–19.

[30] See CRCA 2005, s 18; *Fleet Street Casuals* (n 25) 636H (Lord Diplock).

[31] *R (Ingenious Media and McKenna) v HMRC* [2016] UKSC 54, [2016] 1 WLR 4164, [35] (Lord Toulson).

dictate everyday decisions or become involved in an individual taxpayer's affairs).[32] The provision alone does not constrain HMRC, but rather HMRC's discretion is limited if the Treasury's power is exercised.[33]

Other items of legislation, some of which might be termed 'constitutional statutes',[34] similarly impose obligations on HMRC. For instance, section 4 of the Bill of Rights Act 1689 requires that HMRC not collect taxes that have not been approved by Parliament.[35] In consequence, HMRC may not exercise its discretion in a manner which would impose taxes which have not been prescribed as due by Parliament.[36] Statutes such as the Human Rights Act 1998 also impose obligations concerning the manner in which HMRC operates its discretion, as it must do so in a manner which is compliant with the European Convention on Human Rights.[37] It follows that HMRC must not purport to exercise discretion in a way which breaches taxpayers' Convention rights, such as the right not to be discriminated against based on sex.[38]

Beyond what we can see directly from statutes, discretion is also subject to a series of principles of interpretation, which have been developed by the courts, through which the exercise of public power is restrained. Though there is much debate about its content, it is uncontroversial to propose that HMRC must operate in conformity with the constitutional principle of the rule of law.[39] In specific circumstances, this would require HMRC to produce guidance to assist taxpayers where the absence of guidance would undermine a taxpayer's human rights.[40] The principle of legality, on the other hand, ensures that any attempt by HMRC to use its discretion to override fundamental rights, such as access to justice,[41] will be regarded as unlawful.[42]

Judicial review principles meanwhile have developed to limit how public authorities may act.[43] As the jurisdiction of the courts[44] in judicial review is supervisory,

[32] See Explanatory Notes to the Commissioners for Revenue and Customs Act 2005, para 71.

[33] See below in text at n 112.

[34] On constitutional statutes, see *Thoburn v Sunderland City Council* [2002] EWHC 195 (Admin), [2003] QB 151, [60]–[70] (Laws LJ).

[35] *Attorney-General v Wilts United Dairies Ltd* (1921) 38 TLR 781 (CA).

[36] Though Article 4 was not mentioned in the House of Lords judgment in *Vestey v IRC* (n 24) this could have been used to resolve the case.

[37] See Human Rights Act 1998, s 6.

[38] This argument was tried but failed in the case of *R (Wilkinson) v IRC* [2005] UKHL 30; [2006] STC 270 because the matter did not fall within HMRC's discretion (*Wilkinson*).

[39] See Freedman and Vella, 'HMRC's Management of the UK Tax System' (n 6) 95.

[40] See *R (on the application of Nicklinson) v Ministry of Justice* [2014] UKSC 38, [2014] 3 WLR 200; *R (Purdy) v Director of Public Prosecutions* [2009] UKHL 45, [2010] 1 AC 345 (HL). This was tried but failed in *Privacy International v HMRC* [2014] EWHC 1475 (Admin), [2015] STC 948.

[41] *R (Haworth) v Revenue and Customs* [2019] EWCA Civ 747, [2019] 1 WLR 4708 [36] (Newey LJ); *R (UNISON) v Lord Chancellor* [2017] UKSC 51, [2017] 3 WLR 409, [66]–[85] (Lord Reed).

[42] On the principle of legality, see: *R v Secretary of State for Defence Ex p Smith* [1996] QB 517 (CA), 554E–G (Bingham LJ); *R v Lord Chancellor Ex p Witham* [1998] QB 575 (DC), 581E–F (Laws LJ); *R v Secretary of State for the Home Department Ex p Pierson* [1998] AC 539 (HL), 575 (Lord Browne-Wilkinson).

[43] The categorisation of the different grounds on which judicial review may be brought is not universally agreed. See M Elliott and R Thomas, *Public Law*, 3rd edn (Oxford, Oxford University Press, 2017) 497. See *CCSU v Minister for the Civil Service* [1985] AC 374 (HL) for the famous tripartite categorisation.

[44] See now also Senior Courts Act 1981, s 31A which allows the High Court to transfer judicial review proceedings to the Upper Tribunal. Where references are made to the courts in respect of judicial review in this chapter, it should be taken that this also includes the Upper Tribunal.

these principles generally only permit the courts to check whether proper processes have been followed when decisions are made. For instance, the tax authority must not exercise its discretion for an improper purpose.[45] The tax authority should take into account relevant considerations and disregard irrelevant considerations.[46] The courts may nevertheless also assess the merits of a decision where the decision arrived at is *unreasonable*,[47] as occurred in the case of *R v Inland Revenue Commissioners, ex parte Unilever*.[48] A court will only regard the purported exercise of discretion as unreasonable, however, in 'exceptional circumstances'.[49] As Bingham LJ (as he then was) put it in *R v IRC, ex p MFK Underwriting Agents Ltd*:[50] 'the revenue's judgment on the best way of collecting tax should not lightly be cast aside'.[51] What is critical when determining reasonable action, as a result, is whether a good reason (or good reasons) can be provided or inferred which can relate the action to the desired aim, though the courts will not interrogate the reasoning in depth.

B. A Range of Choices

Provided that HMRC is acting within these limits, then the actions of the body taken pursuant to its managerial discretion will be respected by the courts. Three seminal judgments from the UK's highest court dealt with the specific issue of how the discretion *may* be exercised. But the courts in these cases were not seeking to lay down a rule about how the discretion must be exercised; instead, they were simply affirming why the manner in which the discretion was exercised in the three cases was lawful. To interpret these cases otherwise would remove the range of choices that are supposed to be inherent in the exercise of discretion.

In *IRC v National Federation of Self-Employed and Small Businesses Ltd* (*Fleet Street Casuals*),[52] a case concerning an agreement between the Inland Revenue and print workers about past and future tax liabilities, the House of Lords endorsed the agreement on the basis that it fell within the Revenue's discretion. Lord Diplock explained that:

> [T]he board have a wide managerial discretion as to the best means of obtaining for the national exchequer from the taxes committed to their charge, the highest net return that is practicable having regard to the staff available to them and the cost of collection.[53]

In *R (Wilkinson) v IRC* (*Wilkinson*),[54] the House of Lords rejected a taxpayer argument that HMRC should exercise its discretion to extend by way of 'concession' a relief for widows to widowers. After quoting Lord Diplock's statement, Lord Hoffmann held that

[45] *Padfield v Minister of Agriculture, Fisheries and Food* [1968] AC 997 (HL), 706 (Lord Morris).
[46] *UK Uncut Legal Action v HMRC* [2013] EWHC 1283 (Admin), [2013] SWTI 1849.
[47] *R v Secretary of State for the Home Department ex parte Doody* [1994] 1 AC 531 (HL), 560 (Lord Mustill).
[48] See *R v Inland Revenue Commissioners, ex parte Unilever plc* [1996] STC 681 (CA).
[49] *The United Policyholders Group v The Attorney General of Trinidad and Tobago* [2016] UKPC 17, [2016] 1 WLR 3383, [93] and [144] (Lord Carnwath).
[50] *R v IRC, ex p MFK Underwriting Agents Ltd* [1990] 1 WLR 1545 (QBD) (*MFK Underwriting*).
[51] ibid 1568.
[52] *Fleet Street Casuals* (n 25).
[53] ibid 626.
[54] *Wilkinson* (n 38).

it was not within HMRC's discretion to extend an 'allowance which Parliament could have granted but did not grant'.[55] The scope of the discretion is more limited:

> This discretion enables the commissioners to formulate policy in the interstices of the tax legislation, dealing pragmatically with minor or transitory anomalies, cases of hardship at the margins or cases in which a statutory rule is difficult to formulate or its enactment would take up a disproportionate amount of Parliamentary time.[56]

Finally, in *Gaines-Cooper*, several taxpayers sought to rely upon HMRC guidance to argue that they should be treated as non-resident. The argument was rejected by a majority of the Supreme Court. In doing so, Lord Wilson (who wrote the majority judgment) similarly affirmed Lord Diplock's statement and confirmed that HMRC could exercise its managerial discretion according to cost–benefit analysis:

> [T]he Revenue is entitled to apply a cost–benefit analysis to its duty of management and in particular, against the return thereby likely to be foregone, to weigh the costs which it would be likely to save as a result of a concession which cuts away an area of complexity or likely dispute.[57]

In each of these cases, the courts were not seeking to lay down rules about how HMRC *must* exercise its managerial discretion. The principal statute, now the CRCA 2005, does not dictate that it would be appropriate for HMRC to seek always to obtain the best practicable return for the exchequer, or put another way to maximise revenues due. Nor would it be appropriate for HMRC only to issue concessions in the categories set out by Lord Hoffmann, namely to deal pragmatically with minor or transitory anomalies, cases of hardship at the margins or cases in which a statutory rule is difficult to formulate or its enactment would take up a disproportionate amount of parliamentary time. Nor finally is it required that HMRC use cost–benefit analysis to manage resources as per Lord Wilson.

Rather, HMRC *may* make decisions that maximise revenues due. Under this guiding objective, it is a rational use of discretion in the circumstances to produce guidance as in *Gaines-Cooper*, or settle a dispute as in *Fleet Street Casuals*, or issue concessions in the limited scenarios outlined by Lord Hoffmann. In each case, there are good reasons given or inferred which connect the tax authority's decision to a chosen objective. But lawfulness in the context of discretion does not dictate discrete answers. It is inherent in the nature of legal discretion that there is a range of lawful options from which to choose. The subtlety of this point was not lost on Bingham LJ in *MFK Underwriting*. The Inland Revenue sought to argue in that case that its discretion could only be exercised 'for the better, more efficient and more economical collection of tax and not otherwise'.[58] Bingham LJ rejected this interpretation as being too narrow.[59] He followed this by stating that the Inland Revenue could equally act in a manner which is uncooperative and

[55] ibid [21] (Lord Hoffmann).
[56] ibid.
[57] *Gaines-Cooper* (n 7) [26].
[58] *MFK Underwriting* (n 50) 1567B. Though see L Beighton, 'The Finance Bill Process: Scope for Reform?' [1995] *BTR* 33, 41.
[59] *MFK Underwriting* (n 50) 1568F.

that this too would fall within the scope of its managerial discretion, thereby implicitly rejecting the idea that discretion must be used to maximise revenues due:

> The revenue might stick to the letter of its statutory duty, declining to answer any question when not statutorily obliged to do so … and maintaining a strictly arm's length relationship with the taxpayer.[60]

Accordingly, HMRC's managerial discretion need not only be exercised in a manner conducive to maximising revenues due. HMRC to this end has long understood that it has discretion not to collect taxes, not where this would be conducive to maximising revenues due, but rather where it would lead to 'hardship'. For instance, a Treasury Minute from 1897 notes that the Inland Revenue was dispensing with the collection of taxes in individual cases on 'the motive of equity or from compassion'.[61] Over the years the justification for such dispensation evolved from compassion to 'poverty or other grounds' in 1936, then 'comparative hardship' in 1971[62] and simply to its modern incarnation of 'hardship'.[63] Today the practice of granting relief for hardship continues and the amounts remitted are highlighted in the annual reports.[64] In 2018–19, HMRC made £794 million of remissions.[65] In its annual report for that year, HMRC defined remission as the 'process used to identify and separate money owed to HMRC which we have decided not to pursue – for example, on the grounds of value for money'.[66] Though the definition does not mention hardship, HMRC's policy was explained later in the accompanying Comptroller & Auditor General Report, where it is noted that remission is where HMRC decides not to pursue the liability on value-for-money or hardship grounds,[67] thereby separating 'value for money' from 'hardship'. In *Vrang v HMRC*,[68] HMRC documents put the meaning of hardship in the following terms:

> [C]ircumstances where keeping the charge in place would cause significant hardship and result in a situation which a court would view as grossly unfair to the individual paying the charge, as a result of actions entirely beyond that person's control.[69]

[60] ibid 1568F–G. See also ibid 1572H (Judge J).

[61] Treasury Minute dated 31 December 1897 on the Reports relating to Civil and Miscellaneous Accounts, 1895–96 in Public Accounts Committee, *Second report from the Committee of Public Accounts* (HC 1897–98, 261) 147–49.

[62] Inland Revenue, *Report of the Commissioners of Her Majesty's Inland Revenue for the year ended 31st March 1971: Hundred and Fourteenth Report* (Cmnd 4838, 1972) 9.

[63] J Booth, 'Inland Revenue Concessions: Convenience or just Illegal?' (2000) 27 *Amicus Curiae* 23, 23. See for instance Inland Revenue, *Report of the Commissioners of Her Majesty's Inland Revenue for the year ended 31st March 1980: One Hundred and Twenty-Third Report* (Cmnd 8160, 1981) 52 which uses just the phrase 'hardship'. The final Annual Report to mention comparative hardship was: Inland Revenue, *Report of the Commissioners of Her Majesty's Inland Revenue for the year ended 31st March 1976: One Hundred and Nineteenth Report* (Cmnd 6734, 1977) 41. However, it was subsequently mentioned in Parliamentary Commissioner for Administration, *First Report-Session 1991–92: Selected Cases 1992-Volume 1* (HC 1991–92, 195) 24, though this was the latest reference to the phrase that the author could find on www.parlipapers.proquest.com.

[64] See HMRC, *HM Revenue and Customs Annual Report and Accounts 2018–19 (For the year ended 31 March 2019)* (HC 2394, 2019) 182.

[65] ibid 182.

[66] ibid 158.

[67] ibid R14, para 1.10.

[68] *Vrang v HMRC* [2017] EWHC 1055 (Admin), [2017] STC 1192.

[69] ibid [42].

In that case, monies were levied in accordance with the UK–Swiss Agreement on Cooperation in the Area of Taxation.[70] The Agreement could have the effect whereby taxpayer inaction could result in monies being collected from Swiss bank accounts even though no tax was due (as occurred in the case of the taxpayer Karin Vrang).[71] HMRC devised a system which resulted in taxpayers being repaid monies because of the financial hardship caused by the levying of the monies or where the levying of the monies was caused by inaction (or an error) brought about by personal hardship.[72] For Ousley J, the power to promulgate such a policy, justified as it was on the basis of hardship, 'undoubtedly' fell within HMRC's discretion,[73] thereby confirming the lawfulness of exercising managerial discretion on a basis other than maximising revenues due.

III. How HMRC Ought to Act

HMRC is vested with an overarching managerial discretion as to how it goes about the task of collecting taxes due. It follows that HMRC may decide how to allocate resources internally. Of course, HMRC cannot go so far as dismissing the collection of certain taxes. But, given that not every penny of any tax due must be collected, HMRC may make choices as to how to allocate resources to the collection of different taxes. In practice HMRC can delay having to make such choices. For instance, it can lobby the government for more money, become more efficient, or seek to outsource some of the collection activities as we witness in the collection of VAT, PAYE and NICs for instance.[74] However, in the end, the hurdle of resource constraints must be confronted. These constraints are caused by decisions regarding how much money should be provided and by factual limitations like the fact that there are only so many tax inspectors, computers, even hours in the day.[75]

In this regard, the courts have indicated that the objective of maximising revenues due may drive the choices regarding the allocation of resources to collect taxes. However, it does not follow that HMRC may *only* act in a way which does so; the question of what HMRC *may* do therefore is distinguishable from the question of what HMRC normatively *ought* to do. The priorities that HMRC sets, whether expressly or impliedly, to guide the allocation of resources to the task of collecting taxes, will embody these normative choices. The field of moral ethics seeks to provide, if not specific directions

[70] Agreement between the United Kingdom of Great Britain and Northern Ireland and the Swiss Confederation on Cooperation in the area of Taxation (London, 6 October 2011).

[71] She may have owed some interest and perhaps some tax, but it was nothing on the scale of monies taken from her bank account in Switzerland.

[72] *Vrang v HMRC* (n 68) [89]–[95].

[73] ibid [123].

[74] This outsourcing is particularly interesting given the proportion of the tax base that these three taxes take up – see for instance HMRC, *Annual Report and Accounts 2018–19* (n 64) 24. Most tax it seems is collected without the tax authority lifting a finger!

[75] This (unclear antecedent) is well acknowledged in the field of health care. See for instance J Bickenbach, 'Disability and Health Care Rationing' (*Stanford Encyclopaedia of Philosophy*, 29 January 2016); K Bærøe, 'Priority-Setting in Healthcare: A Framework for Reasonable Clinical Judgements' (2009) 35 *Journal of Medical Ethics* 488, 488.

about how one ought to act, at least pathways to figuring it out.[76] Through understanding the ethical underpinnings of different choices, we can also appreciate any resulting ethical limitations. Consequently, these lessons can be applied to critique the explicit priorities set by HMRC.

A. Moral Ethics

The classic starting point in moral ethics, when determining how one ought to act, is to consider the issue from the perspectives of deontology and consequentialism.[77] The former prescribes that the rightness of an action can be judged by the inherent features of the act, whilst the latter ascribes judgement of the rightness or wrongness to the outcomes produced by an action. Kantian ethics, the most well-known strand of deontology, requires that to do good, one must do one's duty (the categorical imperative). Such a duty arises if the action can be universalised and thereby should be performed by all persons in all situations ('will that it should become universal law'). Humans, meanwhile, in any situation, should not be used as a means to an end. Tax collection based on Kantian ethics would seek to respect the choices of individual taxpayers, treating them as autonomous, rational agents. The application of such an approach can be seen in the provision of free advice to taxpayers, for instance, in the form of rulings or guidance, to enable them to make autonomous, rational choices.[78] The focus on personal or financial hardship in the case of *Vrang v HMRC*[79] similarly can be understood as an application of Kantian ethics: to cause hardship would be to remove or undermine autonomy.

Utilitarianism, meanwhile, is perhaps the most famous strand of consequentialism. An action will be judged good if it maximises utility. There are three essential elements to utilitarianism.[80] First that it is consequentialist; second that it focuses on consequences that are conducive to the utility of those affected, where utility is generally regarded as happiness or welfare; third that it aggregates – where there is a choice 'between the welfare of one lot of people and the welfare of another lot, we should choose the action which maximizes the welfare … in aggregate'.[81] The objective of maximising revenues due in tax collection could be understood as utilitarian, if 'utility' were to be defined in

[76] Others have written about ethics and tax, but not in the context of the ethics in tax administration, see for instance: I Lindsay, 'The Ethics of Tax Policy' in A Lever and A Poama (eds), *The Routledge Handbook of Ethics and Public Policy* (Routledge, Abingdon, 2018); J Frecknall Hughes and P Moizer, 'Taxation and Ethics' in M Lamb, A Lymer, J Freedman and S James (eds), *Taxation: An Interdisciplinary Approach to Research* (Oxford, Oxford University Press, 2004); L Murphy and T Nagel, *The Myth of Ownership: Taxes and Justice* (Oxford, Oxford University Press, 2002) in particular, ch 3.

[77] For an overview of different theories and how they are applied in healthcare, see I Williams, S Robinson and H Dickinson, *Rationing in Health Care: The Theory and Practice of Priority Setting* (Bristol, Policy Press, 2011) ch 2.

[78] This approach aligns with the overarching principle of the rule of law. On which see S Daly, *Tax Authority Advice and the Public* (Oxford, Hart Publishing, 2020) ch 3.

[79] See above in text at n 69.

[80] Adopting, but departing slightly in relation to utility, RM Hare's approach. See RM Hare, 'A Utilitarian Approach' in H Kuhse and P Singer (eds), *A Companion to Bioethics*, 2nd edn (West Sussex, Blackwell Publishing, 2009) 87. See also N Simmonds, *Central Issues in Jurisprudence: Justice, Law and Rights*, 5th edn (London, Sweet & Maxwell, 2018) 18–19.

[81] Hare (n 80) 87.

terms of revenues alone (which itself would be to make hefty assumptions about the role of money in society).[82] In any event, the objective is consequentialist. An example of this strand of ethics applied in practice would be risk-rating, wherein a tax authority allocates resources according to the consequent risk posed to public finances.[83]

Other theoretical approaches include egalitarianism, whereby all persons are to be treated equally, and paternalism where decision-making is vested in somebody other than the individual concerned, such as an expert. Aspects of each are evident in tax collection also. Egalitarianism, for instance, could be seen as requiring the allocation of resources according to need, thereby implying a more significant role for the assistance of less sophisticated taxpayers.[84] A paternalistic approach to priority-setting in tax collection can explain 'nudging', whereby HMRC seeks to nudge taxpayers towards compliance behaviour, such as with deadline reminders.[85]

Each theory will have some undeniable attraction. Deontology and egalitarianism leave the reader with a distinct sense of respect for the individual; consequentialism and paternalism provide an efficient means of progressing towards a desired end. Further, each theory will have normative boundaries that must be accepted. For instance, Kantian ethics requires that we not base decisions on consequences, something which in certain circumstances will be instinctively unappealing[86] or practically unacceptable. For instance, as humans should never be used as a means to an end, Kantian ethics would dictate that tax authorities should avoid placing pressure on one taxpayer to give over the information of another taxpayer who has assisted in tax evasion.[87] A system based on consequentialism would give little guidance where two different actions produce the same aggregate outcome.[88] How should resources be allocated where the same amount of revenue can be collected by expending the same level of resources on the collection of two different taxes, or on the provision of two different offices? In this way, consequentialist theories neutralise differences where those differences may be material. Consequentialism could lead to ignoring differences across taxes and taxpayers, even though taxpayers are not a homogenous group and taxes are geared towards objectives other than raising revenue. Egalitarianism, on the other hand, is unlikely to

[82] To this end, Richard Posner has written that utilitarianism and wealth maximisation are not equivalent, given that not all scholars would equate utility with economic value. See R Posner, 'Utilitarianism, Economics, and Legal Theory' (1979) 8 *Journal of Legal Studies* 103.

[83] See further HMRC, *HMRC Internal Manual: Tax Compliance Risk Management* (30 September 2019), available at: www.gov.uk/hmrc-internal-manuals/tax-compliance-risk-management; J Freedman, G Loomer and J Vella, 'Corporate Tax Risk and Tax Avoidance: New Approaches' [2009] *BTR* 74.

[84] Given that the bulk of taxes are collected without HMRC having to lift a finger, we see that this assistance has mostly been outsourced, but at least it evidences the role of assisting less sophisticated taxpayers in practice.

[85] See Kate Palmer, 'Psychology and "nudges": Five tricks the taxman uses to make you pay £210m extra' *The Telegraph* (9 October 2014).

[86] The classic example is that it is a duty to be truthful. For instance, it would be wrong to lie to a murderer at the door about the whereabouts of a person hiding inside a house.

[87] HMRC does, in fact, do so. See: HMRC, *Code of Practice 9* (30 June 2014) 5, available at: www.gov.uk/government/publications/code-of-practice-9-where-hm-revenue-and-customs-suspect-fraud-cop-9-2012.

[88] Bickenbach, 'Disability and Health Care Rationing' (n 75); N Daniels and J Sabin, 'Limits to Health Care: Fair Procedures, Democratic Deliberation, and the Legitimacy Problem for Insurers' (1997) 26 *Philosophy and Public Affairs* 303, 319.

be palatable to policymakers, given that it will not necessarily generate a significant amount of revenue. Further, paternalism can be viewed as undermining autonomy.

Inevitably any given theory will have its advantages and disadvantages as well as winners and losers when it comes to the allocation of scarce resources in the performance of a public duty. Further, in a pluralistic society, it is incredibly difficult and perhaps even impossible[89] to reach a consensus on the moral principles that should guide our actions.[90] To this end, a pluralist principle-based approach provides an attractive starting point. A principle-based approach holds 'that some general moral norms or action guides are central in moral reasoning'.[91] The principles need not stem from a single theory such as deontology or consequentialism.[92]

B. Priority-Setting by HMRC

HMRC engages in the process of explicit priority-setting. The Department's Single Departmental Plan,[93] which has been developed in agreement with the Treasury, sets out its three strategic objectives:

- Collect revenues due and bear down on avoidance and evasion.
- Transform tax and payments for our customers.
- Design and deliver a professional, efficient and engaged organisation.

These objectives appear to reflect consequentialist principles, given that the focus is on aggregate consequences. However, no evident supremacy is granted to one set of consequences over another. More generally, this consequentialist approach has distinct operational benefits as it grants clear guidance to officials within HMRC as to the outcomes that are to be pursued.

Understanding the ethics underlying this approach, however, reveals problems with the composition. For instance, it is misleading to have, as a single objective, collecting revenues due on the one hand, and bearing down on avoidance and evasion on the other, as it suggests that there are no choices that have to be made between the two. To the contrary, choices have to be made given finite resources between collecting taxes from those who are liable to make accidental errors, those that look to bend the rules, and those who are fraudulent. A costly exercise to clamp down on evasion, for instance, will come at the expense of an initiative to change the behaviour of tax avoiders or to assist taxpayers who are liable, but without intent, to get their taxes wrong.

[89] B Williams, *Moral Luck* (Cambridge, Cambridge University Press, 1981) ix–x.

[90] S Holm, 'Policy-Making in Pluralistic Societies' in B Steinbock (ed), *The Oxford Handbook of Bioethics* (Oxford, Oxford University Press, 2009).

[91] J Childress, 'A Principle-based Approach' in H Kuhse and P Singer (eds), *A Companion to Bioethics*, 2nd edn (West Sussex, Blackwell Publishing, 2009).

[92] ibid 68.

[93] HMRC, *HM Revenue and Customs Single Departmental Plan* (1 October 2019), available at: www.gov.uk/government/publications/hm-revenue-and-customs-single-departmental-plan/hm-revenue-and-customs-single-departmental-plan--2.

A further downside to this approach is that it gives no guidance per se on the choices made, or those which will be made, where the objectives conflict. Tie-breaking rules are required to deal with the conflicts, such as 'effectiveness, proportionality, necessity, least infringement, and public justification'.[94] Given that HMRC is accountable to Parliament through ministers,[95] who are accountable, in turn, to the public, it would be entirely legitimate to adopt *public justification*, for instance, as a tie-breaking rule. It is, however, unsatisfying that no tie-breakers are provided publicly by HMRC, much less the reasons which reveal how conflicts have been and are resolved. As a matter of law, it is arguable that HMRC has an obligation to set out reasons to demonstrate how the exercise of discretion relates to the objectives pursued.[96] However, more broadly, the publication of tie-breakers and the reasoning would demonstrate a public commitment to rationality in administration, thereby enhancing the legitimacy of the outcomes of the allocation of resources.[97]

More fundamentally, the adoption of a consequentialist approach leads to the aggregation of outcomes and therefore ignores, at some level, the differences between taxes and taxpayers. As correctly identified by Freedman and Vella,[98] this approach can lead to the dedication of fewer resources to taxes which are difficult to collect. However, those taxes, for instance, inheritance tax – which is relatively costly to collect[99] but is, in essence, a tax on wealth – may serve broader functions that would simply be ignored in a consequentialist regime. A consequentialist approach has an impact on equity across taxpayers.[100] On the one hand, a greater share of resources should be dedicated to those who pose the highest risk to the Exchequer, which on the whole would be larger businesses and the wealthier. This difference in the allocation of resources according to risk is evidenced by the contrast between the fact that the largest businesses in the UK each have a dedicated Customer Compliance Manager[101] and the fact that other taxpayers are provided with helplines (wherein HMRC's goals are to answer the phone within five minutes and to leave no more than 15 per cent of callers waiting for more than 10 minutes to speak to an adviser).[102] At the same time, however, the larger taxpayers

[94] J Childress et al, 'Public Health Ethics: Mapping the Terrain' (2002) 30 *Journal of Law, Medicine & Ethics* 170, 173.

[95] The Chief Executive and Permanent Secretary is responsible to Parliament for the department's expenditure and performance: HMRC, *Resolving Tax Disputes* (n 27) 13. Meanwhile, the Financial Secretary to the Treasury has been delegated responsibility for oversight of HMRC by the Chancellor of the Exchequer: HMRC, *Annual Report and Accounts 2018–19* (n 64) 72.

[96] See above in text at n 46; A Le Sueur, 'Legal Duties to Give Reasons' (1999) 52 *Current Legal Problems* 150, 155.

[97] M Elliott, 'Has the Common Law Duty to Give Reasons Come of Age Yet?' [2011] *Public Law* 56, 61–63.

[98] See above in text at n 8.

[99] HMRC, *Pocket Guide 2013: Facts and Figures about what we do* (14 March 2014) 61, available at: www.gov.uk/government/publications/pocket-guide-2012.

[100] Freedman and Vella, 'Revenue Guidance' (n 5) 195. This [unclear antecedent- what is 'this' referring to? The argument? The consequentialist approach? Perhaps consider re-wording for clarity] appears to have been accepted by Lord Scarman, in that 'good management' decisions could justify discrimination between taxpayers: *Fleet Street Casuals* (n 25) 651 (Lord Scarman).

[101] HMRC, *How HMRC works with large businesses* (9 April 2018), available at: www.gov.uk/guidance/hm-revenue-and-customs-large-business.

[102] HMRC, *Annual Report and Accounts 2018–19* (n 64) 38.

might find it more difficult to settle disputes given that HMRC may litigate cases it believes it is unlikely to win where there is a large amount of tax at stake.[103]

Meanwhile from at least 2014[104] to 2019,[105] HMRC's allocation of resources was driven by a single overarching objective, namely 'maximising revenues due'.[106] Singling out an objective in this way requires robust justification. Why should maximising revenues due take precedence over other potentially desirable ends, such as the importance of the rule of law,[107] the perceived fairness of administration[108] and the integrity of the tax system?[109] It may be the case that these other considerations can be accommodated within a framework of maximising revenues due without entailing a trade-off[110] but that would be to make assumptions about the impact of these objectives on the overall tax yield: assumptions which are open to empirical challenge or perhaps impossible to back up with evidence. The latter, which adopts an 'article of faith', is difficult to square with a commitment to rationality in administration. It would seem preferable, instead, to have accepted a pluralist approach and to have used 'maximising revenues due' as a tie-breaking rule where the objectives came into conflict.[111]

IV. How HMRC Can Act

Moral ethics can provide guidance as to how discretion ought to be exercised. The study of moral ethics further highlights the normative merits and limitations of different

[103] HMRC, *Resolving Tax Disputes* (n 27) para 18.

[104] See HMRC, *HMRC Business Plan 2014–16* (14 April 2016), available at: www.gov.uk/government/publications/hmrcs-business-plan-2014-to-2016. There was no mention of maximising revenues due in previous publications outlining HMRC objectives. For instance, HMRC, *Business Plan 2012–2015* (31 May 2012), available at: www.gov.uk/government/publications/business-plan-2012-15; HMRC, *HMRC Purpose, Vision and Way* (3 November 2008), available at: www.gov.uk/government/publications/hmrc-purpose-vision-and-way.

[105] There was a change from maximising revenue due to collecting revenue due in May 2019: HMRC, *HMRC Stakeholder Engagement Research 2018 Research Conducted by Populus among HMRC Stakeholders in 2018–2019* (July 2019) 4, fn 1.

[106] See for instance HMRC, *Annual Report and Accounts 2017–18 (For the year ended 31 March 2018)* (HC 1222, 2018) 8. Though it may not be apparent from reading the previous strategic objectives that any one of the objectives took priority over the others, HMRC officials confirmed this to be the case to the author.

[107] In the sense of equality before the law. See for instance R de la Feria, 'Tax Fraud and Selective Law Enforcement' (2020) 47 *Journal of Law and Society* (forthcoming).

[108] In this respect, HMRC has contemplated exercising its managerial discretion to relieve the taxpayers as a response to the possible public perception that it would be otherwise 'unduly harsh and disproportionate', see Letter from Jim Ferguson to the Exchequer Secretary, 'UK – Swiss Tax Cooperation Agreement: Repayments' (12 July 2013) 38 [letter shared with author by Karin Vrang].

[109] Elsewhere, HMRC has stressed the importance of integrity in the tax system in relation to the exercise of managerial discretion. See HMRC and Cabinet Office, *Memorandum of Understanding Between HMRC and Cabinet Office: For access to information from HMRC to assist honours committees in making decisions about awarding honours to individuals* (21 March 2017) para 2.3(iii).

[110] See for instance HMRC's 'risk framework' which HMRC uses in order to manage risks to the achievement of the strategic objectives: HMRC, *Annual Report and Accounts 2017–18* (n 106) 71–75. These 'risks' include 'External perception/loss of trust' and are said to potentially impact 'levels of confidence in the department', 'our reputation with the public' and ultimately 'revenues for the Exchequer'.

[111] For an example of justification based on maximising revenues due, which appears forced, see HMRC, *ADML1300 Incorrect Advice to Customers: When incorrect advice can be binding* (30 January 2018), available at: www.gov.uk/hmrc-internal-manuals/admin-law-manual/adml1300.

approaches to the allocation of resources. However, whilst moral ethics illuminates different choices, the selection of any one of which would be lawful, how HMRC *can* act is limited by the Treasury. Section 11 of CRCA 2005 requires HMRC to comply with Treasury directions of a general nature, and in practice, the Treasury exercises its power to set tax collection policy.[112] HMRC and the Treasury together have a 'policy partnership' arrangement whereby the Treasury leads on strategic tax policy and policy development. HMRC leads on policy maintenance and implementation.[113] HMRC's Single Departmental Plan is an example of this policy partnership arrangement in practice. This Plan is a joint venture between the Financial Secretary to the Treasury and HMRC's Permanent Secretaries and sets out HMRC's objectives and how it is intended they shall be achieved.[114] To this end, whilst neither the CRCA 2005 nor the dicta from the courts interpreting the provisions of CRCA 2005 dictate that HMRC must pursue a particular strategy, the direction from the Treasury that it should removes HMRC's control of the explicit priority-setting process. Further, the Single Departmental Plan also determines the choice of key performance indicators that test HMRC's success in meeting its objectives. Accordingly, the choice of principles and performance indicators is a matter for HMRC and the Treasury together rather than HMRC alone. Of course, this means that any criticisms should be directed at both HMRC *and* the Treasury and further that any proposed reforms can only be instituted by the bodies jointly rather than HMRC alone.

It becomes clear then that to describe HMRC as having a 'wide managerial discretion' is misleading.[115] The statement may be true as a matter of law; however, since the Treasury exercises its powers in respect of setting priorities for the allocation of resources, the discretion is circumscribed as a matter of practice. The study of moral ethics provides blueprints for checking that discretionary decisions are rationally connected to the ends pursued. To that end, the courts are comfortable with accepting that a consequentialist approach is a rational exercise of power but should equally be comfortable with accepting a different approach, such as one which accounts for hardship, provided there is a reasonable connection with the desired aims. Given that the Treasury is involved in the setting of express priorities, however, it is clear why some approaches, such as prioritising generating revenues, will always be favourable to other approaches, such as those that prioritise egalitarianism. These observations clearly lead to the conclusion that legal, moral and practical boundaries of discretion are interwoven. How HMRC's managerial discretion is exercised is a question which can only be answered by combining all three.

[112] It could be argued that this statutory provision need not be invoked in order to constrain decision-making decisions in respect of resource allocation. HMRC receives its funding from Treasury and Treasury is entitled to apply conditions to the use of that money. Whilst HMRC, in theory, may not be legally bound to follow these conditions (though it would be practically advised to do so), the conditions would be a relevant consideration for HMRC to take into account. It would not be unlawful therefore, even absent the statutory provision to that effect, for HMRC to follow these directions.

[113] HMRC, *Annual Report and Accounts 2018–19* (n 64) 72.

[114] HMRC, *HM Revenue and Customs Single Departmental Plan* (n 93).

[115] The author must thank Clair Quentin for highlighting this point during a meeting.

V. Conclusion

Henry Louis Mencken famously wrote that 'there is always a well-known solution to every human problem – neat, plausible, and wrong'.[116] Freedman too in her writings regularly argues against the thinking that complex problems are amenable to simple solutions – when it comes to the gig economy, the solution is not 'an incremental approach to a problem that requires structural reform';[117] 'an appropriate solution to the problem of taxing multinational corporations' will only be forthcoming when we 'ask fundamental questions about what we are taxing and why';[118] and answers to the issue of public confidence in the tax system are not found by lurching 'from one improvised response to another after each perceived scandal'.[119]

The questions raised by Freedman and Vella's observations on the logical conclusion of a cost–benefit approach to tax collection similarly do not yield themselves to simple answers. Instead, they bring up issues in respect of the legal, normative and practical boundaries of HMRC's managerial discretion, an investigation of which reveals that the boundaries are interwoven.

The fact that a legal discretion arises in HMRC's hands necessarily requires that HMRC should be entitled to choose the decision that it will make from a range of options. Once acting within its legal boundaries, the exercise of discretion will be lawful. Lord Diplock's influential judgment in *Fleet Street Casuals*, later affirmed by the UK's highest court in *Wilkinson* and *Gaines-Cooper*, masks this fact. However, other approaches, for instance one which places importance on alleviating individual hardship, will be accepted as lawful provided that there is a rational connection with the desired aims. The law however leaves open the question of how HMRC *ought* to act, though lessons can be drawn from the study of moral ethics. Different theories will have advantages, but also limitations. In explaining the breadth of HMRC's discretion, Lord Diplock adopted the language of a consequentialist approach, which has the advantage of providing operational certainty but is limited because it obscures differences across taxes and taxpayers. HMRC's current strategy is one by way of which no single objective is obviously prioritised above others. However, it gives little guidance as to how conflicts are resolved. In practice, however, HMRC's ability to determine the allocation of resources is restricted by its relationship with the Treasury. The explicit setting of priorities is a task undertaken by both of these bodies rather than HMRC alone. What discretion HMRC has, therefore, is far from 'wide' in this respect. What HMRC may do and what HMRC ought to do will be circumscribed accordingly by what HMRC in practice can do.

[116] HL Mencken, *Prejudices: Second Series* (New York, Alfred A Knopf, 1920) 158.
[117] Judith Freedman, 'Three myths about tax and the self-employed' *The Financial Times* (10 March 2017).
[118] Michael Devereux and Judith Freedman, 'The system must change' *The Guardian* (9 February 2009).
[119] Judith Freedman, 'We should create a tax system that reassures the public' *The Financial Times* (9 February 2016).

15

Trends in Tax Administration

MICHAEL WALPOLE

I. Introduction

It is remarkable what profound changes in tax administration are discernible in the early twenty-first-century experience of the relationship between tax advisers and the revenue authorities in many countries especially, for this chapter, in Australia and the United Kingdom (UK). In the UK, in particular, there has been increased public scrutiny of multinational corporations and how Her Majesty's Revenue and Customs (HMRC) has dealt with them. From this writer's perspective, HMRC has been subjected to wave after wave of critical outburst in the press and online. Groups such as Tax Justice Network have prosecuted a highly effective campaign to make both taxpayers and the custodians of the tax collection system more accountable. For HMRC and the Australian Taxation Office (ATO), a balance is always required. A laissez-faire tax system herds most taxpayers into compliance through a light touch and encourages voluntary compliance through perceptions of fairness and decency. In contrast, a more heavy-handed and forceful approach runs the risk of making an enemy of the tax adviser and taxpayer thus undermining the necessary faith and mutual commitment of those from whom and through whom the revenue is raised.

The result appears to be a tax system that leaves much less opportunity for tax minimisation and an attitude to the profession that is much less tolerant of any inclination to serve clients' interests above the interests of the public purse. Professor Judith Freedman has pointed out elsewhere that '[s]ystems dependent purely on coercion generally do not work in the long term'.[1] She has urged 'that sustainable tax systems must [also] rely on trust to a considerable degree'.[2] Whether there will be a continued trend to coercion or whether the pendulum will swing back in favour of taxpayer freedom to (within bounds) reduce their tax liability remains to be seen. This chapter will discuss selected changes in law and practice and will provide opportunities for reflection on where society is headed in terms of controlling tax minimisation and the power of the government. The critical question that is asked is whether more emphasis on compliance will impact adversely on morale.

[1] Judith Freedman, 'Restoring Trust' *Tax Adviser* (1 June 2016).
[2] ibid.

II. A Change of Rhetoric and Culture

Examples abound of increased pressure on government and HMRC to reduce the opportunities to avoid tax. Few could forget the highly personal attack on the then Second Permanent Secretary of HMRC under such headlines as 'How Vodafone made tax dodging respectable' in *The Guardian* apparently relying on a report in *Private Eye*.[3] The criticism was more widespread and spread to trusted tax advisers.[4] Large sections of the public were swayed by calls to boycott Vodafone itself (the main object of the earlier criticisms).[5] The boycott was highly effective in terms of publicity and inconvenience, and at one point in 2010, Vodafone closed its Oxford Street store for hours.[6] Other protests affected Top Shop[7] and Marks & Spencer.[8] The Tax Justice Network and the UK Uncut tax advocacy groups maintained pressure on the authorities and taxpayers (and continue to do so). The Public Accounts Committee of the UK Parliament, especially under the chairmanship of Dame Margaret Hodge, took a keen interest in the response of HMRC to tax avoidance, and in the role of advisers in tax minimisation on behalf of their clients.[9] The resultant report of the Public Accounts Committee entitled *Tax Avoidance: The Role of Large Accountancy Firms* concluded, amongst other things, that

> HM Revenue & Customs (HMRC) appears to be fighting a battle it cannot win in tackling tax avoidance. Companies can devote considerable resource[s] to ensure that they minimise their tax liability. There is a large market for advising companies on how to take advantage of international tax law, and on the tax implications of different global structures. The four firms employ nearly 9,000 people and earn £2 billion from their tax work in the UK and earn around $25 billion from this work globally. HMRC has far fewer resources. In the area of transfer pricing alone there are four times as many staff working for the four firms than for HMRC.[10]

Tax minimisation had become so unpalatable that on occasion the mere hint of it could cause extreme public reactions. A high-water mark of this was the reaction of the public to allegations in 2012 that the US multinational Starbucks had used tax minimisation techniques to pay no corporate tax in the UK for many years and in the response by

[3] Nick Cohen, 'How Vodafone Made Tax Dodging Respectable' *The Guardian* (14 November 2010) www.theguardian.com/commentisfree/2010/nov/14/vodafone-tax-evasion-revenue-customs.

[4] Richard Brooks, 'Tax, Lies, and Videotape' *Private Eye*, Special Report, Issue 1494 (20 September 2013), available at: www.private-eye.co.uk/special-reports/tax-lies-and-videotape.

[5] See 'Boycott Vodafone Until they Repay their 6bn Tax Bill' (*Facebook*, 23 October 2010, 6:24am AEST), available at: www.facebook.com/Boycott-Vodafone-until-they-repay-their-6bn-tax-bill-153153704726686/.

[6] Ed Monk, 'Vodafone Closes Oxford St Store at £6bn Tax Protest' (*This is Money*, 28 October 2010), available at: www.thisismoney.co.uk/money/news/article-1706973/Vodafone-closes-Oxford-St-store-at-6bn-tax-protest.html.

[7] Tracy McVeigh, 'UK Uncut Targets Topshop and Vodafone over Tax Arrangements' *The Guardian* (4 December 2010), available at: www.theguardian.com/politics/2010/dec/04/uk-uncut-protest-topshop-vodafone.

[8] Alastair Jamieson and Ben Leach, 'Marks and Spencer Targeted as Tax Protests Widen' *The Telegraph* (19 December 2010), available at: www.telegraph.co.uk/finance/newsbysector/retailandconsumer/8212040/Marks-and-Spencer-targeted-as-tax-protests-widen.html.

[9] See Tom Bergin, 'MPs Press Accountants on Tax Avoidance' *Reuters* (1 February 2013), available at: uk.reuters.com/article/uk-britian-tax-accountants/mps-press-accountants-on-tax-avoidance-idUKBRE90U0SG20130131.

[10] Public Accounts Committee, *Tax Avoidance: The Role of Large Accountancy Firms* (HC 2012–13, 44) 3.

Starbucks. It was alleged that in 15 years of operating in the UK, Starbucks had paid corporate income tax in only one of them. Starbucks UK was accused of '[u]sing a combination of legal tax avoidance practices (eg, transfer prices, royalty payments, interest expense)' such that it 'had effectively shifted taxable income to other Starbucks subsidiaries where it would be taxed at lower rates'.[11]

In 2012 there was a media furore over this, which became a public relations problem. At risk of facing a boycott, the managing director of Starbucks UK stated, in an open letter on the company website, and in a speech, that Starbucks would voluntarily abandon certain UK tax deductions associated with transfer pricing and thus pay an extra £20 million in corporate tax in 2013 and 2014 'above what is required by law'.[12]

The hounding of a corporation into paying tax in excess of its legal obligations (there was never any suggestion that Starbucks had acted illegally) is an unfortunate and undesirable outcome in a media war over tax avoidance by multinational companies. Better that legal obligations be properly incurred and collected.

It is little wonder that amid such concerted media interest in tax advice and the management of compliance by HMRC, attitudes to the payment of tax changed. This attitude change provided fertile ground for governments and revenue bodies to change laws to provide more tools with which to control aggressive tax behaviour by taxpayers, and by their advisers.

III. Government and HMRC Responses

Over the years, as the tax avoidance debate and numerous scandals raged on in the public eye, the UK authorities have responded in various ways. One of the first of these was the general anti-abuse rule (GAAR) which took effect from 17 July 2013 (Finance Act 2013) and which was amended and strengthened in the Finance Act 2016. The UK had been unusual amongst major economies for the absence of a general anti-avoidance law. Australia (admittedly not a major economy) has had its Part IVA of the Income Tax Assessment Act 1936 since May 1981 and prior to that had section 260 of that Act. The latter had been hobbled by the development of the jurisprudence around what was a simple and clear principle-based piece of drafting. The legislative purpose, as the Explanatory Memorandum to the new Part IVA explained, was partly to remove the constraint of the predication test in the decision on section 260 in *Newton v Commissioner of Taxation (Cth)*.[13] In that case, the Privy Council found that section 260 would only apply if an observer would predicate, based on the taxpayer's actions, that the taxpayer took those actions for the purpose of avoiding tax. Part IVA establishes an entirely objective test of purpose, using distinct objective criteria to be weighed in order to determine whether it can be concluded by reference to eight factors that the scheme in question was entered into for the purposes of avoiding tax.

[11] K Campbell and D Helleloid, 'Starbucks: Social Responsibility and Tax Avoidance' (2016) 37 *Journal of Accounting Education* 38, 38.

[12] 'Starbucks Agrees to Pay More Corporation Tax' *BBC* (6 December 2012), available at: www.bbc.co.uk/news/business-20624857.

[13] *Newton v Commissioner of Taxation (Cth)* (1958) 98 CLR 1.

Although Part IVA was in place more than 10 years before a suitable case concerning the section reached the High Court, and although the Commissioner of Taxation lost that first case (*FCT v Peabody*),[14] Part IVA, despite being a measure of last resort, was and still is a highly effective bulwark against tax avoidance in Australia. Its precision and breadth, and the careful exclusion of considerations of the actual purpose of the taxpayer are such that it is a powerful weapon in the hands of the Commissioner of Taxation. From this writer's perspective, it is a more specific and harder-hitting measure than the UK GAAR, which is an anti-abuse rule (as Professor Freedman has pointed out)[15] – not an anti-avoidance rule, and which relies on deterrence from the most abusive and contrived schemes, 'leaving the clear centre ground of tax planning undisturbed'.[16] The test of whether a tax arrangement is 'abusive' is that it cannot be reasonably regarded as a reasonable course of action – the so-called 'double reasonableness test'. The legislation sets up for particular attention when concluding such things, factors such as consistency with the policy behind the legislation, the existence or otherwise of contrived or abnormal steps, and intention to exploit loopholes in the law. Tax arrangements are not 'abusive' where they are consistent with 'general practice' which HMRC has indicated that it accepts. There may also be comfort for taxpayers in the fact that an opinion on the reasonableness of a taxpayer's actions is made by an independent Advisory Panel rather than by HMRC officers solely.

An interesting, but essentially different, parallel may be drawn with the Australian use of an ATO-convened extra-statutory 'Part IVA Panel' which advises the Commissioner on the applicability or otherwise of Part IVA to a particular 'scheme' (a close equivalent to the UK's 'tax arrangement'). This panel is a step self-imposed by the Commissioner not based in law, but a Part IVA determination is not made without this review by the panel. As in the UK (where the GAAR Panel does not give an opinion on whether the GAAR should apply) the panel does not itself determine whether Part IVA applies, it merely advises the Commissioner.[17] There are other similarities and parallels in relation to these anti-avoidance measures. For instance, both have been (fairly) recently amended to strengthen the hand of the revenue authorities in the respective jurisdictions.

In 2013 Part IVA was amended[18] to reorganise and tighten elements of the 'tax benefit' test. The most significant change was the removal of an argument derived from the case law that a tax benefit cannot have been obtained in breach of Part IVA if the alternative to the action taken by the taxpayer would have been to do nothing. A new section 177CB requires consideration of whether a tax benefit has been obtained under the scheme to assume that only the events or circumstances that happened or existed

[14] *FCT v Peabody* [1994] HCA 43.

[15] J Freedman, 'United Kingdom' in M Lang et al (eds), *GAARs – A Key Element of Tax Systems in the Post-BEPS Tax World* (Amsterdam, IBFD, 2016).

[16] PwC, 'Recent Global Developments in General Anti-Avoidance Rules' (*Tax Insights from Tax Controversy and Dispute Resolution*, 14 October 2016), available at: www.pwc.com/gx/en/tax/newsletters/tax-controversy-dispute-resolution/assets/pwc-TCDR%20Insights-GAAR-recent-developments.pdf 16.

[17] For a full explanation, see Australian Taxation Office, 'Part IVA: The General Anti-Avoidance Rule for Income Tax: Basic Principles about how and when it Applies' (Guide to the Part IVA of the Income Tax Assessment Act 1936, Australian Taxation Office December 2005). See also 'Public Statement Law Administration (PSLA) 2005/24' (Guide to the Application of General Anti-Avoidance Rules, available at: www.ato.gov.au/law/view/document?DocID=PSR/PS200524/NAT/ATO/00001&PiT=99991231235958).

[18] Tax Laws Amendment (Countering Tax Avoidance and Multinational Profit Shifting) Bill 2013 (Cth).

took place and to assume that any alternative action that might have been taken was reasonable. Thus if, for example, the offensive tax scheme took place in the context of a company reorganisation it must be assumed (to determine whether there has been a tax benefit) that the alternative action of the taxpayer would have been to achieve a company reconstruction. It cannot be argued that the taxpayer's only action could have been to either do what it did or do nothing. Some find this change disturbing as it stacks the cards heavily in favour of the Commissioner of Taxation.

A further change to Part IVA in 2016 has been the inclusion within it of the Australian Multinational Anti-Avoidance Law (MAAL). It is quite similar to the UK's Diverted Profits Tax (DPT) although Australia now also has its own DPT.[19]

The MAAL brings Part IVA into effect when a foreign entity, part of a global group having annual income worldwide in excess of $A 1 billion makes a supply to an Australian group member customer for gain, and activities are undertaken in Australia 'directly in connection' with that supply either by an Australian resident or the local branch of a foreign entity. It is a condition that the local entity or local branch is either an 'associate' or 'commercially dependent' on the foreign entity. A further condition is that some or all of the income or gain the foreign supplier earns from supplies to Australian customers is not attributable to an Australian Permanent Establishment (PE) of the foreign supplier, and the taxpayer obtains an Australian tax benefit and the person who executed the scheme (based on several factors to be taken into account) did so to enable this. The factors boil down to five (complex) key tests which tackle schemes designed to obtain tax benefits through the avoidance of the establishment of a PE and transfer pricing activities designed to attribute an insufficient proportion of global profits to an Australian PE.

Although the MAAL is housed in Part IVA, it applies to relevant schemes more straightforwardly in that it is easier to attribute the schemer's purpose. Whereas Part IVA generally requires the tax benefit to be the 'sole or dominant purpose' of the scheme, the standard in the MAAL is lower in that securing the tax benefit must have been only 'one of the principal purposes' of entering into the scheme.

The consequences of the MAAL applying would be that a foreign entity that has no Australian PE would be deemed to have one. The deemed PE would be regarded as having earned the profit that the Australian entity doing the activities would have earned as well as some of the profit earned outside Australia, thus imposing a greater liability to tax on the company in Australia.

The MAAL legislation[20] has also made a change to the penalty provisions in Part IVA. For a taxpayer that is part of a global group with annual worldwide income exceeding AUD 1 billion the penalty for having undertaken a Part IVA scheme (not only a MAAL scheme) is not 50 per cent of the tax as is the case for other taxpayers, but twice that amount, whether or not the taxpayer is an Australian resident.

Although the Australian MAAL was seen as a jump ahead of agreed OECD/G20 Base Erosion and Profit Shifting (BEPS) initiatives, Australia was behind the UK in some of the steps taken in controlling multinational avoidance. The Finance Act 2015

[19] The DPT was introduced via the Diverted Profits Bill 2017 which received Royal Assent on 4 April 2017.

[20] Tax Laws Amendment (Combating Multinational Tax Avoidance) Act 2015.

had already introduced a DPT effective from 1 April 2015 imposing a rate of 25 per cent tax on profits that are artificially diverted from the UK. Reserved for large corporations, the UK DPT is a discrete tax which applies to diverted profits. It comes into play where:

- there are arrangements between connected parties within a group that has a UK subsidiary or PE which arrangements 'lack economic substance' and which exploit tax mismatches; or
- a non-resident company carries on activity in the UK connected with supplies of goods services or property, designed to ensure that the non-resident does not create a PE in the UK, done for the main purpose of avoiding UK tax in such a way as to 'avoid a UK taxable presence' or to secure a tax mismatch to reduce the total derived from UK activities.

The application of the DPT in the UK seems confined to structures contrived to achieve the 'diverted profit' tax benefit. There will not be an avoidance of a UK taxable presence if the UK activity was being undertaken by someone acting as an independent agent or the activity was for alternative finance arrangements. The parallels between the Australian MAAL and the UK DPT will be obvious.

Australia later introduced a DPT of its own by way of yet another inclusion in Part IVA. The DPT applies[21] to large taxpayers (the same ones as the MAAL companies with a global annual income of over $1 billion) defined as a 'significant global entity', which is:

- a 'global parent entity' whose 'annual global income' is AUD 1 billion or more.
- a member of a group of entities consolidated (for accounting purposes) where the global parent entity has an annual global income of AUD 1 billion or more.[22]

The DPT imposes a tax rate of 40 per cent on amounts derived through such schemes from 1 July 2017. It is an, as yet, untested weapon available to the Commissioner. A taxpayer is liable to the DPT from a scheme in relation to a 'DPT tax benefit' – on the 'DPT base amount' applicable to that 'DPT tax benefit'. The taxpayer can be liable if the provision applies to a scheme concerning more than one 'DPT tax benefit' (ie, on the sum of the 'DPT base amounts' for those DPT tax benefits). There is no discretion in the imposition of the DPT and DPT liability may be assessed up to seven years from the date of assessment to income tax for a relevant year.

The essence of the provision is what is the 'DPT base amount' for a 'DPT tax benefit'?[23] The provision lists five 'tax benefit' requirements and a set of eight exclusions. If these requirements are satisfied the tax benefit in question is a 'DPT tax benefit'.

The requirements are:

- DPT tax benefit has or would be obtained in connection with the scheme; and
- the scheme has been entered into for the principal purpose of deriving the relevant tax benefit;[24] and

[21] Income Tax Assessment Act 1936 (Cth), s 177P.

[22] 'Significant Global Entities' (Australian Taxation Office, 19 February 2018), available at: www.ato.gov.au/Business/Public-business-and-international/Significant-global-entities/. The term is defined in Income Tax Assessment Act 1997 (Cth), s 960-U.

[23] ibid s 177J.

[24] ibid s 177J(2).

- the taxpayer is a 'significant global entity' (discussed above); and
- the taxpayer has a 'foreign entity associate'; and
- the foreign entity is the person or one of the persons who carried out the scheme or part of it or is otherwise connected with the scheme/part.

The principal purpose test, as for the MAAL, departs from the usual Part IVA 'sole or dominant purpose' test and includes extra-jurisdictional taxes because it considers whether the person or one of them, who entered into or carried out the scheme did so for a principal purpose (or for more than one principal purpose that includes a purpose) of:

i. enabling the relevant taxpayer to obtain a tax benefit, or both to obtain a tax benefit and to reduce one or more of the relevant taxpayer's liabilities to tax under a foreign law, in connection with the scheme; or
ii. enabling the relevant taxpayer and another taxpayer (or other taxpayers) each to obtain a tax benefit, or both to obtain a tax benefit and to reduce one or more of their liabilities to tax under a foreign law, in connection with the scheme.

Furthermore, the test requires one to have regard, inter alia, to 'the result, in relation to the operation of any foreign law relating to taxation, that (but for this Part) would be achieved by the scheme'. Thus, the benefits in question recognise benefits obtained outside Australia in the form of a reduction of a taxpayer's foreign tax liabilities, so the extra-jurisdictional ambit of the DPT is considerable. The writer believes this might lead to a constitutional challenge one day.

The principal purpose test in the DPT is objective, as it is for the general anti-avoidance provisions in Part IVA. A purpose that offends these provisions of the Act will be found where one may objectively conclude that the 'principal purpose' of at least one person who entered into or carried out the scheme was to obtain the relevant DPT tax benefit. This conclusion must be based on a consideration of the eight matters listed in Part IVA plus the three matters that are additional for the DPT, viz:

- the extent to which there are quantifiable non-tax financial benefits that are, have or will result (or may be expected to result) from the scheme;
- the result in relation to the operation of any foreign tax laws, that would be achieved in relation to the scheme; and
- the amount of the tax benefit in question.

The DPT attacks the shifting of profits from Australia to other jurisdictions through related-party transactions. It focuses on tax planning arrangements or excessive payments that lack economic substance. There are exclusions from the DPT. Five categories of taxpayers are excluded from the operation of the DPT.[25] The categories excluded are managed investment trusts, widely held foreign collective investments, sovereign funds of foreign governments, complying superannuation entities and foreign pension funds. It would seem that these are the types of entities unlikely to be engaged in related-party transactions.

[25] ibid s 177J(1)(f).

Also excluded from the DPT are taxpayers in circumstances where it is reasonable to conclude that any of three conditions are met.[26] These cover off small entities via a $25 million income test;[27] a 'sufficient foreign tax test'[28] (where the increase in the foreign tax liabilities of foreign entities resulting from the scheme is 80 per cent or more of the reduction in the Australian tax liability); or where the profit made as a result of the scheme, by the relevant taxpayer and its associates, reasonably reflects the economic substance of the entity's activities in connection with the scheme.[29]

Another interesting (but threatening for taxpayers) feature of the DPT is a departure from normal due process in that it is not limited by the standard rules associated with the review of assessments. The time in which review may be sought is shorter under the DPT and the evidence that may be used for purposes of the review is restricted. A DPT notice of assessment may be subject to review only within 12 months of the date of the DPT notice. In the event of a challenge using the usual route to seek review of an assessment by the Administrative Appeals Tribunal or/and the Federal Court,[30] the taxpayer may rely on information or documents within its control or custody *only* if the Commissioner also had those documents in his control or custody during that period.

IV. Other Controls on Avoidance

Also aimed at discouraging avoidance and evasion have been the UK's 'enablers' provisions. These are not a long way from the Australian 'promoter penalties' rules.[31] It imposes a penalty on a person who is an 'enabler' of use of a tax arrangement that is later defeated because it is 'abusive'. This provision highlights the distinction between the Australian and UK GAAR in that the former applies to 'mere' avoidance whereas the UK GAAR does require that the actions be an abuse of the law which imports a level of reprehensibility that is not obvious in avoidance. On the other hand, an 'enabler' finding arises sometime after the actions are taken.

The term 'enabler' might, at first glance, imply that the person involved in the abusive tax scheme is the governing mind behind the scheme. The definition of 'enabler'[32] seems to attach liability to some of the more passive roles in a particular tax scheme.

The Part explains that:

> 7(1) A person is a person who 'enabled' the arrangements mentioned in paragraph 1 if that person is –
>
> (a) a designer of the arrangements (see paragraph 8),
> (b) a manager of the arrangements (see paragraph 9),
> (c) a person who marketed the arrangements to … [the taxpayer] (see paragraph 10),
> (d) an enabling participant in the arrangements (see paragraph 11), or
> (e) a financial enabler in relation to the arrangements (see paragraph 12).
>
> (2) This paragraph is subject to paragraph 13 (excluded persons).

[26] ibid s 177J(1)(g).
[27] ibid s 177K.
[28] ibid s 177L.
[29] ibid s 177M.
[30] A challenge under pt IVC of the Income Tax Assessment Act 1936 (Cth).
[31] Finance Act (No 2) 2017.
[32] ibid pt 4, sch 16.

It would appear from this that even remote participation in the scheme may expose persons who satisfy these definitions to the risk of penalties. It is noticeable that there is protection based on lack of *mens rea* only for an aspect of the actions of designers of arrangements who are subject to the 'knowledge condition'.[33]

This 'knowledge condition' is met if advice has been given that makes a person a designer under the statute and

> when the advice was provided, the person providing it knew or could reasonably be expected to know –
>
> that the advice would be used in the design of abusive tax arrangements or of a proposal for such arrangements, or
>
> that it was likely that the advice would be so used.[34]

There is a further protection for designers in the further requirements that the advice in question is 'relevant advice' being

> (a) advice or any part of it [that] suggests arrangements or an alteration of proposed arrangements, and (b) it is reasonable to assume that the suggestion was made with a view to arrangements being designed in such a way that a tax advantage (or a greater tax advantage) might be expected to arise from them.

The conditions for the application of this shelter seem to be cumulative. There seems to be no similar protection for managers, marketers, participants or financial enablers. It will be interesting to see what a court will make of this.

Penalties for breach of the enabler rules are the amount of consideration received for the thing(s) that they did to enable the offensive arrangements. This provision effectively removes any gain available to tax advisers for the promotion of abusive tax schemes. The risk they are under is however shared by a broader range of persons who might be party to the marketing or operation of the abusive tax scheme.

In comparison, the Australia 'promoter penalties rules' seem a close parallel. A scandal involving mass-marketed ineffective tax avoidance 'investment' schemes in the 1990s in Australia[35] resulted, inter alia, in the introduction of penalties for the promotion of such schemes.[36] The changes have deterred the promotion of tax exploitation schemes by way of a civil penalty regime.

The legislative provisions deter:

- The promotion of tax avoidance and evasion schemes (referred to in the legislation as 'tax exploitation schemes').
- The implementation of schemes that have been promoted on the basis of conformity with a product ruling, in a way that is materially different to that described in the product ruling.

The Commissioner is able, under the rules, to request that the Federal Court imposes a civil penalty on a scheme promoter or implementer. The maximum penalty the Federal

[33] ibid para 8.
[34] ibid pt 4, sch 16, para 8(4).
[35] A representative example is described in the 'Budplan scheme' in *Howland-Rose v Commissioner of Taxation* [2002] FCA 246. The deduction associated with a purported investment in an agricultural scheme was disallowed.
[36] Div 290 was introduced into the Tax Administration Act 1953 (Cth) with effect from April 2006.

Court can impose is the greater of 5,000 penalty units (currently equal to $1,050,00) for an individual or 25,000 penalty units (currently equal to $5.25 million) for a body corporate *and* twice the consideration received or receivable, directly or indirectly, by the entity or its associates in respect of the scheme).

The Commissioner is also able to seek an injunction to stop the promotion of a scheme or implementation of a scheme not in conformity to its product ruling and may enter into voluntary undertakings with promoters or implementers about how schemes are being promoted or implemented.

The *mens rea* element is addressed in the Australian rules by means of a requirement that the Federal Court not apply for the imposition of a penalty

> if the entity satisfies the Court that the entity did not know, and could not reasonably be expected to have known, that the entity's conduct would produce … [a] result [in the form of the promotion of the scheme or non-conforming implementation of a product ruling].[37]

The meaning of 'promoter' of a 'tax exploitation scheme' seems narrower under the Australian rules than it is under the UK enablers law. Defined in section 290-60, an entity is a 'promoter' of a 'tax exploitation scheme' if

> (a) the entity markets the scheme or otherwise encourages the growth of the scheme or interest in it; and
>
> (b) the entity or an *associate of the entity receives (directly or indirectly) consideration in respect of that marketing or encouragement; and
>
> (c) having regard to all relevant matters, it is reasonable to conclude that the entity has had a substantial role in respect of that marketing or encouragement.
>
> (2) However, an entity is not a ***promoter*** of a * tax exploitation scheme merely because the entity provides advice about the * scheme.
>
> (3) An employee is not to be taken to have had a substantial role in respect of that marketing or encouragement merely because the employee distributes information or material prepared by another entity.

The application seems to be confined to marketing or encouragement of the scheme for remuneration and not as a mere employee. There seems to this writer to be less comfort in the UK rules.

A 'tax exploitation scheme' is different to the UK's idea of an arrangement that is abusive. The threshold is lower as there is no requirement that it be 'abusive' there need only be a tax benefit. The conditions present that may lead to a scheme (a term already broadly defined in Part IVA) being a 'tax exploitation scheme' are set out in s290-65:

> '290-65 Meaning of tax exploitation scheme[38]
>
> (1) A *scheme is a tax exploitation scheme if, at the time of the conduct mentioned in subsection 290-50(1):
>
> (a) one of these conditions is satisfied:
>
> (i) if the scheme has been implemented – it is reasonable to conclude that an entity that (alone or with others) entered into or carried out the scheme did

[37] Tax Administration Act 1953 (Cth) sch 1, s 290-55.

[38] Tax Administration Act 1953 (Cth) sch 1, s 290-65. Note that, in Australian taxation Acts, the presence of * next to a word or term indicates that it is defined.

so with the sole or dominant purpose of that entity or another entity getting a * scheme benefit from the scheme;

(ii) if the scheme has not been implemented – it is reasonable to conclude that, if an entity (alone or with others) had entered into or carried out the scheme, it would have done so with the sole or dominant purpose of that entity or another entity getting a scheme benefit from the scheme; and

(b) one of these conditions is satisfied:

(i) if the scheme has been implemented – it is not *reasonably arguable that the scheme benefit is available at law;

(ii) if the scheme has not been implemented – it is not *reasonably arguable that the scheme benefit would be available at law if the scheme were implemented'.

A few features stand out from a reading of this definition. One is that unlike the UK rules which apply after a finding that the arrangement was abusive and (presumably) had been carried out, the Australian rules seem to apply to an attempted tax exploitation scheme because of the conditions related to what might have occurred if the scheme had been implemented. Another feature is that it seems to be a defence that the scheme benefit is derived from a 'reasonably arguable' position. The Tax Administration Act 1953 defines 'reasonably arguable' as a position in which 'it would be concluded in the circumstances, having regard to relevant authorities, that what is argued for is about as likely to be correct as incorrect, or is more likely to be correct than incorrect'.[39] Although this means that the assumption of a position that is probably incorrect will attract the consequences of the Act, this writer suggests that this may include schemes which would not be readily seen as abusive.

In deciding what penalty is appropriate, the Federal Court can have regard to all matters it considers relevant, including the amount of loss or damage incurred by scheme participants and the role of honest mistake, the cooperation of the promoter etc.[40]

The Explanatory Memorandum accompanying the Bill noted that the civil penalty regime is not intended to inhibit the provision of independent and objective tax advice, including advice regarding tax planning. Some commentators have, however, expressed serious reservations about the potential impact on tax advisers providing tax planning advice, as well as expressing concerns about many other aspects of the promoter penalty provisions.[41] That the promoter penalties rules have been effective cannot be doubted. Mass marketed schemes have, since their introduction, disappeared from view. One assumes that the schemes that are being used are bespoke and possibly unique to each client.

Another weapon in the arsenal of HMRC in the UK is the regime known as POTAS (Promoters of Tax Avoidance Schemes). When read together with all that has been described above, some might regard the cumulative effect as overkill.[42]

[39] ibid s 284-15.

[40] ibid s 290-50(5).

[41] See, eg, J King, 'New Measures Deterring the Promotion of Tax Exploitation Schemes' (2006) 35 *Australian Tax Review* 163.

[42] POTAS is found in pt 5 of the Finance Act 2014.

POTAS steps are more targeted than other measures in the UK in that they are intended to deter an apparently 'small and persistent minority of promoters of avoidance schemes who exhibit certain behaviours'.[43] These rules look to have been made somewhat redundant by the enabler provisions, but there will be circumstances in which actions under POTAS will be more appropriate. The POTAS rules require promoters that have been identified for monitoring purposes to disclose to HMRC details concerning their products and their clients and disclose to clients that they have been identified for monitoring.

POTAS identifies advisers that are high risk by means of a series of threshold conditions. If these conditions are met, HMRC may issue conduct notices on such advisers and impose conditions upon them. In the event of a breach of the conditions, HMRC may apply to the First-Tier Tribunal for the issue of a monitoring notice. If one is issued, the adviser in question is subjected to monitoring and publicity of their status. The threshold conditions that must be met before conduct notices are issued are summarised as follows:

1. HMRC publishing information about the promoter as a deliberate tax defaulter;
2. The relevant person has been named in a report under the Code of Practice on Taxation for Banks because of promoting arrangements which they cannot reasonably have believed achieved a tax result which was intended by Parliament;
3. The promoter is given a conduct notice as a dishonest agent;
4. The promoter fails to meet DOTAS obligations (reasonable excuse is ignored for these purposes);
5. The promoter is charged with a relevant criminal offence (even if not yet found guilty);
6. Arrangements that the adviser has promoted are regarded as unreasonable by a majority of the GAAR advisory panel;
7. A professional body of which the promoter is a member takes disciplinary action against him;
8. A regulatory authority imposes certain sanctions on the promoter;
9. The promoter fails to comply with an information notice;
10. The promoter imposes certain restrictive contractual terms on clients; and
11. The promoter continues to promote arrangements despite being given a stop notice in respect of those arrangements.[44]

The imposition of a conduct notice is apparently not subject to appeal (presumably it may be subject to review), but the imposition of a monitoring notice by the Tribunal is appealable and has no effect until the appeal remedies have been exhausted. The POTAS regime works in concert with the longer established Disclosure of Tax Avoidance Schemes (DOTAS) regime. The latter is not entirely dissimilar to the Australian rules regarding 'reportable tax positions' which require large businesses to disclose their tax positions that are most material and most contestable.

These rules are described and discussed below.

[43] Andy Wood, 'POTAS: Promoters of Tax Avoidance Schemes' (*ETC Tax*, 25 May 2018), available at: www.etctax.co.uk/potas-promoters-of-tax-avoidance-schemes/.

[44] 'PCRT Help Sheet: DOTAS, Follower Notices, Accelerated Payment of Tax and POTAS' (Chartered Institute of Taxation), available at: www.tax.org.uk/professional-standards/professional-standards-%E2%80%93-full-listing/professional-conduct-relation-0#POTAS.

V. Disclosure of Tax Positions

Both Australia and the UK have long had a practice of requiring taxpayers to alert the Revenue to contentious tax positions that they are adopting. In the UK, the DOTAS regime has been important for HMRC to garner intelligence on tax avoidance practices. It was introduced in 2004 and has been amended from time to time since. DOTAS is broad. It covers schemes involving income tax; capital gains tax; corporation tax; National Insurance contributions; stamp duty land tax; some aspects of inheritance tax; VAT (under its own subset of rules); and now even the apprenticeship levy.

DOTAS requires the declaration by a promoter of a tax scheme, to HMRC, of the details of a scheme that will (or might be expected to) enable a person to obtain a tax advantage that is the, or a main benefit of the arrangement entered into provided the tax arrangement in question bears the hallmarks that have been set down in regulation.

The hallmarks will differ from tax to tax and the arrangements that apply to them. This chapter will not deal in detail with the legislation and Guidance[45] but an example of 'hallmarks' of a tax scheme can be found in those involving the creation of losses by wealthy individuals.[46] The Guidance tells us that the hallmark applies where there is a promoter of such arrangements and when:

1. 'Test 1 … the promoter expects that there will be more than one individual client for each set of arrangements having the same, or substantially the same, form';
2. It would be reasonable to expect an informed observer to conclude that the provision of losses is one of the main (thus not insignificant nor insubstantial) benefits expected to accrue to one or more of the individuals participating;
3. It would be reasonable to expect an informed observer to conclude that it '[w]ould … be unlikely the arrangements, or any element of the arrangements, would have been entered into were it not for the provision of the losses'.[47]

Where the hallmarks applicable to a DOTAS arrangement are met the promoter, or in some cases, the user of an arrangement is required (within five days of it being made available to a user) to report it to HMRC which will issue a DOTAS number which the user must supply with its tax return. HMRC will monitor the scheme and may terminate it through legislation. Failure to disclose the arrangements leaves the promoter open to penalties and users open to penalties where they fail to supply their DOTAS number when appropriate.

There are similarities between DOTAs and the Australian promoter penalties rules in that they apply to similar types of tax arrangements – being ones that might be profitably marketed and replicated. However, DOTAS commenced as a way of identifying schemes, whereas the promoter penalties in Australia are intended to take the incentive out of marketing them to clients and little else.

The ATO obtains intelligence concerning schemes from the Reportable Tax Position (RTP) scheme. Whereas DOTAS is founded in specific anti-avoidance legislation and has extensive application, the RTP expectation is imposed only on large businesses.

[45] 'Guidance: Disclosure of Tax Avoidance Schemes (DOTAS)' (HM Revenue and Customs (HMRC), 20 April 2018), available at: assets.publishing.service.gov.uk/government/uploads/system/uploads/attachment_data/file/701190/DOTAS-March.pdf.

[46] ibid 55–57.

[47] The Guidance suggests there is a Test 4, but the Guidance does not deal with it.

Further, the RTP takes the form of a schedule to the company income tax return submitted as part of the Australian self-assessment process. It is not so much based in statute as imposed by a directive by the Commissioner under the 'general power of administration'.[48] Not every company must complete an RTP schedule, only large companies.[49] The ATO directs such taxpayers to do so. The power of the RTP is that in the event that a taxpayer has not declared an RTP, there are consequences in the form of amplified penalties should they be discovered by the ATO to have engaged in tax avoidance that is not declared through an RTP or that has been declared in a manner that is false or misleading. Penalties in cases of RTP lodgement failure are one hundred times higher for 'significant global entities' (above) than other companies, highlighting the concern Australia shares with the UK about tax avoidance by large corporations.

The taxpayer required to lodge an RTP schedule is thus placed in the position that it must disclose its questionable tax arrangements to the ATO lest the consequences of their discovery lead to hefty penalties. Three categories of arrangement must be disclosed.

'Category A' disclosures concern 'uncertainty in your income tax return'. This category arises where the tax position argued for by the taxpayer is 'about as likely to be correct as incorrect, or is less likely to be correct than incorrect'. The advice is that this excludes a 'reasonably arguable position' (see above) in which 'what is argued for is more likely to be correct than incorrect'.[50] A position may be reasonably arguable, but if it is about as likely to be correct as incorrect, it is Category A.

'Category B' disclosures involve a position in which the uncertainty about taxes payable is recognised in the financial statements of yourself or of related party or parties. The ATO explains:

> Uncertainty about taxes payable or recoverable exists where there is a difference between your position and the measurement and/or recognition of the taxes payable or recoverable in respect of that position as adopted in your or a related party's financial statements. A Category B RTP is material if this difference is equal to or exceeds your materiality amount.[51]

Materiality amounts are identified as follows:

Your materiality amount is 5% of your Australian current tax expense, except where:

- 5% of your Australian current tax expense exceeds A$30 million – the materiality amount is then A$30 million.
- 5% of your Australian current tax expense is less than A$3 million – the materiality amount is then A$3 million.
- You have no Australian current tax expense – the materiality amount is then A$3 million.[52]

[48] Income Tax Assessment Act 1936 (Cth), s 8.

[49] Companies in public or international economic groups with a turnover greater than $250 million.

[50] 'What is a Reportable Tax Position?' (Australian Taxation Office, 11 February 2019), available at: www.ato.gov.au/Forms/Guide-to-reportable-tax-positions 2018/?page=3#What_is_a_reportable_tax_position.

[51] ibid.

[52] 'Guide to Reportable Tax Positions 2017 Definitions' (Australian Taxation Office, 11 February 2019), available at: www.ato.gov.au/Forms/Guide-to-Reportable-Tax-Positions-2017/?page=10.

A 'Category C' disclosure is required where the answer to a set of Category C questions is affirmative. These questions are set out in the Guidelines, and at present, there are 23 of them. They include such questions as:

> Did you fund a special dividend or a share buy-back through an equity raising event at a similar time, where the arrangement is a type of arrangement or variation of an arrangement described in Taxpayer Alert TA 2015/2?[53] [in Question 2; and]
>
> At any stage during your income year, did you have a cross border financing arrangement with a related party (including via back to back arrangements through third parties) where you claimed a tax deduction for interest or an amount in the nature of interest and interest withholding tax was not remitted because a withholding tax liability is not expected to arise within the next 18 months.[54] [In Question 17]

These questions are updated through the year, and there must be a compliance cost in remaining current.

The RTP requirement is unpopular with taxpayers and advisers but is presumably very effective.

VI. Controls on Evasion

Aside from avoidance, the UK has recently seen the introduction of rules to discourage involvement in evasion of tax, ie, the new corporate offence of failure to prevent the criminal facilitation of tax evasion. The offence came into force in September 2017.

Evasion is not a focus of this chapter partly for reasons of space and partly because evasion in the sense of fraudulent behaviour cannot be defended and actions intended to defeat it possibly merit less scrutiny than actions set to control behaviour that is legal although undesirable.

VII. Controls on the Revenue

In 2016 in Australia a study was undertaken by the office of the Inspector-General of Taxation of practices associated with taxpayer charters and 'taxpayer rights'.[55] That review concluded, inter alia, that:

> [T]he IGT's research of the legislative regimes of comparable jurisdictions indicated that none of these jurisdictions had a comprehensive legislated charter or taxpayer bill of rights and Australia compared favourably in terms of legislative protections. Moreover, the IGT noted that whilst legislated rights would provide the highest degree of protection, it is unlikely to be

[53] 'Guide to Reportable Tax Positions 2018 Section C: Category C Reportable Tax Positions' (Australian Taxation Office, 11 February 2019), available at: www.ato.gov.au/Forms/Guide-to-reportable-tax-positions-2018/?page=6.

[54] ibid.

[55] 'Review of Taxpayer Rights and Taxpayer Protections' (Inspector-General of Taxation (Cth)), 2016), available at: igt.gov.au/publications/reports-of-reviews/taxpayers-charter-and-taxpayer-protections-review/.

of significant assistance to taxpayers who are unable to enforce such rights due to the costs associated with doing so.[56]

In compiling base data for the report, this writer and the principal researcher found few actual 'rights' in the Australian tax law.

The 'Report to the Inspector-General of Taxation on Taxpayer Rights'[57] explained that there were 30 'key enforceable rights' in Australian law that apply to the administration of the income tax. These arise principally under statute although some are based in common law:

> [T]he majority of the enforceable rights relate to the ability to seek reasons for ATO decisions and to challenge certain decisions through the objection and appeal processes pursuant to Part IVC of the *Taxation Administration Act 1953* .... Other enforceable rights include those relating to the issue of refunds and the right to having interest paid on overpayments. The common law rights include those relating to claims for legal professional privilege, procedural fairness and damages for pure economic loss due to wrongful ATO conduct.

This body of 'rights' is relatively narrow. They are expensive to enforce because of the costs of litigation, and rights such as legal professional privilege are fragile. The Report to the Inspector-General identified other categories of protection that taxpayers might expect (the Report was at pains to distinguish these from legitimate expectations in the legal sense) and these have no greater status than 'presumptions' that the ATO will act fairly in certain circumstances. They are set out below.

Table of taxpayer presumptions[58]

Under certain circumstances, an administrative penalty may be reduced by between 20 and 100% if certain criteria are met	Reduce administrative penalties	Divisions 284– 98 TAA	Section 3.13
Taxpayers will be treated in terms of the taxpayer's charter and other forms of non-binding advice	To be treated fairly	Common-law	Section 9.2
The Commissioner will act in such a way as to recognise a taxpayer's human rights	To ensure the taxpayer is treated fairly	Australian Human Rights Commission Act 1986 and common-law	Section 15
Taxpayers have a presumption they will be treated in terms of the model litigant rules	To be treated fairly when litigating against the ATO	Section 55ZF of JA read with Appendix B to Legal Services Directions 2005 – F2006L00320, [2]	Section 1

[56] ibid, Executive Summary.
[57] Kalmen Datt, Appendix 2 of 'Review into the Taxpayers' Charter and Taxpayer Protections' (n 55).
[58] ibid 154–55.

As will be evident from the use of the term 'presumptions' these are not entitlements, and they are difficult to enforce. Elements will no doubt be observed in cases of judicial review and administrative review, but there are no guarantees. Take, for example, the surprise expressed in academic circles at the outcome of the *Donoghue* case. Whereas the Federal Court had made a finding of conscious maladministration on the part of the Commissioner,[59] the Full Federal Court[60] found that the use by the ATO of privileged documents in assessing the taxpayer who had been subjected to blackmail by his legal adviser who then handed over documents to the ATO was not an issue of privilege:

> Once the confidentiality of the communications was lost, legal professional privilege could not apply, and the ATO was free to use those documents as the basis for an assessment. Indeed, … the Full Court held that s 166 of the *ITAA 1936* imposes an overriding *duty* on the Commissioner to use whatever information he has in his possession to make an assessment.[61]

Of even greater interest at this time is the *Glencore* case. In *Glencore International AG and Others v FCT and Others*[62] the international mining company and others in the Glencore Group sought a High Court order for the delivery by the ATO of documents that form part of the 'Paradise Papers' which they say were created as part of their 'Project Everest' when they sought advice from a Bermudan law practice on a corporate restructure. They sought an injunction against the ATO using the documents. Counsel for the applicants argued that:

> The principal question which arises in these proceedings, your Honours, is whether legal professional privilege is a self-sufficient basis for an injunction to restrain the use of privileged documents and for an order for delivery up of those documents.[63]

The applicants' submission was that although the documents are no longer confidential (they are on a website) they were at the time of communication when they were created, and privilege over them persists. Privilege is a rule of substantive law, and the privilege protection applies not only to the rules of evidence but also to investigatory procedures.

The application was heard on 17 April 2019 and a decision handed down in October 2019 in *Glencore International AG v Commissioner of Taxation*.[64] The application failed with the High Court finding that although the documents were privileged they could still be used by the Commissioner in the exercise of his statutory powers as they were already in his possession. Privilege affords immunity from powers to compel the disclosure of privileged communications. It does not undermine the legality of the use of the privileged documents once they have come into the hands of the office that must use them to come to a decision. To put it another way, legal professional privilege is a shield, not a sword.[65]

[59] *Donoghue v FCT* [2015] FCA 235, [71]–[72] (Logan J).

[60] *FCT v Donoghue* [2015] FCAFC 183 (Kenny and Perram JJ – joint judgment; Davies J).

[61] R Woellner and J Bevacqua, 'The ATO, Conscious Maladministration, and Stolen Information' (2017) 46 *Australian Tax Review* 26, 39–40. See also R Woellner, 'Problems in Paradise: Conscious Maladministration in the ATO' (2015) 8 *Journal of the Australasian Law Teachers Association* 129.

[62] *Glencore International AG and Others v FCT and Others* S256/2018.

[63] IM Jackman SC [2019] HCA Trans 082, 2.

[64] *Glencore International AG v Commissioner of Taxation* [2019] HCA 26.

[65] IM Jackman SC [2019] HCA Trans 082 at 75. Counsel was arguing the opposite.

The Taxpayers' Charter is another example of the limits of the rights of taxpayers. There have been no instances in which a court has recognised the Charter as a document creating rights under which a taxpayer can take action to control the actions of the ATO.[66]

In *Harts Fidelity Pty Ltd v Chapman, Deputy Commissioner of Taxation*[67] the taxpayer was unable to rely on the Charter in arguing that it was entitled to deferral of tax due. In *Engler v Commissioner of Taxation (No 3)*[68] the applicant was unsuccessful in trying to base certain allegations of bad faith on the part of the Commissioner in alleged breaches of the Charter. In *McLaren v Deputy Commissioner of Taxation*[69] the applicants argued that, inter alia, the Commissioner had failed to meet the legitimate expectations arising under the Charter. The application was dismissed without the court discussing the Charter and the possibility of such expectations arising under it. Charter arguments were seemingly ignored in *Engler v Commissioner of Taxation (No 2)*[70] and another *Engler v Commissioner of Taxation.*[71] Similarly, there have been several cases in the Administrative Appeals Tribunal (AAT) where the ATO's departure from the terms of the Taxpayers' Charter has been alleged, but no decision of the AAT seems to have turned on this.

The value in a charter, in Australia, is the manner in which it is observed internally by the revenue authority. It is not its enforceability that is the most important feature; it is the fact that it is followed. Its power is in the context of organisational culture.

In the UK, there is more substance in the expectations that arise from the Taxpayers' Charter. The Inspector-General of Taxation's Report explains how in the UK the first taxpayers' charter was published in 1986, was superseded and revised in 1991 and that after HMRC was formed a new *Your Charter* was adopted in 2009. Like the Australian version the *Your Charter* identifies what taxpayers might expect from HMRC and what HMRC might expect in return. In other words, both the Australian and the UK charters set out obligations along with the 'rights' afforded taxpayers.

Your Charter was 'refreshed' in 2016, and the Report notes that

> HMRC has also sought to strengthen its charter governance by creating a sub-committee of its Board, namely: the Charter Committee. The Charter Committee is chaired by a HMRC non-executive director whilst the majority of the other members are external to HMRC.122 The HMRC has also appointed nine senior staff members as Charter Champions to assist the Charter Committee in its oversight work.[72]

In light of the point made above that the real value of a charter is in its being followed, it is worth noting that:

> The Charter Champions also promote *Your Charter* within the organisation and ensure its principles are considered in developing HMRC processes and policy design. A number of

[66] M Walpole, 'The Australian Taxpayers Charter: A Review of 'Unchartered' Waters' in S Van Thiel (ed), *The Confederation Fiscale Europeenne at 50 years* (Confédération fiscale européenne, 2009) 270–73.

[67] *Harts Fidelity Pty Ltd v Chapman, Deputy Commissioner of Taxation* [1999] FCA 1033.

[68] *Engler v Commissioner of Taxation (No 3)* [2003] FCA 1571.

[69] *McLaren v Deputy Commissioner of Taxation* [2001] FCA 31.

[70] *Engler v Commissioner of Taxation (No 2)* [2003] FCA 411.

[71] *Engler v Commissioner of Taxation* [2002] FCA 226.

[72] Inspector-General of Taxation (Cth) (n 55) 2.56.

> Charter Advocates have also been recruited by Charter Champions to ensure adherence to *Your Charter* principles by HMRC staff.[73]

There is a powerful feature of *Your Charter* not shared by the Australian experience that makes it entirely different, and that is that it is backed by the concept of legitimate expectation. Bevacqua observes that 'while the commitment to treat taxpayers fairly in the newly adopted HMRC Charter closely resembles its counterpart in the Australian Charter, the UK commitment is backed with the weight of judicial precedent'.[74]

Bevacqua is pessimistic about the prospect of Australia's Charter reaching similar levels of enforceability. First because, as he says:

> [T]here is no sign of Australian judges accepting the doctrine of legitimate expectations in Australia or any associated legally enforceable right to fair treatment, with former High Court Chief Justice Sir Anthony Mason extra-judicially observing that '[i]t would require a revolution in Australian judicial thinking to bring about an adoption of the English approach to substantive protection of legitimate expectations'.[75]

Second, he sees European law, and especially the Human Rights Act 1998, as providing the fundamental justiciable norm that the Australian law lacks.

Accordingly, the non-binding HMRC Charter, while modelled on the Australian Charter also has the backing of legislatively entrenched rights as well as rights of appeal to European courts. These options further enhance the potential of the new HMRC Charter to result in real improvements in taxpayer rights despite the Charter itself lacking legislative force. In those circumstances, the need for the Charter itself to create any new legal rights is less pressing than in Australia.[76]

That there might be a need for an enforceable charter of rights is argued by Bevacqua (especially in light of an increasing trend of complaints to the Taxation Ombudsman) and is most recently evidenced in Australia by the diversion of media attention away from tax avoidance by multinationals to allegations of heavy-handed approaches to tax collection by the ATO. The strikingly titled Australian Broadcasting Corporation (ABC) Four Corners report called 'Mongrel Bunch of Bastards'[77] aired in April 2018. It claimed to 'examine … whether the ATO is playing by the rules and acting fairly and ethically'. Headlines and extracts associated with the programme include such statements as:

> '"*You might say that murderers have more rights than taxpayers.*" Tax barrister'.[78]
>
> 'The Australia Taxation Office is a formidable enforcer with extraordinary powers. It can raid your home or business without a warrant, it can compel you to answer questions and treat you as guilty until proven innocent'.[79]

[73] ibid 2.57.

[74] J Bevacqua, 'Redressing the Imbalance – Challenging the Effectiveness of the Australian Taxpayers' Charter' (2013) 28 *Australian Tax Forum* 377, 394–95.

[75] ibid 395.

[76] ibid.

[77] 'Mongrel Bunch of Bastards' *Four Corners* (Australian Broadcasting Corporation, 2018), available at: www.abc.net.au/4corners/mongrel-bunch-of-bastards/9635026.

[78] ibid.

[79] ibid.

> '"*(It) can effectively act like a judge, jury and executioner all rolled up into one. That's the problem.*" Tax barrister'.[80]

> 'While there's strong public support for a crackdown on major multinational corporations to force them to pay their fair share, there is growing concern that the Tax Office is targeting people a long way from the big end of town'.[81]

> '"*They chase low-hanging fruit, people who are being honest and upright, and they whack them with a huge bill and then chase them.*" Small business lobbyist'.[82]

The claims are strong and so have been reactions. The course of this journalistic exercise is a demonstration of how the revenue authorities are expected to toe the line between not being soft on avoidance – but not being so severe that they appear to have gone too far the other way. Heavy-handed methods and stripping of rights to be heard will undermine faith in the essential fairness of the tax system.

VIII. Conclusion

The chapter has attempted to demonstrate that there has been a burgeoning of measures to control the excesses of taxpayers in minimising tax and an apparent change in social expectations. Not only do the authorities have the power to collect more and tolerate less, but there is a political swell demanding that they do so and deep suspicion on the part of some that the rich and powerful companies can 'get away with it' when it comes to tax manipulation and minimisation. Governments have grasped this opportunity to look tough and be tough. To the powers described above may be added a plethora of OECD/G20 BEPS initiatives including far-reaching information-sharing powers. We are in an almost unique period in history where authorities know so much about so many taxpayers.

However, both the UK and Australian models of income taxation are based on voluntary compliance. Willing compliance is essential to such systems because widespread disobedience in tax would be beyond the powers of such agencies to deal with or if brought within powers would be extraordinarily onerous and expensive for government. Whether one is sympathetic to the cause of legal avoidance or not, it is clear from the research that perceptions of fairness are key to the morale of the body of taxpayers. We may be at a point when these perceptions are tested more than ever.

[80] ibid.
[81] ibid.
[82] ibid.

16

True and Fair View and Tax Accounting

ANDRÉS BÁEZ MORENO

I. Introduction

All successive versions of the European Accounting directives[1] incorporate the True and Fair View Principle (TFV). Apart from other less relevant references to the principle, the directives require that annual accounts shall give a TFV of the company's assets, liabilities, financial position and profit or loss,[2] compel them to provide additional information where the application of the provisions of the Directive would not be sufficient to give a TFV,[3] and to depart from any provision in the Directive where in exceptional cases its application is incompatible with the obligation to give a TFV.[4] Most EU Member States[5] have literally incorporated these provisions into their respective national accounting rules. Other (non-EU) accounting regimes[6] contain similar or identical references to the TFV or similar concepts.[7]

[1] [1978] OJ L222/11 Fourth Council Directive of 25 July 1978 based on Article 54 (3)(g) of the Treaty on the annual accounts of certain types of companies (78/660/EEC Directive) and [2013] OJ L182/19 Directive 2013/34/EU of the European Parliament and of the Council of 26 June 2013 on the annual financial statements, consolidated financial statements and related reports of certain types of undertakings, amending Directive 2006/43/EC of the European Parliament and of the Council and repealing Council Directives 78/660/EEC and 83/349/EEC (2013/34/EU Directive).

[2] Article 2(3) of the 78/660/EEC Directive and, with immaterial changes, Article 4(3).1 of the 2013/34/EU Directive.

[3] Article 2(4) of the 78/660/EEC Directive and, with immaterial changes, Article 4(3).2 of the 2013/34/EU Directive.

[4] Article 2(5) of the 78/660/EEC Directive and, with immaterial changes, Article 4(4) of the 2013/34/EU Directive.

[5] There are few exceptions some of which will be referred to later in this contribution.

[6] eg, in Australia at least until 1991 (AS Dunk and A Kilgore, 'The Reintroduction of the True and Fair Override and Harmonization with IASC Standards in Australia: Lessons from the EU and Implications for Financial Reporting and International Trade' (2000) 35 *The International Journal of Accounting* (2000) 213, 214) or New Zealand until 1993 (N Kirk, 'Perceptions of the True and Fair View Concept: An Empirical Investigation' (2006) 42 *Abacus* 205, 206.

[7] Such as the requirement of Fair Presentation (FP) in International Accounting Standards/International Financial Reporting Standards (IAS/IFRS). See: IAS 1 *Presentation of Financial Statements* (IAS 1.15–21). Certain authors have stressed differences between the TFV in the directives and the FP requirement in IAS 1: see, eg, L Evans, 'The true and fair view and the "fair presentation" override of IAS 1' (2003) 33 *Accounting and Business Research* 311, 311–25.

Such widespread legal recognition might suggest that the TFV counts on more or less precise legal contents; however, this intuition would be utterly wrong. Indeed accountants, and to a lesser extent also lawyers, have been arguing for more than 75 years about the TFV.[8] From pure semantic (and rather irrelevant) trivialities to far-reaching discussions on its role and consequences, everything touched by the TFV becomes an accounting and legal battleground. It is therefore hardly surprising to find a good number of defeatist statements among specialised scholars labelling the TFV as: a 'nebulous concept',[9] 'an accounting anachronism',[10] 'a philosophical concept not susceptible to definition by a comprehensive set of detailed rules',[11] 'a formula for international disharmony'[12] or, even worse, as 'an excuse for non-compliance and the worst excesses of creative accounting'.[13] Other descriptions, not being so harsh, amount actually to what some scholars refer as 'non-telling formulations'.[14]

For us (tax) lawyers, this vagueness would be no more than a relief to find that even those dedicated to a discipline so seemingly algebraic and straightforward as accounting must live with principles (sometimes even *slogans*) which all use without anyone knowing what is actually meant by them. However, once more (tax) lawyers cannot relax and watch others struggle. Indeed, there is a host of relations between tax and commercial accounting being perhaps so-called book-tax conformity the most intense among them.[15] Accordingly, if the rules for calculating the taxable income are based upon financial statements, it seems very clear that, at least in principle, a commercial accounting problem automatically becomes a tax (accounting) issue. In this context, TFV could well be a Trojan Horse in tax law. This contribution is an attempt to relativise this alarmist diagnosis arguing that: (i) TFV is nothing different from what lawyers already know under different names; and (ii) not all contents of TFV must have a consequence in tax accounting.

[8] Being the exact wording *true and fair view* was supposed to have been originated in the United Kingdom in the mid-1940s. See BA Rutherford, 'The True and Fair View Doctrine: a Search for Explication' (1985) 12 *Journal of Business Finance & Accounting* 483, 485–86.

[9] FJO Ryan, 'A True and Fair View' (1967) 3 *Abacus* 95, 104.

[10] W McGregor, 'True and Fair View – and Accounting Anachronism' (1992) 62 *Australian Accountant* 71.

[11] D Flint, *A True and Fair View in Company Accounts* (London, Gee and Co for the Institute of Chartered Accountants of Scotland, 1982) 2.

[12] H Andrew and J Blake, 'The True and Fair View Concept – A Formula for International Disharmony: Some Empirical Evidence' (1993) 28 *The International Journal of Accounting* 104.

[13] McGregor (n 10) 71.

[14] Streim refers to qualifiers such as 'magic words', 'term of art', 'matter of ethics and morality' or 'an article of belief, credo, a symbol': see H Streim, 'Die Generalnorm des § 264 Abs. 2 HGB- Eine kritische Analyse' in W Ballwieser, HJ Böcking, J Drukarczyk and RH Schmidt (eds), *Bilanzrecht und Kapitalmarkt. Festschrift zum 65. Geburtstag von Professor Dr. Dr. h.c. Dr. h.c. Adolf Moxter* (Düsseldorf, IDW, 1994) 394.

[15] Of course, not all countries link formally the calculation of business income tax bases to accounting profits. However, even in systems that lack a formal link between commercial and tax accounting rules, there are strong connections between those sets of rules: see, eg, W Schön, 'The David R Tillinghast Lecture. The Odd Couple: A Common Future for Financial and Tax Accounting?' (2005) 58 *Tax Law Review* 111, 120; and J Freedman, 'Aligning Taxable Profits and Accounting Profits: Accounting standards, legislators and judges' (2004) 2 *eJournal of Tax Research* 71, 72. See also, in relation to southern European and Latin American countries, A Báez Moreno and JJ Zornoza Pérez, 'Modelos Comparados de Relación entre Normas Contables y Normas Fiscales en la Imposición sobre el Beneficio de las Empresas' in JR Piza and P Sarmiento (eds), *El Impuesto sobre la Renta y Complementarios* (Bogotá, Universidad Externado, 2010) 432–33.

The rest of this chapter is organised as follows: section II tries to decode what TFV means in legal terms for commercial accounting purposes by analysing what powers the principle assigns and to whom. Section III analyses if the results in the application of this principle as described in section II also apply for tax accounting purposes in book-tax conformity systems. Section IV concludes. The analysis is based upon commercial and tax accounting rules of EU Member States; however, many of the findings in this chapter might be applicable to other jurisdictions with TFV and book-tax conformity links.

II. What Does *True and Fair View* Mean in Strict Legal Terms?

As indicated above, everything concerning TFV and especially its content and corresponding legal consequences is shrouded in mystery. There has been no shortage of well-meaning attempts to put the TFV in more concrete terms and some of which have even achieved a significant degree of acceptance among accounting scholars. This is the case, for example, of Walton's construction describing the possible meaning(s) of TFV using the concepts of a *legal residual clause*, *independent concept* and *generally accepted accounting principles*.[16] Even if this classification has had a significant impact on accounting scholarship,[17] it nevertheless has some technical problems: (i) these categories may overlap rendering the classification relatively imperfect. Indeed a legal residual clause[18] might also entail an independent concept[19] and vice versa. (ii) Some of these concepts mean simply nothing in legal terms. Apart from the term *generally accepted accounting principles*, whose juridical meaning is more or less clear, the legal uncertainty surrounding the concepts of *legal residual clause* and *independent concept* is maximal.

To my mind, the problem with the meaning of TFV is not the difficult conciliation between two distant legal worlds (the Anglo-Saxon and Continental systems) – as is frequently suggested in the academic literature[20] – but actually the introduction in legal documents, such as the European Accounting directives, of terms without any

[16] PJ Walton, *The True and View: A Shifting Concept* (London, Technical and Research Department of the Chartered Association of Certified Accountants, 1991) 29.

[17] Kirk (n 6) 210 and Evans (n 7) 313.

[18] Defined by Walton as a 'sort of clause which is often added to statutes, contracts and other legal documents to cover circumstances other than those specifically foreseen in other clauses of the document': see PJ Walton, 'Introduction: the true and fair view in British accounting' (1993) 1 *European Accounting Review* 49, 50.

[19] Defined by Walton as 'a higher objective to be sought by accountants': see Walton, 'Introduction: the true and fair view in British accounting' (n 18) 49.

[20] In this regard, TFV has been labelled as a 'means to bring English techniques of interpretation in line with Continental traditions' in B Grossfeld, 'Common Roots of the European Law of Accounting' (1989) 23 *International Lawyer* 865, 871; and a 'political tool intended to temper the continental, in particular German, influence on European accounting rules' in A Hopwood, 'Ambiguity, knowledge and territorial claims: some observations on the doctrine of substance over form: a review essay' (1990) 22 *British Accounting Review* 79, 84–85.

clear legal meaning. Therefore, the solution to the TFV conundrum lies in a proper 'translation' into legal categories of terms which are in principle alien to the former. For these purposes it may be best to begin with the literal wording of the main provisions contained in the 2013/34/EU Directive which referred to the TFV:

> The annual financial statements shall give a true and fair view of the undertaking's assets, liabilities, financial position and profit or loss. Where the application of this Directive would not be sufficient to give a true and fair view of the undertaking's assets, liabilities, financial position and profit or loss, such additional information as is necessary to comply with that requirement shall be given in the notes to the financial statements [article 4(3) of the 2013/34/EU Directive].
>
> Where in exceptional cases the application of a provision of this Directive is incompatible with the obligation laid down in paragraph 3, that provision shall be disapplied in order to give a true and fair view of the undertaking's assets, liabilities, financial position and profit or loss. The disapplication of any such provision shall be disclosed in the notes to the financial statements together with an explanation of the reasons for it and of its effect on the undertaking's assets, liabilities, financial position and profit or loss.
>
> The Member States may define the exceptional cases in question and lay down the relevant special rules which are to apply in those cases [article 4(4) of the 2013/34/EU Directive].

Beyond matters of detail, it seems clear that TFV, enshrined in Article 4 of the 2013/34/EU Directive, sets the main objective of the Directive itself.[21] In this context, and even when the Directive has not characterised TFV as a legal principle – something which it has done in relation to so-called 'General Financial Reporting Principles' in its Article 6 – it seems obvious that TFV must be also qualified as such.[22] The qualification of the TFV as legal principle is of key importance in providing the interpreter of the Directive with a legal toolkit to unravel its very content. In particular, it shows how TFV cannot work in isolation but rather is connected with specific accounting rules.[23] Its characterisation as main objective of the accounting system and its operating mode as ancillary of specific accounting rules defines the functions and content of the TFV. These functions are analysed in detail next.[24]

[21] D Tweedie, 'Preface' in RH Parker and CW Nobes (eds), *An International View of True and Fair Accounting* (London, Routledge, 1994) xii. J Hennrichs, *Wahlrechte im Bilanzrecht der Kapitalgesellschaften unter besonderer Berücksichtigung der EG-Bilanz-Richtlinie* (Köln, Dr Otto Schmidt, 1999) 133. This has been also the interpretation of the Court of Justice of the European Union in several important decisions considered later in this chapter: Case C-234/94, *Tomberger*, ECLI:EU:C:1996:252, judgment of 27 February 1996, para 17; Case C-275/97, *DE+ES*, ECLI:EU:C:1999:406, judgment of 14 September 1999, para 26; Case C-306/99, *BIAO*, ECLI:EU:C:2003:3, judgment of 7 January 2003, para 72 (labelling it a 'fundamental principle'); Case C-322/12, *Gimle*, ECLI:EU:C:2013:632, judgment of 3 October 2013, para 30; and Case C-510/12, *Bloomsbury NV*, ECLI:EU:C:2014:154, judgment of 6 March 2014, para 18.

[22] Hennrichs, *Wahlrechte im Bilanzrecht der Kapitalgesellschaften* (n 21) 139–43 correctly describing TFV as a legal, European principle. See also D Alexander and E Jermakovicz, 'A True and Fair View of the Principles/Rules Debate' (2006) 42 *Abacus* 132, 139.

[23] The ancillary character of legal principles is explicitly or implicitly present in all legal scholars dealing with principles as opposed to rules. See, eg, R Dworkin, *Taking Rights Seriously*, Fourth Indian Reprint (New Delhi, Universal Law Publishing, 2008) 14–45.

[24] This contribution is partially based upon the three functions (interpretative, explanatory and overriding) attributed by Gelders to TFV: see G Gelders, 'Image fidèle et consolidation des comptes' in Université de Liège, Commission Droit et Vie des Affaires (ed), *Nouvelle orientations en droit comptable* (1994) unpublished, quoted in K Van Hulle, '"True and Fair View", im Sinne der 4. Richtlinie' in G Förschle, K Kaiser and A Moxter (eds), *Rechenschaftslegung im Wandel. Festschrift für Wolfgang Dieter Budde* (München, Beck, 1995) 319.

A. The Interpretative Function of TFV

The accounting rules in the Directive, and also in local accounting law of Member States, can be very imprecise and thereby generate significant interpretative problems. It goes without saying that if TFV embodies the main objective of the Directive it might prove crucial to resolve these interpretation issues. Indeed, the idea seems simple: if the purpose of a provision is relevant for its interpretation and the TFV sets the purpose of the Directive accounting system as whole, then the first function of TFV must be interpretative. Scholars[25] and, in a more tentative way also the Court of Justice of the European Union (CJEU)[26] seem to have easily accepted this logic. In this context, the CJEU has tried to clarify what TFV means for the interpretation of particular accounting provisions in some passages worth a literal quotation:

> It is clear from those provisions that taking account of all elements of profits made, charges, income, liabilities and losses which actually relate to the financial year in question ensures observance of the requirement of a true and fair view.[27]

And further:

> The principle of a true and fair view requires that the accounts reflect the activities and transactions which they are supposed to describe and that the accounting information be given in the form judged to be the soundest and most appropriate for satisfying third parties' needs for information, without harming the interests of the company.[28]

These statements, and particularly the result of the CJEU decision in *Tomberger* – ie, under certain circumstances profits obtained by a subsidiary must be contemporarily entered in the balance sheet of its parent company – might lead one to believe that TFV imposes information provision as the main objective of the Directive[29] and that all accounting provisions should be interpreted in accordance with this purpose.

[25] This is one of the rare cases in which German and Anglo-Saxon accounting scholars seem to agree. For German scholars see, eg, D Ordelheide, 'True and Fair View: A European and a German Perspective' (1993) 1 *European Accounting Review* 81, 86; Hennrichs, *Wahlrechte im Bilanzrecht der Kapitalgesellschaften* (n 21) 134. For non-German scholars see, eg, JM Gondra Romero, 'Significado y función del principio de "Imagen Fiel" ("True and Fair View") en el Sistema del nuevo Derecho de Balances' in *Derecho Mercantil de la Comunidad Europea. Estudios en Homenaje a José Girón Tena* (Madrid, Civitas, 1991) 580; Van Hulle, 'True and Fair View' (n 24) 321–22; C Nobes, 'Is true and fair of over-riding importance?: a comment on Alexander's benchmark' (2000) 30 *Accounting and Business Research* 307, 307, referring to TFV in a UK context; D Alexander and E Eberhartinger, 'The True and Fair View in the European Union' (2009) 18 *European Accounting Review* 571, 573–76. However, on occasion, the interpretative function of TFV is denied, particularly among German traditional accounting scholars: see H Beisse, 'Die Generalnorm des neuen Bilanzrechts' in B Knobbe-Keuk, F Klein and A Moxter (eds), *Handelsrecht und Steuerrecht. Festchrift fir Dr.Dr.h.c. Georg Döllerer* (Düsseldorf, IDW, 1988) 41–42; H Beisse, 'Die Generalnorm des neuen Bilanzrechts und ihre steurrechtliche Bedeutung' in W Mellwig, A Moxter and D Ordelheide (eds), *Beiträge zum neuen Bilanzrecht. Band 2. Handelsbilanz und Steuerbilanz* (Wiesbaden, Gabler, 1989) 30; H Beisse, 'Zehn Jahre "True and fair view"' in W Ballwieser, A Moxter and R Nonnenmacher (eds), *Rechnungslegung- warum un wie. Festchrift für Hermann Clemm zum 70.Geburtstag* (München, Beck, 1996) 46.

[26] *Tomberger*, judgment (n 21) para 17; *DE+ES* (n 21) para 26.

[27] *Tomberger*, judgment (n 21) para 22, later repeated *verbatim* in *DE+ES* (n 21) para 27.

[28] *BIAO* (n 21) para 123.

[29] W Schön, 'Case C-234/94, *Waltraud Tomberger v. Gebrüder v.d. Wettern GmbH*. 5th Chamber, Judgment of 27 June 1996, not yet reported' (2007) 34 *Common Market Law Review* 681, 691–92.

Beyond the very particular case and facts of *Tomberger*,[30] this conclusion would have a deep impact in practical terms. Take, for example, the case of long-term contracts and the potential use of the percentage of completion method which, in my view, would enable or even impose[31] the aforementioned approach to the content of *Tomberger*. However, putting aside the many mistakes of this decision, I believe there is a more accurate approach to the statements aforementioned and the proper understanding of the interpretative function of the TFV.[32]

It is my understanding that those statements require the financial statements: (i) when accounting rules refer to verifiable natural facts, to truthfully reflect them; or, using the aforementioned language of *BIAO*, 'activities and transactions which they are supposed to describe'; (ii) when accounting rules refer to estimates and forecasts, to take into account all those verifiable natural facts which might lead to a more accurate accounting reflection; or, using the aforementioned language of *BIAO*, 'accounting information be given in the form judged to be the soundest and most appropriate'. Not only is this approach to the content of the TFV most suited to the very semantical formulation of the principle – facts can be *true* whereas estimates can at best be *fair* – but it also allows us to properly understand the interpretative function of the principle.[33] In this context, we may refer to different kinds of accounting rules on which the TFV might deploy its interpretative function.

First, all accounting rules refer ultimately to (economic) facts. In this respect TFV requires not making false references to these facts in the financial statements. This rather trivial statement would not even need to be recognised in the law.

Second, some (crucial) accounting rules neither refer specifically to natural facts nor require the elaboration of estimates and forecasts. This is, in my view, the case for the realisation principle. Article 6.1(c)(i) of the 2013/34/EU Directive imposes that 'only profits made at the balance sheet date may be recognised' whereas Article 6.1(d) of the same Directive adds that 'only profits made at the balance sheet date may be recognised'. Both principles, according to which income will be recognised, do not refer either to natural facts or to estimates or forecasts. Indeed, the combination of both provisions makes clear that profits need to be made in order to be recognised, without clearly defining what must be understood under 'made' but also that this realisation cannot be identified with cash movements.

Consequently, realisation is a pure legal convention which does not require one to investigate natural facts or elaborate estimates or predictions. In this respect it can be concluded that the TFV plays no role in the interpretation of the realisation principle.

[30] Indeed, according to the decision, the circumstances in which this contemporary realisation might be legally possible are very particular to the case: *Tomberger*, judgment (n 21) para 25.

[31] In my view, it is not at all clear whether contemporary realisation in the circumstances provided for in the *Tomberger* decision is an option or an obligation for the parent company. In the same vein, see Schön, 'Case C-234/94' (n 29) 689.

[32] Even if the result in *Tomberger* very much departs from the aforementioned starting point.

[33] In a similar vein, see the Opinion of Advocate General Tesauro delivered on 25 January 1996 in Case C-234/94, *Tomberger*, ECLI:EU:C:1996:16, stating: 'That principle requires the balance sheet to be drawn up so as to give not only a true (even in the relative sense in which that adjective is traditionally and necessarily used as regards balance sheets) but also a fair (essentially with regard to the good faith of the person drawing up the balance sheet) representation of the company's assets and liabilities, its financial position and its profit or loss'.

Realisation, as an expression of the more general principle of prudence, needs to be interpreted according to its goal which is precisely to protect creditors from overly optimistic accounting practices. For this reason, the formula used by German case law – a profit needs to be 'almost sure' (*so gut wie sicher*)[34] to be realised – seems accurate, but it will require further specification normally resorting to the (private law) rules regulating transfer of the risk to the buyer of a good or recipient of a service. And for this reason, too, the conclusion reached by the CJEU in *Tomberger* seems wrong.

The *Tomberger* decision allows the registration in the annual accounts of a parent company of the benefits obtained by a 100 per cent owned subsidiary in the same financial year and logically before the existence of a formal resolution to distribute dividends. Nevertheless, on the fringes of a pure cash approach, which is clearly excluded by Article 6.1(c)(i) of the 2013/34/EU Directive, it must be acknowledged that the income from shares for a parent company becomes 'almost sure' once the subsidiary has formally agreed the distribution of dividends. Indeed, the interpretation of realisation in this case, like in any other, does not require investigating facts or elaborating estimates; it only calls for the identification of the (normally legal) requirements to ascertain whether an income can be considered or not to be almost sure. There is no place for TFV in the interpretation of this kind of rules.

Third, many accounting rules require the elaboration of estimates and forecasts.[35] These rules, as well as any others, can give rise to doubts of interpretation. As we previously stated, TFV would require in these cases to take into account, when interpreting the rules, all those verifiable natural facts which might lead to a more accurate accounting reflection. Obviously estimates and forecasts cannot be true or false in the same sense as natural facts; they can just be fair or not. In this context, when an accounting rule enables several interpretations, TFV requires interpretation of the rule in such a way as to take account of those facts which allow the estimate to be 'more fair' (in line with the 'unknown' reality). The abundance of this kind of accounting rule would offer various examples; however, we will focus on one specific case for the importance it has gained in the accounting case law of the CJEU.

Several decisions of the CJEU have made clear that, despite the principle of separate valuation laid down (at present) in Article 6.1(f) of the 2013/34/EU Directive, the creation of a separate provision for each potential liability could produce a distorted view of the financial position of the company concerned therefore enabling the recognition of a single provision for all such liabilities.[36] Regarding the calculation of these global provisions, the Court has repeatedly stated that the Directive contains no indications as to valuation criteria to be applied or as to the percentage up to which they may be recognised; the regulation of these conditions would therefore be a competence of Member States under national law.[37] However, the valuation criteria laid down by national law must comply with TFV and the rule settled in Article 42(1) of the 78/660/EEC Directive, according to which provisions for liabilities and charges may not exceed in amount the

[34] See for more references D Dauber, *Das Realizationsprinzip als Grundprinzip der steuerrechtlichen Gewinnermittlung* (Frankfurt, Peter Lang, 2003) 132.
[35] Freedman, 'Aligning Taxable Profits and Accounting Profits' (n 15) 75.
[36] *DE+ES* (n 21) paras 28–34; *BIAO* (n 21) para 116.
[37] *DE+ES* (n 21) para 35.

sums which are necessary. This means, according to the Court, that national provisions must therefore allow account to be taken of the reporting company's previous experience, or that of other companies active in the same sector, with warranty claims relating to similar contracts. Accordingly, creation of a global provision for potential liabilities under warranties cannot therefore be limited by the national authorities, *a priori* and in the abstract, to a fixed percentage of the turnover subject to warranties.[38]

I agree with many of the observations made by the Court in relation to global provisions. However, in the same manner in which the Court has limited national competences in relation to *fixed global provisions*, I believe the Court should have considered TFV when deciding the most appropriate method to calculate global provisions for potential liabilities under warranties. Indeed, as indicated by the Court, a provision built upon a fixed percentage of the turnover subject to warranties would, by nature, exceed or fall short of the expenses to be incurred but, by the same token, a provision calculated according to data of other companies in the same sector would be less accurate than one based upon the company's previous experience. Therefore, if reliable data on past claims against the company is available it must be used, according to TFV, particularly where this substantially differs from that usual in the sector concerned.

In the *DE+ES* case, German tax authorities did not deny that the company was under an obligation to put right defects in work regarded as being covered by the provisions for warranty liabilities,[39] yet they refused to accept the amount of the provision recognised by the company – valued at 2 per cent of the turnover subject to warranties. The authorities proposed a provision corresponding to 0.5 per cent of the turnover in the last two years pointing out that, if an undertaking claims a global provision which is higher than that usual in the sector concerned, it must prove that, in the past, claims against it have been above the usual level.[40] This conclusion appears to be unassailable at first glance, and the Court also concluded that national provisions must allow account to be taken of the reporting company's previous experience, or that of other companies active in the same sector – implying that both options would be equally complaint with TFV. As previously stated, however, an interpretation according to TFV requires, when accounting rules refer to estimates and forecasts, taking into account all those verifiable natural facts which might lead to a more accurate accounting reflection. Therefore: (i) national rules on calculation of global provisions should be required to take into account the reporting company's previous experience; and (ii) in the absence of such rules Article 42(1) of the old 78/660/EEC Directive, which imposed that provisions for liabilities and charges may not exceed in amount the sums which are necessary, and current Article 12(12) of the 2013/34/EU Directive, establishing that a provision shall represent the best estimate of the expenses likely to be incurred or, in the case of a liability, that the amount required to meet that liability should be interpreted according to TFV and, again, be required to take into account the reporting company's previous experience.

Fourth, many accounting rules have an optional structure (accounting options), meaning that for the same facts the rule offers different and alternative legal consequences

[38] ibid paras 35–39.
[39] ibid para 14.
[40] ibid para 15.

for which the agent might opt.[41] There are many reasons why the directives or domestic legislation of different Member States would formulate accounting options.[42] In any case, scholars hover between those who, in a more or less nuanced manner, accept that TFV might eventually limit the exercise of these options[43] and those who deem options as not limited by TFV.[44] Although it has been suggested that the decision of the CJEU in *Tomberger* could speak in favour of an eventual limitation of options by TFV,[45] this conclusion is certainly bold taking into account the lack of reasoning in the decision and the fact it was actually not focused on accounting options.[46] However, there are, in my view, strong reasons for advocating that TFV might, under certain circumstances, limit the options contained in accounting rules.

Save for certain arguments very much linked to the (peculiar) transposition of Accounting directives in Germany, German scholars have rejected the power of TFV to restrict accounting options based upon two main grounds. First, and the one that I will focus on for present purposes, is that it makes no sense for a provision to grant options later denied by a principle integrated in the same system.[47] In my view, this argument would make sense for certain kinds of options granted to companies for reasons beyond a reliable and accurate reflection of the undertaking's assets, liabilities, financial position and profit or loss; indeed, some accounting options intend to improve the – too pessimistic – view offered by an orthodox application of the accounting rules,[48] to facilitate the accounting reflection of otherwise too complex accounting methods,[49] or finally to leave recognition or valuation up to the undertaking for certain accounting

[41] In opposition to these 'explicit legal options' German scholars frequently refer to 'factual options' (*factische Wahlrechte*) referring thereby to estimates and forecasts frequently contained in accounting rules: see, eg, H Clemm, '§ 264 und Wahlrechte' in G Förschle, K Kaiser and A Moxter (eds), *Rechenschaftslegung im Wandel. Festschrift für Wolfgang Dieter Budde* (München, Beck, 1995) 146–48. On the interpretation of rules requiring estimates and forecasts, we have already explained our position.

[42] For these motivations see Hennrichs, *Wahlrechte im Bilanzrecht der Kapitalgesellschaften* (n 21) 67–73.

[43] Gondra Romero (n 25) 580; Ordelheide, 'True and Fair View' (n 25) 85; WD Budde, 'Der true and fair view als Generalnorm' (unpublished manuscript, quoted and commented by Clemm (n 41)); Hennrichs, *Wahlrechte im Bilanzrecht der Kapitalgesellschaften* (n 21) 340–344; A Báez Moreno, 'Normas Contables e Impuesto sobre Sociedades' (Pamplona, Thomson-Reuters Aranzadi, 2005) 402–15; Alexander and Eberhartinger (n 25) 579.

[44] This is a frequent statement in traditional German accounting scholars: see, eg, Beisse 'Die Generalnorm des neuen Bilanzrechts' (n 25) 42; Beisse, 'Die Generalnorm des neuen Bilanzrechts und ihre steurrechtliche Bedeutung' (n 25) 30; Beisse 'Zehn Jahre' (n 25) 47. Further references can be found in Hennrichs, *Wahlrechte im Bilanzrecht der Kapitalgesellschaften* (n 21) 330.

[45] B Kropff, 'Vorsichtsprinzip und Wahlrechte' in T Fischer and R Hömberg (eds), *Jahresabschluß und Jahresabschlußprüfung. Probleme, Perspektiven, internationale Einflüsse. Festschrift zum 60. Geburtstag von Jörg Baetge* (Düsseldorf, IDW, 1997) 72.

[46] As recognised by Kropff himself: see Kropff (n 45) 72.

[47] Clemm (n 41) 152; WD Budde and KP Karig in WD Budde et al (eds), *Beck'scher Bilanz-Kommentar* 4th edn (München, Beck, 1999); W Ballwieser in J Baetge, HJ Kirsch and S Thiele (eds), *Bilanzrecht. Handelrecht mit Steuerrecht un den Regelungen des IASB Kommentar* (Bonn, Stollfuβ, 2002) Band 1, § 264 Rz. 59.

[48] We refer to those options labelled by German scholars as 'equity options' (*Billigkeitswahlrechte*) and normally identified with so-called 'accounting supports' (*Bilanzierungshilfen*). For more on this kind of options see T Siegel, 'Wahlrecht' in U Leffson, D Rückle and B Groβfeld (eds), *Handwörterbuch der unbestimmten Rechtsbegriffe im Bilanzrecht des HGB* (Köln, Dr Otto Schmidt, 1986) 420. The controversial concept of 'accounting support' is beyond the scope of this contribution; see, with further Spanish, German and Italian references, Báez Moreno, 'Normas Contables e Impuesto sobre Sociedades' (n 43) 167–73.

[49] We refer to those options labelled by German scholars as 'simplification options' (*Vereinfachungswahlrechte*). On these kinds of options see Siegel (n 48) 420.

problems whose 'proper' treatment has not been agreed by the legal or professional standard-setters.[50] For many of these cases a limitation of the accounting option would make no sense.[51] In effect, it would be absurd to reduce options 'alien to accounting reasons'[52] using precisely the main objective of the Accounting Directive (ie, TFV).

By way of example, it would make no sense to try and reduce an option granted by a Member State according to Article 12(11)3 of the 2013/34/EU Directive to include formation expenses under 'Assets'. If, as defended by a significant part of the accounting scholarship,[53] formation expenses may only be capitalised as a way to improve the otherwise bad results in the early years of an enterprise's existence – they are not real assets – it makes no sense to reduce this option according to the alleged influence of TFV. Things might be different regarding options which aim precisely at taking into account those different fact patterns that might underlay the application of the specific accounting rule and offer the enterprise a chance to select that option which better fits the facts as occurred in reality.

At times, this reality might become evident when exercising an option and it is precisely in these cases in which the option(s) might be reduced according to TFV if, as I believe, the principle requires taking into account all those verifiable natural facts which might lead to a more accurate accounting reflection. Consider two examples: (a) depreciation; and (b) stock valuation. Beginning with depreciation, neither current Article 12(5) of the 2013/34/EU Directive nor Article 35.1(b) of the 78/660/EEC Directive are very specific when it comes to regulating depreciation, merely laying down that historical cost of fixed assets with limited useful economic lives shall be reduced by value adjustments calculated to write off the value of such assets systematically over their useful economic lives. However, national accounting rules of Member States normally refer to depreciation methods, including straight-line, declining-balance or sum-of-the-years' digits.[54] Even if these specific regulations involve the granting of an option, for example, based upon different depreciation schedules of different assets, TFV might impose or, at least, discard certain method(s) if it is indisputable that certain method(s) fit better or do not fit at all the depreciation of a specific asset. Following this logic, the use of

[50] We refer to those options labelled by German Scholars as 'commitment options' (*Kompromißwahlrechte*). On these kinds of options see Siegel (n 48) 421.

[51] J Schulze Osterloh, '*GmbH-Gesetz*' in A Baumbach, A Hueck and L Fastrich (eds), *GmbH-Gesetz: Gesetz betreffend die Gesellschaften mit beschränkter Haftung* 18. erw. und völling überarb. Aufl. (München, Beck, 2006) 907, labelling these as options granted without regard to reflection of the undertaking's assets, liabilities, financial position and profit or loss. See also Hennrichs, *Wahlrechte im Bilanzrecht der Kapitalgesellschaften* (n 21) 341–44.

[52] As labelled by certain German scholars (*Wahlrechten aus bilanzfremden Gründen*): see, eg, J Baetge and D Commandeur in K Küting, C Peter and J Weber (eds), *Handbuch der Rechnungslegung – Einzelabschluss: kommentar zur Bilanzierung und Prüfung* 5. Auflage (Stuttgart, Schäffer-Poeschel, 2004) Band II § 264 Tz. 45.

[53] This is a contentious issue in my opinion: see Báez Moreno, 'Normas Contables e Impuesto sobre Sociedades' (n 43) 167–73; A Báez Moreno and JJ Zornoza Pérez, 'Definition of assets and capitalization problems for CCCTB purposes' in M Lang, P Pistone, J Schuch and C Staringer (eds), *Common Consolidated Corporate Tax Base* (Vienna, Linde, 2008) 294–95. Be that as it may, both the wording of Article 34 of the 78/660/EEC Directive and Article 12(11)3 of the 2013/34/EU Directive seem to adhere to the thesis that formation expenses are not 'real assets': see D Ordelheide, 'True and Fair View: A European and a German Perspective II' (1996) 5 *European Accounting Review* 495, 501.

[54] I refer here just to time-based methods.

the straight-line method or degressive non-linear method must be considered to be in breach of the TFV if applied, for example, to IT equipment.[55]

Turning to my second example, stock valuation, both the 78/660/EEC Directive (Article 40) and the 2013/34/EU Directive (Article 12(9)) offer Member States the possibility of permitting the calculation of historical costs of stocks of goods or fungible items based on weighted average prices, the 'first in, first out' (FIFO) method, the 'last in, first out' (LIFO) method, or a method reflecting generally accepted best practice. Many Member States have maintained this option in their domestic accounting law. Much has been written on this option particularly regarding the LIFO method and the appropriateness of its acceptance for both commercial and tax purposes,[56] and it has even been argued that the option can be considered immune to the limiting effects of TFV.[57] However, projecting the aforementioned content of TFV on this particular option, I am unable to understand why if a particular warehouse follows or does not follow a specific flow pattern, TFV should not impose the selection of the particular method which better fits that flow or the rejection of that method which does clearly not befit that pattern. In this regard, for example, the election of the LIFO method to value perishables[58] would militate against the TFV. Further, despite the fact that experience shows that FIFO better describes the real flow of most warehouses, TFV could also discard this method in (rare) cases where the normal flow follows a LIFO pattern (for example, mineral storage piles).

The second reason developed by German scholars to negate the limiting power of TFV in relation to options is precisely the lack of specific content of the principle itself.[59] In a more elaborated form, it has also been stated that an 'exercise of accounting options in accordance with the facts' cannot be reliably determined.[60] The real possibilities of concretisation for TFV in relation to options have already been dealt with.

B. Gaps in Accounting Law and TFV

Accounting rules might suffer legal gaps, meaning an 'incompleteness of the law contrary to the plan of the legislator or the law itself'.[61] Inasmuch as the purpose of the law is also

[55] Assuming that the systematic allocation of value adjustments to the useful economic lives of fixed assets to which the Directive refers are based upon the depreciation curve of them. Things might be different where depreciation/amortisation aims at reflecting the contribution of an asset to the generation of economic benefits for the enterprise. On this problem see Hennrichs, *Wahlrechte im Bilanzrecht der Kapitalgesellschaften* (n 21) 342.

[56] For more detail see Hennrichs, *Wahlrechte im Bilanzrecht der Kapitalgesellschaften* (n 21) 389–410.

[57] See, for Germany, Hennrichs, *Wahlrechte im Bilanzrecht der Kapitalgesellschaften* (n 21) 410; Báez Moreno, 'Normas Contables e Impuesto sobre Sociedades' (n 43) 234–35.

[58] Or even rapidly deteriorating non-perishable goods.

[59] See the references in Hennrichs, *Wahlrechte im Bilanzrecht der Kapitalgesellschaften* (n 21) 332.

[60] Clemm (n 41) 152.

[61] In its almost standard definition by law theorists and originating in the work of Canaris: see CW Canaris, 'Die Feststellung von Lücken im Gesetz. Eine methodologische Studie über Voraussetzungen und Grenzen der richterlichen Rechtsfortbildung praeter legem' 2, *überarbeitete Auflage* (Berlin, Duncker & Humblot, 1983) 16. The concept has also been used by accounting scholars: see, eg, Alexander and Eberhartinger (n 25) 573–74.

crucial for filling gaps, TFV, as an incarnation of the main objective of the Directive, is also considered the instrument through which analogy operates in accounting law.[62] In my view, however, there are two good reasons to deny this gap-filling function of TFV.

First, the existence of a gap, as previously defined, is a precondition for analogy, meaning the application of the legal consequence attributed to a regulated legal event to similar non-regulated events (gaps or loopholes).[63] If there is an applicable rule then no gap exists and there is obviously no need for analogy. In my view, many of the alleged gaps in accounting law cannot simply be considered as such. Take foreign currency translation as an example. Neither current 2013/34/EU Directive nor its predecessor contain specific rules on this issue and particularly on accounting treatment of short-term and long-term positive differences. This has led some authors to identify a loophole (in the Directive)[64] and some Member States to regulate this in detail in their national accounting rules even allowing the record of both long-term and short-term positive differences as realised profits.[65]

However, it is difficult, if not impossible, to characterise the lack of specific rules on currency translation as an 'incompleteness of the law' and, therefore, as a gap capable of being covered by means of analogy. Indeed, the accounting treatment of (particularly) positive differences derived from foreign currency translation is clearly regulated in Article 6.1(c)(i) of the 2013/34/EU Directive (realisation principle) and Article 6.1(i) of the 2013/34/EU Directive (principle of purchase price or production cost).[66] According to these rules, and beyond their difficult interpretation problems, these gains shall not be included in the profit and loss account until the profit in the underlying asset has been realised according to ordinary rules. Moreover, even accepting this might be a real gap, the result would not be different. Indeed, in the latter case, the only rule to be extended by analogy would be precisely the rule on realisation and valuation at

[62] This is a common position even beyond German scholars: see Gondra Romero (n 25) 581–83; Walton, 'Introduction: the true and fair view in British accounting' (n 18) 50, when referring to TFV as a 'legal residual clause'; J Arden, 'True and fair view: a European perspective' (1997) 6 *European Accounting Review* 675, 677; Nobes (n 25) 307, referring to TFV in a UK context; Van Hulle, 'True and Fair View' (n 24) 321–22, without a clear distinction between interpretation and analogy; Budde and Karig (n 47); Ballwieser (n 47) § 264 Rz. 59; Hennrichs, *Wahlrechte im Bilanzrecht der Kapitalgesellschaften* (n 21) 134–35 without mentioning analogy explicitly but actually referring to the *complement function of TFV* (*Ergänzungsfunktion*); M Lutter and P Hommelhoff, *GmbH-Gesetz Kommentar.* 15. neubearbeitete und erwiterte Auflage (Köln, Dr Otto Schmidt, 2000) 610–11; Schulze Osterloh (n 51) 906–07.

[63] K Larenz, '*Methodenlehre der Rechtswissenschaft*' Dritte, neu bearbeitete Auflage (Berlin, Springer, 1995) 202.

[64] Ordelheide, 'True and Fair View' (n 25) 83; Arden (n 62) 679. Also the Commission when stating: 'The Directive does not specifically address the problem of accounting for the effects of changes in foreign exchange rates' (European Commission, 'Interpretative Communication Concerning Certain Articles of the Fourth and Seventh Council Directives on Accounting' 98/C 16/04, 38).

[65] So the original regulation in Spain (Norma de Valoración 14ª del Plan General de Contabilidad de 1990) and even more intensively in the current regulation (Norma de Valoración 11ª del Plan General de Contabilidad de 2007). Along these lines the European Commission, in an unhesitating contradiction with the prior statement regarding the existence of a gap in the Directive regarding the effects of changes in foreign exchange rates has stated: 'Article 31 of the Directive does not exclude an interpretation whereby positive exchange differences may be included in the profit and loss account' (European Commission' Interpretative Communication', 40).

[66] Tentatively in this direction in relation to the accounting treatment of leasing and long term production contracts: Hennrichs, *Wahlrechte im Bilanzrecht der Kapitalgesellschaften* (n 21) 135.

historical cost.[67] The same goes, in my view, for most alleged accounting gaps, which will normally be nothing more than problems of interpretation of general accounting rules and principles such as realisation or historical cost.[68]

Second, current Article 4(4) of the 2013/34/EU Directive may be used, in exceptional cases, to disapply a provision of the Directive in order to give a TFV of the undertaking's assets, liabilities, financial position and profit or loss. The key aspects of this provision will be analysed later; at this point I merely try to emphasise that the Directive allows the non-application of an accounting provision which might jeopardise TFV. This technique, labelled by law theorists 'teleological reduction',[69] is considered a parallel of analogy. Indeed, analogy requires extending the application of a prima facie non-applicable rule in the light of the purpose of the law; conversely teleological reduction implies rejecting the application of a prima facie applicable rule also in the light of the purpose of the law. Although both techniques differ in their practical operation, both imply development of the law beyond interpretation and therefore might pose serious problems of compatibility with the rule of law. For those reasons, it would make no sense to unrestrictedly allow analogy by means of TFV in Article 4(3) of the 2013/34/EU Directive[70] and regulate, at the same time, the use of teleological restriction in Article 4(4) of the 2013/34/EU Directive in a more cautious manner. In this sense, particularly in those legal fields in which the rule of law acquires greater importance, limits to analogy and teleological restriction – development of the law beyond interpretation – should be common.[71]

C. The Overriding Function of TFV

As aforementioned, Article 4(4) of the 2013/34/EU Directive may be used, in exceptional cases, to disapply a provision of the Directive in order to give a TFV of the undertaking's assets, liabilities, financial position and profit or loss – the 'true and fair view override' (TFVO). This provision, which is substantially different from Article 4(3), second sentence of the 2013/34/EU Directive,[72] is clearly the most contentious aspect of the

[67] In a similar vein see Ordelheide, 'True and Fair View' (n 25) 83.

[68] Things would be different in those cases in which national rules have foreseen provisions deviating from regular accounting standards which are applicable just for certain sectors or undertakings. By way of example, Spanish accounting rules, at least until 2007, imposed, under certain circumstances, the use of the percentage of completion method in long-term production contracts concluded by building companies. In this context, there was a doubt whether companies outside the building sector concluding long-term contracts could or even were obliged to also make use of the percentage of completion method. However, in my view, it should have been ascertained whether or not these special rules were in accordance with the Directive in the first place. For more see Báez Moreno, 'Normas Contables e Impuesto sobre Sociedades' (n 43) 429–31.

[69] K Larenz (n 63) 210–16. It has also been referred to by accounting scholars: see, eg, Alexander and Eberhartinger (n 25) 573–74.

[70] As pretended by all those who consider TFV as a way to cover gaps in accounting law.

[71] On this particular problem see A Báez Moreno, 'Algunas reflexiones sobre la prohibición de analogía en Derecho Tributario' in A Báez Moreno and DJ Jiménez-Valladolid (eds), *Tratado sobre la Ley General Tributaria. Homenaje a Álvaro Rodríguez Bereijo.* Tomo I (Pamplona, Thomson Reuters-Aranzadi, 2010) 466–71.

[72] This provision compels the preparers of annual accounts to provide additional information in the notes to the financial statements where the application of the Directive would not be sufficient to give a true and fair view of the undertaking's assets, liabilities, financial position and profit or loss. The 'so-called' explanation function of TFV (*Erläuterungsfunktion*) contained in this provision is not separately analysed in this contribution as it does not play any role for tax accounting purposes.

content of TFV. In this regard, the wording in Article 4(4) seems to suggest that an accounting treatment in accordance with TFV – whatever this means[73] – might override the treatment contained in a specific accounting rule; or, simply stated, that TFV overrides, in the abstract, accounting rules. The only fact triggering the application of TFVO would be therefore the misalignment between a specific accounting rule and a hypothetical accounting treatment that better reflects the TFV of the undertaking's assets, liabilities, financial position and profit or loss. This understanding of TFVO, which many scholars appear ready to accept,[74] has (almost) provoked anger in some (not only German) professional and academic circles,[75] even resulting in a 'mutilated' transposition of the Accounting Directive in certain Member States.[76]

Be that as it may, it is very difficult to accept, at least according to the legal Continental tradition, that a provision can be disapplied by whatever accounting actor (preparers, auditors, courts or tax authorities) just because its consequences are not in line or are less in line with the evanescent contents, and therefore unknown requirements, of a principle such as TFV.[77] Moreover, the artificial fragmentation in the life of a firm required in accounting leads to a thirst for (also artificial) time allocation conventions on which passing a judgment based upon 'truth' or 'fairness' is very difficult, if not impossible. The somehow mixed purpose (creditor protection and investor information) of European accounting rules (particularly after Directives 2001/65/EC[78] and 2003/51/EC)[79] certainly does not help either to formulate that judgment. In short, there are few if any 'features by nature' in accounting further compounding a radical TFVO that is not a mere exercise of arbitrariness or manipulation.[80] Several decisions of

[73] We are not referring here to the interpretative function of TFV as described above.

[74] Gondra Romero (n 25) 583–86; D Alexander, 'A European true and fair view?' (1993) 1 *European Accounting Review* 59, 62; D Alexander, 'Truer and fairer: uninvited comments on invited comments' (1996) 5 *European Accounting Review* 483, 492; K Van Hulle, 'The true and fair view override in the European Accounting Directives' (1997) 6 *European Accounting Review* 711, 713.

[75] Indeed, German scholars and practitioners reject, with only a very few exceptions, this broad understanding of the TFVO (see, in particular, the bibliographic review by Heinrich Beisse and the literature quoted there: Beisse, 'Zehn Jahre' (n 25) 45–47). However, this understanding of TFVO has also been rejected outside Germany: see Báez Moreno, 'Normas Contables e Impuesto sobre Sociedades' (n 43) 409–10; A Báez Moreno, 'El caso GIMLE: una oportunidad perdida para aclarar el sentido del principio de imagen fiel y sus consecuencias fiscales' (2014) 106 *Revista Técnica Tributaria* 29, 47.

[76] Germany has not incorporated into § 264 of its *Handelsgesetzbuch* the contents of Article 2(5) of the 78/660/EEC Directive (current Article 4(4) of the 2013/34/EU Directive). This is also the case for Austria (on Austrian peculiarities: Alexander and Eberhartinger (n 25) 577–83) and Sweden (S Aisbitt and C Nobes, 'The true and fair view requirement in recent national implementations' (2001) 31 *Accounting and Business Research* 83, 86).

[77] In the same vein see Ordelheide, 'True and Fair View: II' (n 53) 502–03.

[78] Directive 2001/65/EC of the European Parliament and of the Council of 27 September 2001 amending Directives 78/660/EEC, 83/349/EEC and 86/635/EEC as regards the valuation rules for the annual and consolidated accounts of certain types of companies as well as of banks and other financial institutions [2001] OJ L283/1.

[79] Directive 2003/51/EC of the European Parliament and of the Council of 18 June 2003 amending Directives 78/660/EEC, 83/349/EEC, 86/635/EEC and 91/674/EEC on the annual and consolidated accounts of certain types of companies, banks and other financial institutions and insurance undertakings (Text with EEA relevance) [2003] OJ L178.

[80] Nobes argues that TFVO should not be available for preparers as this would be open to abuse: Nobes (n 25) 307. In Australia a TFVO was removed to avoid the opportunistic invocation by directors not wishing to comply with certain accounting rules (Dunk and Kilgore (n 6) 214). Van Hulle reports unreasonable accounting treatments in the financial statements of certain European companies allegedly based upon the

the CJEU – not allowing a radical TFVO in particular cases[81] – reinforce the need for a restrictive approach to Article 4(4) of the 2013/34/EU Directive.

An interpretation leaving a rule void of content cannot be correct, however, and therefore it is necessary to provide TFVO with a precise meaning. In my view, current Article 4(4) of the 2013/34/EU Directive and its predecessor embody a general anti-abuse rule (GAAR) for commercial accounting purposes.[82] Indeed, in any area of law (including accounting) the performance of abusive arrangements implies the execution of facts in a way that a rule either cannot be applied (abuse through avoidance) or is applied even if not intended for cases of the kind (abuse through capture). The legal consequences when a GAAR is applied are to either extend the avoided rule by analogy or (more frequently) to discard the application of the unduly appropriated rule; so the structure of TFVO – allowing the non-application of a provision of the Directive in order to give a TFV[83] – perfectly fits the legal technique underlying GAARs. Even if the CJEU failed to recognise this function of TFVO when it had the opportunity to do so,[84] this interpretation offers considerable advantages.

TFVO (K Van Hulle, 'Harmonization of accounting standards in the EC. Is it the beginning or is it the end?' (1993) 2 *European Accounting Review* 387, 393. McGregor labels TFVO as an excuse for non-compliance and the worst excesses of creative accounting (McGregor (n 10) 71); K Van Hulle, 'Truth and untruth about true and fair: a commentary on "A European true and fair view" comment' (1993) 1 *European Accounting Review* 99, 101.

[81] In *BIAO* (n 21) paras 123–26, the CJEU rejects that the repayment of a loan, which takes place after the balance-sheet date, constitutes a fact necessitating retrospective revaluation of a provision relating to that loan entered on the liabilities side of the balance sheet. However, instead of disapplying Article 31(1)(c)(bb) of the 78/660/EEC Directive – pursuant to which account must be taken, in the balance-sheet date of all foreseeable liabilities and potential losses arising in the course of the financial year concerned – the Court concludes that compliance with the true and fair view principle requires that mention must be made somewhere in the annual accounts of the disappearance or reduction of such a risk. The position of the CJEU in *Gimle* (n 21) paras 36–42 and *Bloomsbury NV* (n 21) paras 25–30 seems even stricter, as the Court held that Article 2(5) of the Directive (ie, TFVO) does not permit the principle of valuation at historical cost to be departed from in favour of a valuation on the basis of their real value, where the acquisition price or the production cost of those assets is manifestly lower than their real value or free of charge.

[82] This is not an entirely new idea and many academics and practitioners establish explicit or implicit links between TFVO and GAARs: see, eg, Arden (n 62) 677; Alexander and Eberhartinger (n 25) 576; JE McEnroe and SC Martens, 'It's time for true and fair view' (2004) 28 *Accounting Forum* 427, 429–30; Báez Moreno, 'El caso GIMLE' (n 75) 47–48. A number of German scholars consider that TFVO might put a brake on artificial exercise of accounting optional rules: see J Baetge and D Commandeur in K Küting, C Peter and J Weber (eds) '*Handbuch*' Band II § 264 Tz. 43; M Hinz, 'Bild der Vermögens-, Finanz- und Ertragslage' in E Castan et al (eds), *Beck'sches Handbuch der Rechnungslegung – HGB und IFRS-* (München, Beck, 2011) Band I, B106, para 47 with references. In any case, in my view, there is no legal reason to limit the nature of TFVO as GAAR just for the purposes of disapplying options and not other accounting rules.

[83] And, in our view, the extension of a prima facie non-applicable provision by analogy.

[84] In *Gimle* (n 21), the CJEU was confronted with an artificial transaction (purchase by a company from a shareholder for a price manifestly lower than the real value) implemented essentially with the intention of shifting taxable gains from the United Kingdom to Belgium. Irrespective of the particular circumstances surrounding the purchase, the CJEU stated that the possibility that certain assets would be undervalued in company accounts where their acquisition value is lower than their real value is merely the necessary corollary of the choice made by the European Union legislature, in Article 32 of the Fourth Directive, to opt for a valuation method based not on the real value of the assets but on their historical cost and denied the application of TFVO in the case. As rightly pointed out by scholars (see, eg, W Schön, 'Verdeckte Einlagen in Kapitalgesellschaten – unsichtbar für den EuGH' (2014) 178 *Zeitschrift für das gesamte Handels- und Wirtschaftsrecht* 373, 374–75) neither the request by local Belgian courts nor the decision of the CJEU take into proper consideration the particular features of the case. Professor Schön has defended that a resort to TFVO or substance over form would not be necessary either in the case of gifts or sales for a symbolic price between a shareholder

First, it is consistent with the ultimate goal of harmonisation underlying the Accounting directives. Indeed, a radical TFVO allowing preparers, legislators, standard-setters and even perhaps tax authorities to simply disregard the application of whatever accounting rules in those (exceptional) circumstances in which these might contravene the requirements of TFV, would undoubtedly lead to undesired dispersion and a corresponding lack of comparability.[85]

Second, the possibility of the TFVO being applied by preparers of the accounts is practically removed. It would make no sense for an abuser to apply an anti-abuse rule, leaving its effective use to auditors and courts.[86] This transforms a creative accounting enhancer into a pure anti-abuse rule.[87]

Third, this interpretation of the TFVO is systematically coherent, or at least more coherent than a radical TFVO, with several provisions of the Accounting directives. To begin, the current and traditional formulation of TFVO in the Accounting directives has invariably called for the application of the override 'in exceptional cases'. The advocates of a radical TFVO cannot of course ignore this legal requirement, but simply do not identify the exceptional cases which trigger the override. It is true that the preconditions upon which a restricted anti-abuse TFVO as the one proposed in this chapter is based are not defined in the law either. However, on the one hand, Article 6(1)(h) of the 2013/34/EU Directive requires items in the profit and loss account and balance sheet to be accounted for and presented having regard to the substance of the transaction or arrangement concerned. Even if discrepancy between form and substance is not a perfectly clear trigger for an anti-abuse rule,[88] it is undeniable that many (EU) countries count on considerable experience in the application of this very broad anti-abuse rule.

On the other hand, the CJEU has long recognised that there is a general principle of EU law that abuse of rights is prohibited.[89] Even if scope, content and limits of the 'prohibition of abuse of law' principle are far from settled,[90] it is also true that since the

and his participated company (Schön, ibid 382, 385. We totally agree in cases of gifts such as the one wrongly analysed by the CJEU in *Bloomsbury NV* (n 21) where a simple application of accounting rules would be enough to include the donated asset under its fair value. However, at least in certain countries such as Spain, where the aforementioned rule applies to gifts and endowments but not to sales for a symbolic price, a TFVO would be needed in order to deviate from the agreed price.

[85] See, implicitly, Van Hulle,'Harmonization of accounting' (n 80) 393. It is highly illustrative that scholars in favour of what we call a radical understanding of TFVO seem to show a quasi-hostile attitude towards accounting harmonisation. In this sense see Alexander: 'A common Europe-wide view of the TFV implies a common and homogeneous European culture. No thanks!': Alexander, 'A European true and fair view?' (n 74) 75.

[86] Eventually also to tax authorities as will be analysed later in this chapter.

[87] As indicated by Nobes: 'This dislike of the over-ride of standards is due to the fear that preparers would use vague Type A criteria [meaning the TFVO] to over-ride Type C rules [meaning specific accounting rules] in order to improve the look of their financial statements': Nobes (n 25) 307.

[88] I have criticised the use substance over form as an alternative for other more detailed GAARs: see A Báez Moreno and JJ Zornoza Pérez, 'Chapter 33: Spain' in M Lang et al (eds), *GAARs – A Key Element of Tax Systems in the Post-BEPS Tax World* (Amsterdam, IBFD, 2015) 33.8.

[89] Case C-321/05, *Kofoed*, ECLI:EU:C:2007:408, judgment of 5 July 2007, is supposed to be the first case in which the CJEU has explicitly stated the existence of this 'general principle of EU law'.

[90] This was one of the main conclusions drawn by Professor Vogenauer from the symposium held at the University of Oxford in October 2008 under the title 'Prohibition of Abuse of Law: A New General Principle of EU Law?': see S Vogenauer, 'The Prohibition of Abuse of Law: An Emerging General Principle of EU Law' in Rita de la Feria and Stefan Vogenauer (eds), *Prohibition of Abuse of Law. A New General Principle of EU Law?*

seminal *Emsland-Stärke* case[91] the lay-out parameters of what exactly constitutes abuse have been gradually pinpointed by the case law of the CJEU. In any event, a broad anti-abuse legal threshold will be far easier to specify than a radical TFVO whose application depends exclusively on an abstract contravention of the (very fussy) requirements of TFV.

In addition, as already stated, Article 4(3), second sentence of the 2013/34/EU Directive (Article 2(4) of the 78/660/EEC Directive) compels the preparers of annual accounts to provide additional information in the notes to the financial statements where the application of the Directive would not be sufficient to give a true and fair view of the undertaking's assets, liabilities, financial position and profit or loss. A radical interpretation of the TFVO in Article 4(4) of the 2013/34/EU Directive (Article 2(5) of the 78/660/EEC Directive) would make it extremely difficult to distinguish when to apply Article 4(3), second sentence of the 2013/34/EU Directive and merely provide additional information in the notes and when to apply Article 4(4) of the 2013/34/EU Directive and disapply a provision. This interpretation would imply the (impossible) distinction between applications of the Directive which 'are not sufficient to give a true and fair view' and applications of the Directive which are 'incompatible with the obligation to give a true and fair view'.

This is the reason why, in my view, accounting scholars have not convincingly explained the different requisites to apply both Article 4(3) second sentence, and Article 4(4) of the Directive or, in other words, when additional information is not sufficient to give a true and fair view enabling any provision of the Directive to be departed from. A restrictive anti-abuse rule based on understanding of the TFVO makes interrelationships between both provisions easier. A strict application of (particularly) prudence-based accounting provisions can result in situations in which additional information in the notes is required in order to provide a true and fair view. One should not forget that prudence imposes a deliberately pessimistic view of the undertaking's assets, liabilities, financial position and profit or loss. An abusive arrangement, for its part, also generates situations of inaccurate information which, however, might not be solved by a mere informative addendum requiring, according to the Directive, a disapplication of a provision with effect on the balance sheet or the profit and loss account.

(Oxford, Hart Publishing, 2011). Years later Martín Jiménez continued to report a similar situation: A Martín Jiménez, 'Towards a homogeneous Theory of Abuse in EU (Direct) Tax Law' (2012) *Bulletin for International Taxation* 288. Advocate General Bobek in his opinion of 7 September 2017 in Case C-251/16, *Cussens*, ECLI:EU:C:2017:648, para 2 expressed a similar view: 'Although it was explicitly confirmed more than a decade ago, and has been since then the object of extensive scholarly discussion and analysis, the detailed operation of that principle, including the precise test to be applied for ascertaining abuse, may be said to be still somewhat underdeveloped'.

[91] Case C-110/99, *Emsland-Stärke*, ECLI:EU:C:2000:695, judgment of 14 December 2000, in which the CJEU settled for the first time the abstract criteria according to which an arrangement might be considered abusive (paras 52–53): 'A finding of an abuse requires, first, a combination of objective circumstances in which, despite formal observance of the conditions laid down by the Community rules, the purpose of those rules has not been achieved. It requires, second, a subjective element consisting in the intention to obtain an advantage from the Community rules by creating artificially the conditions laid down for obtaining it. The existence of that subjective element can be established, inter alia, by evidence of collusion between the Community exporter receiving the refunds and the importer of the goods in the non-member country'.

This also explains why Article 4(3) second sentence does not require, unlike the TFVO, to be applied only in 'exceptional cases'.[92]

Furthermore, Article 4(4), second paragraph of the 2013/34/EU Directive (Article 2(5), second sentence of the 78/660/EEC Directive) provides that Member States may define the exceptional cases in question (those which enable a TFVO) and lay down the relevant special rules which are to apply in those cases. Accounting scholars assuming more or less radical versions of TFVO disagree on almost every detail regarding this provision. In particular, the question whether the TFVO must be applied in relation to a given company[93] or in relation to all or a category of companies[94] has long been the subject of discussions being even claimed that Article 2(5), second sentence (or its current parallel) allows Member States to declare the areas in which a departure might be possible whereas the specific deviation must be applied company by company.[95] The European Commission has even suggested that in order for the TFVO to be applied Member States need to have made use of the entitlement contained in Article 2(5), second sentence of the 78/660/EEC Directive.[96]

Any of these interpretations lead to similar irrational results as a radical TFVO. If TFVO is restricted to merely embody an accounting GAAR, Article 4(4) second paragraph of the 2013/34/EU Directive might well be interpreted as permission for Member States to regulate special anti-avoidance rules (SAARs) which might of course imply a deviation from the accounting rules applicable at first sight. This interpretation would provide the permission with a specific content while serving to provide certainty in relation to several rules (actually accounting SAARs) of Member States whose compatibility with Accounting directives have been traditionally dubious.[97]

III. The Functions of TFV and their Effects on Tax Accounting

In all countries with comprehensive or more or less limited systems of book-tax conformity the tax consequences of TFV have been considered. In this respect there has

[92] This subtle difference between old Articles 2(4) and 2(5) of the 78/660/EEC Directive has been pointed out by accounting scholars: see, eg, Van Hulle, 'True and Fair View' (n 24) 320. Other authors, however, have read an 'inexistent' requirement for application just in exceptional cases also in Article 2(4) of the Directive: see, eg, Hennrichs, *Wahlrechte im Bilanzrecht der Kapitalgesellschaften* (n 21) 135.

[93] Van Hulle, 'The true and fair view override' (n 74) 714.

[94] Alexander, 'A European true and fair view?' (n 74) 73.

[95] Ordelheid, 'True and Fair View' (n 25) 85.

[96] A position that even the CJEU seems to advocate for: see *Gimle* (n 21) para 41. This statement seems to clearly contradict a previous position held by the Commission on Article 2(5) second sentence of the 78/660/EEC Directive when stating: 'As stated in the last sentence of Article 2(5), Member States may define the exceptional cases in question and lay down the relevant special rules. In the interest of harmonization, Member States may however not use the last sentence of Article 2(5) in order to introduce an accounting rule of a general nature which is contrary to provisions of the Directive, nor can they use this sentence to create additional options allowing for accounting treatments which are not in conformity with the Directive' (European Commission, 'Interpretative Communication', 6).

[97] As, eg, the special sale and lease back rule contained in valuation rule 8(3) or the special regime for intra group transactions contained in valuation rule 21 both of the Spanish *Plan General de Contabilidad*.

been no shortage of maximalist positions ranging from those who cannot even detect a single conflict – by merely equating TFV and ability to pay[98] – to those others who claim to maintain TFV, and its alleged fatal consequences, away from tax accounts.[99] However, as is often the case, virtue is (probably) the happy medium. In order to elaborate a measured and dispassionate answer to this problem one should take into account, on the one hand, the functions of TFV as described above and, on the other, the specific tax rules containing the links between commercial accounting and taxable corporate income.

All book-tax conformity systems are based upon a more or less general reference by tax law provisions to accounting rules for the purposes of determining taxable corporate income. It is generally assumed that the referring rule – in this case a tax law provision – incorporates the referred legal materials – in this case the commercial accounting rules – to its own contents. In the simplest terms, the referred rule is converted into a rule of the referring system.[100] Accordingly, the interpretation and general application of the incorporated provisions must be done according to the particular rules of the referring system. With this simple logic, one could conclude that TFV, playing a mere applicative (interpretative and anti-abuse) function for commercial accounting purposes, would be utterly irrelevant for the determination of taxable profits: the incorporated commercial accounting rules would be interpreted and generally applied according to the specific tax rules regarding these issues. This approach, however, might be over-simplistic.

Book-tax conformity systems involve normally much more than a pure normative reference to accounting rules. In one way or another, most (European) book-tax conformity systems link corporate taxable income not just to accounting rules in the abstract but actually to the specific profit or loss calculated by the preparers. This formal link to specific accounting results does not only stem from positive tax rules[101] but is actually coherent with the purposes normally attributed to book-tax conformity:[102] simplification and prevention of accounting/tax abuse.[103] In this context, any accounting result generated by the application of TFV would have an immediate tax effect, except of

[98] A dominant position among Italian scholars. For references and criticism see Báez Moreno, 'Normas Contables e Impuesto sobre Sociedades' (n 43) 127–46.

[99] As defended by traditional German scholars: see, eg, Beisse, 'Die Generalnorm' (n 25) 36; and Beisse, 'Zehn Jahre' (n 25) 52–53.

[100] This is the normal approach to legal references and their effects in German law theory. For references see Báez Moreno, 'Normas Contables e Impuesto sobre Sociedades' (n 43) 267. This is also the approach to the tax rule referring to commercial accounting provisions in Germany: see Báez Moreno, ibid.

[101] In Spain, eg, tax rules settle the 'accounting profit or loss calculated' in accordance with commercial accounting rules as a starting point for the calculation of corporate taxable income: see A Báez Moreno, 'Chapter 12. Accounting and Taxation: Spain' in M Grandinetti (ed), *Corporate Tax Base in the Light of the IAS/IFRS and EU Directive 2013/34* (Alphen aan den Rijn, Wolters Kluwers, 2016) 186–87; for more detail see Báez Moreno, 'Normas Contables e Impuesto sobre Sociedades' (n 43) 45–68. In Germany, in its turn, elections laid down in the accounting rules have to be exercised uniformly also for tax purposes (see Schön, 'The David R Tillinghast Lecture' (n 15) 115).

[102] This is perhaps the reason why this formal link has also been respected in countries in which it could not be so easily inferred from positive tax rules: see E Traversa and S Peeters, 'Chapter 4. Accounting and Taxation: Belgium' in M Grandinetti (ed), *Corporate Tax Base in the Light of the IAS/IFRS and EU Directive 2013/34* (Alphen aan den Rijn, Wolters Kluwers, 2016) 72.

[103] In particular on these purposes see Freedman, 'Aligning Taxable Profits and Accounting Profits' (n 15) 74–75. J Freedman, 'Financial and Tax Accounting: Transparency and "Truth"' in W Schön (ed), *Tax and Corporate Governance* (Berlin, Springer Science, 2008) (accessed in University of Oxford Faculty of Law Legal Studies Research Paper Series Working Paper No 02/2008) 5–6.

course, when a particular tax rule deviation is applicable. However, this general conclusion needs nuances in relation to every particular function of TFV.

First, regarding the interpretative function of TFV, the immediate tax effect of interpretations guided by TFV proves rather straightforward. On the one hand, most jurisdictions assume teleological interpretation of tax law provisions as a natural phenomenon. On the other hand, and regarding a potential disparity between TFV – as the main objective of the accounting system – and ability to pay – as the main goal of tax accounting[104] – I do not think that serious problems can arise here. The necessity of taking into account all those verifiable natural facts which might lead to a more accurate accounting reflection, as the above-mentioned main requirement of a TFV interpretation of accounting rules, may hardly lead to any conflict with the ability to pay principle. Moreover, one should not forget that in those cases in which certain accounting rules may interfere with tax requirements the legislator is always free to introduce a particular deviation. Interpretative TFV effects apply only in those cases in which accounting rules are incorporated by reference to rules on taxable profits where, at least theoretically, a particular tax deviation is not needed. This is all the more so regarding accounting options, if one takes into consideration that these options pose several constitutional problems.[105]

Second, the fact that TFV does not allow an application of accounting rules by analogy must be also welcome from a strict tax (accounting) perspective since a significant number of (European) countries rely on an explicit or implicit ban of analogy in tax law.

Third, a radical TFVO – meaning that an accounting provision can be disapplied by whatever accounting actor (preparers, auditors, courts or tax authorities) just because it is allegedly not in line with TFV – might pose serious constitutional problems for obvious reasons. On the other hand, a restrictive TFVO with mere anti-abusive character would be more readily acceptable for tax accounting purposes. In fact GAARs are a common feature in European tax systems.[106] However, the simple acceptance of an anti-abuse TFVO for tax accounting purposes might prove rushed.

As we have already stated elsewhere,[107] there might be relevant differences between an anti-abusive TFVO and the domestic GAARs of Member States. The application of domestic GAARs is made conditional upon the fulfilment of general – yet at least regulated – abuse thresholds. TFVO, as interpreted in this contribution, does not describe this abusive threshold or, at best, since the adoption of 2013/34/EU Directive, might be identified with the rather untelling concept of 'substance over form'. In addition, domestic GAARs frequently require the application of special procedures whereas these procedures do obviously not apply to TFVO.

[104] For more detail see J Hennrichs, 'Maβgeblichkeitsgrundsatz order eigenständige Prinzipien für die Steuerbilanz' in I Ebling (ed), *Besteurung voin Einkommen* (Köln, Dr Otto Schmidt, 2001) 308–12.

[105] Space limitations prohibit a deeper investigation of this problem, but for more on accounting options and constitutional tax limits see Báez Moreno, 'Normas Contables e Impuesto sobre Sociedades' (n 43) 199–207.

[106] As already found in 2002 by Zimmer only a few countries seem to have neither a statute-based nor a court-based general tax avoidance rule: F Zimmer, 'Form and Substance in Tax Law – General Report' in IFA, *International Fiscal International Cahiers de Droit Fiscal International* (The Hague, Kluwer, 2002) 37–38.

[107] Báez Moreno, 'Chapter 12. Accounting' (n 101) 200–01.

Furthermore, many domestic GAARs exempt criminal charges or even administrative penalties eventually linked to its application. A similar exemption does not exist for the application of TFVO. In this context tax authorities might feel tempted to apply TFVO, instead of the corresponding domestic GAAR, when an accounting rule applicable for the computation of taxable profits has been abused.[108] It might be thought at first glance that this practice could be in line with the formal link between taxable profits and specific accounting results as described above. Additionally, many domestic regimes when regulating the deviations from the material dependence rule merely refer to those contained in corporate income or personal income tax Acts.[109] However, in those systems making a reference to the specific profit or loss calculated by the preparers, it could always be argued that preparers do not apply TFVO (auditors and courts do) so the remission to accounting rules and results would not cover the GAAR.

Finally, I think it is quite obvious that the application of different GAARs to specific taxes or, even worse, of different GAARs on different rules within the same tax does not make much sense and might generate serious constitutional concerns. Nevertheless, this is a rather local problem, which depends essentially on the particular formulation of the dependence rules in every State.

In a nutshell: Much Ado About Nothing. A properly interpreted TFV principle should not pose particular problems in book-tax conformity systems, with the possible exception of the effects of TFVO in certain jurisdictions. These countries would do well to directly intervene in order to clarify the situation and make the particular tax GAAR also applicable to the abuse of accounting provisions.

IV. Conclusion

This chapter is based on many of the conclusions set out at the time by Professor Freedman regarding the general topic of how commercial and tax accounting relate when determining the taxable base of corporate income taxes. Indeed, in the real world there are no systems of pure separation between commercial and tax accounting which leads to partial alignment being the closest thing to a universal solution in this respect.[110] But just because a solution is the most common does not mean it is problem-free. This partial dependence is in fact at the origin of many of the interpretative problems generated by the system.[111]

[108] This was in fact the starting point of the controversy between Belgian tax authorities and the tax payer in the *Gimle* case: see *Gimle* (n 21) paras 11–18.

[109] eg, Article 10.3 of the Spanish Corporate Income Tax Act reads as follows: 'In the direct assessment system the taxable base will be determined by correcting, *according to the special provisions of this law*, the accounting profit or loss' (emphasis added).

[110] As stated by Professor Freedman: 'The overall movement seems to be towards partial alignment. The stereotypical extreme cases do not seem ever to have been entirely accurate and are becoming less so': Freedman, 'Financial and Tax Accounting' (n 103) 11.

[111] As stated again by Professor Freedman: 'The consequence of this partial conformity with accounting standards is that there is no certainty about when the courts will decide that a matter falls within their jurisdiction and when they will follow accounting practice': Freedman, 'Financial and Tax Accounting' (n 103) 25.

However, this chapter also tries to offer arguments to those who want to see in the principle of TFV (and particularly TFVO) an additional argument to end any kind of link between commercial and tax accounting. Indeed, some of the functions attributed to TFV – notably the interpretative function – should not, in my opinion, pose any problems when projected onto tax accounting. On the contrary, if TFVO is interpreted as a general anti-abuse rule for commercial accounting purposes – and this is in my opinion the only logical interpretation for the principle – countries would do well to clarify that for tax purposes (tax accounting) just the specific tax GAARs apply.

Afterword: Professor Judith Freedman: A Short Appreciation from Women in Tax

I am delighted to write this short appreciation of Professor Judith Freedman, on behalf of the Women in Tax network.

Judith has been an inspiring role model and has supported a wide range of women in tax throughout her career. As the first female professor of tax law at a UK university, she has played a leading part in establishing tax law as an important area of research and teaching.

Around five years ago, it began to be noticed that many professional tax events in the UK (and elsewhere) included few, if any, women speakers. On social media platforms, Judith and others started to comment on all-male panels ('manels' in the vernacular), and we asked why women were not more visible. Matters came to a head at one particular event, which both Judith and I attended, where the all-male panel was introduced by the male chairman as a 'balanced panel' because it included both lawyers and accountants. Enough, we decided, was enough.

Judith mentioned the Women in Law network in Oxford and asked whether there was a Women in Tax network – and if not, whether we should start one. From that point, it took us about five months to get the network off the ground and to hold our first debate – on the question of 'What do we mean by a fair tax system?' with Judith on the panel.

Judith encouraged and supported us from the beginning and generously made her expertise and network available to us. While she has not been involved in the detail of the committee's work, she has been very much part of the network and has often suggested to her students that they should get involved.

Four years after that first event, we have a network which meets in London, Bristol, Manchester, Leeds, Birmingham, the East Midlands, the Thames Valley, Cambridge, Edinburgh and Aberdeen – and new groups are being formed regularly. At the IFA Congress in London, in autumn 2019, Women in Tax worked closely with Women in IFA to raise the profile of women attending the event, including a wall of photographs of notable women in tax – which, of course, included Judith's picture.

The impact which Judith has had on the careers of many women in tax is incalculable – Rita de la Feria and Daisy Ogembo, both of whom have been involved in bringing this publication together, are just two examples. Judith exemplifies the values which Women in Tax aims to achieve – to raise the voice of women in tax, and to be a supportive network for all women working in tax, whether in the professions, business, academia, HMRC or elsewhere.

Heather Self

INDEX

www.ingramcontent.com/pod-product-compliance
Ingram Content Group UK Ltd.
Pitfield, Milton Keynes, MK11 3LW, UK
UKHW020233290926
15470UKWH00002B/522

9 781509 929092